D0847820

The Natural Resources Trap

The Natural Resources Trap

Private Investment without Public Commitment

edited by William Hogan and Federico Sturzenegger

The MIT Press
Cambridge, Massachusetts
London, England

For information about special quantity discounts, please e-mail special_sales@mitpress
.mit.edu

This book was set in Palatino on 3B2 by Asco Typesetters, Hong Kong.
Printed and bound in the United States of America.

Library of Congress Cataloging-in-Publication Data

The natural resources trap : private investment without public commitment / edited by
William Hogan and Federico Sturzenegger.
    p. cm.
Includes bibliographical references and index.
ISBN 978-0-262-01379-6 (hbk. : alk. paper)
1. Natural resources—Government policy. 2. Natural resources—Law and legislation.
3. Investments, Foreign. 4. Public—private sector cooperation. I. Hogan, William W.
II. Sturzenegger, Federico.
HC85.N36   2010
333.7—dc22   2009029574

10 9 8 7 6 5 4 3 2 1

Contents

Contributors

Philippe Aghion Robert C. Waggoner Professor of Economics, Harvard University

George-Marios Angeletos Professor of Economics, Massachusetts Institute of Technology

Fernando Candia Castillo Managing Director, EFECE & Asociados

Rafael Di Tella Joseph C. Wilson Professor of Business Administration, Harvard Business School

Juan Dubra Professor of Economics, Universidad de Montevideo

Eduardo Engel Professor of Economics, Yale University

Ramón Espinasa Oil and Gas Specialist, Energy Division, Inter American Development Bank, and former Chief Economist, PDVSA

Ronald Fischer Professor, Centro de Economía Aplicada, Universidad de Chile and Instituto Milenio Sistemas Complejos de Ingeniería

Jeffrey Frankel James W. Harpel Professor of Capital Formation and Growth, Harvard Kennedy School

Nicolás Gadano Procurement Manager, Banco Ciudad de Buenos Aires

Dieter Helm Professor of Energy Policy, University of Oxford

William Hogan Raymond Plank Professor of Global Energy Policy, Harvard Kennedy School

Robert MacCulloch Professor, Imperial College London

Osmel Manzano Adjunct Professor, International Center on Energy and the Environment, IESA, and Universidad Catolica Andres Bello, Venezuela

Francisco Monaldi   Hoover Institution, Stanford University and Director, International Center on Energy and the Environment, IESA

Bijan Mossavar-Rahmani   Chairman, Mondoil Corporation

Erich Muehlegger   Assistant Professor of Public Policy, Harvard Kennedy School

Fernando H. Navajas   Chief Economist and Director, FIEL and Professor, University of La Plata, Argentina

Robert Pindyck   Bank of Tokyo-Mitsubishi Ltd. Professor of Economics and Finance, Sloan School of Management, Massachusetts Institute of Technology

Lucía Quesada   Assistant Professor, Universidad Torcuato Di Tella

Roberto Rigobon   Society of Sloan Fellows Professor of Management, Sloan School of Management, Massachusetts Institute of Technology

Eduardo S. Schwartz   California Professor of Real Estate and Professor of Finance, UCLA

Federico Sturzenegger   President, Banco Ciudad de Buenos Aires

Lawrence H. Summers   Charles W. Eliot University Professor, Harvard Kennedy School

Laurence Tai   PhD Candidate in Public Policy, Harvard University

Michael Tomz   Associate Professor, Stanford University, and Senior Fellow, Stanford Center for International Development

Anders B. Trolle   Swiss Finance Institute Assistant Professor, École Polytechnique Fédérale de Lausanne

Louis Wells   Herbert F. Johnson Professor of International Management, Harvard Business School

Nils Wernerfelt   Research Associate, Harvard Kennedy School

Mark J. Wright   Assistant Professor, University of California, Los Angeles

Richard Zeckhauser   Frank Plumpton Ramsey Professor of Political Economy, Harvard Kennedy School

Jeromin Zettelmeyer   Director for Policy Studies, European Bank for Reconstruction and Development

Preface

Recent years have seen unprecedented volatility in commodity prices. Oil, to mention a paradigmatic case, increased steadily from below $18 a barrel in 1998, to reach an all-time high of $147 by mid-2008. Six months later, however, the price had collapsed back to $40. Such roller-coaster movements have been common for most other commodities: iron, timber, aluminum, soybeans, and corn, all of which have seen their prices skyrocket and then collapse.

Thus the world experienced another trying time for governments and private investors in commodity export projects. During the commodity price upswing, many governments in countries with energy and minerals felt compelled to appropriate a larger share of apparently ever-increasing natural resource revenues. From the United Kingdom and Russia to Bolivia and Venezuela, countries changed the contract rules by which private-sector participation engaged in natural resource production. At the height of the boom, debate reopened even in the United States about the need to socialize a larger share of the oil revenues in the Gulf of Mexico and Alaska. At lower commodity prices, these new contracts appear far less attractive, and the larger state participation, justifiable when prices were high, becomes a burden. It will not be long before private-sector participation is called back in.

The cycle through 2008 stands out for the magnitude and speed of the changes in prices, but the pattern is not new at all, nor is the contractual instability that comes with it. It is precisely the recurrent nature of the cycle of governments opening up to foreign investors, then appropriating the resources, only to start the cycle again sometime later, that we find most intriguing. If it is well known that commodity prices exhibit cycles, why are contracts being renegotiated again and again? Why do these contracts not allow for better mechanisms that could smooth the fluctuations in a way that would provide a more stable commercial framework?

To explore this question, and aware that research on contracts in natural resources had received little attention in recent years, we invited a group of leading scholars to address the issues from different angles. The response was overwhelmingly positive. As a result, the investigations span a number of fields, ranging from Aghion and Quesada's application of contract theory in chapter 2, or Engel and Fischer's analysis of optimal extraction paths and taxation in the presence of expropriation risk in chapter 5, to Rigobon's public finance analysis explaining the relative benefits of royalties in chapter 7. The impact of social beliefs on contract stability is taken up by Di Tella, Dubra, and MacCulloch in chapter 4, and the pricing of expropriation risk is discussed by Schwartz and Trolle in chapter 8, while Tomz and Wright provide a historical analysis of the expropriation cycles in chapter 3.

We expected that the contributions to *The Natural Resources Trap: Private Investment without Public Commitment* would reveal an inherent complexity. It was unlikely that a single model, concept, or idea, such as time inconsistency, could capture by itself the full nature of the problems. If a single model applied, contractual frameworks would be much simpler and sustainable. In fact, the chapters explain some sources of this complexity: how the volatility of the revenue flows justifies particular contractual frameworks, how beliefs about and public perception of the fairness of the contracts are shaped by price instability, how the ability to hedge in financial markets affects government incentives, how lack of credibility reinforces a time-inconsistency problem, and so on, all making it difficult to bring in private participation on reasonable terms.

Anticipating this complexity, we complemented the analytical pieces with a few relevant case studies. Hence, the book includes contributions on the experiences of the United Kingdom, Bolivia, Argentina, Venezuela, and, in Mossavar-Rahmani's final discussion in the epilogue, a broader synthesis of similar dilemmas in other parts of the world. In these country chapters, the authors explore how capital structures of private firms evolved in unexpected directions in the United Kingdom, how social aspirations conspired against reforms in Bolivia, how internal political dynamics played a role in Argentina, and how irrationality may be necessary to explain some of the decisions in Venezuela. Thus the real-world cases added another layer of richness to the analysis.

The papers were presented at a conference at Harvard, November 1–2, 2007. The interaction was both interesting and productive. In one instance, the comments of respondents (Wernerfelt and Zeckhauser, commenting on the paper by Engel and Fischer in chapter 5) grew into a separate and complementary chapter. In every case, the discussion set the stage for revision of the papers into the form contained in this volume.

While we did not uncover a universal "contract" that could solve all the problems, the book provides a review of the main elements. Our introductory chapter locates the subsequent chapters within the context of the literature on natural resource contracting. The results should be a valuable reference for scholars working on the issues and for policymakers trying to grasp the main lessons learned from other countries' experiences.

Lawrence Summers's comments motivated the title of the book. He talks about the privatization trap: the idea that countries with low credibility need to offer attractive terms to the acquiring firm. But these attractive conditions make the contracts politically unviable later on. We draw a parallel to Summers's concept with the notion of the "natural resources trap." Governments with poor credibility need to offer attractive terms to private-sector investors. The more serious the credibility problem of the government, the better the deal it needs to offer the private sector. Building credibility, in turn, would imply abiding by high private rates of return for some time. But these terms become a political liability once a society sees the high rates of return, at which time pressure mounts for renegotiation. This difficulty in building credibility constitutes part of the natural resources trap. Additionally, rewards and punishments are highly asymmetric. A contract that delivers to the government a reasonable outcome in bad times is taken for granted by society, but a contract that delivers a poor outcome in good times is taken as a gift to foreign or private-sector interests. However, if the government appropriates more on the upside it will be forced to absorb more of the losses in bad times. Large losses in bad times are politically costly, but so are large gains to private-sector firms in good times. It is difficult to avoid both, thus adding to the complexity of the natural resources trap. It is these factors, among many others, that have made contractual stability elusive so far. In the short run, the losers are the private investors hurt when their contracts get renegotiated. But investors adjust. In the long run the losers may well be the citizens of the host country that suffers lower investment. Thus the trap and the tragedy.

In putting together this book we received the help of many people and institutions. The Harvard Kennedy School provided the environment in which to carry forward this project. The project was supported by the Mossavar-Rahmani Center for Business and Government and the Consortium for Energy Policy Research.

We thank Jo-Ann Mahoney, who was in charge of the logistics of our conference and supported the preparation of this volume, assisted by Trudi Bostian. Laurence Tai edited the comments. John Covell and Sandra Minkkinen helped smooth the path at the MIT Press. Last but not least, we thank our families for their support and patience while we made this project a reality.

1 Contracts and Investment in Natural Resources

William Hogan, Federico Sturzenegger, and
Laurence Tai

Natural resources have been the source of both prosperity and misery. Some countries have seen their fortunes change overnight with the vagaries of international prices. Some have basked in their newly acquired wealth. Others have moved from heaven to hell as prices plummeted. While it would seem strange to argue that highly valuable resources may lead to negative consequences for any country, the role of natural resources in economic development has been highly controversial. In fact, while many countries have been able to grow harmoniously with their natural resource industries, for others natural resources have been a source of problems. Colonialism, wars, political violence, corruption, and exchange-rate appreciation are among the maladies afflicting countries that find themselves with large riches prior to being able to organize themselves in a way that allows this wealth to be used and shared appropriately. Paradoxically, the abundance of natural resources can produce economic stagnation or even decline, and a large literature suggests that this latter scenario is, in fact, common. Even if the so-called curse of natural resources—the idea that countries better endowed with natural resources tend to grow more slowly than those less well endowed—holds on average, the fact remains controversial. (See Lederman and Maloney 2008 for a survey of the literature.)

In this book, our objective is not to discuss whether natural resources turn out to be good or bad, but rather to address a related issue: the problem that countries face in setting up a credible and stable regime for private investment to exploit these resources. Of course, governments may develop the resources on their own, but many lack the technical knowledge to do so or the large sums of capital required to undertake the investments. As a result, countries may rely on multinational corporations (MNCs) to discover and develop these resources. In doing so they become a host country (HC) to a (foreign) firm. The assistance of a second party introduces an attendant conflict of interest. The MNC needs to recover its costs and would like to keep as much revenue as possible. The HC, on the other hand, wants to secure as much of the proceeds as possible while making sure that the MNC continues to be interested in operating in the country. As Sunley, Baunsgaard, and Simard (2003) succinctly put it, "Both want to maximize rewards and shift as much risk as possible to the other party."

A central and persistent problem here is the limit on enforceability for contracts with a sovereign government. Unlike contracts between private parties that can appeal to the judicial system to enforce the terms, there are only imperfect ways to appeal to third parties to compel a sovereign government to abide by contract terms. Hence, the HC and the MNC must struggle with their competing interests and changing circumstances.

The HC and MNC strive to balance these interests through arrangements that allocate costs and benefits over a project's lifetime. The nature of these arrangements and the associated contracts is the main focus of this book. A remarkable feature is the number of cases in which these contracts turn out to be renegotiated. This is surprising because we know from the corporate finance literature that renegotiations are costly, and we know from the sovereign debt literature that while restructurings do occur, they are not normal occurrences but rare exceptions.[1] However, in natural resources, the phenomenon is more pervasive. There are, of course, reasons why renegotiations occur in natural resource contracts. While foreign direct investment (FDI) occurs in many industries, extractive industries are vulnerable to government theft (to use the terminology that Michael Tomz and Mark L. J. Wright introduce in chapter 3 of this book) because of the timing and nature of investments and payoffs. Typically, many years separate the first capital investment in a project from the first production of a resource, and most investment takes place before any revenue flows. Typically the MNC shoulders the costs for investments. The investment is sunk because it is specific to each field or mine. Most of the capital used for one project cannot easily be shifted to another one, nor can it be used for other purposes than for resource recovery. Furthermore, it can be argued that, once the investment is made, there will be little distortion with respect to the production possibilities if firms are expropriated or taxed more heavily. All this exposes the projects to mounting populist pressures to capture more of the revenue stream ex post than as provided under the ex ante arrangements, particularly when commodity prices go up, making the properties or concessions in the hands of MNC more valuable. In more technical terms, we would say that natural resource extraction contracts are subject to time-inconsistency problems. A contract is set up that seems to work, but as conditions evolve the interests of the parties change and the HC seems more inclined to expropriate for an immediate gain. But, of course, this outcome is anticipated, and this means that the initial contract should already have taken into account that this will happen. Here is where the natural resource trap that we refer to in the title of this book develops. Because MNCs anticipate expropriation, they will offer a contract that compensates them for the risk. But this forces the HC to expropriate; if they do not firms will be rewarded with a windfall gain that may be politically intolerable. It is a double trap, because lack of credibility not only creates a contract that in itself is more vulnerable, but also because it forces even those governments that would prefer to operate in a stable and law-abiding context to fall in the vicious cycle with the rest. In natural resource contracts, the difficulties are compounded by the fact that prices move widely, so that contracts need to deal not only with the lack of credibility but with large and sometimes unexpected revenue swings. This may lead to a cycle of nationalizations and privatizations. At times of high prices HCs are tempted to expropriate. But at times of depressed prices, once HCs experience the costs of running less profitable undertakings, they invite multinationals back on terms favorable to the companies. Then the cycle starts again, with similar costs to both parties as before.[2]

In the short run, the immediate costs of expropriation land in an obvious way on the party expropriated. However, over a longer perspective with rational investors, the costs would be borne by the HCs. There is a direct analogy to the tragedy of the commons in that each expropriation appears beneficial to the particular HC, but the collective effect of the expropriations would be to lower the ex ante returns and thereby lower the investments by MNCs or increase the privileges granted by HCs for their participation, resulting in lower overall resource rents for the HCs. This appears to be the experience over a long period in the parallel case of default on sovereign debt. On average the default costs have been borne by the borrowing countries, not the lenders (Sturzenegger and Zettelmeyer 2006).

Even while aware of these factors and that conditions in natural resource markets change suddenly and significantly, it is surprising that the HC and MNC would not craft contracts that better preserve the interest of intervening parties and avoid the recurrent renegotiations. In the case of natural resources this is particularly puzzling for two reasons. First, it seems that, because of the high rents, one does not need to rely on a high-powered incentive scheme that might be criticized as too favorable to the MNC. Second, one of the main sources of uncertainty is the price of the resource. But the prices of most energy commodities are perfectly observable, traded in liquid markets, and at least partly hedgeable. It seems that this uncertainty is easily quantifiable so that "transactions costs" cannot be an explanation for the lack of completeness of the contract. In short, we see a conceptual puzzle as to why contracts are so incomplete and the outcomes plagued by so much renegotiation.[3]

In the early twenty-first century, the upswing in commodity prices led to a wave of new renegotiations and expropriations, many of which have been in the news.[4] Tables 1.1 and 1.2 show countries and industries involved in acts of expropriation in 2007. Petroleum has been a particularly common target for takeovers: Venezuela again took steps to nationalize its oil industry, and the Russian government took control over Yukos, the largest nonstate oil firm. In 2006, Bolivia began to nationalize oil and gas, and Ecuador also took over the operations of a foreign oil firm by canceling its contract. More moderately, Argentina increased taxes on oil and mining fields, in spite of tax guarantees that precluded doing so. Expropriation has also been a concern for mining projects: it seems to have taken place in Uzbekistan, and firms have brought arbitration cases against Kyrgyzstan and Azerbaijan over this issue.

Furthermore, developing countries are not the only ones considering the taking of natural resources. Canadians favored nationalizing their country's petroleum resources in a 2005 poll (Wyatt 2005), and Alberta unilaterally changed royalties on oil and gas production. The United Kingdom has repeatedly changed the rules on oil exploitation in the North Sea, increasing tax pressure when prices increased (as described Dieter Helm, chapter 9, this volume). Even in the United States, a developed country with strong democratic institutions, there were changes in contractual terms when much more oil than expected was discovered in Prudhoe Bay (Mead 1994), and talks of increasing royalties for fields in the Gulf of Mexico, which had been awarded under favorable terms when oil prices fell below $20 a barrel, also resurfaced when oil prices increased above $50. Several cases of expropriation

Table 1.1
Active cases of direct expropriations in 2007

Country	Industry	Status	Updated*	MNC(s) involved	Action(s) taken
Russia	Gas	In progress	12/27/07	ExxonMobil, Royal Dutch Shell, and others	Took over Sakhalin-2 project, criticized foreign participation in Sakhalin-1
Ecuador	Oil	Confirmed	12/13/07	Occidental Petroleum	Seized Occidental assets
Kyrgyzstan	Mining	Confirmed	3/12/07	Oxus	Continuing dispute over revoked license in Jeeroy gold mine
Congo	Mining	Planned	11/3/07	Various	Seeks contract cancellations and renegotiations
Venezuela	Oil	In progress	11/1/07	ConocoPhillips, ExxonMobil, and others	Nationalizing industry
Uzbekistan	Mining	Confirmed	10/24/07	Metal-Tech, Oxus, and others	Declared joint venture on molybdenum project bankrupt; challenged other projects in court for back taxes
Algeria	Gas	Confirmed	9/5/07	Repsol and Gas Natural	Canceled contract and seeks reparations, alleging delays and cost overruns
Bolivia	Mining	Confirmed	9/12/07	Glencore	Nationalized Glencore's tin smelter
Russia	Oil	Confirmed	5/28/07	Yukos	Seized assets after alleging bankruptcy, auctioned off assets
Bolivia	Oil and gas	In progress	5/11/07	Petrobras and others	Nationalizing industry
Zimbabwe	Mining	Confirmed	1/30/07	African Consolidated Resources	Revoked claim on diamond mine from British firm, gave it to state firm

* "Updated" refers to the date of the last report on the story by Reuters in 2007.
Source: Reuters News search with Factiva. An "active" case is an industry in a country covered by Reuters in 2007, even if it began earlier (e.g., Ecuador and Venezuela's oil industries).

Table 1.2
Active cases of indirect expropriations in 2007

Country	Industry	Status	Updated*	MNC(s) involved	Action(s) taken
Kazakhstan	Oil	In progress	12/25/07	Eni, Royal Dutch Shell, ExxonMobil, and others	Seeks cash payment and larger ownership share
Ecuador	Oil	Confirmed	12/13/07	Repsol, Andes Petroleum	Raised profit tax on other firms
Libya	Oil	Confirmed	12/10/07	Petro-Canada	Increased production share
Ivory Coast	Oil and gas	Planned	12/7/07	Various	Seeks renegotiation
Kyrgyzstan	Mining	Confirmed	11/30/07	Centerra Gold	Assumed greater share of Kumtor gold mine
Congo	Mining	Planned	11/3/07	Various	Seeks contract cancellations and renegotiations
Alberta	Oil	Confirmed	10/26/07	Various	Increased revenue share
Argentina	Oil	In progress	9/6/07	Shell Argentina	Prevented exportation, shut down refinery because of pollution concerns
Bolivia	Mining	Planned	7/25/07	Various	Plans to raise taxes on profits
Algeria	Oil	Confirmed	3/21/07	Various	Enacted oil windfall tax
Mongolia	Mining	Confirmed	3/6/07	Various	Raise taxes on projects, state can buy into deposits

*"Updated" refers to the date of the last report on the story by Reuters in 2007.
Source: Reuters News search with Factiva. Some countries are involved in both direct and indirect expropriations in the same industry, often targeting different firms.

are discussed in more depth in this book (Dieter Helm discusses the United Kingdom in chapter 9; Fernando Navajas, Bolivia in chapter 10; Nicolás Gadano, Argentina in chapter 11; and Osmel Manzano and Francisco Monaldi, Venezuela in chapter 12).

Of course, expropriations in extractive industries are not a new phenomenon. The "direct" or "total" kind, in which the MNC is forced to surrender control of an enterprise to the government, dates back at least as far back as Bolivia's 1937 takeover of Standard Oil's properties (Geiger 1989), among developing countries. Later in the century, data compiled by Minor (1994) indicates that expropriations of this type were especially common in the 1960s and 1970s but had declined in frequency to zero by the mid-1980s. However, total expropriations have seen a comeback, as evidenced by the examples listed in table 1.1. Figure 1.1, taken from chapter 3 of this book, makes these points by showing data for expropriations over the century (both in total numbers and as a share of countries in the sample with external liabilities).

Less dramatic actions, such as increased taxation and more stringent regulations targeted against a foreign firm, have been termed "indirect" or "creeping" expropriation. Table 1.2 points out some recent cases (those recorded for 2007), including cases in which the government assumes a larger share of a project, that can also be included in this category. These changes can be initiated not only through forced renegotiation, but also through legislation that affects an entire industry. Unlike total expropriation, creeping expropriation does not involve seizure of physical property and allows continued MNC participation. However, expropriation is a valid term for both types of actions because they both result in a reduction of MNC profitability unanticipated at the signing of the contract.

Takings of the indirect type are not included in Minor's data set, nor do statistics appear to have been compiled by any other researchers. While the cases in table 1.2 appear fairly uncontroversial, counting such incidents is challenging because it is often unclear what constitutes an expropriation. A policy change that makes a field or mine less profitable to the MNC may be an intentional attempt by the HC to obtain more resource rents, but the tax increases could also be motivated by a legitimate public interest such as environmental protection. Guidelines for making this distinction in international law exist, but are still in the process of being made consistent (Reinisch 2006). And, since indirect expropriations are more difficult to detect than direct ones, the former type is probably more prevalent in reality.

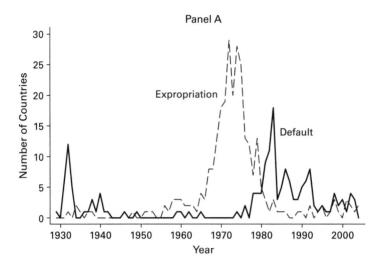

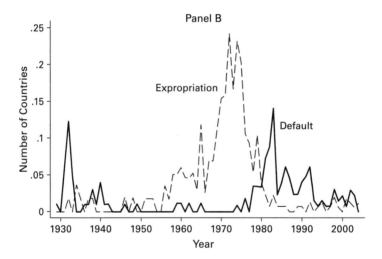

Figure 1.1
"Sovereign theft" since 1930. Panel A lists the absolute number of countries with sovereign theft, while panel B expresses these instances in terms of the proportion of countries with the potential for sovereign theft.
Source: Figure 3.16, this volume

Just as expropriations have a significant history, scholarship on expropriations also dates back decades. Raymond Vernon's (1971) influential work on MNC-HC relationships, *Sovereignty at Bay*, described the MNC-HC contract as an "obsolescing bargain." Among the reasons he identified that these bargains obsolesce and lead to expropriation are the following: (1) uncertainty about the viability of a mine or field is forgotten when a project turns out to be profitable (see Schwartz and Trolle, chapter 8, this volume), (2) the country and its government budget become increasingly dependent on resource revenues, (3) expropriation allows politicians to make statements of independence from foreign influence, and (4) MNCs often lose market control or their technological advantage over time, making the host country less dependent on the foreign firm (pp. 46–59). While Vernon did not fully realize that these issues had to be taken into consideration from the outset, the identification of factors seems to suggest that even if taken into account, the resulting contract was not shielded from political pressures—in other words, that the time-inconsistency problem has always been present.

Since Vernon's work, much has been written to understand MNC-HC contracts and to seek solutions to expropriation and renegotiation issues. Several strands of literature can be identified. First, there is a literature that describes the various possibilities for contracts in terms of how they divide revenues and profits between the two parties. Changing the method of allotment agreed to in a contract affects the MNC's incentive to invest, the profitability of the project, as well as the level of populist pressure.

Vernon's obsolescing bargain has also been the subject of formal work in the context of contract theory. Models in this area, the second strand of literature we will review, have focused on the issue of time inconsistency (also referred to as the holdup problem) and assume that neither party can credibly commit to take less than the maximum that is available to it at any time. Thus, the only possible contracts are self-enforcing contracts. A closely related literature is on sovereign debt, which considers why investments known to be subject to default risk occur in the first place.

Another literature emphasizes inflexibility in contracts as the main problem. Rather than devising a contract that does not need to be changed over its lifetime, research in this area asks how contracts can allow for change without leaving either party at an undue disadvantage. In this area, one focus is on renegotiation clauses, which allow for contract revisions and also structure the way these changes are decided. Another focus is on MNC-HC informal relationships outside the written contract, dealing with "governance" models. This literature implicitly assumes that contracts are partially enforceable as a last resort by arbitration, to which unresolved disputes are to be directed.

Finally, there is a line of research that goes beyond the relationship between a developing country and foreign firms to consider how one of the parties can improve its financial standing separately from the contract. On the firm side, we discuss analyses that incorporate political risk into firm models, as well as the use of local partners and political-risk insurance. Host countries can also independently shield their payoffs in two main ways. First, they can potentially improve the selection of MNCs through competitive bidding. Second, countries can reduce the macroeconomic impact of fluctuating resource rents with stabilization funds and by hedging against future commodity prices.

The remainder of this chapter summarizes these four strands of literature, introducing the following chapters where appropriate, and concludes with a preview of the country cases in this book.

1.1   Contractual Allocation of Benefits, Costs, and Risks

Knowing when and how money is apportioned to the HC and MNC according to the terms of different kinds of contracts currently in use provides a realistic starting point from which to consider alternative schemes. A significant literature has been devoted to improving this allocative feature of contract designs, but most of it seems to have focused on maximizing profit or government take without considering the risk of expropriation. This section begins by describing current contract designs and their perceived flaws in terms of underinvestment, followed by alternative designs that attempt to correct for this distortion. Some of the proposed alternative contract designs prove difficult to apply in developing countries with credit constraints and risk of expropriation. Thus, the section concludes by discussing Eduardo Engel and Ronald Fischer's solution to this issue via an alternative design (see chapter 5, this volume).

Up to the middle of the twentieth century, natural resource contracts tended to be quite similar. (See Vernon 1971 for a history of MNC-HC contracts, and see Bindemann 1999 for a more updated history of petroleum contracts.) The foreign firm would own the land and any resulting production, of which the government would collect only royalties and tax revenue. Some governments, like that of Mexico under Porfirio Díaz, even allowed tax exemptions to increase production for domestic consumption (Haber, Maurer, and Razo 2003). (Similarly favorable conditions for investors also obtained in the period between 1909 and 1943 in Venezuela, described by Manzano and Monaldi, chapter 12, this volume). In recent decades, new types of agreements have been negotiated, particularly production-sharing agreements (PSAs), whose terms have become ever more diverse (Bindemann 2000). Research describing the ways governments can extract rent from natural resource projects reveals that there are more ways to do so than can be listed here (Baunsgaard 2001; Sunley, Baunsgaard, and Simard 2003). However, a few of the more common ways can be summarized. In addition to the two types of contracts mentioned above, there are also pure service contracts and joint ventures. Figure 1.2 shows a typology from Johnston 2003, which provides a more detailed treatment of this topic.

In royalty/tax (R/T) systems, the MNC develops a tract at its own risk (maybe after auctioning for a certain amount of investment commitments or money). If a field is productive, the government takes some initial percentage of each period's production, the royalty. On top of this royalty, the government levies a tax on the remaining revenues, after allowable deductions. Typically this consists of the standard corporate tax rate in the country and may include a special tax rate on natural resources. Since the tax rate is usually constant, the government ends up receiving a lower overall share of profits as a project becomes more profitable. As a result, the R/T system is a regressive method of extracting rent. Other taxes paid by producers include payments to the owners of the land (typically companies do not operate in land they own) and, in some cases, export taxes.

While some countries still use R/T systems, most other countries in recent decades have opted for contractual-based systems, which come in two forms: production-sharing contracts (or agreements), under which payment is in production, and service agreements, under which payment is in cash. The first PSA was signed in 1966 by Indonesia. In a PSA, the MNC assumes all the cost of exploring for developing a resource tract, and then the MNC and HC share production in up to four ways. First, the government sometimes, though not always, takes some percentage of production as a royalty. Second, the firm is allotted up to some maximum percentage of production to recover its cost. Third, the remaining production is considered profit and is split

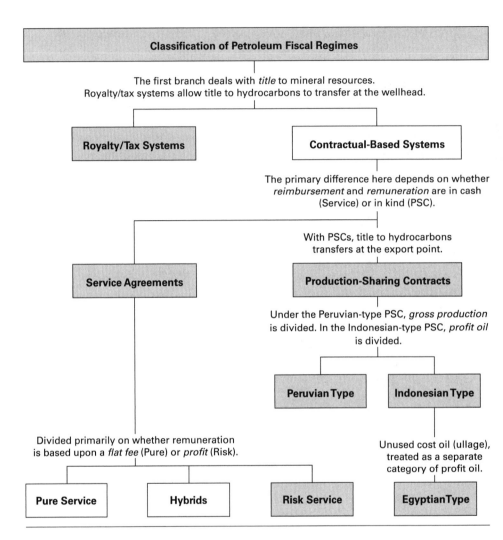

Figure 1.2
Typology of petroleum fiscal regimes
Source: Reproduced from Johnston 2003, 10

between the two parties, at a ratio that may increase in favor of the government as total production increases (i.e., a sliding scale). Finally, the firm pays income tax as it would in an R/T system on its share from the third step. PSAs now come in a variety of categories. There is a Peruvian type, in which gross production is divided between the HC and MNC, and an Indonesian type, in which profit oil is divided. Egyptian-type PSAs, a subset of Indonesian-type PSAs, treat unused cost oil as a separate category of profit oil in dividing proceeds.

Compared to the R/T system, the PSA has the potential to be progressive if it has a sliding scale, although a PSA with a royalty also contains a regressive element. Regressivity can also occur when the cost-recovery limit binds (and is less than 100 percent); for these low profit levels, the PSA is taking a constant percentage of something more than just profits.[5] If the MNC retains a constant percentage of profit oil, the cost-recovery limit is 100 percent, and there is no royalty, the PSA functions like an income tax, which still distorts if there is no compensation to the MNC for an unprofitable project. Because actual costs are difficult to measure, distortions also arise whenever what the PSA counts as production for cost recovery differs from the true cost of production. Since the specific percentages and collection methods for each step vary widely among PSAs, it is difficult to characterize them as generally progressive or regressive.

Johnston (2003) mentions three other possibilities in the category of service agreements. The first is a pure service contract, under which the HC pays the MNC a flat fee for exploring and developing a tract, regardless of the resulting production. Here, the HC assumes all risk and reward. These contracts are fairly uncommon, though. A more popular alternative, particularly when handing over an existing oil field, is a risk service contract, in which the MNC produces for the government, and the government promises a price for each unit of production. (Thus, a risk service contract is similar to a PSA in that it recovers its costs based on production, except that a risk service contract pays in cash.) Here, risks are more evenly distributed, but, to the extent that the government commits to a given price, it takes on itself the whole risk of price fluctuations (assuming it has not hedged this risk away, which is the standard situation). To reduce this risk, the payment is typically related to the international price of oil. With a constant discount on international prices, this contract becomes similar to a standard royalty. Also, hybrids between pure service and risk service contracts are possible.

Finally, the government can implicitly extract rent through joint ownership of a project with the foreign firm. In theory, such a system should be neutral with respect to profits, but it could be effectively progressive or regressive depending on the specific terms. In these joint ventures, the HC typically only assumes partial ownership when there is a discovery; meanwhile, the firm bears all exploration costs and risks.

Because MNCs typically have better technical knowledge than HCs about exploiting natural resources, a moral-hazard problem arises from the difficulty that HCs have in verifying that MNCs are developing a field in a way that maximizes government take. Economists have been concerned that nonneutral contracts cause distortions and underinvestment that reduce profitability. Royalties, in particular (Leland 1978), tend to depress production over the lifetime of the project (Baunsgaard 2001). Also, because they are charged on the full price of production and not only on profits, they distort an extra margin relative to income taxes.[6] Manzano (2006), using a Hotelling framework, shows that royalties affect more strongly the production of higher-productivity fields. Of course, more progressive PSAs also cause underinvestment as firms receive a decreasing percentage of marginal profits as profits increase (see Blake and Roberts 2006).

Under a pure service contract, the foreign firm receives the same amount regardless of how productive a tract is and thus has little incentive to invest optimally for the government's benefit. The firm has more incentive when it receives a per-unit price for production that varies with the world price of the resource. Finally, if, in a joint venture, a MNC bears all exploration costs in an unprofitable project but earns only some of the profit in a lucrative project after the government assumes an ownership share, the firm will be inclined to underinvest.

To mitigate underinvestment, three types of neutral taxation have been conceived as alternatives to current contract designs: a resource rent tax (RRT), a Brown tax, and a pure auction (Sunnevåg 2000). These systems are neutral in the sense that, over the life of the project, the MNC receives the same percentage of net profit regardless of the level of net profit. Because a constant percentage of net profit is transferred to the HC, the MNC has no reason to invest more or less than it would without taxes, and thus joint profits for the project are maximized. One might suppose that, by maximizing the profit to be shared, these fiscal systems minimize the incentive for expropriation. In practice, however, they are unlikely to solve the expropriation problem for two reasons. The first two systems have features that are infeasible for developing countries, and all three are subject to ex post populist pressure, which has continued to result in government takings.

First, some PSAs are already formulated as an RRT. With the RRT early losses are carried over with discounting until revenues accrue to offset the loss (Sunnevåg 2000). Then some percentage tax is applied to the remaining revenues. The government gains nothing unless a project is successful, and even then it gains revenue only toward the end of its lifetime. A delayed revenue stream hinders the growth of a credit-constrained developing country. Politically, citizens may not appreciate that the government has no cash flow while the first production occurs. The government also assumes the information challenge of choosing the interest rate on which the tax is calculated to match the true discount rate. While choosing a rate too low disincentivizes investment, a rate too high denies the government a source of needed revenue and can also add to populist pressure. Similar problems can be identified with the so-called R-factor tax, under which taxes are applied to additional revenue when the ratio of cumulative revenue to cumulative expenses exceeds one. (If the tax rate changes with the R-factor, neutrality is also lost.)

Second, a so-called Brown tax takes a constant percentage of positive or negative cash flows in each period and is tantamount to making the government a partner in the prospect (Brown 1948). The scheme is virtually distortion free, but has the drawback that under the Brown tax, the government partially reimburses the firm during the first years when the firm incurs investment costs (Blake and Roberts 2006) and may pay out in the case of unsuccessful ventures. Very few countries use Brown taxes, although Norway comes close in its Petroleum Taxation Law. Developing countries find it difficult to apply this tax. Financially, many countries cannot afford to reimburse early expenses incurred in a project. Also, firms have an incentive to inflate costs, making it difficult to collect rent or to justify the payments early on. Politically, it is doubtful whether government cash flows to foreign firms would be well received, particularly when domestic firms in nonextractive industries do not receive this benefit. That government loses money on unprofitable projects under this cash flow tax only exacerbates political tensions.

The problems associated with late streams of government revenue from resource rent and Brown taxes could be mitigated if developing countries' credit constraints were relaxed, at least for natural resource development purposes. However, these countries would still have to deal with revenue losses from unprofitable projects. While some might contend that these difficulties are mitigated by averaging gains over losses (see Osmundsen 1999), there are two reasons to doubt this argument. First, the averaging effect may not matter from a populist standpoint, because citizens pay attention only to the profitable projects. Furthermore, the averaging effect may not even exist. Small countries, in particular, may not be able to subdivide their oil, gas, or mineral reserves into many parcels (Baunsgaard 2001), and the geological information they have may be particularly uncertain (Blitzer, Lessard, and Paddock 1984). Populist pressure in the HC would be especially salient when firms argue they have reasonable overall profitability because they did poorly in another country. Thus, in different ways, these methods of neutral taxation probably pose too much risk for MNCs while also depressing interest in the fields.

The final type of neutral contract would entail not taxing production at all in the traditional sense but relying entirely on auction payments as the "tax" revenue in what is called bonus bidding. This procedure has been recommended for oil and gas leases in the United States (Mead 1994) because, again, it leads to no distortions. This system is the inverse of a pure service contract, in which the government pays the firm and reaps all revenues. Financially, it may be attractive for developing countries since it guarantees positive and immediate cash flows, provided that there are bids. Also, after the auction is concluded, the government has no revenue risk, since it knows how much it is receiving. At first glance, this type of contract seems ideal for credit-constrained, risk-averse host countries.

However, this scheme presents risks during the auctioning process from two sources. First, there is significant ex post political risk in that governments may be pressured by citizens or their representatives to raise taxes on an especially profitable project despite prior commitments to the contrary.[7] Mead (1994) notes the importance and challenge of making the terms of an auction absolutely final. If they are not final or are perceived not to be final, firms anticipate the political pressures; then their anticipation depresses the price and increases, in turn, the likelihood of expropriation. To rely solely on auction revenue thus seems extremely difficult. A government must resist the temptation to extract more revenue as the resource is produced, and the firm also faces the threat that a future government will not respect contracts of the previous government.

More recently, contracts have attempted to match production to government cash flow, but they have also been insufficient to prevent expropriation. These characteristics can be seen in royalty/tax (R/T) systems. In chapter 7 of this book, Roberto Rigobon observes that royalties provide a fairly steady income stream, much more than that arising from income taxes. Thus, countries with little access to other mechanisms for smoothing income will be strongly inclined to use royalties. For Rigobon this provides a paradox, because royalties also increase the probability of expropriations if commodity prices increase. He models a potential vicious cycle in which increases in prices increase the probability of expropriation to the point that makes the fields less attractive to the private firm in a sort of "Laffer curve" effect. Fernando Navajas, in his description of Bolivia in chapter 10, discusses, on the contrary, a problem with income taxes. In a context of high levels of initial investments, taxable income remained low for several years during which counterreform pressures built up.

These problems have drawn attention to and support for PSAs. Many small countries have uncertain levels of reserves, which make them rightfully risk averse (Baunsgaard 2001). The PSA shifts some of this risk from the HC to the MNC, which can better adjust for risk with investments in many countries and is therefore arguably closer to risk neutral. (Compare Leland 1978; Blitzer, Lessard, and Paddock 1984; Mead 1994; and Osmundsen 1999.) As a result, this type of contract may allow a government to reap revenue from its resources even though they have been produced at a loss overall. The lessee accepts the loss but offsets it with gains in other countries.

In theory, PSAs are inefficient contracts, in the sense that they distort investment decisions quite significantly (Blitzer, Lessard, and Paddock 1984; Bindemann 1999; Pongsiri 2004). But the attractiveness of PSAs lies in the sharing of risks. These countries face a trade-off between reducing risk and incentivizing investment. No single solution exists for every country; instead, the right type of taxation needs to account for country-specific financial situations, geological uncertainties, and political risks. That solutions should be adapted to each country has been readily admitted (Sunley, Baunsgaard, and Simard 2003). However, the extent to which populist pressures may be high under the more efficient schemes explains why some form of PSA is probably the best for many host countries, and why we see it so often.

But cases of expropriation due to populist pressure appear even among PSAs. Paradoxically, high taxes or a sliding scale may also increase the risk of expropriation if underinvesting by the MNC becomes an issue. The government may be tempted to undertake investment itself or find another firm that agrees to invest more heavily. For example, the government of Kyrgyzstan alleged underinvestment when it denied Oxus its license to mine gold (Bell 2006). This type of vicious cycle is akin to the one emphasized by Rigobon in chapter 7. Thus, the reality of expropriations under current contracts and the probability of these incidents under other contract designs that have been considered point to the need for a clearer solution.

One potential solution may be found in chapter 5 by Engel and Fischer. They consider the optimal contract when there is a risk of expropriation as the profitability of a tract increases. They observe that, when losses in a project are possible, expropriations cannot be eliminated entirely. However, the government maximizes its take and minimizes the chance of expropriation with a contract consisting of an auction that is complemented by windfall taxes. The two components combined do not amount to neutrality with respect to profits, but they do keep the returns to the firm at a level that reduces the occurrence of expropriation and renegotiation.

1.2   Unenforceable Contracts

The frequent occurrence of expropriations and forced renegotiations in natural resource projects indicates that the contracts have largely been unenforceable in any practical sense. In a bilateral contract, the party that incurs costs for investment is commonly vulnerable to opportunistic behavior by the other party in what is known as the time-inconsistency or holdup problem. A significant body of research has considered how contracts can be designed to be self-enforcing and thereby avoid holdup issues. However, adapting these solutions to the unique investment characteristics of natural resource contracts is challenging. Typically, extralegal forms of punishment explain when and why investment occurs despite the risk of expropriation, but before discussing these solutions, this section begins by detailing how these MNC-HC relationships present holdup problems.[8]

One feature that distinguishes these relationships from other business deals is that a sovereign party and a private party are involved, as opposed to two private parties. Adelman (1970) notes the significance of the government as a party. If the firm were in a contract with a private landlord in the same country, the government could enforce the revenue-sharing arrangement agreed to ex ante in the contract and prevent expropriation. However, no such enforceability exists when a sovereign government is one of the parties. Because governments are inherently responsive to contemporaneous pressures of politics, they find it very difficult to credibly commit to abstain from acts that improve their future state (Rodrik and Zeckhauser 1988).

A substitute for the lack of a binding legal framework is the alternative of international arbitration. But opinions vary as to the effectiveness of arbitration provisions commonly found in contracts. According to some accounts, some governments seem deliberately to ignore arbitration awards (Jensen 2006), or they accept arbitration in principle but need to make changes in their legal system to make it fully operational (Brunet and Lentini 2007). Others find that arbitration can often be "too" effective, in the sense that courts' decisions may favor corporate interests (Wells 2005). Even if arbitration becomes sufficiently enforceable and unbiased, the long delays and administrative costs it entails would still make preventing expropriation more attractive than correcting for it after it has occurred.

The difficult MNC-HC relationship, in which sunk costs incurred by the MNC are followed by potential opportunism by the HC, can thus be understood as an example of the time-inconsistency or holdup problem in contract and game theory. It is a problem in which the property of renegotiation proofness does not apply because countries cannot credibly commit not to expropriate if a project becomes more profitable. The holdup problem has been studied extensively, but mostly in situations in which the two parties are in the same legal system. (See Bolton and Dewatripont 2005 for an overview.) The typical holdup problem involves a contract that is incomplete because a relationship-specific investment is not contractable. (In the literature, typically at least some aspect is enforceable by an outside authority.) In our case, with no real binding authority for sovereign countries, expropriations and renegotiations need to reflect contracts that are unenforceable in their entirety, even if the details are verifiable as well as observable. Thus, the role played by a sovereign party in the contract leads to an extreme version of holdup.

The lack of an enforceable legal system renders a larger number of solutions to the holdup problem inapplicable to natural resource FDI. For example, in one solution, the seller (equivalent to the MNC) has the option to deliver some good or not to do so and makes the payment of the buyer (equivalent to the HC) dependent on the seller's decision (Nöldeke and Schmidt 1995). However, this solution assumes that a court can enforce the buyer's payment based on the option (Nöldeke and Schmidt 1995), which is not the case for an HC buyer. Other solutions that require a higher legal authority include vertical integration and allocation of property rights. (See Che and Sákovics 2004 for a summary of various solutions.) Because one of the parties is the legal authority, these options are not possible.

Then there are solutions that require no outside enforcement but that assume an investment problem with characteristics that may differ from those in resource projects. One approach suggests that the buyer initially sell the project to the seller while retaining the option to repurchase it later at a preagreed price (Nöldeke and Schmidt 1998). Another solution (Guriev and Kvasov 2005), using a sequence of fixed-term contracts, or termination with advance notice, requires zero negotiation costs, though this may be unrealistic for ventures of this scale. A similar problem occurs in a model with gradual investments and gradual payments until the good is produced (Pitchford and Snyder 2004); to analogize, the HC would have to pay the MNC for initial investment, which, in many cases, is precluded by its credit constraint.

Thus, the inapplicability of general solutions to holdup problems in this context and the incompleteness of solutions for FDI-specific holdup suggest the need for more work that directly addresses this issue in natural resource contracts. In the next chapter, Philippe Aghion and Lucía Quesada provide an analysis that combines the holdup problem of sunk investments with other challenges for these contracts mentioned earlier—the allocation of risks between the two parties, the moral-hazard problems associated with asymmetric information, and the lack of enforcement because one of the parties is a sovereign government. They also incorporate ex post grievances produced by changes in preferences when conditions change. According to Aghion and Quesada it is this complex combination of features that makes contracts in natural resources so difficult to write and thus eventually so fragile.

Still a puzzle remains: if holdup is so difficult to avoid and expropriation and forced renegotiation are so likely, why do foreign firms invest so heavily in developing countries' resource reserves? Some answers may possibly lie in the sovereign debt literature that has dealt with a similar set of issues: how to support a contract in which one party is a sovereign and thus not subject to the scrutiny of a common legal system. Like the contracts mentioned above between two private parties, debt contracts in the corporate world are enforced by the courts. A corporation cannot simply repudiate—that is, decide not to repay. If it tried, it would be sued and courts would force it to hand over assets to the creditor, restructure, or (in the limit) shut it down and liquidate its remaining assets. As in MNC-HC contracts, this enforcement mechanism is lacking in sovereign debt. Thus, there is an analogous question of why private creditors are willing to lend to sovereigns in the first place.

In general, the solution may lie in punishments that are neither enforced by a legal system nor limited to just the two parties involved. The sovereign debt literature, however, has considered methods of punishment that extend beyond the sphere of a single contract to explain the continuation of private lending. A short summary follows with analogies to natural resource contracts where applicable.

An influential contribution by Eaton and Gersovitz (1981) asked whether there would be a sovereign debt market (investment) if creditors (MNCs) had no direct control over debtors (HCs) whatsoever, and their only means of retaliating in the event of default (expropriation) would be through the denial of future credit (investments). The analogy in our case would be whether, in response to expropriation, no further investments by MNCs as a whole would be sufficient to induce HCs to respect contracts. Eaton and Gersovitz showed that under some assumptions, the answer is yes. If debtors have no way of insuring against output shocks (in our case HCs have no other way of producing the resources) other than through borrowing, and default triggers permanent exclusion from credit markets, then the threat of losing access to credit markets is a sufficient reason for repaying, up to a certain maximum level. This level is higher, the bigger the variance of output, and the more the borrowing country values the insurance function of international capital markets for given fluctuations in output.

A similar setup in the context of FDI is a model that produces a contract not subject to renegotiation only if the promise for future investment is sufficiently strong (Thomas and Worrall 1994). In each period, investment by the MNC precedes a return divided between the HC and MNC. Similarly to the Eaton and Gersovitz assumption, it is assumed that the MNC can punish the HC by not investing in future projects (i.e., that the HC has no other way of financing the investment). The model applies to extractive industries only if time periods are represented by different projects over the very long run, each with the initial sunk investment. Similarly, Schnitzer (1999) assumes that the MNC has a large sunk cost at the start of the project and that it has investments outside the particular HC. This outside option allows the MNC to punish the HC by shifting investments outside the HC if it expropriates. Here technology spillovers from the MNC to the HC increase the set of feasible investment levels, as do stochastic returns in the outside option. However, this set may be empty, which means that making investment without expropriation is sometimes unachievable. Also, while this model usefully identifies some determinants of expropriation risk, it is difficult to conceive of policy changes that would mitigate this risk. Technology spillovers appear not to be a choice variable. Moreover, since the outside option is itself in another host country, how one would reduce expropriation risk in all countries is an unresolved question.

Though highly influential, Eaton and Gersovitz's result was quickly criticized because the assumption that a default could be punished through permanent exclusion from future credit seemed unrealistic. The problem is that in such a situation both parties—creditors and debtors—are generally worse off than in a situation in which lending (investment) resumes or is resumed by new parties. In technical parlance, a lending equilibrium sustained by the threat of a permanent embargo on future lending is not "renegotiation-proof," in the sense that after a default both parties potentially benefit from reaching a new agreement involving positive lending (investment). But if such renegotiation is anticipated, then this undermines the expected punishment that was sustaining positive lending in the first place (see Kletzer 1994 for details). These objections posed a powerful challenge to the notion that the threat of exclusion from credit markets, by itself, makes sovereign borrowing possible (in our context that MNC withdrawal will not be replaced by new FDI).

Broadly speaking, the literature evolved in three directions. A first group of papers, including Sachs and Cohen 1982, Bulow and Rogoff 1989a, and Fernandez and Rosenthal 1990, focused on direct punishments as the reason for repayment. Direct punishments are generally interpreted as interference with a country's current transactions—that is, trade and payments—either through seizure outside the country's borders or through the denial of trade credit. Recent examples include the use of trade sanctions and embargoes that purportedly cause damage to the country they are imposed on. Renegotiations are explicitly modeled in these papers. In Bulow and Rogoff 1989a, for example, contracts can be renegotiated at any time. The amount that a country can borrow is determined by the proportion of the debtor's output that creditors can expect to extract in this renegotiation. The fact that they can extract anything at all hinges critically on the assumption that inflicting a sanction not only harms the debtor, but also benefits the creditor directly (e.g., the creditor receives a share of the debtor country's trade payments). Thus, the threat that in the event of nonpayment the creditor will actually impose the sanction is credible. This would not be the case if imposing the sanction hurts both debtors and creditors. However, both in the context of sovereign debt (see Sturzenegger and Zettelmeyer 2006) and in our discussion on arbitration above, it seems that sanctions may play only a limited role. In particular, energy resources appear too precious to induce sanctions, witness the response of Europe to Russia's expropriation actions in the Sakhalin concession in 2007. In short, it appears it is not the threat of sanctions that explains why MNCs still engage in operations within the HC, though Wells (2005) and Wells and Ahmed (2007) find that arbitration and political-risk insurance agencies exact too much from host countries.[9]

A second line of research attempts to rescue the idea that governments repay because they are worried about the repercussions of a default in the credit market (i.e., worried about the prospects for future investment by MNCs). Most of these papers no longer rely on enforcement through the (implausible) threat of permanent exclusion from credit markets, and some explicitly address the renegotiation problem. One group of papers, including Cole and Kehoe 1995, Eaton 1996, and Kletzer and Wright 2000, assume that just like the debtor countries themselves, financial institutions may not be able to commit to future payments, at least not to countries that have defaulted (e.g., because past lenders could attempt to interfere with such payments as a way of enforcing their claims). In the jargon of this literature, the "one-sided commitment problem" assumed by the sovereign debt literature of the 1980s is replaced by a "two-sided commitment problem." This said, with multiple lenders, an equilibrium sustained by credit-market sanctions could still unravel if a new lender refuses to participate in the sanctions. In Kletzer and Wright's model, this is deterred by the original lender's offer to "pardon" the debtor (i.e., to let the debtor return to the original lending relationship) in exchange for defaulting on any new lender. As a result, potential new lenders "will respect the punishment of the borrower in equilibrium"—that is, a defaulter will not be able to find new positive surplus lending relationships. Most recently, Wright (2002) shows that sovereign debt can be sustained if countries can have lending relationships with more than one bank at a time—syndicated lending, which offers banks a profit relative to competitive lending—because this creates an incentive for lenders to collude in punishing default. Banks that defect by engaging in financial relationships with a defaulting country are punished by exclusion from future syndicated lending. These interpretations have a clear parallelism with MNC and FDI. To the extent that oil production is tackled by a consortium of large firms, and that these firms interact in a complex network of associations across countries, then it is likely that there are costs of committing investments to countries that have expropriated other firms, for the simple reason that these firms are likely to be your own partner in some other venture. Thus, the threat of exclusion appears somewhat more likely in the context of energy resources with large firms. (Also new players may come in, for example, the Chinese are moving to exploit natural resources in some unstable countries in Africa, while there is relatively little interest from MNCs.)

Amador (2003) considers a political motive to respect contracts. He poses a model in which governments undersave because they know that they may lose power, but at the same time wish to retain access to capital markets since they count on being returned to power eventually. This fits a situation in which several established parties alternate in power. This combination—a desire for insurance, combined with a chronic lack of cash that could be used to make a deposit or finance a cash-in-advance insurance contract—means that the threat of exclusion from future borrowing is sufficient to sustain sovereign lending.

A third strand of literature focuses on the reputation losses from default and expropriation. Eaton (1996) presents a finite-horizon model in which there is incomplete information about the borrower's type: "bad" types will strategically default if this is optimal, while "good" types will always try to repay. Borrowers cannot save or buy insurance. Lenders try to distinguish between the two types by observing the borrower's default history. If there is no uncertainty about the borrower's ability to pay, then observing a default identifies the borrower as a "bad" type. This leads to exclusion from credit markets. If there is extraneous uncertainty, default does not imply that a borrower is necessarily bad, but it increases the probability. This leads to higher interest rates. Either way, "bad" borrowers have an incentive to build a good credit history, at least at low levels of debt. The analogy with our case again is clear: a government may be inclined to expropriate, but to the extent that it needs to rely on MNCs down the road it will try to build a good reputation in the short run.

The reputation arguments can rely on the idea that a default could have much broader adverse effects on a lender's reputation than just through the lender's standing in credit markets. This was first raised as a possibility by Bulow and Rogoff (1989b) and is developed by Cole and Kehoe (1998). Like Eaton (1996), Cole and Kehoe assume that there are two types of debtor-country governments: "honest" governments that always repay, and "normal" governments. Suppose, however, that there is another relationship in which the government's partners (say, workers) also have incomplete information about the government's true type. Both workers and lenders make inferences about the government's true type from the way the government behaves in the other relationship as well as in their own. Default, vis-à-vis lenders, tarnishes the government's reputation with its workers. This provides a powerful new incentive to repay. This reputation story may be a plausible mechanism, because it could explain the why debt crises are typically associated with domestic contractions in the midst of capital flight and confidence losses. The intuition is that while the need to preserve a good reputation vis-à-vis the creditors may not be essential, it is essential for preserving a good reputation in other relationships. Think of a miser riding in a cab. If he is alone, he will not tip the driver. He does not care if this exposes him as a miser, since he does not depend on this particular cab driver for future rides. But if he is with his girlfriend, he will tip the driver in order to maintain a reputation of generosity vis-à-vis her.

In summary, the classic theory of sovereign debt suggests that incentives to repay sovereign debt might include credit-market incentives, worries about reductions in trade and legal harassment, and broader reputational concerns. The analogies to the case of natural resource contracts are straightforward, at least from a theoretical point of view. Tomz and Wright tackle this issue head on in chapter 3. In fact, they compare sovereign defaults and expropriations, two actions that they refer to as "sovereign theft." The interesting feature of Tomz and Wright's discussion is that they find that sovereign debt and expropriation waves do not occur at the same time. This is interesting because it discards some of the theories used to support sovereign debt. For example, if reputation is the issue, why did FDI continue in spite of sovereign debt defaults? Wouldn't expropriation or sovereign debt make either type of investment in the country infeasible? And so on. In fact, if reputation is important, Tomz and Wright's results suggest it is fairly fragmentary. A government can repudiate its debt but keep a good standing vis-à-vis its foreign investors and vice versa.

In any case, some type of implicit punishment does seem to explain the persistence of MNC-HC contracts in natural resource development in the face of expropriation risk. Duncan (2006a) confirms empirically that HCs incur significant costs after direct or indirect expropriation of natural resource projects. As noted at the beginning of this section, punishment among MNCs as a whole is an important deterrent. As Duncan argues, these costs may explain why expropriation is not more common than is currently observed.

1.3 Contract Complexity, Renegotiation Clauses, and Governance Models

One source of contract incompleteness arises because important aspects are observable but not verifiable by a court. Contracts can also be incomplete because the future possibilities are too complex to be knowable ex ante. For instance, many contingencies could occur while developing a new product (Bolton and Dewatripont 2005). The same can be said for oil, gas, or mineral contracts that begin at the point of exploration. Contingencies multiply due to uncertainties in geological viability, commodity prices, economic conditions, and political climate. Thus, it is extremely difficult, or at least very costly, to identify all the possible contingencies in a contract.

The previous two strands of literature focused on how contracts are set up, in some cases so that expropriation is less likely, as well as on understanding how the contracts could be self-enforcing. But other scholars have doubts that fixed contracts are the solution and propose allowing explicit contract terms to vary in a controlled way after they have initially been signed. Two types of solutions have been discussed: renegotiation clauses and a so-called governance model.

While two parties can always renegotiate a contract, the purpose of renegotiation clauses is to protect firms from expropriation. Firms invoke these clauses to ensure that, when changes in laws or regulations occur, they are left at least able to share in the changed financial circumstances. Parties are encouraged to discuss new terms for the contract by the threat of arbitration, which is riskier for both parties, if negotiations fail to reach a resolution. The literature in this area is not entirely in agreement about the necessity of renegotiation clauses and there is a debate regarding the relative utility of renegotiation clauses and stabilization clauses, which we will briefly review here. (Compare Berger 2003 and Al Qurashi 2005 to Coale 2002.)

Stabilization clauses seek to protect MNCs in the opposite way from renegotiation clauses. They essentially dictate that changes in laws that adversely affect the profitability of a project do not apply to it. While such clauses are still widely included in contracts, it is not clear whether they are or should be followed. In theory, stabilization clauses may not be respected by arbitration courts (Berger 2003; Al Qurashi 2005). (In that case they are included only by convention and do not have binding force.) Stabilization clauses produce a conflict between two competing principles of international law: sanctity of contracts should support stabilization clauses, but national sovereignty allows countries to freely change their laws.[10] In practice, these clauses have sometimes had an impact, but only after balancing the two principles (Coale 2002). Compared to the ambiguities surrounding stabilization clauses despite their stated function, any ambiguity surrounding the function of renegotiation clauses can at least be anticipated due to the definition of renegotiation.

From a normative standpoint, it is also problematic to weigh sanctity of contracts more heavily. Wells (2005) has argued that arbitration courts have been too willing to adhere to other terms of contracts because domestic courts would have been less strict about analogous contracts. Wells and Ahmed (2007) suggest that international arbitration law might imitate domestic law and modify contracts for reasons like "changed circumstances" rendering a contract irrelevant or economically inefficient, "unconscionable terms," failure to satisfy a "'just and reasonable' test," and "compulsion or corruption" (pp. 285–288). Interestingly, they perceive these measures as protecting governments from opportunistic firm behavior. Applying these criticisms of contract sanctity to stabilization clauses suggests that they do not account for contingencies that validly dictate some policy changes in the way renegotiation clauses do. However, determining when this may be the case remains controversial.

Renegotiation clauses prescribe a goal of mitigating HC policy changes while leaving the method of achieving this goal up to the two parties' discretion. These clauses also have the advantage of structuring renegotiations by conditioning them on so-called trigger events. The resulting renegotiations can then occur without breaking trust between the two parties (Atsegbua 1993). Despite these benefits, questions remain about the specific design and implementation of renegotiation clauses. Uncertainties exist as to which events should be allowed to trigger renegotiation, whether renegotiations must lead to resolution, what legal consequences follow failure to renegotiate, and whether renegotiation must take place before arbitration can occur (Berger 2003). Empirically, these uncertainties may explain why renegotiation clauses have not been used too frequently (Gotanda 2003). Two specific concerns are that trigger events under the control of one of the parties can be used to its advantage and that the arbitrator may not know how to adapt the terms of the contract (Gotanda 2003). Clearly, structuring uncertainty and conflict inherently complicates renegotiation clauses. What is not considered in such a critique, though, is the alternative: given the greater challenge of specifying all contingencies, organizing disagreements may be better than trying to avoid them.

A similar logic underlies the "governance model," described by Orr (2006). In this model, decision making is "incremental," possibly involves other stakeholders, and is "constrained within defined parameters" (Orr 2006). This model has been proposed in contradistinction to the "contractual model," for the MNC-HC contracts in infrastructure projects that have often been breached. Contracts are still a necessary part of interaction between foreign firms and developing countries, but now decision making outside the contract proper is to be more structured.

One application is a setting in which "relational governance" may complement "formal contracts" (Poppo and Zenger 2002). The former refers to "social processes that promote norms of flexibility, solidarity, and information exchange" (p. 710). Complementarities occur as formal contracts provide the foundation for informal relations and generate expectations for future cooperation, while relational governance allows more specific contracts as time passes (p. 713). Since Poppo and Zenger use questionnaire data to support their theory, specific details on structure seem lacking in their study. While their results might be adequate for business executives in the United States sharing a common corporate culture, application to MNC-HC relationships, which are cross-cultural, will be more difficult. Overall, the study suggests that models like the governance model are worth pursuing but does not indicate how they should be defined.

One example of broadly structuring conflict comes from a brief passage in an article by Wells and Gleason (1995), who cite the example of the Paiton power project in Indonesia. The agreement allows for different dispute mechanisms for various levels of dispute, including "mutual discussion" and "referral to expert," as well as "arbitration" (p. 55). Overall, the governance model holds promise but still needs development before becoming a useful or general solution. Unlike in infrastructure projects, the focus of Orr's work, the public value of natural resource contracts derives from the share of profits that goes to the government, rather than from any public good that is explicitly produced. Thus, it may be particularly difficult for a governance model or a public-private partnership to succeed in extractive industries.

Given the flexibility and informality of structures suggested by these solutions, societal beliefs regarding these contracts gain importance, especially in light of potential populist pressure. Rafael Di Tella, Juan Dubra, and Robert MacCulloch discuss this issue in chapter 4 of this book, using models in which beliefs are produced endogenously from the features of the economy. For example, volatility in an economy, which these authors believe applies to societies that rely primarily on a few commodities for production, generates a "morale" incompatible with the development of a work ethic, because most of the outcomes in such societies are the product of luck rather than of effort. Similarly, societies in which the wealth-creation process depends on the movements in commodity prices produce a sense of unfairness. Either way, natural resource–dependent societies are associated with lesser confidence in effort and capitalism and a larger demand for redistribution. The authors discuss a paradoxical interpretation: the business community may favor nationalization of the oil industry to reduce the arbitrariness of economic wealth, thus enhancing the support for capitalism in the rest of the economy. The role of beliefs adds an additional layer of complexity to the issue of natural resource contracts.

1.4 Nonstrategic Options for MNCs and HCs

The last category of solutions exists entirely outside the contract between a developing country and a foreign investor. Thus, they are not direct solutions to the problem but perhaps may be considered substitutes until the strategic interaction can be altered. We refer to actions in which the firm assumes the existence of expropriation risk and tries to adjust accordingly but does not attempt to reduce the risk. Measures for the host country reduce the positive and negative impacts of fluctuations in resource prices and production but only indirectly reduce the temptation to expropriate, although the same could be said for the reallocation of risk and reward. MNC possibilities are discussed first, followed by potential HC actions.

First, recent decades have seen significant advances in the analysis of profit maximization in resource extraction industries. The traditional approach, based on discounted cash flows (DCFs) (or net present-value calculation), has been shown to be insufficient in accounting for the wide range of uncertainties in projects in oil, gas, and minerals (Brennan and Schwartz 1984). Two alternative methods that have arisen to account for uncertainty involve dynamic programming (or decision analysis) (e.g., Stensland and Tjostheim 1991) and options valuation (or contingent claims analysis), in which mineral projects are treated as if they were financial options to the extent possible (Paddock, Siegel, and Smith 1988). Efforts have been made to integrate the two methods (Smith and McCardle 1998; Chorn and Shokhor 2006), although there have also been claims that one is better than the other (Lund 2000; Insley and Wirjanto 2006). In chapter 8 of this book, Eduardo Schwartz and Anders Trolle use the options model to value the expropriation risk directly, providing a new tool to evaluate the risks faced by an MNC as it moves into a new contract. This follows a previous literature that derived an options valuation method to price the risk of expropriation into the value of a project (Mahajan 1990; Clark 2003).

Other methods of valuing expropriation risk include adjustments to the discount rate in the DCF method. Davis (2001) adjusts for a constant risk of nationalization of South Africa's mineral assets, and Bunn and Mustafaoglu (1978) have attempted to do so based on expert opinion on probabilities. Overall, adoption by firms of either decision analysis or contingent claims, with or without political risk incorporated, constitutes an improvement over DCF. However, Moyen, Slade, and Uppal (1996) observed that Canadian mining firms had continued to use variations of the DCF rather than adopting newer methods, even though by then the newer methods had existed for some years.

The results found by Schwartz and Trolle, an example using new methods, indicate that the option to expropriate depends quite dramatically on the conditions of energy markets. When prices are low or when they are high but with strong signals from the future market that they will decline, the expropriation option is inconsequential. The reason for the low valuations is that Schwartz and Trolle assume that the government is less efficient in running the fields, and thus they require prices to go up and stay there for expropriation to make sense. However, when prices are high and expected to remain high, the expropriation option can be sizable. In one example using actual data for the recent upswing in oil prices they find that the expropriation option can trim close to 40 percent of the field value, thus confirming the fear that lack of commitment can have significant effects on firm valuation (eventually increasing the probability of expropriation).

Better valuation does not mitigate the risk, beyond providing measures of its relevance. Two measures that firms have adopted to protect from risks are the incorporation of local partners and the use of political-risk insurance. More recently the use of credit default swaps (CDSs) has become the principal vehicle to hedge political risk. Local partners can provide a multinational domestic protection from government intervention. Woodhouse (2006) found that in infrastructure projects, firms with local partners tended to avoid renegotiation more often. However, local partners are effective only as long as they remain politically favored. A change in power can turn a local partner into a liability, since it can bring charges of favoritism or corruption (Moran 1998; Wells and Gleason 1995).

Political-risk insurance provides payouts in the event of expropriation, usually of the total kind. Organizations that provide political-risk insurance are the Overseas Private Investment Corporation, of the U.S. government, and the Multilateral Investment Guarantee Agency, part of the World Bank Group. An important issue to be resolved is whether political-risk insurers too readily award claims damages. Because political-risk insurers are often allowed to claim damages from host countries, they have less incentive to scrutinize MNC claims of expropriation before awarding damages (Wells 2005). This constitutes an example of moral hazard in addition to the usual one associated with riskier action under insurance (Wells 2005). If insurers do claim damages, then efforts to reduce the incidence of expropriation worldwide risk losing credibility. Thus, while individual firms may benefit from political-risk insurance, firms as a whole have to face the reaction of developing countries to what they would perceive as injustice. CDSs provide a more elliptic, but also relevant, hedge for expropriation. Because CDS premiums are likely to increase in the event of a real asset expropriation, CDS can be used as a hedging instrument. Given its liquidity and ease of trade, CDS use today has increased in importance relative to other forms of political-risk insurance.

As for HC actions, much of the discussion has surrounded how to change behavior or contract terms with a particular foreign firm. What has not been discussed is the choice the HC can have in selecting a firm to contract with in the first place. Much support in the literature exists for competitive bidding among qualified firms, followed by more specific contract negotiations (Wells and Gleason 1995; Sunnevåg 2000; Woodhouse 2006). This partial solution is like the auctioning described above, except that auctioning includes payments by firms during production as well as at the time of the auction. In addition to introducing competition, bidding undermines populist accusations that a contract was signed corruptly.

Bidding may not select the most efficient operator in the face of anticipation of renegotiation or expropriation. As noted before, contracts must be absolutely final (Mead 1994). If a firm could count on renegotiation at a lower price after the auction, it would raise its price during the auction (Mead 1994). In Latin American infrastructure projects, Guasch (2004) found that competitive bidding statistically increased the incidence of renegotiation (consisting mostly of firms extracting better terms). In these cases, firms underbid the price they would accept to perform services and then asked for more later on. As Guasch put it, a bidding process might result in "selection not of the most efficient operator but the one most skilled in renegotiation" (p. 92).

However, in the case of extractive industries, the opposite scenario is most likely. As discussed above, firms fear expropriation or renegotiation by the government and therefore will bid less than they would have, even if the government has no intention of expropriating. At the same time, governments may become frustrated in underbids and engage in total or creeping expropriation. Anticipation of future problems, even nonexistent ones, can influence both the incidence of expropriation and the selection of lessees. This is the natural resource trap we discussed at the beginning of the chapter.

Another option for developing countries with large natural resource endowments is the use of stabilization funds or hedging of resource rents (Everhart and Duval-Hernandez 2001). Because production and commodity prices fluctuate and influence GDP, these funds can be used to reduce the extent of these fluctuations. Stabilization funds consist of funds accrued during years of high revenue and spent during years of lower revenue. Hedging implies securing prices for commodities in the future so as to leave sales of resources less susceptible to short-term market fluctuations. If the macroeconomic volatility is a cause of expropriation (Vernon 1971), then either of these instruments might reduce the temptation to expropriate.

A key advantage of a stabilization fund is that it is easy to administer (Daniel 2002), but it may be politically difficult not to spend the fund early (Everhart and Duval-Hernandez 2001), as occurred in Ecuador or Venezuela in recent years. Populist pressures are significant, even in a developed country like Norway, which has a large stabilization fund from oil revenues (Listhaug 2005; Røed Larsen 2006) and has been forced to commit the resources to balance its pension program. Also, stabilization funds only smooth income over time if a commodity price is ultimately mean-reverting, which may or may not be the case (Devlin and Titman 2004).

Hedging instruments, on the other hand, are risky for policymakers who, while midly praised when producing some stability, will definitely be under strong pressure when their hedging strategies implies a short-run loss. (See Lawrence Summers's commentary on chapter 2 of this book. Summers cites this asymmetry in benefits and costs of hedging for policymakers as the explanation for why hedging is seldom used.) Furthermore, the use of hedging instruments requires more financial knowledge, and the markets need to exist (Everhart and Duval-Hernandez 2001). Devlin and Titman (2004) also observe that it would be challenging to find buyers for the large magnitude of commodity futures that would be produced if many countries began to engage in this financial technique. They suggest that international agencies and institutional investors could combine to form these markets. Such markets do not seem to be forming yet.

Finally, another way to reduce contractual uncertainty is to follow the route already implemented in Alaska, where the royalties are partially shared through direct payments to the population. This changes the political dynamics by having the population feel that it participates in oil rents, thus reducing the risk of expropriation. Such a government is akin to the MNC practice of including local partners in its strategy.

1.5   Country Cases

The issues discussed above have provided a fairly wide overview of the complexities involved in writing natural resource contracts that are more stable, self-enforcing, and convenient for all parties involved. In the book we discuss four country experiences that provide further examples of additional complexities.

Helm addresses the United Kingdom and considers the similar case of investment in capital-intensive utilities where a sovereign government is the de facto party to the contract. In his description of the United Kingdom's RPI-X regulation of the electricity sector, Helm concludes that the rules were frequently broken, resulting in a system that eventually replicated the perverse system it was trying to replace (a simple rate-of-return regulation). But the surprising feature of his discussion is his analysis of how the new system dramatically affected the incentives in terms of the financing structure for the firm. In fact, the new system increased dramatically the return of equity (particularly before all the subsequent changes), incentivizing a sharp increase in leverage, again an unintended consequence of a particular way of writing contracts.

A similar surprise is provided in Navajas's description of the reform process in Bolivia. Here a reform process that was quite well conceived and that was very successful in adding reserves for the country was based heavily on two factors: income taxation and 50 percent ownership by the pension funds in the companies. Large investments, however, led to relatively low taxable income in the initial years of the reform (the reforms permitted steep depreciation allowances), thus generating a window where the population observed large gross income and low net income. The sense of unfairness skyrocketed, undermining the reform process.

Gadano, discussing the Argentina experience, relies on an internal mechanism to explain the dynamics. According to Gadano, reforms were pushed by the urgency of short-run needs (an economic crisis in the early 1950s, mounting oil imports in the late 1950s, and hyperinflation in the late 1980s). In all cases reforms were implemented by politicians that initially had won their election by advocating against FDI. Thus, when the sense of urgency abated the underlying political preferences resurfaced (typically not on the part of the same politician but of someone who would have come to defend "true national preferences"), reversing the reform process.

Finally, Manzano and Monaldi provide an extensive review of the three main periods of Venezuela's oil history. There was an initial period of low taxes starting in 1909, but a new law in 1943, during World War II, renegotiated the contracts under the auspices of the United

States. The period after 1943 was characterized by constant tax renegotiations, leading to the nationalization of the industry in 1976. Finally, there has been another cycle of deregulation (in the 1990s) and renationalization (in the 2000s). In the latest bout of invitations for foreign companies, some past lessons had been learned and some of the tax schemes were highly progressive (with close to 100 percent of proceeds going to the government if prices increased sharply). Yet, in some of the renegotiations in these areas the government accepted less progressivity, and thus a worse deal. Because this change is difficult to explain given the conditions in the oil market at the time of nationalization, one can only conclude that ideology or irrationality may also intrude in the process, making the analysis all the more difficult.

1.6   Summary

How can we understand the pervasiveness of the phenomenon of expropriation and contractual renegotiation, and what lessons apply for policy going forward? The discussion of arbitration and of hedging alternatives illustrates again that there is no escaping the lack of a contract "protective framework," be it legal or financial, that may help explain why these investments occur at all. In other words, very much as in the sovereign debt literature, these contracts will exist to the extent that they are mutually beneficial and self-enforcing.

There are reasons for such contracts to achieve these minimally required conditions. As found in the sovereign debt literature, MNCs can always threaten to withhold new investment projects down the road or to come back, but only on very unfavorable terms to the HC. Additionally there may be sanctions, though as with debt, these have seldom been used and if so, they have been rather ineffectual. Finally, a plausible supporting reason for respecting contracts, at least broadly, has to do with the reputational spillovers. Governments interact not only with MNCs but in many other dimensions and with many different parties. Each of these participants constantly looks at what the government is doing. Thus contractual breaches may damage the government in multiple other dimensions, both external and local, providing the incentives for minimizing these reputationally damaging contractual renegotiations.

Our review of several country cases also revealed the complexities of the various schemes as well as the many variables that interact, sometimes in an unpredictable way. Bolivia seems to have done it right, but failed to factor in the delay that large amortization allowances created until companies reported positive net income. The Argentina experience suggests the role of ideological and historical considerations as almost unavoidable determinants. Venezuela's case even suggests irrationality because some contractual changes defied any logical justification. The UK experience hints at dramatic and unanticipated changes in corporate financing that contributed to distorting, and eventually undermining, the reform process. In other words, the idiosyncratic conditions in countries add to the general complexity. There is not a textbook case or a simple textbook contract.

The theoretical chapters point to yet a number of other conceptual justifications for why expropriation and renegotiations should not be expected to go away. Rigobon's chapter (chapter 7), for example, shows that royalties are preferred for governments without alternative income sources, but royalties are a regressive form of taxation, thus stimulating expropriation at high commodity prices. Schwartz and Trolle demonstrate in chapter 8 that expropriation is not a relevant concern under stable or declining oil prices and may therefore be ignored by companies in the first place. In chapter 4, Di Tella, Dubra, and MacCulloch show that other business sectors may support expropriation of the commodity price industry if they believe it may reduce the arbitrariness of wealth creation, thus avoiding the shift to left-wing politics created by large windfalls in private-sector gains. An auction may be the least distorting way to lease a field, but it maximizes expropriation incentives when prices go up. In other words, the complexity of objectives of policymakers themselves implies that a zero-expropriation-risk contract is likely never to be the optimal solution.

The question then is who gains from such a state of affairs. On the one hand it is clear that if the game is one shot, a country that finds itself with its optimal investment in place would gain from expropriating. But such a case is seldom found in the real world. First of all, this is a repeated game: there are always new fields to explore and there is always additional production to be developed. And then there are the externalities that we referred to above, which impose a cost regardless of whether the government may win from expropriating a specific contract or even a whole sector. The analogy with debt default suggests that even if some countries may gain by defaulting, the asset class (which in the case of sovereign debt would be emerging-market debt) does pay a price. It is found that ex post investors in emerging-market debt do earn a spread on developed-country debt, which means that defaults did not serve to benefit the class of emerging countries as a whole. If the analogy is correct, as with the tragedy of the commons, it means that a specific country may get ahead through expropriation but that both poor and emerging countries may have done better individually and collectively by sustaining a more credible and predictable contractual framework.

The case studies provide examples of the national political conditions that can set the stage for expropriation. The theoretical studies reinforce the notion that in the most profitable cases, ex post, the temptation of expropriation may be irresistible, and rational investors incorporate this expectation in their investment choices. In the long run, everyone would gain from reinforcing a regime to make contracts more enforceable and expropriations more the exception.

Notes

1. One could argue, as Roberto Rigobon does in chapter 7 in this book, and as has been argued in the sovereign debt literature (Grossman and Van Huyck 1988), that renegotiations are an anticipated possibility, dealing with unexpected contingencies that are impossible to anticipate in a written contract. If so, renegotiations would have relatively little costs. Grossman and Van Huyck use this concept, which they refer to as "excusable defaults," to explain why countries that eventually default are not punished in credit markets. However (as Tomz and Wright mention in chapter 3), in contrast with sovereign debt, renegotiations in natural resources occur during good times (when resources are more valuable), making the renegotiations less excusable at least from a strict economic point of view.

2. Perhaps because of data limitations, very little empirical work analyzing the determinants of expropriations in natural resource projects has been done. The only examples seem to be Duncan 2006b, which attributes mineral expropriations primarily to government opportunism when commodity prices are high, and Boyarchenko 2007, which considers "the exchange rate and long-term foreign liabilities" and other contributing factors (p. 13). Guasch (2004) found that other factors also mattered, like macroeconomic shocks and the amount of competition in selecting a contractor, but his study was on infrastructure projects.

3. Here, renegotiation is not used in the sense of attempts to implement a Pareto-improving outcome when circumstances change, but in the sense of attempts by one of the parties to take a larger share of the pie.

4. Less prominent are instances in which foreign firms initiate renegotiation, which are significant, though not as highly publicized. Such occurrences do not seem as common or as likely in natural resource contracts, compared to contracts in other sectors, such as infrastructure, as is explained later in this chapter.

5. For example, suppose total production and price are fixed, so that revenue is fixed. Forty percent is the cost-oil limit, and the government takes 50 percent of profit oil. If the true cost is 40 percent, true profits and profit oil are both 60 percent. Thirty percent of revenue goes to the HC, and the effective tax rate on profits is 50 percent. If the true cost

is 50 percent, the true profit is 50 percent of revenue, but profit oil is still 60 percent. Since 30 percent of total revenue is still given to the HC, the effective tax rate on profits is 60 percent. Thus, a tax rate that increases as profits decline means that a PSA can be regressive when the limit on cost oil binds.

6. With just income tax rate t, the MNC earns $(1 - t)[pq - c(q)]$, where p is price, q is quantity, and c is the cost function. With royalty rate r, MNC earns $(1 - t)[(1 - r)pq - c(q)]$. The royalty is applied to gross revenue, whereas the income tax is applied to net profit.

7. Gadano and Sturzenegger (1998) discuss the experience of Argentina with auctioning of oil fields. They find that in spite of a great dispersion in the internal rate of returns of individual projects, the average returns obtained at the different rounds of auctions matched surprisingly well with the yields on government bonds at the time, suggesting that reserves were sold are a fairly high price.

8. Among projects with high sunk costs and delayed revenues, natural resource projects are different from infrastructure projects. In empirical and theoretical research on these infrastructure ventures, MNCs initiate renegotiations as much as governments do (Guasch 2004; Guasch, Laffont, and Straub 2006). But two characteristics of infrastructure projects confer additional bargaining power on MNCs in this area compared to MNCs in extractive projects. First, whereas oil, gas, and minerals are often intended primarily for export, infrastructure is entirely for domestic consumption. This means foreign firms in infrastructure can threaten to deny citizens access to the services in a way their counterparts in natural resources cannot. Thus, foreign investors are possibly most vulnerable to total and creeping expropriation by their hosts when they are involved in extractive industries.

9. Wells (2005) offers as examples HC-MNC projects in Indonesia to build geothermal power plants. When these projects were not completed, arbitration courts awarded foreign investors "the full amount the investors put up so far plus some large fraction of the net present value of future earnings (at least 30 years' worth, in some cases), even when contracts had been broken for economic reasons" (p. 94). These are infrastructure projects, however, and we have not found a similar pattern for natural resource contracts.

10. What is typically argued in arbitration is that sovereign countries have the liberty to change their taxes but not on investments that were committed under a different tax regime.

References

Adelman, M. A. "Economics of Exploration for Petroleum and Other Minerals." *Geoexploration* 8 (1970): 131–150.

Al Qurashi, Zayed A. "Renegotiation of International Petroleum Agreements." *Journal of International Arbitration* 22, no. 4 (2005): 261–300.

Amador, Manuel. "A Political Economy Model of Sovereign Debt Repayment." Unpublished Paper, Stanford University, 2003.

Atsegbua, Lawrence. "Acquisition of Oil Rights under Contractual Joint Ventures in Nigeria." *Journal of African Law* 37, no. 1 (Spring 1993): 10–29.

Baunsgaard, Thomas. *A Primer on Mineral Taxation*. IMF Working Paper WP/01/139, 2001.

Bell, Simon. "Gold Miner Oxus Stops Glittering in Central Asia." *Sunday Times* (London), August 27, 2006, Business section, 7.

Berger, Klaus Peter. "Renegotiation and Adaptation of International Investment Contracts: The Role of Contract Drafters and Arbitrators." *Vanderbilt Journal of Transnational Law* 36, no. 4 (October 2003): 1347–1380.

Bindemann, Kirsten. *Production-Sharing Agreements: An Economic Analysis.* Oxford Institute of Energy Studies WPM 25, October 1999.

Bindemann, Kirsten. *The Response of Oil Contracts to Extreme Price Movements.* Economics Discussion Paper No. 29 [Oxford University], 2000.

Blake, Andon J., and Mark C. Roberts. "Comparing Fiscal Petroleum Regimes under Price Uncertainty." *Resources Policy* 31 (2006): 95–105.

Blitzer, C. R., D. R. Lessard, and J. L. Paddock. "Risk Bearing and the Choice of Contract Forms for Oil Exploration and Development." *Energy Journal* 5, no. 1 (January 1984): 1–29.

Bolton, Patrick, and Mathias Dewatripont. *Contract Theory.* Cambridge, MA: MIT Press, 2005.

Boyarchenko, Nina. *Turning Off the Tap: Determinants of Expropriation in the Energy Sector.* SSRN Working Paper 963779, February 15, 2007.

Brennan, Michael J., and Eduardo S. Schwartz. "Evaluating Natural Resource Investments." *Journal of Business* 58, no. 2 (April 1984): 135–157.

Brown, E. Cary. "Business Income, Taxation, and Investment Incentives." In L. A. Metzler et al., *Income, Employment, and Public Policy: Essays in Honor of Alvin H. Hansen,* 300–316. New York: Norton, 1948.

Brunet, Alexia, and Juan Agustin Lentini. "Arbitration of International Oil, Gas, and Energy Disputes in Latin America." *Northwestern Journal of International Law and Business* 27, no. 3 (Spring 2007): 591–630.

Bulow, Jeremy, and Kenneth Rogoff. "A Constant Recontracting Model of Sovereign Debt." *Journal of Political Economy* 97, no. 1 (February 1989a): 155–178.

Bulow, Jeremy, and Kenneth Rogoff. "Sovereign Debt: Is to Forgive to Forget?" *American Economic Review* 79, no. 1 (March 1989b): 43–50.

Bunn, D. W., and M. M. Mustafaoglu. "Forecasting Political Risk." *Management Science* 24, no. 15 (November 1978): 1557–1567.

Che, Yeon-Koo, and József Sákovics. "A Dynamic Theory of Holdup." *Econometrica* 72, no. 4 (July 2004): 1063–1103.

Chorn, L. G., and S. Shokhor. "Real Options for Risk Management in Petroleum Development Investments." *Energy Economics* 28 (2006): 489–505.

Clark, Ephraim. "Pricing the Cost of Expropriation Risk." *Review of International Economics* 11, no. 2 (2003): 412–422.

Coale, Margarita T. B. "Stabilization Clauses in International Petroleum Transactions." *Denver Journal of International Law and Policy* 30, no. 2 (2002): 217–238.

Cole, Harold L., and Patrick J. Kehoe. "Models of Sovereign Debt: Partial versus General Reputations." *International Economic Review* 39, no. 1 (February 1998): 55–70.

Cole, Harold L., and Patrick J. Kehoe. "The Role of Institutions in Reputation Models of Sovereign Debt." *Journal of Monetary Economics* 35, no. 1 (February 1995): 46–64.

Daniel, Philip. "Petroleum Revenue Management: An Overview." Paper presented at [ESMAP] Workshop on Petroleum Revenue Management, Washington, DC, October 23–24, 2002.

Davis, Graham A. "The Credibility of a Threat to Nationalize." *Journal of Environmental Economics and Management* 42 (2001): 119–139.

Devlin, Julia, and Sheridan Titman. "Managing Oil Price Risk in Developing Countries." *World Bank Research Observer* 19, no. 1 (Spring 2004): 119–139.

Duncan, Roderick. *Costs and Consequences of the Expropriation of FDI by Host Governments.* Working Paper, January 2006a.

Duncan, Roderick. "Price or Politics: An Investigation of the Causes of Expropriation." *Australian Journal of Agricultural and Resource Economics* 50, no. 1 (March 2006b): 85–101.

Eaton, Jonathan. "Sovereign Debt, Reputation and Credit Terms." *International Journal of Finance & Economics* 1, no. 1 (January 1996): 25–35.

Eaton, Jonathan, and Mark Gersovitz. "Debt with Potential Repudiation: Theoretical and Empirical Analysis." *Review of Economic Studies* 48, no. 2 (April 1981): 289–309.

Everhart, Stephen, and Robert Duval-Hernandez. *Management of Oil Windfalls in Mexico.* World Bank Policy Research Working Paper No. 2592, 2001.

Fernandez, Raquel, and Robert W. Rosenthal. "Strategic Models of Sovereign-Debt Renegotiations." *Review of Economic Studies* 57, no. 3 (July 1990): 331–349.

Gadano, Nicolás, and Federico Sturzenegger. "La Privatización de Empresas en el Sector Hidrocarburífero: El Caso de Argentina." *Revista de Análisis Economico* 13, no. 1 (1998): 75–116.

Geiger, Linwood T. "Expropriation and External Capital Flows." *Economic Development and Cultural Change* 37, no. 3 (April 1989): 535–556.

Gotanda, John Y. "Renegotiation and Adaptation Clauses in Investment Contracts, Revisited." *Vanderbilt Journal of Transnational Law* 36, no. 4 (October 2003): 1461–1473.

Grossman, Herschel I., and John B. Van Huyck. "Sovereign Debt as a Contingent Claim: Excusable Default, Repudiation, and Reputation." *American Economic Review* 78, no. 5 (December 1998): 1088–1097.

Guasch, J. Luis. *Granting and Renegotiating Infrastructure Concessions: Doing It Right.* Washington, DC: World Bank, 2004.

Guasch, J. Luis, Jean-Jacques Laffont, and Stéphane Straub. "Renegotiation of Concession Contracts: A Theoretical Approach." *Review of Industrial Organization* 29, no. 1–2 (September 2006): 55–73.

Guriev, Sergei, and Dmitriy Kvasov. "Contracting on Time." *American Economic Review* 95, no. 5 (December 2005): 1369–1385.

Haber, Stephen, Noel Maurer, and Armando Razo. "When the Law Does Not Matter: The Rise and Decline of the Mexican Oil Industry." *Journal of Economic History* 63 (2003): 1–32.

Insley, M. C., and T. S. Wirjanto. *Contrasting Two Approaches in Real Options Valuation: Contingent Claims versus Dynamic Programming.* Working paper, 2006.

Jensen, Nathan. *Political Regimes and Political Risk: Democratic Institutions and Expropriation Risk for Multinational Investors.* Working Paper, 2006.

Johnston, Daniel. *International Exploration Economics, Risk, and Contract Analysis.* Tulsa, OK: PennWell, 2003.

Kletzer, Kenneth M. "Sovereign Immunity and International Lending." In F. van der Ploeg, ed., *The Handbook of International Macroeconomics*, 439–479. Oxford: Blackwell, 1994.

Kletzer, Kenneth M., and Brian D. Wright. "Sovereign Debt as Intertemporal Barter." *American Economic Review* 90, no. 3 (June 2000): 621–639.

Lederman, Daniel, and William F. Maloney. "In Search of the Missing Resource Curse." Paper presented at 17th Economia Panel Meeting, Yale University, New Haven, CT, May 2–3, 2008.

Leland, Hayne E. "Optimal Risk Sharing and the Leasing of Natural Resources with Application to Oil and Gas Leasing of the OCS." *Quarterly Journal of Economics* 92, no. 3 (August 1978): 413–438.

Listhaug, Ola. "Oil Wealth Dissatisfaction and Political Trust in Norway: A Resource Curse?" *West European Politics* 28, no. 4 (September 2005): 834–851.

Lund, Morton W. "Valuing Flexibility in Offshore Petroleum Projects." *Annals of Operations Research* 99 (2000): 325–349.

Mahajan, Arvind. "Pricing Expropriation Risk." *Financial Management* 19, no. 4 (Winter 1990): 77–86.

Manzano, Osmel. *Tax Effects upon Oil Field Development in Venezuela.* MIT Center for Energy and Environmental Policy Research WP-2000-006, September 2006.

McPherson, Charles. "National Oil Companies: Evolution, Issues, Outlook." Paper presented at National Oil Companies Workshop, World Bank, Washington, DC, May 27, 2003.

Mead, Walter J. "Toward an Optimal Oil and Gas Leasing System." *Energy Journal* 15, no. 4 (October 1994): 1–18.

Minor, Michael S. "The Demise of Expropriation as an Instrument of LDC Policy." *Journal of International Business Studies* 25, no. 1 (1994): 177–188.

Moran, Theodore H. "The Changing Nature of Political Risk." In Theodore H. Moran, ed., *Managing International Political Risk*, 7–14. Malden, MA: Blackwell, 1998.

Moyen, Nathalie, Margaret Slade, and Raman Uppal. "Valuing Risk and Flexibility: A Comparison of Methods." *Resources Policy* 22 (1996): 63–74.

Nöldeke, Georg, and Klaus M. Schmidt. "Option Contracts and Renegotiation: A Solution to the Hold-Up Problem." *RAND Journal of Economics* 26, no. 2 (Summer 1995): 163–179.

Nöldeke, Georg, and Klaus M. Schmidt. "Sequential Investments and Options to Own." *RAND Journal of Economics* 29, no. 4 (Winter 1998): 633–653.

Orr, Ryan J. "Investment in Foreign Infrastructure: The Legacy and Lessons of Legal-Contractual Failure." Background paper presented at the 2nd General Counsels' Round-table, Collaboratory for Research on Global Projects, Stanford University, Stanford, CA, February 10–11, 2006.

Osmundsen, Petter. "Risk Sharing and Incentives in Norwegian Petroleum Production." *Energy Policy* 27 (1999): 549–555.

Paddock, James L., Daniel R. Siegel, and James L. Smith. "Option Valuation of Claims on Real Assets: The Case of Offshore Petroleum Leases." *Quarterly Journal of Economics* 103 (1988): 479–508.

Pitchford, Rohan, and Christopher M. Snyder. "A Solution to the Hold-Up Problem Involving Gradual Investment." *Journal of Economic Theory* 114 (2004): 88–103.

Pongsiri, Nutavoot. "Partnerships in Oil and Gas Production-Sharing Contracts." *International Journal of Public Sector Management* 17, no. 5 (2004): 431–442.

Poppo, Laura, and Todd Zenger. "Do Formal Contracts and Relational Governance Function as Substitutes or Complements?" *Strategic Management Journal* 23 (2002): 707–725.

Reinisch, August. "Expropriation." Paper presented to International Law Association [ILA] Committee on International Law on Foreign Investment at ILA Conference, Toronto, Canada, June 2006. Available at http://www.ila-hq.org/pdf/Foreign%20Investment/ILA%20paper%20Reinisch.pdf.

Rodrik, Dani, and Richard Zeckhauser. "The Dilemma of Government Responsiveness." *Journal of Policy Analysis* 7, no. 4 (Autumn 1988): 601–620.

Røed Larsen, Erling. "Escaping the Resource Curse and the Dutch Disease? When and Why Norway Caught Up with and Forged Ahead of Its Neighbors." *American Journal of Economics and Sociology* 65, no. 3 (July 2006): 605–640.

Sachs, Jeffrey D., and Daniel Cohen. *LDC Borrowing with Default Risk.* NBER Working Paper No. 1925. Cambridge, MA: National Bureau of Economic Research, 1982.

Schnitzer, Monika. "Expropriation and Control Rights: A Dynamic Model of Foreign Direct Investment." *International Journal of Industrial Organization* 17 (1999): 1113–1137.

Smith, James E., and Kevin F. McCardle. "Valuing Oil Properties: Integrating Option Pricing and Decision Analysis Approaches." *Operations Research* 46, no. 2 (March 1998): 198–217.

Stensland, Gunnar, and Dag B. Tjostheim. "Optimal Decisions with Reduction in Uncertainty over Time—An Application to Oil Production." In Diderik Lund and Bernt Øksendal, eds., *Stochastic Models and Option Values: Applications to Resources, Environment, and Investment Problems*, 267–291. Contributions to Economic Analysis 200. Amsterdam: North-Holland, 1991.

Sturzenegger, Federico, and Jeromin Zettelmeyer. *Debt Defaults and Lessons from a Decade of Crises.* Cambridge, MA: MIT Press, 2006.

Sunley, Emil M., Thomas Baunsgaard, and Dominique Simard. "Revenue from the Oil and Gas Sector: Issues and Country Experience." In Jeffrey M. Davis, Rolando Ossoski, and Annalisa Fedelino, eds., *Fiscal Policy Formulation and Implementation in Oil-Producing Countries*, 153–183. Washington, DC: International Monetary Fund, 2003.

Sunnevåg, Kjell J. "Designing Auctions for Offshore Petroleum Lease Allocation." *Resources Policy* 26, no. 1 (March 2000): 3–16.

Thomas, Jonathan, and Tim Worrall. "Foreign Direct Investment and the Risk of Expropriation." *Review of Economic Studies* 61, no. 1 (January 1994): 81–108.

Vernon, Raymond. *Sovereignty at Bay: The Multinational Spread of U.S. Enterprises*. New York: Basic Books, 1971.

Wells, Louis T. "The New International Property Rights: Can the Foreign Investor Rely on Them?" In Theodore H. Moran and Gerald T. West, eds., *International Political Risk Management: Looking to the Future*, 87–102. Washington, DC: World Bank, 2005.

Wells, Louis T., and Rafiq Ahmed. *Making Foreign Investment Safe: Property Rights and National Sovereignty*. Oxford: Oxford University Press, 2007.

Wells, Louis T., and Eric S. Gleason. "Is Foreign Infrastructure Investment Still Risky?" *Harvard Business Review*, September–October 1995, 44–55.

Woodhouse, Erik J. "The Obsolescing Bargain Redux? Foreign Investment in the Electric Power Sector in Developing Countries." *New York University Journal of International Law and Politics* 122 (2006): 121–219.

Wright, Mark L. J. "Reputation and Sovereign Debt." Unpublished paper, Stanford University, 2002.

Wyatt, Nelson. "Canadians in Favour of Nationalizing Gas Resources, Companies, New Poll Suggests." *Canadian Press*, September 5, 2005.

I Theoretical Papers

2 Petroleum Contracts: What Does Contract Theory Tell Us?

Philippe Aghion and Lucía Quesada

2.1 Introduction

In recent years we have witnessed the case of local governments (for example, in Bolivia) that have reneged on past agreements with oil or gas companies on the grounds that the past agreements were unfair. Are they justified in doing so, because of the terms of the initial contracts, on the basis of economic conditions, or in light of the political context in which the initial contract was negotiated?

In this chapter we briefly describe the main characteristics of contracts between oil companies and local governments, and then we draw from existing contract theory to rationalize these contractual forms, to assess their strengths and weaknesses, and to explain their recent evolution. In particular, we are concerned with understanding why governments may indeed be justified in reneging on past agreements and why contracts have evolved toward more flexible sharing rules. We argue that Hart and Moore's recent model of "contracts as a reference point," adapted to the situation where the initial contract is negotiated by a government with specific (short-term, private benefits) interests, is best suited for that purpose.

2.2 Prevailing Contracts between Countries and Oil Companies

Existing contracts between countries and oil companies are mainly distinguished by the allocation of ownership of the oil and gas to be extracted. This, in turn, has an influence on the way they allocate financial returns between the parties. The four most prominent types of contracts are production-sharing agreements (PSAs), concession contracts, risk service agreements, and joint ventures, with the first two now being the most common. There are two parties to the contract: an international oil company (IOC) and the government, usually represented by a national oil company (NOC).

2.2.1 Production-Sharing Agreements

PSAs were first introduced in Indonesia in 1966 and since then have become the most important type of petroleum contract, especially in developing countries. The key feature of PSAs is that the state owns the resource and all the installations and plants, and the IOC is hired to explore, exploit, and develop the resource in exchange for a share of production.[1] In general, PSAs establish a partnership between the state and the IOC that monitors operations and decides on production.

Under this form of contract, the risk of exploration is entirely borne by the IOC. After discovery and extraction the IOC has to pay a royalty to the government, levied on gross production. This royalty guarantees a minimum revenue flow to the government that is independent of the profitability of the project.

In a second step, the contract allows the operator to recover its costs by retaining a certain percentage of production (with a prespecified ceiling, usually between 30 and 50 percent of production). This is the so-called cost oil. Cost oil is supposed to recover not only production costs, but also costs of exploration and drilling.

Production exceeding the cost oil, called profit oil, is shared between the IOC and the NOC following a predetermined scheme, which could be linear (fixed shares) or could depend on total production or the firm's rate of return (sliding scales).[2] Typically, the state gets the largest share of profit oil.

Finally, the IOC has to pay income taxes on its share of profit oil, as well as other taxes. In some cases, it is the NOC that pays taxes on behalf of the IOC.

2.2.2 Concession Contracts

Initially, petroleum exploration, production, and marketing activities were governed by concession contracts. These contracts grant exclusive rights to explore, develop, and export petroleum in a specific territory and for a specific period of time.

In such concession contracts, the state transfers ownership of the mineral resources to the IOC, as well as all managerial and decision-making rights over petroleum exploration and production activities. The IOC has to secure the entire financing and technological capabilities and bears all exploration and production risks. Revenues for the government come mainly from royalties and income taxes. The royalties to be paid are a portion of petroleum production, and are computed based either on surface area granted to IOC (surface royalty) or on petroleum production (proportional royalty).

2.2.3 Risk Service Contracts

Under this particular arrangement, the IOC supplies services and know-how to the state in exchange for an agreed-on fixed fee or some other form of compensation. In a pure service contract, the IOC is paid a flat fee, and hence bears no exploration cost. In risk service contracts, however, the IOC bears all the exploration costs. The state remains the owner of the oil produced, but in some cases the IOC has the option to buy oil back at world prices. Moreover, payments to the IOC are usually made in oil. This makes actual risk service contracts very similar to PSAs.

2.2.4 Joint Ventures

In joint ventures, ownership of production is shared according to the participation of the IOC and the government in the venture. The government and the IOC participate actively in the operation of the oil field. Thus, the government is entitled to a share of profits, but it also bears a share of development and operation costs. However, in many cases, the company bears all the exploration costs and the government enters the venture only after commercial discovery.

2.3 A Basic Model of Petroleum Contracts

In this section, we develop a very simple model of petroleum contracts that highlights the uncertainties and nonverifiability issues inherent in this relationship. We will use this model to illustrate the main problems that may affect the efficiency of contracting.

There are two parties to the contract, the company (C) and the state (G). There are three periods: an exploration period ($t = 0$) and two production periods ($t = 1, 2$). In period $t = 0$ a contract is signed between the company and the state. The contract assigns control rights and a profit-sharing rule. After the contract has been signed, exploration begins. Thus to start exploration, a sunk, noncontractible investment I has to be made. An oil reserve is discovered with probability $q(I)$; $q(\cdot)$ is increasing and concave and converges to $\bar{q} < 1$ when I goes to infinity. Conditional on discovery, the size of the reserve, R, is observed by the parties but is not verifiable. In periods $t = 1, 2$, extraction occurs (conditional on discovery). Extraction in period t requires a noncontractible effort e_t, which costs $\psi(e_t, I)$, increasing and convex in e_t, decreasing and concave in I, and with $\psi_{eI} < 0$.[3] Production y_t is obtained according to a cdf $F(y_t|e_t, R_t)$, and pdf $f(y_t|e_t, R_t)$, with $F_e < 0$ (high production is a signal of high effort), where R_t is the size of the reserve left under the surface in period t. Thus, $R_1 = R$ and $R_2 = R - y_1$. We also assume that $F_R < 0$ (with a higher reserve, the probability of higher production increases). Petroleum prices are uncertain at $t = 0$ but become common knowledge at the beginning of each period. At the end of each period, the IOC pays income taxes at a rate equal to i_t.

Under a *concession contract* the initial investment I and the effort levels (e_1, e_2) are chosen by the company. Moreover, at the end of periods 1 and 2, C pays royalties, T_t, to G. Royalties can be a fixed amount (surface royalties) $T_t = T$ or computed as a proportion of production in period t (proportional royalties), $T_t = \gamma y_t$, $\gamma \in (0, 1)$. The government take is $u_t = T_t + i_t(p_t y_t - T_t)$ and the firm take is $\pi_t = (1 - i_t)(p_t y_t - T_t) - \psi(e_t, I)$.

Under a *production-sharing agreement* the initial investment I is chosen by the company, but both the company and the state make effort decisions at the production stages (production effort and monitoring effort). Moreover, at the end of periods 1 and 2, a part of production is separated as cost oil, to compensate the company for the investment. Cost oil in period $t = 1$ is $c_1 = \min\{I/p_1; \beta y_1\}$. Cost oil in period $t = 2$ is $c_2 = \max\{0; \min\{(I - \beta p_1 y_1)/p_2; \beta y_2\}\}$. The remainder production in each period is profit oil, $\tilde{\pi}_t = y_t - c_t$. Profit oil is shared between C and G in a proportion α_t for the state and $1 - \alpha_t$ for the company. The share of profit oil can be $\alpha_t = \alpha$ (linear scheme) or $\alpha_t = \alpha(y_t)$ (sliding scales). This share is intended to compensate the company for production effort. The government take is $u_t = \alpha_t p_t(y_t - c_t) + i_t p_t(y_t - \alpha_t(y_t - c_t))$ and the firm take is $\pi_t = (1 - i_t) p_t(y_t - \alpha_t(y_t - c_t)) - \psi(e_t, I)$.

2.4   Potential Sources of Contractual Inefficiencies

In this section we use contract theory to understand the potential sources of contractual inefficiencies and how actual contracts between governments and oil companies address each of them. We will then try to identify the issues that may lead governments to renege on past agreements.

2.4.1 Moral Hazard and Risk Sharing

Investments in the oil industry are very risky from many different perspectives. First, the existence, size, and quality of the oil field are very difficult to anticipate at the moment of the initial investment. Second, drilling costs change with the characteristics of the field. Thus, even when a deposit is discovered, it is not always economically viable. Finally, in all countries except the United States, the government owns petroleum resources under the surface (ground or sea). Thus, the chances are that a new government in power will expropriate the oil company or will force contract renegotiations in the name of sovereignty.

To achieve risk diversification, large IOCs simultaneously drill wells in many different locations in a country and across different countries. For this reason, we can assume that IOCs are essentially risk neutral. On these grounds, concession contracts that allocate all the risk (and residual claims) to the company may be justifiable insofar as the company is exerting efforts (e_1, e_2) and can bear all the risk because it is (almost) risk neutral.

To illustrate the moral-hazard problem, suppose that the only non-verifiable variable is effort, that there is only one period, and that there are no income taxes $(i = 0)$. In period 1, the IOC chooses its effort e_1 in order to maximize its take

$$\max_e \int (p_1 y_1 - T_1) f(y_1 | e, R) \, dy_1 - \psi(e, I),$$

in the case of concession contracts and

$$\max_e \int (p_1 y_1 - \alpha_t (y_1 - c_1)) f(y_1 | e, R) \, dy_1 - \psi(e, I),$$

in the case of PSAs.

First-best effort e_1^*, on the other hand, maximizes the aggregate surplus and is independent of the specific contract. Indeed, e_1^* is the solution to

$$\max_e \int p_1 y_1 f(y_1 | e, R) \, dy_1 - \psi(e, I).$$

From the first-order conditions, it is straightforward to see that the first-best level of effort is only achieved under a concession contract with constant (surface) royalties. Indeed, in that case, the company is made residual claimant and appropriates all the benefits of its effort.

Moral hazard in itself seems not to be a significant problem at the exploration stage. In the production phase, however, moral hazard can be a relevant issue under PSAs. Indeed, the company does not appropriate all the benefits of its production effort. For that reason, contracts include a work program that reflects the company's commitments in terms of drilling and production.

However, in the following subsections, we draw on more recent contract theory to argue that concession contracts miss important characteristics of the actual contractual context between companies and local governments.

2.4.2 Assets Specificity and Holdup

Investments in oil exploration I are large and highly specific in nature. The IOC is in charge of this investment in all existing contractual arrangements. It is then exposed to opportunistic behavior and holdup once a discovery is made.[4] Usually, to make the deal attractive to the company, the state offers generous contract terms (low royalties, fast investment recovery, and so on). Once production begins, the state may want to change the agreement to increase its take. This is usually done through adjustments in the tax system, although sometimes expropriations occur, as in Venezuela and Bolivia. The company anticipates this possibility of holdup and underinvests.

Suppose that the contract does not specify anything about the tax rate i. This implies that the state can adjust i at any time and, in particular, after the initial investment I is sunk. Suppose also that adjusting the tax system (increasing i) involves a political cost $\phi(i)$, increasing and convex.[5] In period 1, once I is sunk, the IOC chooses its effort e_1 and the state chooses its tax rate i_1. To make our point, it is enough here to assume that there is only one production period. In the Nash equilibrium, each party maximizes its take, taking as given the choice of the other party. That is, e_1 is chosen to solve

$$\max_e \int (1 - i_1)(p_1 y_1 - x_1) f(y_1 | e, R) \, dy_1 - \psi(e, I),$$

while i_1 is chosen to solve

$$\max_i \int (x_1 + i_1(p_1 y_1 - x_1)) f(y_1 | e, R) \, dy_1 - \phi(i),$$

where $x_1 = T_1$ in a concession contract and $x_1 = \alpha_1 p_1(y_1 - c_1)$ in a PSA. The Nash equilibrium levels of effort and tax rate are $(\hat{e}(I), \hat{i}(I))$ functions of the initial (sunk) investment I. Moreover, under reasonable conditions the tax rate increases with I—that is, $\hat{i}' > 0$.

In period 0 the IOC chooses its investment I in order to maximize its expected profit, taking into account how I affects effort and tax rate in period 1. The problem that the company solves in period 0 is

$$\max_{I} \; q(I)\left[\int (1 - \hat{i}(I))(p_1 y_1 - x_1)f(y_1|\hat{e}(I), R)\, dy_1 - \psi(\hat{e}(I), I)\right] - I. \qquad (1)$$

Call $\hat{I}$ the solution of this problem. On the other hand, conditional on the effort level $\hat{e}(I)$, the optimal investment level, I^*, maximizes the aggregate surplus:

$$\max_{I} \; q(I)\left[\int (p_1 y_1 - x_1)f(y_1|\hat{e}(I), R)\, dy_1 - \psi(\hat{e}(I), I)\right] - I. \qquad (2)$$

It is easy to see from the first-order conditions of problems (1) and (2) that $\hat{I} < I^*$ if the tax rate increases with I, and this is independent of the particular contract form.

The holdup problem is addressed by contractual provisions in different ways. First, provisions can be made to reduce the degree of asset specificity or the extent of sunk cost. For instance, exploration costs may be deductible for income tax purposes or the state may agree to reimburse part of the company's exploration costs. These provisions aim at making the state a partner in the exploration phase. This implies, however, that the state actually agrees to share the risk of exploration with the company, which may reduce the latter's incentives to exert effort.

Second, some safeguard clauses are made in the spirit of Grossman and Hart 1986, which suggests that underinvestment can be overcome by assigning residual control rights to the IOC. One possible approach is by including a stabilization clause whereby the state commits not to change its laws in ways that may affect the terms of the contract. A second instrument is a convertibility clause allowing the IOC to convert the revenues it may receive in local currency into U.S. dollars or its own currency. This, however, does not protect the company from the possibility of holdup through the country's exchange-rate policy.[6] For that reason, some arrangements allow the company to sell its entire share of produced oil in the international market, so that changes in the domestic exchange-rate policy have less impact on the company's revenues.

Finally, another way to get around the holdup problem is through appropriate renegotiation design. Indeed, Aghion, Dewatripont, and Rey (1994) show that the underinvestment problem disappears if the contracts include renegotiation rules that determine default options and allocate bargaining power. This issue becomes especially important in the context of petroleum contracts given the unique position of the state, which is in control of the executive and legislative powers and sometimes even the judiciary. To incorporate this idea, some contracts include a renegotiation clause that makes explicit the conditions under which renegotiation may occur. Moreover, the duration of the contract is usually structured in short-term phases (two or three years), and often the company can opt to terminate the contract at the end of each phase.

Note that our discussion so far does not provide any justification for countries unilaterally reneging on the initial contract. It only justifies moving toward more flexible contracts.

2.4.3   Poor Enforcement

The issue of contractual enforcement is key in this type of relationship for several reasons. In general, contracts between a foreign company and a country (in particular, the rules for sharing revenues and ownership rights) are not fully enforceable because it is not always easy to find an impartial third party within the country's judiciary system. The problem is worsened in the context of oil reserves because resources in the ground are considered the property of the state. The related sovereign risk has three main components: the possibility that the state will unilaterally change the terms of the contract, the possibility of an ex post expropriation of the company by the state, and the extent to which the state has given up its rights over the resource for the duration of the contract.

To illustrate the enforcement problem, suppose that there is a positive probability, η, that the contract is not enforced. Here we assume that η is fixed, but it could actually depend on the terms of the contract (higher if the contract terms are very generous) and on the political party in power when the contract is signed. Suppose also that nonenforcement means expropriation.[7] Under expropriation, the company loses its assets and its rights to future profits. Suppose also that expropriation can only occur after production has began. In our model, this implies that the risk of expropriation is borne only in the second period.

Under these conditions, the company takes into account the probability of expropriation when it chooses its investment level I and its effort in period 1, e_1. To simplify, we assume that there are no income taxes. Indeed, in period 1 the firm chooses e_1 to solve

$$\max_e \int \{(p_1 y_1 - x_1) + (1 - \eta)E_{y_2,p_2}[(p_2 y_2 - x_2 - \psi(e_2^*, I))|y_1]\}$$

$$\times f(y_1|e, R)\, dy_1 - \psi(e, I),$$

where $E_{y_2,p_2}[(p_2 y_2 - x_2 - \psi(e_2^*, I))|y_1]$ is the expected profit in period 2, given the optimal choice of effort in period 2 and conditional on period 1 production. Note that when y_1 increases, the expected profit in period 2 decreases (for any effort in period 2, the probability of a high y_2 is lower). From the first-order conditions we can show that the first-period effort increases with η. The reason is that when the probability of expropriation in period 2 increases, the firm wants to maximize profits in period 1 (before expropriation) and thus increases effort. With a similar argument, it is easy to show that investment in period 0 decreases when η increases. Indeed, in period 0 the company solves

$$\max_I q(I)E_{y_1,p_1}\{p_1 y_1 - x_1 - \psi(e_1^*, I)$$

$$+ (1 - \eta)E_{y_2,p_2}[(p_2 y_2 - x_2 - \psi(e_2^*, I))|y_1]\} - I.$$

Since the expected (total) profit decreases with η, the marginal benefits of the initial investment are lower and investment decreases. This effect is of course higher if the risk of expropriation also exists in the first period.

Therefore, enforcement problems are associated with inefficient levels of initial investment (low I) and too quick extraction rates (high e_1).

Given the importance of enforcement considerations, a large set of safeguard clauses are often included in any contract aiming at creating a mechanism to resolve disputes (reduce η). The IOC usually wants disputes to be solved outside the state's judiciary system. The idea is to find a credible and fair third party to mediate between the company and the state. To this end, contracts usually establish that any dispute concerning the original agreement will be resolved through international commercial arbitration, whose decisions will in turn be enforced through multilateral treaty mechanisms. A related issue concerns the choice of the law that governs the oil contract. Most of the contracts are governed by host-state law, but sometimes the company manages to impose a combination of international law and host-state law.

Two complementary, extracontractual, tools to mitigate the enforcement problem are, first, reputation concerns on the state's side, and second, the threat of not reinvesting in the country by the company. Compliance with the terms of a contract helps the local government build a good reputation, which can be used to eliminate the need for the safeguard clauses just mentioned. If one thinks that the government will survive forever and cares about the possibility of having other companies exploit new wells, then reputation concerns provide enough incentives to comply with the contract terms. However, if one takes the view that governments are short-lived by nature, reputation concerns lose power as a solution to the enforcement problems. The second (related) idea is based on Bolton and Scharfstein 1990. They argue that in a dynamic debt contract, better incentives can be given by threatening to terminate funding if performance is poor. Using a very similar argument, the threat of not reinvesting in the country should make the local government less prone to unilaterally changing the original contract. Note, however, that once oil has been found, it may be relatively easy for a state to acquire another investor to take over the production stage.

2.4.4 Ex Post Uncertainty and Grievance

A new idea introduced by Hart and Moore (2008) is that contractual performance depends to some extent on the contracting parties' willingness to cooperate ex post on some aspects of the agreement that are not ex ante contractible. Hart and Moore (2008) distinguish between performance "within the letter of the contract" (perfunctory performance) and performance "within the spirit of the contract" (consummate performance). Only perfunctory performance is enforceable. The original contract works as a reference point for the parties' perceptions of entitlement. The party who ex post receives less than what he or she feels entitled to, feels aggrieved and reduces his or her cooperation ex post (shading)—that is, provides only perfunctory performance, generating a deadweight loss. Under uncertainty, grievance creates a trade-off between rigid and flexible contracts. A flexible contract makes it possible to adjust the outcome to the state of the world, but leaves room for disagreements and grievances. In the context of the petroleum contracts, the IOC can shade ex post by cutting the quality of the oil delivered or by delaying royalty payments. The state can shade by imposing excessive controls, by changing regulations so that they affect the company adversely, or by generating hostility in the local population toward foreign companies.

We will use our formal model to illustrate this problem. To keep things simple and make the point clear, suppose that the tax rate is 0, effort is verifiable, and the enforcement problem has been taken care of. Suppose also that the date 0 contract between the IOC and the state specifies that the company has to pay an amount $x_t \in [\underline{x}, \bar{x}]$ in period t. x_t is the royalty payment in the case of concession contracts, and the cost oil and the company's share of profit oil in the case of a PSA. The exact payment will be defined in period t. At date 1, production begins and the payment has to be specified. The parties bargain over the price and agree on the average price $(\underline{x} + \bar{x})/2$. However, since the contract specifies that any price in $[\underline{x}, \bar{x}]$ could be chosen, the company feels aggrieved because it feels entitled to pay only $\underline{x}$. Similarly, the state feels entitled to be paid $\bar{x}$ and also feels aggrieved. Then both parties shade. Suppose that shading is proportional to the degree to which a party feels aggrieved. Hence, shading by the company is $\theta(\bar{x} - \underline{x})/2$ and shading by the government is $\theta(\bar{x} - \underline{x})/2$, where $\theta \in (0,1)$ is a constant of proportionality.[8] Total deadweight loss is equal to $\theta(\bar{x} - \underline{x})$, and this is independent of which payment in the interval is actually chosen (a higher payment would reduce shading by the government but increase shading by the company).

In a world with no uncertainty, Hart and Moore (2008) show that rigid contracts are optimal. If the date 0 contract specifies a payment of $x_t = x$ in period t, then both parties feel entitled to x and when x is realized, nobody feels aggrieved. Indeed, if the terms of the contract are fixed, there is nothing to argue about ex post and therefore no party feels aggrieved. There is neither shading nor deadweight loss ex post $(\bar{x} - \underline{x} = 0)$.

This is no longer true if there is uncertainty, as is the case in the petroleum industry. In the petroleum industry, at the contracting date, there is uncertainty about the size of the well (R) and the quality of the oil. These uncertainties translate into uncertainties about production costs and the monetary value of oil produced. Flexibility may then be necessary to guarantee that production is efficient and to avoid contract renegotiations. Suppose that the contract is rigid (it specifies a payment $x_t = x$). But the well could be very small and the company may not be able to afford a payment of x. The quality of the oil could also be very high, and the lowest price at which the state is willing to give up the oil production is now higher than x. Under those circumstances the parties will need to renegotiate the contract. Note that any contract renegotiation implies that at least one party is not getting what he or she felt entitled to according to the original contract (the newly agreed-on payment is higher or lower than x), and thus induces inefficient shading.

Traditional concession contracts with surface royalties are rigid by assumption. Thus these contracts are more likely to be renegotiated as uncertainty unfolds—for example, if the well turns out to be more profitable than expected (the firm take is way above 0) or if profitability turns out to be lower than expected (the firm cannot cover its costs). Traditional PSAs with linear schemes for sharing profit oil are more flexible than traditional concessions, but yet they may be too rigid, given the degree of uncertainty in which the contracting parties operate. This in turn may account for the observed increase in the flexibility of both types of contracts in recent years. Flexibility in concession contracts is obtained by using a progressive royalty scheme, where the royalty is based on some profitability indicators (production, location, and so on). In PSAs, flexibility is introduced by a nonlinear scheme for sharing profit oil (sliding scales or shares based on the firm's rate of return). With this increased flexibility, the government agrees to get less on marginal fields and more on very profitable ones. Note also that this flexibility has been obtained to account for the production uncertainties, but once those uncertainties are resolved, the contract specifies a fixed payment. Hence, grievance is actually minimized.

An additional advantage of greater flexibility in the contracts between governments and oil companies—one that sheds light on why some local governments unilaterally renege on previous resource contracts—has to do with political economy. Governments tend to be short-termist and to disregard the welfare of future generations. This, in turn, represents a major departure from the Hart and Moore 2008 world in which the contracting parties remain the same ex ante and ex post. More concretely, suppose that the company faces two successive governments that only care about maximizing their current "private benefits" from holding power. The first government may then be willing to sign a contract ensuring high levels of bribes to government officials, but these could be largely detrimental to the country in the long run. Implicitly here, we assume that officials in the first local government have limited ability to use the oil contract to borrow against future revenues and then enjoy free use of the corresponding funds. In that case, even in the absence of additional uncertainty, implementation of the initial contract may cause grievance on the part of the country. In other words, because the initial contract may not have been negotiated under the same degree of ex ante competition as implicitly assumed in Hart and Moore 2008, this contract may no longer be a suitable reference point that reduces the scope for ex post grievance, particularly if the contract is rigid. This points to an interesting avenue for future research: the relationship between ex ante democracy, and the extent to which more rigid initial contracts between local governments and (foreign) companies limit the scope for ex post shading.

2.5   Conclusion

In this chapter we have discussed the pros and cons of various types of contracts between oil companies and local governments in light of recent contract theory. In particular, we have tried to explain the observed evolution toward more flexible contracts in resource extraction. Let us mention two main limitations of our analysis. First, our discussion appears to suggest that contracts have evolved toward greater flexibility, mainly because contract theory has only recently made us understand the drawbacks of rigid contracts. In practice, however, analytic considerations are intertwined with political considerations, in particular regarding the balance of power between the developed countries in which oil companies originate and the developing countries in which these companies operate. Developing countries are increasingly asserting their rights, and the propensity for colonial intervention by developed countries has clearly been receding in recent decades. The second aspect has to do with time-consistency issues. For example, to what extent do local governments need to impose fairer deals in order to convince others that they will not renege in the future? Or, on the other hand, do they always undermine their future credibility by imposing unilateral renegotiations? These and other equally important issues await further analysis.

Notes

1. Actual PSAs vary a lot from country to country and even within the same country. Hence, here we will describe a typical PSA. For a more detailed description of PSAs, see Bindemann 1999.

2. For instance, the state retains a proportion α_0 of profit oil if production is lower than Y and a proportion $\alpha_1 > \alpha_0$ if production is higher than Y.

3. The assumption that the cost of effort depends on I is made to reflect the fact that a larger investment increases future profits. The same idea could be introduced by assuming that I affects the distribution function F or reduces production costs (which in this stylized model are assumed to be equal to 0).

4. See Williamson 1975.

5. For instance, the efficiency of the whole tax system may be reduced or an increase in i requires higher collection effort.

6. See Tirole 2003 for a similar argument in the context of foreign borrowing.

7. Of course, expropriation is just an extreme case. In general, nonenforcement implies increased royalties in the case of concession contracts or a reduction in the company's share of profit oil in the case of PSAs.

8. For simplicity, we assume that θ is the same whether the shading party is the state or the company.

References

Aghion, P., M. Dewatripont, and P. Rey. 1994. "Renegotiation Design with Unverifiable Information." *Econometrica*, 62(2), 257–282.

Behn, D. 2007. "Sharing Iraq's Oil: Analyzing Production-Sharing Contracts under the Final Draft Petroleum Law." Ms., Tulane University School of Law.

Bindemann, K. 1999. *Production-Sharing Agreements: An Economic Analysis*. Oxford Institute for Energy Studies WPM 25.

Bolton, P., and D. S. Scharfstein. 1990. "A Theory of Predation Based on Agency Problems in Financial Contracting." *American Economic Review*, 80(1), 93–106.

Brinsmead, S. 2007. "Oil Concession Contracts and the Problem of Hold-Up." Ms., Australian National University.

Grossman, S. J., and O. D. Hart. 1986. "The Costs and Benefits of Ownership: A Theory of Vertical and Lateral Integration." *Journal of Political Economy*, 94(4), 691–719.

Hart, O., and J. Moore. 2007. "Incomplete Contracts and Ownership: Some New Thoughts." *AEA Papers and Proceedings*, 182–186.

Hart, O., and J. Moore. 2008. "Contracts as a Reference Point." *Quarterly Journal of Economics*, 123(1), 1–48.

Pongsiri, N. 2004. "Partnerships in Oil and Gas Production-Sharing Contracts." *International Journal of Public Sector Management*, 17(5), 431–442.

Tirole, J. 2003. "Inefficient Foreign Borrowing: A Dual- and Common-Agency Perspective." *American Economic Review*, 93(5), 1678–1702.

Williamson, O. 1975. *Markets and Hierarchies: Analysis and Antitrust Implications*. New York: Free Press.

Commentary

Lawrence H. Summers

Aghion and Quesada's chapter presents a contract theoretic model of how and why natural resource contracts often lead to expropriation. However, the chapter's modeling of potential solutions is not as comprehensive as the modeling of the problem. Indeed, the search for a better contract within the theory of contracts is likely to be a substantially less fruitful exercise than the derivation of a relevant theory that accommodates the institutional realities of this situation. Future models need to develop the complex motivations of other parties—including both individuals and institutions—that influence natural resource contracts without directly enforcing them.

My comment considers three aspects of third-party interactions that could be incorporated into future models. First, I examine what I call the "privatization trap"—the challenges faced by developing countries that lack credibility in bringing private-sector participation on reasonable terms. Second, I discuss a number of specific agency problems faced by government officials. Third, I describe the challenges of soliciting the assistance of third-party entities such as the World Bank or the U.S. government, which can influence the parties even though they cannot enforce the contract directly. In discussing these avenues for future research, I will draw significantly from my experiences at the World Bank, the Treasury Department, and Harvard.

The Privatization Trap

Let me start by discussing the "privatization trap," a term I used when I was at the World Bank and in government. Consider the case of a well-intentioned, well-meaning representative of a country that has a telephone company it wishes to privatize. Suppose that this country has had a history of changing governments with some frequency and a history of expropriating investors in ways that were not contemplated in the investors' contracts. The country faces a profoundly difficult problem in the following sense: Will any corporation pay a price for my telephone company such that if the government does not expropriate down the road, the company will earn a reasonable rate of return?

The answer is "no." If the corporation pays an amount such that it will earn a 10 percent rate of return, it is acting foolishly because there is a 50 percent chance that the government will expropriate. There thus is no reason it should make that investment. As a result, the corporation will not be willing to pay a reasonable price for this phone company. Instead it might be prepared to buy the phone company only at a price-earnings ratio of 3. In this situation, if the government does not expropriate and keep its promises, then a windfall profit is likely, in which case people will criticize the government. They will say that it was foolish to sell the phone company and to give rich foreigners an unjust windfall. These protests certainly contain a strong internal political logic. They may even have a strong moral logic as well, given that the windfall return could amount to 600 percent or more.

Once a country has worked itself into a position of being noncredible, it is rather difficult to achieve a satisfactory privatization outcome where other parties judge both the country and the foreign firm to have come out in a reasonable economic place. If a country is credible, it enjoys a good reputation, and there are incentives to maintain that reputation. Once the country is noncredible, very powerful incentives are created. It quickly finds itself burdened with a bad reputation that is difficult to shake. A bad reputation presents a particular challenge because getting rid of it requires the government to give away money to people who are not entitled to an extraordinary return.

In sovereign debt contracts, often a country wants to borrow money but is not credible, so it has to pay a 10 percent risk premium to do so. If the investment pays out over ten years, has the country given away an enormous amount of money, paying back usurers in this most outrageous of ways? Or has the country decided that it needs to renegotiate the debt downward and is going to reschedule it?

In exactly the same way, there is no good answer in natural resource contracts. The essence of this problem is that if everybody expects that a government is going to expropriate, then that government will have to give a share of production, a share of profits, or a royalty to the investor. If it in fact does not expropriate, the investor is going to have found its investment to be a spectacularly good one.

The key challenge is to escape this lack of credibility. Unfortunately, the answer that seems most attractive on the surface fails for the same reason that it is attractive in the first place. The government could pay in advance for a natural resource company to build facilities for extraction and then keep all the profits. Then the government has no actions to take, so no expropriation is possible.

But to state this answer is, in a sense, to explain why it does not work. An important part of the reason that a developing country is a developing country is its extremely high discount rate. Judged from the government's perspective, the outcome—pay a lot of money now, while its successors get a great deal of revenue down the road—is not terribly attractive.

Leaders in many settings experience the challenges of a high discount rate. When I became president of Harvard, for example, I was involved in a certain amount of fundraising and development activity. I noticed that the Development Office would set up many more meetings with people of my father's generation than with people of my generation. I inquired as to the wisdom of this practice and suggested that perhaps I could meet with people my own age. Somebody very wise in the Development Office, who grew a little tired of hearing me on this theme, said to me: "Larry, you have a very important question to decide: either you can raise money for your presidency, or you can raise money for your successor's. You can do it either way, but your strategy will raise money for your successor, and our strategy will raise money for you. Take your pick."

The privatization trap is the first aspect that traditional contract theory considerations do not capture at the highest order. From my perspective, this combination of high discount rates, limited resources, and credibility issues seems to capture the essence of the problem more than reframing the terms *royalty* and *production sharing*, as section 2.3 of the chapter does. The main problem is that if a country is not credible, you really cannot expect ex post to meet the dual conditions of not being an expropriator and not being a windfall giver.

Agency Problems

The second aspect is that governments are not monoliths. Governments consist of a collection of actors, and each actor has a different set of incentives. Each actor must be responsive to different sets of citizens who score their performance differently from what standard contract theory might suggest. Two examples from my professional experience demonstrate the types of considerations that future models must take into account.

When I was at the World Bank in the early 1990s, I was quite seized with the idea that the World Bank and others should work with governments to avoid uncertainty and reduce risk by engaging in strategic planning around export price volatility. This concern was particularly important considering that when governments had a lot of money to spend fast, they wasted it for all kinds of agency reasons, and cutbacks brought excruciating political consequences. It was obvious that locking in prices to some degree was the right thing to do.

While the liquidity of the markets surely would not permit everybody, most people, or even Saudi Arabia to hedge a large fraction of its activities, it was clear that the liquidity of the markets would permit more hedging than was the case at the time. On that issue I was somewhat more equation-oriented as an economist than I am today, and I was absolutely mystified that so little hedging occurred. As I moved out of the two-dimensional world of equations and increasingly acquainted myself with government finance officers in the real world, it became absolutely clear to me why the answer deviated so dramatically from the theory.

Consider a government official who decides to mitigate risk and uncertainty regarding future income from the export of her country's commodity by purchasing insurance. She faces two possibilities. One is that the price of her country's commodity will go down, in which case everybody would be moderately appreciative of the decision to purchase insurance. The other is that the price of her country's commodity will go up, in which case she would, ex post, be criticized for spending money unnecessarily by having purchased the insurance. Thus, there are asymmetrical rewards and punishments for the individual agent responsible for this type of decision.

A second example might be understood as a negotiation version of the Hart-Moore reference point feature of contracts. In most negotiation theory pieces by game theorists or economists, the goal of each party is to get as good an outcome as it possibly can from the negotiation. The utility function is about the negotiation.

Time at the Treasury Department in the Clinton Administration, however, taught me that the goal was not to do as well as possible in absolute terms, but to do as well as possible compared with expectations. Our negotiation strategy was heavily conditioned by the fact that the way we were going to be scored by the broader world was not in terms of the ultimate outcome we achieved, but rather in terms of the aspirations we had established for our outcome. If we ever said our goal was to do X, and then we only achieved 70 percent of that goal, then we had achieved an undesirable outcome. Therefore, the type of negotiation pattern that emerged depended substantially on how ambitious the aspirations for the negotiation were.

Closely related is a hypothetical example in which the agency and the intertemporal aspect come together. Consider a government agent in China in 2007 who is contemplating discussions of the exchange rate and trade with the United States. She would be intensely aware of the fact that the new administration in January 2009 would need to see itself as being successful with her. More specifically, the new administration would not be scored based on the state of trade relations in July 2009; instead, it would be scored based on how much talks had progressed between January and July. In other words, new governments are scored not in terms of the aggregate welfare that exists, but in terms of what they have achieved. This achievement mentality creates a further incentive for expropriation activities and for maximizing similar kinds of problems.

Third-Party Influences

Finally, what is the role of third parties in facilitating better outcomes in these situations? One interesting feature of chapter 2 as well as the other chapters is that there is almost no discussion of U.S. tax law. Some of the issues dealing with contractual arrangements—such as what form cash streams take—are not only about reducing expropriation risk, but also about domestic laws as to what is credited, what is deducted, and what can be counted as a cost. The shaping of these arrangements in U.S. tax law may be intellectually uninteresting, but from a practical perspective, it is a very important aspect for consideration in future models. It would be at least worth thinking about whether the biases that those taxes induce are positive or negative from the point of view of the contracts that we want to achieve.

More fundamental is the question of public hostages around various kinds of private investment deals, a question that first occurred to me while I was at the World Bank. My experiences came up a little more with respect to debt, but the same point could be made in this context. For example, if a country defaults and is dealing not just with Exxon but also with the U.S. government, it becomes much more problematic to expropriate. If ex ante it will become much more problematic to expropriate, the country will then be able to structure contracts that give it less good deals ex post. However, less good deals ex post mean that the ex post incentive to expropriate is increased. Thus, in order to drive more efficient and more able transactions, there is a very strong incentive to associate those with good enforcement technology and those that it is harder and more costly to expropriate with these transactions.

To what extent should it become the business of the World Bank or the U.S. government to associate little bits of its preferred creditor status with a large number of projects so as to improve their enforcement and produce better outcomes? The idea is tempting, but a few questions remain. One is something that I used to call the "realtor squeeze" in the context of IMF programs. On each of the occasions when I have bought or sold a house, there were two levels of negotiation. At one level, the other party and I were opposed to each other, each striving for the best price. At another level, there was a kind of choreography between us to not come to complete agreement and threaten to walk away. The only way the realtors could get any commission was to chip in the last 1 percent and take a 4 percent commission rather than their standard 5 percent commission.

Now consider the same situation, but replace the realtors with the public sector. A similar situation arises, for example, when Ukraine is negotiating with its creditors. Both sides want to get to a place where there just cannot be an agreement, and the whole economy will collapse, and then neither will get paid unless the IMF comes in with $10 billion. Something very similar would likely start to occur if governments or international agencies involved themselves to a larger extent with these projects.

Second is the question of the broad geopolitics of natural resources. After all, we tend, almost universally in American history classes, to make fun of General Smedley Butler, who proudly invaded Honduras on behalf of United Fruit. To endorse such militaristic policies in the name of having a better enforcement technology so there can be more foreign direct investment so there can in turn be better development investment might be, to put it mildly, to miss some important elements of the situation.

Such policies raise a third question: What is the relative benefit of more involvement by the World Bank? If the World Bank associated itself with two-thirds of the foreign investment that took place in countries, it would presumably stop being a preferred creditor, and that would have a set of collateral consequences. I am not yet ready to endorse such a move as a major systematic strategy for dealing with this problem.

Conclusion

To the extent that the model presented in Aghion and Quesada's chapter is representative of contract theory, contract theory seems to tell us that natural resource contracts are fundamentally between two parties that seek to maximize their own utility. By highlighting three alternative aspects of these contractual relationships, this comment suggests that the opposite is true. The two main parties, the government and the foreign firm, are concerned about the opinions of onlookers, and agents are concerned about the opinions of their principals. Since a solution within contract theory still seems elusive, a general suggestion for theoretical research in this area would be to model the contracts in less elaborate ways and to model the contracting parties and their motivations in more elaborate ways. The chapter has taken a useful step in this direction by adopting Hart-Moore reference points in its model, but motivations should be integrated significantly more in future models.

3 Sovereign Theft: Theory and Evidence about Sovereign Default and Expropriation

Michael Tomz and Mark L. J. Wright

All investments are subject to political risk: the possibility that, after investments have been sunk, governments will enact policies that reduce the payoffs to investors. Political risk is particularly severe in the case of foreign investments, where the absence of supranational courts limits legal remedies and where an investor's foreign nationality limits redress through domestic political institutions.

In this chapter we study the most extreme forms of political risk (default and expropriation, which we refer to collectively as *sovereign theft*) and their effect on the two most important forms of foreign investment (sovereign debt and direct investment). We first review the theoretical literature about sovereign theft. We then use a series of formal models to analyze how the incentives to engage in sovereign theft vary with the state of the economy, the risk aversion of political leaders, and the nature of punishments for default and expropriation.

Finally, we document patterns of sovereign theft and foreign investment across much of the twentieth century. Our research, based on a new data set, reveals a striking asynchronicity: defaults and expropriations have occurred in alternating, rather than coincident, waves. We further show that the overall level of foreign investment has increased, but the composition has alternated between debt and direct investment. We conclude by discussing the implications of our theoretical and empirical work for future research about sovereign theft.

3.1 Theoretical Perspectives on Sovereign Theft

When deciding whether to engage in sovereign theft, a government must weigh the benefits of taking resources from investors against the potential costs, such as a loss of access to future investments or exposure to other penalties. The balance of costs and benefits will depend on the type of investment, as well as on the economic and political circumstances the government faces. In this section we provide a nontechnical review of the theoretical literature about the incentives to default on foreign debts and/or expropriate the assets of direct investors. In the following section we offer a more technical analysis, based on a suite of formal models.

3.1.1   The Short-Run Benefits of Sovereign Theft

A simple debt contract specifies a fixed return that investors are entitled to receive, whereas a simple equity contract specifies a variable return that is proportional to the profits from the enterprise. In practice, debt and equity contracts come in more elaborate forms. This is particularly true of international bonds, which may be issued in different currencies and at different maturities, may be indexed to inflation, and may even specify that returns should vary with commodity prices or the gross domestic product of the economy (for example, the Brady bonds of Mexico and Bulgaria, or the Argentine bonds in the 2005 restructuring). Likewise, equity contracts may vary in the details by which investors and the host country share revenues and costs. Notwithstanding this rich variation, one can gain valuable insights by examining debt and equity contracts in their purest forms.

First consider a simple debt contract, which requires the country to pay a fixed amount no matter whether economic times are good or bad. Leaders will be most tempted to default on such a contract when their value for resources is highest. During a recession, for example, tax revenues are often low, and residents of the country often place a heavy burden on the welfare state. In hard times like these, political leaders need resources and might be especially inclined to withhold interest and principal from foreigners.

The incentives to engage in sovereign theft are somewhat different with equity contracts. Suppose that a project financed by foreign direct investment (FDI) has returns that correlate perfectly with the business cycle. The desire to expropriate is then determined by a trade-off between two forces: "desperation" and "opportunism" (Cole and English 1991). If leaders place a high value on resources in recessions, they will be most tempted to expropriate out of desperation during recessions, even though the required payments to foreign investors would be lowest at those times. If, on the other hand, the leaders value resources in recessions about the same as in booms, they will be most tempted to expropriate opportunistically in booms when payments to investors (and hence the amount to be gained from expropriation) would be highest. As we show formally below, the trade-off between desperation and opportunism depends crucially on the risk aversion of political leaders.

3.1.2   The Long-Run Benefits of Sovereign Theft

The benefits of sovereign theft typically extend beyond the period in which the theft occurs. By defaulting completely on a debt contract, the country can gain all interest and principal payments that were scheduled to have occurred in the future; by completely expropriating direct investments, the country can appropriate the future stream of revenues that would otherwise have gone to foreign investors.

The long-run benefits of sovereign theft depend, however, on the nature of the investment. Direct investments, unlike loans, typically involve some transfer of control over the operations of the project and some transfer of complementary goods, assets, or factors of production from foreign investors to the host country. Some of these transfers are irrevocable. For example, once the domestic workforce has been trained to operate the project, it may continue long after the direct investor has departed. In this case, the future gains from expropriation can be large. Other transfers must occur repeatedly. A project may, for example, require goods from some other arm of the multinational firm or managerial inputs that are vested in foreign employees. When factors of production must be sent repeatedly, expropriation will significantly reduce the value of the project, especially if disgruntled foreign investors deny access to these factors and the factors are not available from other sources.[1]

3.1.3   The Costs of Sovereign Theft: Loss of Access to Future Investments

We have considered the principal benefit of sovereign theft: the country can retain resources it otherwise would have paid to foreigners. If there were no costs to sovereign theft, countries would always default on debts and expropriate foreign direct investments, and consequently we would never observe foreign investments of any kind. There is substantial disagreement among scholars about the costs of sovereign theft. Indeed, some authors have posed this as a puzzle: Why do we ever observe foreign investments in practice?

Perhaps countries honor their contracts to preserve access to future investments. They might, for example, fear that sovereign theft would trigger *retribution*, in which investors would withhold funds in order to punish the country for breaking the contract. Eaton and Gersovitz (1981b) formalized this idea in the context of sovereign borrowing. They modeled a repeated game in which lenders deterred the sovereign from defaulting by threatening to retaliate against a single act of default by permanently excluding the perpetrator from future borrowing. Other authors have used similar logic to explain why countries refrain from expropriating direct investments (e.g., Cole and English 1991, 1992a, 1992b; Albuquerque 2003).[2]

It is not obvious that the threat of permanent exclusion from future investments would be credible, however. If a country is excluded from capital markets, potential gains from trade are being left unexploited. Investors other than the party that was directly affected by the act of sovereign theft might, therefore, be tempted to cooperate with the country, instead of participating in the punitive embargo. Bulow and Rogoff (1989b) showed, for example, that a country could take the payments it would have made to foreign lenders and invest them with foreign financial institutions in such a way as to duplicate the gains it could have attained from future borrowing. To avoid the costs of default, then, the country need not convince foreign creditors to lend; it need only convince financiers to accept deposits.

A growing literature establishes the limitations of the Bulow-Rogoff critique. As Kletzer and Wright (2000) show, limits on the ability of financial institutions in creditor countries to guarantee repayment can restore the threat of exclusion. Wright (2001) finds conditions under which even competitive financial institutions (in the sense of making zero profits in equilibrium) can coordinate to exclude a defaulter from access to all capital markets. Amador (2004) adds that leaders in politically unstable countries may be unwilling to save in ways that would help them evade punishment for default. Foreign direct investment may be even less vulnerable to the Bulow-Rogoff critique. As already noted, direct investments often involve the transfer of skills and factors of production. If these are in limited supply, competitors may not be able to undermine the threat of exclusion, and hence the threat may be effective in deterring expropriation.

Sovereign theft might not only trigger retribution but also sully a country's *reputation*. International investments take place in a context of incomplete information, in which investors cannot fully know the preferences of foreign governments. If a government engages in sovereign theft, foreigners may infer that the government is a "bad type" that assigns a low value to future loans and good relations with foreign investors. Having learned about the government's preferences, foreigners refrain from making new investments, not because they are participating in a coordinated retaliatory embargo, but simply because they now think that further investment would be a money-losing proposition. Given what they know about the government's type, the risk of sovereign theft would be too great to warrant future investment (see, for example, Cole, Dow, and English 1995; Sandleris 2008; and Tomz 2007, with the latter documenting the importance of reputation throughout history).

Some models emphasize the possibility of reputational spillovers: a government's behavior in one area of world affairs could reveal its type more generally, thereby affecting all its international relations (Cole and Kehoe 1998; Rose and Spiegel 2009). Such models predict that a government should commit all acts of sovereign theft simultaneously, instead of spacing them across time. Essentially, there is no reason to continue repaying debts in the hope of preserving a good reputation if, by expropriating foreign direct investments, a government has already revealed itself to be unreliable. The country should expropriate and default at the same time to get the maximum benefit for the same reputational cost. Other models allow defaults and expropriations to signal different things about the government, such that defaults and expropriations need not coincide.

3.1.4 The Costs of Sovereign Theft: Other Considerations

Sovereign theft could entail other costs, beyond the loss of access to future investments. Kaletsky (1985) and Bulow and Rogoff (1989a) suggest that sovereign theft could trigger direct sanctions, such as trade embargoes or gunboat diplomacy. Rose (2005) finds that countries that defaulted on their debts experienced a decline in foreign trade, perhaps because creditors were imposing trade sanctions. Mitchener and Weidenmier (forthcoming) and Ahmed, Alfaro, and Maurer (2007) add that during the nineteenth and early twentieth centuries, creditors used the threat of military retaliation to deter countries from defaulting. These views remain controversial, however. Martinez and Sandleris (2008) show that the trade declines identified by Rose (2005) are unrelated to the pattern of creditor holdings of debt. Moreover, in a study of sovereign debt across three centuries, Tomz (2007) finds no evidence that trade sanctions were explicitly used to punish defaulters and uncovers little proof that creditors ever used—or even threatened to use—military intervention to enforce debt contracts.

Would the prospect of direct sanctions be more effective in protecting foreign direct investment than in compelling countries to honor debt contracts? Much depends on who owns the debt versus the direct investment. If a sovereign government owes debts to other governments or to supranational institutions, as is sometimes the case today, it seems plausible that those public creditors would apply diplomatic or commercial sanctions in response to default. It is less obvious that governments would take military or commercial action against countries that reneged on contracts with private citizens. Research by Platt (1968) and Tomz (2007) shows that, before World War II, governments occasionally used force to help private citizens recover their foreign direct investments, but they did not take similarly punitive steps to assist holders of foreign government bonds.

Counterbalancing the possibility of direct sanctions, there may be sizable direct benefits to developing countries that expropriate foreign investments in politically sensitive natural resource projects, where nationalist sentiment often makes foreign investment unwelcome. Domínguez (1982), for example, documents the tide of "business nationalism" that contributed to expropriations in Latin America during the 1970s.

Finally, the liquidity of investments may affect the costs of sovereign theft. Broner, Martin, and Ventura (2006) have argued that the development of liquid secondary markets in debt may reduce a country's temptation to default. If, through the operation of secondary markets, debts that were once owned by foreigners become the property of citizens in the borrowing state, the government may be reluctant to default, since such action would hurt its own constituents. Provided that debts are more liquid than direct investments (see Fernández-Arias and Hausmann 2001, Hausmann and Fernández-Arias 2001), debts might be less vulnerable to sovereign theft. Spiegel (1994), however, has argued the opposite: that direct investments have a liquidity advantage and are, therefore, more secure vehicles for international capital.

In summary, the costs and benefits of sovereign theft are likely to vary with economic and political conditions, and with the type of foreign investment. We explore these differences formally in the next section.

3.2 Models of Sovereign Theft

We model relations between international investors and a country that needs foreign capital for production. The decisions of the country's residents are assumed to be captured by the decisions of a representative agent who is risk averse, and may, therefore, seek foreign funds not only to increase production but also to insure against production risk. We develop several models that differ according to the assets through which the country can access international financial markets and the punishments the country would suffer for breach of contract. All the models share several basic features, which we now outline.

3.2.1 Assumptions in All the Models

Consider a small open economy with a production opportunity that requires foreign capital. Investing k units of foreign capital produces $\theta f(k)$ units of output. Here f is a standard neoclassical production function that is bounded, strictly increasing, and strictly concave in k, and $\theta > 0$ is a random productivity shock with probability density function $g(\theta)$. The function $g(\theta)$ is common knowledge, but the realization of θ is not known to either the country or to international investors at the time investments take place. Thus, investments in the country are intrinsically risky, independent of any potential for sovereign theft.

The country's representative agent is risk averse and evaluates consumption levels according to a strictly increasing and strictly concave utility function, $U(c)$. As long as contracts are honored, the country will be rewarded with an extra utility prize P that depends on the investment environment and represents the benefits associated with honoring contracts (e.g., future access to foreign finance and trade, and favorable diplomatic relations with creditor countries).

The country can obtain capital from a large group of risk neutral international investors. Competition among members of this group ensures that they earn, on average, no more than the opportunity cost of their funds, which is given by the constant international interest rate r^w. The models that follow differ in the limitations, if any, on the country's ability to interact with international investors.

3.2.2 First-Best Contracts

Suppose the country could commit to honoring all possible contracts, including but not limited to debts and direct investments. In this case, investment will be at the *first-best level*, which maximizes the expected value of production less the opportunity cost of funds to international investors. That is, the first-best level of investment, k^{FB}, solves

$$1 + r^w = E[\theta] f'(k^{FB}),$$

where E is an expectation operator that captures the expected value of the productivity shock θ. This equation says that in a first-best world, investment occurs up to the point where the expected marginal product of investment equals the gross world interest rate.

Under the assumption that international capital markets are competitive, the country retains all gains from dealing with foreign investors and can insure itself perfectly against fluctuations in production. It therefore earns the certain return (measured in utility units) of

$$U^{FB} = U(E[\theta] f(k^{FB}) - (1 + r^w) k^{FB}).$$

In what follows, we examine how limitations on the assets available to the country, and on the country's ability to commit to honoring contracts, affect the level of investment and the country's welfare.

3.2.3   Defaultable Debt

Suppose the only asset available to the country is defaultable debt. That is, the country can raise capital only by issuing an amount b of zero-coupon bonds at price $q(b)$ per bond, where q is a function of b. The capital the country receives from issuing these bonds, $k = bq(b)$, can be invested in the project. At the end of the period, the country chooses whether to honor the contract by paying the non-state-contingent amount b to investors, or to default completely and retain all resources for itself.

If the country repays the debt, it consumes $\theta f(k) - b$ and also receives a utility prize P^D for maintaining good relations with lenders. If, on the other hand, the country defaults, it consumes the entire output $\theta f(k)$ but forgoes the utility prize P^D. As a result, after observing the productivity shock θ, the country defaults if

$$U(\theta f(k)) > U(\theta f(k) - b) + P^D.$$

The bond price $q(b)$ is determined by competition in the capital market and reflects expectations about the likelihood of default. Denote the probability of default as

$$\pi(b) = \Pr\{\theta | U(\theta f(bq(b))) > U(\theta f(bq(b)) - b) + P^D\},$$

where we have substituted $bq(b)$ for k to make clear that the probability of default depends on b, the size of the promised repayment.

Investors will demand a price $q(b)$ that makes them indifferent between lending to the country and receiving b with probability $1 - \pi(b)$, versus investing in an alternative asset that pays $(1 + r^w)k$ with certainty. Setting these quantities equal to each other and solving for $q(b)$, we get

$$q(b) = \frac{1 - \pi(b)}{1 + r^w}.$$

The country chooses b (which implies a level of k), taking into account b's effect on the price of the bonds.

This model belongs to the class of defaultable debt models introduced by Eaton and Gersovitz (1981b) and exploited by Arellano (2008), Aguiar and Gopinath (2006), and Tomz and Wright (2007), among others. In contrast to these models, it adds production—as opposed to just consumption smoothing—as a motivation for international borrowing. For simplicity, the direct utility benefit of repayment is taken as exogenous, unlike in the papers by Yue (2006), Pitchford and Wright (2007), and Benjamin and Wright (2009), who model these payments as the outcome of bargaining between creditors and debtors.

We solve the model numerically using a version of the following algorithm:

Algorithm 1 (Defaultable Debt Model)

1. For every promised repayment b, every bond price q, and every productivity realization θ, compute whether it is optimal for the country to default.

2. Given the result of step 1, compute the expected return to the investor (averaging over the probability distribution of θ) for each combination of b and q.

3. Find the combination of b and q that maximizes the expected utility of the debtor country,

$$E[\max\{U(\theta f(bq)), U(\theta f(bq) - b) + P^D\}],$$

subject to the constraint that the combination gives the investor an expected return at least as large as the risk-free rate.

For this model, we have found that our algorithm converges faster than the usual iterative method, even when implemented on very fine grids of possible promised repayments.

3.2.4   Expropriable Direct Investment

The previous model assumed that the country could obtain foreign capital only by borrowing. Suppose instead that the country's only option is to sell an equity stake that entitles investors to a proportion α of net output. The country will expropriate the equity stake if

$$U(\theta f(k)) > U((1 - \alpha)\theta f(k)) + P^E,$$

where P^E represents the direct prize from honoring equity contracts. This prize may differ from P^D if, for example, a direct investor contributes factors to the production process that make the project less valuable in the event of an expropriation.

Let Θ^* be the set of all θ such that the contracts are not expropriated. In equilibrium, the shareholding α necessary to raise k resources must satisfy

$$(1 + r^w)k = \alpha f(k) \int_{\Theta^*} \theta g(\theta) \, d\theta,$$

in order to ensure that foreign investors break even.

As with the defaultable debt model, we solve the expropriable direct investment model numerically using a grid-search algorithm.

Algorithm 2 (Expropriable Direct Investment Model)

1. For every level of capital k, every shareholding proportion α, and every productivity realization θ, compute whether it is optimal for the country to expropriate.

2. Given the result of step 1, compute the expected return to the investor (averaging over the probability distribution of θ) for each combination of k and α.

3. Choose the combination of k and α that maximizes the expected utility of the debtor country,

$$E[\max\{U(\theta f(k)), U((1 - \alpha)\theta f(k)) + P^E\}],$$

subject to the constraint that the combination gives the investor an expected return at least as large as the risk-free rate.

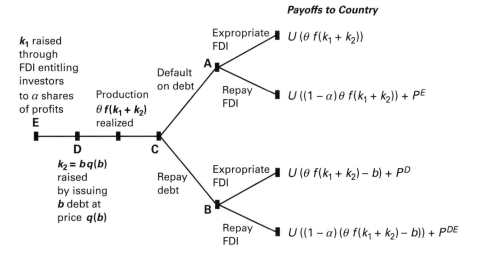

Figure 3.1
A model of defaultable debt and expropriable direct investment

3.2.5 Defaultable Debt and Expropriable Direct Investment

Having considered scenarios in which the country can issue either
defaultable debt or expropriable equity, we now develop a model in
which the country can issue both. This allows us to consider the optimal mix of debt and equity, and how the mix evolves in response to
the economic and political environment.

To create room for both debt and equity, we need to specify the timing with which different types of capital are raised and repaid (or not).
We assume that direct investments occur before loans are contracted,
and that loans are repaid before profits are distributed to direct investors. The resulting environment, in which decisions are taken in successive stages, is displayed in figure 3.1. First, an amount of capital k_1 is
raised by issuing shares that entitle direct investors to a proportion α
of the profit from the project. Next, more capital k_2 is raised by issuing
debt (a promise to repay b at the end of the project) at bond price q. The
total, $k_1 + k_2$, is devoted to production. The production shock θ is then
observed, and production $\theta f(k_1 + k_2)$ is realized. The country next
decides whether to default on its debts, and finally chooses whether
to expropriate the earnings of direct investors. The size of the "prize"
associated with honoring contracts is P^{DE} if the country repays both
debt and equity, and is either P^D or P^E if only one of the two contracts
is upheld. If neither contract is honored, the country receives no prize.

The model is solved by backward induction. Consider the decision of a country that has already defaulted and is now weighing whether to expropriate the equity stake of foreign direct investors. At this stage of the game (stage A in figure 3.1), the country expropriates if and only if

$$U(\theta f(k_1 + k_2)) > U((1 - \alpha)\theta f(k_1 + k_2)) + P^E.$$

Let

$$V^A(\theta, k_1, k_2, \alpha) = \max\{U(\theta f(k_1 + k_2)), U((1 - \alpha)\theta f(k_1 + k_2)) + P^E\}$$

be the optimum value to the country from ending up at stage A, and let $\phi^A(\theta, k_1, k_2, \alpha)$ be an indicator function for an expropriation at this stage in state θ.

Next consider a country that has not defaulted and must decide whether to expropriate (stage B in figure 3.1). If the country expropriates, it receives the total output net of the repayment of debt, $\theta f(k_1 + k_2) - b$, whereas if it honors the direct investment contract it receives a fraction $1 - \alpha$ of this amount. Hence, a country at stage B expropriates if and only if

$$U(\theta f(k_1 + k_2) - b) + P^D > U((1 - \alpha)[\theta f(k_1 + k_2) - b]) + P^{DE}.$$

Let

$$V^B(\theta, k_1, k_2, \alpha, b) = \max\{U(\theta f(k_1 + k_2) - b) + P^D,$$

$$U((1 - \alpha)[\theta f(k_1 + k_2) - b]) + P^{DE}\}$$

be the optimum value to the country from stage B, and let $\phi^B(\theta, k_1, k_2, \alpha, b)$ be an indicator function for expropriation at that stage in state θ.

Working backward, consider the country's decision to default or not (stage C). If it repays its debts, it gives up b resources today and moves on to stage B; if it defaults, it keeps those resources and moves on to stage A. Hence, a country in state θ defaults if and only if

$$V^A(\theta, k_1, k_2, \alpha) > V^B(\theta, k_1, k_2, \alpha, b).$$

The value to the country from choosing optimally at stage C is, therefore,

$$V^C(\theta, k_1, k_2, \alpha, b) = \max\{V^A(\theta, k_1, k_2, \alpha), V^B(\theta, k_1, k_2, \alpha, b)\}.$$

If $\phi^C(\theta, k_1, k_2, \alpha, b)$ is an indicator function for default at stage C in state θ, then the probability that the country defaults is

$$\pi(k_1, k_2, \alpha, b) = \int \phi^C(\theta, k_1, k_2, \alpha, b)g(\theta)\,d\theta,$$

where $g(\theta)$ is the probability density of θ.

Next consider stage D, where the country can issue some amount of debt b at price $q(b; k_1, \alpha)$, where q is set taking into account not only b but also the direct investment contract, if any, that exists when loans are raised. At this point, the country has not observed the outcome of the production shock, θ, and hence must maximize its expected payoffs. The optimum value to the country at stage D is

$$V^D(k_1, \alpha) = \max_b \int V^C(\theta, k_1, bq(b; k_1, \alpha), \alpha, b)g(\theta)\,d\theta,$$

where we have replaced the amount the country has borrowed, k_2, with $bq(b; k_1, \alpha)$. Denote the level of capital raised through debt issuance, as a function of k_1 and α, as $k_2^*(k_1, \alpha)$.

Competition among lenders implies that the bond price satisfies

$$q(b; k_1, \alpha) = \frac{1 - \pi(k_1, k_2, \alpha, b)}{1 + r^w}$$

$$= \frac{1 - \pi(k_1, bq(b; k_1, \alpha), \alpha, q)}{1 + r^w},$$

where r^w is the risk-free world interest rate. Note the self-referential nature of this equation: bond prices affect the probability of default, which in turn affects bond prices. This opens the possibility of multiple equilibria.

At stage E, the starting point of the game, equity is issued to maximize the country's welfare, $V^E(k_1, \alpha(k_1))$, where α, now expressed as a function of k_1, is determined by competition among equity investors. That is, $\alpha(k_1)$ must solve

$$(1 + r^w)k_1 = \alpha(k_1) \int \{\phi^C(\theta, .)(1 - \phi^A(\theta, .))\theta f(k_1 + k_2^*(k_1))$$

$$+ (1 - \phi^C(\theta, .))(1 - \phi^B(\theta, .))[\theta f(k_1 + k_2^*(k_1)) - b]\}g(\theta)\,d\theta,$$

where we have suppressed the arguments of the ϕ's for simplicity.

This model is more complex than the previous two, because it combines elements of each. It is solved by the following algorithm:

Algorithm 3 (Combined Model: Defaultable Debt and Expropriable Direct Investment)

1. For every level of capital raised from foreign direct investment k_1, every shareholding level α, every promised debt repayment b, every bond price q, and every productivity realization θ, compute whether it is optimal for the country to
(a) Default on its debts and expropriate foreign direct investments;
(b) Default on its debts and honor its foreign direct investments;
(c) Repay its debts and expropriate its foreign direct investments; or
(d) Repay its debts and honor its foreign direct investments.

2. Given the result of step 1, compute the expected return to a bondholder, and to a foreign direct investor, for each combination of k_1, α, b, and q.

3. Find the combination of k_1, α, b, and q that maximizes the expected utility of the debtor country,

$$E[\max\{U(\theta f(k_1 + qb)), U((1 - \alpha)\theta f(k_1 + qb)) + P^E,$$

$$U(\theta f(k_1 + qb) - b) + P^D, U((1 - \alpha)\theta f(k_1 + qb) - b) + P^{DE}\}],$$

subject to the constraint that foreign direct investors and bondholders each earn an expected return at least as large as the risk-free rate.

3.3   Analysis of the Models

In this section we use the defaultable debt model, the expropriable direct investment model, and the combined model to study the incentives of sovereign governments and foreign investors. We show how the temptation to engage in sovereign theft (and hence the willingness of foreigners to make investments) varies with the state of the economy, the risk aversion of decision makers, and the nature of the prizes for respecting contracts.

3.3.1   Defaultable Debt vs. Expropriable Direct Investment
When the only source of foreign investment is defaultable debt, sovereign theft should be more likely to occur in bad times than in good ones. Recall that the country's utility function, U, is strictly concave

and that the promised debt repayment, b, must be greater than or equal to zero. It follows that, if a country defaults at some productivity level θ^*, it will default for all $\theta < \theta^*$. This result holds for all countries, regardless of the leader's attitude toward risk.

In the direct investment model, by contrast, the effect of economic conditions on sovereign theft depends on the risk aversion of leaders. Recall that expropriation occurs when

$$U(\theta f(k)) > U((1 - \alpha)\theta f(k)) + P^E.$$

Suppose the country has a constant relative risk aversion (CRRA) utility function

$$U(c) = \begin{cases} \frac{c^{1-\sigma}}{1-\sigma}, & \text{for } \sigma > 0, \ \sigma \neq 1 \\ \log c & \text{for } \sigma = 1. \end{cases}$$

If $\sigma \neq 1$, then, the country will expropriate if

$$\theta^{1-\sigma} > \frac{(1-\sigma)P^E}{[1 - (1-\alpha)^{1-\sigma}]f(k)^{1-\sigma}}.$$

This inequality formally establishes the aforementioned trade-off between "desperation" and "opportunism" (Cole and English 1991).[3] The left side of the inequality is decreasing in θ when $\sigma > 1$ but is increasing in θ when $\sigma < 1$. Thus, highly risk-averse leaders (leaders with $\sigma > 1$), who are very reluctant to forgo consumption when output is low, will expropriate out of desperation when θ is small. In contrast, leaders who are not especially risk averse (i.e., ones with $\sigma < 1$) will expropriate shareholdings opportunistically when θ is high. In the intermediate case of $\sigma = 1$, these two forces exactly balance and offset, making the decision to expropriate independent of θ.

These results highlight important similarities and differences between sovereign debt and direct investment. When leaders are relatively risk averse, debt and equity are similar in the sense that leaders are most tempted to engage in sovereign theft when output is low. When leaders are relatively neutral about risk, though, the two types of investments differ: leaders remain most likely to default when output is low, but they are least likely to expropriate in those same situations.

To illustrate these patterns and obtain other results, we assign values to parameters and solve the models numerically. Let the production function be Cobb-Douglas, such that

$f(k) = k^\eta$,

where η, the output elasticity of capital, takes on a standard value of 1/3. Suppose the productivity level θ follows a discrete-state approximation to a lognormal distribution with coefficient of variation equal to 10 percent. Finally, let the world interest rate r^w be 5 percent. In the analyses that follow, we vary either the risk aversion of leaders or the rewards for honoring contracts.

Figures 3.2a–3.2d display the effect of risk aversion on country-investor relations when only one type of capital—either a loan or a direct investment—is available. To construct the figures, we varied the coefficient of relative risk aversion, σ, from a nearly risk-neutral value of 1/5 to a highly risk-averse value of 5. We further set the prize for respecting each type of contract at 35 percent of the first-best utility value, U^{FB}, scaled by $(1 - \sigma)$ to ensure positive prizes.

Figure 3.2a shows, for each value of σ, the set of productivity levels (θ's) at which the country would find it optimal to default. When σ is small, the country has little desire to smooth its consumption and engages in sovereign theft only in the most adverse states of the world, when productivity levels are at a minimum. As σ rises, the country becomes more risk averse and therefore less tolerant of repaying during bad times. Investors respond by increasing interest rates, further heightening the incentive to default. Eventually, at a coefficient of relative risk aversion of just under 4, default occurs in all states and the market for debt shuts down.

Figure 3.2b plots the analogous set of circumstances under which the country would expropriate. Consistent with the analytical derivations, expropriations occur in good times when the country is relatively risk tolerant and in bad times when the country is relatively risk averse. Consequently, the probability of expropriation (see figure 3.2c) is nonmonotonic, falling as σ climbs toward one and rising thereafter, whereas the probability of default increases steadily with σ.

Moreover, the probability of default exceeds the probability of expropriation for all but the lowest values of σ. There are two reasons why a relatively risk-averse leader would be more likely to default than to expropriate in bad states of the world. The main reason is that, during hard times, debt contracts afford the country less slack than equity contracts. Simple debt contracts require the same payment regardless of circumstances, whereas equity contracts require smaller payments when productivity is low.

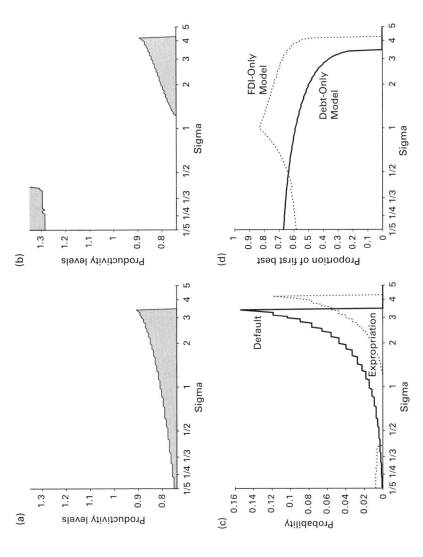

Figure 3.2
The effect of risk aversion (debt-only model vs. FDI-only model): (*a*) set of default states as a function of sigma; (*b*) set of expropriation states as a function of sigma; (*c*) probability of sovereign theft as a function of sigma; (*d*) investment levels (relative to first-best investment) as a function of sigma.

The second reason is more indirect and subtle. In bad times, debt contracts stipulate larger repayments than equity contracts. When sovereign theft occurs, therefore, lenders forgo more (relative to what they were promised) than direct investors. Knowing this, lenders demand much higher interest rates to compensate for the risk of default, whereas direct investors require only a slightly larger shareholding to indemnify themselves against the risk of expropriation. Because the average repayment rises faster for debt than for equity, the temptation to default increases faster than the temptation to expropriate.

What implications do these findings have for the level of investment? Figure 3.2d displays investment as a proportion of the first-best amount, k^{FB}, for different values of σ. Again, the pattern for direct investment is nonmonotonic, with the largest investments when σ is close to one. The money the country receives from lenders, on the other hand, declines with σ.

These patterns have implications for the welfare of countries. Unless leaders are nearly risk neutral, they can obtain more investment in the FDI-only world than in the debt-only world, because leaders are less willing to expropriate than to default for these parameter values. The relationship reverses for highly risk-tolerant leaders (ones with $\sigma < 1/2$); such leaders can raise more money from a world of lenders than from a world of direct investors. Relative welfare follows a similar pattern: risk-averse leaders achieve higher welfare in the equity-only world than in the debt-only world, whereas the opposite is true for leaders who are fairly neutral about risk.

Our findings deepen a well-known puzzle about international finance. Levels of international debt typically exceed levels of direct investment. Scholars have argued that this pattern is not optimal for insuring countries against production risk. After all, equity contracts by their very nature are state-contingent, whereas debt contracts typically are not. Our analysis reinforces this puzzle. In a world where risk-averse countries cannot commit to honoring their contracts, an equity-only environment should lead to more investment than a debt-only environment. Equity investors should be willing to supply this additional capital because, in bad states, the probability of expropriation is lower than the probability of default. Our results thus make the prevalence of debt over equity even more puzzling.

Investor-government relations depend not only on risk aversion but also on the prize for honoring contracts, as shown in figures 3.3a–3.3d. To construct these figures, we set $\sigma = 2$ and varied the prize for

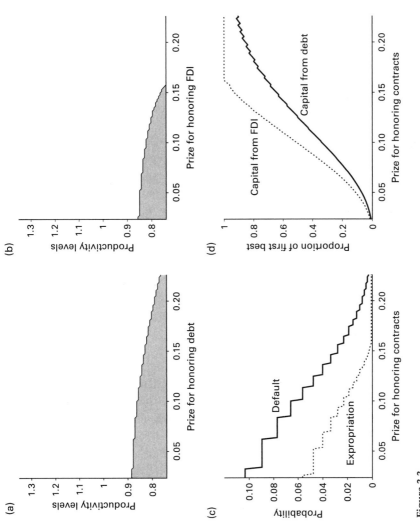

Figure 3.3
The effect of the prize for honoring contracts (debt-only model *vs.* FDI-only model): (*a*) set of default states as a function of the prize; (*b*) set of expropriation states as a function of the prize; (*c*) probability of sovereign theft as a function of the prize; (*d*) investment levels (relative to first-best investment) as a function of the prize.

repaying debts in the debt-only model or the prize for eschewing expropriation in the FDI-only model from 5 to 45 percent of our benchmark level, $(1 - \sigma)U^{FB}$. Recall that, when $\sigma > 1$, both the debt-only and the FDI-only models predict that governments will honor contracts in good times but practice sovereign theft in bad times. Figures 3.3a and 3.3b illustrate this prediction, while also demonstrating that sovereign theft occurs in fewer states of the world as the prize for honoring contracts increases.

Interestingly, our simulations show that, for any given prize, default is more common (occurs for a larger set of θ's) than expropriation. Figure 3.3c shows this explicitly: at each prize level, the probability of default exceeds the probability of expropriation. A given prize should, therefore, support more FDI than loans. Figure 3.3d confirms this prediction. Once the prize exceeds about 30 percent of the benchmark level, the incentive to expropriate disappears and the amount of direct investment approximates the first-best level that the country would attain if it could commit to honoring all contracts. In contrast, loans never rise to the first-best level for the range of prizes displayed in figure 3.3d. It is, therefore, even more puzzling why debt levels have historically exceeded direct investment levels.

3.3.2 Defaultable Debt and Expropriable Direct Investment

To analyze the combined model, one must specify a relationship between the prize from not defaulting on debt and the prize from not expropriating direct investment. We first consider *narrow symmetric prizes*. By narrow, we mean that an act of default or expropriation has no spillovers to other investment relationships, such that the prize for honoring both contracts is the sum of the prizes from honoring each. By symmetric, we mean that the prize from honoring debts matches the prize from honoring direct investments. Formally, $P^{DE} = P^D + P^E > 0$ and $P^D = P^E$. To facilitate comparison with our previous results, we let P^D and P^E each equal 35 percent of the benchmark level, $(1 - \sigma)U^{FB}$, and allowed σ to range between $1/5$ and 5.

With these assumptions, the combined model produces lower rates of sovereign theft and higher levels of international investment than a world with only one type of foreign investor. The combined model has these effects because it allows the government to raise an optimal mix of debt and FDI. For very low levels of σ, the optimal mix involves more debt than equity. At $\sigma = 1/5$, for example, the country raises 58 percent of its capital from lenders and gets the balance from direct

investors. As the country becomes more risk averse, FDI rises to dominate debt. The relationship between σ and composition of the portfolio
is not monotonic, though; the largest role for FDI occurs at around
$\sigma = 4/3$, when direct investors supply 69 percent of the country's funds.

Although the contributions of debt and FDI in our simulations
varied with σ, the sum of these two types of investment was nearly
constant and almost exactly equal to the first-best level. Moreover, sovereign theft almost never occurred. By raising two types of capital,
loans and direct investments, the country kept the amount of each
small enough that theft was not a tempting option. In equilibrium,
only the most risk-averse leaders (those with $\sigma > 4$) ever defaulted
and/or expropriated, and they did so no more than 4 percent of the
time.

These findings suggest lessons about the structure of international
capital markets. If the prize for honoring debt contracts is equal in
magnitude to, but also independent from, the prize for respecting direct investments, then all parties are better off in a world with both
debt and FDI than in a world that offers only one type of investment.
Laws that limit either type of investment will, therefore, reduce welfare
by preventing the sovereign government from attracting the optimal
level and mix of debt and equity.

For more insight about the model with narrow symmetric punishments, we next cut the prizes in half, such that P^D and P^E each stood
at only 17.5 percent of the benchmark level. With smaller prizes,
investor-government relations more closely resembled the patterns
from the debt-only and equity-only models. Specifically, the probability of default increased monotonically with σ, whereas the probability
of expropriation declined as σ approached 1 and increased thereafter
(see figures 3.4a and 3.4b). Moreover, at low levels of σ, the country
raised relatively more capital from debt than from direct investment,
whereas the opposite was true when σ exceeded 1. Overall, the total
amount of capital never exceeded 70 percent of the first-best level (see
figure 3.4c).

Finally, we examined the possibility of *broad symmetric prizes*. By
broad, we mean that any act of sovereign theft would undermine all
the country's investment relationships. Spillovers could arise through
retribution, in which lenders and direct investors coordinate their retaliatory strategies, or through reputation, in which a country that seizes
some types of investments signals that it would seize other types as
well. Our concept of broad symmetric prizes implies that the reward

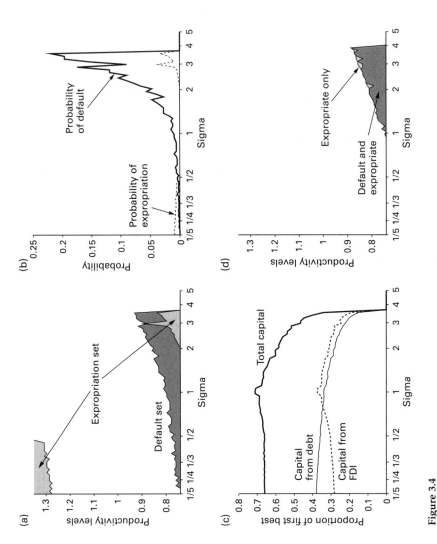

Figure 3.4
The effect of risk aversion (combined model: debt and FDI): (*a*) set of theft states when prizes are narrow and symmetric; (*b*) probability of sovereign theft when prizes are narrow and symmetric; (*c*) investment levels when prizes are narrow and symmetric; (*d*) set of theft states when prizes are broad and symmetric.

from honoring both types of contracts exceeds the sum of rewards from honoring either in isolation—that is, $P^{DE} > P^D + P^E > 0$. In our simulations, we set $P^D = P^E = P^{DE}/6$, where P^{DE} was 35 percent of $(1 - \sigma)U^{FB}$.

In such a world, defaults and expropriations almost always coincided. Figure 3.4d displays, for each level of σ, the productivity levels at which the country found it optimal to steal from foreign investors. At low levels of risk aversion, the country honored both types of contracts, no matter what state of the world it encountered. At about $\sigma = 1$, though, the country began responding to adverse productivity shocks by defaulting and expropriating simultaneously. The country occasionally expropriated at θ's that were too high to warrant default, but most of the time the two acts of sovereign theft were perfectly coordinated. We return to the theme of narrow versus broad prizes later in the chapter, when we use a new data set to test whether defaults and expropriations have coincided in practice.

3.4 The Optimal Self-Enforcing Contract

In this section we retain the assumption that the country cannot commit to honoring contracts, but we remove all restrictions on the types of contracts that can be issued. Rather than specifying all possible contracts, we find the optimal "self-enforcing" contract—the best possible contract that the country has an incentive to respect.

3.4.1 The Model

The optimal contract specifies the investment level k, the country's state-contingent consumption $c(\theta)$, and payments $t(\theta)$ that the country will make to foreign investors. Assuming that, due to competition, investors earn no profits, the best contract maximizes the country's expected welfare $E[U(c(\theta))]$, subject to three types of constraints: a sequence of feasibility constraints

$$c(\theta) + t(\theta) \leq \theta f(k)$$

for all θ, which imply that the output retained by the country, plus the output transferred to foreign investors, cannot be larger than the total production; a single zero-profit constraint for foreign investors,

$$E[t(\theta)] = (1 + r^w)k;$$

and a sequence of "no sovereign theft" constraints

$$U(c(\theta)) + P^{DE} \geq U(\theta f(k))$$

for all θ, which require that the country receive enough consumption to deter it from engaging in sovereign theft in all states of the world.

If we define $\pi(\theta)\mu(\theta)$ to be the Lagrange multipliers on the feasibility constraints, λ to be the multiplier on the zero-profit constraint, and $\pi(\theta)\gamma(\theta)$ to be the multipliers on the "no sovereign theft" constraints, then the first-order necessary conditions[4] for an optimum include

$$(1 + \gamma(\theta))U'(c(\theta)) = \mu(\theta),$$

$$\mu(\theta) = \lambda,$$

$$\lambda(1 + r^w) = f'(k)E[\theta\mu(\theta) - \theta\gamma(\theta)U'(\theta f(k))].$$

3.4.2   Analytical Results

What do these first-order conditions imply about the behavior of sovereign governments and foreign investors? If the "no sovereign theft" constraints do not bind in any state of the world—that is, $\gamma(\theta) = 0$ for all θ—then

$$U'(c(\theta)) = \lambda$$

for all θ, and the consumption of the country is perfectly smoothed. In addition, investment is at the first-best level

$$1 + r^w = f'(k)E[\theta].$$

In any state where the "no sovereign theft" constraint binds, we have

$$U'(c(\theta)) = \frac{\lambda}{1 + \gamma(\theta)} < \lambda.$$

This shows that the optimal contract deters default or expropriation by awarding the country more consumption (and hence a lower marginal utility of consumption) when the "no sovereign theft" constraint binds than when it does not. From this, a simple variational argument shows that these constraints bind only in high-θ states of the world. Intuitively, the country would like to smooth its consumption completely and only fails to do so in states of the world where the constraint on repayment binds. But this constraint is tighter in states of the world where production is higher (high θ). This suggests that equity should improve on debt in the contractual structures considered above, at least when agents are not too risk averse.

To see how the optimal self-enforcing contract relates to agreements observed in practice, it is instructive to consider the logarithmic utility case. As we argued above, the optimal contract specifies a fixed amount of consumption for the country in bad times (when the "no sovereign theft" constraint does not bind), and allows consumption to rise with the level of production in good times (when the constraint binds). In good times, then, the amount of consumption is determined by

$$U(c(\theta)) = U(\theta f(k)) - P^{DE},$$

which, for logarithmic preferences, can be rearranged to get

$$c(\theta) = e^{-P^{DE}} \theta f(k).$$

This shows that, in good times, the country receives a fixed share $e^{-P^{DE}}$ of output, as in some royalty contracts. The share it receives in good times is decreasing in the size of the prize for honoring contracts, whereas the amount it receives in bad times increases in the size of this prize. Intuitively, a bigger prize deters sovereign theft, so the country is insured against fluctuations in output to a greater degree.

Although in equilibrium the country honors the optimal self-enforcing contract in all states of the world, the mere option of sovereign theft (the inability to commit to honoring contracts) affects the amount of capital that investors are willing to supply. Rearranging the first-order condition in k yields

$$1 + r^w = f'(k)E\left[\theta - \frac{\theta \gamma(\theta)}{\lambda} U'(\theta f(k))\right].$$

The term within the expectation operator is less than θ in high-θ states of the world. This decreases the expected return and means that investment will be below the first-best level when the country cannot commit to honoring its contracts.

3.4.3 Numerical Results

To say more about the features of the optimal self-enforcing contract, we solve the model numerically. Substituting for $t(\theta)$ from the feasibility constraints and rearranging, the problem involves choosing k and $c(\theta)$ to maximize $E[U(c(\theta))]$, subject to the single zero-profit constraint for investors,

$$(1 + r^w)k = E[\theta f(k) - c(\theta)],$$

and a sequence of "no sovereign theft" constraints

$$c(\theta) \geq U^{-1}(U(\theta f(k)) - P^{DE})$$

for all θ.

The following two-stage algorithm solves the model:[5]

Algorithm 4 (Optimal Self-Enforcing Contract Model)

1. For every level of capital k, find the optimal sequence of state-contingent consumption levels $c(\theta)$ subject to the constraint that investors make no profits and that the country would willingly honor the contract. This solution implies a sequence of state-contingent transfers to investors, $t(\theta)$.

2. From the results from step 1, choose the level of k that maximizes the expected value to the country.

Figures 3.5a and 3.5b compare the optimal self-enforcing contract with the equilibrium contracts from the other models. The figures show the proportion of output that the country retains for itself in each model, under the assumption that $\sigma = 2$ (figure 3.5a) or $\sigma = 1/2$ (figure 3.5b).[6]

In the debt-only model, the country's share of output follows a Z-shaped pattern. When output is low, the country defaults and thus keeps 100 percent of the resources. As output rises, though, the prize for maintaining good relations with lenders eventually overwhelms the temptation to default. At that point the country transfers a proportion $b/\theta f(k)$ of output to lenders and retains the complementary proportion $1 - b/\theta f(k)$ for itself. With b fixed, any further increases in output go directly to the country, thereby raising its share of the total. The FDI-only model produces a similar Z-shaped pattern. With $\sigma = 2$, the country expropriates out of desperation and thus seizes all the output in bad times. Once output reaches a sufficiently high level, though, the country starts remitting the proportion α of direct investors and retaining the balance at home. With $\sigma = 1/2$ and other parameters at our benchmark levels, the country never expropriates. Consequently, the country's share of output is constant and equal to $1 - \alpha$.

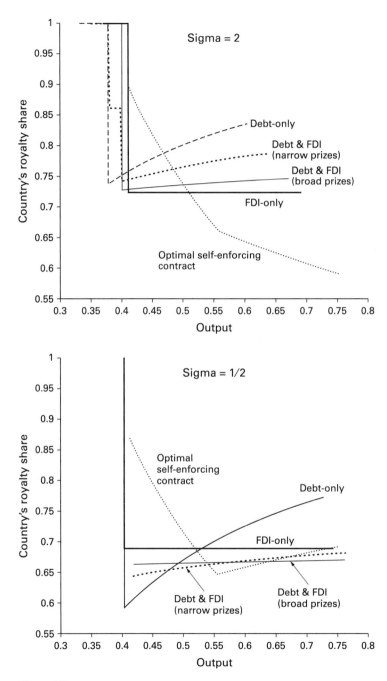

Figure 3.5
Country's royalties, by model

The combined model, which includes both debt and equity, blends features from each type of investment. When prizes are narrow and $\sigma = 2$, the country violates both types of contracts when output is low, violates only debt contracts at intermediate output levels, and respects both types of contracts at high output levels. When prizes are broad, the pattern is similar, except the country either violates or honors both contracts simultaneously. When $\sigma = 1/2$, neither default nor expropriation occurs in equilibrium. The country's royalties therefore increases with output, at a rate proportional to the share of debt in the country's portfolio of liabilities.

Thus, in a world of debt contracts, equity contracts, or a mix of the two, the relationship between output and the country's share is either flat or increasing everywhere, except in the region of sovereign theft. This demonstrates the role of sovereign theft in providing partial (and costly) insurance against bad economic outcomes.

The optimal self-enforcing contract is fundamentally different. In bad times, the country's consumption under the optimal contract is constant, and hence declines as a function of output. In better times the country's consumption rises with output at a rate that depends on the value of σ. In the relatively risk-averse case of $\sigma = 2$, consumption during good times rises more slowly than output, and hence the royalty curve continues to slope downward. Risk sharing is, therefore, more extensive with the optimal self-enforcing contract than with debt and/ or equity. In the more risk-tolerant case of $\sigma = 1/2$, consumption during good times accelerates faster than output, causing the royalty curve to turn upward. The curve most closely resembles a debt contract, which helps explain why debt outperforms equity at low levels of risk aversion. The shape of the curve also helps explain why, when σ is low, expropriation tends to occur in good states, because this is the only way for FDI to produce patterns of payments that approximate the optimal self-enforcing contract.

3.5   Sovereign Theft and Foreign Investment in History

We now document historical patterns of sovereign theft and foreign investment, in order to shed new light on theoretical debates about these phenomena. Our analysis proceeds in three steps. We construct a new data set about sovereign theft since the late 1920s, use the data to identify key patterns of default and expropriation, and finally study how the level and composition of foreign investment have varied over time.

3.5.1 Measures of Sovereign Theft

To determine which countries owed debts to foreign bondholders and commercial banks, we employed the methods in Tomz and Wright 2007. For each year from 1929 and 1970, we classified a country as indebted if it, according to Adler 2005, had outstanding obligations to foreign bondholders. For the years from 1970 to the present, we counted a country as indebted if the World Bank (2007) listed it as owing money to foreign private creditors, excluding trade creditors.

Having determined which countries owed debts, we next documented cases in which defaults took place. A default occurred whenever a county failed to pay interest or repay principal within the allowable grace period. We also regarded a country as having defaulted if, in the case of sovereign bonds, it made an exchange offer that contained terms "less favorable than the original issue," or if, in the case of bank credits, the parties rescheduled the principal and/or interest at "less favorable terms than the original loan" (Beers and Chambers 2004). In our data set, a default started when the government first missed a payment or rescheduled a loan, and it ended when most creditors agreed to settle with the country.[7]

Our measure of default, like our measure of indebtedness, focuses entirely on transactions with private creditors. It therefore differs from Paris Club reschedulings and other defaults involving public-sector lenders. Moreover, to keep the focus on *sovereign* theft, we document defaults of national governments while omitting defaults by cities or provinces. Data on defaults are from Beers and Chambers 2004 and Suter 1990.

We used similar methods to document the potential for and the occurrence of expropriation. A country was regarded as having expropriable FDI in a particular year if, in that year, U.S. citizens held direct investments in the country. We obtained data on FDI positions from 1929 to the present through a comprehensive search of reports by the U.S. Commerce Department and the U.S. Bureau of Economic Analysis. The resulting country-year panel of FDI positions is, to our knowledge, the most extensive in existence. Nonetheless, it omits countries that received direct investments entirely from non-U.S. sources. Future research could expand the coverage to include other suppliers of direct investment.

Following Kobrin 1980 and 1984, we adopted a broad definition of expropriation that embraces any of the following actions: (1) nationalization, defined as action by a government to take ownership of a foreign firm; (2) coerced sale, in which the government threatens or takes actions that induce foreigners to sell part or all of their direct investments to the government or to domestic citizens; (3) intervention or requisition, in which the government takes control of foreign direct investments without proclaiming itself the rightful owner; or (4) renegotiation, in which the government compels direct investors to accept substantial changes in a contract or a concession. We regard these acts as expropriation, regardless of whether the government offers compensation to affected investors.

Our inventory of expropriations covers much of the twentieth century. We gathered data for the years 1929–1960 by combing through a wide range of primary and secondary sources.[8] We then augmented our newly collected data with existing inventories by Kobrin (1984) for the period 1960–1979, Minor (1994) for the years 1980–1992, and Hajzler (2007) for the years 1993–2004. The resulting database, although still preliminary, provides a unique long-run perspective on sovereign theft.

3.5.2 Patterns of Sovereign Theft

Figure 3.6 displays trends in sovereign theft over nearly a century. Figure 3.6a shows, for each year from 1929 to 2004, the number of sovereign countries in the world that expropriated at least some foreign direct investment or initiated default on at least one loan from private foreign lenders. Figure 3.6b reexpresses the same data as a share of all countries with the potential for sovereign theft.

Two patterns emerge immediately. First, sovereign theft has occurred in waves. In some historical periods, many countries have taken property that belonged to foreign investors, but in other periods, countries generally have refrained from defaulting and/or expropriating. Second, waves of default and expropriation have not coincided. Defaults were most common during the Great Depression of the 1930s and during the economic crises that struck developing countries in the 1980s. Expropriations, in contrast, were most prevalent during the 1970s, with smaller surges in the 1960s and at the end of the sample period.

These alternating waves of default and expropriation have interesting implications for theories of sovereign theft. As noted earlier, some authors argue that sovereign theft has spillover effects: by cheating one type of investor, a country spoils its relations with other types of investors. Spillovers could arise through a process of retribution, in which lenders and direct investors coordinate their retaliatory

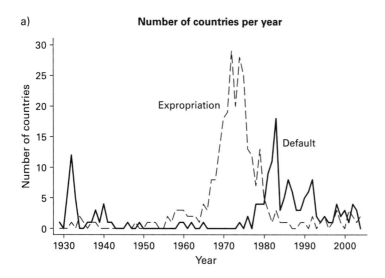

a)

Number of countries per year

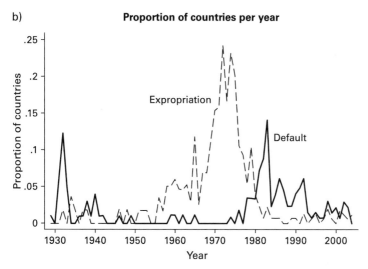

b)

Proportion of countries per year

Figure 3.6
Sovereign theft in history

strategies. Spillovers could also arise via a reputational mechanism in which, for example, default would signal that a government is a "bad type" that would also expropriate direct investments. With spillover effects or "broad prizes," expropriations and defaults should cluster together in time.[9] The global oscillation between the default and expropriation seems at odds with the spillover hypothesis.

Although defaults and expropriations have not coincided in the aggregate, there is an interesting country-level relationship between these two types of sovereign theft (see table 3.1). The countries in the upper-left quadrant of the table neither defaulted nor expropriated at any point in the years 1929–2004, whereas the countries in the lower-right quadrant both defaulted and expropriated, although usually not simultaneously. Overall, nearly 70 percent of countries occupy one of those two quadrants, versus only 30 percent that expropriated without ever defaulting or defaulted without ever expropriating. The chi-squared statistic for table 3.1 is 28 with 1 degree of freedom. In a sample of this size, the probability of observing such a strong relationship between default and expropriation purely by chance is less than 1 in 1,000.

It seems, therefore, that most countries fall into one of two categories: they consistently refrain from default and expropriation, or they willingly practice both types of sovereign theft. Future research should examine the factors that distinguish no-theft from pro-theft countries, and that explain why some countries practice one form of sovereign theft but not the other.

Setting aside the correlation between default and expropriation, it is both theoretically and practically important to ask whether sovereign theft occurs more often in good times or in bad. A detailed analysis of this question must await future research, but figure 3.6 suggests some lessons. The largest waves of default occurred during the Great Depression and the 1980s, periods of severe economic hardship for developing countries. There were far fewer defaults during periods of relative economic growth. This pattern is consistent with the hypothesis that countries default more often in bad times than in good, although Tomz and Wright (2007) show that the relationship between economic performance and default is weaker than previous scholars had assumed.

In theory, the relationship between economic conditions and expropriation should depend on the risk aversion of political leaders. Those who feel relatively neutral about risk will expropriate opportunistically during good times, whereas those who are highly risk averse will

Table 3.1
Sovereign theft by country (1929–2004)

	No expropriation	Expropriation
No default	Armenia, Australia, Azerbaijan, Bangladesh, Barbados, Belarus, Belgium, Belize, Botswana, Burundi, Canada, Cyprus, Czech Republic, Denmark, Djibouti, Estonia, Fiji, Finland, France, Georgia, Germany (reunified), Grenada, Hong Kong, Iceland, Ireland, Israel, Korea (South), Kyrgyzstan, Latvia, Lithuania, Luxembourg, Mali, Mauritius, Netherlands, New Zealand, Norway, Papua New Guinea, Portugal, Rwanda, Saint Kitts and Nevis, Saint Lucia, Saint Vincent and the Grenadines, Samoa, Singapore, Slovakia, Solomon Islands, Spain, Sweden, Switzerland, Tunisia, United Kingdom, Uzbekistan, Vanuatu	Benin, Chad, India, Kazakhstan, Lebanon, Lesotho, Malaysia, Nepal, Oman, Somalia, Sri Lanka, Swaziland, Syria, Thailand
Default	Albania, Austria, Bosnia, Bulgaria, Burkina Faso, China, Croatia, Czechoslovakia, Dominica, Germany (prewar), Germany (West), Greece, Guinea Bissau, Italy, Jordan, Korea (North), Macedonia, Moldova, Nauru, Nigeria, Paraguay, Poland, Romania, Russia, Serbia, Seychelles, Slovenia, South Africa, Turkey, Ukraine, Uruguay, USSR, Vietnam, Yemen (North), Yemen (unified)	Algeria, Angola, Antigua and Barbuda, Argentina, Bolivia, Brazil, Cameroon, Central African Republic, Chile, Colombia, Congo (Brazzaville), Congo (Kinshasa), Costa Rica, Cuba, Dominican Republic, Ecuador, Egypt, El Salvador, Ethiopia, Gabon, Gambia, Ghana, Guatemala, Guinea, Guyana, Haiti, Honduras, Hungary, Indonesia, Iran, Iraq, Ivory Coast, Jamaica, Japan, Kenya, Liberia, Madagascar, Malawi, Mauritania, Mexico, Morocco, Mozambique, Myanmar, Nicaragua, Niger, Pakistan, Panama, Peru, Philippines, Senegal, Sierra Leone, Sudan, Tanzania, Togo, Trinidad and Tobago, Uganda, Venezuela, Yugoslavia, Zambia, Zimbabwe

expropriate out of desperation during hard times. Figure 3.6 shows a massive surge in expropriations during the 1970s, a period often classified as a boom for developing countries (especially those that were exporting commodities). Expropriations began before commodity prices began to soar, however. There is, therefore, some evidence that leaders expropriate opportunistically, but the correlation is not perfect.

The patterns of sovereign theft that we have uncovered can be rationalized within our suite of models under two auxiliary assumptions. If prizes are narrow, one can rationalize asynchronous defaults and expropriations. And if leaders are relatively neutral to risk, one can rationalize an apparent tendency to default in bad times but to expropriate in good times.

3.5.3   Patterns of Foreign Investment

Our models have implications not only for sovereign theft, but also for the level and composition of foreign investment. No detailed data exist on the global stock of debt versus direct investment over the past century. One can, however, gain insight from the work of Lane and Milesi-Ferretti (2007), who calculate net foreign asset and liability positions beginning in 1973, and break them down into debt, foreign direct investment, and portfolio investment. We partition the data into two country groupings: the "developed countries," defined as the 1973 membership in the Organization for Economic Cooperation and Development (OECD), and all other countries, which are classified as "developing."

Figure 3.7 decomposes the major classes of gross foreign liabilities of developed countries (figure 3.7a) and developing countries (figure 3.7b). For both groups of countries, debt is on average at least as important as FDI, which is consistent with our theory provided that leaders are relatively risk tolerant. Interestingly, though, the proportion of foreign liabilities due to debt is "hill-shaped": rising at the start of the period, reaching a peak in the mid-1980s, and falling in recent years. This hill-shaped pattern could reflect changes in the values of P^D and P^E, the prizes for honoring debt and equity contracts, respectively. Our model predicts a positive association between the ratio P^D/P^E and the share of debt in countries' foreign liabilities. If P^D/P^E rose through the early 1980s but retreated thereafter, one would expect debt to rise and fall in importance, as shown in figure 3.7.

We next consider patterns of total liabilities, scaled by gross domestic products. As figures 3.8a–3.8d show, both measures of liabilities

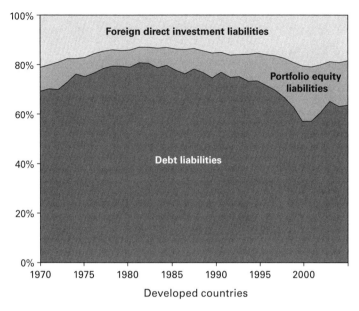

Developed countries

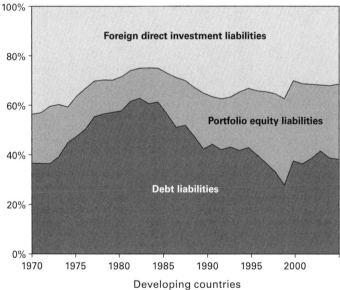

Developing countries

Figure 3.7
Gross liabilities by asset class

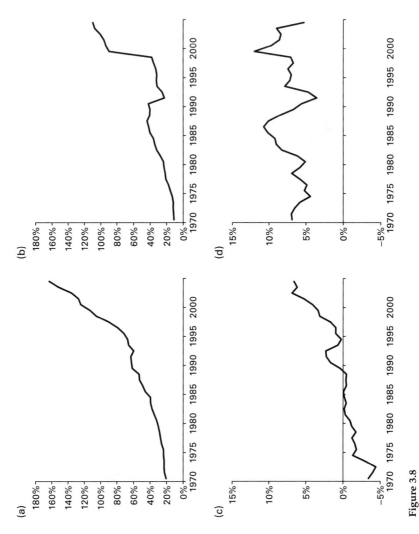

Figure 3.8
Gross and net liabilities as a percent of GDP: (*a*) gross liabilities of developed countries; (*b*) gross liabilities of developing countries; (*c*) net liabilities of developed countries (*d*) net liabilities of developing countries.

have trended upward, with developed countries showing the fastest growth in gross liabilities and developing countries experiencing the fastest growth in net liabilities. These figures also expose a danger associated with the use of international investment position statistics. By the end of the period, both the developing and developed countries were net debtors, implying (illogically) that the world was in net debt to someone else. Although one must, therefore, be cautious in interpreting the data, the rising pattern of liabilities is stark, and is probably robust to corrections in the measurement of net positions. Such growth in both gross and net foreign investment positions could arise, for example, if the overall level of prizes increased over time.

As noted earlier, though, sovereign theft has occurred in alternating waves, with expropriations in the 1970s and defaults in the 1980s. We would expect such behavior if, for instance, P^E fell at the beginning of the sample period and P^D fell subsequently.

In summary, we observe a hill-shaped pattern in the level of debt, an overall increase in liability positions, and oscillation between expropriation and default. Reconciling these facts is a delicate exercise. Perhaps the prizes for repaying debt and honoring equity have moved in opposite directions, with rises in P^D outstripping declines in P^E prior to the 1980s, and with rises in P^E more than compensating for reductions in P^D from the 1980s to the present. Future research should investigate, in more detail, how the prizes for honoring debt and equity have evolved over time.

3.6   Conclusion

Foreign investments in both debt and equity are subject to the risk that the foreign government may, directly or indirectly, interfere with their repayment. Despite this similarity, and despite substantial literatures devoted to examining the phenomena of sovereign default and expropriation of direct investments separately, little has been done to compare and contrast the two. In this chapter, we have made a first attempt at examining the interrelationship between default on debt and the expropriation of direct investment—what we have referred to as sovereign theft—in both theory and practice.

Our models show that, at least in theory, the incentives for sovereign theft and patterns of foreign investment depend crucially on the state of the economy, the risk aversion of political leaders, and the nature of punishments for default and expropriation. Defaults are more likely in bad times than in good. Expropriations, on the other hand, will arise out of desperation in bad times if leaders are risk averse, but will occur out of opportunism in good times if leaders are relatively risk tolerant. Naturally, cooperation between investors and sovereign governments will improve with the prizes for honoring contracts. Nonetheless, much depends on whether prizes are broad or narrow. If prizes are broad, such that a single act of sovereign theft spills over to affect all of a country's investment relations, countries should default and expropriate simultaneously, instead of honoring one type of contract while violating the other.

Using a new data set about sovereign theft across much of the twentieth century, we found that defaults and expropriations have been remarkably asynchronous. One possible explanation is that prizes are, in fact, relatively narrow: seizing from one type of foreign investor does not spoil relations with other types of investors. A different explanation focuses on shifts in the composition of the foreign liabilities in developing economies, first away from direct investment toward debt, and more recently back to direct investment and portfolio equity. In the 1970s, when direct investment was a greater proportion of foreign liabilities, expropriations reached their historical peak. In the decade that followed, foreign investments were increasingly channeled into sovereign lending, which culminated in the debt crisis of the 1980s. Perhaps partly in response to this crisis, direct investment and portfolio equity have reemerged as an important source of foreign liabilities for developing economies.

Our theories have abstracted from many issues that affect the level of direct investment and the incentives to expropriate. One is the fact that countries use different sources of capital—loans versus FDI—to fund different types of projects. If the risk properties of these investments differ, our models would make different predictions about the likelihood of observing defaults and expropriations at different points in the economic cycle.

Another issue that we have mostly abstracted from is that direct investment typically brings with it some control over the project's operations.[10] In future analyses, therefore, one could relax the assumption of symmetry and allow the direct penalties associated with expropriation to exceed those associated with debt default. Control may be important in other respects as well. It may, for instance, be an additional motive for expropriation, particularly when the control extends to assets with special national or strategic significance.

The issue of control is also related to deeper questions about the design of financial contracts and the incentives they give to managers of firms. Much of the corporate finance literature has examined the incentive of firms to issue debt versus equity, and has emphasized the trade-off between agency costs and monitoring costs. These issues are no doubt important for thinking about FDI versus debt. To the best of our knowledge, no one has examined the effect of political risk on this trade-off. This should be a focus of future work.

Notes

We thank our discussant at the Populism and Natural Resources Workshop, Jeromin Zettelmeyer, the editors William Hogan and Federico Sturzenegger, the conference participants, and Stephen Kaplan, Thomas Plümper, and Christoph Trebesch for helpful comments. We are grateful for financial support from the Stanford Center for International Development and the National Science Foundation (CAREER Grant SES-0548285).

1. This argument has been made in various forms by many authors, including Eaton and Gersovitz (1981a, 1984), Thomas and Worrall (1994), and Albuquerque (2003).

2. The magnitude of punishments may vary with the degree of sovereign theft. For example, Schnitzer (2002) argues that retribution is less likely when countries engage in "creeping expropriation" of FDI than when they engage in outright nationalization.

3. In deriving the inequality, note that the factor $(1 - \sigma)$ in the numerator and the factor $1 - (1 - \alpha)^{1-\sigma}$ in the denominator both change signs as σ crosses the threshold from being less than one to being greater than one.

4. The problem is not convex because of the presence of concave U and f on the right-hand side of the "no sovereign theft" constraint. Hence, the first-order conditions are not, in general, sufficient to guarantee a solution.

5. We break the solution into two stages to guarantee that the first stage is a well-behaved convex programming problem.

6. We let P^{DE} equal 35 percent of $(1 - \sigma)U^{FB}$ when $\sigma = 2$, and 100 percent of $(1 - \sigma)U^{FB}$ when $\sigma = 1/2$. All other parameters were at our benchmark levels.

7. A country is defined to be in default in a given year if it was in default for any month of that year, with the exception of defaults that are settled in January of a given year, which are assumed to imply that the country is not in default for that year.

8. The following sources were especially useful for expropriations before 1960: Lipson 1985; Truitt 1974; U.S. Congress, House Committee on Foreign Affairs 1963; White 1961; and Wilkins 1970.

9. The two types of sovereign theft should also cluster in time if leaders are highly risk averse $(\sigma > 1)$, because such leaders would find both default and expropriation attractive in periods of low economic productivity.

10. The issue of control is at the heart of the decision to invest directly in a foreign firm, as opposed to licensing a technology to that firm, as discussed in Antras, Desai, and Foley 2009.

References

Adler, Michael. 2005. *Sovereign Bond Database*. New York: Graduate School of Business, Columbia University.

Aguiar, Mark, and Gita Gopinath. 2006. "Defaultable Debt, Interest Rates and the Current Account." *Journal of International Economics* 69:1, 64–83.

Ahmed, Faisal, Laura Alfaro, and Noel Maurer. 2007. *Gunboats and Vultures: Market Reaction to the "Enforcement" of Sovereign Debt*. Working paper, Harvard University.

Albuquerque, Rui. 2003. "The Composition of International Capital Flows: Risk Sharing through Foreign Direct Investment." *Journal of International Economics* 61:2, 353–383.

Amador, Manuel. 2004. *A Political Economy Model of Sovereign Debt Repayment*. Working paper, Stanford University.

Antras, Pol, Mihir A. Desai, and C. Fritz Foley. 2009. Multinational Firms, FDI Flows and Imperfect Capital Markets." *Quarterly Journal of Economics* 124:3, 1171–1219.

Arellano, Cristina. 2008. "Default Risk and Income Fluctuations in Emerging Economies." *American Economic Review* 98:3, 690–712.

Beers, David T., and John Chambers. 2004. "Sovereign Defaults: Set to Fall Again in 2005." *Standard and Poors*, September 28.

Benjamin, David, and Mark L. J. Wright. 2009. *Recovery Before Redemption: A Model of Delays in Sovereign Debt Renegotiations*. Working paper, SUNY-Buffalo and UCLA.

Broner, Fernando, Alberto Martin, and Jaume Ventura. 2006. *Sovereign Risk and Secondary Markets*. Cambridge, MA: National Bureau of Economic Research Working Paper 12783.

Bulow, Jeremy, and Kenneth Rogoff. 1989a. "A Constant Recontracting Model of Sovereign Debt." *Journal of Political Economy* 97:1, 155–178.

Bulow, Jeremy, and Kenneth Rogoff. 1989b. "Sovereign Debt: Is to Forgive to Forget?" *American Economic Review* 79:1, 43–50.

Cole, Harold Linh, James Dow, and William B. English. 1995. "Default, Settlement, and Signalling: Lending Resumption in a Reputational Model of Sovereign Debt." *International Economic Review* 36:2, 365–385.

Cole, Harold Linh, and William B. English. 1991. "Expropriation and Direct Investment." *Journal of International Economics* 30:3–4, 201–227.

Cole, Harold Linh, and William B. English. 1992a. "Direct Investment: A Doubtful Alternative to International Debt." *Federal Reserve Bank of Minneapolis Quarterly Review* 16:1, 12–22.

Cole, Harold Linh, and William B. English. 1992b. "Two-Sided Expropriation and International Equity Contracts." *Journal of International Economics* 33:1–2, 77–104.

Cole, Harold Linh, and Patrick J. Kehoe. 1998. "Models of Sovereign Debt: Partial versus General Reputations." *International Economic Review* 39:1, 55–70.

Domínguez, Jorge I. 1982. "Business Nationalism: Latin American National Business Attitudes and Behavior toward Multinational Enterprises." In Jorge I. Domínguez, ed., *Economic Issues and Political Conflict: U.S.–Latin American Relations*. Boston: Butterworth Scientific.

Eaton, Jonathan, and Mark Gersovitz. 1981a. "Country Risk: Economic Aspects." In Richard J. Herring, ed., *Managing International Risk*. New York: Cambridge University Press.

Eaton, Jonathan, and Mark Gersovitz. 1981b. "Debt with Potential Repudiation: Theoretical and Empirical Analysis." *Review of Economic Studies* 48:2, 289–309.

Eaton, Jonathan, and Mark Gersovitz. 1984. "A Theory of Expropriation and Deviations from Perfect Capital Mobility." *Economic Journal* 94:373, 16–40.

Fernández-Arias, Eduardo, and Ricardo Hausmann. 2001. "Capital Inflows and Crisis: Does the Mix Matter?" In Jorge Braga de Macedo and Enrique V. Iglesias, eds., *Foreign Direct Investment versus Other Flows to Latin America*. Paris: Interamerican Development Bank and OECD.

Hajzler, Chris. 2007. *Expropriation of Foreign Direct Investments, Trends from 1993 to 2006*. Working paper, University of Western Ontario.

Hausmann, Ricardo, and Eduardo Fernández-Arias. 2001. "Foreign Direct Investment: Good Cholesterol?" In Jorge Braga de Macedo and Enrique V. Iglesias, eds., *Foreign Direct Investment versus Other Flows to Latin America*. Paris: Interamerican Development Bank and OECD.

Kaletsky, Anatole. 1985. *The Costs of Default*. New York: Priority Press.

Kletzer, Kenneth M., and Brian D. Wright. 2000. "Sovereign Debt as Intertemporal Barter." *American Economic Review* 90:3, 621–639.

Kobrin, Stephen J. 1980. "Foreign Enterprise and Forced Divestment in LDCs." *International Organization* 34:1, 65–88.

Kobrin, Stephen J. 1984. "Expropriation as an Attempt to Control Foreign Firms in LDCs: Trends from 1960 to 1979." *International Studies Quarterly* 28:3, 329–348.

Lane, Philip R., and Gian Maria Milesi-Ferretti. 2007. *The External Wealth of Nations Mark II: Revised and Extended Estimates of Foreign Assets and Liabilities, 1970–2004. Journal of International Economics* 73:2, 223–250.

Lipson, Charles. 1985. *Standing Guard: Protecting Foreign Capital in the Nineteenth and Twentieth Centuries*. Berkeley: University of California Press.

Martinez, Jose Vicente, and Guido Sandleris. 2008. "Is it Punishment? Sovereign Defaults and the Decline in Trade." Working paper, University of Oxford, Johns Hopkins University, and Universidad Torcuato Di Tella.

Minor, Michael S. 1994. "The Demise of Expropriation as an Instrument of LDC Policy, 1980–1992." *Journal of International Business Studies* 25:1, 177–188.

Mitchener, Kris James, and Marc D. Weidenmier. Forthcoming. "Supersanctions and Sovereign Debt Repayment. *Journal of International Money and Finance*.

Pitchford, Rohan, and Mark L. J. Wright. 2007. *Restructuring the Sovereign Debt Restructuring Mechanism*. Working paper, UCLA.

Platt, Desmond Christopher Martin. 1968. *Finance, Trade, and Politics in British Foreign Policy, 1815–1914*. Oxford: Clarendon Press.

Rose, Andrew K. 2005. "One Reason Countries Pay Their Debts: Renegotiation and International Trade." *Journal of Development Economics* 77:1, 189–206.

Rose, Andrew K., and Mark M. Spiegel. 2009. "Non-Economic Engagement and International Exchange: The Case of Environmental Treaties." *Journal of Money Credit, and Banking* 41:2–3, 337–363.

Sandleris, Guido. 2008. "Sovereign Defaults: Information, Investment and Credit." *Journal of International Economics* 76:2, 267–275.

Schnitzer, Monika. 2002. "Debt vs. Foreign Direct Investment: The Impact of Sovereign Risk on the Structure of International Capital Flows." *Economica* 69:273, 41–67.

Spiegel, Mark M. 1994. "Sovereign Risk Exposure with Potential Liquidation: The Performance of Alternative Forms of External Finance." *Journal of International Money and Finance* 13:4, 400–414.

Suter, Christian. 1990. *Schuldenzyklen in der Dritten Welt: Kreditaufnahme, Zahlungskrisen und Schuldenregelungen peripherer Länder im Weltsystem von 1820 bis 1986.* Frankfurt a.M.: Anton Hain.

Thomas, Jonathan, and Tim Worrall. 1994. "Foreign Direct Investment and the Risk of Expropriation." *Review of Economic Studies* 61:1, 81–108.

Tomz, Michael. 2007. *Reputation and International Cooperation: Sovereign Debt across Three Centuries.* Princeton, N.J.: Princeton University Press.

Tomz, Michael, and Mark L. J. Wright. 2007. "Do Countries Default in 'Bad Times'?" *Journal of the European Economic Association* 5:2–3, 352–360.

Truitt, J. Frederick. 1974. *Expropriation of Private Foreign Investment.* Bloomington: Graduate School of Business, Division of Research, Indiana University.

U.S. Congress, House Committee on Foreign Affairs. 1963. *Expropriation of American-Owned Property by Foreign Governments in the Twentieth Century.* Washington, DC: U.S. Government Printing Office.

White, Gillian. 1961. *Nationalisation of Foreign Property.* London: Stevens and Sons.

Wilkins, Mira. 1970. *The Emergence of Multinational Enterprise: American Business Abroad from the Colonial Era to 1914.* Cambridge, MA: Harvard University Press.

World Bank. 2007. *Global Development Finance.* Washington, DC: World Bank.

Wright, Mark L. J. 2001. *Reputations and Sovereign Debt.* Working paper, Stanford University.

Yue, Vivian Z. 2006. *Sovereign Default and Debt Renegotiation.* Working paper, New York University.

Commentary: Expropriations, Defaults, and Financial Architecture

Jeromin Zettelmeyer

Michael Tomz and Mark L. J. Wright's chapter is both elegant and highly instructive, and it also makes some important new points. This commentary is structured as follows. First, it describes some of the key contributions of the chapter. Second, it shows lessons that can be drawn from the chapter for crises in emerging markets. Finally, it mentions a few limitations, which are not meant as criticisms, but rather as an acknowledgement that this field is an open one, and that there are critical issues that must still be grappled with. Concluding impressions of the chapter follow.

Contributions of the Chapter

The chapter makes three important contributions. First, it establishes a key stylized fact about expropriations and defaults. Second, it offers a simple framework for thinking about the determinants of expropriations and defaults that is capable of explaining this stylized fact. Third, it takes a step away from the real-life contracts that are subject to expropriation and default—namely, foreign direct investment and debt, respectively—and asks how the contractual relationship between foreign investors and recipient countries would need to be structured to optimally deal with sovereign risk. As I will explain, this last step has some important implications for the debate on how to reform, or develop, the "international financial architecture" governing capital flows to emerging markets.

The key stylized fact is that expropriations and defaults are not synchronized. Since World War I, there have been two main clusters of sovereign defaults: in the 1930s and in the 1980s. These major default clusters were followed by a smaller wave between 1998 and 2003. These were cyclical "bad times" for emerging markets: the Great

Depression; the 1980s bust triggered by a fall in commodity prices and high U.S. interest rates; and the aftermaths of the Asian and Russian crises, which raised the cost of capital throughout the emerging economies. In contrast, as the chapter shows, expropriations were concentrated in the late 1960s and particularly the 1970s—that is, cyclical good times—with high commodity prices. This is surprising: If expropriations and defaults are both forms of "sovereign theft," why are they not more correlated? Some economic theories of defaults—first and foremost, the idea that what deters defaults is a *generalized* loss of reputation—suggest that they should be. If an expropriation has already ruined your reputation, why not default too (and vice versa)?

The answer, suggested by the chapter, may be that any "punishments" associated with sovereign theft are in fact more narrowly tailored to the "crime" (expropriation or default) than a generalized loss of reputation would be. If this is assumed, the different cyclical properties of defaults and expropriations can be rationalized fairly easily. The effort that governments must exercise to repay debt is higher in recessions, but the benefit of repayment—avoiding a future punishment of some kind—is not. Hence, the temptation to default—out of "desperation," as it were—is highest in bad times. A similar temptation exists with regard to expropriation, since expropriations also raise consumption at the time when it is needed the most. But this is balanced by another temptation: to capture the larger share of output (or commodity revenue) that goes to foreign direct investors in *good* times. If the country is not too risk averse—meaning that the pain of reducing consumption in bad times is not too great—this "opportunistic" motive will dominate, governments will prefer to expropriate in good times (if at all), and expropriations will hence be procyclical. This idea resonates well with the most recent wave of expropriations in the natural resource area, in which governments have tried to capture an increasing share of the "windfall" of much higher commodity prices.

This brings us to the third main contribution of the chapter: it addresses how general investment contracts between foreign investors and governments should be structured so as to remove any incentive to default and expropriation. Based on the argument made so far, it is intuitive that investment contracts need to stipulate relatively low payments to foreign investors in bad times—below the threshold that would trigger a default. As output rises, payments to investors can rise more than proportionately without triggering defaults out of desperation, leading to a decline in the share of output that is kept by the country. Provided governments are not very risk averse, however, there will be an output threshold beyond which the temptation to expropriate for "opportunistic" reasons becomes dominant. The only way to counter this temptation is through an *increase* in the share of output that remains in the country. In other words, beyond a certain level of output (or commodity price), the share of the "pie" that a government must pay in good times must decline as the overall size of the "pie" increases, so that the payments that a government could keep by breaking its contract are never high enough to make a default/expropriation worthwhile. A contract that specifies a fixed royalty share of output or commodity revenue does not have this feature, and as such is at risk of expropriation when output is very high.

Relevance for Emerging Market Crises

The general optimal contract in chapter 3 is not just of academic interest. It provides an interpretation of why expropriations occur in good times even though the benefits of these good times are shared under typical natural resource contracts (see chapter 1 in this volume). The contract rationalizes the idea that to avoid such expropriations, the country's share must rise more than proportionally once commodity prices exceed a certain threshold.

Beyond this point, Tomz and Wright's chapter contains an important message that has direct relevance for the policy debate on how to reduce the costs of emerging market crises. This angle is not pursued in the chapter, and it arguably involves a bit of an intellectual detour. However, the applicability of this chapter to this other issue shows that it is useful beyond the topic it was designed to address.

There is a strong intellectual tradition in economics that sees costly debt crises as the manifestation of an incomplete-contracts problem (see Sturzenegger and Zettelmeyer 2007, chap. 12, for a survey). Importantly, this incomplete-contracts problem must go beyond sovereign risk—that is, the sovereign's inability to contractually commit to making payments to investors. As Grossman and Van Huyck (1988) famously argued, there could be sovereign risk and still no costly crises. The reason for this is that the punishments that enforce debt repayment do not necessarily need to arise in equilibrium, because the contract could be designed in a way so that governments will never repudiate (i.e., default, for opportunistic reasons). Governments may still default—but only in situations that are "excusable" in the eyes of investors, and hence do not merit punishment. There is some evidence for this view: defaults that are not viewed as "justified" by fundamentals are punished more harshly by capital markets when they are (Tomz 2007, chap. 5). At the same time, it is clear that the view that only "excusable" defaults occur, and that they are costless, is a huge overstatement.

Why is this the case? The most plausible view is that the boundary between "excusable" defaults and repudiations is blurred in practice, because it depends on policy actions taken long before the default actually materializes. From an investor point of view, sovereign debt involves not one but (at least) *two* moral-hazard problems. One is about sovereign risk in a narrow sense: the willingness-to-pay problem that the sovereign debt literature focuses on. The other has to do with crisis prevention. Perhaps it is true that almost all defaults are excusable to some degree, in the sense that they occur in bad times only. But those bad times themselves may be the result of debtor actions. Economic management in normal times has huge implications for whether pressures to default will build up or not.

The solution, in principle, is more complete debt contracts. Contracts could be more complete both by conditioning on specific debtor actions, such as maintaining debt at low levels and keeping the macroeconomy stable, and by conditioning on specific exogenous (or near-exogenous) events. For example, if times are bad because of a bad shock, then payments would simply be lower. If times are good, they should be higher. Rather than having to default and renegotiate, with the ensuing reputational and practical costs, state-contingent payments would be built into the contract. Debt would become more equitylike.

So far, so good. In pushing for more equitylike contracts, however, one must address a fundamental objection and a concern. The objection is obvious: contracts may be incomplete for a reason. It is not clear that it may be possible to write more complete contracts, at least not without creating better institutions that somehow provide commitment or improve information. This said, such reforms may be feasible, over time, either domestically or at the international level. The concern is more subtle. If one introduces significant state contingency in contracts, might this not bring back the repudiation problem? Equitylike contracts are fine for risk sharing, but they could also create incentives to expropriate in good times. If so, are we not just shifting the problem?

As I read it, Tomz and Wright's chapter speaks directly to this second point. It first shows, both theoretically and empirically, that sovereign risk may indeed be an issue in equity contracts. However, it also
shows that—for symmetric costs of default and expropriation—it is
actually less of an issue than in debt contracts: because of the state contingency of payments, the risk premiums that equity investors need to
charge are lower, and hence so is the temptation to expropriate. And
most importantly, their analysis of the optimal contract shows that
any remaining expropriating risk could in fact be removed by fine-
tuning the risk-sharing rules embedded in the contract—specifically,
by making equitylike contracts even more state-contingent, in a
way that balances the "desperation" and "opportunism" motives for
default.

Limitations

I end by pointing out a few limitations, which should be understood
not so much as limitations of this specific chapter, but rather as limitations of the field.

First, as the authors themselves point out, their model (or suite of
models) work best for a specific parameterization of country risk aversion (the $\sigma < 1$ case). In this parameter range, the model delivers all the
important stylized facts: expropriations tend to happen in good states
and defaults in bad states, and debt could be higher than FDI for symmetric punishments. It also implies that in the optimal self-enforcing
contract country "royalties" need to increase as a share of revenue
once output or commodity prices exceed a certain threshold. Unfortunately, however, $\sigma < 1$ is not usually viewed as the relevant parameter
space in parameterized macroeconomic models, where σ is usually set
in the neighborhood of 2. This could mean three things: (1) there is a
puzzle, in the sense that a reasonably parameterized Tomz and Wright
model cannot explain important stylized facts; (2) σ is in fact lower
than usually assumed; and (3) developing-country governments, in
deciding about expropriations and defaults, act as if they were less
risk averse than we are generally used to from representative consumers. I lean toward the third interpretation. What we need to understand
better is why governments would behave in this way. Political economy must be a part of the answer, but the question is how and why.

Second, there is a question as to whether the finding that expropriations and defaults are not positively correlated (or even inversely cor-

related) in the time dimension is really robust. As explained at the beginning, this finding is enormously important for the literature on sovereign risk because it conflicts with the "reputational spillover" view of sovereign debt crises, which otherwise seems quite attractive (in particular, because it offers an interpretation for some of the observed domestic costs of default; see Sturzenegger and Zettelmeyer 2007, chap. 11, and Panizza, Sturzenegger, and Zettelmeyer 2009). The reason to perhaps doubt the robustness of this finding is that it is based, in effect, on a single boom-bust cycle, namely, the cycle of the 1970s–1980s. If one were to cut off Tomz and Wright's data sample in the late 1960s (i.e., concentrate on the 1929–1969 period, for example) the stylized fact seems to go away.

This still leaves the question of why countries did not default in the 1970s when they were already ruining their reputations by expropriating. The answer could be simply that they did not, at that time, have much debt to private creditors, so there wasn't much of a point in defaulting. Conversely, why were there not more expropriations in the 1980s? Well, although there were reputational spillovers, countries might nevertheless have had an incentive to contain such spillovers through "good behavior" in other areas. Hence, the evidence may be consistent with the existence of reputational spillovers, provided they are not full in the sense that defaulting inevitably and to the same extent tarnishes a country's reputation with respect to FDI, for example.

This leads to a third and related, point. Aside from the risk-aversion parameter σ, the results from Tomz and Wright's model are highly sensitive to the assumptions that are made about default and expropriation costs to the country. Depending on these parameters, the model can produce results that resonate with what we seem to observe, or it can lead us to conclude that there are puzzling discrepancies between theory and reality. Unfortunately, the empirical basis for judging alternative assumptions on default costs remains weak and largely inconclusive: basically, we still do not have a good answer to the question of why countries do not default more often (Panizza, Sturzenegger, and Zettelmeyer 2009). Evidence on the costs of expropriation and how they relate to the costs of default is even less developed.

Conclusion

Tomz and Wright's chapter on "sovereign theft" advances our understanding in three ways. First, it provides an accessible conceptual survey of economic thinking on sovereign risk. Using variants of the same canonical model, this analysis elegantly answers the question of how the sovereign risk problem differs across debt and equity contracts, what the implications are for when we should expect to observe defaults or expropriations, and what relative levels of debt and foreign direct investments can be sustained in the presence of sovereign risk.

Second, the chapter has made at least two significant, substantive contributions to the literature, one empirical and one theoretical. The empirical contribution is to document a lack of synchronization—indeed, an apparent inverse correlation—between expropriations and defaults, at least in the postwar era. The theoretical contribution is to characterize the optimal self-enforcing contract between sovereign debtors and foreign investors in the presence of sovereign risk and to show how it differs from both debt and standard equity contracts. By doing so, it has shed light on a key problem of financial architecture, and, in my view, strengthened the intellectual position of those who argue for richer state-contingent contracts in international finance.

Finally, it has taken us to the empirical frontier of the field and illustrated some tensions between theory and evidence. Ultimately, the predictions of their model depend on parameter assumptions about which we have either little information or information that appears to contradict what we need in order to generate sensible results. It is to be hoped that the recognition of these tensions will spur new empirical work, less stylized models, or a combination of both.

Note

The views expressed in this commentary are the author's only and should not be attributed to the European Bank for Reconstruction and Development.

References

Grossman, Herschel I., and John B. Van Huyck. 1988. "Sovereign Debt as a Contingent Claim: Excusable Default, Repudiation, and Reputation." *American Economic Review* 78(5): 1088–1097.

Panizza, Ugo, Federico Sturzenegger, and Jeromin Zettelmeyer. 2009. "The Economics and Law of Sovereign Debt and Default." *Journal of Economic Literature* 47(3): 651–698.

Sturzenegger, Federico, and Jeromin Zettelmeyer. 2007. *Debt Defaults and Lessons from a Decade of Crises.* Cambridge, MA: MIT Press.

Tomz, Michael. 2007. *Reputation and International Cooperation: Sovereign Debt across Three Centuries.* Princeton, NJ: Princeton University Press.

4   A Resource Belief Curse? Oil and Individualism

Rafael Di Tella, Juan Dubra, and Robert MacCulloch

Like all the men of Babylon, I have been proconsul; like all, I have been a slave.
I have known omnipotence, ignominy, imprisonment. . . .

I owe that almost monstrous variety to an institution—the Lottery—which is
unknown in other nations. . . .

A slave stole a crimson ticket; the drawing determined that that ticket entitled the bearer to have his tongue burned out. The code of law provided the
same sentence for stealing a lottery ticket. Some Babylonians argued that the
slave deserved the burning iron for being a thief, others, more magnanimous,
that the executioner should employ the iron because thus fate had decreed.
There were disturbances, there were regrettable instances of bloodshed, but
the masses of Babylon at last, over the opposition of the well-to-do, imposed
their will; they saw their generous objectives fully achieved.

—Jorge Luis Borges, excerpts from "The Lottery in Babylon," 1941

4.1   Introduction

Markets, privatizations, and other capitalist ideas do not seem to be
appreciated by the public at large. Outside the United States, and a
few countries where communism made people's life really miserable,
capitalism, at least without strong regulations, is not in high demand
around the world. Several survey measures attest to this. A 2005 survey in twenty countries showed that 65 percent of respondents
endorsed the view that "the free enterprise system and free market
economy work best in society's interests when accompanied by strong
government regulations." Beyond opinions, data on the platforms and
names of political parties reveal that left-wing parties are more common in poor countries than in rich countries. Figure 4.1 illustrates
the typical pattern.[1] This is unfortunate for economists because our
own enthusiasm for markets relies on the assumption that people are
rational. Thus, explaining the public's antipathy toward our preferred

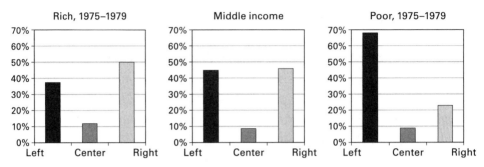

Figure 4.1
The distribution of party ideology around the world, 1975–1997, by income
Note: From Di Tella and MacCulloch 2002. Data on parties comes from Beck et al. 2001 and refers to the color of the Chief Political Officer (prime minister or president). A similar picture emerges using largest government party. *Right*: Parties on the right are those with the term conservative or Christian democratic in their names, or that are labeled right-wing in their sources. *Left*: Similarly, parties are classified as left if their names reveal them to be communist, socialist, or social democratic or if the sources label them as left-wing. *Center*: Similarly, centrist parties are those called centrist by their sources or if their proposed policies can best be described as centrist (e.g., because the party advocates strengthening private enterprise but also supports a redistributive role for government).

solution to the world's material problems appears to be of importance to economics.

Beyond this general point, antipathy toward markets has become particularly acute in Latin America, where a series of "surprise right-wing reformists" had emerged during the 1990s.[2] Of course, the left-wing wave eventually coincided with particularly high prices for oil and primary commodities after 2000. In Bolivia, Venezuela, Ecuador, and Argentina, policymakers have focused their antimarket energies and attention on natural resource companies, renegotiating their contracts in several cases. Accordingly, a more specific question for economists concerns the possible connection between natural resource dependence and ideological inclination. Believers in the advantages of free markets for economic development might be inclined to ask the question differently: Is the curse of the "resource curse" a tendency for people to become left wing when natural resources are important in the economy?

A basic explanation for the general phenomenon is provided in an influential paper by Piketty (1995). He showed that beliefs concerning the income-generating process could be central in determining the form of economic organization. In particular, he emphasized how rational agents would increase taxes when luck is important. In contrast, when effort plays a large role, rational agents fearing adverse incentive effects would moderate taxes. Interestingly, Piketty argued that, even if there was one unique reality (given by the technology), a shock could make one belief particularly important at a point in time. If taxes had to be set at that moment, agents with different beliefs might not converge as long as it was difficult/costly to find credible information to generalize from their own experience. In fact, he argued that information on how much effort really pays is not easy to observe (given that effort input is not observable), and that eventually agents would settle on some belief about the likely value of these parameters and stop experimenting (a form of bandit problem). He emphasized that there are mechanisms that would reinforce these beliefs: where effort does not pay and luck dominates, agents would tend to vote on high taxes and luck would then really dominate. Other papers that give a central role to beliefs include Bénabou and Ok 2001 on upward mobility, Alesina and Angeletos 2005b on fairness, Di Tella and Dubra 2008 on punitiveness, Bénabou and Tirole 2006 on belief in a just world, and Alesina and Angeletos 2005b as well as Di Tella and MacCulloch 2002 on corruption. Denzau and North 1993 also gives a central role to beliefs in discussing institutions as "shared mental models" (see also Greif 1994).

In this chapter we develop adaptations of models predicting that oil dependence leads to beliefs and attitudes that lean toward the left end of the spectrum. We then present evidence of a negative correlation between individualist beliefs and oil dependence, using survey evidence from the U.S. General Social Survey and the share of oil in a state's GDP for the period 1983–2004. The first theoretical mechanism delivering the correlation is quite simple: when the price of oil increases, people feel richer and want to increase the amount of money they give to the poor. We call this the "charity model"; it is related to (the spirit of) Meltzer and Richard 1981. In principle, a similar process might be affected by other primary commodities, and one could "test" whether charity (or some other factor specific to oil) is driving the push to the left by looking at the effect of other commodity prices and establishing whether they have the same effect as oil.[3] However, it is perhaps significant that oil is visible in political debates and occupies a place of some importance in the popular imagination (influencing, for example, the perception of whether individuals are living in a rich country), so the dynamics affecting oil might be different from those affecting other commodities.

The second model introduces an important cost of these redistributions, namely, that higher taxes reduce the amount of effort that agents put forth, as argued in Piketty 1995. The basic assumption is that the effort elasticity of income in the oil sector is smaller (or is perceived to be smaller) than in the nonoil sector. We model this by assuming that the elasticity in the oil industry is actually zero, which leads to the extreme result that full nationalization of the oil industry is good for the economy because it leads to lower taxes in the rest of the economy, and to lower distortions overall. Trivially, in more sophisticated settings, where oil companies have to invest heavily to maintain production, this result changes. But the model raises an important issue, namely, that as long as the voters have an image of oil industries effortlessly extracting a natural resource, the demand for taxes and state intervention in the sector will be high.[4] This reasoning also applies to exogenous increases in the price of oil. Presumably, exogenous movements in the price of oil redistribute income and reduce people's faith in their estimate of the effort elasticity of income (these movements will increase the standard error of their estimates of how income responds to effort). Note that, to the extent that the oil industry is owned by (and affects) actors outside the state, changes in employment in the oil industry observable within the state are particularly relevant. A related point is that in an economy where oil is an important export, changes in the price of oil lead to changes in capital inflows and macroeconomic volatility more generally. Again, if income in the economy behaves like earnings in a casino, it will be hard for voters to be convinced of the idea that one has to be careful about raising taxes because it might affect effort (and income).

The third model we present is built around the idea that oil dependence may affect the perception of fairness in the economy. This matters in the model of Alesina and Angeletos 2005b, which gives a central role to an individual's perception of fairness in the economy, although the version we use here is heavily modified. This perception is increased when people are seen to "get what they deserve and deserve what they get." Accordingly, they focus on how talent and effort affect income relative to random shocks. We adopt a similar assumption concerning how unfairness reduces utility, and assume income in the oil sector is particularly noisy, leading to an increased perception of unfairness in the economy. By increasing taxes when oil prices are high, voters are able to reduce the amount of undeserved (because talent and effort play a small role) income among the rich. Again, directing the taxes to the oil sector would improve the efficiency (and fairness) in the economy, although in circumstances in which high oil prices bring about capital inflows, such ability to target taxes to particular sectors might be of limited use.

Finally, it is worth mentioning that oil dependence is positively correlated with perceptions of corruption within countries. Corruption is correlated with a desire for higher taxes, both generally, in the fairness models of Alesina and Angeletos (2005b), and specifically as it relates to how the income of capitalists is derived, in the model of commercial legitimacy of Di Tella and MacCulloch 2002. More broadly, the idea that beliefs, in particular beliefs about the income-generating process, play an important role in the determination of the economic system goes back at least to De Tocqueville's work emphasizing economic opportunities and status as derived from material position. It also goes back to Frederick Jackson Turner's work on the the frontier in American history and its significance for the determination of American culture in cities far away from the frontier itself. Later work, particularly by Seymour Martin Lipset, emphasized the role of beliefs about mobility independent of the amount of mobility itself. Evidence on the patterns of beliefs has been gathered by Hochschild (1981), Inglehart (1990), Ladd and Bowman (1998), Hall and Soskice (2001), Corneo and Gruner (2002), Fong (2004), and Di Tella, Schargrodsky, and Galiani (2007), among others. Closer to the question we ask, concerning the statistical correlation between beliefs and oil, is the more recent work by Alesina and Glaeser (2004), who find left-wing views to prevail in countries small in size or with electoral systems based on proportional representation, and the papers by Di Tella, Donna, and MacCulloch (2006) (on the correlation between beliefs and oil dependence, macroeconomic volatility, and crime) and Giuliano and Spilimbergo (2007) (on the effects of growing up in a recession on your beliefs).

As a reference, we present the results from Di Tella, Donna, and MacCulloch 2006 in figure 4.2. The figure shows that average right (left) self-placement in the country is negatively correlated with Fuel Exports ("Fuel exports as % of merchandise exports") and Ores ("Ores and metals exports as % of merchandise exports"), controlling for country and year fixed effects in a sample of forty-nine countries included in the World Values Survey. For illustration purposes, we rerun the base regression with Fuel Exports as the independent variable using a probit, and set the other variables at their average levels, forcing the data so that there is an even split of beliefs when Fuel Exports

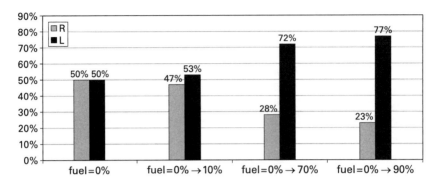

Figure 4.2
Average left-right self-placement predicted in the country for different levels of dependence on oil exports. Based on Di Tella, Donna, and MacCulloch 2006.

are equal to zero. When Fuel Exports increase to 10 percent, self-placement on the left exceeds that on the right by 6 percentage points (i.e., 53 to 47 percent). We also show increases in Fuel Exports of up to 90 percent because, in our sample, the Fuel Exports in Nigeria in 1997 are 96 percent.

In the next section we discuss the three simple models that help us interpret the relationship between oil dependence and beliefs. In section 4.3 we present evidence on this correlation using panel data for the United States for the period 1983–2004. The final section concludes the chapter.

4.2   Three Models Connecting Oil and Beliefs

4.2.1   Charity
We start by exploring a simple mechanism directly connecting income and beliefs (or more generally, ideology). The literature starting with Meltzer and Richard 1981 has emphasized the role of material gains from redistribution in more unequal societies (in terms of income). In particular, income inequality has a big role to play because the median voter has more to gain from taxing citizens that are farther away in terms of income. A problem with this approach is that it is well known that this mechanism fails to explain even the basic properties of cross-country data. For example, the United States is more unequal than France and seeks to redistribute less (instead of more). Still, the natural reaction when faced with governments that recontract when the price of oil goes up is related to material incentives: these governments are

taking advantage of the good times to get a bigger piece of the pie for themselves. The "charity model" presented here also gives a central role to increases in income because it makes people more willing to help others.[5] The connection with "helping others" follows the empirical evidence that we have available on why and how people give to charity, or help in the charitable provision of public goods (see Morgan 2000 and the references there). In brief, the section seeks to illustrate why a higher oil price might increase the desire to help the poor, through an income effect. The intuition is simple enough: concavity of the utility function implies that a given transfer costs less in utils for a richer person.

There are two people in the state, the representative worker and the "poor person." Output in the manufacturing industry is fixed at m, and nominal output in the oil industry is $p.q$. All the output (which equals profits) is owned by the worker, who is taxed an amount t, and the receipts of the tax are transferred to the poor person. The utility of the poor person is $v(t)$ and that of the representative worker is $u(pq + m - t) + v(t)$ (he or she cares about the poor person).[6]

Proposition 1 If $u'' \leq 0$, the optimal tax is increasing in the price of oil.

Proof We use monotone comparative statics (see Milgrom and Shannon 1994). It is easy to see that since the choice variable t is one dimensional, the utility function of the worker is quasisupermodular in t. It will therefore suffice to show that it satisfies the single crossing property: for $p' > p$ and $t' > t$,

$$u(pq + m - t') + v(t') \geq u(pq + m - t) + v(t)$$

$$\Rightarrow u(p'q + m - t') + v(t') \geq u(p'q + m - t) + v(t)$$

(and similarly with strict inequalities). The idea is that if the worker prefers raising taxes for a low price, he or she also prefers doing so for a high price. Rearranging terms, the above condition is equivalent to

$$u(pq + m - t') - u(pq + m - t) \geq v(t) - v(t')$$

$$\Rightarrow u(p'q + m - t') - u(p'q + m - t)$$

$$\geq v(t) - v(t').$$

So it is enough that

$$u(p'q + m - t') - u(p'q + m - t) \geq u(pq + m - t') - u(pq + m - t)$$

which is ensured if u is concave (note that in this case, u being concave is not a "cardinal" property, because the worker's utility is $u + v$, so one cannot transform u "at will" as would be the case if v was not there). To see this, note that $u'' \leq 0$ implies that for all $s \in [t, t']$, $u'(p'q + m - s) \leq u'(pq + m - s)$, which implies

$$\int_t^{t'} u'(p'q + m - s) \, ds \leq \int_t^{t'} u'(pq + m - s) \, ds \Leftrightarrow$$

$$u(p'q + m - t') - u(p'q + m - t) \geq u(pq + m - t') - u(pq + m - t)$$

as was to be shown.   ∎

Notice that the intuition for the result corresponds exactly with the statement of the proposition: if u is concave, a given transfer costs less in utils for a richer person. If we used more "traditional" methods, however, we would also have to assume that $v'' \leq 0$. With traditional methods, the first-order condition for the optimal tax is $u'(pq + m - t(p)) = v'(t(p))$, so that

$$u''(pq + m - t(p))(qdp - t'dp) = v''(t(p))t'dp \Leftrightarrow$$

$$t' = \frac{u''(pq + m - t(p))q}{u''(pq + m - t(p)) + v''(t(p))}.$$

If $v'' \leq 0$ and $u'' \leq 0$, we obtain $t' \geq 0$ (but note that we need more conditions, not just $u'' \leq 0$).

Finally, we note that the roles of p and q are symmetric in the utility function of the worker. Therefore, optimal taxes would also increase after an increase in q. We do not push this point further, because in this simplified model we have assumed that there is no cost to extracting output in the oil industry. In a richer model that incorporates the realistic assumption that extracting oil has a cost, the roles of p and q would not be symmetric anymore, and an increase in output would not lead necessarily to an increase in taxes. In addition, here p and q are taken as given, but in a richer model, p would be exogenous, while q would be a choice variable.

4.2.2   Efficiency

The features discussed in this model follow Piketty's discussion in the context of alternative economic systems, but it is a general approach that goes back to Ramsey (1927) and his insights about the relationship between elasticities and taxes.[7] The basic idea that drives our results in this section is that output in the oil industry, being driven primarily by luck and not effort, is less sensitive to taxes than output in the manufacturing industry. Hence, efficiency dictates that taxes in the oil industry should be higher. This translates into two different effects. First, if taxes are uniform across industries, the tax rate in a society will be higher the higher the share of oil in the GDP. Second, if tax rates are allowed to vary across industries, a nationalization (expropriation) of the oil industry may be optimal.

There are two sectors in the economy, the Oil industry and the Manufacturing industry, and time is discrete $t = 0, 1, 2 \ldots$.

1. At the start of each period the tax rate for the period and the proportion of people earning income from the oil industry are fixed.

2. Then, people in the manufacturing industry choose effort, and incomes are realized: pretax incomes can be either y_0 or $y_1 > y_0 > 0$; in the oil industry, the probability of y_1 is a fixed exogenous π, whereas in the manufacturing industry the probability of y_1 is e, the worker's effort.

3. After the choices of effort, and the realization of the income shocks, nature chooses for the next period (through its choice of the price of oil) whether the proportion of people in the economy earning income from the oil industry is q_l or $q_h > q_l$ (higher price leads to more investment and more hiring by the oil firms).

4. A tax rate that maximizes the income of (the next period's) poor workers is set.[8]

The worker's utility when income is y and effort e is

$$U = y - \frac{e^2}{2a}$$

(where $a > 0$ is a parameter such that $a(y_1 - y_0) \in [0, 1]$). We also add the restriction that the oil sector is not too large in the economy to ensure that the optimal tax rate is not full expropriation: $a(y_1 - y_0) \geq \pi q/(1 - q)$ for all q (we have assumed that there are only two levels of q, but the model can be immediately generalized to an arbitrary set of q's in $\mathbf{R}$).

Income is taxed at a rate τ and tax revenue is redistributed in a lump-sum way to all workers, so that if total income is Y, after-tax income is either $(1 - \tau)y_0 + \tau Y$ or $(1 - \tau)y_1 + \tau Y$. When choosing his or her effort level, the worker takes Y as given (there is a continuum many workers), so that the worker's effort is

$$e(\tau) = \arg\max_e e[(1 - \tau)y_1 + \tau Y] + (1 - e)[(1 - \tau)y_0 + \tau Y] - \frac{e^2}{2a}$$

$$= \arg\max_e e(1 - \tau)(y_1 - y_0) - \frac{e^2}{2a} = a(y_1 - y_0)(1 - \tau) \quad (1)$$

By our assumption that $a(y_1 - y_0) \in [0, 1]$, then optimal effort lies between 0 and 1, and hence the probability of the high income in the manufacturing industry (which is exactly e) is also between 0 and 1.

Then, the income of the poor workers in the next period (if today a tax rate of τ is chosen for tomorrow and a proportion q of the population will be in the oil industry) is

$$(1 - \tau)y_0 + \tau\{q[\pi y_1 + (1 - \pi)y_0] + (1 - q)[e(\tau)y_1 + (1 - e(\tau))y_0]\}$$

which, after simplification, becomes

$$y_0 + (y_1 - y_0)\tau\{q\pi + (1 - q)e(\tau)\}. \quad (2)$$

Note first that the poor worker's income is his or her production, y_0, plus a proportion τ of the incremental income of the rich, $y_1 - y_0$, multiplied by the proportion of rich people $\{q\pi + (1 - q)e(\tau)\}$. Of course, if the effort were fixed at e^*, the optimal τ would be 1, since $q\pi + (1 - q)e^* > 0$ (it would be optimal to completely equalize incomes). But since taxing reduces effort, such a high tax rate is not optimal because eventually it becomes counterproductive.

Proposition 2   The optimal tax rate is

$$\tau = \frac{a(y_1 - y_0) + \pi\frac{q}{1-q}}{2a(y_1 - y_0)} \quad (3)$$

which is increasing in q.

Proof   Substituting the expression of the optimal effort rate $e(\tau) = a(y_1 - y_0)(1 - \tau)$ into equation (2), we obtain the objective function

$$y_0 + (y_1 - y_0)\tau\{q\pi + (1 - q)e(\tau)\}$$

$$= y_0 + (y_1 - y_0)\tau\{q\pi + (1 - q)a(y_1 - y_0)(1 - \tau)\}$$

that is maximized for the tax rate in equation (3). Also, we note that the expression for the optimal tax rate is increasing in q, and that the tax rate is between 0 and 1, because of our assumption that $a(y_1 - y_0) \geq \pi q/(1-q)$. ∎

The previous proposition can be interpreted more generally in the context of the "curse of natural resources": if a country's income relies heavily on activities in which taxes are not "very" distortionary, taxes will tend to be higher. Note that the problem arises because the same tax is applied to all sectors. If the tax on the two sectors could be different, the oil sector would be taxed at a 100 percent rate (because there is no effort cost, and no inefficiency associated with the tax), providing a rationale for nationalizations. Thus, it is best for the rest of the capitalists (and the economy) to nationalize the oil industry. This result is presented in the next proposition, but before we continue, a word about what it means to nationalize an industry is in order. Our "operational" definition of a nationalization is that all oil workers' income is equated to the income of the poor workers in the manufacturing industries; all income in excess of that of poor workers in other sectors is expropriated. Formally, after a nationalization, the poor workers' income (irrespective of the sector) is the sum of their posttax income, plus the government transfers arising from the oil industry, plus the transfers arising from the manufacturing sector:

$$(1 - \tau)y_0 + q(\pi(y_1 - (1 - \tau)y_0) + (1 - \pi)\tau y_0)$$
$$+ \tau(1 - q)(ey_1 + (1 - e)y_0). \tag{4}$$

With other (reasonable) definitions of a nationalization, the result that taxes are lower after a nationalization continues to hold. The reason is simple: after the nationalization, the tax rate is applied only to sectors where the taxes are distortionary, while before the nationalization, it also applied to the oil sector where no distortions would arise.

Proposition 3 The optimal tax rate falls after a nationalization of the oil industry.

Proof After a nationalization, the income of the poor workers is as in equation (4), which simplifies to $y_0 + (\pi q + \tau e(1 - q))(y_1 - y_0)$. Substituting the optimal effort from equation (1), we obtain the expression to be maximized:

$$y_0 + (\pi q + \tau a(y_1 - y_0)(1 - \tau)(1 - q))(y_1 - y_0)$$

This expression is maximized for $\tau = 1/2$, which is smaller than the tax rate (3) before the nationalization, as was to be shown.   ∎

As argued above, since proposition 3 shows that taxes would fall in the rest of the economy after a nationalization of the oil industry, it provides both a political economy and an efficiency rationale for nationalizing the oil industry (assuming that output in the industry would not fall if the sector is managed by the government).

4.2.3   Fairness: Adapting Alesina-Angeletos

An alternative channel through which oil might influence the desire to distribute income is by its effect on the perception of the degree to which people live in a fair society. A natural question is how fairness is going to be defined.[9] We assume people can feel disutility when they find out that they live in a society where people consume more than what they "deserve," where this is the amount that their effort and talent would command. This is broadly the approach followed in Alesina and Angeletos 2005b (henceforth AA), although our specification differs in several respects (see below for a detailed discussion).[10]

Finally, it is worth pointing out that with the present definition of fairness, oil dependence increases the perception that unfairness prevails because it generates income that is not tied to effort or talent. As explained earlier, we do not have evidence concerning this assumption (i.e., we do not have evidence that there is such a widespread perception that effort plays such a small role in the extraction of oil, or, more precisely, that the effort elasticity of production in the oil sector is smaller than in manufacturing). Again, we view this as a broad issue, where the discovery of oil (or an increase in its price) may lead to an increase in capital inflows and changes in relative prices (in particular in the exchange rate), which can be seen as unexpected and tied to luck.

There are two sectors in the economy, the Oil industry and the Manufacturing industry, and time is discrete $t = 0, 1, 2 \ldots$.

1. At the start of each period the proportion of people earning income from the oil industry is fixed (by nature) and known. Nature then chooses two shocks for each individual: an ability shock and a luck shock. The latter is identically 0 for the manufacturing industry.

2. Taxes are set by majority voting.

3. Then people choose effort.

4. After the choice of effort, nature chooses for the next period whether the proportion of people in the economy earning income from the oil industry is q_l or $q_h > q_l$. This is a reduced form formulation for a broader model in which nature chooses demands or tastes in the economy that induce variations in the price of oil; then if, for example, nature chose a high price, that would lead to more investment and more hiring by the oil firms.

The economy is populated by a measure 1 continuum of individuals $i \in [0, 1]$. For each individual i, and industry $j = O, M$, total pretax income y_i is

$$y_i = A_i e_i + \eta_i^j$$

where A is talent, e is effort, and η_i^j is "noise" or "luck" for individual i in industry j. We assume that η^O has 0 mean and a symmetric distribution, that η^M is always 0, and that the distribution of A^2 is symmetric (we also assume that $2A^2$ is greater than the maximum element in the support of A_i^2). The shocks A and η are independent among them, and across agents.

The government imposes a flat tax rate τ on income and redistributes the proceeds in a lump-sum fashion, so that the individual's consumption is

$$c_i = (1 - \tau)y_i + G$$

for government transfer $G = \tau \int_i y_i$.

Let u_i be the private utility from one's own consumption and effort; γ the "distaste for unfair outcomes"; and Ω a measure of the social injustice in the economy. Then, with $u_i = V(c_i, e_i) = c_i - e_i^2/2$ being the private utility of consumption and effort, individual preferences are

$$U_i \equiv u_i - \gamma\Omega \equiv V(c_i, e_i) - \gamma\Omega \equiv c_i - \frac{e_i^2}{2} - \gamma\Omega.$$

Social injustice is

$$\Omega = \int_i (u_i - \hat{u}_i)^2$$

where u_i is the actual level of private utility, and $\hat{u}_i$ is a measure of the "fair" level of utility the individual should have (deserves) on the basis of talent and effort. This follows Alesina and Angeletos 2005b, which in turn follows a considerable literature in philosophy and morality on "just deserts." We note, however, that there are two differences between A and η. The first is that although one tends to view ability as a fairly permanent shock and luck as a transitory shock, in the model both are transitory shocks. Still, in our definition of unfairness (which follows Alesina and Angeletos's), we have assumed that people see a shock to talent as fair and a luck shock as unfair; this assumption that a permanent shock is "fair" and a transitory one not, seems at odds with our perception of what people see as fair.

The second difference between A and η is that the ability shock A affects the agent's optimal choice of effort, while the luck shock does not. This second feature of our assumption of the interaction between shocks and effort is simply a reflection of how one usually thinks about talent and luck. Given the unobservable nature of "talent" and "luck," it would be impossible to gather evidence suggesting whether effort applied to the permanent shock has more impact on income than if applied to the temporary shock (in favor of our assumption, however, one can think of situations in which an individual with high talent could acquire education that affects the quality of the effort). We now define the fair level of utility $\hat{u}_i$ as the level of utility an individual would have after consuming all his or her income, minus the income gained from a luck shock: $\hat{u}_i = V_i(\tilde{c}_i, e_i) = \tilde{c}_i - e_i^2/2$ for

$$\tilde{c}_i = \tilde{y}_i = (1 - \tau)A_i e_i + G.$$

For the purposes of comparison, recall that individual consumption is $c_i = (1 - \tau)(A_i e_i + \eta_i^j) + G$.

The individual maximizes

$$u_i = (1 - \tau)A_i e_i + (1 - \tau)\eta_i^j + G - \frac{e_i^2}{2} \tag{5}$$

with respect to e, to obtain $e_i = (1 - \tau)A_i$. Let $\bar{\eta}$ be the mean and median of η, and let $a_i = A_i^2$ and $a_m = \int A_i^2$. Substituting into the utility function, and using

$$G = \tau \int y_i = \tau \int A_i e_i + \eta_i^j = \tau(1 - \tau) \int A_i^2 + \tau\bar{\eta} \equiv \tau(1 - \tau)a_m + \tau\bar{\eta},$$

we get

$$u_i = \frac{a_i}{2}(1 - \tau^2) + \eta_i + \tau(\bar{\eta} - \eta_i) + \tau(a_m - a_i)(1 - \tau)$$

$$= \frac{a_i}{2}(1 - \tau^2) + (1 - \tau)\eta_i + \tau(a_m - a_i)(1 - \tau)$$

Using our definition of fair consumption, $\tilde{c}_i = (1 - \tau)A_i e_i + G$, we get

$$\Omega = Var(c_i - \tilde{c}_i) = Var((1 - \tau)y_i - (1 - \tau)A_i e_i)$$

$$= Var((1 - \tau)(y_i - A_i e_i)) = Var((1 - \tau)\eta_i)$$

But since only people in the oil industry have nonzero η_i shocks, and they are a proportion q of the population, letting σ_η^2 stand for the variance of η, social injustice is

$$\Omega = (1 - \tau)^2 q \sigma_\eta^2.$$

Then, $U_i = u_i - \gamma\Omega$ implies

$$U_i = \frac{a_i}{2}(1 - \tau^2) + (1 - \tau)\eta_i + \tau(a_m - a_i)(1 - \tau) - \gamma\Omega$$

$$= \frac{a_i}{2}(1 - \tau^2) + (1 - \tau)\eta_i + \tau(a_m - a_i)(1 - \tau) - \gamma(1 - \tau)^2 q \sigma_\eta^2 \tag{6}$$

The next theorem identifies who the median voter is, in terms of the underlying shocks: given our symmetry assumptions, the individual whose preferred tax rate is the median of the distribution of preferred tax rates, is the individual with the median values of the shocks a and η.

Theorem 1 The median voter is the individual with the median values of the shocks. That is, the tax rate preferred by the individual with the median values of the shocks, $(a_i, \eta_i) = (a_m, 0)$, is a Condorcet winner: it beats every other tax rate by simple majority voting.

Proof From equation (6) we obtain

$$\frac{dU_i}{d\tau} = -a_i\tau - \eta_i + (a_m - a_i)(1 - 2\tau) + 2\gamma(1 - \tau)q\sigma_\eta^2$$

and then

$$\frac{d^2 U_i}{d\tau^2} = a_i - 2a_m - 2\gamma q\sigma_\eta^2.$$

The optimal tax rate for an individual with shocks (a_i, η_i) is determined by $\frac{dU_i(\tau^*)}{d\tau} = 0$ if $\tau^* \in (0, 1)$:

$$\frac{dU_i}{d\tau} = -a_i\tau - \eta_i + (a_m - a_i)(1 - 2\tau) + 2\gamma(1 - \tau)q\sigma_\eta^2 = 0 \Leftrightarrow$$

$$\tau^* = \frac{-\eta_i + a_m - a_i + 2\gamma q\sigma_\eta^2}{2a_m - a_i + 2\gamma q\sigma_\eta^2}$$

If the numerator is negative, the optimal tax rate for the individual is 0, and if τ^* thus calculated is greater than 1, the optimal tax rate is 1.

To finish solving the model, notice that we have assumed that $a_i - 2a_m \leq 0$ for all a_i in the support, so that $d^2U_i/d\tau^2 < 0$ and preferences are single peaked; then the median-voter theorem applies. We now show that the median voter (the individual whose preferred tax rate accumulates $1/2$ of the peaks to each side) is the individual who receives the median shocks $a_i = a_m$ and $\eta_i = 0$. Note that an individual's preferred tax rate is larger than the preferred tax rate of the voter with the median shocks iff

$$\frac{-\eta_i + a_m - a_i + 2\gamma q\sigma_\eta^2}{2a_m - a_i + 2\gamma q\sigma_\eta^2} \geq \frac{2\gamma q\sigma_\eta^2}{a_m + 2\gamma q\sigma_\eta^2} \Leftrightarrow \eta_i \leq \frac{a_m(a_m - a_i)}{a_m + 2q\gamma\sigma_\eta^2}.$$

Let f denote the density of a_i and g that of η. Recalling that a_m is the mean of a_i, we assume that for all x, $f(a_m - x) = f(a_m + x)$, and that $g(-x) = g(x)$. With this assumption, a_m is not only the mean of a_i but also its median. Let

$$S = \left\{ (a_i, \eta_i) : \eta_i \leq \frac{a_m(a_m - a_i)}{a_m + 2q\gamma\sigma_\eta^2} \right\}$$

so that the proof will be complete if we show that $\Pr(S) \geq 1/2$.

We have that for $c \equiv a_m/(a_m + 2q\gamma\sigma_\eta^2)$

$$\Pr\{S\} = \int_{-\infty}^{\infty} \left[\int_{-\infty}^{(a_m-a_i)c} g(\eta)\, d\eta \right] f(a)\, da$$

$$= \int_{-\infty}^{a} \left[\int_{-\infty}^{(a_m-a_i)c} g(\eta)\, d\eta \right] f(a)\, da + \int_{a}^{\infty} \left[\int_{-\infty}^{(a_m-a_i)c} g(\eta)\, d\eta \right] f(a)\, da \quad (7)$$

Define $z(a) = a - a_m$, the density h of z is such that $h(z) = f(z + a_m)$, so that by the symmetry assumption on f, we have $h(z) = f(z + a_m) =$

$f(a_m - z) = h(-z)$. Then, equation (7) and the change of variable $z(a) = a - a_m$ imply that

$$\Pr\{S\} = \int_{-\infty}^{0} \left[\int_{-\infty}^{-zc} g(\eta)\, d\eta \right] h(z)\, dz + \int_{0}^{\infty} \left[\int_{-\infty}^{-zc} g(\eta)\, d\eta \right] h(z)\, dz \qquad (8)$$

but symmetry of g implies that

$$\int_{-\infty}^{-zc} g(\eta)\, d\eta = \int_{zc}^{\infty} g(\eta)\, d\eta$$

so that equation (8) becomes

$$\Pr\{S\} = \int_{-\infty}^{0} \left[\int_{-\infty}^{-zc} g(\eta)\, d\eta \right] h(z)\, dz + \int_{0}^{\infty} \left[\int_{zc}^{\infty} g(\eta)\, d\eta \right] h(z)\, dz$$

Since g is symmetric, the pdf of g, G, is such that for all x, $G(-x) = 1 - G(x)$. Therefore

$$\Pr\{S\} = \int_{-\infty}^{0} G(-zc) h(z)\, dz + \int_{0}^{\infty} [1 - G(zc)] h(z)\, dz$$

$$= \int_{-\infty}^{0} [1 - G(zc)] h(z)\, dz + \int_{0}^{\infty} [1 - G(zc)] h(z)\, dz$$

so for $w = -z$, using $h(-w) = h(w)$ and $1 - G(-wc) = G(wc)$ we obtain

$$\Pr\{S\} = \int_{-\infty}^{0} [1 - G(zc)] h(z)\, dz + \int_{0}^{\infty} [1 - G(zc)] h(z)\, dz$$

$$= \int_{0}^{\infty} [1 - G(-wc)] h(w)\, dw + \int_{0}^{\infty} [1 - G(zc)] h(z)\, dz$$

$$= \int_{0}^{\infty} G(wc) h(w)\, dw + \int_{0}^{\infty} [1 - G(zc)] h(z)\, dz = \int_{0}^{\infty} h(z)\, dz = \frac{1}{2}.$$

This completes the proof. ∎

The previous theorem establishes whose preferences will prevail. The next result is the main result of this section: it characterizes the tax rate preferred by the median voter; it establishes the equilibrium tax rate, and indicates the comparative statics of the equilibrium tax rate with respect to how important oil is in the economy. The theorem shows that as the oil industry becomes more important in a society, its tax rate will increase.

Theorem 2   The Condorcet winner, the equilibrium tax rate, is

$$\tau^* = \frac{2\gamma q \sigma_\eta^2}{a_m + 2\gamma q \sigma_\eta^2} \tag{9}$$

so that an increase in q leads to an increase in the tax rate desired by society.

Proof   Substituting the median shocks in equation (6) and optimizing with respect to τ, we obtain the tax rate preferred by the individual with median shocks given in equation (9). Theorem 1 then ensures that this is the tax rate adopted by society.   ∎

Our model is loosely based on Alesina and Angeletos's. Given the importance of that paper, in the next section we detail the differences between our model and theirs. In particular, the model of AA has a few mistakes, some of which are important both for their paper and ours.

4.2.3.1   Differences between Our Model and That of Alesina and Angeletos   A first difference is that we corrected some small algebraic mistakes that lead AA to conclude that preferences are single peaked. Our assumption that $a_i - 2a_m \leq 0$ for all a_i in the support is necessary for single peakedness (see the proof of theorem 1).

A second difference from the AA model is that even if one assumes that $a_i - 2a_m \leq 0$ for all a_i in the support, so that preferences are single peaked and the median-voter theorem applies, their analysis of the equilibrium is problematic. In particular, they claim that the individual with the median values of the shocks is the median voter, which is not always true. As a consequence, they predict (for example) a 0 tax rate when the tax rate that arises in equilibrium (the Condorcet winner) is positive. To fix this problem in our model, we have made some symmetry assumptions on the distributions, which ensure that the individual with the median shocks is indeed the median voter.[11]

Finally, and most important, their definition of what constitutes a "fair level of consumption" is unattractive. Individual consumption is $c_i = (1 - \tau)(A_i e_i + \eta_i^j) + G$; the AA definition of fair consumption (adapted to this model without capital) is $\hat{c}_i = A_i e_i$; and our definition of fair consumption is $\tilde{c}_i = (1 - \tau)A_i e_i + G$. The "current" situation of the economy is $c_i = (1 - \tau)(A_i e_i + \eta_i^j) + G$, so when asking ourselves what a fair society would look like—that is, what life would be like without luck shocks, the natural comparison seems to be with $\tilde{c}_i = (1 - \tau)A_i e_i + G$ (the current situation, with luck shocks set to 0, but with taxes and government still in place). AA, however, define fair consumption as consumption with 0 luck shocks, but also without government: $\tau = G = 0$. An important point to note is that while defining fair consumption as we do, or as AA do, has no relevant consequences for our model, it has critical consequences for AA: the multiplicity of equilibria disappears.[12] Also, this problem with the definition of fair consumption has the unnatural consequence that even if there is no unfairness in society ($\eta_i = 0$ for all i), changes in the preference for fairness (changes in γ) that should have no effect on the equilibrium tax rate (because there is no unfairness) *do* change the amount of redistribution that society wants. That is, the wedge between the "verbal" definition of fairness and the technical one affects the optimal tax for reasons unrelated to fairness.

4.3 Empirical Illustration Using U.S. Data

4.3.1 Data and Empirical Strategy

4.3.1.1 Data
We use two primary sources of data and discuss each in turn. First, because we are trying to explain the determinants of a subjective preference (i.e., left- versus right-wing), we need to acquire survey data on this attribute of an individual. The data we use for this purpose are repeated cross-sections of randomly sampled Americans from the United States General Social Survey (GSS) from 1983 to 2004. The sample is reasonably continuous over time (although there are some holes—there are no GSS data for 1992, 1995, 1997, 1999, and 2001). There are, however, data for 1973 but they were discarded given that it is separated by ten years from the rest of our sample. Each survey is an independently drawn sample of English-speaking persons eighteen years of age or over, living in the United States. One of the basic purposes of the GSS is to gather data on contemporary American society in order to monitor and explain trends and constants in attitudes, behaviors, and attributes.

The particular variable that we use from the GSS is called *Help Poor* − R_{ist}, which is a categorical variable that is the answer (by individual i, living in state s and year t) to the following question:

"Some people think that the government in Washington should do everything possible to improve the standard of living of all poor Americans; they are at Point 1 on this card. Other people think it is not the government's responsibility, and that each person should take care of himself; they are at Point 5. Where would you place yourself on this scale, or haven't you made up your mind on this?" The possible answers are "1 (Gov't actions), 2, 3 (Agree with both), 4, 5 (People help selves)."

We assign the "R" extension to the variable name since higher values of this variable are usually associated with response often linked with parties on the right end of the political spectrum, which assume that the poor themselves should be responsible for their own well-being, without government intervention.

Second, as a proxy for the relative role of luck versus effort in the determination of income we use $Luck_{st}$, which is defined as the price of oil (in U.S. dollars) multiplied by the share of the oil industry in the total GDP of the state. States that are heavily dependent on oil revenues, and consequently on the price of oil, are assumed to experience economic outcomes that are more determined by luck.

4.3.1.2 Empirical Strategy   We estimate an ordered logit regression of the following form:

$$HelpPoor - R_{ist} = \alpha \, Luck_{st} + \beta \, Personalcontrols_{ist} + State_s$$

$$+ \, Year_t + StateTimeTrends_{st} + \varepsilon_{ist}$$

where the dependent variable, $HelpPoor - R_{ist}$, and our primary explanatory variable of interest, $Luck_{st}$, are both defined above. Note that exogeneity concerns should be mitigated because of the oil price (and relative size of the oil industry) being primarily determined by factors outside the control of individual preferences. $Personalcontrols_{ist}$ include the respondent's marital status, gender, income, and age. Income is the response to the GSS question "In which of these groups did your total family income, from all sources, fall last year, before taxes that is? Just tell me the letter." There are twelve possible categorical responses corresponding to different income ranges, so we use dummy variables that correspond to each of them.

All the regressions include state fixed effects, and we also report results that control for year fixed effects, $Year_t$, as well as state-specific time trends, $StateTimeTrends_{st}$. The error term, ε_{ist}, is assumed to be logistic (and identically, independently distributed). For more information, see the appendix.

4.3.2 Results

Our main results are reported in table 4.1. Column 1 reports the base specification in which the determinants of $HelpPoor - R$ are estimated. State dummies are included though there are no other controls. The negative sign is suggestive of a relationship whereby higher oil prices within states drive people away from the right-wing and more toward the left-wing preference that the government should help the poor, although the effect is insignificant. As we argued above, this may be expected when people start believing that luck (not effort) plays an important role in the economy. In column 2 we add year dummy variables and obtain a similar result.

The third column adds state-specific time trends (in addition to state and year dummies). The negative effect of *Luck* on an individual's survey response as to whether the poor should help themselves becomes significant at the 5 percent level. In the base scenario, the cutoff points leave 16.0 percent of the population in the bottom $HelpPoor - R$ category (i.e., Gov't actions), 13.4 percent in the second to last, 45.7 percent in the third, 14.6 percent in the fourth, and 10.3 percent in the top category (i.e., People help selves). When *Luck* increases by an amount equivalent to a shift from a state that has no dependence on oil (e.g., Vermont) to the state with the highest dependence on oil in the sample (Wyoming), the median person has the same response to $HelpPoor - R$ as the person at the 36th percentile of the distribution in the base scenario. Figure 4.3 illustrates the alternative scenarios. That is, they become more supportive of government intervention to help the poor. This calculation assumes that the other explanatory variables are at their average levels in the sample. This does not seem like a very large effect. The exercise assumes a large change in oil dependence, which corresponds to an increase in *Luck* of $1,248 (in constant 2000 dollars), when the standard deviation of *Luck* is $117 (see table 4.5 in appendix A).

In an attempt to provide another metric for these changes, we can focus on the top two categories of $HelpPoor - R$ (where people favor self-help for the poor). When *Luck* increases by an amount equivalent to a shift from (no-oil) Vermont to (oil-dependent) Wyoming, 8.9 percentage points of people no longer report themselves in one of the top two categories of $HelpPoor - R$. That is, the proportion preferring the poor to bear responsibility for helping themselves drops from 24.9 to 16.0 percent as people lean more toward the view that the government should help. Alternatively, a one-standard-deviation increase in

Table 4.1
How beliefs about helping the poor vary with luck; Ordered logit regressions; U.S. General Social Surveys, 1983–2004

Dependent variable: *Help Poor-R*		(1)	(2)	(3)	(4)
Luck		−4.25e-04	−1.70e-04	−4.48e-04**	−6.48e-04***
		(3.13e-04)	(2.82e-04)	(2.09e-04)	(1.99e-04)
Marital Status	Widowed				0.0837
					(0.0751)
	Divorced				−0.0845*
					(0.0496)
	Separated				−0.2764***
					(0.0907)
	Never married				−0.0512
					(0.0346)
Female					−0.2550***
					(0.0293)
Personal Income	Income 2				−0.4826**
					(0.1902)
	Income 3				−0.5495***
					(0.1802)
	Income 4				−0.7108***
					(0.2069)
	Income 5				−0.6494***
					(0.2066)
	Income 6				−0.5890***
					(0.2027)
	Income 7				−0.4243*
					(0.2189)
	Income 8				−0.2874
					(0.1935)
	Income 9				−0.1644
					(0.1944)
	Income 10				−0.0680
					(0.1893)
	Income 11				0.1712
					(0.1934)
	Income 12 (top)				0.4121**
					(0.1909)
Age					0.0093***
					(0.0011)
Year dummies		No	Yes	Yes	Yes
State-specific time trends		No	No	Yes	Yes
Pseudo R-sq		0.0042	0.0062	0.0077	0.0240
No. of states		44	44	44	44
No. of years		15	15	15	15
No obs.		17,401	17,401	17,401	17,401

Note: See appendix B.

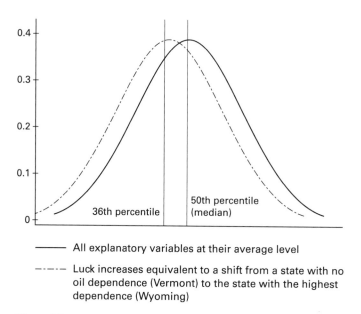

——— All explanatory variables at their average level

—·—·— Luck increases equivalent to a shift from a state with no
oil dependence (Vermont) to the state with the highest
dependence (Wyoming)

Figure 4.3
The probability density function of *Help Poor* − R_{ist}

Luck leads 1.0 percent of people to no longer report themselves in one of the top two categories of *HelpPoor* − *R*.

Similar results are obtained in column 4 once we add personal controls for each individual's marital status, gender, age, and income level. As may be expected, whereas those with low incomes are strongly in favor of more government help for the poor, those with higher incomes are more disposed toward the view that the poor should look after themselves. The coefficients range from significantly negative in the low-income categories to significantly positive in the top couple of categories. Older people are also in favor of the poor having to help themselves. The size of the effect of Luck on *HelpPoor* − *R* becomes somewhat more negative with this full set of controls. Figure 4.4 provides an illustration of the results in this column, using an approach that can be compared with the country-panel results in Di Tella, Donna, and MacCulloch 2006 that are presented in figure 4.2. The sizes of the effects within the United States are clearly smaller; in the present chapter the exercise uses a much larger scale to display similar-size effects, with a value of *Luck* of $1,248 (because that is the value adopted in Wyoming in 1983).

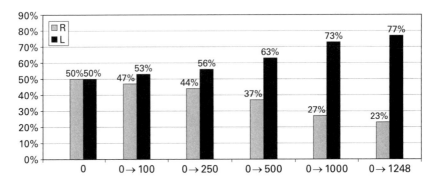

Figure 4.4
Average Belief (Help-Poor) predicted in the state for different shares of the oil industry in state GDP (times the price of oil), using the coefficient in column 4 in table 4.1

Robust regressions using the same specifications as above are done in table 4.2. In the base specification in column 1, more *Luck* drives significantly fewer people to report that the poor should help themselves. The sign of the coefficient on *Luck* remains negative throughout all of the other specifications, though in contrast to table 4.1, the effect loses significance in columns 2–3. In the most general specification reported in column 4, more *Luck* has a negative effect on *HelpPoor – R* at the 5 percent level of significance, and its size is not significantly different from the corresponding (nonrobust) coefficient reported in column 4 in table 4.1.

One simple way of distinguishing the charity channel from the luck channel (for both the Piketty-based model of section 4.2.2 and the Alesina-and-Angeletos-based model of section 4.2.3) is by including income in the regression. Since the charity channel depends only on income, and not on luck specifically, if the luck coefficient continues to be significant, it suggests that there is a role for the belief-based arguments in the models of sections 4.2.2 and 4.2.3. The regression in column 4 does that by controlling for individual income. If oil affects beliefs through the charity mechanism, then any increase in income affects the desire to give to the poor because the concavity of the utility function implies that a given transfer costs less in utility for a richer person. An alternative to the same test is to include GDP per capita in the state at the same time as *Luck*. We do this in tables 4.3 and 4.4. We find that GDP per capita does not have a robust correlation with *HelpPoor – R*, whereas *Luck* is still negative and, in the most complete

Table 4.2
How beliefs about helping the poor vary with luck; Robust OLS regressions; U.S. General Social Surveys, 1983–2004

Dependent variable: *Help Poor-R*		(1)	(2)	(3)	(4)
Luck		−2.94e-04**	−1.22e-04	−2.92e-04	−4.08e-04**
		(1.23e-04)	(1.35e-04)	(1.79e-04)	(1.77e-04)
Marital Status	Widowed				0.0534
					(0.0375)
	Divorced				−0.0527*
					(0.0283)
	Separated				−0.1824***
					(0.0506)
	Never married				−0.0317
					(0.0266)
Female					−0.1596***
					(0.0187)
Personal Income	Income 2				−0.3159***
					(0.1111)
	Income 3				−0.3589***
					(0.1100)
	Income 4				−0.4589***
					(0.1080)
	Income 5				−0.4187***
					(0.1061)
	Income 6				−0.3761***
					(0.1081)
	Income 7				−0.2731**
					(0.1065)
	Income 8				−0.1822*
					(0.0999)
	Income 9				−0.1003
					(0.0913)
	Income 10				−0.0342
					(0.0921)
	Income 11				0.1229
					(0.0917)
	Income 12 (top)				0.2748***
					(0.0884)
Age					0.0059***
					(0.0007)
Year dummies		No	Yes	Yes	Yes
State-specific time trends		No	No	Yes	Yes
R-sq		0.0119	0.0176	0.0219	0.0672
No. of states		44	44	44	44
No. of years		15	15	15	15
No obs.		17,401	17,401	17,401	17,401

Note: See appendix B.

Table 4.3
How beliefs about helping the poor vary with luck; controlling for GDP per capita;
Ordered logit regressions; U.S. General Social Surveys, 1983–2004

Dependent variable: *Help Poor-R*		(1)	(2)	(3)	(4)
Luck		−3.14e-04	−3.1e-04	−3.91e-04	−5.74e-04**
		(2.69e-04)	(2.92e-04)	(2.89e-04)	(2.79e-04)
GDP per capita (US$ 2000)		2.21e-05***	1.37e-05	−6.19e-06	−7.98e-06
		(5.07e-06)	(1.26e-05)	(2.46e-05)	(2.44e-05)
Marital Status	Widowed				0.0838
					(0.0751)
	Divorced				−0.0845*
					(0.0495)
	Separated				−0.276***
					(0.0907)
	Never married				−0.0512
					(0.0346)
Female					−0.255***
					(0.0292)
Personal Income	Income 2				−0.483**
					(0.1903)
	Income 3				−0.5493***
					(0.18)
	Income 4				−0.7106***
					(0.2069)
	Income 5				−0.6493***
					(0.2066)
	Income 6				−0.589***
					(0.2027)
	Income 7				−0.4244**
					(0.219)
	Income 8				−0.2876
					(0.1937)
	Income 9				−0.1644
					(0.1944)
	Income 10				−0.0683
					(0.1894)
	Income 11				0.1712
					(0.1934)
	Income 12 (top)				0.4121
					(0.1909)
Age					0.0093**
					(0.0011)
Year dummies		No	Yes	Yes	Yes
State-specific time trends		No	No	Yes	Yes
Pseudo R-sq		0.0049	0.0062	0.0077	0.0240
No. of states		44	44	44	44
No. of years		15	15	15	15
No obs.		17,401	17,401	17,401	17,401

Note: See appendix B.

Table 4.4
How beliefs about helping the poor vary with luck; controlling for GDP per capita; Robust OLS regressions; U.S. General Social Surveys, 1983–2004

Dependent variable: *Help Poor-R*		(1)	(2)	(3)	(4)
Luck		−2.2e-04*	−2.11e-04	−2.46e-04	−3.58e-04*
		(1.23e-04)	(1.58e-04)	(2.19e-04)	(2.16e-04)
GDP per capita (US$ 2000)		1.43e-05***	8.79e-06	−4.95e-06	−5.46e-06
		(2.31e-06)	(8.10e-06)	(1.36e-05)	(1.34e-05)
Marital Status	Widowed				0.0534
					(0.0375)
	Divorced				−0.0527*
					(0.0283)
	Separated				−0.1824***
					(0.0506)
	Never married				−0.0317
					(0.0266)
Female					−0.1596***
					(0.0187)
Personal Income	Income 2				−0.316***
					(0.1111)
	Income 3				−0.3589***
					(0.1100)
	Income 4				−0.4589***
					(0.1080)
	Income 5				−0.4187***
					(0.1061)
	Income 6				−0.3761***
					(0.1081)
	Income 7				−0.2731**
					(0.1065)
	Income 8				−0.1822*
					(0.0999)
	Income 9				−0.1003
					(0.0913)
	Income 10				−0.0342
					(0.0921)
	Income 11				0.1229
					(0.0917)
	Income 12 (top)				0.2748***
					(0.0884)
Age					0.0059***
					(0.0007)
Year dummies		No	Yes	Yes	Yes
State-specific time trends		No	No	Yes	Yes
R-sq		0.0119	0.0176	0.0219	0.0672
No. of states		44	44	44	44
No. of years		15	15	15	15
No obs.		17,401	17,401	17,401	17,401

Note: See appendix B.

specification that controls for personal characteristics and state-specific time trends, is also significant.

4.4 Conclusions

We start from the observation that capitalism is not as widespread as economists might hope. Data from surveys of public opinion, as well as on the distribution of political parties, confirm the idea that capitalism does not flow to poor countries. In some countries, antimarket sentiment has increased in recent years, a period where the prices of oil and other primary commodities have soared. The combination (of antimarket sentiment and high oil prices) has led, not surprisingly, to renegotiations of oil contracts and even nationalizations in some countries such as Bolivia and Venezuela. Of course, it is tempting for economists trained in the theory of political capture to argue that this is just another instance where special interests exploit the circumstances to make an extra dollar. Given that these nationalizations are often popular with the majority of voters, we resist this temptation and ask if there are explanations where a positive correlation emerges between voter's desired tax rates and dependence on oil.

We present three models where this association is natural. For example, in our adaptation of Alesina and Angeletos 2005b, oil dependence increases the perception that luck rather than effort matters and high taxes are introduced to increase "fairness." One implication is that non-oil sectors benefit from a nationalization of the oil industry because people's desired taxes go down. The link is based on the idea that the nationalization "removes" the sector where luck prevails from the determination of income in the country. Of course, several assumptions are needed for this result. For example, the oil sector in the hands of the government will generate rents to some groups and this might again undermine the notion that effort pays, this time because connections and corruption drive income instead of effort. Thus, the results require that perceptions of corruption do not immediately become widespread (Di Tella and MacCulloch (2002) present evidence that corruption perception leads to a desire to regulate).

We then present suggestive evidence for the period 1983–2004 from the United States, where answers to a question about whether the poor should be helped by the government (versus helping themselves) tend less toward the individualist end of the spectrum when the share of the oil industry in a state increases. This holds in some specifications that control for income shocks. Thus, at least some connection seems to exist between dependence on oil and receptivity to populist rhetoric that is both natural in economic models and has some support in the data. Critics of left-wing ideas might see this connection as another version of the "resource curse" whereby countries that are well endowed with natural resources fail to develop, often due to populist policies. Since the emergence of populist policies in our context is due to people's beliefs about the relative importance of luck and effort, we call this a "resource belief curse."

Appendix A

Survey Descriptions GSS 1972–2006 Cumulative Data File

The General Social Surveys (GSS) are designed as part of a program of social indicator research, replicating questionnaire items and wording in order to facilitate time-trend studies. This collection is a cumulative data set that merges all data collected as part of the General Social Surveys from 1972 to the present. Among the new items added for the 2002 surveys are topical modules on prejudice, doctors and patients, quality of working life, employee compensation, altruism, adult transitions, and mental health. Also included are cross-national modules, conducted under the aegis of the International Social Survey Program (ISSP), on the role of government, social support and equality, family and gender, national identity, religion, the environment, and work.

This cumulative data file merges all twenty-five General Social Surveys (1972–1978, 1980, 1982–1991, 1993, 1994, 1996, 1998, 2000, 2002, 2004) into a single file with each year or survey acting as a subfile. This arrangement of the data facilitates trend analysis on repeated questions over the thirty-two-year period. Each survey is an independently drawn sample of English-speaking persons eighteen years of age or over, living in noninstitutional arrangements within the United States. Block quota sampling was used in the 1972, 1973, and 1974 surveys and for half of the 1975 and 1976 surveys. Full probability sampling was employed in half of the 1975 and 1976 surveys and in the 1977, 1978, 1980, 1982–1991, 1993–1998, 2000, 2002, and 2004 surveys. The basic purposes of the GSS are to gather data on contemporary

American society in order to monitor and explain trends and constants in attitudes, behaviors, and attributes; to examine the structure and functioning of society in general as well as the role played by relevant subgroups; and to compare the United States to other societies in order to place American society in comparative perspective and develop cross-national models of human society. See http://www.disc.wisc .edu/newcatalog/study.asp?tid=13995&id=8093).

Individual-Level Variables

Help Poor-R: A categorical variable that is the answer to the question, "Some people think that the government in Washington should do everything possible to improve the standard of living of all poor Americans; they are at Point 1 on this card. Other people think it is not the government's responsibility, and that each person should take care of himself; they are at Point 5. Where would you place yourself on this scale, or haven't you made up your mind on this?" The possible answers are 1 (Govt actions), 2, 3 (Agree with both), 4, 5 (People help selves).

Age: Respondent's age in years.

Gender: Respondent's gender.

Marital Status: Respondent's marital status: married, widowed, divorced, separated, never married.

Income: The answer to the question, "In which of these groups did your total family income, from all sources, fall last year, before taxes that is? Just tell me the letter." The possible answers are 1 if "LT $1,000," 2 if "$1,000 to 2,999," 3 if "$3,000 to 3,999," 4 if "$4,000 to 4,999," 5 if "$5,000 to 5,999," 6 if "$6,000 to 6,999," 7 if "$7,000 to 7,999," 8 if "$8,000 to 9,999," 9 if "$10,000 to 14,999," 10 if "$15,000 to 19,999," 11 if "$20,000 to 24,999," 12 if "$25,000 or more," 13 if "Refused." Refused values are treated as missing values in the regressions.

State-Level Variables

Oil Price(t): Refers to annual average crude oil price per barrel (real US$) and is obtained from the U.S. Energy Administration.

Oil Share(s,t): Refers to oil industry share as a percentage of GDP (US$ current) and is obtained from the U.S. Bureau of Economic Analysis, www.bea.gov.

Luck(s,t): Computed as *Oil Price(t)*Oil Share(s,t)*, where *Oil price(t)* denotes oil price at time t, *Oil Share(s,t)* refers to oil share in state *s* at time *t*, and *Luck(s,t)* denotes luck in state *s* at time *t*.

Table 4.5
Summary statistics for the aggregate variables

Variable		Obs.	Mean	Std. dev.	Min.	Max.
Help Poor-R		Total = 17,401	2.90	1.16	1	5
	between	n = 95		0.28	2	3.82
	within	T-bar = 183.168		1.16	0.55	5.90
Oil Price		Total = 17,401	22.47	8.54	11.27	40.16
	between	n = 95		6.87	14.61	38.25
	within	T-bar = 183.168		7.91	9.30	39.83
Oil Share		Total = 17,401	1.33	3.75	0	31.21
	between	n = 95		5.43	0	26.67
	within	T-bar = 183.168		2.94	−5.26	31.19
$Luck(s,t) = Oil\ Price(t)$		Total = 17,401	34.62	116.93	0	1248.16
$* Oil\ Share(s,t)$	between	n = 95		151.21	0	837.34
	within	T-bar = 183.168		96.76	−425.55	1250.46

Appendix B

Notes to Tables 4.1 and 4.3

1. All regressions are ordered logistic regressions. Cut points (standard errors) in table 4.1: for column 1 are as follows: $c_1 = -1.73$ (0.10), $c_2 = -0.95$ (0.11), $c_3 = 1.02$ (0.11), $c_4 = 2.07$ (0.11). Cut points for column 2: $c_1 = -1.51$ (0.12), $c_2 = -0.73$ (0.13), $c_3 = 1.24$ (0.13), $c_4 = 2.29$ (0.14). Cut points for column 3: $c_1 = -6.50$ (0.39), $c_2 = -5.72$ (0.39), $c_3 = -3.74$ (0.39), $c_4 = -2.68$ (0.39). Cut points for column 4: $c_1 = -5.90$ (0.47), $c_2 = -5.09$ (0.47), $c_3 = -3.04$ (0.46), $c_4 = -1.97$ (0.46).

Notes to Tables 4.2 and 4.4

1. In all regressions we utilize the robust regression method using iteratively reweighted least squares (Huber and Tukey biweights) with rreg routine in Stata.

Notes to all Tables

1. All regressions include state dummies.

2. Name of dependent variable has R (L) extension if higher numbers mean more Right (Left).

3. *Help Poor-R*: is a categorical variable that is the answer to the question, "Some people think that the government in Washington should do everything possible to improve the standard of living of all poor Americans; they are at Point 1 on this card. Other people think it is not the government's responsibility, and that each person should take care of himself; they are at Point 5. Where would you place yourself on this scale, or haven't you made up your mind on this?". The possible answers are "1 (Govt actions), 2, 3 (Agree with both), 4, 5 (People help selves)." Help Poor-R is obtained from the GSS.

4. *Luck(s,t) = Oil Price(t)*Oil Share(s,t)*. Oil Price refers to Annual Average Crude Oil Price per Barrel (Real US$) and is obtained from the U.S. Energy Administration. *Oil Share* refers to Oil Industry share as a percentage of GDP (US$ current) and is obtained from U.S. Bureau of Economic Analysis, www.bea.gov.

5. Personal Controls reported in column 4: marital status, gender, income, and age.

6. *Income* is the answer to the GSS question, "In which of these groups did your total family income, from all sources, fall last year, before taxes that is? Just tell me the letter." The possible answers are: 1 if "LT $1,000," 2 if "$1,000 to 2,999," 3 if "$3,000 to 3,999," 4 if "$4,000 to 4,999," 5 if "$5,000 to 5,999," 6 if "$6,000 to 6,999," 7 if "$7,000 to 7,999," 8 if "$8,000 to 9,999," 9 if "$10,000 to 14,999," 10 if "$15,000 to 19,999," 11 if "$20,000 to 24,999," 12 if "$25,000 or more," 13 if "Refused." Refused values are treated as missing values in the regressions.

7. Standard errors (adjusted for clustering) in parentheses.

8. * significant at 10%; ** significant at 5%; *** significant at 1%.

Notes

We thank our discussant, George-Marios Angeletos, as well as the editors of this book (William Hogan and Federico Sturzenegger) for very helpful suggestions. For helpful conversations or comments we thank Rawi Abdelal, Sebastian Galiani, Ernesto Schargrodsky, and seminar participants at the Harvard Kennedy School Conference on "Contractual Renegotiations in Natural Resources" on October 30, 2007. We also thank Javier Donna and Jorge Albanesi for excellent research assistance.

1. This is shown in Di Tella and MacCulloch 2002, using data on political parties from Beck et al. 2001. Survey data comes from the 2005 GlobeScan Report on Issues and Reputation, http://www.globescan.com/news_archives/pipa_market.html.

2. Interestingly, these surprise reforms were all cases of left or center politicians turned free marketers (including Menem in Argentina, Fujimori in Peru, and Lula in Brazil). In contrast, in rich countries, there are more cases of surprises in the other direction (i.e.,

left-wing actions by politicians elected on right-wing platforms), including the case of "Nixon going to China." See Lora and Olivera 2005 as well as Queirolo 2006 for the electoral fate of the reformers.

3. If the "profits" generated by other commodities depend more on effort than do the profits from oil, a rise in the price of these commodities might lead to less effort, however.

4. There is evidence that expropriation rhetoric pays attention to this aspect. For example, Venezuelan president Hugo Chávez announced in 2005 a plan to expropriate approximately 1,800 enterprises that were deemed unproductive. See, for instance, "Otro Controvertido Plan del Gobierno de Chávez," *La Nacion,* July 19, 2005.

5. We assume altruistic preferences, whereas Meltzer and Richard (1981) assume agents that care only about their own material payoffs. Strangely enough, altruism is relatively uncommon in the political economy literature as a motivation. But see Rotemberg 2003.

6. It is possible to write this model with standard selfish preferences by assuming that one decides on taxes before the revelation of income.

7. In the first version of this chapter we incorrectly claimed that the approach originated in Piketty 1995. We thank George-Marios Angeletos for pointing this out, as well as for other useful comments.

8. Why focus on income and not utility? There are at least two reasons for this choice. First, utility is unobservable, while income may be observed (possibly imperfectly). Second, in this model utility is different depending on the sector (workers in one sector exert effort, while in the other they do not). Therefore, while the simplification of oil's production being just luck and manufacturing's probability of high output just effort is good for highlighting our point, it would be incorrect to make it play an additional role (as it would do if we considered the cost of effort in the maximization).

9. Another question is why oil dependence would make society more unfair. We retain our assumption from the previous model, that output in the oil industry is more connected to luck than is output in the rest of the economy Hence, in a broad sense, the models in this and the previous section can be seen as having the same underlying structure on the firms' side. But higher taxes arise for efficiency reasons in the previous model, and for fairness reasons in this model.

10. We note that reasonable alternatives to the definition of what is fair and what is not include Levine 2001 and Rotemberg 2008, which focus on reciprocal altruism; Di Tella and MacCulloch 2002 use these preferences to analyze why capitalism does not flow to countries where capitalists are perceived to be corrupt.

11. We note that the symmetry assumptions that ensure that the median voter is the voter with the median values of the shocks are not necessary to apply the median-voter theorem, or the methods of theorem 1. The model can easily be generalized to situations with asymmetric distributions of shocks.

12. To obtain multiplicity again, one has to give a very complicated definition of Ω, the aggregate level of unfairness in society.

References

Alesina, Alberto, and George-Marios Angeletos. 2005a. "Corruption, Inequality and Fairness." *Journal of Monetary Economics* 52(7): 1227–1244.

Alesina, Alberto, and George-Marios Angeletos. 2005b. "Fairness and Redistribution." *American Economic Review* 95(4): 960–980.

Alesina, Alberto, and Edward L. Glaeser. 2004. *Fighting Poverty in the U.S. and Europe: A World of Difference.* New York: Oxford University Press.

Alesina, Alberto, Ed Glaeser, and Bruce Sacerdote. 2001. "Why Doesn't the US have a European Style Welfare State?" *Brookings Papers on Economic Activity* 2: 187–277.

Beck, Thorsten, George Clarke, Alberto Groff, Philip Keefer, and Patrick Walsh. 2001. "New tools in comparative political economy: The Database of Political Institutions." *World Bank Economic Review* 15: 1, 165–176.

Bénabou, Roland, and Efe A. Ok. 2001. "Social Mobility and the Demand for Redistribution: The Poum Hypothesis." *Quarterly Journal of Economics* 116(2): 447–487.

Bénabou, Roland, and Jean Tirole. 2006. "Belief in a Just World and Redistributive Politics." *Quarterly Journal of Economics* 121(2): 699–746.

Borges, Jorge Luis. 1944. La Loteria de Babilonia. In Jorge Luis Borges, *Ficciones.* Buenos Aires: Editorial Sur.

Corneo, Giacomo, and Hans Gruner. 2002. "Individual Preferences for Political Redistribution." *Journal of Public Economics* 83(1): 83–107.

Davis, James A., Tom W. Smith, and Peter V. Marsden. 2005. "General Social Surveys, 1972–2004: [Cumulative file] [Computer file]. 2nd ICPSR version." Chicago: National Opinion Research Center [producer], 2005. Storrs, CT: Roper Center for Public Opinion Research, University of Connecticut / Ann Arbor, MI: Inter-university Consortium for Political and Social Research / Berkeley, CA: Computer-Assisted Survey Methods Program (http://sda.berkeley.edu), University of California [distributors].

Denzau, A., and Douglass North. 1993. *Shared Mental Models: Ideologies and Institutions.* Economic History Working Paper No. 9039003.

Di Tella, Rafael, Javier Donna, and Robert MacCulloch. 2006. "Oil, Macro Volatility and Crime in the Determination of Beliefs in Venezuela." In Ricardo Hausmann and Francisco Rodríguez, eds., *Venezuela: Anatomy of a Collapse.* Cambridge, MA: Harvard University Press.

Di Tella, Rafael, and Juan Dubra. 2008. "Crime and Punishment in the 'American Dream.'" *Journal of Public Economics* 92(7): 1564–1584.

Di Tella, Rafael, and Robert MacCulloch. 2002. "Why Doesn't Capitalism Flow to Poor Countries?" Ms., Harvard Business School.

Di Tella, Rafael, Ernesto Schargrodsky, and Sebastian Galiani. 2007. "The Formation of Beliefs: Evidence from the Allocation of Land Titles to Squatters." *Quarterly Journal of Economics* 122, no. 1 (February): 209–241.

Fong, Christina. 2001. "Social Preferences, Self Interest and the Demand for Redistribution." *Journal of Public Economics* 82: 225–246.

Fong, Christina. 2004. "Which Beliefs Matter for Redistributive Politics? Target-Specific versus General Beliefs about the Causes of Income." Ms., Carnegie Mellon University.

Giuliano, Paola, and Antonio Spilimbergo. 2007. "Growing Up in a Recession: Beliefs and Macroeconomic Shocks." Ms., Harvard University and the IMF.

Greif, Avner. 1994. "Cultural Beliefs and the Organization of Society: A Historical and Theoretical Reflection on Collectivist and Individualist Societies." *Journal of Political Economy* 102(5): 912–950.

Hall, Peter, and David Soskice. 2001. *Varieties of Capitalism.* Oxford: Oxford University Press.

Hochschild, Jennifer. 1981. *What's Fair? American Beliefs about Distributive Justice.* Cambridge, MA: Harvard University Press.

Inglehart, Ronald. 1990. *Culture Shift in Advanced Societies.* Chicago: University of Chicago Press.

Ladd, Everett Carll, and Karlyn Bowman. 1998. *Attitudes towards Economic Inequality.* Washington, DC: AEI Press.

Levine, D. K. 1998. "Modelling Altruism and Spitefulness in Experiments." *Review of Economic Dynamics* 1: 593–622.

Lora, Eduardo, and Mauricio Olivera. 2005. "The Electoral Consequences of the Washington Consensus." *Economia* 5(2): 1–61.

Meltzer, A., and S. Richard. 1981. "A Rational Theory of the Size of Government." *Journal of Political Economy* 89(5): 914–927.

Milgrom, P., and C. Shannon. 1994. "Monotone Comparative Statics." *Econometrica* 62(1): 157–180.

Morgan, J. 2000. "Financing Public Goods by Means of Lotteries." *Review of Economic Studies* 67(4): 761–784.

North, Douglass. 2005. *Understanding the Process of Economic Change.* Princeton, NJ: Princeton University Press.

Piketty, Thomas. 1995. "Social Mobility and Redistributive Politics." *Quarterly Journal of Economics* 110(3): 551–584.

Queirolo, Rosario. 2006. "The Impact of Neoliberal Economic Reforms on Latin Americans' Voting Behavior (1980–2004)." Doctoral dissertation, Department of Political Science, University of Pittsburgh.

Ramsey, F. P. 1927. "A Contribution to the Theory of Taxation." *Economic Journal* 37: 47–61.

Rotemberg, Julio. 2003. "Commercial Policy with Altruistic Voters." *Journal of Political Economy* 111: 174–201.

Rotemberg, Julio. 2008. "Minimally Acceptable Altruism and the Ultimatum Game." *Journal of Economic Behavior and Organization* 66(3–4): 457–476.

Commentary

George-Marios Angeletos

The chapter by Di Tella, Dubra, and MacCulloch examines how an economy's share of natural resources, in particular of oil, affects political attitudes toward redistribution and toward regulation of the oil sector. In so doing, it offers a very interesting example of how important it is to study the two-way interaction between economic conditions, on the one hand, and social beliefs and political attitudes, on the other. Recent work—including some of mine with Alberto Alesina—has emphasized how the codetermination of economic outcomes, social beliefs, and political choices may be crucial for understanding the cross-country variation in social perceptions regarding inequality and political choices regarding redistribution and regulation in the economy. Rafael Di Tella and his coauthors have also made important contributions in this area of research, and this chapter falls in this line of work.

The chapter has two sections, theoretical and empirical. My commentary starts by discussing the chapter's theoretical section, which provides three simple stories to illustrate why the demand for redistribution and regulation might be higher in economies in which the share of the oil sector is higher. It then proceeds to discuss the empirical section, which provides some supporting evidence using U.S. state-level data. The empirical results are particularly surprising and arguably constitute the most valuable contribution of this chapter.

Theoretical Section of the Chapter

The chapter's theoretical section includes three models. The key ingredient of the first model is altruism. First, it is assumed that rich people are altruistic toward the poor and that redistribution is the outcome of such altruism. Second, it is assumed that altruism is a normal good, so that the richer the rich are, the more they wish to redistribute. And finally, it is assumed that a bigger oil sector makes the rich richer. It then follows that a bigger oil sector leads to more redistribution.

In my view, the empirical underpinnings and the interpretation of this model are problematic. First, it is doubtful that this mechanism is empirically relevant. It is well known that in the United States the propensity toward charity strongly increases with income, but it is also known that attitudes toward charity are very different from attitudes toward redistribution. Second, whereas the author suggests that this model represents the spirit of Meltzer and Richard 1981, it actually has nothing to do with it. That model is about selfish political choices— namely, how a poor median voter may push for redistribution or regulation even if this is distortionary because this will transfer wealth from the richer people to him or her—not about altruism. That being said, a true Meltzer-Richard model could also share the prediction that a bigger oil sector could lead to more redistribution. This would be true as long as this increases the gap between the median and the mean of the income, and hence the scope for redistribution—a channel that seems more likely to be empirically relevant.

The second model is based on efficiency considerations. The key assumption is that the elasticity of labor supply or investment is lower in the oil sector than in other sectors, so that the distortionary effects of taxation and regulation are less severe in the oil sector than in other sectors. It then follows from a Ramsey-type efficiency argument that the extent of redistribution and regulation is likely to be greater the bigger the oil sector.

One issue of interpretation here is whether more taxation or regulation of the oil sector will spill over to more overall redistribution or simply remain limited within the oil sector. The model delivers this sort of spillover effect by restricting the tax so that it is the same across sectors, but this need not be the case. Another issue is that, although the mechanism sounds quite plausible, it would be helpful to have more direct evidence for it. Is it known whether labor and investment are really less elastic in the oil sector?

Finally, the third model is a variant of the one in Alesina and Angeletos 2005b. (In fact, this variant also corrects a small mistake in that earlier paper.) Like Alesina and Angeletos 2005b, the third model focuses on the two-way feedback between economic outcomes and social perceptions. The core idea is that people care not only about how much inequality there is per se, but also to what extent this inequality is a fair or unfair outcome.

How exactly people draw a distinction between what is considered a fair economic outcome and what is not, is a delicate question that is not yet fully understood. However, there is plenty of evidence from both the psychology literature and the experimental economics literature that people believe that others should deserve what they get (what they earn), and that they should get what they deserve. And there seems to be a notion that if income is driven more by talent and hard work, then this is income that you deserve to keep. If, on the other hand, it's income that is driven by random luck, political connections, corruption, fraud, unfair market activities, and the like, then this component of income should be taxed away.

Now, consider how this line of reasoning could affect perceptions of the oil sector. In 2007, oil prices have gone up for reasons completely exogenous to the effort and investment choices of oil companies—for example, because of increased demand from China—and this has made certain people much richer. Because this increase in wealth is not a reward for talent or effort, it is likely to be perceived as a completely unfair outcome. Provided that most people have the type of preferences concerning fairness that I discussed above, it then follows that the demand for taxation and regulation of the oil sector will increase.

This explanation is very plausible, but again, a small qualification about the interpretation of the results is needed. As in the previous model, this effect need not spill over to a higher demand for more regulation and redistribution in the entire economy, to the extent that people can direct their anger toward the oil sector. But this effect appears to be intended from the model's interpretation, and it also appears to have occurred recently in the United States, during the spike in oil prices in late 2007 and early 2008: many people are angry about the oil executives and demanding more regulation and taxation of the oil sector precisely because their big fortunes are considered totally unfair, the outcome of pure luck.

Empirical Results of the Chapter

The empirical results are quite intriguing, and arguably more important that the theoretical contribution of the chapter. Although they do not provide any direct evidence on the particular mechanisms behind the chapter's three models, they do provide quite strong evidence in favor of its core theme.

The evidence is based on a panel of U.S. states over the period 1983–2004. The left-hand variable is a measure of beliefs and political attitudes, while the right-hand side is a measure of "luck." In particular, this variable is the interaction of the share of the oil sector in each state (a number varying in the cross-section of states) with the U.S. oil price (a number varying in the time series). Various state and time controls are included. The key finding is that the aforementioned measure of luck has a strong and quite robust impact on beliefs.

This finding is quite intriguing. Although the theoretical arguments are plausible, I would have bet before seeing the chapter that such an effect would not appear in the data. Moreover, the effect seems to be quite strong, at least in relative terms. If one looks at a panel of individuals and tries to explain the variation in beliefs across individuals on the basis of variation in individual characteristics, individual income turns out to have a rather small effect. Hence, relative to the other documented determinants of these beliefs, what the authors are finding is actually a pretty big number.

It's important to note that this result is not driven by any observable individual characteristics, because in the last regressions the authors control for individual characteristics. Also, it is great that the authors did not merely provide cross-state evidence, because then one would not have been able to include state-specific effects, which would have made the results much less reliable. For then the fraction of the oil sector in the state may be correlated with other things in the state, so it was important that the chapter could control for this by having state-fixed effects. That is, I think the chapter should emphasize a bit more where the identification comes from: it is precisely the time variation in oil prices interacting with the state-specific value of impact of that time variation in the state, as measured by the size of the oil sector.

Given that these empirical are findings very interesting, it would be nice to see some more. There are alternative measures of political attitudes and social beliefs; there are other questions that solicit more attitudes toward the poor, attitudes toward the rich, and more generally about regulation and distribution of the economy. It would be helpful to see whether the results are robust across these alternative measures. Moreover, one could consider a similar exercise with a panel of countries instead of the panel of U.S. states considered by the authors.

Conclusion

This chapter makes an important contribution to the economics of natural resources, highlighting the interplay between social perceptions, taxation, and regulation. The theoretical part provides valuable insights into the workings and implications of this interplay. More empirical work could be done in terms of understanding whether the desire to tax or regulate is targeted to a specific sector (the oil sector) or spills over more broadly in the economy. Nevertheless, the empirical findings of this chapter are quite surprising, especially in showing a strong relationship between fortuitous profit and political attitudes. I expect, and hope, that these findings will fuel more research into the aforementioned interplay within the context of natural resources.

5 Optimal Resource Extraction Contracts under Threat of Expropriation

Eduardo Engel and Ronald Fischer

We have nationalized copper by unanimous decision of Parliament, where the parties supporting the government are in the minority. We want the whole world to understand that we have not confiscated the large foreign mining companies. In keeping with a constitutional amendment, we have redressed an historical iniquity by subtracting from the compensation due to the firms, the profits accrued since 1956 that are in excess of a 12% annual rate.

The profits of some of the nationalized firms were so outrageous that when applying the reasonable annual profit rate of 12%, their compensations were subject to substantial deductions.

—Salvador Allende, speech to the United Nations, December 4, 1972

5.1 Introduction

Natural resource–rich countries are prone to expropriating investors in those sectors in good times, when prices of resources are considerably above the long-run average price. The temptation for governments is large, because in the future prices will be lower, and thus any punishment by investors in terms of reduced future investment is low relative to the immediate gains of expropriation. Moreover, the short time frame of democratic governments also leads to high discounting of future losses of investment. Apart from these considerations, profits under a bonanza may be so high that populist pressures for redistribution can compel governments to act. Hence in recent years, high commodity prices have led to outright expropriation or to sectoral tax increases, which also amount to a form of expropriation.[1]

This type of behavior is especially common in industries with large sunk investments, such as oil and mining. These plants normally operate at capacity, except when prices are so low that they shut down. Therefore, it is especially galling for the public when profits rise substantially, without change in output, solely because of higher international prices. If the investors are foreign and have little political support, it seems to the public that they are exploiting the generous conditions offered them.[2] In addition, the investments are sunk, so it appears to be a case of there being little or no cost to the government from expropriation.

We therefore observe a cycle in which, when prices are high, investors receive less than the amounts stipulated in their contracts, and when prices are low, they are offered especially favorable conditions to induce them to invest. These special conditions are not credible, since investors realize that they will be expropriated—or at least receive smaller profits than would have existed under the original contracts—when times are good again. The resulting policies lead to lower investment than under certainty, and of a stop-go variety, which is inefficient.[3]

The boom in natural resources that peaked in 2008 is an example: Venezuela, Ecuador, and Bolivia have expropriated investors, Peru imposed "voluntary contributions" worth US$757 million, and Chile (before the rise in prices) imposed a small royalty. Even developed countries have used windfall taxes (the United States imposed an oil windfall tax post-1973) or increasing royalties (Australia, Canada, and the United Kingdom) after perceived increases in profits in the natural resource sector.

The standard mining contract does not provide for the possibility of expropriation. From the point of view of the foreign investor, it is an additional risk of investment. Attempts have been made to introduce profit-sharing mechanisms to reduce the temptation to expropriate, but in practice they are often abused by transfer pricing, creating a negative effect on public opinion, which in turn increases the probability of expropriation.

Hence it appears that the appropriate contracts for this type of environment are different from those currently in use. It is possible to describe hypothetical scenarios where all parties, including the foreign investor, are better off if the contract is such that taxes paid by the firm are highly progressive, since this may lower the probability of expropriation in high price scenarios (by reducing the gains from expropriation), while increasing the expected profits of the firm, because of the reduced risk of expropriation. And even if firm's rents are dissipated through some competitive mechanism, the deadweight loss associated with expropriations may be reduced through such a contract.

The object of this chapter is to present a family of models that formalize this intuition by proposing an environment in which expropriations cannot be ruled out, because of ex post political pressures. We derive general conditions that characterize the optimal ex ante contract, in the sense that the government maximizes social welfare under the threat of expropriation. We also show how the optimal contract can be implemented using a competitive auction.

In our model, the government has a natural resource project that requires up-front sunk investment, as in the case of a mining or oil extraction project. Since the problem of expropriation usually arises with foreign investment, profits are not included (or have a lower weight) in the welfare function of the planner, and because the good is not consumed at home but exported, the government only cares about the revenues it can obtain from the project.

The present value of raw profits of the project (i.e., if we disregard the possibility of expropriation) depends on the price, which is random, so profits are described by a probability density.[4] In a dynamic model, governments are replaced by new governments that do not necessarily respect the commitments of previous governments, or they may be subject to political pressures that make them renege on previous agreements not to expropriate or renegotiate natural resource contracts. We deal with these sources of dynamic inconsistency in our model via a reduced form: we assume that there is a predefined function, known to all parties, of the probability of expropriation, which depends on the firm's present discounted profits.[5]

We assume that the expected value of profits in each state (i.e., given the possibility of expropriation) increases with raw profits, but at a decreasing rate. Furthermore, we assume that expropriations cause a deadweight loss that is proportional to the firm's loss—that is, to the difference between contractual and effective profits. This deadweight loss can be interpreted as a measure of the country's respect for property and contract law. In a country in which contracts are broken continually, there is little trust in them and firms cannot impose a large cost on government when they are expropriated. On the other hand, countries where contract and property rights are respected are those where firms can impose a large cost on the government when they are expropriated.

The question for the planner is to determine a contractual profit schedule for the firm that depends on the present value of raw profits and the expropriation function, subject to a participation constraint: given the known expropriation probability, the investor must at least break even on its investment. Initially, we assume that there is no unobservable effort the firm can exert to increase profits (i.e., there is no moral hazard in effort), or to reduce the probability of expropriation (no political moral hazard).

In the simple setup without moral hazard, we show that a contract that eliminates all risk for the firm, while granting it no rents, is optimal in the case in which operating profits cover investment costs in all states of demand in finite time (*high-demand* scenario). The optimal contract then entails no expropriation. On the other hand, if the project cannot be financed using a transfer schedule that avoids expropriations, a case we refer to as an *intermediate-demand* scenario, the optimal contract is characterized by a cap on the firm's present discounted revenues. This cap is not binding in low-demand states, and the firm collects all revenue in those states. By contrast, in high-demand states all revenues above the cap accrue to the government. The threshold is chosen so that ex ante expected profits, net of expropriation, are zero.[6] In an ordinary natural resource contract, the firm would receive all of the upside in the good states, making it prone to expropriation. In the optimal contract, there is an upper bound to the operating profits of the firm, and this reduces, by the optimal amount, the probability of expropriation in high-demand states. Note that this is equivalent to a windfall tax, because in the good states, the residual revenues go to the government.[7] In both the high- and intermediate-demand cases the optimal contract can be implemented via an auction where firms bid on the maximum present value of operating profits they would obtain in the good states of the world, and the minimum bid wins the auction. The planner does not need to know the expropriation probability or the firm's sunk investment cost in order to implement this auction.[8]

We extend the model in several directions. First we consider the possibility that the government provides subsidies in the bad states of the world. Second, we extend the model to the case of moral hazard in effort—that is, when the firm can exert costly effort that increases the probability of the good states of the world (the price distribution mentioned above now becomes a distribution of net revenue where marginal costs depend on effort exerted by the investor up front). Finally, we consider the possibility that the firm can exert effort to reduce the probability of expropriation (by lobbying, targeted social expenditures, and so on) and consider the optimal contract in that case.[9]

Subsidies in bad states are not unusual in countries characterized by a probability of expropriation in the good states of the world. These subsidies usually cost society more than they benefit the firm, as in the case in which they involve relaxing environmental or labor regulations in bad states.[10] We find that the optimal contract with distortionary subsidies involves a minimum operating profit guarantee coupled to a maximum bound to profits: the government subsidizes the firm in the worst states (in which there is no expropriation), sets a maximum value to operating profits in the good states of the world, and has an intermediate range of states where the firm receives all the revenue generated by the project, but is not subsidized.

In the case of moral hazard in effort, effort influences the results of the project, by reducing marginal costs throughout the life of the project. In a mining project, for example, as the grade of the ore declines, marginal costs tend to increase until they become higher than operating costs, and the mine closes down. By reducing marginal costs, the amount of minerals extracted before the mine has to close down is higher, and this is more valuable when prices are high. Here the optimal contract does not set a fixed cap on the operating profits of the firm, since that would lead to insufficient effort. Nevertheless, as in the benchmark model, the optimal contract lowers the firm's profits, as compared to the standard contract in high-demand scenarios. In this case it does so by imposing a revenue sharing agreement similar to progressive taxation when operating profits exceed predetermined values. Thus, the government trades off the deadweight cost associated with expropriation in high-revenue scenarios against incentives that make these scenarios more likely.[11]

We also consider the case in which the firm faces political moral hazard and can exert costly effort to reduce the probability of expropriation. The optimal contract is similar to that in the simpler case with no political moral hazard. It stipulates that in bad states the firm operates the franchise forever, while in better states the contract lasts until a fixed amount of operating profits, common to all these states, is collected. The reason is that, in contrast to the case of moral hazard in effort, here effort affects the probability of expropriation across states, but does not increase the probability of higher-income states. Hence there is no conflict between reducing the probability of expropriation by limiting contracted profits and the provision of incentives to increase the probability of higher-income states.

Finally, we come to the issue of implementation. It would be politically infeasible to have a contract in which the government collects nothing while accumulated profits are lower than the limiting amount of profits, and receives all the residual afterward, with all the attendant complications for the government of operating the mine. Consider then the following schematic proposal to determine the windfall tax in a given period. Each period, an independent agency makes the best estimate of future discounted profits given current information. This estimate plus the profits accrued and taxes already paid leads to an estimate of the present value of taxes that needs to be paid in the future so as to comply with the contract. The firm then pays a tax proportional to this amount—for example, the fraction that, if paid indefinitely, would lead, in expectation, to paying the windfall tax stipulated in the contract. In the absence of uncertainty about future profits, this tax rate leads to a tax burden that remains constant over time. Given the existence of uncertainty, it may be desirable to have a lower tax rate, set so that the probability of the firm earning less than the contracted amount is a predetermined and small value.

The remainder of the chapter is organized as follows. In the next section, which can be skipped without loss of continuity, we relate this chapter to the literature. Section 5.3 describes the basic model and derives the main results, including how to implement the optimal contract using a competitive auction with realistic informational assumptions. Section 5.4 considers various extensions. The last section concludes.

5.2   Relation to the Literature

There is an extensive literature on optimal taxation of exhaustible natural resources to which this chapter is related (see Heaps and Helliwell 1985, Gillis 1982, and Boadway and Flatters 1993 for classical references).[12] Also related to this chapter is Bohn and Deacon 2000, which explores both theoretically and empirically the effects of insecure ownership on investment and natural resource use. They show that investment falls with insecure ownership and therefore the net effect on depletion of natural resources is ambiguous. Finally, Fraser and Kingwell 1997 compares the performance of resource rent taxes and ad valorem royalties on investment levels, but the effects the authors describe are due to risk aversion, whereas in our case the investors are risk neutral.

There are two justifications to tax resource rents over and above the levies implicit in general income taxes. One is the efficiency-based argument that resource rents are not distorting (but note that this argument requires positive ex ante and not ex post rents). The other reason is an equity-based argument that suggests that natural resource rents should accrue to the population at large, not to a few private individuals. We assume that the private firm is paid no rent at all when solving the planner's problem (i.e., rents receive no weight in the social welfare function), which is consistent with the assumption that the firm is foreign. However, the characteristics of the optimal contract remain unchanged when the planner weighs firm's profits in the objective function, as long as this weight is not too large (see Result 3 for a formal statement).

Our contribution to this literature is to incorporate, in admittedly reduced form, the probability of expropriation and the deadweight loss associated with this event into the planner's objective function. Also, in contrast to most of that literature, the taxes that are implicit in our contract are on the present value of firm's profits, and not on flow profits—that is, we assume away the dynamic issues. This simplifies our analysis considerably and explains why we can implement the planner's optimal contract via a competitive auction with realistic informational requirements.

As noted by Boadway and Flatters (1993), there are three "ideal" approaches for government to divert rents to the public sector. One approach is a full-fledged cash flow tax, which implies that tax liabilities will be negative at initial stages of exploitation of the natural resource, making governments reluctant to adopt this option. A second approach is that the government takes a share of equity in the firm. The third approach is for governments to capture rents by having firms bid for the rights to exploit the resource. The winning firm provides an up-front payment in exchange for the perpetual right to extract the resource. This option is not credible, precisely because of the time inconsistency in government policy—that is, because of ex post expropriation. The policy proposals that emerge from this chapter lie within this third group, even though the bidding variable that implements the planner's optimal contract is the firm's present discounted profit. This has the advantage that no up-front payments by the firm to the government are needed, but motivates extending our model to incorporate moral hazard, since the firm's incentives to extract the resource efficiently are reduced by the fact that under our contract it is not the residual claimant of revenues generated by the contract.[13]

The planner's problem considered in this chapter has much in common with the problem facing the planner who designs the optimal public-private partnership contract in Engel, Fischer, and Galetovic 2007, and therefore the results we obtain share the flavor of the results obtained in that paper as well. Interestingly, we do not need to assume a risk-averse firm here, since the possibility of expropriation combined with a deadweight loss associated with expropriations leads the planner to view a risk-neutral firm's behavior as if it were risk averse, at least for high-demand realizations.

5.3   The Main Model

A natural resource project ("mining project" in what follows) requires a fixed amount of up-front investment I common across firms. The present value of operational profits generated by the project are described by a probability density $f(v)$, with support $[v_{\min}, v_{\max}]$ and c.d.f. $F(v)$. Operational profits are equal to revenue minus operating costs minus standard income taxes; in what follows we refer indistinctly to *revenues* and *operational profits*. The density f summarizes exogenous price uncertainty—that is, the project sells its product in a large world market over which it has no influence.[14]

A contract is characterized by a schedule $R_c(v)$ that defines the firm's present discounted remuneration as a function of discounted revenues generated by the project, v; the subscript c emphasizes that this is the remuneration stipulated in the contract, thereby ignoring the possibility that the contract will be cut short by expropriation and realized revenues may be lower. The only source of remuneration for the firm are revenues generated by the project, therefore $0 \leq R_c(v) \leq v$. The government is the residual claimant of revenues generated by the project, so that, according to the contract, in state v it receives $v - R_c(v)$.[15]

At the time of contracting, expropriations are random events, both as to when they happen and as to the amount expropriated. Because of this, in state v, the firm may end up receiving present discounted profits that can lie anywhere between $-I$ (when the government expropriates all its revenue) and $R_c(v) - I$ (when no expropriation takes place). Since the government and the firm are risk neutral, all we need to know about expropriations is expected profits that accrue to the firm in state v *after* expropriation. We denote this function by $\Pi_e(R_c(v) - I)$, and refer to it as the *effective profit* function. In general, $\Pi_e(x)$ denotes the present value of the firm's expected ex post discounted profits, when the contract entitles it to profits equal to x. This function summarizes, admittedly in reduced form, all the (common) knowledge available to the planner and the firm about future expropriation scenarios when signing the resource extraction contract. Will the next president be market friendly or a diehard nationalist? And if she turns out to be a diehard nationalist, will the firm be successful bribing the upcoming administration to avoid expropriation?

In this section Π_e is determined exogenously—that is, the current planner and firm's actions have no effect on this function.[16] We make the following assumptions regarding this function:

Assumption 1 (Effective Profit Functions)   The effective profit function, $\Pi_e(x)$, has a continuous second derivative, and there exists an $x_E \geq 0$, referred to as the *expropriation threshold*, that satisfies

1. $\Pi_e(x) = x$ for $x \leq x_E$.
2. $\Pi_e'(x) > 0$ and $\Pi_e''(x) < 0$, for all $x > x_E$.

The first property says that there exists a threshold for effective profits below which expropriation cannot take place: expropriations are possible only when discounted profits are positive, larger than x_E.[17] The second property implies that, beyond this threshold, the firm's effective profit increases with the discounted profits it is entitled to according to the contract, albeit at a decreasing rate.

The above properties assume that expropriation depends on the profit rate—that is, on $(R_c(v) - I)/I$, which is linear in $R_c(v)$. The quote at the beginning of this chapter, from Salvador Allende's 1972 speech at United Nations, is consistent with this assumption. If the firm earns five times its investment, so that its profit rate is 400 percent, it expects to lose a much larger fraction of its profit because of expropriation than if its profit rate is only 20 percent. This is captured by the first assumption. Furthermore, if the firm expects to lose half of every additional dollar generated by the project when the profit rate increases from 200 to 210 percent due to expropriation, then the second assumption implies that the government will grab more than half of every additional dollar of profit when the profit rate goes from 210 to 220 percent.

Our final assumption relates to the cost of expropriations. We assume that when a mining project is expropriated, the firm challenges the decision in (possibly international) court, thereby imposing a cost on the government of defending itself. This deadweight loss is a fraction μ of the expropriated value of the project, where $0 < \mu < 1$.[18]

5.3.1   Planner's Problem
In the benchmark model there is no moral hazard, and therefore no need to provide incentives for performance. In order for firms to be

willing participants in the project, the contract offered by the planner must satisfy the firm's participation constraint:

$$\int \Pi_e(R_c(v) - I) f(v) \, dv > 0.$$

Since the government is the residual claimant of revenues generated by the mining project, in state v its expected revenue is the difference between net (of investment) revenues generated by the project, $v - I$, and profits accrued to the firm, $\Pi_e(R_c(v) - I)$:

Expected government revenue $= v - I - \Pi_e(R_c(v) - I)$,

while the average loss to the firm due to expropriation is the difference between profits it was entitled to in the contract and actual profits:

Revenue loss for the firm due to expropriation

$$= R_c(v) - I - \Pi_e(R_c(v) - I).$$

Because of the deadweight loss mentioned above, only a fraction $(1 - \mu)$ of the revenue lost by the firm due to expropriation is received by the government, hence the planner maximizes

$$\int [v - I - \Pi_e(R_c(v) - I) - \mu\{R_c(v) - I - \Pi_e(R_c(v) - I)\}] f(v) \, dv.$$

And because the term $\int (v - I) f(v) \, dv$ is independent of the actions of the government, the planner's problem is equivalent to solving

$$\min_{R_c(v)} (1 - \mu) \int \Pi_e(R_c(v) - I) f(v) \, dv + \mu \int R_c(v) f(v) \, dv, \tag{1a}$$

$$\text{s.t.} \quad \int \Pi_e(R_c(v) - I) f(v) \, dv \geq 0, \tag{1b}$$

$$0 \leq R_c(v) \leq v. \tag{1c}$$

As mentioned above, the effective profit function, Π_e, is exogenous, while the firm's contractual revenue function, R_c, is the planner's decision variable.

It follows from (1a) that the government's objective is to minimize a weighted average of the operating profits effectively received by the firm and those profits it had contracted to pay according to the original contract. The former enters for obvious reasons, since less money for the firm means more money for the government. The latter is more interesting, and reflects the fact that, other things being equal, a contract that promises higher returns to the firm leads to larger losses when the firm is expropriated and therefore larger losses for the government as well.

Note that there is another interpretation, mentioned in the introduction: the higher the cost the firm can impose on the government by challenging the expropriation decision (via a higher μ), the more weight the government gives to the terms of the original contract in the objective function—that is, to $R_c(v)$. In other words, the more secure the property rights of the foreign firm, the more the government concentrates on reducing the contractual profits, while if property rights are insecure (small μ), the government is willing to offer more generous terms in the original contract, since it knows that the costs of expropriation are lower.

5.3.2   Optimal Contract

We first consider projects that can be financed with operating profits below the expropriation threshold (so that, if desired, they could be financed while avoiding any risk of expropriation) and show that the optimal contract indeed considers no expropriation. When the firm's participation constraint can be satisfied without incurring an expropriation risk, any contract that avoids expropriation altogether and for which the firm's participation constraint is satisfied with equality is optimal (these are the *high-demand* projects we referred to in the introduction). Expropriation *should* be avoided when it *can* be avoided.

Result 1 (Projects Where Expropriation Can Be Avoided)   Denote by x_E the expropriation threshold defined in Assumption 1 above and assume that

$$\int_0^{x_E} vf(v)\,dv + x_E(1 - F(x_E)) \geq I. \tag{2}$$

Then any contract that satisfies the firm's participation constraint with equality and for which $R_c(v) \leq I + x_E$ for all v, is optimal. In particular, the contract with $R_c(v) \equiv I$ is optimal.

Proof   The following string of equalities and inequalities shows that the planner's objective function is bounded from below by μI for any schedule $R_c(v)$ that satisfies the firm's participation constraint:

$$\int R_c(v) f(v)\, dv = I + \int [R_c(v) - I] f(v)\, dv$$

$$= I + \int \Pi_e^{-1}(\Pi_e(R_c(v) - I)) f(v)\, dv$$

$$\geq I + \Pi_e^{-1}\left(\int \Pi_e(R_c(v) - I) f(v)\, dv \right)$$

$$\geq I + \Pi_e^{-1}(0)$$

$$= I.$$

The first and second equalities are trivial. The first inequality follows from Jensen's inequality (Assumption 1 implies that Π_e^{-1} is convex), while the second inequality is justified by the firm's participation constraint. Finally, the last equality follows from the assumption that $\Pi_e(0) = 0$ (which follows from Assumption 1).

Next note that any schedule with $R_c(v) \leq I + x_E$ that satisfies the firm's participation constraint with equality attains a value of μI for the planner's objective function (1a) and therefore is optimal.

Finally, note that the first inequality is strict unless the function $\Pi_e(x)$ is linear in the range of values taken by $R_c(v) \leq I + x_E$. Thus the set of optimal policies derived above is the set of all optimal policies. ∎

The intuition for this result is the following: When the planner can design a contract that avoids expropriations and satisfies the firm's participation constraint with equality, this contract is optimal, since it avoids the deadweight loss associated with expropriations. Even though the firm is indifferent between this and a wide variety of contracts where its expected profits, net of expropriation risk, are zero, the planner prefers the contract without expropriations.

The next result analyzes the case in which the expropriation risk is unavoidable (*intermediate-demand* projects according to the introduction). It confirms the intuition that the planner wants this risk to be as small as possible.

Result 2 (Projects with Unavoidable Expropriation) Assume that there exists no contract that avoids expropriation risk altogether—that is,

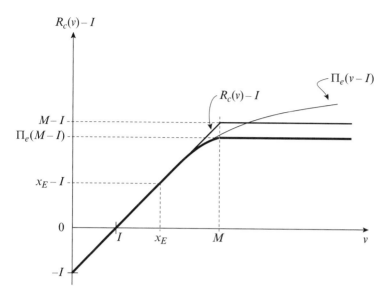

Figure 5.1
The optimal contract in the case where expropriation is unavoidable

$$\int_0^{x_E} vf(v)\,dv + x_E(1 - F(x_E)) < I. \tag{3}$$

Also assume that the firm's participation constraint can be satisfied:

$$\int_0^{\infty} \Pi_e(v - I)f(v)\,dv > 0.$$

Then M defined via

$$\int \Pi_e(\min(M, v) - I)f(v)\,dv = 0, \tag{4}$$

is finite and larger than x_E. More important, $R_c(v) = \min(v, M)$ characterizes the optimal contract (see figure 5.1). That is, operational profits of the firm in the optimal contract are limited to a cap M defined in (4).

Proof Even though a proof based on the problem's Lagrangian and complementary slackness conditions is straightforward, we believe the following informal argument provides more insight.

It is obvious that the firm's participation constraint will hold with equality in the optimal contract. Also, increasing by one dollar the firm's revenues stipulated in the contract in state v increases the firm's expected revenue by $\Pi_e'(R_c(v) - I)f(v)$, while it increases the objective function the planner wishes to minimize by $[(1 - \mu)\Pi_e'(R_c(v) - I) + \mu]f(v)$. It follows that the rate at which the objective function increases with the money being collected by the firm is

$$\rho(v, R_c(v)) \equiv (1 - \mu) + \frac{\mu}{\Pi_e'(R_c(v) - I)}. \tag{5}$$

The smallest value $\rho(v, R_c(v))$ can take is one, and it takes this value if and only if $R_c(v) \leq x_E$ (and $R_c(v)$ is feasible, i.e., $0 \leq R_c(v) < v$). The planner first uses up socially cheaper dollars to satisfy the firm's participation constraint—that is, dollars with $\rho(v, R_c(v)) = 1$. If the firm's participation constraint can be satisfied this way, the optimal contract belongs to the family described in the previous proposition.

In the case we are considering here, however, the planner falls short of satisfying the firm's participation constraint after exhausting all transfers from schedules with $\rho(v, R_c(v)) = 1$, and must resort to socially more expensive revenues with $\rho(v, R_c(v)) > 1$. Since Assumption 1 implies that $\rho(v, R_c(v))$ is increasing in $R_c(v)$ for given v, it follows that in the optimal contract

$$\rho(v, R_c(v)) = \begin{cases} \rho_0, & \text{if } \rho(v, v) \geq \rho_0, \\ (1 - \mu) + \frac{\mu}{\Pi_e'(v-I)}, & \text{if } \rho(v, v) < \rho_0, \end{cases}$$

where ρ_0 is chosen to satisfy the firm's participation constraint with equality. The optimal contract now follows immediately, with M defined via $\rho_0 = (1 - \mu) + \mu/\Pi_e'(M - I)$.   ∎

The optimal contract, depicted in figure 5.1, caps the firm's upside risk. In doing so, the planner minimizes the deadweight loss associated with expropriation. The social cost of transferring an additional dollar to the firm increases with the amount already transferred, hence the planner has incentives to keep the firm's profits as low as possible. The planner keeps away from high values of $R_c(v)$ because they entail higher expropriation probabilities, and therefore larger gaps between expected (under the contract) and realized profits for the firm. Large "disappointments" by the firm are costly, since they imply larger losses for the planner.

Two extensions follow immediately for both results above. First, if the planner gives weight α to the firm's profits, the optimal contract remains unchanged, as long as $\alpha \leq 1 - \mu$, for in this case the planner minimizes

$$(1 - \mu - \alpha) \int \Pi_e(R_c(v) - I) f(v) \, dv + \mu \int R_c(v) f(v) \, dv$$

and the above proofs go through without change as long as $1 - \mu - \alpha \geq 0$.

Second, if the firm's participation constraint requires a predetermined level of rents, so that

$$\int \Pi_e(R_c(v) - I) f(v) \, dv \geq \Pi_0 > 0,$$

the proofs of both results above continue holding with only minor modifications.

Result 3 (Optimal Contract for the Main Model)   If the planner gives weight $\alpha \leq 1 - \mu$ to the firm's profit, the firm's participation constraint is

$$\int \Pi_e(R_c(v) - I) f(v) \, dv \geq \Pi_0,$$

with $\Pi_0 \geq 0$, and the firm's participation constraint can be satisfied:

$$\int \Pi_e(v - I) f(v) \, dv \geq \Pi_0.$$

Define M via

$$\int \Pi_e(\min(M, v) - I) f(v) \, dv = \Pi_0.$$

Then the contract $R_c(v) = \min(M, v)$ solves the planner's problem, and this is the only optimal contract if $M \geq x_E$. By contrast, if $M < x_E$, any contract with $R_c(v) = \min(M, v)$ in states with $v \geq x_E$ that collects $\int_0^{x_E} \Pi_e(\min(M, v) - I) f(v) \, dv$ in states with $v \leq x_E$ is optimal.

5.3.3   Implementation
We have shown that a threshold contract that specifies a particular cap on discounted profits for the firm is the optimal contract when expropriation is possible. We show next how this contract can be implemented via a competitive auction. Following this result, we

discuss some practical implementation issues that are ignored by our framework.

Result 4 (Implementation)   Many identical firms exist for which

$$\int \Pi_e(v - I)f(v)\, dv \geq \Pi_0, \tag{6}$$

with Π_0, $\Pi_e(x)$, $f(v)$ and Π_0 defined earlier.

The following auction then implements the optimal contract: Firms bid on the present value of revenue they are entitled to by the contract; the firm that bids the lowest value, β, wins. The contract stipulates that the winning firm collects β if $v > \beta$ and v otherwise.[19] The firm bears demand (i.e., price) and expropriation risk under the ensuing contract.

The planner does not need to know the ex ante probability density $f(v)$, the expropriation probabilities (and therefore the effective profit function $\Pi_e(x)$), the up-front investment I, or the outside option Π_0 to implement the optimal contract via a competitive auction. The planner needs to observe operating profits, since it needs this information to enforce the contract (in high-demand scenarios it must determine when the firm has collected M). Finally, no firm will bid in the auction if the project is not privately profitable—that is, if (6) does not hold.

Proof   Given a winning bid β, the firm's profit in state v is $\beta - I$ if $v \geq \beta$ and $v - I$ otherwise. Thus the winning firm's expected profits are

$$\int \Pi_e(\min(\beta, v) - I)f(v)\, dv.$$

This expression is continuous, negative for low values of β, positive for large values of β (because of (6)), and strictly increasing in β. Hence a unique $\bar{\beta}$ exists for which

$$\int \Pi_e(\min(\bar{\beta}, v) - I)f(v)\, dv = \Pi_0.$$

This bid wins the auction (in the sense that it defines the Nash equilibrium), and it is trivial to see that $\bar{\beta}$ is equal to the threshold M that characterizes the optimal contract in Result 3 (note that $M = I$ in the case of a project with avoidable expropriation, as in Result 1).   ∎

Working with discounted revenues has provided tractability, at the expense of avoiding dynamic issues. There are many revenue trajectories for the firm and government that will implement the optimal contract, in that they satisfy the condition that their present values are those stipulated in the contract. This motivates discussing, at least informally, which of this multitude of trajectories are more attractive in practice.

One possibility is to allow the firm to collect all revenues from the project until their discounted value adds up to M or it is expropriated. There are several problems with this approach. First, the government collects windfall taxes only late in the contract. Contracts with long gestation periods before the government collects any windfall tax, even in high-demand scenarios, are likely to lead to a higher expropriation risk, thus lowering the effective profit function, $\Pi_e(v)$, and therefore are unattractive. Second, the government has to operate the project once the threshold of the firm's profits is attained, which is not appealing.

An alternative implementation, which we believe to be more attractive, is to define by contract a windfall tax schedule that increases with the firm's accumulated discounted profits at the date of taxation and decreases with the amount of windfall taxes paid. We present a simple example of such a schedule.

Example 1   Production is constant over time (and equal to one), production costs are zero, and the price of the natural resource follows a random walk:[20]

$$P_t = P_{t-1} + \epsilon_t,$$

where the ϵ_t are i.i.d. with zero mean and variance σ^2. The discount rate is constant over time and denoted by r.

Unless indicated otherwise, all discounted values are expressed as of time zero. Denoting expected discounted revenues between period s and u by R_s^u, and by $E_t R_s^u$ the corresponding expected value conditional on information available in period t (given the random walk assumption, this is equivalent to conditioning on P_t), we have:

$$E_t R_t^\infty = (1+r)^{-t} \sum_{k \geq 0} (1+r)^{-k} E_t P_{t+k}$$

$$= (1+r)^{-t} \sum_{k \geq 0} (1+r)^{-k} P_t = \frac{1}{r(1+r)^{t-1}} P_t.$$

Hence

$$E_t R_0^\infty = R_0^t + \frac{1}{r(1+r)^{t-1}} P_t.$$

Denote by T_s^u discounted windfall taxes paid by the firm between periods s and u and by M the revenue threshold that characterizes the optimal contract. If $\sigma = 0$—that is, if there is no price uncertainty—we have that the windfall tax schedule in period t dollars defined by

$$T_t = \frac{r}{1+r}[E_t R_0^\infty - T_0^{t-1} - M]$$

implements the optimal contract with a constant tax payment in all periods.

In general, when $\sigma > 0$ and we have uncertainty, defining

$$T_t = \frac{\delta r}{1+r}[E_t R_0^\infty - T_0^{t-1} - M],$$

with $\delta \in (0,1]$, provides a family of plausible windfall tax schedules. The parameter δ should decrease as σ increases, to ensure that the probability that the firm's discounted payment of windfall taxes exceeds $v - M$ is small.   ∎

The auction that implements the optimal contract differs in important ways from the standard auction considered in the literature to dissipate the rents of natural resource projects. While the standard auction involves an up-front payment to the government by the firm, the auction derived in this chapter does not. In the case of this auction, the firm's bid is linked to the degree of progressivity of the windfall tax faced by the firm. More aggressive bids are associated with higher expected profits and lead to more progressive taxation.

5.3.4   Welfare Gain
As noted in section 5.2, the standard auction proposed in the literature to dissipate the rents of an exhaustible natural resource project has firms bid for the perpetual right to extract the resource. Next we compare the welfare implications of this auction ("standard auction" in what follows) with those of the optimal auction under threat of expropriation derived above.

Since both auctions dissipate the firm's rents (we assume that the firm's outside option, Π_0, does not depend on the auction), in both cases the project's rents accrue exclusively to the government. It follows that the auction that is most attractive for the government is the one that leads to the smallest average deadweight loss from expropriation. With the standard auction, the deadweight loss is given by

$$\mathcal{L}_{\text{st}} = \mu \int [v - I - \Pi_e(v - I)] f(v) \, dv,$$

while for the optimal auction derived in this section the loss is

$$\mathcal{L}_{\text{opt}} = \mu \int [R_c(v) - I - \Pi_e(R_c(v) - I)] f(v) \, dv.$$

Since $R_c(v) = \min(M, v)$ for the optimal contract,[21] we have

$$\mathcal{L}_{\text{opt}} = \mu \int_0^M [v - I - \Pi_e(v - I)] f(v) \, dv + \mu \int_M^\infty [M - I - \Pi_e(M - I)] f(v) \, dv.$$

Subtracting $\mathcal{L}_{\text{opt}}$ from $\mathcal{L}_{\text{st}}$ leads to the following expression for the government's gain from using the optimal auction:

$$\text{Gain} \equiv \mu \int_M^\infty [v - I - \Pi_e(v - I) - \{M - I - \Pi_e(M - I)\}] f(v) \, dv. \tag{7}$$

Note that the Gain is positive only for states where prices are sufficiently high that revenues are larger than M. The optimal contract provides no gain in relatively low demand states. Define the "grab function" $G(x) \equiv x - \Pi_e(x)$.[22] We have that $G(x) = 0$ for $x \le x_E$, while $G(x)$ is strictly increasing for $x > x_E$, with $G'(x) = 1 - \Pi'_e(x) > 0$ in this range. It then follows that

$$\text{Gain} = \mu \int_M^\infty [G(v - I) - G(M - I)] f(v) \, dv$$

and since the integrand is strictly positive, the gain from using the optimal contract is strictly positive as well.

The intuition for why the contract derived above is better than the standard contract is the following: The optimal contract avoids, to the extent allowed by the firm's participation constraint, scenarios where expropriations are more costly, in terms of deadweight loss, thereby leading to higher welfare than the standard auction. Welfare gains are larger when the threshold M is lower—that is, for example, when the firm's outside option Π_0 is lower.

Even in the case where the distribution of revenue from the project is highly skewed, welfare gains from the optimal auction can be significant. Consider, for instance, an exploratory prospect where the probability of success is π and I corresponds to investment in exploration. Conditional on successful exploration, the distribution of revenue is described by a probability density $f(w)$ (with c.d.f. $F(w)$) that takes values between w_m and w_M. The revenue threshold that characterizes the optimal contract, M, then solves

$$\int_{w_m}^{M} \Pi_e(w - I)f(w)\,dw + \Pi_e(M - I)(1 - F(M)) = \frac{(1 - \pi)}{\pi}I. \tag{8}$$

Revenue uncertainty is usually large in such a project, even conditional on successful exploration, which amounts to a large variance of $f(w)$. It then follows that the threshold M will be much smaller than w_M if the project is highly profitable ex ante; and welfare gains associated with moving from the standard to the optimal contract can be expected to be considerable. For example, if $\pi = 0.1$, the r.h.s. of (8) suggests that return on investment will average 900 percent when exploration is successful, yet realized profit rates may still vary substantially, say between 500 and 2000 percent, as is likely to be the case for most natural resource projects. Gains from the optimal contract are negligible only for a project where the firm's participation constraint holds for a value of M close to w_M.

The following result summarizes our result on the welfare gain from the optimal contract:

Result 5   Welfare under the optimal auction derived in this section is higher than under the standard auction where firms bid on the right to extract the resource indefinitely. The welfare gain from the optimal auction is equal to

$$\text{Gain} = \mu \int_{M}^{\infty} [v - I - \Pi_e(v - I) - \{M - I - \Pi_e(M - I)\}]f(v)\,dv > 0.$$

5.4   Extensions

In this section we examine two extensions of practical importance. First, we study the case in which the government provides subsidies to the firm in bad states of the world. In the context of this chapter, subsidies usually translate into laxer application of environmental or labor regulations and sometimes into direct cash transfers. The second extension incorporates moral hazard—for example, it could be that by exerting costly effort, the foreign investor can reduce unobservable costs and increase revenues. The question is how to design a contract that provides optimal incentives.

5.4.1 Subsidies

The main problem of subsidies is that they cost governments more than the benefit they provide to firms. If labor and environmental regulations are meant to correct externalities, the social cost of the laxer regulations is higher than the private benefit perceived by the foreign investor.

Hence we assume that a subsidy $S(v)$ has a social cost of $\zeta S(v)$, $\zeta > 1$, so that the objective function maximized by the planner now is

$$\int [v - I - \Pi_e(R_c(v) + S(v) - I) - (\zeta - 1)S(v)$$

$$- \mu\{R_c(v) + S(v) - I - \Pi_e(R_c(v) + S(v) - I)\}]f(v)\,dv, \qquad (9)$$

where the term $(\zeta - 1)S(v)$ captures the social cost of the subsidy, beyond its private value. Two schedules are available to the planner now to achieve her objective, the revenue schedule $R_c(v)$ and the subsidy schedule $S(v)$.[23]

The problem facing the planner is equivalent to

$$\min_{R_c(v),S(v)} (1 - \mu) \int \Pi_e(R_c(v) + S(v) - I)f(v)\,dv$$

$$+ \mu \int R_c(v)f(v)\,dv + (\mu + \zeta - 1) \int S(v)f(v)\,dv, \qquad (10a)$$

s.t. $$\int \Pi_e(R_c(v) + S(v) - I)f(v)\,dv \geq 0, \qquad (10b)$$

$$0 \leq R_c(v) \leq v, \qquad (10c)$$

$$S(v) \geq 0. \qquad (10d)$$

To solve this problem, note that as in the proof of Result 2, the participation constraint (10b) holds with equality. Hence the problem is similar to that in section 3 of Engel, Fischer, and Galetovic 2007, with the expropriation function Π_e playing the role of the firm's concave utility function u.[24] The only difference is that $\Pi_e(x)$ is linear in net profits for $x \leq x_E$, while the utility function considered in Engel, Fischer, and Galetovic 2007 is strictly concave everywhere.

Hence, the results of that paper apply to this case, with slight modifications. For example, $R_c(v) < v$ and $S(v) > 0$ cannot be optimal, since achieving the firm's participation constraint via subsidies has a higher cost for the government than achieving it via the income generated by the project. Also, demand states can be classified into high, intermediate, and low demand. In high-demand states the optimal contract stipulates $R_c(v) < v$ and $S(v) = 0$. Expropriation is most likely in these states; the optimal contract assigns the same value of $R_c(v)$ to all states in this group (denote it by $\tilde{M}$); and the government collects a windfall tax equal to $v - \tilde{M}$. Similarly, $R_c(v) = v$ and $S(v) > 0$ in low-demand states. In these states there are no expropriations and no windfall taxes. Finally, a range of intermediate-demand states exist, where $R_c(v) = v$ and $S(v) = 0$. There are no windfall taxes in these states, yet expropriations can happen but are less likely than in high-demand states.

Result 6 (Optimal Contract with Subsidies)   Consider the planner's problem described by (10a)–(10d). If a finite M exists that satisfies

$$\int \Pi_e(\min(M, v) - I) f(v)\, dv = 0, \tag{11}$$

and $\Pi'_e(M - I) > \mu/(\mu + \zeta - 1)$, then the optimal contract is either the one described in Result 1 (if $\Pi'_e(M - I) = 1$) or the one described in Result 2 (if $\mu/(\mu + \zeta - 1) < \Pi'_e(M - I) < 1$).

Otherwise—that is, either if (11) has no solution or M solving this equation satisfies $\Pi'_e(M - I) < \mu/(\mu + \zeta - 1)$—the optimal contract is characterized as follows:

Define $\tilde{M}$ via $\Pi'_e(\tilde{M} - I) = \mu/(\mu + \zeta - 1)$. Clearly $M > \tilde{M} > x_E$. The optimal contract then satisfies $R_c(v) = \min(\tilde{M}, v)$ (figure 5.2 shows the resulting contract). Furthermore, subsidies are handed out only in states where $v < x_E$ and

$$\int_0^{x_E} S(v) f(v)\, dv = -\int \Pi_e(\min(\tilde{M}, v) - I) f(v)\, dv. \tag{12}$$

Proof   As mentioned above, $S(v) > 0$ and $R_c(v) < v$ cannot be optimal. Hence states can be classified into three categories: (a) $R_c(v) < v$ and $S(v) = 0$; (b) $R_c(v) = v$ and $S(v) = 0$; and (c) $R_c(v) = v$ and $S(v) > 0$.

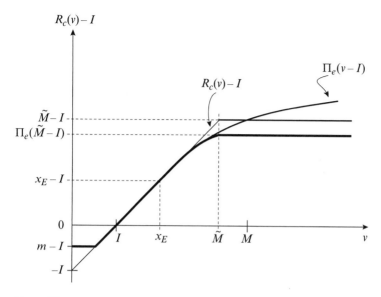

Figure 5.2
The optimal contract in the case of subsidies

Next we extend the argument used to prove Result 2. The planner's cost of providing an additional dollar of revenues to satisfy the firm's participation constraint, is

$$\rho_R(v, R_c(v)) = (1 - \mu) + \frac{\mu}{\Pi'_e(R_c(v) - I)},$$

where we have used that $S(v) = 0$ since additional revenue from the project can be provided to the firm only if $R_c(v) < v$.

Similarly, the planner's per-dollar cost of providing an additional dollar via subsidies is

$$\rho_S(v, R_c(v)) = (1 - \mu) + \frac{\mu + \zeta - 1}{\Pi'_e(v + S(v) - I)},$$

where this time we used that $R_c(v) = v$ when $S(v) > 0$. In particular, this cost is lowest (and equal to ζ) when $v \leq x_E$.

In the optimal contract the planner resorts to more expensive options to satisfy the firm's participation constraint only once cheaper options are exhausted. Since the social cost of financing the firm with subsidies is ζ, and there is no limit to the resources available to finance the firm with this option, the planner will use revenues as long as their social cost is smaller than ζ and will then resort to subsidies to complete the amount needed to satisfy the firm's participation constraint.

It follows that the planner sets $R_c(v) = \min(\tilde{M}, v)$ since this assigns to the firm all the revenue with marginal cost less than or equal to ζ. From the assumptions we know that the income obtained in this way is not enough to satisfy the firm's participation constraint, because it adds up to $\int \Pi_e(\min(\tilde{M}, v) - I)f(v)\, dv < 0$. Thus the firm obtains the remaining income needed to satisfy its participation constraint via subsidies in states where expropriations are impossible.   ∎

Implementation   A simple two-threshold auction, analogous to the one derived in Engel, Fischer, and Galetovic 2007, implements the optimal contract in this case.

Result 7 (Implementation with Subsidies) The following two-threshold, scoring auction implements the solution to the planner's problem (10a)–(10d):

• The government announces the probability density of expected discounted profit flow from the project, $f(v)$, and the parameter ζ that summarizes the social cost of subsidies.

• Firms bid on the minimum revenue guarantee, m, and the cap on their user-fee revenue, M, so that, in case of winning: $R_c(v) = \min(M, v)$ and $S(v) = \max(m - v, 0)$.

• The firm that bids the lowest value of the scoring function

$$W(m, M) = \mu M(1 - F(M)) + \mu \int_m^M vf(v)\, dv$$

$$+ (\mu + \zeta - 1)mF(m) - (\zeta - 1)\int_0^m vf(v)\, dv$$

wins the contract.[25]

Proof   We first note that the optimal contract can be implemented via a contract characterized by the threshold pair (M, m), where M denotes the revenue cap, and m the minimum revenue guarantee. In the first scenario described in Result 6, M is defined via (11) and m can be any number less than or equal to $v_{\min}$ (recall that the support of $f(v)$ is $[v_{\min}, v_{\max}]$). In the second scenario in Result 6, M is defined via

$$\Pi'_e(M - I) = \frac{\mu}{\mu + \zeta - 1}$$

and m via

$$\int_0^m (m - v)f(v)\,dv = -\int \Pi_e(\min(M, v) - I)f(v)\,dv. \tag{13}$$

It is easy to see that in a Nash equilibrium the winning bid minimizes the scoring function, subject to the firm's participation constraint, among all contracts in the two-threshold family described above. Since the scoring function differs from the planner's objective function only in a term proportional to the firm's expected profits, and this term is equal to zero for the optimal contract, the optimal contract also solves the planner's problem constrained to the family of two-threshold contracts described above. The proof concludes by noting that this family includes the optimal contract.   ∎

What is the intuition underlying this result? Note first that the planner's problem is equivalent to minimizing an objective function that does not require knowledge of I or Π_e. The objective function only depends on the probability distribution of the present value of revenue that the project can generate and the distortions associated with government expenditures, as summarized by ζ. By awarding the contract to the bidder that maximizes his objective function, and assuming competitive bidding, the planner induces firms to solve society's problem without knowing the cost of the project or the expropriation risk.

As before, in the case of a high-demand project—that is, a project where the firm's participation constraint can be satisfied without expropriation risk—the two-threshold auction is equivalent to a PVR auction. In this case any bid with $M = I$ and $m \leq I$ wins the auction, and no subsidies are paid out.

5.4.2   Moral Hazard in Effort

The possibility of expropriations may lead firms to spend less on upfront investments that reduce costs during the exploitation of the natural resource. The framework developed in this chapter is not needed to make this point, because it can be made with the simpler, static model discussed in the appendix. Yet it is instructive to derive this result within the framework developed in this chapter, and explore the extent to which the results of previous sections continue holding. That is what we do in this section. We show that, loosely speaking, the optimal contract combines the two effects, by providing incentives for effort (investment) while lowering the probability of costly expropriation—that is, it resembles a progressive tax above a predetermined operating profit threshold.

5.4.2.1 The Planner's Problem   We embed the benchmark model of section 5.3 in a simple moral-hazard framework. The Firm's marginal extraction costs are decreasing in the firm's effort, ϵ, exerted at the time the up-front investment I is made. This can be summarized by assuming that the probability density describing the firm's discounted profits is determined by $\epsilon \geq 0$, so that we may write $f(v|\epsilon)$. The impact of effort is larger when price turns out to be higher, since optimal production can be expected to be higher in this case. Thus the monotone likelihood ratio property (MLRP) holds, so that $\ell(v,\epsilon) \equiv \frac{\partial f}{\partial \epsilon}(v|\epsilon)/f(v|\epsilon)$ is increasing in v for all ϵ—that is, effort increases the probability of higher realizations of demand. Effort ϵ costs the firm $k\epsilon$, $k > 0$, so that its expected profit in state v, net of expropriation, is $\Pi_e(R_c(v) - I) - k\epsilon$. Since it is necessary to ensure that the firm provides effort, we need to introduce an incentive compatibility constraint in the planner's program.

The planner chooses effort ϵ and a revenue schedule $R_c(v)$ to solve the following program:

$$\min_{\{R_c(v),\epsilon\}} \int [\mu(R_c(v) - I) + (1-\mu)\{\Pi_e(R_c(v) - I) - (v - I)\}]f(v|\epsilon)\,dv \quad (14a)$$

$$\text{s.t.} \quad \int \Pi_e(R_c(v) - I)f(v|\epsilon)\,dv \geq k\epsilon, \quad\quad\quad\quad\quad (14b)$$

$$\epsilon = \arg\max_{\epsilon'}\left\{\int \Pi_e(R_c(v) - I)f(v|\epsilon')\,dv - k\epsilon'\right\}, \quad\quad (14c)$$

$$0 \leq R_c(v) \leq v. \quad\quad\quad\quad\quad\quad\quad\quad\quad\quad (14d)$$

Comparing program (1a)–(1c) with program (14a)–(14d), it can be seen that the term $v - I$ can no longer be dropped because effort affects the p.d.f. of revenue (or operating profit). Constraint (14b) is the firm's participation constraint, and (14c) is the incentive compatibility constraint.

Under standard assumptions,[26] we can use the First Order Approach to examine the properties of the solution. The concessionaire's incentive compatibility constraint then can be replaced by

$$\int \Pi_e(R_c(v) - I)\ell(v, \epsilon)f(v|\epsilon)\, dv = k. \tag{15}$$

Denoting by $\gamma > 0$ the multiplier associated with (14b), which will hold with equality, and by $\tau > 0$ the multiplier associated with (15), we have that the Lagrangian of the problem is

$$\mathcal{L} = \int [\mu(R_c(v) - I) + (1 - \mu)\{\Pi_e(R_c(v) - I) - (v - I)\}]f(v|\epsilon)\, dv$$

$$- \gamma \left[\int \Pi_e(R_c(v) - I)f(v|\epsilon)\, dv - k\epsilon \right]$$

$$- \tau \int \Pi_e(R_c(v) - I)\ell(v, \epsilon)f(v|\epsilon)\, dv. \tag{16}$$

The first-order condition w.r.t. to ϵ, combined with (15), provides an expression for τ where the multiplier for the participation constraint does not appear:

$$\tau = \frac{\int [\mu(R_c(v) - I) + (1 - \mu)\Pi_e(R_c(v) - I) - (v - I)]\ell(v, \epsilon)f(v|\epsilon)\, dv}{\int \Pi_e(R_c(v) - I)\frac{\partial^2 f}{\partial \epsilon^2}(v, \epsilon)\, dv}.$$

If $0 < R_c(v) < v$ the first-order condition for $R_c(v)$ derived from the Lagrangian yields

$$\Pi_e'(R_c(v) - I) = \frac{\mu}{(\mu + \gamma - 1) + \tau\ell(v, \epsilon)}. \tag{17}$$

The MLRP then implies that $R_c(v)$ is strictly increasing in v. Furthermore, the solution is interior if and only if the denominator in the expression on the right-hand side is positive (which ensures that $v > 0$) and

$$\Pi_e'(v - I) < \frac{\mu}{(\mu + \gamma - 1) + \tau\ell(v, \epsilon)},$$

which ensures that $R_c(v) < v$.

Standard arguments used for moral-hazard models (as in the proof of Proposition 5.2 in Laffont and Martimort 2002) can be used to show that $\mu + \gamma - 1 > 0$ and $\tau > 0$. This, combined with the MLRP, implies that for sufficiently large v the denominator in the right-hand expression in (17) is positive. It then follows that if $\Pi_e'(v - I)$ tends to zero faster than $\ell(v, \epsilon)$ tends to infinity, in the sense that for all positive constants a and b

$$\lim_{v \to \infty} \Pi'_e(v - I)[a + b\ell(v, \epsilon)] = 0, \tag{18}$$

then there exists a threshold M such that $R_c(v) < v$ for all $v \geq M$.

For example, if $\Pi_e(x) = 1 - \exp(-cx)$, for $x > 0$, with $c > 0$, and $f(v|\epsilon)$ is exponential with mean $\theta(\epsilon)$ and $\theta'(\epsilon) > 0$, then

$$\lim_{v \to \infty} \Pi'_e(v - I)[a + b\ell(v, \epsilon)] = \lim_{v \to \infty} ce^{-c(v-I)}[a' + b'v] = 0,$$

where a' and b' denote constants that depend on a, b, θ, and θ'. Condition (18) then holds and the optimal contract involves a windfall tax when profits are high enough.

5.4.3 Political Investment

There is an additional way that a firm may exert effort in order to increase its profits: it can invest in political support, either by lobbying politicians or by trying to influence the press, in order to reduce the probability of expropriation.[27] This can also be treated as a moral-hazard model, but in this case effort affects the probability of expropriation and hence expected profits, rather than the probability of high-profit states directly.

5.4.3.1 The Planner's Problem

Assume then that political effort can be described by ϵ and that expected profits are $\Pi_e \equiv \Pi_e(x, \epsilon)$, which we assume satisfies

$$\frac{\partial \Pi_e}{\partial \epsilon} \geq 0, \quad \frac{\partial^2 \Pi_e}{\partial \epsilon^2} < 0, \quad \frac{\partial^2 \Pi_e}{\partial v \partial \epsilon} > 0, \quad \frac{\partial^3 \Pi_e}{\partial v^2 \partial \epsilon} > 0$$

and where $\partial \Pi_e / \partial \epsilon = 0$ for $v \leq 0$ because $\Pi_e(v, \epsilon) = v$ for $v \leq 0$.[28] Using the first-order approach, the problem for the planner can be stated as

$$\min_{\{R_c(v), \epsilon\}} \int [\mu(R_c(v) - I) + (1 - \mu)\{\Pi_e(R_c(v) - I, \epsilon) - (v - I)\}]f(v) \, dv \tag{19a}$$

s.t. $$\int \Pi_e(R_c(v) - I, \epsilon) f(v) \, dv \geq k\epsilon, \tag{19b}$$

$$\int \frac{\partial \Pi_e}{\partial \epsilon} (R(v) - I, \epsilon) f(v) \, dv = k \tag{19c}$$

$$0 \leq R_c(v) \leq v. \tag{19d}$$

Denoting by $\gamma > 0$ the multiplier associated with (19b), which will hold with equality, and by $\tau > 0$ the multiplier associated with (19c), we have that the Lagrangian of the problem is

$$\mathcal{L} = \int [\mu(R_c(v) - I) + (1 - \mu)\{\Pi_e(R_c(v) - I, \epsilon) - (v - I)\}] f(v) \, dv$$

$$- \gamma \left[\int \Pi_e(R_c(v) - I) f(v) \, dv - k\epsilon \right] - \tau \int \frac{\partial \Pi_e}{\partial \epsilon} (R_c(v) - I, \epsilon) f(v) \, dv. \quad (20)$$

The first-order condition w.r.t. to ϵ, and using (19c), lead to

$$\int (1 - \mu - \gamma) \frac{\partial \Pi_e}{\partial \epsilon} (R_c(v) - I, \epsilon) f(v) \, dv + \gamma k - \tau \int \frac{\partial^2 \Pi_e}{\partial \epsilon^2} (R_c(v) - I, \epsilon) f(v) \, dv$$

$$= (1 - \mu)k - \tau \int \frac{\partial^2 \Pi_e}{\partial \epsilon^2} (R_c(v) - I, \epsilon) f(v) \, dv$$

from which we derive an expression for τ:

$$\tau = \frac{(1 - \mu)k}{\int \frac{\partial^2 \Pi_e}{\partial \epsilon^2} (R_c(v) - I, \epsilon) f(v) \, dv} < 0.$$

Now consider the first-order conditions with respect to $R(v)$:

$$\mu + (1 - \mu - \gamma) \frac{\partial \pi_e}{\partial v} (R_c(v) - I, \epsilon) = \tau \frac{\partial^2 \Pi_e}{\partial v \partial \epsilon} (R_c(v) - I, \epsilon). \quad (21)$$

Recall that $0 < \mu < 1$, that $\tau < 0$, and that $\partial \Pi_e / \partial v > 0$ and $\partial^2 \Pi_e / \partial v \partial \epsilon < 0$, and therefore $\gamma > 1 - \mu > 0$. Now consider the function

$$\mathcal{H}(R(v)) \equiv \tau \frac{\partial^2 \Pi_e}{\partial v \partial \epsilon} (R_c(v) - I, \epsilon) - (1 - \mu - \gamma) \frac{\partial \Pi_e}{\partial v} (R_c(v) - I, \epsilon),$$

where (21) is equivalent to $\mathcal{H}(R(v)) = \mu$. The conditions we imposed at the beginning of the section ensure that $\partial \mathcal{H}(v) / \partial v < 0$. Let M be the value where $\mathcal{H}(v) = \mu$. Then if $v > M$, we have that the Lagrangian is maximized at $R(v) = M$, and if $v \leq M$, the Lagrangian is maximized at $R(v) = v$.

We have shown that there is a bound M such that the optimal contract is

$$R(v) = \begin{cases} v & \text{if } v \leq M, \\ M & \text{if } v > M. \end{cases}$$

Hence, in contrast to the case of moral hazard, in the case of political investment, the planner does not provide incentives to the firm, except in the range $v \in [0, M]$. The reason is that effort affects the probability of expropriation across all states, but does not increase the probability of higher-income states v, hence there is no conflict between reducing the probability of expropriation by limiting $R(v)$ and providing incentives in order to increase the probability of higher states. The resulting contract belongs to the family of threshold contracts that are optimal in the absence of moral hazard, even though the threshold itself will usually be different.

5.5   Conclusion

Developing countries need foreign investment in order to develop their natural resources. In order to attract investment, they offer favorable conditions. When prices rise and revenues increase beyond expectations, there are often calls to change the terms of the original contracts, or to expropriate the investment and appropriate the windfall profits. This can be costly because the investor will try to defend the original contract in local and international courts. Moreover, there will be less investment in the next price cycle. We have proposed an alternative contract that improves welfare by reducing the attraction of expropriation by lowering profits in the good states of the world. This implies that there is a smaller cost of expropriation directly, because there will be less expropriation, and indirectly, because the expropriated assets are less profitable and therefore worth less to the foreign firm, which will not fight as forcefully to retain the project.

We have shown that in the case of high-demand projects, which are always profitable (though some states may be better than others), the optimal contract can be achieved by a present-value-of-revenue (PVR) auction and there will be no expropriation. In the case in which the project is profitable in expected value, but has bad states in which it never recovers the investment, the first best is achieved by setting a cap on profits, and this can be implemented fairly easily via an auction. We have shown that this is analogous to a lump-sum windfall tax on profits. Next, we showed that in the case when the government has the possibility of subsidizing the firm in the bad states of the world by relaxing regulations, the first best is achieved by a system of subsidies in bad states of the world and caps on profits in good states. Again, we found that the first best can be implemented via an auction. We

examined the case in which the firm can invest in lobbying or other political activities (regional subsidies, for example) and showed that the
optimal contract is of the same type as before.

The most interesting case, however, is when there is moral hazard
and the firm can perform unobservable (or partially observable) effort
that increases the likelihood of the high-revenue states. Here the planner must provide incentives, which implies that a constant cap on
revenues is inappropriate. The optimal contract involves progressive
taxation of revenues above a predetermined value, thus combining
some incentives to attain higher-revenue states with a reduction in the
attraction of expropriation, as well as its associated costs.

Note, however, that these measures—lump-sum windfall profits or
progressive taxation—must be incorporated in the original contracts
and must not be imposed ex post. Finally, we showed that there is
positive welfare gain from our contract, and that the gain is due solely
to the better behavior of the government in the good states of the
world, above the cap.

Appendix: The Effect of a Positive Expropriation Probability: A Simple Model

Consider the following simple model that describes the effect of potential expropriation on investment. For simplicity, we assume that
the firm's present discounted profits, as a function of price p and unobservable effort F, are given by

$$\Pi(p, F) = pq(F) - F,$$

with $q > 0$, $q' > 0$, and $q'' < 0$. Price uncertainty is described by a probability density $g(p)$ with c.d.f. $G(p)$.

No Expropriation

Rents are dissipated via an up-front payment to the government in a
competitive auction; all firms are the same.

Once it wins the auction, the firm solves

$$\max_{F} \int pq(F)g(p)\, dp - F$$

which leads to

$$q'(F) = \frac{1}{\int_0^\infty pg(p)\,dp}.$$

(22)

Denote the optimal value of F by F_{ne}.

Expropriation

If $p > \bar{p}$, the firm is expropriated and receives no income at all. The firm is aware of this when deciding how much to invest in effort, so that the price distribution it considers has mass $1 - G(\bar{p}) > 0$ at $p = 0$ and density $g(p)$ for $0 < p < \bar{p}$.

The same derivation that led to (22) now yields

$$q'(F) = \frac{1}{\int_0^{\bar{p}} pg(p)\,dp}.$$

(23)

Denote the solution by F_e. Since, trivially, the denominator in (23) is smaller than the one in (22), concavity of $q(F)$ implies that $F_e < F_{ne}$.

As before, ex ante rents are dissipated via an up-front payment to the government and all firms are the same. The up-front payment that wins is smaller than in the case without expropriation, for two reasons. First, the firm expects fewer rents since it realizes there is a probability of being expropriated. Even if the firm exerts effort F_{ne}, the up-front payment to the government by the firm would be smaller, by exactly the amount the government expects to collect via expropriation. Furthermore, as $F_e < F_{ne}$ we also have an efficiency loss to society, since the firm exerts less effort and therefore social welfare—which is equal to the sum of what the government collects from the firm up front and via expropriation—is lower.

Result 8 Expropriation when price realizations are high lowers social welfare because it induces the firm to do less unobservable, yet socially desirable, investment up front.

This conventional analysis has a limited scope, and it is difficult to obtain additional results. The approach used in the chapter leads to stronger results.

Notes

Fischer thanks the support of the Complex Engineering Systems Institute. E-mails: eduardo.engel@yale.edu, rfischer@dii.uchile.cl. We thank William Hogan and Federico

Struzenegger for proposing this research topic, and Richard Zeckhauser for an insightful discussion of the first version of this chapter. We also thank William Nordhaus and participants in the Populism and Natural Resources Workshop for comments and suggestions.

1. "Ecuadorean President Rafael Correa has signed a decree giving the state a greater share of profits from foreign oil companies working in his country. He said the 50% of windfall oil profits stipulated in a law passed last year was not enough, and the state should now receive 99%" (BBC News, October 5, 2007). "Algeria is to levy a windfall tax on the profits of oil companies, as it tries to retain more of the economic benefits of its recent energy boom.... From early 2007, profits accrued by firms when prices are above $30 a barrel will be taxed at between 5% and 50% depending on total output" (BBC News, October 15, 2006).

2. See epigraph, corresponding to a previous cycle of high prices and expropriation.

3. "Zambia, meanwhile, plans to cash in on the stratospheric price of copper by renegotiating the generous terms it gave to foreign firms when it privatised its copper mines in 2000. Then the price was low. Although these investors rescued an industry close to collapse, Zambia now wants to increase royalties and other taxes.... Governments intent on reworking contracts or imposing new taxes clearly feel that they have the upper hand at the moment. When prices were depressed and profits scarce, foreign firms had to be lured with generous terms that now rankle" (*The Economist*, October 4, 2007).

4. Though profits are unobservable in general, we denote by operating profits the difference between the revenues of the firm and costs that are based on observable variables. These are the profits that are prespecified in the initial contract.

5. In general terms, this probability should depend on institutional aspects of the country such as the degree of belief in the sanctity of contracts, the impact of public pressure on governments, and so on.

6. We do not analyze the possibility of a project that does not break even in expected value—that is, one that impoverishes the country.

7. This may lead to procyclical government income, which should be addressed via a countercyclical spending rule.

8. This auction is similar to the present-value-of-revenue auction analyzed in Engel, Fischer, and Galetovic 2001.

9. The study of this case was suggested by our discussant in the Populism and Natural Resources Workshop, Richard Zeckhauser.

10. Since the revenue collected by the government from the project can be used to reduce distortionary taxation elsewhere in the economy, the deadweight loss associated with subsidies for the firm financed via taxes does not provide a rationale for this result. For a formal derivation of this insight, see the Irrelevance Result in Engel, Fischer, and Galetovic 2007.

11. If the moral-hazard effect dominates the expropriation effect, the standard contract that provides full residual rights to the private firm is again optimal.

12. There also is an extensive literature, going back to Hotelling 1931, that derives the price of an exhaustible natural resource as an equilibrium outcome resulting from optimal extraction (see, for example, Devarajan and Fisher 1981, Salant 1995, and the references

cited there). We depart from this literature by assuming *exogenously* given demand uncertainty—that is, a small-country assumption—as well as by omitting the dynamic issue of optimal resource extraction. Moreover, we search for the optimal contract when expropriation is possible and depends on the price realization.

13. Osmundsen (1998) considers the case of optimal dynamic taxation with adverse selection in the firm's cost structure. By contrast, we assume identical firms.

14. The case where f responds to actions taken by the firm is considered when studying moral hazard in section 5.4.

15. In section 5.3.3 we discuss alternative options for how the government actually collects its share.

16. We relax this assumption in section 5.4.

17. Many of the results we derive are simpler if we assume $\Pi_e(x)$ strictly concave for all x—that is, when expropriations are possible for all realizations of v. In this case the planner's problem is analogous to the one considered in Engel, Fischer, and Galetovic 2007.

18. Alternatively, the value of the revenue stream is reduced because the new management is less efficient, or because experienced personnel leaves. Finally, there could be a cost due to an increase in the perceived riskiness in the country for foreign investment.

19. The resulting auction is analogous to the present-value-of-revenue (PVR) auction studied in Engel, Fischer, and Galetovic 2001.

20. What follows can be extended easily to the case where the price of the natural resource (or its log) follows a more general process—for example, a first-order autoregressive process.

21. The unique optimal contract takes this form when expropriation cannot be avoided (see Result 2), and one of many optimal contracts takes this form when expropriation can be avoided (see Result 1).

22. The "grab function" terminology was suggested by Richard Zeckhauser.

23. We assume no transfers from general funds are possible; these could be incorporated following the approach used in Engel, Fischer, and Galetovic 2007 without affecting the qualitative nature of the results we obtain.

24. The fact that here $\int \Pi_e(R_c(v) + S(v) - I) f(v) \, dv$ shows up in the objective function, while the utility function does not show up in the objective function in Engel, Fischer, and Galetovic 2007, is irrelevant, since the firm's participation constraint implies that this term is equal to zero.

25. Note that M here corresponds to $\tilde{M}$ in Result 6.

26. For instance, strict concavity of the agent's utility as a function of ϵ and the convexity of the distribution function condition (see, e.g., Proposition 5.2 in Laffont and Martimort 2002).

27. This section was suggested by our discussant, Richard Zeckhauser, at the Populism and Natural Resources Workshop.

28. In an abuse of notation, we have written $\frac{\partial \Pi_e}{\partial v}$ for the partial derivative with respect to the first argument of Π_e.

References

Boadway, R., and F. Flatters. *The Taxation of Natural Resources: Principles and Policy Issues.* Working Paper No. 1210, World Bank, 1993.

Bohn, H., and R. Deacon. "Ownership Risk, Investment, and the Use of Natural Resources." *American Economic Review* 90, no. 3 (2000): 526–549.

Devarajan, S., and A. Fisher. "Hotelling's 'Economics of Exhaustible Resources': Fifty Years Later." *Journal of Economic Literature* 10, no. 1 (1981): 65–73.

Engel, E., R. Fischer, and A. Galetovic. *The Basic Public Finance of Public-Private Partnerships.* NBER Working Paper No. 13284, August 2007.

Engel, E., R. Fischer, and A. Galetovic. "Least-Present-Value-of-Revenue Auctions and Highway Franchising." *Journal of Political Economy* 109, no. 5 (October 2001): 993–1020.

Fraser, R., and R. Kingwell. "Can Expected Tax Revenue Be Increased by an Investment-Preserving Switch from Ad Valorem Royalties to a Resource Rent Tax?" *Resources Policy* 23, no. 3 (1997): 103–108.

Gillis, M. "Evolution of Natural Resource Taxation in Developing Countries." *Natural Resources Journal* 22 (July 1982): 620–648.

Heaps, T., and J. Helliwell. "The Taxation of Natural Resources." In Alan J. Auerbach and Martin Feldstein, eds., *Handbook of Public Economics*, vol. 1, 421–472. Amsterdam: North-Holland, 1985.

Hotelling, H. "The Economics of Exhaustible Resources." *Journal of Political Economy* 39 (1931): 137–175.

Laffont, J. J., and D. Martimort. *The Theory of Incentives.* Princeton, NJ: Princeton University Press, 2002.

Osmundsen, P. "Dynamic Taxation of Non-renewable Natural Resources under Asymmetric Information about Reserves." *Canadian Journal of Economics* 31, no. 4 (1998): 933–951.

Salant, W. "The Economics of Natural Resource Extraction: A Primer for Development Economists." *World Bank Economic Observer* 10 (1995): 93–111.

6 Denying the Temptation to GRAB

Nils Wernerfelt and Richard Zeckhauser

6.1 Introduction

On March 18, 1938, Mexican President Lázaro Cárdenas expropriated the oil facilities of all foreign investors in Mexico. As in most cases of expropriation, the justification was shady, and it involved the combined efforts of several branches of the Mexican government. In light of the government's coup, every March 18 Mexico celebrates the "Expropiación Petrolera" (the "Oil Expropriation"). While having a national holiday celebrating expropriation does not send a positive message to foreign investors, the story of Mexico in 1938 has been repeated countless times in countries throughout the world, and continues to thrive in modern times.[1] And this cautionary tale does not just apply to the oil industry. All forms of natural resources are at risk, ranging from coal mines to beachside resorts. Indeed, though our focus is on natural resources, any concentration of fixed assets, such as a steel plant or even a bank, is subject to confiscation. In the developing world, where expropriation problems are most severe, few resource-laden countries have a strong enough rule of law to make investors confident. Only a few more have a history of protection sufficient that their reputation alone offers protection.

If the rule of law or reputations were strong enough to ensure contracts would be honored, then the situation would be very different. The government could sell development rights at the outset, or impose lump-sum taxes on resource deposits, and thereby avoid distorting the firm's incentives to go about its activities efficiently, to the benefit of the country. Alternatively, the government could simply tax a constant fraction of company earnings, taking proper account of capital costs. Either way, the government could prevent most future bad experiences abroad by overseas investors. Unfortunately, given real-world contractual insecurities, for many nations such secure sale or tax arrangements will remain theoretical niceties.

Foreign investment in natural resources is both expensive and widespread, and often requires significant private-sector skills.[2] It is disturbing that there are very few cases where private firms and developing-country governments work in harmony, thus enabling firms to pursue efficiency and confidently plan for the long run. Expropriation risks produce a portfolio of problems. The firm may not merely slacken its efforts; it may change its whole investment strategy.

This chapter is part of the general literature on insecure property rights and their consequences for economic efficiency. (See, for example, Shleifer and Vishny 1994; Che and Qian 1998.) The literature points out that there are other modes of expropriation or partial expropriation beyond merely taking over the firm. Sharp rises in taxation play this role; so do regulations that say labor must be paid far above its competitive wage.

In this literature, the tools of modern contract theory have opened the door for analyses of contracts that are optimal given unavoidable expropriation risk should certain conditions arise (Bohn and Deacon 2000; Engel and Fischer 2008; Schwartz and Trolle 2010; Mahajan 1990). A prime factor promoting expropriation is higher net returns to the government if the asset is in its hands. In some instances counterthreats may prevent expropriation. Thus, the country whose firm has been expropriated can retaliate by blocking assets or imposing trade sanctions or other forms of international pressure.[3] However, if such measures fail to deter, and the ongoing stream of expropriations suggest that they often do, the firm whose property has been taken will be a severe loser. As a consequence, any firm with a big asset at stake will anticipate, and seek to reduce, the factors that would lead to expropriation. Usually, such firm actions will hurt the host country.

Similarly, such firm actions may affect other countries as well, and the benefits or costs to the uninvolved countries might depend on a number of factors, including firm size. A larger firm, for example, might be able to afford to place refineries and other secondary processing plants in safer countries, whereas a new firm might not have that luxury. This would benefit the country that receives these plants at the cost of harming the alternative host country. To illustrate how a negative effect might be experienced by an outside country, assume that a South American country expropriated a mining property. Then firms might be less likely to invest in South America in general, thereby harming the entire continent. This reputational externality would ideally be controlled by groups of resource-rich countries trying to constrain their members' tendencies to expropriate.

As with any agency problem, agency losses will be shared. Hence both the principal (the government) and the agent (the firm) have an interest in reducing such losses, at least before any contracts are drawn or investments are undertaken. In theory, for example, the firm bids at the outset to develop a resource. Bids will be lower if expropriation is a risk, implying the government as well as the firm will gain if the temptation to expropriate can be partially or completely denied.

Assuming the occasional expropriation is unavoidable, the literature has focused on contracts designed to implement a given investment. Engel and Fischer (2010) prove the insightful result that a contracted cap on a firm's profits, equivalent to a super windfall tax, can act as a safeguard against expropriation in high states of profit.[4] The existing literature has mostly focused on moral hazard on the magnitude of the investment. Following earlier work, Engel and Fischer posit that firms bid competitively for the contract by announcing the lowest cap they would accept. If the firm's choice is only how much to invest, this approach secures maximal monies for the government, and also has the lowest-cost firm develop the resource.

Our analysis builds on this work by introducing a number of responses that the firm and then the government might take to dampen expropriation risk. In particular, we look at firms' willingness to severely sacrifice expected return to avoid projects yielding the types of high payoffs that might lead to confiscation. In this vein, firms may also inefficiently smooth profits over time. We also address situations where two or more phenomena interact. When the problems just mentioned intrude, preferred contracts may diverge substantially from the second-best optimal contracts for cases where the straightforward problem is mere discouragement of investment.

We first outline the potential factors that influence the government's decision to expropriate the resource. We label these relationships the GRAB function, where *GRAB* has its normal meaning: "get hold of or seize quickly and easily."[5] It is also an acronym for Gain and Retain Another's Belongings—in other words, to expropriate. Then, taking this GRAB function to be exogenous, as we do throughout, we examine what effect its hovering presence will have on the firm and its investment decisions. Specifically, we consider how firms select lotteries over profits, and then examine how moral hazard and adverse selection complicate matters. Then we examine how the government can address the aforementioned issues. The government basically has two approaches. It can induce the firm to take more favorable actions despite expropriation risk, or it can find measures that tamp down its own temptation to GRAB. Finally, we look at some policies the firm can undertake to improve the situation, basically by making a GRAB less likely.

We should note at the outset that our analysis is stylized. It often invokes simplified models to facilitate intuition and understanding. At times we play put and take with assumptions, thus dealing with one phenomenon at a time. Some of our results are merely presented as figures, in geometric terms. Given our simplifications, some of the measures we identify to reduce temptation would be difficult or impossible to implement politically. However, their structure often points in appropriate directions.

The rest of the chapter is organized as follows. Section 6.2 discusses the nature of the government's commitment problem and the nature of the GRAB function. Section 6.3 discusses how the firm distorts its investments when a GRAB threatens. Section 6.4 details how the government might induce firms to invest more and more appropriately when they confront the threat of a GRAB. Section 6.5 discusses the challenge of hidden information. Section 6.6 describes mechanisms available to the government and then the firm to reduce the temptation to GRAB. Section 6.7 concludes the chapter.

6.2   The GRAB Function

Expropriation is almost always a probabilistic threat as opposed to a certainty over the relevant range of investor decisions. Otherwise, the investor or firm—the two terms are used interchangeably here— would not create the conditions for expropriation, since payment in case of expropriation rarely comes close to making the firm whole.[6] As is common in the literature, we posit that the probability of expropriation rises with the magnitude of profits the investor is securing. That is because the government's benefits from expropriation rise with profits, but its accompanying costs likely rise less rapidly, as we explain below.

The government's decision to expropriate may not result from a straight financial cost-benefit calculation; it may also be subject to populist pressures that we would expect to rise with the magnitude of the investor's profits. In this light, populist pressures could arise from nationalist desires to have full control over the country's resources—for example, the belief that these resources should belong to the people, not to some multinational firm. More pragmatically, they could be stirred by desires for increased funds for the government to allocate within the country, or for better treatment of its workers.

Cognizant of the power of populism, however, populist pressures may also be stirred by those in power with the ultimate goal of rationalizing expropriation. Others may stir them to enhance their chance of securing power, and the corrupt may push them as a means to get more resources under their control, thereby increasing their private wealth.

As a first step in developing a model for expropriation, call the investor's profits, Π, the amount the government would get if it could run the operation as effectively as the firm and with no other consequences. Π is computed on a discounted expected value basis. Additional costs to the government, should it take over the operation, fall into three categories: efficiency costs, reputation costs, and payment costs. The efficiency costs are incurred because the government cannot produce as efficiently as the investor. Reputation costs, namely a reduced ability to get other firms to invest in the future, increase with the magnitude of profits, but far less than proportionally. A $200 million expropriation sends more shivers to the investor community than does a $100 million expropriation but hardly twice as many. Payment costs rise with Π because even expropriating governments usually pay something absolutely and at the margin, albeit invariably far less than fair market value. These categories of cost will come onstage occasionally below, but for the most part we just assume that they are positive and substantial.

Beyond these benefits and costs, a third factor influences the expropriation decision, namely the potential populist benefits from expropriating. These too are put into a financial equivalent term to simplify exposition.[7] Putting all of these elements together produces the function $f(\Pi)$, which gives the probability of expropriation, where it should be reemphasized that Π is what the firm loses, not what the government reaps. We expect $f'(\Pi) \geq 0$—that is, a greater pot of resources creates a greater likelihood of a GRAB. Though $f(\Pi)$ can equal 1 for high values of Π, the investor would be unlikely to choose such a Π, since, as mentioned, payment is likely to be woefully insufficient. However, such Π values may occur by chance after a prudent investment decision, say if mine exploration discovers a mammoth deposit.[8] One reason why $f(\Pi)$ is probabilistic is that many of these costs and benefits are quantities that are hard to assess. Moreover, they are subjectively judged by the government, the potential seizer of assets.

The government certainly will not show its hand in advance—for example, by saying what level of profit will make expropriation likely. We take $f(\Pi)$ to be subjectively assessed by the firm. In a more elaborate game-theoretic analysis, we could think of the government as determining $f(\Pi)$ as part of a game, where it would trade off the need to get firms to build up the value of their assets against the benefits it receives when expropriations do and do not take place.[9]

From the standpoint of investors, the relevant GRAB function is the one they believe. That makes it the relevant function for the government as well, at least to the extent that it is worried about investor behavior. In the parlance of game theory, the GRAB function in the eyes of an investor should be common knowledge. The investor is trying to guess how the government will behave. And both parties are attempting to assess a range of factors from future profits to efficiency losses given expropriation, from uncertainties about benefits and costs to evolving populist pressures. In short, the two players are engaged in a highly conjectural game about the behavior of the other, of what nature will do, and of third-party sentiment.

The elaborate game that emerges is summarized in the $f(\Pi)$ function. For example, when investor decisions are being made, we can expect the government to provide reassuring words, attempting to lower the perception of the $f(\Pi)$ function. These words may be something more than what economists call "cheap talk," namely mere platitudes with no consequence. Such words in some sense are quasi promises. Schelling (1960, 117) observes that a player's public proclamations that she will return the favor assuming another party does something beneficial for her puts her reputation on the line and changes her payoffs. They make it worthwhile for her to carry out the promise. Quasi promises surely change payoffs, but both parties understand that they may not do so sufficiently when the temptation to renege (in this case to expropriate) gets sufficiently great. Reassuring words about expropriation that are spoken softly may provide only modest reassurance (i.e., only slightly lower $f(\Pi)$), but when provided effectively and widely disseminated the shift will be greater, since breaking a widely broadcast commitment will discourage other potential investors.

The consequence of an $f(\Pi)$ whose value is not simply 0 is that investor decisions can be distorted in many ways. The most discussed, to be sure, is the simple discouragement of investment. Engel and Fischer provide an insightful treatment of the discouragement problem in chapter 5. We consider a range of important complementary distortions.

6.3   When GRABs Threaten, Moral Hazard

Whenever an arrangement provides for a transfer from A to B depending on the outcome, and when A has some control over the outcome, moral hazard intrudes. A will no longer take the actions he would in the absence of the contract. In our context, the arrangement is the $f(\Pi)$ function, A is the firm, and B is the government. Given $f(\Pi)$, the firm will no longer make the efficient investment, since B will be grabbing some of his profits. Such a deviation is called moral hazard.

The investor's expected loss from expropriation is $f(\Pi)\Pi$. In a scenario where there is neither a GRAB function nor risk aversion, the investor simply maximizes $E(\Pi)$. Take the simplest case where there is no investment decision to be made, and there is no uncertainty about profits. The investor can just select profits from a range. Maintaining the assumption of risk neutrality but introducing a GRAB function, the investor now maximizes $E(\Pi(1 - f(\Pi)))$. Since $f(\Pi)$ ranges from 0 to 1, we can see that the expectation will be lower here. As long as $f(\Pi)$ is increasing over the relevant range, the expected profits from a higher Π will be countered with a smaller $1 - f(\Pi)$ term. Thus, the firm will simply select a lower profit level than it would absent a potential GRAB.

If we drop the risk-neutral assumption and assume risk aversion, we are then maximizing $E[U(\Pi)]$ in the situation where there is no GRAB function, and $E[U(\Pi(1 - f(\Pi)))]$ when there is a GRAB function. Note that since the utility function is concave, risk aversion further reduces these values compared to their corresponding values in the risk-neutral setting. The potential for a GRAB reinforces any mean-reducing propensity of risk aversion. This should be understood in what follows, where for simplicity we assume risk neutrality.

6.3.1   Discouraged Development: Certain Profits

Let us return to the case where firms have to invest up front to produce profits, and can invest at variable levels. If there is the prospect of

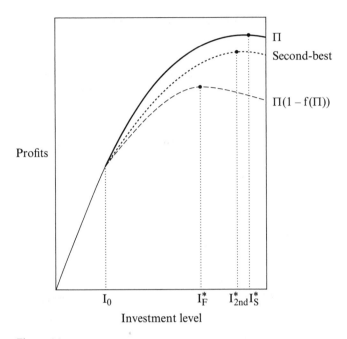

Figure 6.1
The certainty case

losing their investment—particularly if as we both assume and expect, likelihood increases with the magnitude of future profitability—investment will be discouraged. Sometimes they will not invest at all. In others, they will simply invest less than they otherwise would. The first case we treat has profits expressed as a certain function of the magnitude of investment (see figure 6.1). In this figure, three curves are shown. The solid curve shows profits if expropriation is ruled out. The dashed curve shows the expected return to the firm, $\Pi(1 - f(\Pi))$. The point I_0 shows where $f(\Pi)$ begins to be positive. The social optimum, assuming no possible GRAB, is at I_S^*. The firm's optimum is at I_F^*.

If the government expropriates, we will assume that it receives profits $b\Pi$, where $0 < b < 1$. The dotted curve indicates the expected returns to the government and firm together given the presence of $f(\Pi)$. Thus, the dotted curve takes into account the sacrifice in efficiency because the government will sometimes operate the resource. The formula for the dotted curve is

$$\Pi(1 - f(\Pi)) + b\Pi f(\Pi) = \Pi(1 - (1 - b)f(\Pi)).$$

The second-best optimum is at I^*_{2nd}. We assume $f'(\Pi) \geq 0$ when $f(\Pi > 0)$. The three curves and the three optimality points will have the relationship shown, where the optimal investment for the firm will be below the optimal second-best investment given the $f(\Pi)$ function, which in turn will be less than the optimal social investment assuming that the government would never GRAB. In short, the firm will underinvest.

This analysis leaves aside three other benefits that the government secures from the investment: (1) It may sell the concession at the outset. (2) It may impose ordinary taxes and possibly some severance taxes on the firm. (3) The operation of the firm yields benefits to the citizens of the country, and presumably the government counts these as a benefit. In each case, these extra considerations make it worse for the government to have its potential GRAB reduce the firm's investment. We will not discuss these extra considerations further below, though in virtually all cases they reinforce the desirability of each of our recommended policy measures. In short, even when profits are certain, the government would welcome temptation-inhibiting measures, which if put in place would enhance the firm's profitability and its investment.

6.3.2 Distribution Distortion: Uncertain Profits

For most real-world cases, there will be substantial uncertainty in the profit level. Most models of moral hazard simply assume that investors determine how much to invest. However, the investor may also be able to influence the distribution of returns. For example, in exploring for oil in a particular field, one has a choice of drilling strategies. Strategy S may be the "safe" strategy, offering a higher probability of a smaller find than strategy R, the "risky" strategy, which has a higher expectation but more variable returns.

In a potential expropriation situation, more variable returns are not welcome, since they increase the expected cost of expropriation holding mean returns and mean expropriation probability fixed. To see this, consider two equally likely levels of profits, $\Pi_1 < \Pi_2$, with respective expropriation probabilities $f(\Pi_1) < f(\Pi_2)$. The expected GRAB will be $[\Pi_1 f(\Pi_1) + \Pi_2 f(\Pi_2)]/2$. By contrast, if there were a certain profit level equal to $\Pi_c = [\Pi_1 + \Pi_2]/2$, with $f(\Pi_c) = [f(\Pi_1) + f(\Pi_2)]/2$, the expected GRAB would be less by $0.25[\Pi_2 - \Pi_1][f(\Pi_2) - f(\Pi_1)]$. Note that this quantity is strictly positive, because each term is positive. In effect, an expected GRAB is a rectangle, where the width is the profit level and the height is the probability of expropriation. With variable

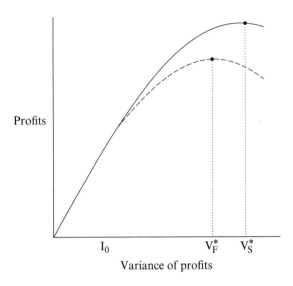

Profits

I_0 V_F^* V_S^*
Variance of profits

Figure 6.2
Uncertainty case; investment of I

returns, a weighted average of the areas of these rectangles is computed, where the weights are the likelihoods of each profit level, to get
a total expected GRAB. Holding the expected probability of a GRAB
and the expected cost of a GRAB fixed, the more variable profits become, the more bigger widths are multiplied by bigger heights, resulting in a larger total expected GRAB.

To simplify in the uncertain profits case, we will assume that the
firm is risk neutral, and only one level of investment is possible. The
firm invests I at step 1, probabilistic profits Π are realized at step 2,
and whether there is a GRAB is determined at step 3. The firm is able
to make more or less risky investments and thus selects the distribution from which Π is drawn. Since the government is more likely to
GRAB when Π is high, the firm will have an incentive to invest in
ways that are too conservative—that is, in ways that sacrifice mean
profits so as to reduce variance.[10] Figure 6.2 illustrates this point. The
solid curve shows profits as a function of variance, assuming no
GRAB. The dashed curve subtracts the expected GRAB from the solid
curve. The firm will optimize at V_F^*, whereas the social optimum
assuming no GRAB is at V_S^*. The firm will invest too little.[11]

The term *distribution distortion* refers to situations where such dis-
proportionate sharing—in this case between the government and

the agent—causes an agent to depart from what would be his optimal action. This phenomenon is very general, and influences the behavior of executives with stock options, investors with confiscation threats, and asset owners who have insurance. In each of these cases, the outside party—respectively shareholders, the government, and the insurance company—have a nonlinear claim on returns. The term distribution distortion was developed for insurance contexts (Zeckhauser 1996), where someone with insurance may accept a small risk of a larger loss to avoid a larger risk of a small loss despite this leading to a larger expected loss, since the larger loss gets a greater percentage compensation from the insurance. Here the expected returns to the outside party are quite the reverse and lead to excess risk avoidance, not excess risk taking.[12]

6.3.3 Delayed Development

The investor has to be concerned that Π becomes sufficiently large that the government will find it worthwhile to expropriate. Posit an extreme case where only the investor has the ability to discover and exploit a mine, though the government can expropriate the resource once discovered and developed. In this extreme case, the investor will then find it worthwhile to constrain the discovery and development process to deter a GRAB. The most likely way this would be done would be to dribble investment over time, even though the firm would invest much more rapidly if the assets developed were secure.

Suppose, for example, that the firm can extract the entire profit X in a single period but also can spread it over several periods. If there are substantial fixed costs of operation per period, or if current prices—as with oil in June 2008—are above expected future prices, or merely because money is worth more today than tomorrow, the former is most efficient. However, if $f(X)$ is much greater than $f(X/2)$, the firm will extract over two periods and thus sacrifice efficiency. An asset subject to expropriation is like a store in a high-crime neighborhood; it is imprudent to have too much inventory on hand.

6.4 Government Measures to Promote Appropriate Investment

The government suffers when firms respond in the ways described in the previous section. First, the government will probably sell concessions, say to develop resources, at the outset. If profitability will be lower, firms will pay less. Second, the government may collect

ordinary taxes on a firm's profits and the economic activity it generates. Third, the government, representing its citizens, will care about
payments to other entities. Fourth, given that it will sometimes expropriate, the government has a self-interest in a higher profit level. In this
section we discuss incentives the government can provide to induce
firms to invest more and more appropriately. We assume that if the
government does end up expropriating, such incentives are not paid.
That is, expropriation is total.

We next analyze the government's ability to optimally constrain its
propensities to GRAB in the context of models that successively incorporate different considerations. The models assume that the parties can
contract on profits (e.g., on a tax or royalty program, or indeed on payments that go from the government to the firm) that would pertain in
the absence of expropriation. We realize that some such contracting
may be difficult in practice—for example, the government may not
want to incur the wrath of the populace by negotiating contracts that
hand over large payments to a foreign firm.

6.4.1   The Optimal Constrained Payment Schedule When I* Is Observable

Consider first the simplest conceivable situation in which only one
type of investment is possible, though the investment amount can
vary and the amount invested, I, can be inferred or observed. Given
everything, the government has an ideal investment level, I^*, for the
firm. There is no problem if the firm will reach this level when optimizing for itself. Assume that it will invest too little. The simplest solution
is for the government to compensate the firm enough that it covers the
cost up to I^* if and only if it is undertaken. If any payment were politically acceptable, and if payments did not affect the likelihood of a
GRAB, the government would merely pay an amount P if $I \leq I^*$,
where P was just sufficient to make the investment worthwhile for the
firm.

Given that profits are uncertain, this arrangement would entail paying the firm in cases where profits are very low and also when they
were very high. The former would be politically unpalatable; the latter
would surely promote a GRAB. A more feasible solution might thus be
to have the payment depend on profits. Specifically, if profits are Π,
and there is no GRAB, then the firm could get $P = p(\Pi)$ along with Π,
if and only if the desired investment is undertaken. But what would
$p(\Pi)$ look like? The distribution of profits assuming that I^* is invested

is $g(\Pi \mid I^*)$. The firm will get paid by the government an amount $p(\Pi)$, a payment that is employed to get the firm to invest more than it otherwise would, but an amount that can sometimes be negative. Thus, assuming no GRAB, the firm receives $\Pi + p(\Pi)$. With a GRAB it gets nothing. The firm and the government have a common interest in avoiding extremely high profits for the firm, lest there be a GRAB, which creates a deadweight loss. Presumably the government is selling a concession at the outset, or otherwise extracting a significant portion of the firm's return, say through a royalty payment. Hence, it wishes to minimize the deadweight loss. As Engel and Fischer show, looking at the case where only the firm pays the government, the optimal program, taking account of $f(\Pi)$, caps the firm's profits. Hence, the firm pays the government when big profits are realized—that is, at the top. The government has a constraint at the bottom as well. For political reasons, it cannot pay the firm for investing when little has been produced in terms of profits. The firm's maximum payment function, is indicated as $MAX(\Pi)$. (Note that this formulation prevents the government from paying some or all investment costs up front.) Finally, the sum of $p(\Pi) + \Pi$ cannot be decreasing with Π, since the firm can always throw away some profits. Figure 6.3 shows the optimal constrained payment schedule from the standpoint of the government. It is indicated as the heavy curve. To compute the expected payoff going to the firm, the values on the curve would be integrated over $g(\Pi \mid I^*)$.

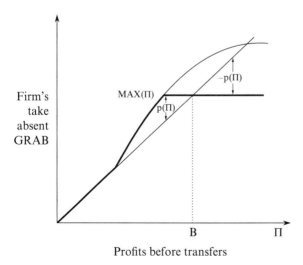

Figure 6.3
The optimal constrained payment schedule

As before, the firm's profits, including its payment from the government, might be GRABbed.

One critical constraint is that the firm must be securing enough expected payment from the government to cover its investment cost. That is why the structure cannot simply cap profits. Given investment I^*, the firm's expected payoff is

$$\int p(\Pi)g(\Pi \mid I^*)(1 - f(\Pi))\, d\Pi + \int \Pi g(\Pi \mid I^*)(1 - f(\Pi))\, d\Pi,$$

where the first term is the expected net transfer from the government and the second term is its own expected profits. This sum must be at least equal to I^*.[13]

6.4.2 The Optimal Constrained Schedule When I* and Investment Type Are Observable

Things are more challenging if the firm can choose not merely the magnitude of the investment, but its type, as indicated say by its variance, V. We capture the nature of the investment by the distribution of returns it will produce. Concern for distribution distortion was covered in section 6.3. Fortunately, and not surprisingly, if both the amount and nature of investment are contractible, a first-best outcome is achievable, assuming the government can just make a payment when it gets the result it wishes. Basically, the government just solves the problem of what pair I^*, V^* yields the social optimum. It then "pins" this outcome by offering to pay the amount $Q = q(I^*, V^*)$ if $I \leq I^*$ and $V = V^*$, thereby giving the firm the minimum incentive that gets it to invest the socially optimum amount. The solution to the case will be just like the case where the government pays P if $I < I^*$.

In fact, of course, this solution is likely no more feasible in practice than was the simple payment of P. The government is constrained in what it can pay, and it also must be concerned with $f(\Pi)$. Given that, it will simply replicate the solution outlined in figure 6.3. It will base payments on profits, will provide for MAX(Π) over a range, and then will cap the total returns to the firm.

6.4.3 Optimal Payments When the Investment Type Cannot Be Observed

We now move on to the more realistic situation in which the firm and government cannot contract over the choice of investments. As before, we posit that $f(\Pi)$ is exogenously given. Rarely will the first best be achievable. Hence, we often must settle for second best. Throughout this section, to keep things as simple as possible, we assume that the amount of investment, I, is exogenously given at I^*.[14] Because the parties cannot contract on the type of investment, they will write a contract promising the firm a payment $P = p(\Pi)$, since Π is the only thing that can be observed.

This sets the stage for a very interesting conflict. The government wants to reward the firm for high values of Π in order to implement risky investments, but the firm wants to avoid such realizations in order to prevent expropriation. But it should be recognized that the firm and government, despite disparate interests, are really partners. They both wish to find the $p(\Pi)$ function that yields a second-best outcome, given the $f(\Pi)$ function and the investment possibility curve. The optimal $p(\Pi)$ function may depend on the relative benefits being accorded to the firm and the government. The anchor points of the Pareto frontier are the respective levels of welfare if the government does nothing, and the firm simply optimizes against $f(\Pi)$. But there is a range of outcomes where both parties do better. If the government can choose $p(\Pi)$, obviously it will pick the function that is best for itself, subject to the constraint that the firm will participate (i.e., not be a loser).

6.4.3.1   Example Involving Two Technologies   Whether or not the government can provide appropriate incentives will depend on the distribution of profits and the nature of the GRAB function. We illustrate with an extreme example, with only two possible technologies. Technology 1 gives profits Π_1 for sure, while technology 2 gives profits Π_2/μ with probability μ and 0 with probability $1 - \mu$, where $\Pi_1 < \Pi_2$. So technology 2 is more efficient, and its choice would be the government's goal. If the GRAB function $f(\Pi)$ is such that $f(\Pi_1) = 0$ while $f(\Pi_2/\mu) > 1 - \Pi_1/\Pi_2$, no $p(\Pi)$ can implement technology 2. Thus, technology 1 will be chosen.

With other parameter values, incentives can implement the preferred outcome. Let $\Pi_1 = 1$, $\Pi_2 = 1.5$, and $\mu = 0.5$. Thus, if the firm selects technology 2, there is a 0.5 chance of a payoff of 3. If $f(3) = 0.5$, the expected profit to the firm is $3(0.5)(0.5) + p(3)/2$, or $0.75 + p(3)/2$. Thus, for $p(3) > 0.5$, the firm will choose technology 2.

6.4.3.2   Continuous Choice of Technologies   Let us return to an earlier example where the firm has a continuous choice reflecting a trade-off between mean and variance. The government receives considerable benefit from the firm's profits—including possibly selling the concession at the outset—for a variety of reasons. Thus, it promises the firm an additional payment $p(\Pi)$ to induce it to invest for a higher mean. Otherwise, the firm will simply choose too compressed an earnings distribution. We begin with five assumptions:

1. The maximum government payment to the firm is capped due to populist pressures.

2. The maximum government payment is small relative to the firm's expected loss from expropriation.

3. Given that the government is seeking to have the firm produce more profits, it is politically unacceptable to pay the firm more when profits are low than when profits are high.

4. When profits are high, the higher they are the more likely it is that the firm in fact chose a high variance–high mean investment. (This is the monotone likelihood assumption.)

5. The government's payment, $p(\Pi)$, is treated as equivalent to Π. Thus, the argument of the GRAB function is $f(\Pi + p(\Pi))$.

If there were no potential for a GRAB, the government would simply pay the firm a big amount when revenues were high. For any given expected payment by the government, this turns out to be the instrument that gets the firm to push for the highest mean return. Essentially, the government is making its payoff as high as possible when it is most likely that the firm has done what it wishes. We know from extensive work on monotone likelihood models, that high payoffs in the tail provide the most incentive bang for the buck. This payment is indicated as "ideal" in figure 6.4.

The cap on the government payment, of course, prevents an extremely high (and politically infeasible) payment way out in the tail. Thus, the nature of the optimal contract, absent the GRAB threat, might give the firm $50 million (the maximum feasible prize) if profits reach or exceed $300 million.[15] This payment is indicated as "capped" in figure 6.4.[16]

Alas, a GRAB is a threat, and any payments through $p(\Pi)$ help to promote a GRAB. Thus, the government must attend to this when choosing the $p(\Pi)$ function. We address this situation, but leave aside the cap and $MAX(\Pi)$, which would complicate the analysis. Three important factors come into play: (1) The firm's payoff, $\Pi + p(\Pi)$, cannot

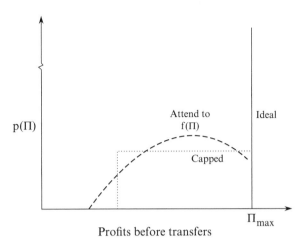

Figure 6.4
Optimal payment schedules

be decreasing, lest it capitalize on free disposal. (2) The goal should be to have $p(\Pi)$ high when Π is high in order to counteract the firm's tendency to compress the revenue distribution as it seeks to avoid a GRAB. (3) A countervailing consideration to (2) is to hold down $p(\Pi)$ when Π is high to reduce the probability of a GRAB, for the GRAB threat also leads the firm to avoid high outcomes.

Putting these three factors together, we know first that the $p(\Pi)$ function cannot focus payments in the lower tail as a means to promote a high variance. Second, it will be designed to reduce the likelihood of a GRAB. The optimal function will be optimal at every point. Thus, in looking at the GRAB propensity at two points, one relevant consideration for increasing $p(\Pi)$ at either will be $f'(p(\Pi) + \Pi)$ at those two points, namely the cost that comes from increasing the GRAB likelihood. To illustrate, we will assume that over the relevant range $f'' > 0$, there are increasing marginal costs in terms of GRAB likelihood.[17] This factor will be a force for having $p(\Pi)$ decline with Π. But we also know that the monotone likelihood consideration will make it desirable to have $p(\Pi)$ be highest for larger values, producing a tension. The dashed curve in figure 6.4—indicated as "Attend to $f(\Pi)$"—shows one possible resolution of these forces. Its initial rise phase reflects the desirability of putting density on higher values. Ultimately it begins to decline in response to the ever-increasing marginal effect of $p(\Pi)$ on the GRAB likelihood.

6.5   Hidden Information

Kenneth Arrow (1985) proposed the phrase "hidden information" to describe situations where one party has knowledge the other does not. The term more commonly applied to such situations is "adverse selection." But that term is inferior for our circumstances, since it is usually applied in insurance contexts, and since it implies a particular type of action, namely choosing whether to insure (and at what value). Our ultimate concern here is whether the firm should invest, and if so how much and in what way. Our intermediate concern is how the government can structure contracts to produce the best possible outcome given the information situation. The amount of investment I may be unobservable. If so, it will be subject to moral hazard. But that does not mean that the situation is hopeless.

6.5.1   The Expected Externalities Solution: Two-Sided Asymmetric Information

Fortunately, the government has some tools at its disposal to extract private information. Thus, for example, it can extract information by asking the firm to declare its type, and making future payments contingent on its declaration. The declaration will also guide the government in choosing what temptation-control measures to put in place. A transfer payment (sometimes negative) will go from the government to the firm depending on the firm's declaration and the government's response to it. The nexus of this mechanism is to have the parties pay one another the expected cost each imposes on the other due to its choice, whether that declaration is about information or an action. This approach is called paying the expected externality (Pratt and Zeckhauser 1987).

The government, not merely the firm, may have hidden information. If so, two-sided problems of asymmetric information may arise. This situation can be modeled in simple and stylized form by assuming that a firm already has a concession, and that two resource development projects are possible, Little and Big. The Little project will do no environmental damage. But the Big project will afflict the environment, producing damages of D, which the government values fully. The firm knows its potential profits. Using this information, and any incentives to which it is subject, it chooses the project to be undertaken to maximize its profits net of incentives. The direct profits from the Little project will be 2; the direct profits for the Big project are known to the firm, but not the government. The damages, D, which are fully valued by the government, are known only to the government. It is common knowledge that the Big project profits are uniform on $[2, 4]$, and that damages are uniform on $[0, 1]$. There is no chance the Little project will be expropriated. If the Big project is built, it is 20 percent likely to be GRABbed. If it is GRABbed, the government gets an incremental benefit of 0.5Π. Thus, the government's expected profit if the Big project is built is $(0.2)(0.5)\Pi = 0.1\Pi$.

The payoffs going forward are as follows:

	Little project	Big project
Firm	2	0.8Π
Government	0	$0.1\Pi - D$

The social optimum, subject to the constraint that the GRAB probability cannot be altered, is for the government to signal D honestly, and for the firm to invest in Big if $.8\Pi + .1\Pi - D > 2$. Thus, the formula for the social optimum is

$$\frac{1}{2}\int_0^1 \int_{(D+2)/.9}^4 .9\Pi - D d\Pi\, dD + \frac{1}{2}\int_0^1 \int_2^{(2+D)/.9} 2\, d\Pi\, dD = 2.359$$

The firm contributes 2.414 of this value, meaning the government receives $-.055$, assuming no side payments.

We will compute three outcomes with three mechanisms: no externality payment, the one-way externality payment, and the two-way externality payment. We will compare the results they achieve to this social optimum. The analysis follows the traditional economic approach of charging parties for the externalities they impose, with two extensions that comprise the foundation of the expected externalities mechanism. First, parties are charged for their declarations as well as their actions. Second, where information is not public, charges are made on an expected value basis using common priors.

6.5.1.1 No Externality Payment Suppose first that the firm must determine which project to undertake with no further knowledge of environmental damages. If $0.8\Pi > 2$, it will build the Big project, namely if $\Pi > 2.5$. The firm's payments will be given by $(0.25)(2) + 0.5\int_{2.5}^4 (.8\Pi)\, d\Pi = 2.45$, and the government's by $0.5\int_{2.5}^4 .1\Pi\, d\Pi - 0.75\int_0^1 D\, d\Pi = -.13125$. Thus, the total social surplus is $-.13125 + 2.45 = 2.319$.

6.5.1.2 One-Way Expected Externality Payment by Firm The traditional economic approach will charge the firm for the expected environmental damage it imposes on the government, which is 0.5. Given this, the firm will build the Big project when $0.8\Pi > 2.5$, namely when $\Pi > 3.125$.

Appropriate accounting for externalities will recognize that the government also benefits when it GRABs. Thus, the government must pay the firm the net expected externality it receives when the firm builds Big. This payment could in theory be negative or positive, since it has both a negative (environmental externality) and positive (GRAB potential) element. That expected externality is $0.1\Pi_B - D$, where Π_B is the expected value of Π when it is worthwhile for the firm to build Big. The firm will find the value Π^* such that $0.8\Pi^* + 0.1E(\Pi \mid \Pi > \Pi^*) - 0.5 = 2$ or $0.85\Pi^* = 2.3$. That value is $\Pi^* = 2.706$. Then $\Pi_B = 3.353$. The expected externality that the firm conveys to the government when it builds the Big project is thus $0.1(3.353) - D$. On average, D will equal 0.5. Therefore, the expected externality that the firm conveys to the government when it builds the Big project is $0.335 - 0.5 = -0.165$. Paying this amount to the firm when it builds the Big project produces the optimal outcome absent communication. The firm will build Big if $0.8\Pi - 0.165 = 2$, or if $\Pi > 2.706$, which appropriately is the Π^* found above. The expected payoffs to the two players will thus be $0.5 \int_2^{2.706} 2 \, d\Pi + 0.5 \int_{2.706}^4 .8\Pi - 0.5 + 0.1\left(\frac{4+2.706}{2}\right) d\Pi$ $= 2.335$ for the firm, and $0.5 \int_0^1 \int_{2.706}^4 D - .1\left(\frac{4+2.706}{2}\right) + .1\Pi - D \, d\Pi \, dD = 0$ for the government. Total social surplus is thus simply 2.335.

6.5.1.3 Two-Way Expected Externality Payments and Communication The two-way expected externality approach takes advantage of communication. The government first announces D^*, and then pays the firm the expected externality. That payment is equal to the change in the firm's expected profit from some base case. We take the base case to be that D^* is announced as 0. It is important to note that the announcement creates two different externalities to the firm. First, the announcement may induce the firm to build Little rather than Big; the greater D^* is, the more likely this is to happen. Second, D^* affects the subsequent externality payment the firm will pay to the government if it does build Big. Both of these effects would be taken into account in computing the expected externality that the government pays for making its declaration. After it hears the announcement and receives the payment from the government, the firm decides to build Big or Little. Its choice will take into account its own profits plus what it must pay the government for its decision. The firm then pays the government for its Big or Little decision. Little is taken to be the base case.

Thus the firm pays 0 if it chooses Little. The profit-maximizing firm will build Big for any value of $\Pi \geq \Pi^*(D^*)$. At this marginal (cutoff) value Π^*, the firm conveys an externality to the government of $0.1\Pi^* - D$ should it build Big. Thus, efficiency is served if the firm pays the government the amount $D^* - 0.1\Pi^*$ when it does build Big, assuming that the firm maximizes its profits after payment. It will build Big, as appropriate, if and only if $\Pi \geq \Pi^*$.

Obviously, this two-way externality format can be streamlined by subtracting the second payment (firm to government) from the first (government to firm), and computing the net payment by the government to the firm for the announcement of D^* given the choice of Big or Little.

The value of $\Pi^*(D^*)$ is given by $.8\Pi^* - D^* + .1\left(\frac{2+D^*}{.9}\right) = 2$. Thus, the cutoff value is $\Pi^*(D^*) = \frac{20}{9} + \frac{10}{9}D^*$. In light of this second-stage action, the government at stage 1 will select D^* to maximize its payoff. Specifically, it can compute the change in the firm's profits from announcing $D = 0$ versus $D = D^*$, the amount it will have to pay to the firm. This comes out to be $-\frac{20}{81}(D^*)^2 + \frac{64}{81}(D^*)$. Being subject to this expected externality, the government, maximizing its expected return, calculates

$$\max_{D^*} -\frac{20}{81}(D^*)^2 + \frac{64}{81}(D^*) + \frac{1}{2}\left(4 - \frac{2+D^*}{.9}\right)$$

$$\times \left(D^* - .1\Pi^* - D + .1\left(\frac{1}{2}\right)\left(4 + \frac{2+D^*}{.9}\right)\right)$$

Note that this quantity is equal to the initial lost payment to the firm plus the probability of the firm's building Big times the firm's payment to the government minus the environmental damage, and plus the expected value to the government of a potential GRAB. Solving this for $D(D^*)$, we see that the government sets $D^* = D$. Thus, the government correctly reports the environmental damage from building Big. Furthermore, from this equation, we can see that the formula for Π^* is the same as it is in the social optimum. Thus, we know we must be able to implement the first best.

The total expected payoffs are

$$\int_0^1 \left(\frac{1}{2}\int_2^{(20/9+10/9D)} 2\,d\Pi + \frac{1}{2}\int_{(20/9+10/9D)}^4 -D + .9\Pi\,d\Pi\right)dD = 2.359\ldots$$

Similarly, the government's payoff is

$$\int_0^1 \left(\frac{20}{81} D^2 - \frac{64}{81} D + \frac{1}{2} \int_{20/9+10/9D}^4 .1\Pi - \frac{2}{9} - \frac{D}{9} d\Pi \right) dD = -.273\ldots$$

A similar expression for the firm yields profits to it of roughly 2.632. We now compute the efficiency performance for the various schemes. We take the social optimum (constrained to recognize the GRAB function) to be 100 percent, and the outcome in the absence of any externality payment to be 0. The expected payoffs are

Payments	Firm	Government	Total payment	Efficiency
None	2.450	−0.131	2.319	0
One-way EE	2.335	0	2.335	39.986%
Two-way EE	2.632	−0.273	2.359	100%
Social optimum	2.414	−0.055	2.359	100%

The relevant efficiency indicator is given by the fourth column. The distribution of payoffs between the government and the firm in the table should be given little weight, since they could be shifted from the firm to the government without any loss through an up-front concession charge, or by changing the base cases from which externality payments are computed. Similarly, if multiple firms bid for the concession, excess profits to the winning firm will be competed away. The critical finding is that one-way expected externality payments are far below the social optimum, and that two-way externality payments can achieve the social optimum despite the information asymmetry.[18]

6.5.2   Moral Hazard, Distribution Distortion, and Hidden Information

Our analysis thus far has addressed government self-control mechanisms that work well when one or two of the key problems of moral hazard, distribution distortion, and hidden information are part of the picture. However, often all three are present. Consider a situation where a firm has hidden information about the state of the world. Using a variation of the example from section 6.3.2, suppose that there are two possible states. Thus, the firm knows whether a project is reasonably safe or quite risky. In state 1, the project gives profits Π_1 for sure if and only if an investment of I_1 is made, where $I_1 \geq I_a$ and $I_a < \Pi_1$. In state 2, it gives profits Π_2/μ with probability μ and 0 with probability $1 - \mu$ if and only if an investment I_2 is made, where $I_2 \geq I_b$ and $I_b < \Pi_2$. We assume that $\Pi_2/\mu > \Pi_1$ and that $\Pi_2/\mu - I_b > \Pi_1 - I_a > 0$. This implies that for either state the projects are profitable, but the project yields greater expected value in state 2.

Unfortunately, GRABbing is also more likely in state 2. Assume now that the GRAB function $f(\Pi)$ is deterministic, namely that $f(\Pi) = 0$ for $0 < \Pi \leq S$, and $f(\Pi) = 1$ for $\Pi > S$, where $I_a < S < \Pi_1$ and $S < I_b$. In this case, the government can implement investment in state 1 by simply doing nothing. But there is nothing the government can do to implement investment in state 2 because positive profits in that state, along with any payment from the government, are sure to generate a GRAB.

Under some circumstances the government can solve this problem by paying some of the firm's investment costs up front. This significantly tilts the firm toward being a contractor rather than an independent entrepreneur. For example, the firm might be given a choice to simply proceed on its own or to take a contract under which it is paid J up front and T if $\Pi > 0$. The firm will accept this contract in state 2 if $\mu T - I_b + J > 0$. It will simply proceed on its own in state 1 if profits going alone are greater, namely if $\Pi_1 - I_a > T + J$.

6.6 Temptation-Reducing Mechanisms

6.6.1 Government's Mechanisms
The government has several other tools at its disposal beyond those analyzed above. For example, to make the firm less fearful about expropriation, to lower the $f(\Pi)$ curve, it can voluntarily choose to implement a future hand-tying mechanism against expropriation.[19] Schelling-type promises would have this effect, since they would put the credibility of the government on the line, or the international reputation of its leader, and lower the government's payoff should an expropriation be undertaken.

A promise may not have long-term credibility if governments turn over, particularly between parties with different ideologies. This suggests that competitive democracies may have more trouble reassuring investors than governments that tend to stay in power over long periods. Fortunately, the current government may have some tools that can even tie up future governments of a quite different complexion. For example, the country could allow, indeed encourage, the firm to put in place machinery for which the country could not get spare parts.

The limiting case would make the efficiency loss total. That would entirely remove the temptation to GRAB.

Alternatively, the government could post a bond, presumably with
some impartial overseas organization. Of course, it would be prohibi-
tively costly to post a separate bond for each investment in a nation.
Presumably, the bond would cover a broad panoply of investments
within the country. The government would end up a loser if it expropriated one or two properties. This assumes that the government cannot confiscate everything at once. Thus, it might have ten different
firms in different areas, with a mean profit of $1,000 in each area, but it
might only have to put up $3,000 to ensure reasonable security. Part of
the security comes because not all assets are susceptible to GRABs at
the same time. This situation bears parallels to an insurance arrangement, where not everything bad happens at once. The bond would be
paid off by a third party, presumably some independent agency overseas, to the extent that the government violated the contract. The contract might even give the government the right to GRAB above some
point, which might be necessary with populist sentiment, even if it
would mean forfeiting something on the bond. The bond method
could be extended to effective GRABs, such as measures that dramatically raise taxes, force the employment of local workers, set excessively
high wages, and so on. It would only be essential that such developments or effects be spelled out in the contract, or be subject to the determination of the third-party agency. Note that the agency is not acting
as an insurer, only as an adjudicator and payment agent. Ideally, such
an adjudicator would build up a reputation for fairness over time, and
would deal with many nations, playing somewhat the role that a court
does in commercial disputes in the United States.

Governments, of course, have other measures that may represent
partial confiscations and that can provide feedback to affect firm behavior. Among tools in the category of tax policy, it is important to
note the distinction between taxing price and taxing quantity. A windfall tax on "excess price" merely promotes moral hazard, say lowered
investment; a windfall tax on "excess production," however, promotes
both moral hazard and distribution distortion. Moral hazard can be
fought through governmental contribution to the investment, by insuring price on the downside, or if a binding forward contract is possible
with the market, the firm can hedge its price. Price is readily observable. Production, and particularly optimal production, may be less observable. Thus, in an optimal arrangement, the firm will keep a greater

share of "excess profits" that come from unexpected production than from unexpected price.

6.6.2 Firm's Mechanisms

6.6.2.1 Extra Payments Thus far we have looked at the problem mostly from the standpoint of the government trying to get the firm to behave in an efficient fashion, even though the government itself cannot commit to refrain from efficiency-damaging expropriation. But the firm may seize the initiative and seek to make it worthwhile for the government not to expropriate. It can do this by agreeing to give the government greater profits than it otherwise would receive in the dangerous circumstances when the profits are great.[20] Posit that the $f(\Pi)$ function is immutable, where Π gives the profits the firm will reap. For simplicity, let us posit also that all investments and investment decisions have been made, and the firm is just waiting for probabilistic profits to be realized. Despite having no obligation, the firm may find it desirable to grant the government some profits for any value of Π so as to discourage a GRAB. Let $q(\Pi)$ be the positive profits granted to the government if Π eventuates.[21] The relevant GRAB function then becomes $f(\Pi - q(\Pi))$. Note that from the government's standpoint, this is equivalent to magnifying the inefficiencies it suffers if it conducts the firm's business. Thus, if the country only operates oil wells half as efficiently as the firm, that imposes a cost of 0.5Π on the government and makes a GRAB less likely. The firm cannot pick the government's efficiency level, but it can enhance the benefits to the government should it refrain from a GRAB. Here the firm picks $q(\Pi)$ to maximize its own expected profits:

$$q^*(\Pi) = \arg\max_{\Pi}[\Pi - q(\Pi)][1 - f(\Pi - q(\Pi))]$$

For example, if $0 < \Pi < 1$ and $f(\Pi) = \Pi$, then $q^*(\Pi) = \Pi - 0.5$ if $\Pi > 0.5$, and otherwise $q^*(\Pi) = 0$, since the payment to the government cannot be negative. This solution is general for any $f(\Pi)$ function. The firm in effect plots its expected after-GRAB profits as a function of actual profits, leaving aside $q(\Pi)$. Over any interval where that function dips, it pays the government an amount that places it at the bottom of the interval—that is, at the prior peak. Note that the $q(\Pi)$ function is independent of the distribution of profits.

This maximization can be envisioned as follows. The firm can draw its expected profits curve. Over any interval where it expects its after-GRAB take to diminish, it can continue across the dip on a horizontal line, thereby making the function monotonically increasing. The difference between the horizontal lines and Π will be paid out to the government. For example, consider the following scenario: $\Pi \in [0, 10]$, with $f(\Pi) = 0$ for $\Pi \leq 6$ and for $\log(\Pi - .5)/2$ for $\Pi > 6$. Here, the expected payoffs dip around 7, which can be smoothed over by a horizontal $q(\Pi)$ function.

6.6.2.2 Extralegal Solutions Firms subject to holdup may reduce the likelihood of a GRAB by influencing the behavior of leaders. This can be done in one of two ways: (1) making it less likely that an expropriation-prone leader is chosen, or (2) affecting the behavior of whichever leader is in office. Experience from Peru, Venezuela, and so on illustrates such actions by firms. It is important to note that such activity, albeit having strong distasteful elements, could actually be in the country's interest.

Another counterintuitive way the country could benefit is through the use of certain types of bribes. The GRAB function may depend not merely on profits but also on the leader's actions. A firm's ex ante anticipation that it will bribe a leader not to GRAB can benefit the country. To be sure, the expected cost of the bribe will come out of what the firm will pay for a concession; this produces a loss in profit for the country, a direct cost. But if a leader can switch the outcome from GRAB to not GRAB in a sufficiently broad range of circumstances, the resources saved may more than offset the profit loss from the bribe. The critical question, of course, is how large the bribe has to be to get the leader to change. Note that the outcome with optimal bribes is not equivalent to having the ruler(s) of the country merely own the resource, as they do in many oil-rich nations. Then they will still have the incentive to expropriate. The critical element of a bribe is that party A pays party B to give away party C's property. In our context, party C (the citizens of the country) cannot prevent this from happening.

6.7 Conclusion

Firms will respond in a self-interested manner to a government's temptation to GRAB their assets. The literature has analyzed the general inhibition of investment, but GRAB threats will induce firms to change their types of investments as well—for example, by compressing the distribution of payoffs at the expense of the mean. Fortunately, the forward-looking firm or government has tools available that can influence the future division of any profits, and thereby boost the expected payouts to both the firm and the country. If confiscations threaten, favorable outcomes will be served if effective controls are put in place before temptation looms.

Notes

The authors would like to thank Bijan Mossavar-Rahmani for his insightful ideas and remarks, and Laurence Tai for his able research assistance.

1. For example, on April 30, 2008, Venezuelan President Hugo Chávez expropriated a foreign steelmaking plant.

2. Though our discussion throughout is of a foreign firm as the investor, it applies equally well to domestic firms, which also do get expropriated.

3. There is even a premise with precedent called extraterritoriality, which allows country A to interfere in country B's companies that operate in country C, if country A is sufficiently opposed to the company's functioning there.

4. We should note that this chapter grew out of the authors' discussion of Engel and Fischer's piece at the 2007 Harvard conference. Their effort was so stimulating that we asked if we could write a paper inspired by it.

5. From wordnet.princeton.edu/perl/webwn.

6. For example, in the aforementioned case from Venezuela, the Venezuelan government appraised the foreign firm's assets at $800 million, whereas the firm reports they were worth between $3 and $4 billion.

7. A fuller exposition might treat this as a two- or multivariable utility function, but that would offer little gain in comprehension, and at best a modest gain in reality.

8. In some instances, the investor may be able to hide the magnitude of a big find, and thereby reduce the likelihood of expropriation.

9. It is important to note that the expropriation decision is essentially an option problem. Once the government expropriates, it cannot go back. However, if it does not expropriate, it can always do so in the future—that is, it retains option value. This implies, for example, that if there is a modest discounted expected surplus from expropriating now, it is likely to be worthwhile to wait. Such considerations, and the difficulty for the firm in judging how the government thinks about them and weighs them, help create the uncertainty surrounding $f(\Pi)$. Consider the following numerical example, with all costs and benefits computed on a discounted expected value basis. Current benefits are 100, and costs are 98. But posit that benefits are uncertain and that there is a 50-50 chance that benefits will go to 110 or 90. Expropriating now gives an expected surplus of 2, namely $100 - 98$. But waiting, and only expropriating if benefits go to 110, gives an expected

surplus of $0.5(110 - 98) = 6$. As with option problems in general, the greater future uncertainty is, the more worthwhile it is to preserve one's option, in this case not to expropriate now.

10. Our use of variance implicitly assumes that the profit distribution has just two parameters.

11. Note also the interaction with an auction on a profit cap as envisioned by Engel and Fischer. If firms can influence the distribution of returns, or if different firms will have different distributions for the same resource, such an auction may be inefficient. It will tend to select a firm that has compressed returns or can easily compress returns.

12. If the function relating expected return to risk is well behaved—that is, the same increment in risk reduction entails a greater loss in expected return the further the return is from the maximum return—risk aversion will compound the losses due to GRAB avoidance.

13. It also must be that the firm does not have another investment level that yields a greater expected return. Given that the government can monitor investment, it could presumably penalize an alternative superior investment level.

14. Matters would be more complex, but not fundamentally different, if I were also subject to choice.

15. The alert reader will have noticed the importance of our assumptions. If the government could have paid off more, basically it would have made an enormous payment in very unlikely circumstances. Beyond the political problem with such a scheme, it would induce the firm to choose an investment to the right of the mean-maximizing variance, hardly what the government wants. Our assumption that the government payment is small relative to expected losses from a GRAB also prevents this problem. Absent assumption 3, the government should provide some of its incentive in the lower tail of outcomes, outcomes that are also more likely when a high-variance investment is made. Payments for lower-tail outcomes would bring additional complications—for example, if firms had the ability to reduce their profits (i.e., free disposal).

16. If the curve relating mean to variance has an internal maximum, there is the danger that the firm would choose a variance above V^*, the level that maximizes the mean. The government would counter this by paying a high amount for a high realization, but penalizing even more highly a slightly more extreme low realization. This would prevent the firm from "shooting" by choosing an excessively high variance. With careful choice of payoffs in both tails, the government can ensure that the firm chooses V^*.

17. Obviously, f'' cannot be positive everywhere, because otherwise f would ultimately exceed 1.

18. The expected externality approach normally does not allow one player's private and unverifiable information to enter another player's payoff function. Our example got around that problem by charging the firm when it built Big for the cost of its externality for the marginal value of Π^*. This system will work unless the government's direct payoff from the firm's private information both falls as the firm's direct payoff rises, and also falls more rapidly than the firm's payoff rises.

19. Note that not only does the magnitude of the $f(\Pi)$ curve matter, but so does its slope in critical regions.

20. This is the flip side of the Engel-Fischer approach of having the government cap the firm's profits.

21. The function $q(\Pi)$ is actually identical to the $p(\Pi)$ function met earlier when $p(\Pi)$ is negative, as it is for larger Π in figure 6.3.

References

Arrow, Kenneth J. 1985. "The Economics of Agency." In J. Pratt and R. Zeckhauser, eds., *Principals and Agents: The Structure of Business*, 37–51. Cambridge, MA: Harvard Business School Press.

Bohn, Henning, and Robert T. Deacon. 2000. "Ownership Risk, Investment, and the Use of Natural Resources." *American Economic Review* 90(3): 526–549.

Chatterjee, Kalyan, John W. Pratt, and Richard J. Zeckhauser. 1978. "Paying the Expected Externality for a Price Quote Achieves Bargaining Efficiency." *Economics Letters* 1(4): 311–313.

Che, Jiahua, and Yingyi Qian. 1998. "Insecure Property Rights and Government Ownership of Firms." *Quarterly Journal of Economics* 113(2): 467–496.

Di Tella, Rafael, Juan Dubra, and Robert MacCulloch. 2007. *A Resource Belief-Curse: Oil and Individualism*. Harvard Business School Working Paper No. 08-035.

Engel, Eduardo M. R. A., and Ronald D. Fischer. 2008. *Optimal Resource Extraction Contracts under Threat of Expropriation*. NBER Working Paper No. W13742.

Engel, Eduardo M. R. A., Ronald D. Fischer, and Alexander Galetovic. 2001. "Least-Present-Value-of-Revenue Auctions and Highway Franchising." *Journal of Political Economy* 109(5): 993–1020.

Jacoby, Hanan G., Guo Li, and Scott Rozelle. 2002. "Hazards of Expropriation: Tenure Insecurity and Investment in Rural China." *American Economic Review* 92(5): 1420–1447.

Luttmer, Erzo F. P., and Richard J. Zeckhauser. 2008. *Schedule Selection by Agents: From Price Plans to Tax Tables*. NBER Working Paper No. W13808.

Mahajan, Arvind. 1990. "Pricing Expropriation Risk." *Financial Management* 19(4): 77–86.

Pratt, John W., and Richard Zeckhauser. 1987. "Incentive-Based Decentralization: Expected-Externality Payments Induce Efficient Behaviour in Groups." In George R. Feiwel, ed., *Arrow and the Ascent of Modern Economic Theory*, 439–483. New York: New York University Press.

Rodrik, Dani, and Richard Zeckhauser. 1988. "The Dilemma of Government Responsiveness." *Journal of Policy Analysis and Management* 7(4): 601–620.

Schelling, Thomas C. 1960. *The Strategy of Conflict*. Cambridge, MA: Harvard University Press.

Schwartz, Eduardo S., and Anders B. Trolle. 2008. "Pricing Expropriation Risk in Natural Resource contracts: A Real Options Approach." Paper prepared for Conference on Populism and Natural Resources, John F. Kennedy School of Government, Harvard University, November 1–2, 2007.

Shleifer, Andrei, and Robert W. Vishny. 1994. "Politicians and Firms." *Quarterly Journal of Economics* 109(4): 995–1025.

Tomz, Michael, and Mark L. J. Wright. 2008. *Sovereign Theft: Theory and Evidence about Sovereign Default and Expropriation?* CAMA Working Papers 2008-07. Australian National University, Centre for Applied Macroeconomic Analysis.

Walter, Matthew. 2008. "Venezuela's Chavez Decrees Takeover of Ternium Unit." April 30. http://www.bloomberg.com/apps/news?pid=20601086&sid=aFkcqZ4TOZNc&refer =latin_america.

Zeckhauser, Richard. 1996. "Insurance and Catastrophes." *Geneva Papers on Risk and Insurance: Issues and Practice* 78: 3–21.

7   Dealing with Expropriations: General Guidelines for Oil Production Contracts

Roberto Rigobon

7.1   Introduction

In the last decade, a new round of renegotiation of contracts occurred in the oil industry. In fact, most contracts involved some form of expropriation, and certainly all of them implied some degree of conflict. Bolivia and Venezuela were perhaps the most notorious ones. In these cases their governments violated significant portions of the production contracts, and sizable expropriations took place. On the other hand, less publicized cases (such as England) mostly changed the corporate tax rates. This is not the first round of contract renegotiations that has taken place in the industry, nor the last. Contracts in the oil industry are indeed as volatile as its prices.

One attitude toward the recontracting is simply that contracts are meant to be violated. In other words, it is possible to argue that writing a complete contract is extremely difficult (or impossible), and therefore it is well understood, ex ante, that it will be violated.[1] In this sense, renegotiation is just the natural outcome of the incompleteness. However, there are several features of the oil industry that hint at alternative explanations. First, the renegotiation of these contracts seems to be more disruptive than with other private ones. In fact, institutions that deal with the "exceptions" are not guaranteeing the rights of one of the agents involved in the transaction. Most of these renegotiations are occurring between governments and foreign firms, which are not equally treated (or represented) within the judicial system in several of these countries. Second, renegotiations occur within heavily politicized environments—which usually leads to the most visible action as opposed to the most efficient renegotiation. For instance, new governments with populist messages are the ones expropriating. Third, and equally important, when contracts are analyzed in detail, several potential ways of reducing the incentives for expropriation become apparent. In fact, the mixture of taxes and transfers is always regarded as one of the most important areas for improvement. One typical line of argument is that the optimal taxation of the oil industry is one where the taxes are fully procyclical. This is a very simplistic view, because two problems arise. First, when there is investment and in certain price paths the investment is not recovered, the optimal tax involves subsidies to the oil industry. Second, governments care about the variance of the revenue stream when they are unable to hedge the price risk. The optimal tax, in this regard, implies variances that are even higher than the volatility of the price itself. For these two reasons governments might find it convenient to deviate from the erstwhile optimal tax.

In this chapter, I am concerned with understanding the motives behind the contracting problem faced by the government, trying to rationalize the choices of instruments that are used in practice, and finding areas of improvement in the "typical" contract. Primarily, the objective is to rationalize some of the mixture of taxes we observe. At the outset it is important to emphasize that this is a simulation exercise; therefore, it is not precise enough to offer implications for actual contract formulations. The objective is to indicate how some elements of the contract can be introduced in the discussion in order to reduce the incentives to renegotiate, and to reduce their disruptions.

Of course this task cannot take into consideration all possible elements—nor activities in the oil industry. The first simplification is that I will concentrate exclusively on production contracts. The exploration and development of oil fields is an important activity in the industry. However, the problems in those areas are different from those pertaining to production. Furthermore, most of the expropriations and renegotiations affect production activity alone. Thus this chapter focuses on the latter and is not concerned with exploration and development.[2]

Which elements would I consider in the design of a contract for the production of hydrocarbons? First, efficiency. The production of hydrocarbons is heavily distorted by the choice of taxes. Indeed, hydrocarbon contracts always involve an overtax, and the private response to such a structure significantly affects production plans. Most of the time, this distortion is reflected in underexploitation of the natural resource. This is costly because recovery operations are very expensive, and so resources left under the ground are likely to remain there. One important question is why oil contracts need the overtax. I discuss this in detail in the chapter, but the short explanation is that when a project is being auctioned to the private sector, governments collect less than its social value. The government has credibility and commitment problems, and the private sector pays less than the social value in anticipation of a renegotiation. In this environment, the private sector assigns a probability of default that lowers the revenue collected by the government, making expropriation a desirable social outcome. This is one reason the private sector generates abnormal returns; it also helps explain why governments try to extract those rents through the tax system. Those taxes create inefficiencies, and choosing the optimal structure is an important part of contract design.

The second feature of the contract under discussion is rents. The main motivation behind expropriation is the perception (by the public sector) that the private sector is receiving "excessive" rents under some conditions. This is in general why the round of expropriations usually happens when commodity prices are very high,[3] and it is why the recontracting is permeated with a heavy load of politics and populism. In fact, contracts that leave "too many" rents in the hands of the private sector, at least in some circumstances, are more likely to be renegotiated when it becomes evident that those circumstances appear. A good contract is one that leaves reasonable rents in the hands of the private sector in all states of nature, reducing the incentives of both sides to renegotiate.

A third component of the contract is stability of revenues. Several countries design their tax systems to smooth revenues. Although fiscal revenue stability might be a desired feature of any economy, it is not clear why the smoothness should be achieved through the tax system as opposed to other institutions providing the necessary insurance. In other words, stabilization funds and transactions in future markets are clearly more efficient mechanisms to stabilize revenues than the tax code. Nevertheless, few governments use alternative institutions to stabilize fiscal revenues, and most of the stability objectives end up affecting the way tax codes are designed. For instance, one of the most often cited benefits of royalties is that a sales tax is more stable than income taxes, which can be affected by agency costs and other sources of fluctuation. Whether or not this argument is valid, the point is that in general, the pursuit of stabilization has affected the contract design.

In this chapter I take this last point seriously. I look at how contracts are affected by the stabilization objective, and study how they interact with expropriations. In fact, these two objectives are inherently at odds with each other. A very simple example will highlight this tension. Assume that the only uncertainty is in prices, and for simplicity assume that production is fixed. The most stable revenue is that in which the government collects a fixed tax per unit of production. However, this means that when prices are very high the firm will have large profits. This could motivate an expropriation based on the fact that the firm is earning "too much." On the other hand, assume that the government collects taxes in such a way that the firm receives a fixed profit in all circumstances. In this contract the firm has constant profits and will never be expropriated (or will be unlikely to be), but all the uncertainty of the price fluctuation is borne by the government revenues. In this example, minimizing the probability of expropriation increases the revenue variance, while minimizing the volatility of taxes increases the probability of expropriation. In this paper I extend this simple intuition to the case when the firm is solving a dynamic stochastic problem in choosing its production level.

Agency costs represent a final component of the contract. Taxes and rents transferred to the public sector can be significantly reduced by companies' expenditure and investment behavior. For instance, several oil and gas contracts have incentives for investment, which are (mis)-used by the private sector to reduce the tax burden. The case of Bolivia is one of the most interesting in this regard. The contracts on gas included investment incentives that the firms used when prices were increasing as a means of reducing the tax pressure. For instance, the fiscal burden was 37 percent of the international price between 1996 and 1998, when international prices were relatively low. It decreased to 24 percent between 1999 and 2001, and further down to 15 percent between 2002 and 2004. The effective tax rate as a percentage of the price was declining with price increases! Given that an important part of the taxation were levied on profits, this can only be explained if the costs increased faster than international prices in the last decade. This is unlikely. The most plausible explanation is that in times of high prices, the firms found easier to undertake large investment projects that reduced the tax burden. Some of these investments might have been profitable, but some responded to tax issues rather that social or private returns.[4]

The chapter starts with a simple setup where income taxes are non-distortionary and there is almost no efficiency lost. The problems begin when the government is concerned about revenue stabilization. Income taxes produce a more volatile revenue than royalties, and a government worried about revenue volatility shifts the tax mixture toward royalties—a more distortionary tax. Not only are production plans affected, but more importantly, private profits become more extreme, and price paths in which private profits are "extremely" large become more likely. This increases the probability of expropriation.

The chapter makes the following core recommendations:

1. Use a stabilization fund to deal with revenue uncertainty. Changes in the tax structure to provide income insurance produce undesirable outcomes. Nevertheless, it is understood that stabilization funds are costly and will never provide full stabilization and hence they have to be complemented.

2. Build a local constituency to mitigate the expropriation incentives. If the transfers to the locals are procyclical—which is equivalent to having a procyclical tax rate—then expropriation incentives are reduced.

3. Joint private and government ownership has been highlighted as a possible way of reducing agency costs. This assumes that the government incurs lower agency costs than the private sector—which seems a strong assumption. The problems of agency costs are reduced by relying on sales taxes, and indeed that has been the response of several governments. The elimination of investment subsidies and depreciation subsidies will go a long way toward reducing the agency costs that plague the industry, and those steps are more efficient than involving the government in the production process or shifting to less than optimal taxes.

In the end, the chapter argues that even though the optimal tax from an efficiency point of view involves a procyclical tax rate, from a political and social point of view this is hard to implement. The fact that governments are concerned with the volatility of the revenue stream, as well as with the presence of agency costs, implies that the mixture of taxes deviates from an efficient one to a tax that relies more heavily on more distortionary—but more stable—taxes. This in turn creates paths where excessive profits are too large for the government to avoid the temptation to expropriate. Hence, expropriation and inefficient taxes are to be expected.

As mentioned above, two issues have been excluded from the analysis. First, the political economy of the expropriation process has been greatly simplified. I assume that expropriation occurs when private profits are "too large." This is clearly part of the expropriation decision, but certainly it is not the whole picture. As discussed in many places in this book, issues related to the fairness, efficiency, and composition of investment are indeed part of the expropriation process. Second, the model I solve has no investment at all. Exploration and development are results of some of those investments. This is an important simplification. A first step toward understanding the optimal contract requires analyzing the simplest problem when investment is not part of the decision problem, although future research has to address this important issue.

The paper is organized as follows: section 7.2 presents the simple model and discusses the assumptions by summarizing the relevant theoretical and empirical literature. Section 7.3 presents the results of the simulations. Section 7.4 concludes the paper.

7.2 A Simple Organizing Framework

Assume that a foreign firm contracts with a government to produce a mineral, which for most of the discussion is going to be oil. Abstract from all interactions at the firm level. Indeed, several problems that arise in the exploitation of natural resources refer to externalities at the firm level. I abstract from all those issues and consider exclusively the problem between the firm and the government.

7.2.1 Setup

An infinitely lived firm is a price taker in the international markets and can only make the choice of production, and as discussed later in this paper, this may include "wasted expenditures." The firm has a known amount of reserves to exploit. These reserves are certain and cannot be changed. The decision to engage in exploration and development of oil fields, for example, relaxes this assumption. This is an important simplification of this paper—I do not deal with the problems that arise from the investment in reserves. Hence, in the baseline model, the firm just chooses how much to produce.

7.2.1.1 Prices   Assume the price of the commodity is described by a random walk with no drift. This assumption is not essential for the analysis, although mean reversion might diminish some of the effects highlighted here. Prices are given by

$$p_t = \begin{cases} p_{t-1} + \delta & \text{w.p.} \quad \alpha \\ p_{t-1} - \delta & \text{w.p.} \quad 1 - \alpha \end{cases}$$

where $p_t = 0$ is an absorbing barrier. I assume that there is a maximum price $\bar{p}$ that is also an absorbing barrier. This price is large enough that the firm will produce the entire field in one period, meaning that higher prices are just not interesting for the present analysis. Furthermore, I initialize the model and simulations at a point at which the upper bound price is never reached.

7.2.1.2 Cost Structure The firm has a cost of production that has increasing marginal costs on two arguments: the production in each period and the amount of reserves left. The idea of the second assumption is to capture the fact that in general the marginal cost of production increases, the deeper the reserves are underground. Not only is this assumption reasonable given the properties of most natural resource exploitation, but most importantly, it is a crucial assumption to generate significant distortions by the different taxes.

The cost function is

$$c(q_t, Q_t, \bar{Q}) = c_0 \cdot q_t + c_1(Q_t/\bar{Q}) \cdot q_t^2 \tag{1}$$

where q_t is the quantity produced at time t, Q_t is the cumulative production that has occurred until time t, and $\bar{Q}$ is the total original reserves in the field. I assume that the cost function is convex and that its degree of convexity is what changes when the reserves are being depleted.

From a practical point of view, making the function c_1 increasing is enough to capture the distortions the chapter is trying to highlight.

7.2.1.3 Taxes in the Typical Contract One of the objectives of this chapter is to study the impact that different taxes have on the production plan, the tax revenue volatility, and the profits left in the hands of the private sector. There are literally thousands of possible taxes and arrangements between the private sector and the government. Just to indicate some of the diversity, table 7.1 summarizes some features of oil and gas contracts in Latin America. Trying to design the optimal contract by looking at the actual clauses is an impossible task. Contracts usually involve taxes (sales, royalties, assets, and income), depreciation clauses, investment incentives, participation shares, and fees—far too many dimensions to consider.

In this chapter, I concentrate on two forms of taxation: royalties and income taxes. These are possibly the two most prevalent forms of taxation in natural resources. The royalties are taxes levied on sales.

Table 7.1
Typical contracts. Author's summary of contract's descriptions

	Argentina	Bolivia	Colombia	Peru	Venezuela
Fees exploration	~20$ per sq.km.				
Fees production	~420$ per sq.km.	~200$ per sq.km.			
Royalties oil	12%	18%		15% to 35%	20%
Royalties gas	15% to 30%	18%	5% to 25%	15% to 35%	20%
Income tax	35%	25%	35%	30%	34%
Depreciation development	10% straight line	20% straight line	20% straight line	20% straight line	Unit of production
Depreciation facility	10% straight line	12.5% straight line	14.3% straight line	20% straight line	
Sales tax	1% to 3%	13% (VAT)	0.2% to 0.7%		
Asset tax	1%				
Participation or profit shares		25%	30% after royalties		35%
Investment uplift		100%			

Source: Several World Bank reports.

Sometimes they are a fixed payment per unit produced, similar to fees, but nowadays most royalties are similar to sales taxes, where the tax rate is constant. The other tax, income tax, is always part of the contract. Sometimes the tax rate is the same as with corporate taxes; however, many contracts specify an overtax.

These contracts do not include all the possible mechanisms now used. For instance, profit-sharing arrangements are becoming more prevalent—in the form of joint ventures, or specific sharing rules. From a taxation point of view, a profit-sharing rule might seem similar to an income tax, but the contrast between mandatory taxes and discretionary dividends makes the distortions of the second arrangement smaller. Having a government as a partner in the production of oil and gas leads to other distortions that I do not discuss in this chapter. Indeed, it is not clear that the literature has reached a consensus on the types of distortions that might arise because of joint ventures.

The other important ingredient missing in the discussion are investment incentives; given that I do not consider investment, subsidies would be irrelevant. Nevertheless, I will try to capture the "bad" aspect of those subsidies, meaning the agency costs that arise from them. The reason is that income taxes and investment incentives create similar behavior by the firm, and I can capture these effects with the income tax alone.

In summary, I consider the choice of two tax rates: royalties levied on total sales, and income taxes levied on total private profits. I assume that the tax rates are not contingent on prices, production, or reserves, which is mostly how contracts are specified in reality.

7.2.1.4 Royalties and Income Taxes   The problem of taxation of the oil industry has, in general, a very simple answer from the point of view of economists: procyclical dividend transfers. For instance, the optimal contract is one in which the firm pays its costs and can retain a "reasonable" return on its capital. If the firm is subject to enough regulation such that it does the optimal investment and uses the factors optimally, then all the other sources of revenue constitute the rent and should be transferred to the government—preferably in the form of dividends, which are less distortionary than taxes. This is indeed the basis of optimal regulation.

However, there are two problems with this mechanism. First, when oil prices are low enough it is possible that the firm will need subsidies. In other words, the oil companies need subsidies when oil prices are too low and investment is not recovered. The likelihood of this happening in an emerging market is essentially zero. In fact, the contribution by Engel and Fischer in this book (see chapter 5) deals with this aspect of the optimal contract under investment. Second, and equally important, the optimal transfer is more volatile than oil prices and sales. If the government is concerned with revenue stability because it is costly to hedge, or the cost of borrowing increases when oil prices decrease, then the optimal tax for efficient production is not optimal for the government. These two reasons imply that the optimal tax from the efficiency point of view is almost never implemented. In the setup developed below the optimal tax (for efficiency) is one that depends entirely on income tax (or corporate taxes); when the volatility concerns are introduced, the implication is that the government implements a different mixture, where royalties and other forms of sales taxes are favored.

As table 7.1 shows, contracts in Latin America have royalties and fees for production and exploration, and almost all have either asset or sales taxes. In comparison, England and Alaska depend almost exclusively on corporate taxes. One reason is that in those areas, oil revenues are a smaller share of all fiscal income and therefore they need less stabilization than in Venezuela or Equatorial Guinea; a second reason is that England and Alaska have access to better financial and insurance markets and hence have the luxury of implementing a better tax mixture.

7.2.2   Maximization Problem

The firm maximizes expected profits given prices, taxes, and total reserves. The firm initially operates under the assumption that there is no default on the contract. The objective is to analyze the impact of the different taxes on the production plan, expected profits, and so on.

The firm solves the following Bellman equation

$$V(Q_t, p_t) = \max_q \left(\pi(q_t, Q_t, \bar{Q}, p_t, \tau_r, \tau_\pi) + \frac{1}{1+\beta} E[V(Q_t + q_t, p_t') \mid p_t] \right)$$

where τ_r is the royalty tax rate, and τ_π is the income tax rate. Profits at the firm level are given by

$$\pi(q_t, Q_t, \bar{Q}, p_t, \tau_r, \tau_\pi) = [p_t q_t (1 - \tau_r) - c(q_t, Q_t, \bar{Q})](1 - \tau_\pi)$$

I solve this standard maximization problem by discretization of the state space and solving for the fixed-point problem of the value and policy functions.

7.2.2.1 Agency Costs When I add agency costs to the problem I assume that the firm can take actions that are costly from a profit standpoint, but can lower the tax burden.

In reality those actions involve deviating from the optimal investment plan or increasing expenditures. They mostly reduce the burden of income taxes and rarely have an impact on royalties. Indeed, several policymakers indicate that one of the benefit of royalties is the fact that they are subject to less manipulation by the firms.

In this chapter I capture the agency costs in a very stark form. I assume that the firm can take an action that has a cost in terms of private profits, but that reduces the income taxes that have to be paid. My assumption is that these actions are useless from the production point of view, because they only reduce the tax burden.

7.2.2.2 Government's Problem The theoretical public finance literature studies tax choices and tax incidence problems by specifying an objective function that tries to minimize the distortion introduced by taxation, and where one of many constraints is to achieve the desired level of taxation. Sometimes the problem formulation actually maximizes the consumer's utility. This is the case when there are several distortions and deciding among them is difficult. In the example discussed in this paper, there is no consumer and the most important distortion that arises is the change in production plans.[5]

The goal of the government is to determine which combination of taxes maximizes its objective function. I assume that in the maximization problem, tax revenues, stabilization objectives, and the probability of renegotiation enter the objective function.

I also assume that the government chooses a fixed tax rate—fixed in terms of the state variable, which includes the price of the commodity. In fact, the optimal contract would always imply a contingent income tax, where the tax burden is procyclical.[6] However, as is clear from section 7.2.1.3, production contracts involve constant fees and tax rates. I retain this assumption throughout the paper.

Assume that the government cares about the efficiency (minimizes the distortion in the production plan) subject to a minimum expected tax revenue and a maximum expected variance in the tax revenue constraints. This is indeed the standard objective function used in public finance.

For simplification, and to be able to solve the model in the simulations, I assume that the only distortion the government is concerned

with is how taxes affect the production plan. The distortion in my case will be one in which the government compares the expected production path of the field with taxes (q_t) and without taxes (q_t^0).[7]
Specifically,

$$\min_{\tau_r, \tau_\pi} E \sum_{t=0}^{\infty} \frac{1}{(1+\beta)^t} (q_t - q_t^0)^2 \qquad (2)$$

$$E \sum_{t=0}^{\infty} \frac{1}{(1+\beta)^t} \tau_t \geq \bar{\tau}$$

$$Var\left(\sum_{t=0}^{\infty} \frac{1}{(1+\beta)^t} \tau_t \right) \leq \bar{v}$$

where $\bar{\tau}$ is the target tax collection, and $\bar{v}$ is the maximum variance the government is willing to suffer. In this problem I have not specified how agency costs enter the problem and how the probability of expropriation affects the government choices. I leave that extension for later, when I clarify how the expropriation decision is made. Let me concentrate for the moment on how concerns about stabilization affect the tax mixture.

In the setup, the optimal tax is the one that reduces the distortion when stabilization is not a concern $(\bar{v} \to \infty)$. This taxation implies a mixture where only income taxes are used. The reason is that income taxes do not change the first-order condition of the firm, while royalties do. However, in this model income tax revenues are more volatile than royalty revenues. Therefore, when the variance constraint binds, the optimal choice of taxes is extremely simple: royalties are increased and income tax rates are reduced to keep total revenue constant and reduce its variability. The solution is always a corner solution given the assumptions I have made.

7.3 Simulations

The first step in the simulation is to show the degree of distortion that the different taxes—and mixture of taxes—generate. The second step is to solve the government's problem and examine the volatility of the tax revenues, efficiency, and probability of default.

In the simulation I assume that the price of the commodity fluctuates between 0.1 and 2, where the initial price is 1. I assume that the step in the random walk (δ) is 0.1 every period. The probabilities of increases and decreases are equal $(1/2)$, hence there is no drift. The discount rate is assumed to be equal to 5 percent. The initial reserves are equal to 20, and the cost function has parameter $c_0 = 0.75$, while the function c_1 is $0.1\left(1 + \frac{Q_t}{Q}\right)$. As mentioned above, the choice of the c_1 function highlights the increasing marginal cost when reserves are depleted.

The first step in the simulation is to solve the firm problem given taxes and the parameters and functional choices just highlighted. The solutions to the problem are not discussed here, nor are the value function or the policy functions for the no-tax case.[8] Rather than studying the policy functions and their changes when taxes are modified, here I analyze how the pattern of production and tax revenues changes in a Monte Carlo exercise. The simulation consists of 500 histories of 100 periods each. All simulations start at the same state (price of commodity and reserves left).

7.3.1 Tax Distortions

The first step is to highlight the different distortions that the taxes produce in the firm's decision. These aspects have been heavily discussed in the regulatory literature. Here, I indicate the different problems that appear. The simulation involves two exercises. First, assuming that the income taxes are zero, royalties are increased from zero to 30 percent. Second, I set royalties to zero and vary income taxes in the same range.

After solving for the value and policy functions for each tax rate, I simulate the dynamic response of the firm using the Monte Carlo technique. The price process feed to all simulations is exactly the same; hence the only differences arise from the firm's responses. Each history has 100 periods and starts at exactly the same point.

7.3.1.1 Measures There are several measures I am interested in evaluating. First, what is the expected total production? As I said in the beginning, the firm starts with twenty units under the ground. The question is, how much of that is actually extracted for each price path? Assuming all paths are equally likely, it is possible to compute the total expected quantity being exploited. This is an important measure of the distortions that the tax system produces. In fact, most of the distortions are reflected in underexploitation of the field. If investment incentives are included in the discussion and they affect the development of reserves, then overproduction is possible. Nevertheless, here I am more concerned with understanding the degree of the distortion rather than its direction.

Second, what is the expected net present value of tax revenues? This is a measure of how much is unconditionally collected by the government. One salient issue is the Laffer curve that arises in the royalty case. This is because at a certain tax level the amount of distortion is so severe that it reduces total revenues.

Finally, I study how the different combinations of taxes affect the volatility of the tax revenues. In this case, I compute the taxes for each of the Monte Carlo simulations, and compute the net present value for each of them. The variance is then computed across all 500 paths. In other words, I do not compute the time-series variation as part of this measure. The reason is that I believe that governments are primarily concerned with the total collection of taxes first, and then the timing second. This is clearly an assumption, but I wanted to concentrate on only one of the sources of variation. Otherwise the analysis becomes cumbersome and it is hard to identify what is actually changing the variance of the tax revenues. In this case, I am certain the variation is across the different paths of prices.

7.3.1.2 Results The first set of results are concerned with the distortions created by the different taxes. From the government's standpoint, the distortion is measured as the net present value deviation of the production plan with and without taxes. There is another interesting dimension of the distortion, which is the total amount of barrels extracted. The first set of results is presented in figure 7.1 and the second, in figure 7.2.

Figure 7.1 shows the net present value of the production plan change as computed by equation (2). The thick continuous line is the distortion generated by increasing the corporate tax rate, while the thin dashed line is the distortion when the royalties are increased. Tax increases produce larger distortions in both cases. However, as can be seen, the increase in the distortion due to the income tax is extremely small in comparison to the distortion that occurs when the royalties are raised. A larger portion of the distortion comes from the fact that royalties decrease the absolute value of the total production. In other words, for a given amount of reserves, increases in royalties reduce the total barrels extracted.

Indeed, figure 7.2 shows the expected total production for the different royalties and income taxes. On the x-axis I present the tax rate (for both the royalties and the income taxes). The continuous line

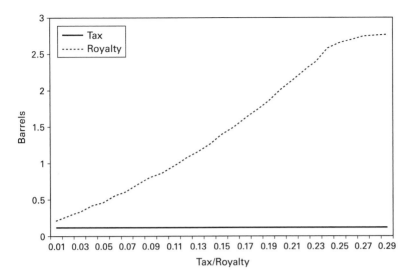

Figure 7.1
Expected net present value of production plan change

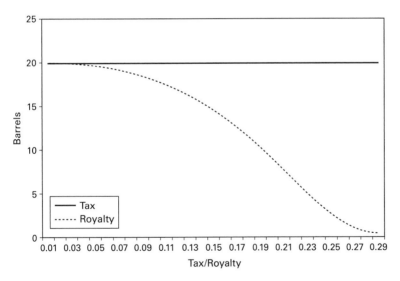

Figure 7.2
Expected total production

corresponds to the expected production under income taxes, while the dashed line is the total expected production for the royalty case.

Even in the absence of taxes, the firm leaves some resources under ground. Given the parameters chosen, the optimal total extraction is 19.86. Some resources are left because there are some paths along which the prices are so low that they do not pay the marginal cost. Furthermore, the more that has been exploited, the larger the marginal cost of the next unit—exacerbating the problem.

As can be seen, the income taxes have a negligible distortion. This is by construction. The way income taxes enter is by proportionally changing all profits in all states of the world, not affecting the first-order conditions faced by the firm. Indeed, the small differences that actually exist in the simulation are of the fourth order of magnitude, and I believe they are mostly the outcome of the approximation.

On the other hand, notice the severe distortion that exists when royalties are levied. In fact, there are tax rates that are so high that almost no production takes place. For taxes above 30 percent, production is indeed zero. This is a standard problem in the regulation of natural resources.

Having seen the impact of the tax rates on the firm' choices, it should be obvious that a Laffer curve exists for royalties. Figure 7.3 shows the

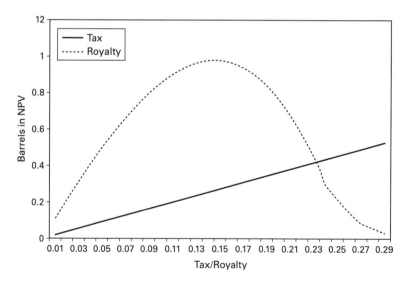

Figure 7.3
Expected tax revenues

net present value tax revenue for each simulation. The x-axis is as before, and as in the previous graph the continuous line reflects the tax revenues from using only income taxes, while the dashed line indicates the tax revenues from royalties.

As should have been expected, notice the Laffer curve in the royalties. Nevertheless, also notice that the collection of revenues is much faster—and more effective—using royalty taxes rather than income taxes. An important question that arises is whether the Laffer curve actually exists in reality. The case of Bolivia in recent years suggests that some Laffer curve indeed exists. In this case, the increase in prices was accompanied by increases in investments and tax credits such that the effective tax rate actually came down rather than rising. The case of Venezuela in the late 1960s provides more evidence, though this is mostly anecdotal. During that period, increases in taxes reduced investment and tax collection. In fact, most oil experts (such as Ramón Espinasa) believe that the tax-system debacle provided an important impetus to nationalization.

Finally, figure 7.4 illustrates the volatility of those taxes. I computed the coefficient of variation of the tax revenues for each choice of taxes. As the figure shows, for relatively large tax rates (very large indeed) the royalty is more volatile than the income tax is. However, for the

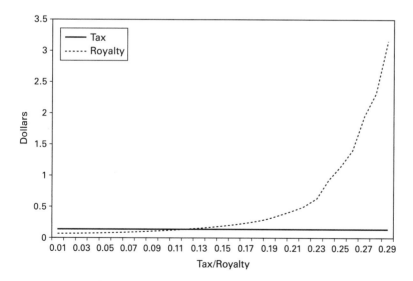

Figure 7.4
Expected volatility of tax revenues computed as the coefficient of variation

range of taxes in which it is usually fluctuating, the royalty is less volatile than the corporate tax.

This is a raw comparison between the two taxes. The real step that
needs to be taken in comparing the two different forms of taxation is
to fix the expected total revenues collected, and compare the variances.
This is the objective of the next subsection.

7.3.2 Volatility, Private Profits, and Expropriation

In this subsection as opposed to changing independently the two taxes,
I establish the total expected tax revenues (I choose 0.75), and determine the different mixtures of taxes that achieve this revenue level. I
vary the royalties from 0 to 10 percent, and compute the income tax
that will match the expected revenue with the target.

This is a very time-consuming process. The optimization is done by
searching along a range of income taxes. For each proposed tax the
whole value and policy functions are solved, the Monte Carlo exercises
are computed, and the expected revenue is calculated. That means that
each proposed pair requires the full solution of the problem.

7.3.2.1 Impact of Taxes on Private Profits The tax mixtures are
shown in figure 7.5. The thick continuous line at the top is the expected
total taxes (almost constant at 0.75; the only errors are for numerical

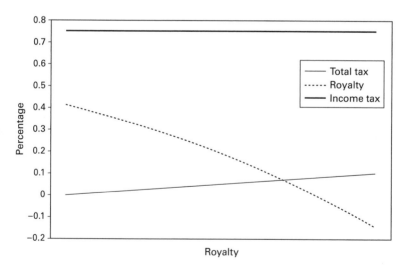

Figure 7.5
Tax mixtures and expected total tax revenues

approximation and are of the order of the fourth decimal). The thin continuous line is the royalty tax rates, and the dashed line is the income taxes.

Notice that for very high royalties there is actually an income subsidy. This is innocuous in terms of the message that the section is intended to convey. As the royalties are increased, as should be obvious, income taxes are reduced.

The next step is to compare the tax revenue volatility and the sensitivity of the production plan. Figure 7.6 shows the variance of tax revenues (the thick line measured on the right axis) and the variance of the production plan (the dashed line measured on the left axis). The variance in tax revenues is computed path by path. Interestingly, when royalties are increased, the variance in tax revenues drops. The intuitive explanation for this result is that because they are levied on sales, royalties are less volatile than profits. In fact, the coefficient of variation of royalties is smaller than the coefficient of variation of income taxes.[9]

At the same time, the variance in the quantity produced increases with the royalties. The reason is that when royalties are higher, quantities are more sensitive to price fluctuations. In fact, there are several paths in which quantities are severely reduced—almost zero. This sensitivity of the quantities produced is reflected in the increase in the unconditional variance of the total production.

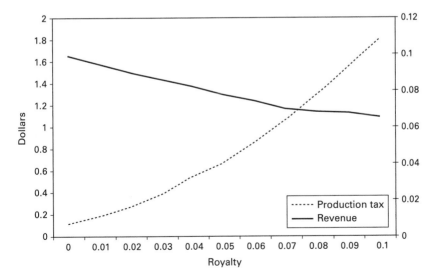

Figure 7.6
Tax mixtures and volatility: Tax revenues and production plans

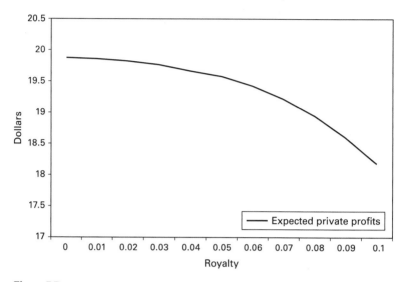

Figure 7.7
Tax mixtures and expected private profits

In general, governments care more about the variance in the tax revenues as opposed to the volatility of production and the degree of inefficiency. In other words, here it can be seen that an increase in the reliance of royalties stabilizes fiscal revenues—some stabilization—sacrificing on efficiency—lower production and higher sensitivity of production to price fluctuations. Because the cost of the inefficiency is mostly borne by the private sector, the government cares very little about it.

In figure 7.7 I present the expected private profits. As should have been expected, they decrease with the royalty rate. This is an indication that the private sector is the one paying for the distortion.

There is, however, another dimension that the royalty affects negatively. In figure 7.8 I present two measures of the profits of the firm that reflect extreme events. The thick continuous line represents the number of times the profits in the private sector are excessively high.[10] The thick line is measured on the left vertical axis. The dashed line indicates the maximum profit across all times and paths and is measured on the right vertical axis. As the figure shows, even though the average profit by the private sector drops with the increase in the royalty rate, the "extreme" events are more frequent. As noted earlier, if the probability of expropriation depends on conditional private profits,

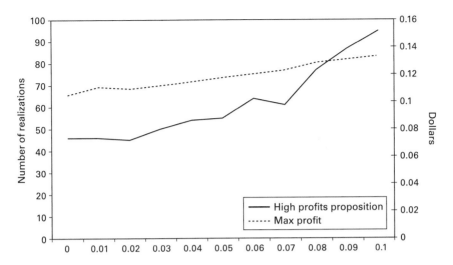

Figure 7.8
Tax mixtures and expropriation. Maximum profit and number of path with profits larger than threshold.

the trend in the tax mixture toward royalties increases the frequency of larger profits, raising the likelihood of expropriation.

In summary, the shift from pure income taxes toward royalties has one advantage—so far. The royalties provide a more stable source of income to the government. On the other hand, they bring bigger distortions in the production plan and higher dispersion of private profits, which might end up implying more probability of default. In the following section I extend the present model to discuss another "positive" aspect of the royalties—mainly the interaction between the tax code and the agency costs.

7.3.2.2 New Maximization Problem When the probability of default or expropriation is introduced in the problem, the maximization that the firm and the government face is as follows:

$$V(Q_t, p_t) = \max_q \left(\pi(q_t, Q_t, \bar{Q}, p_t, \tau_r, \tau_\pi, \Phi_t) + \frac{1}{1+\beta} E[V(Q_t + q_t, p'_t) \,|\, p_t] \right)$$

$$\pi(q_t, Q_t, \bar{Q}, p_t, \tau_r, \tau_\pi) = [p_t q_t(1 - \tau_r) - c(q_t, Q_t, \bar{Q})](1 - \tau_\pi)\Phi_t$$

$$\Phi_t = \phi(q_t, Q_t, \bar{Q}, p_t, \tau_r, \tau_\pi)$$

where Φ_t is the probability of expropriation. I assume that the firm loses everything and collects zero after the expropriation takes place.

The government solves the exact same problem as before

$$\min_{\tau_r, \tau_\pi} E \sum_{t=0}^{\infty} \frac{1}{(1+\beta)^t} (q_t - q_t^0)^2$$

$$E \sum_{t=0}^{\infty} \frac{1}{(1+\beta)^t} \tau_t \geq \bar{\tau}$$

$$Var\left(\sum_{t=0}^{\infty} \frac{1}{(1+\beta)^t} \tau_t\right) \leq \bar{\nu}$$

where it cares about the expropriation only to the extent that it affects the distortion, the tax revenues, and its volatility.

As noted earlier, the expropriation decision has been simplified

$$\exp = \begin{cases} 1 & if \quad \pi_t > \bar{\pi} \\ 0 & o.w. \end{cases}$$

where $\bar{\pi}$ is some threshold. The idea is that the expropriation (or default on the contract) occurs when the government perceives that the private sector is receiving "excess" profits. An alternative specification (proposed by Ricardo Hausmann during the discussion of the conference paper) is to base the expropriation decision on the value of the firm. In other words, rather than making decisions on the profits in some period of time, it makes sense that the expropriation occurs when the value of the firm is higher than some threshold. The reason I chose the specification above is twofold. First, it tremendously simplifies the problem of simulation. I am already computing the value function, but conditioning the probability of expropriation in some state of nature only on current profits is much simpler. Second, and probably more important, is the fact that in this problem I am solving the problem of only one project that has finite reserves—which means that the value function is decreasing in expected value. This implies that almost all expropriation occurs at time zero if the expropriation rule is based on the value function.

Notice that the risk of expropriation only affects the firm's choices. Because the expropriation is very costly for the firm, it chooses a production plan that makes profits in all states of the world less than or equal to $\bar{\pi}$.

When this constraint is added to the maximization problem, it is possible that no solution can be found for particular price paths. The intuition is as follows: Assume there are only two price paths, one that implies very high profits and the other very low profits. Because tax rates are not contingent on price level, expropriation takes place when prices are high. The firm reduces its profits in that path by cutting down production, which reduces tax revenue. If the government wants to keep taxes constant and volatility at the limit, then it has to increase both taxes, but royalties more than income taxes. The change in the tax mixture increases the probability of entering a default state, and depending on parameter values this increase can be so large that the shift reduces the probability of default. In those cases, for the tax revenue target there is no solution. Obviously, in those circumstances government will restrict its objectives—until it finds a solution.[11]

7.3.3   Introducing Small Agency Costs

In this section, I introduce small agency costs. The main reason I concentrate on smaller costs is because if agency incentives are severe, then the income tax also exhibits a Laffer curve, significantly complicating the analysis.

The idea behind the agency costs is to model private decisions that are wasteful but are able to reduce the tax burden. As I have argued earlier, most of those actions are "expenditures" and therefore affect the efficiency of income taxes more than sales taxes. In this chapter, wasteful expenditures are costly in terms of profits but reduce the tax burden proportionally to the tax rate. Therefore, if the income tax rate is high, the benefits of the wasteful expenditures are greater and the firm finds it profitable to incur them.

The only source of inefficiency that I consider is the tax reduction that takes place because of the agency costs. Figure 7.9 shows the ratio between the tax collection without agency costs and the tax collection when agency costs are present. This figure is similar to those in section 7.3.1.2. Each tax was increased independently from zero up to 15 percent. The tax rate is presented on the x-axis. The thick continuous line is the tax reduction when income taxes are used and the dashed line is the ratio when royalties are used.

Notice that the drop in taxes when royalties are present is extremely small. It is always less than 1.2 percent. The reason this drop is not exactly zero is that there are some paths in which the reduction in taxes is beneficial given the extremely high price level. This reduction in taxes allows for further production, and therefore the firm only finds it profitable to throw away money at those extremes.

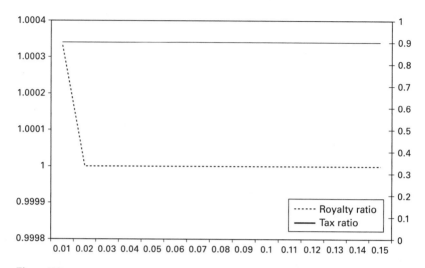

Figure 7.9
Reduction in expected tax revenues when small agency costs are introduced

On the other hand, when income taxes are in place, the distortions are much larger. All taxes drop by more than 10 percent, and the drop increases with the tax rate, meaning that higher tax rates motivate worse behavior.

7.4   Policy Lessons

The previous simulations can be summarized as follows. First, when governments have problems dealing with the volatility of tax revenues, the optimal regulation of oil and gas activities implies a tax mix that deviates from the one that would minimize the distortions. In the example developed in this chapter, corporate taxes represent the optimal taxation from an economic point of view, but because these taxes tend to be very volatile, the government shifts taxation toward sales and royalties, which are less volatile but more distortionary.

Second, this tax mix implies more volatile private profits. The reason is simple: tax mixtures that imply a more stable stream of tax revenues transfer the volatility to private profits. The increase in the volatility of private profits implies states of nature when profits are "extremely" large that culminate in a renegotiation of the contract or an expropriation.

Third, to avoid expropriation the firm reduces production—distorting the production plan even further—or incurs agency costs to reduce profits and the tax burden.

In summary, royalties are more distortionary and might create a greater risk of expropriation, but they are more stable and mitigate agency costs. On the other hand, corporate or income taxes are move volatile and induce agency costs, but they are more efficient and reduce the chances of expropriation. In this chapter, income taxes are exactly the same as any form of government ownership, hence the benefits and costs of joint ventures are also transferrable to the setup analyzed here.

In this section, I would consider another possibility. To avoid expropriation, the firm would be willing to keep production at the optimum level and pay additional taxes. This is clearly Pareto improving. Why wouldn't the firm do it? Because paying taxes in good times would increase the volatility of taxes, violating one of the constraints on the government. In fact, in this model, the anticipation of that "additional" transfer would change the tax mixture ex ante. Therefore, the firm is willing to make a transfer but it cannot do it to the government given the volatility concerns. One possibility is to make the transfer to the society directly. This can take the form of financing NGOs that will then deliver important improvements to society or the environment. It is crucial to remember that these transfers to the NGOs are extremely volatile; this is not a recurring expenditure but occurs only in booms and fluctuates with private profits. Nevertheless, it creates a local constituency that might defend the oil and gas industry at the time an expropriation is likely to occur. In other words, the transfers to the NGOs are greatest when the government is ready to expropriate the industry (during booms). This alternative, although not formally studied, produces less inefficiencies than the ones highlighted in this chapter—which involves changing the production plan.

7.5   Conclusions

This paper has discussed how optimal taxation is affected by three factors that are likely to appear in natural resource extractions: the desire to stabilize revenues, the need to reduce agency costs, and the expropriation incentive. I argue that those factors have negative effects on efficiency, and that trying to find a solution by changing the mixture of taxes is probably inappropriate, although this is the solution most countries pursue.

The paper has shown that problems start when the government is concerned about revenue stabilization. Indeed, one lesson from this exercise is that stabilization should be achieved by a different institution. Taxes, in the case of natural resource extraction, cannot handle the task. The implementation of a stabilization fund is crucial to be able to design a proper production contract. If the stabilization fund does not exist or is not credible, the implication is that the government will have incentives to distort the tax mixture, making agency costs and expropriation more likely.

The problem of expropriation cannot be solved using the standard contracting tricks; taxes are contingent, and profits in the private sector are driven to zero. Both are unrealistic, which means that in the end other arrangements are required. Government will set fixed taxes, and therefore it is in the best interest of the firms to create a local constituency that could be severely damaged in case of an expropriation. Some oil companies indeed spend on local services, but the experience in Alaska might suggest that transferring lump sums to local agents could be a more efficient and long-lasting strategy. Furthermore, if those transfers are tax deductible (like expenditures), it is in the best interest of the firm to actually develop local support.

Finally, sharing ownership has been highlighted as a possible vehicle for mitigating agency costs. This assumes that the government incurs less in agency costs than the private sector.[12] The problems of agency costs are reduced by relying on sales taxes, and indeed, that has been easily one of the most important benefits of sales taxes. Although this is an alternative, it is clear that future research should continue in this area. Nevertheless, the elimination of investment subsidies as well as of depreciation subsidies will go a long way in reducing the agency costs that plague the industry.

Notes

I would like to thank William Hogan and Federico Sturzenegger for their support and encouragement. I would also like to thank the participants at the Populism and Natural Resources Workshop for all their comments. Any remaining errors are mine.

1. See chapter 2 of this book.

2. See Manzano 2000 for a comprehensive discussion of the exploration and development of reserves. Future research should continue examining these important topics.

3. See Manzano and Monaldi 2008 for a political-economy explanation of this phenomenon.

4. See Manzano and Monaldi 2008 for a detailed description of the events.

5. This procedure is the standard one followed in the public finance literature and the one I use in this paper.

6. See, for instance, Rigobon 2004.

7. In an earlier version of the paper, I concentrated on the total production distortion. In other words, the objective function was

$$\min_{\tau_r, \tau_\pi} \left(\bar{Q} - E \sum_{t=0}^{\infty} q_t \right)$$

Notice that in this objective function, increasing production at one time and reducing it later has no impact on the optimization. Here the government is uniquely concerned with the total cumulative production.

The objective function that I have now puts weight on the total production but also on the timing. I thank all the discussants at the conference who pointed this improvement out to me.

8. There is nothing particularly interesting in the policy choices. The solutions are very standard. The interesting question is how those policy choices interact with the taxes, and that question is what is highlighted in the paper.

9. By forcing the tax mixture to collect exactly the same amount of resources, the exercise is comparing the implicit coefficients of variation.

10. In this simulation the assumption is that the profits are above 0.10 in any given period.

11. I thank Federico Sturzenegger and William Hogan for raising this point.

12. Maybe possible in Switzerland, but hard to believe in Latin America.

References

Emerson, C., and R. Garnaut. 1984. Mineral leasing policy: Competitive bidding and the resource rent tax given various responses to risk. *The Economic Record* 60: 133–142.

Garnaut, R., and A. Clunies. 1975. Uncertainty, risk aversion and the taxing of natural resource projects. *The Economic Journal* 85: 272–287.

Garnaut, R., and A. Clunies. 1979. The neutrality of the resource rent tax. *The Economic Record* 55: 193–201.

Giavazzi, F., J. Sheen, and C. Wyplosz. 1988. The real exchange rate and the fiscal aspects of a natural resource discovery. *Oxford Economic Papers* 40: 427–450.

Heaps, T., and F. Helliweel. 1985. The taxation of natural resources. In A. Aurbach and M. Feldstein, eds., *Handbook of Public Economics*, vol. 1. Amsterdam: North-Holland.

Karp, L., and J. Livernois. 1992. On efficiency-inducing taxation for a non-renewable resource monopolist. *Journal of Public Economics* 49: 219–239.

Kemp, A. 1989. Development risks and petroleum fiscal systems: A comparative study of the UK, Norway, Denmark and the Netherlands. *The Energy Journal* 13: 17–39.

Kemp, A., and D. Rose. 1984, Investment in oil exploration and production: The comparative influence of taxation. In: D. Pearce, H. Siebert, and I. Walter, eds., *Risk and the Political Economy of Resource Development*. New York: St. Martin's Press.

Krautkraemer, J. 1990. Taxation, ore quality selection, and the depletion of a heterogeneous deposit of a non-renewable resource. *Journal of Environmental Economics and Management* 18: 120–135.

Livernois J. 1991. A note on the effect of tax brackets on non-renewable resource extraction. *Journal of Environmental Economics and Management* 22: 272–280.

Manzano, Osmel. 2000. Tax effects upon oil field development in Venezuela. Center for Energy and Environmental Policy Research Working Papers Series Number 2000-006. Center for Energy and Environmental Policy Research at MIT, Cambridge.

Manzano, Osmel, and Francisco Monaldi. 2008. The political economy of oil production in Latin America. *Economia* 9, no. 1, Brookings/LACEA Publications, Washington.

Mueller, D. 1989. *Public Choice*. 2nd ed. Cambridge: Cambridge University Press.

Rigobon, Roberto. 2004. Comments on: "When it rains, it pours," by Graciela Kaminsky, Carmen Reinhart, and Carlos Vegh. *NBER Macro Annual*.

Rose, A., B. Stevens, and G. Davis. 1988. *Natural Resource Policy and Income Distribution*. Baltimore: John Hopkins University Press.

Rowse J. 1997. On ad valorem taxation of nonrenewable resource production. *Resource and Energy Economics* 19: 221–239.

Sansing, R. 1993. A note on alternative petroleum taxation. *Resource and Energy Economics* 15: 243–246.

Semmler, W. 1994. On the optimal regulation of an extractive industry. *Journal of Economics and Bussiness* 46: 409–420.

Sibley, D. 1989. Asymmetric information, incentives and price-cap regulation. *RAND Journal of Economics* 20: 392–404.

Spiegel, Y. 1996. The choice of technology and capital structure under rate regulation. *International Journal of Industrial Organization* 15: 191–216.

Train, K. 1991. *Optional Regulation: The Economic Theory of Natural Monopoly*. Cambridge, MA: MIT Press.

Vogelsand, I. 1988. A little paradox in the design of regulatory mechanisms. *International Economic Review* 29: 467–476.

Zhang, L. 1997. Neutrality and efficiency of petroleum revenue tax: A theoretical assessment. *The Economic Journal* 107: 1106–1120.

Commentary

Erich Muehlegger

Introduction

Contracts for resource extraction between firms and governments are often complex. In some respects, a contract between a firm and a government acts in similar ways to a contract between two private parties—the structure of the payments from the firm to the government affects the firm's incentives for production, investment, and exploration. In other respects, the relationship between the two parties is different—unlike a private party to a contract, the government can choose to "renegotiate" the contract at its choosing, by expropriating the assets of the firm. Roberto Rigobon's paper examines the merits of two methods of tax remittance common to resource extraction contracts: income taxes and revenue-proportional royalty payments. In particular, the paper investigates the incentives created by the two methods of tax remittance, emphasizing the trade-off between efficient incentives and the risk of expropriation.

Contracting with the risk of expropriation is similar to the problem of regulating a natural monopoly. Different methods of price regulation vary in the degree to which they allow the firm to earn profits as an inducement for cost savings or efficient production. Some methods of regulating prices provide good incentives but leave substantial rents to the firm, while other methods of regulating prices limit the profits a firm could earn but provide much weaker incentives for efficient production. Just as the government may expropriate the assets of a resource extraction firm, the regulator may choose to renegotiate the regulated price a firm is able to charge, essentially expropriating any cost-saving investment. Although ex ante welfare is improved if the regulator can commit to regulating prices in a way that provides strong incentives, the threat of renegotiation undermines the incentives of otherwise efficient contracts. Thus, policies that reduce the likelihood of renegotiation benefit both the firm and the regulator.

This commentary first summarizes the results Rigobon derives from his theoretical model. It then draws the analogy between the resource extraction with the risk of asset expropriation and the regulation of natural monopoly. Two stylized mechanisms, fixed-price and cost-plus regulation, are more extreme versions of the contracts that Rigobon analyzes and provide useful insight into the trade-off made when selecting the form of the contractual arrangement. In addition, the intuition about regulation of natural monopoly maps nicely to the case of expropriation and sheds some light on how government and firms may act to mitigate the risk of expropriation.

Overview of Rigobon's Paper

Rigobon compares the merits of two stylized contracts: an income tax levied on the profits earned by the firm, and a revenue-proportional royalty, whereby the firm remits a percentage of its revenues (rather than profits) to the government. To simplify the problem, he focuses on the production decision of the firm rather than on investment or exploration decisions. In this model, the government contracts with a firm to extract a finite, depletable resource. In each period, the firm observes the price of the resource in the current period, and knows the likelihood with which the price will rise or fall in all subsequent periods.[1] Since the future price is uncertain, the firm solves a dynamic optimization problem to determine the optimal production in the current period. On the margin, the solution equates its marginal profit in the current period with the present value of the profit it would expect if it saved the marginal unit of the resource for a later period. After producing, the firm reports its production and profits to the government and remits the appropriate taxes.

The model allows for two additional considerations important in actual resource extraction contracts. First, the firm faces some risk that the government will expropriate the assets—in the model, if the firm's profits exceed a fixed, known threshold, the government will expropriate firm assets (and all future profits from the resource) with certainty. Second, the firm can "misrepresent" its fixed costs to make it appear less profitable to the government. Agency costs, arising either through explicit fraud or through failure to exert an effort to reduce costs, are a common regulatory challenge.

To compare the contracts, Rigobon numerically simulates firm production and government revenues along the distribution of possible future price paths. The paper conducts two sets of analyses to compare income taxes and revenue-proportional royalties. First, it considers how firm behavior and government tax revenues change as the income tax rate and royalty rate vary. Rigobon then runs a set of simulations holding the expected government tax revenues constant, but allowing the government to select a contract that extracts tax revenue through a mix of income taxes and revenue-proportional royalties.

Rigobon evaluates the contractual arrangements along four dimensions. Of primary interest to the government, he first estimates the variability of government tax revenues—in particular, how much variation the government should expect to earn over the life of the resource for each of the contractual forms.[2] Rigobon finds that, holding the expected tax revenue constant, a revenue-based royalty provides the government with more certain total tax revenues over the life of the resource.

In addition, the simulations examine three sources of production distortion: (1) direct distortion from the contract changing optimal firm behavior, (2) indirect distortion affecting a firm's incentives to control costs (agency costs), and (3) indirect distortion arising from expropriation risk. The intuition for direct distortions follows from considering how the incentives created by the two tax systems differ from the incentives of a hypothetical firm that owned the resource outright. To induce the firm to extract at the efficient rate, the contract must provide the firm with identical intertemporal incentives to a firm owning the resource. To the extent that a contract provides different incentives, a firm may not only extract the resource at an inefficient rate, but may ultimately leave the resource underutilized. While an income tax reduces firm profits, it proportionally reduces both the current and future value of the resource—the dynamic solution does not change with the income tax rate. The revenue-proportional royalty, on the other hand, does distort production away from efficient behavior. As an example, when the resource price is just above the marginal cost of production, a firm owning the resource (or one subject to an income tax) would find it profitable to begin production. Since a firm facing a revenue-proportional royalty would have to pay taxes on revenues rather than profits, it will only find it profitable to produce when after-tax marginal revenue exceeds the marginal cost.[3]

The risk of expropriation and the ability of the firm to misrepresent its profits create two additional sources of distortion. The risk of expropriation will distort production in any situation in which the probability of government expropriation is positively correlated with firm profits. In Rigobon's model, the threat of expropriation distorts firm production if optimal firm production would generate profits that surpass the fixed, known expropriation threshold.[4] With a sufficiently high discount rate, the threshold acts as an upper bound on firm profits—a firm will produce up until the point at which profits equal the threshold. If profits from optimal production exceed the threshold, the firm will suboptimally produce so as not to trigger expropriation by the government. Consequently, contractual forms that generate high variance in firm profits will tend to distort firm production more than contractual firms that generate low-variance profits. Rigobon finds that, conditional on expected tax revenues, a revenue-proportional royalty leads to more volatile firm profits. Intuitively, since revenues exceed profits, the tax rate required to achieve a certain level of tax revenue in expectation is lower for a royalty than an income tax. Thus, in high-price periods, the firm retains a greater proportion of profits under a revenue-proportional royalty than an income tax.[5]

Agency costs arise in any case in which the regulator cannot reliably determine the efficient cost of production. Absent accurate observation, the regulator cannot determine whether the firm is producing in the most cost-effective way, or exerting optimal effort to keep costs low. Rigobon accounts for agency costs by allowing the firms to misrepresent the fixed cost of production to the regulator, and thus understating their profits to the government. If the tax schedule chosen by the government does not make the firm the residual claimant on the cost it reports, the contract will not provide efficient incentives for cost savings.[6] That is, if a firm's payoff does not change on a one-for-one basis with the cost of production reported to the government, the firm will lack the incentive to exert optimal effort to control costs, or in Rigobon's formulation, a firm will have the incentive to misrepresent the cost of production to the government. Under a revenue-proportional royalty, the firm's remittance is unrelated to fixed costs—thus, the contract provides efficient incentives for cost control. On the other hand, an income tax does not provide correct incentives. Facing an income tax, a firm only partially captures the benefits of a cost reduction, since a firm's taxes rise with profit.

The Analogy of Price Regulation

Rigobon's problem, the creation of an effective contract for resource extraction, is similar to a related, heavily studied problem in regulation, the setting of price in a regulated market. When regulating prices, the regulator faces challenges analogous to those the government faces when designing a resource extraction contract. On the one hand, the regulator (like the government) wants to create strong incentives for the firm to produce efficiently and to keep costs low. In order to provide the firm with efficient incentives, though, the regulator (again, like the government) must allow the firm the potential to earn substantial rents as a reward for efficient production or cost reductions. The primary challenge is that if a firm earns a "reward," the regulator now has an incentive to revisit the contract. As an example, if the firm identifies a way to substantially reduce the cost of production and earn substantial rents, the regulator (like Rigobon's government) has an incentive to renegotiate the contract, thereby expropriating the firm's innovation. As a result, the threat of renegotiation can distort firm behavior, just as the threat of expropriation can distort firm production decisions.

The two canonical mechanisms for setting price in a regulated industry, fixed-price regulation and cost-plus regulation, share similar benefits to the revenue-proportional royalty and the income tax. In setting a fixed price, the regulator allows the firm to be the residual claimant on cost savings achieved. That is, if the firm can identify ways to lower costs, fixed-price regulation allows the firm to claim the full amount of cost savings as additional profit. Consequently, the fixed-price contract provides excellent (and efficient) incentives for production and cost saving, but has the potential to leave substantial rents for the firm, as a reward for lowering the cost of production. This in turn creates an incentive for the regulator to renegotiate the contract postinnovation.

Using cost-plus regulation, the regulator reviews a firm's costs and sets a price to allow the firm to recoup a reasonable rate of return on its investment. If the costs of the firm change (either through innovation or agency costs), the regulated price adjusts so as to always leave the firm with a reasonable rate of return. In contrast to the fixed-price regulation, cost-plus regulation clearly provides very poor incentives for cost control. Any change to a firm's cost directly affects the regulated price it is able to charge—hence a firm receives no reward for an innovation that reduces production costs. Unlike fixed-price regulation,

Table 7.2
Relative merits of various contracts

	Fixed-price contract	Revenue-proportional royalty	Income tax	Cost-plus contract
Production distortion	No	Yes	No	Yes
Expropriation risk	Highest	High	Low	Lowest
Agency costs	No	No	Yes	Yes
Variability of tax revenue	Lowest	Low	High	Highest

though, cost-plus regulation closely controls the profits a firm is able to earn. In principle, it guarantees that the firm earns a precisely fair rate of return on any investment. Although it provides very poor cost-saving incentives—the firm only earns a fair rate of return—the regulator never has an incentive to try to capture firm profits through renegotiation.

In the context of resource extraction, fixed-price and cost-plus regulation correspond to a per-unit royalty (or auctioned extraction rights) and a contract in which the government essentially rents the capital from the firm. In fact, the two forms of regulation are more extreme than the revenue-proportional royalty and income tax studied by Rigobon. Table 7.2 compares royalties and income taxes with the contractual forms analogous to fixed-price and cost-plus regulation along each of the four dimensions of interest to Rigobon. A fixed-price contract provides excellent incentives for the firm. Since the firm becomes the residual claimant on cost-saving and production decisions, the firm has no direct incentive to distort production or misrepresent costs to the regulator. In addition, a fixed-price contract provides the least variable tax revenues.[7] Since the firm is the residual claimant on profits, though, the risk of expropriation is greatest. On the other hand, a cost-plus contract, in which the government pays the firm a fair rate of return on the investment and then sells the extracted resource to generate revenue, provides very poor incentives. The firm has little incentive to extract at an efficient rate and has a strong incentive to misrepresent its costs. In addition, since the government revenue comes entirely from resource sales, tax volatility is greatest with a cost-plus contract. The benefit, though, is that there is very little risk of expropriation—the firm only receives a fair rate of return on its cost of extraction.

Lessons for Resource Extraction

The analogy of price regulation provides a clear way in which resource extraction contracts can be improved. The fixed-price contract (or per-unit royalty) provides better incentives for extraction than an income tax or cost-plus contract. In addition, agency costs are less of a concern and the variability of tax revenue is lower with a fixed-price contract than with an income tax or equivalent cost-plus contract. Absent expropriation risk, the fixed-price contract provides strictly better incentives than cost-plus style contracts and is strictly preferable from a welfare perspective.

Fundamentally, expropriation risk arises because the current government cannot credibly commit future governments to honor the contract, even though both the firm and the current government would be better off if such commitment were possible. Future governments have an ex post incentive to revisit the contract after the firm has either made investments or captured rents through cost savings. This potential threat of renegotiation distorts firm behavior away from the optimum. Thus, policies that reduce the risk of expropriation reduce distortion for a given contract, as well as allowing the regulator to credibly select contracts ex ante that provide better incentives.[8]

In his conclusions, Rigobon discusses how the firm can reduce the risk of expropriation, and thereby reduce the production distortion. Specifically, he discusses the importance of establishing local relationships as a hedge against expropriation. In periods of high profit, the firm can make transfers to local communities to build support among the local constituency, which in turn might protect the firm from government expropriation. A particularly attractive aspect of this strategy is that transfers occur during high-profit periods—the very periods in which government expropriation is most likely to occur. Fundamentally, local relationships reduce the risk of expropriation by increasing the cost associated with it; when the firm transfers rents a local community, expropriation harms both the firm and the local constituency.

The literature on price regulation suggests additional strategies a government could adopt to reduce the risk of expropriation. These strategies focus on making it easier for the regulator to intertemporally commit to honoring the extraction contract at a later date. In cases in which government contracts are renewed at regular intervals, maintaining a credible reputation for honoring contracts may be a sufficient incentive to prevent expropriation. Negotiating with a reputable government, a firm faces less of a chance that its assets will be expropriated—hence it may be willing to sign a contract more favorable to the government than it would if it felt there was a high chance of expropriation. In some cases, such as parcel-level oil leases, the incentive to maintain a credible reputation in future negotiations may be sufficient to deter government expropriation. Alternatively, the government could offer concessions to the firm at the time of contracting that make expropriation less attractive to future governments. For example, the government could offer arbitration in an international court—if arbitration is a credible commitment, or if it increases the costs of expropriation, such a concession could raise the expropriation threshold and reduce the accompanying distortion.

Notes

1. Storage costs are assumed to be sufficiently high so that a firm has no incentive to extract the resource in one period and hold it until a later period.

2. Rigobon focuses on variability of total government tax revenue over the life of the resource. Although partially captured in the risk of expropriation, if tax revenues play a fiscal role, governments likely also care about the expected variation over time as the resource is extracted. An interesting extension to the model could also consider the degree of variation as the resource is extracted.

3. Although Rigobon finds that, conditional on expected total tax revenues, the variance associated with the total tax revenues from revenue-proportional royalties is lower than that from an income tax, the production distortion suggests that it is possible for the intertemportal variance in tax rates to be greater under revenue-proportional royalties. Specifically, revenue-proportional royalties provide lower-variance tax revenues when the firm chooses to produce, but increase the probability that the firm decides to leave the resource idle.

4. Rigobon measures the risk of expropriation as the frequency with which an unconstrained firm operating under a particular contract would exceed the threshold. Alternatively, the risk of expropriation could be measured as the variability of firm profits.

5. Any contract splits the price uncertainty between the firm and the government. An alternative intuition for why the risk of expropriation is greater with the revenue-proportional royalty follows from realizing that the uncertainty borne by the government tends to be lower with the royalty—hence the uncertainty (in profits) borne by the firm is greater.

6. Alternatively, in Rigobon's formulation an inefficient contract creates the incentive for the firm to misrepresent its cost of production to the regulator.

7. In principle, auctioned rights provide completely certain total tax revenues—in a second-price auction, each firm's optimal strategy is to bid the net present value of the future stream of expected profits.

8. In the model, reducing the risk of expropriation is analogous to raising the profit threshold above which the government will expropriate with certainty.

8 Pricing Expropriation Risk in Natural Resource Contracts: A Real Options Approach

Eduardo S. Schwartz and Anders B. Trolle

8.1 Introduction

There are many dimensions to the study of expropriation risk in natural resources including political, environmental, sociological, and economic issues. In this chapter we abstract from most of these aspects and concentrate on some of the important economic trade-offs that arise from the government having an option to expropriate the resource.

We show how to use the real-options approach in valuing a natural resource project, in particular an oil field, exposed to expropriation risk.[1] We view the government as holding an option to expropriate the oil field.[2] The government faces a trade-off. By expropriating, it will receive all future profits from the oil field rather than just a fraction of the profits through taxes. However, there are also costs associated with expropriating, and we consider three such costs. First, a state-run company may produce oil less cost-efficiently than a private firm. Second, the government may have to pay compensation to the firm. Third and perhaps most important, there may be "reputational" costs in the sense that investors will perceive the government as being more likely to renege on other contracts as well, and will therefore be more reluctant to make new investments in the country, particularly in capital-intensive natural resource projects, negatively affecting the overall economy.

The dynamics of the crude-oil spot price, futures prices, and volatility that we use for the analysis is described by a model proposed in Trolle and Schwartz 2009. This model has several attractive features. Futures prices are driven by two factors, with one factor affecting the spot price of the commodity and another factor affecting the slope of the futures curve through the cost of carry. Futures (and spot) price volatility is stochastic and is driven by a third factor, which implies that options are driven by three factors and that the model features "unspanned stochastic volatility" (that is, volatility risk cannot be completely hedged by trading in futures contracts) consistent with the data. The model has quasianalytical prices of European-style options on futures contracts, enabling fast calibration to liquid plain-vanilla exchange-traded derivatives. Finally, the dynamics of the futures curve can be described in terms of four state variables (three stochastic and one deterministic) jointly constituting an affine state vector, which makes the model ideally suited for pricing complex commodity derivatives, including real options, such as the expropriation option, by simulation.[3]

In Trolle and Schwartz 2009, the model was estimated and tested on NYMEX[4] crude-oil derivatives using an extensive panel data set of 45,517 futures prices and 233,104 option prices from January 2, 1990, until May 18, 2006, ensuring that the model provides a realistic description of the dynamics of the crude-oil market. This allows us to make not only qualitative, but also quantitative, predictions about the value of the expropriation option in various scenarios.

The expropriation option is an American-style option, since it can be exercised at any time during the life of the project. To value the option by simulation we use the Least Squares Monte Carlo (LSM) approach developed by Longstaff and Schwartz (2001). At every point in time, the government must compare the value of immediate exercise (expropriation) with the conditional expected value (under the risk-neutral measure) from continuation. The conditional expected value of continuation, for each simulated path at each point in time, can be obtained from the fitted value of the linear regression of the discounted value (at the risk-free rate) of the cash flows obtained from the simulation following the optimal exercise policy in the future, on a set of basis functions of the state variables. It is a recursive procedure starting from the maturity of the option, and the outcome is the optimal exercise time for each path in the simulation. Knowing the optimal exercise time for each path, the expropriation option can then be easily valued. We can also estimate the value of the oil field to the government and to the firm both in the presence and absence of expropriation risk.

We find that, for a given contractual arrangement, the value of the expropriation option increases with the spot price, the slope of the futures curve, and futures (and spot) price volatility. For a given set of state variables the value of the expropriation option decreases with the tax rate and with the various expropriation costs. Under realistic conditions, the value of the expropriation option is substantial and expropriation risk has a significant impact on the value of the oil field to the government and to the firm. We also find that if the government switches from corporate income taxes to royalty taxes in such a way that the value of the oil field to the government in the absence of expropriation risk is unchanged, the value of the expropriation option increases. Finally, from the firm's point of view there is an "optimal" corporate income tax rate, which may be quite high in order to reduce the incentive for the government to expropriate.

With rational expectations, the firm will anticipate the situations under which the government expropriates. This implies that the increase in the oil field's value to the government due to expropriation risk is smaller than the decrease in the field's value to the firm, since oil may be extracted at a higher cost after the government expropriates and since there may be "reputational" costs to the government. In this sense, there is a "deadweight loss" associated with the possibility of expropriation. The reduction in the field's value to the firm due to expropriation risk is exactly matched by a reduction in the amount that the firm will be willing to bid during the process when the government auctions off the lease for the field. Hence, the total value that the government can extract from the field is smaller in the presence of expropriation risk than in the absence of expropriation risk. It would therefore be optimal for the government to commit itself to not expropriating the field, although such a commitment is not believable in countries without a credible legal framework to enforce contracts.

In our analysis, we will abstract from the various operational options that are typically embedded in natural resource projects. These include options to adjust production as prices increase or decrease and the option to abandon the project if prices become too low. Because of the flexibility of the LSM approach, such options could be incorporated into the analysis. However, in the interest of parsimony, and because a wide variety of operational options have already been analyzed in the literature (see, e.g., Brennan and Schwartz 1985 for an early paper), we do not include them here.

A couple of other papers also view expropriation risk through the lens of option pricing. These include Mahajan 1990 and Clark 2003, which both value an American-style expropriation option. However, in these papers the underlying models of uncertainty are highly stylized in order to obtain closed-form solutions for the expropriation option.[5]

The structure of the paper is as follows. Section 8.2 discusses the pricing of expropriation risk. Section 8.3 analyzes a stylized illustrative example. Section 8.4 concludes. Appendix A briefly describes the modeling of the crude-oil market. Appendix B describes the LSM procedure used for pricing the expropriation option.

8.2   Pricing Expropriation Risk

We assume that the oil field has a life of T years. For the purpose of valuation we divide the T years into N periods, each with a length of $\Delta t = T/N$, and define $t_n = n\Delta t$, $n = 0, 1, \ldots, N$. We assume that oil produced during period n (i.e., from t_{n-1} to t_n) is sold at the end of the period. The amount sold at time t_n is denoted $Y(t_n)$.

Let $S(t_i)$ be the time t_i spot price of crude oil and $F(t_i, t_n)$ be the time t_i price of a futures contract maturing at time t_n. The dynamics of $S(t_i)$ and $F(t_i, t_n)$ are given by the model proposed and estimated in Trolle and Schwartz 2009. For completeness, this model is summarized in appendix A.

Let r be the (constant) interest rate, τ_{inc} the corporate income tax rate, τ_{roy} the royalty tax rate, and C_{firm} and C_{gov} the cost of producing one barrel of oil for the private firm and the state-run company, respectively. We assume that the private firm may produce oil more cost-efficiently than the state-run company (i.e., $C_{firm} \leq C_{gov}$), and that the government may pay a compensation to the firm, $K_1(t_i)$, and incur "reputational" costs, $K_2(t_i)$, if expropriating the oil field at time t_i.

Harrison and Kreps (1979), Harrison and Pliska (1981), and others have shown that the absence of arbitrage implies the existence of a probability distribution such that securities are priced based on their discounted (at the risk-free rate) expected cash flows, where the expectation is taken under this risk-neutral probability measure (also called the "equivalent martingale measure"). When futures contracts exist, futures prices are the expected spot prices at the maturities of the futures contracts under this risk-neutral measure.

If the government expropriates the oil field at time t_i, it will lose future tax receipts from the firm and may pay a compensation to the firm and incur "reputational" costs. This has a present value of

$$V_{cost}(t_i) = \sum_{n=i+1}^{N} e^{-r(t_n - t_i)}[(F(t_i, t_n)(1 - \tau_{roy}) - C_{firm})\tau_{inc} + F(t_i, t_n)\tau_{roy}]$$

$$\times\, Y(t_n) + K_1(t_i) + K_2(t_i). \tag{1}$$

Instead it will receive all future profits from the oil field, which may now have higher production costs, with a present value of

$$V_{gain}(t_i) = \sum_{n=i+1}^{N} e^{-r(t_n-t_i)}(F(t_i,t_n) - C_{gov})Y(t_n). \tag{2}$$

Let $\Pi(t_i)$ denote the (undiscounted) payoff from exercising the expropriation option at time t_i. It is given by

$$\Pi(t_i) = \max(V_{gain}(t_i) - V_{cost}(t_i), 0). \tag{3}$$

The option is of the American type since it can be exercised at any time before the oil field has been depleted. In particular, we assume that it can be exercised at time t_n, $n = 1,\dots,N-1$.[6] Let $P(t_i)$ denote the value of the option at time t_i, given that it has not already been exercised. At time t_{N-1} the option value is simply

$$P(t_{N-1}) = \Pi(t_{N-1}). \tag{4}$$

At time t_i, $i = 1,\dots,N-2$ the value is given by

$$P(t_i) = \max_{n=i,\dots,N-1} E_{t_i}^Q[e^{-r(t_n-t_i)}\Pi(t_n)]$$

$$= \max(\Pi(t_i), E_{t_i}^Q[e^{-r(t_{i+1}-t_i)}P(t_{i+1})]). \tag{5}$$

In other words, prior to t_{N-1} the option value is equal to the maximum of exercising the option immediately and the (risk-neutral) expected discounted value of keeping the option alive. This means that we can value the option by a backward iterative procedure starting with (4) to obtain $P(t_{N-1})$, then applying (5) recursively to obtain $P(t_{N-2})$, $P(t_{N-3})$, and so on until we reach $P(t_1)$. Then $P(t_0) = e^{-r(t_1-t_0)}P(t_1)$.

The main problem is how to compute the conditional expectation in (5). This is a nontrivial matter with a high-dimensional state vector such as the one used in this chapter. A simple and powerful procedure for pricing American options was suggested by Longstaff and Schwartz (2001). It is a simulation-based procedure called Least Squares Monte Carlo. We describe the procedure in more detail in appendix B. It yields an estimate of the option price as well as an estimate of the optimal exercise strategy.

Suppose we simulate M paths.[7] Let t_{Z_m} denote the estimated time of expropriation along path m (with $Z_m = N$ if no expropriation takes place) and $S_m(t_n)$ the spot price at time t_n along path m. Then, the value of the oil field to the firm in the presence of expropriation risk is

$$
V_{firm}^{exp}(t_0) = \frac{1}{M} \sum_{m=1}^{M} \left(\sum_{n=1}^{Z_m} e^{-r(t_n - t_0)} (S_m(t_n)(1 - \tau_{roy}) - C_{firm})(1 - \tau_{inc})Y(t_n) \right.
$$

$$
\left. + e^{-r(t_{Z_m} - t_0)} K_1(t_{Z_m}) \right),
\tag{6}
$$

while the value of the oil field to the government is

$$
V_{gov}^{exp}(t_0) = \frac{1}{M} \sum_{m=1}^{M} \left(\sum_{n=1}^{Z_m} e^{-r(t_n - t_0)} [(S_m(t_n)(1 - \tau_{roy}) - C_{firm})\tau_{inc} \right.
$$

$$
+ S_m(t_n)\tau_{roy}]Y(t_n) - e^{-r(t_{Z_m} - t_0)}(K_1(t_{Z_m}) + K_2(t_{Z_m}))
$$

$$
\left. + \sum_{n=Z_m+1}^{N} e^{-r(t_n - t_0)}(S_m(t_n) - C_{gov})Y(t_n) \right).
\tag{7}
$$

In the absence of expropriation risk, the value of the oil field to the firm and the value to the government are given analytically. The value to the firm is

$$
V_{firm}(t_0) = \sum_{n=1}^{N} e^{-r(t_n - t_0)}(F(t_0, t_n)(1 - \tau_{roy}) - C_{firm})(1 - \tau_{inc})Y(t_n),
\tag{8}
$$

while the value to the government is[8]

$$
V_{gov}(t_0) = \sum_{n=1}^{N} e^{-r(t_n - t_0)} [(F(t_0, t_n)(1 - \tau_{roy}) - C_{firm})\tau_{inc} + F(t_0, t_n)\tau_{roy}]Y(t_n).
$$
$$
\tag{9}
$$

8.3   Illustrative Example

8.3.1   Baseline Parameters

We consider a medium-sized oil field with an annual production of 10 million barrels for ten years. In the baseline case, we make the following assumptions: In case of expropriation, the government incurs "reputational" costs of US$1.0 billion and pays the firm a compensation of US$50 million times the remaining life of the oil field measured in years.[9] Furthermore, the private firm has a production cost of US$10

Table 8.1
Parameter estimates of the pricing model

	Estimate	Standard error
κ_v	1.0125	0.0123
σ_v	2.8226	0.0212
α	0.1365	0.0024
γ	0.7796	0.0011
σ_S	0.2275	0.0017
ρ_{12}	−0.8797	0.0040
ρ_{13}	−0.0912	0.0018
ρ_{23}	−0.1128	0.0116
φ	0.0054	0.0001

Note: The table shows maximum-likelihood estimates of the pricing model outlined in appendix A, based on daily data of NYMEX crude oil futures and options. For details, see Trolle and Schwartz 2009. This table is an excerpt from their table 1.

per barrel (bl), while the state-run company has a production cost of US\$15/bl, the corporate income tax rate is 60 percent, and the royalty tax rate is zero.[10] The sensitivity of the results to these assumptions will be examined later. Finally, we assume an interest rate of 5 percent and that expropriation can take place monthly. In the notation of section 8.2 we have $T = 10$, $N = 120$, $Y(t_i) = \Delta t \times 10$ million bls, $K_1(t_i) = (T - t_i) \times$ US\$50 million, $K_2(t_i) =$ US\$1,000 million, $C_{firm} =$ US\$10/bl, $C_{gov} =$ US\$15/bl, $\tau_{inc} = 0.60$, $\tau_{roy} = 0$, and $r = 0.05$. Table 8.1 displays parameter estimates of the pricing model outlined in Appendix A.

In the following, we will focus on four statistics:

1. The dollar value of the expropriation option: $P(t_0)$.

2. The "deadweight loss" associated with the possibility of expropriation: $(V_{gov}(t_0) + V_{firm}(t_0)) - (V_{gov}^{exp}(t_0) + V_{firm}^{exp}(t_0))$. The "deadweight loss" is due to the "reputational" costs and the fact that oil is extracted at a higher cost after the government expropriates. This implies that the increase in the oil field's value to the government because of the expropriation risk is always smaller than the decrease in the oil field's value to the firm.

3. The percentage increase in the oil field's value to the government when taking into account the expropriation possibility: $V_{gov}^{exp}(t_0)/V_{gov}(t_0) - 1$.

4. The percentage decrease in the oil field's value to the firm when taking into account the expropriation possibility: $-(V_{firm}^{exp}(t_0)/V_{firm}(t_0) - 1)$.

8.3.2   Results

8.3.2.1   Expropriation Risk as a Function of State Variables   We first investigate how these key statistics depend on the state variables. Figure 8.1 shows the state variables over the period January 2, 1990, to May 18, 2006, as estimated by Trolle and Schwartz 2009. $S(t)$ is the spot price, $x(t)$ determines the slope of the futures curve through the cost of carry, $v(t)$ determines futures (and spot) price volatility, and $\phi(t)$ is a locally deterministic state variable that enables the dynamics of the futures curve to be described by a Markov process.

We first vary $S(t)$ and $x(t)$, holding $v(t)$ constant at its long-run mean of 2.79 over the sample. Based on figure 8.1, a realistic range for $S(t)$ is US\$20/bl to US\$80/bl,[11] while a realistic range for $x(t)$ is −3 to 3. To give a sense of how $S(t)$ and $x(t)$ affect the futures curve, figure 8.2 shows the futures curve at four extreme combinations of $S(t)$ and $x(t)$: (US\$20/bl, −3), (US\$20/bl, 3), (US\$80/bl, −3), and (US\$80/bl, 3). Clearly, the futures curve is strongly in backwardation (downward sloping) when $x(t) = -3$, while the futures curve is strongly in contango (upward sloping) when $x(t) = 3$. Since the correlation between innovations to $S(t)$ and $x(t)$ is strongly negative (the estimate of ρ_{12} is −0.88 in table 8.1), it is most likely that $x(t)$ decreases as $S(t)$ increases. That is, the futures curve is most likely to be in contango (upward sloping) when the spot price is low and in backwardation when the spot price is high.

Figure 8.3 shows how the key statistics depend on $S(t)$ and $x(t)$. Not surprisingly, the dollar value of the expropriation option, the "deadweight loss," and the increase (decrease) of the oil field's value to the government (firm) all rise with $S(t)$ and $x(t)$. When the spot price is low there is little incentive to expropriate given the various expropriation costs. The incentive is even smaller if the futures curve is in backwardation, since in that case spot prices are expected (under the risk-neutral measure) to decrease in the future. In contrast, when the spot price is high and the futures curve is in contango, the incentive to expropriate is higher since the prospect of receiving all the profits rather than a fraction of the profits may dominate the expropriation costs. For high spot prices and upward-sloping futures curves, the value of the expropriation option and the "deadweight loss" are very large. Keep in mind, though, that a scenario where the futures curve is strongly in contango at high spot prices is not very likely given the historical dynamics.

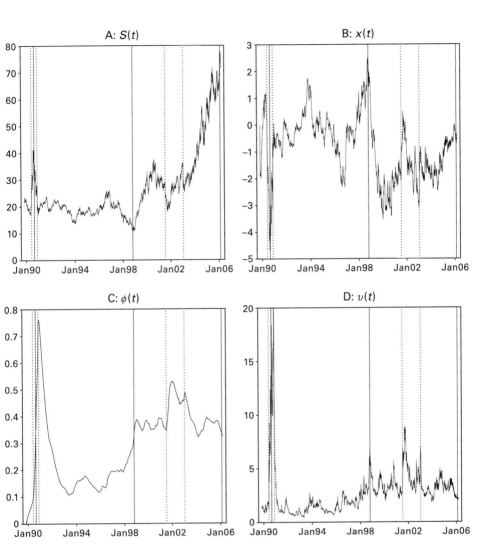

Figure 8.1
Time series of state variables. The figure shows time series of the state variables as estimated by Trolle and Schwartz (2009). The vertical dotted lines mark the Iraqi invasion of Kuwait on August 2, 1990; the beginning of the U.S.-led liberation of Kuwait ("Operation Desert Storm") on January 17, 1991; the September 11, 2001, terrorist attacks; and the U.S.-led invasion of Iraq on March 20, 2003, respectively. The vertical gray lines mark the three dates that we investigate further in table 8.2: October 11, 1990; December 21, 1998; and April 21, 2006. Each time series consists of 4,082 daily observations from January 2, 1990, to May 18, 2006.

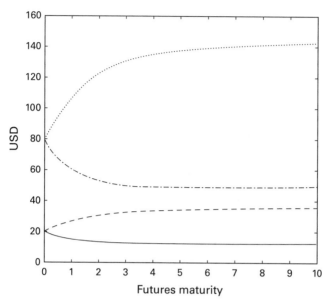

Figure 8.2
Futures curves. The figure shows the futures curves for different combinations of $S(t)$
and $x(t)$. ——— corresponds to $S(t) = 20$ and $x(t) = -3$, --- corresponds to $S(t) = 20$ and
$x(t) = 3$, -·- corresponds to $S(t) = 80$ and $x(t) = -3$, and ······ corresponds to $S(t) = 80$
and $x(t) = 3$.

To give a sense of expropriation risk under reasonable market conditions, we analyze the following three specific dates in the sample: October 11, 1990, December 21, 1998, and April 21, 2006 (in figure 8.1
these dates are marked by vertical lines). The first date is the date
when the spot price reaches its maximum during the first Gulf War
and also corresponds to the date where $x(t)$ attains its minimum during the sample period. The second date is the date when the spot price
reaches its minimum and $x(t)$ reaches its maximum during the sample
period. These two dates clearly illustrate the inverse relationship that
normally exists between the spot price and the slope of the futures
curve. The last date corresponds to the date when the spot price
reaches its maximum during the sample period. Note that the futures
curve is not strongly backwardated at this date, reflecting the fact that
the slope of the futures curve also exhibits variation that is independent of the spot price. Table 8.2 shows the values of the state variables
and a number of statistics related to the possibility of expropriation on
these three dates. On the first two dates, the value of the expropriation

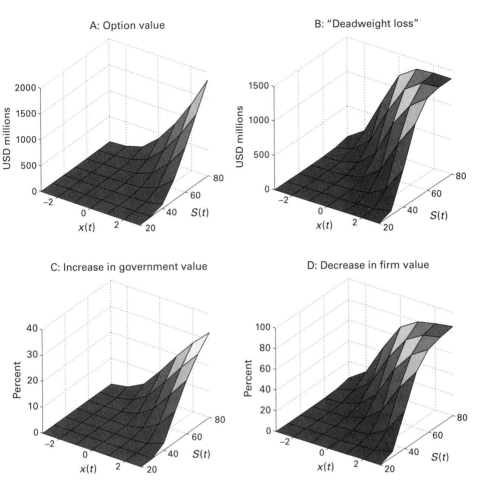

Figure 8.3
Expropriation risk as a function of $S(t)$ **and** $x(t)$**.** Panel A shows the value of the expropriation option, panel B shows the "deadweight loss," panel C shows the percentage increase in the oil field's value to the government when taking into account the expropriation possibility, and panel D shows the percentage decrease in the oil field's value to the firm when taking into account the expropriation possibility.

Table 8.2
Expropriation risk on three specific dates

	Oct. 11, 1990	Dec. 21, 1998	April 21, 2006
$S(t_0)$	41.26	10.62	78.03
$x(t_0)$	-4.67	2.49	-0.78
$\phi(t_0)$	0.29	0.33	0.33
$v(t_0)$	13.72	7.11	2.17
$P(t_0)$, US\$ million	0.55	0.05	159.18
$V_{gov}(t_0)$, US\$ million	557.45	296.74	2966.30
$V_{gov}^{exp}(t_0)$, US\$ million	558.00	296.78	3125.49
$V_{gov}^{exp}(t_0)/V_{gov}(t_0) - 1$, %	0.10	0.02	5.37
$V_{firm}(t_0)$, US\$ million	371.63	197.82	1977.53
$V_{firm}^{exp}(t_0)$, US\$ million	370.66	197.64	993.06
$V_{firm}^{exp}(t_0)/V_{firm}(t_0) - 1$, %	-0.26	-0.09	-49.78
"Deadweight loss," US\$ million	0.42	0.14	825.29

Note: The table shows, on three specific dates, the values of the state variables; the value of the expropriation option $(P(t_0))$; the oil field's value to the government without and with expropriation possibility and the percentage change in value $(V_{gov}(t_0), V_{gov}^{exp}(t_0),$ and $V_{gov}^{exp}(t_0)/V_{gov}(t_0) - 1$, respectively); the oil field's value to the firm without and with expropriation possibility and the percentage change in value $(V_{firm}(t_0), V_{firm}^{exp}(t_0),$ and $V_{firm}^{exp}(t_0)/V_{firm}(t_0) - 1$, respectively); and the "deadweight loss"—that is, $(V_{gov}(t_0) + V_{firm}(t_0)) - (V_{gov}^{exp}(t_0) + V_{firm}^{exp}(t_0))$.

option and the "deadweight loss" are very small. On the third date, however, expropriation risk is high. The value of the expropriation option is US\$159 million and the valuation of the oil field is significantly affected.[12] The value of the field to the firm (government) is US\$1,978 (US\$2,966) million in the absence of expropriation risk compared with US\$993 (US\$3,125) million in the presence of expropriation risk. For the firm, this is a decrease in value of almost 50 percent. There is also a very large "deadweight loss" of US\$825 million.

We next vary $S(t)$ and $v(t)$, holding $x(t)$ constant at zero (corresponding to a slightly upward-sloping futures curve). Figure 8.1 shows that $v(t)$ reached almost 20 at the beginning of Operation Desert Storm in 1991—a time of extreme market stress. Therefore, we vary $v(t)$ between 0 and 20. Figure 8.4 shows how the key statistics depend on $S(t)$ and $v(t)$. Consistent with standard option pricing theory, the dollar value of the expropriation option, and therefore the increase in the oil field's value to the government, rises with volatility. However, the oil field's value to the firm and the "deadweight loss" are not necessarily increasing in volatility. In fact, for high spot prices they are decreasing in volatility since the likelihood of expropriation may decrease.

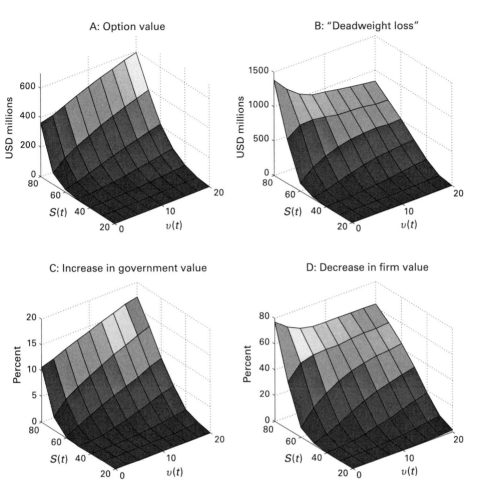

Figure 8.4
Expropriation risk as a function of $S(t)$ **and** $v(t)$. Panel A shows the value of the expropriation option, panel B shows the "deadweight loss," panel C shows the percentage increase in the oil field's value to the government when taking into account the expropriation possibility, and panel D shows the percentage decrease in the oil field's value to the firm when taking into account the expropriation possibility.

8.3.2.2 Expropriation Risk as a Function of Tax Rate and Expropriation Costs   We now investigate how, for a given set of state variables, the statistics depend on the tax rate and the expropriation costs.[13] Figure 8.5 shows how the key statistics depend on τ_{inc} and K_2, when we vary τ_{inc} between zero and 100 percent and K_2 between zero and US\$2,000 million. The dollar value of the expropriation option and the increase (decrease) in the oil field's value to the government (firm) all decline with τ_{inc} and K_2. When the tax rate is 100 percent, the government never expropriates, since it receives all profits from the oil field. In contrast, for low tax rates and low "reputational" costs, the government almost certainly expropriates. In these instances, the value of the expropriation option may easily exceed US\$1 billion.

For a given K_2, the "deadweight loss" decreases with τ_{inc} since the expropriation likelihood decreases with τ_{inc}. However, for a given τ_{inc}, the "deadweight loss" as a function of K_2 is "hump shaped." The reason is that there are two opposing forces: although the expropriation likelihood decreases with K_2, the inefficiency is greater when expropriation occurs. For low tax rates and high (although not extreme) "reputational" costs, the "deadweight loss" may also exceed US\$1 billion.

Figure 8.6 shows how the key statistics depend on K_2 and C_{gov}, when we vary K_2 between US\$0 and US\$2,000 million and C_{gov} between US\$10/bl (i.e., equal to C_{firm}) and US\$20/bl. Except for the "deadweight loss," figure 8.6 is qualitatively similar to figure 8.5. However, the "deadweight loss" now exhibits a hump shape along both dimensions. When $K_2 = 0$ and $C_{gov} = $ US\$10/bl, the government almost certainly expropriates, but there is no inefficiency. As K_2 and/or C_{gov} increase, the expropriation likelihood decreases, but the inefficiency, when expropriation does occur, increases.

8.3.2.3 Royalties vs. Corporate Income Taxes   We now investigate how the choice between royalty tax and corporate income tax affects the value of the expropriation option. So far we have assumed that the government relies exclusively on corporate income taxes. We now compare this with the opposite case where the government relies exclusively on royalties. We do this for the same combinations of $S(t)$ and $x(t)$ as in figure 8.3. In the baseline case we had $\tau_{inc} = 0.60$ and $\tau_{roy} = 0$. Here, we first set $\tau_{inc} = 0$ and compute the τ_{roy}, which, in the absence of expropriation risk, gives the same value of the oil field to the government. Next, we compute the value of the expropriation option with this τ_{roy}.

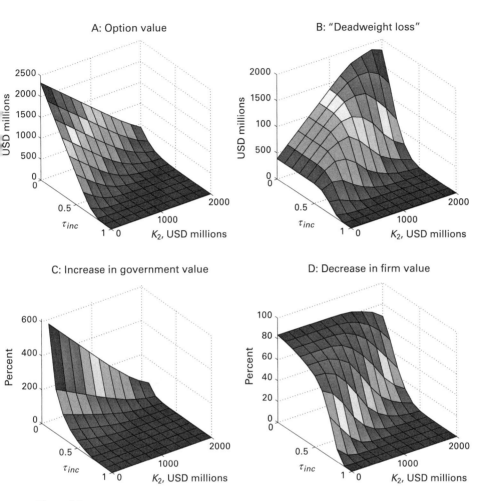

Figure 8.5
Expropriation risk as a function of tax rate and "reputational" costs. Panel A shows the value of the expropriation option, panel B shows the "deadweight loss," panel C shows the percentage increase in the oil field's value to the government when taking into account the expropriation possibility, and panel D shows the percentage decrease in the oil field's value to the firm when taking into account the expropriation possibility.

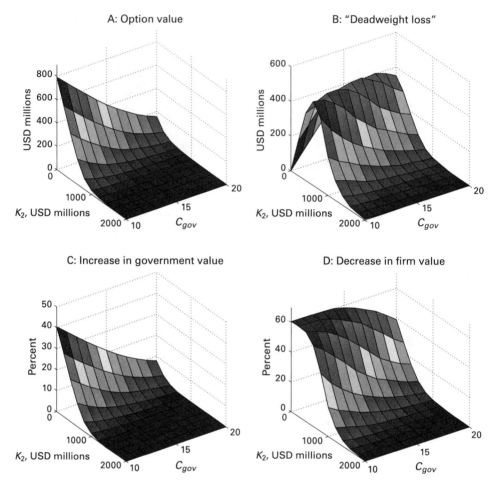

Figure 8.6
Expropriation risk as a function of "reputational" costs and state-run company's production cost. Panel A shows the value of the expropriation option, panel B shows the "deadweight loss," panel C shows the percentage increase in the oil field's value to the government when taking into account the expropriation possibility, and panel D shows the percentage decrease in the oil field's value to the firm when taking into account the expropriation possibility.

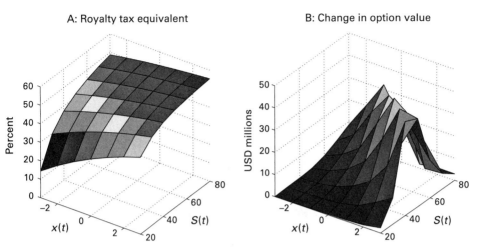

Figure 8.7
Change in option value when shifting from corporate income taxes to royalties. Panel A shows the τ_{roy} which, in the absence of expropriation risk, gives the same value of the oil field to the government as $\tau_{inc} = 0.60$. Panel B shows $P_{roy}(t_0) - P_{inc}(t_0)$, where $P_{roy}(t_0)$ and $P_{inc}(t_0)$ denote the values of the expropriation option when the government relies exclusively on royalties and corporate income taxes, respectively.

Panel A of figure 8.7 shows τ_{roy} while panel B shows $P_{roy}(t_0) - P_{inc}(t_0)$, where $P_{roy}(t_0)$ and $P_{inc}(t_0)$ denote the values of the expropriation option when the government relies exclusively on royalties and corporate income taxes, respectively. The value of the expropriation option is always larger with royalties than with corporate income taxes. The reason is that the royalty tax rate is always lower than the corporate income tax rate of 60 percent, which implies that for high oil prices the revenues from royalties are lower than from corporate income taxes, making expropriation more profitable. The differences in the value of the expropriation option are largest for combinations of state variables where there is some probability of expropriation. The differences are low when $S(t)$ and $x(t)$ are both low or when $S(t)$ and $x(t)$ are both high. In the former case, the government never expropriates, while in the latter case, the government almost surely expropriates regardless of whether it relies on royalties or corporate income taxes.

8.3.2.4 The "Optimal" Tax Rate for the Firm In the absence of expropriation risk, it is optimal for the firm to negotiate the most favorable terms under which to exploit the oil field. In our case, this means

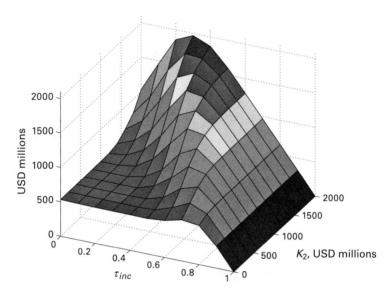

Figure 8.8
Oil field's value to the firm in the presence of expropriation risk as a function of tax rate and "reputational" costs. The figure shows the dollar value of the oil field to the firm in the presence of expropriation risk, i.e., $V_{firm}^{exp}(t_0)$.

obtaining the lowest possible tax rate. However, in the presence of expropriation risk, the firm must take into account that the incentive to expropriate is higher for lower tax rates. For simplicity, we return to the case where the government relies exclusively on corporate income taxes. Figure 8.8 shows the oil field's value to the firm as a function of τ_{inc} and K_2. For low values of K_2 the "optimal" tax rate that maximizes the project's value to the firm is quite high, around 70 percent. As K_2 increases, the "optimal" tax rate decreases, since the incentive to expropriate decreases.

8.3.2.5   Who Bears the "Deadweight Loss"?   Suppose t_0 is the time when the government auctions off the lease for the oil field. Furthermore, assume that extraction requires an initial investment of I. In the absence of expropriation risk, a firm would be willing to pay up to $V_{firm}(t_0) - I$ for the lease, while in the presence of expropriation risk, it would only be willing to pay up to $V_{firm}^{exp}(t_0) - I$.[14] If the government could commit itself, ex ante, not to expropriate, it would be able to extract a value of up to $V_{gov}(t_0) + V_{firm}(t_0) - I$ from the oil field. However, in the absence of a legal framework to enforce contracts, such a commitment is not credible, since, ex post, after the firm has paid for the lease and made the initial investment, it will be optimal for the government to renege on its promise in some states of the world. A rational firm will anticipate this behavior, and the maximum value that the government can extract from the field will be $V_{gov}^{exp}(t_0) + V_{firm}^{exp}(t_0) - I$. Ultimately, therefore, it is the government that bears the "deadweight loss" associated with the possibility of expropriation.

8.3.3   Implementation

When implementing the framework for actual valuation, the analyst must choose a set of reasonable parameters. The parameters and state variables of the Trolle and Schwartz 2009 model can be obtained by calibrating it to, say, NYMEX futures and options prices.[15] Tax rates are given and reserve size and production can be estimated. The main problem is estimating the government's expropriation costs. While it may be possible to infer production costs for a state-run oil company, it is harder to estimate the compensation to the firm in case of expropriation and even more difficult to estimate the "reputational" costs. Figures 8.5 and 8.6 show that the results are sensitive to these costs, and any conclusions drawn should reflect this uncertainty.

8.4   Conclusion

In this paper we develop a framework for pricing expropriation risk in natural resource projects in general and in an oil field in particular. The government is viewed as holding an American-style option to expropriate the oil field. Expropriation is not costless, however, and we consider three possible expropriation costs for the government: A state-run company may produce oil less cost-efficiently than a private firm, the government may have to pay compensation to the firm, and perhaps most importantly, there may be "reputational" costs because investors will lose confidence in the government's willingness to honor contracts. The dynamics of key variables—the spot price, futures prices, and volatility—are described by a model proposed and estimated in Trolle and Schwartz 2009, and the expropriation option is valued by simulations using the LSM approach developed by Longstaff and Schwartz 2001.

We find that the value of the expropriation option increases with the spot price, the slope of the futures curve, and futures (and spot) price volatility, while it decreases with the corporate income tax rate and the various expropriation costs. For reasonable parameter values and under market conditions not too different from those that have prevailed in recent years, the value of the expropriation option can be substantial. The value of the expropriation option increases if the government switches from corporate income taxes to royalty taxes in such a way that the value of the oil field to the government in the absence of expropriation risk is unchanged. In order to reduce the incentive for the government to expropriate, from the firm's point of view there is an "optimal" tax rate on corporate profits that may be quite high. Furthermore, when firms act rationally, the possibility of expropriation leads to a decrease in the total value that the government can initially extract from the oil field.

To keep the analysis focused, we have assumed an exogenous production process.[16] An interesting extension would be to make production endogenous and take into account the various operational options that are typically embedded in natural resource projects. This should be feasible, given the flexibility of the LSM approach.

Furthermore, although we have discussed royalties versus corporate income taxes, the tax structure remains very simple. It would be interesting to study the optimal resource extraction contract within our setup, perhaps drawing on some of the results in Engel and Fischer's chapter in this book (chapter 5).

Appendix A: The Trolle and Schwartz 2009 Model

Here, we briefly review the model of Trolle and Schwartz 2009.[17] The model is based on the Heath, Jarrow, and Morton 1992 framework for interest-rate dynamics and takes the initial futures curve or, equivalently, the initial cost of carry curve as given. $S(t)$ denotes the time-t spot price of the commodity, $\delta(t)$ denotes the time-t instantaneous spot cost of carry, $y(t, T)$ denotes the time-t instantaneous forward cost of carry at time T, and $v(t)$ denotes the volatility state variable. The general specification of the model is given by

$$\frac{dS(t)}{S(t)} = \delta(t)\,dt + \sigma_S \sqrt{v(t)}\,dW_1^Q(t) \tag{10}$$

$$dy(t, T) = \mu_y(t, T)\,dt + \sigma_y(t, T)\sqrt{v(t)}\,dW_2^Q(t) \tag{11}$$

$$dv(t) = \kappa_v(\theta - v(t))\,dt + \sigma_v \sqrt{v(t)}\,dW_3^Q(t), \tag{12}$$

where $W_1^Q(t)$, $W_2^Q(t)$, and $W_3^Q(t)$ denote correlated Wiener processes under the risk-neutral measure with pairwise correlations given by ρ_{12}, ρ_{13}, and ρ_{123}, and the drift term in (11) is given by

$$\mu_y(t, T) = -v(t)\sigma_y(t, T)\left(\rho_{12}\sigma_S + \int_t^T \sigma_y(t, u)\, du\right) \tag{13}$$

to ensure that the model is arbitrage-free.

We obtain a highly tractable model by specifying $\sigma_y(t, T)$ as

$$\sigma_y(t, T) = \alpha e^{-\gamma(T-t)}. \tag{14}$$

In this case futures prices are exponentially affine in the three state variables $s(t) \equiv \log(S(t))$, $x(t)$, and $\phi(t)$, which, along with $v(t)$, jointly constitute an affine state vector. In general, the model is time-inhomogeneous but we obtain a time-homogeneous model by assuming that the initial forward cost of carry curve, $y(0, t)$, is flat and equal to a constant, φ. Let $F(t, T)$ denote the time-t price of a futures contract maturing at time T. Then we have

$$F(t, T) = \exp\left\{\varphi(T - t) + s(t) + \frac{\alpha}{\gamma}(1 - e^{-\gamma(T-t)})x(t)\right.$$

$$\left. + \frac{\alpha}{2\gamma}(1 - e^{-2\gamma(T-t)})\phi(t)\right\}, \tag{15}$$

where $s(t)$, $x(t)$, and $\phi(t)$ evolve according to

$$ds(t) = \left(\varphi + \alpha x(t) + \alpha\phi(t) - \frac{1}{2}\sigma_S^2 v(t)\right)dt + \sigma_S\sqrt{v(t)}\,dW_1^Q(t) \tag{16}$$

$$dx(t) = \left(-\gamma x(t) - \left(\frac{\alpha}{\gamma} + \rho_{12}\sigma_S\right)v(t)\right)dt + \sqrt{v(t)}\,dW_2^Q(t) \tag{17}$$

$$d\phi(t) = \left(\frac{\alpha}{\gamma}v(t) - 2\gamma\phi(t)\right)dt. \tag{18}$$

Appendix B: Pricing the Expropriation Option by the LSM Algorithm

Here we briefly explain how to price the expropriation option using the LSM algorithm of Longstaff and Schwartz 2001.

1. Simulate M paths of X_t. Let $X_m(t_i)$, $\hat{P}_m(t_i)$, and $\Pi_m(t_i)$ denote the value of the state vector, the estimated option value, and the option payoff, respectively, at time t_i along the mth path. Furthermore, let $\mathcal{I}_i$ denote the subset of paths for which the option is in-the-money at time t_i.

2. At time t_{N-1} the value of the option is equal to its immediate exercise value. Therefore, $\hat{P}_m(t_{N-1}) = \Pi_m(t_{N-1})$, $m = 1, \ldots, M$.

3. Apply backward induction from $i = N - 2$ to $i = 1$.

• At time t_i the value of the option is equal to the maximum of its immediate exercise value and its expected continuation value. Longstaff and Schwartz (2001) suggest approximating the expected continuation value by the fitted value of a cross-sectional least squares regression where the ex post realized cash flows from continuation are regressed on a set of basis functions of the state variables. In other words, we run the regression

$$e^{-r(t_{i+1}-t_i)}\hat{P}_m(t_{i+1}) = \sum_{j=1}^{J} \beta_j \psi_j(X_m(t_i)) + \epsilon_m, \quad m \in \mathcal{I}_i \tag{19}$$

where ψ_j denotes the jth basis function.[18] Note that we only use the paths for which the option is in-the-money at time t_i since it is only on these paths that the government may choose to exercise. The fitted value of this regression

$$\hat{C}_m(t_i) = \sum_{j=1}^{J} \hat{\beta}_j \psi_j(X_m(t_i)), \quad m \in \mathcal{I}_i \tag{20}$$

is an efficient unbiased estimate of the expected continuation value.

• Update the estimated option value along each path as

$$\hat{P}_m(t_i) = \begin{cases} \Pi_m(t_i), & \Pi_m(t_i) \geq \hat{C}_m(t_i) \\ e^{-r(t_{i+1}-t_i)}\hat{P}_m(t_{i+1}), & \Pi_m(t_i) < \hat{C}_m(t_i), \end{cases} \tag{21}$$

for $m \in \mathcal{I}_i$ and

$$\hat{P}_m(t_i) = e^{-r(t_{i+1}-t_i)}\hat{P}_m(t_{i+1}) \tag{22}$$

for $m \notin \mathcal{I}_i$.

4. Compute the estimated option value as

$$\hat{P}(t_0) = e^{-r(t_1 - t_0)} \frac{1}{M} \sum_{m=1}^{M} \hat{P}_m(t_1). \tag{23}$$

In general, we obtain a lower bound on the option value, since we approximate the continuation value. Clément, Lamberton, and Protter (2002) prove that the LSM algorithm converges to the true option price as $M \rightarrow \infty$.

As part of the LSM algorithm we also obtain the early exercise strategy. Let t_{Z_m} denote the estimated time of expropriation along path m. We start by setting $Z_m = N$ for $m = 1, \ldots, M$, corresponding to no expropriation along any of the paths. Then we move backward from $i = N - 1$ to $i = 1$. If at time t_i along path m it is optimal to exercise the option, we set $Z_m = i$.

Notes

We thank Robert Pindyck (the discussant at the Populism and Natural Resources Conference), Federico Sturzenegger, William Hogan, and seminar participants for extensive comments. Anders Trolle thanks the Danish Social Science Research Council for financial support. Eduardo Schwartz: UCLA Anderson School of Management, 110 Westwood Plaza, Los Angeles, CA 90095-1481. E-mail: eduardo.schwartz@anderson.ucla.edu. Anders Trolle: Ecole Polytechnique Fédérale de Lausanne, Swiss Finance Institute, Extranef 216, CH-1015 Lausanne, Switzerland. E-mail: anders.trolle@epfl.ch.

1. For a comprehensive exposition of the real-options approach to valuation, see Dixit and Pindyck 1994.

2. Throughout the chapter, we consider the risk of the state taking over the entire oil field. The framework could be modified to consider the risk of a partial expropriation through a forced renegotiation of existing contracts involving, for instance, an increase in taxes or the state taking a certain stake in the oil field.

3. Alternatively, we could use one of the more parsimonious models in Schwartz 1997 to describe the dynamics of crude-oil spot and futures prices. However, none of these models incorporate stochastic volatility, making them inferior to the Trolle and Schwartz 2009 model in terms of pricing options. Furthermore, since we price the expropriation option by simulation, there are only minor computational advantages of using a more parsimonious model.

4. New York Mercantile Exchange.

5. Our paper is also related to Rigobon's contribution (see chapter 7, this volume). In his model, the firm chooses the optimal production plan, which, given the tax rates and the risk of expropriation, maximizes profits, while the government optimally chooses the royalty and income tax rates subject to certain restrictions. However, the commodity price process is highly simplified (a random walk) and he uses a simplified exercise strategy of the expropriation option (the government expropriates if profits rise above a fixed threshold). In contrast, in our framework, the production plan and tax rates are

exogenous. Instead we provide a realistic model for the evolution of commodity prices and compute the optimal exercise strategy of the expropriation option.

6. We exclude current time t_0 from the set of exercise opportunities. We also exclude t_N since at that time the oil field has been depleted.

7. Throughout the paper, we use 10,000 paths and antithetic variates in the simulations.

8. Note that we may alternatively compute the value of the oil field to the government in the presence of expropriation risk as the value in the absence of expropriation risk plus the value of the expropriation option—that is, $V_{gov}^{exp}(t_0) = V_{gov}(t_0) + P(t_0)$.

9. For instance, if the government expropriates the oil field after seven years, the firm will receive a compensation of US$150 million.

10. For simplicity, we assume that production, production costs, and tax rates are constant throughout the life of the oil field. However, these could easily be made time and state dependent. For instance, it is likely that annual production decreases and the marginal production cost increases as the oil field gets depleted.

11. However, after the end of our sample period, crude-oil trading on NYMEX for a time exceeded US$100/bl.

12. The risk-neutral likelihood that the field will get expropriated during its ten-year life-span is 62 percent.

13. In the rest of the chapter, unless otherwise noted, the state variables are given by $S(t) = 50$, $x(t) = 0$, and $v(t) = 2.79$.

14. For simplicity, we abstract from the option to defer the initial investment.

15. The price of crude oil from a particular oil field will usually differ from the price at NYMEX (which refers to the benchmark West Texas Intermediate blend) because of differences in quality. However, the correlation with the NYMEX price is likely to be very high, which implies that one can calibrate the model to NYMEX derivatives and subsequently adjust the spot price to reflect the actual crude-oil quality.

16. In our example, production is constant. However, it is straightforward to make production time and state dependent.

17. In fact, in that paper we propose two models, one model with one volatility factor and another model with two volatility factors. We show that the latter model outperforms the former, particularly in terms of pricing short-term derivatives. However, for pricing real options with long maturities, the performances of the models are likely to be similar. In the interest of parsimony, we therefore work with the model with one volatility factor.

18. We use the following set of functions: 1, $s_m(t_i)$, $s_m(t_i)^2$, $x_m(t_i)$, $x_m(t_i)^2$, $v_m(t_i)$, $v_m(t_i)^2$, $s_m(t_i)x_m(t_i)$, $s_m(t_i)v_m(t_i)$, and $x_m(t_i)v_m(t_i)$. Adding higher-order terms does not change the results.

References

Brennan, M. J., and E. S. Schwartz. 1985. Evaluating natural resource investments. *Journal of Business* 58:135–157.

Clark, E. 2003. Pricing the cost of expropriation risk. *Review of International Economics* 11:412–422.

Clément, E., D. Lamberton, and P. Protter. 2002. An analysis of the least squares regression algorithm for American option pricing. *Finance and Stochastics* 6:449–471.

Dixit, A., and R. Pindyck. 1994. *Investment under Uncertainty*. Princeton, NJ: Princeton University Press.

Harrison, M., and D. Kreps. 1979. Martingales and arbitrage in multiperiod securities markets. *Journal of Economic Theory* 20:381–408.

Harrison, M., and S. Pliska. 1981. Martingales and stochastic integrals in the theory of continuous trading. *Stochastic Processes and Their Applications* 11:215–260.

Heath, D., R. Jarrow, and A. Morton. 1992. Bond pricing and the term structure of interest rates: A new methodology for contingent claims valuation. *Econometrica* 60:77–105.

Longstaff, F., and E. Schwartz. 2001. Valuing American options by simulation: A simple least-squares approach. *Review of Financial Studies* 14:113–147.

Mahajan, A. 1990. Pricing expropriation risk. *Financial Management* 19:77–86.

Schwartz, E. S. 1997. The stochastic behavior of commodity prices: Implications for valuation and hedging. *Journal of Finance* 52:923–973.

Trolle, A. B., and E. S. Schwartz. 2009. Unspanned stochastic volatility and the pricing of commodity derivatives. *Review of Financial Studies* 22:4423–4461.

Commentary

Robert Pindyck

In their paper, Eduardo Schwartz and Anders Trolle use a real options framework to examine the welfare implications of expropriation risk. The basic idea is that the government has an option to expropriate a privately held oil (or other natural resource) reserve, and the question is when the government will exercise that option. The reason that the government does not expropriate the reserve immediately is that (by assumption) the cost of production for the government is greater than the firm's cost of production, that is, the firm is a more efficient producer. The objective in this paper is to value the expropriation option and determine the government's optimal exercise rule. Knowing the value of the expropriation option is important because it allows the firm and the government to rationally negotiate a revenue-sharing contract. Likewise, it is important to know at what point expropriation is likely to happen.

An important issue addressed in this paper is the deadweight loss resulting from the possibility of expropriation. The fact that the government has a higher production cost is what generates the deadweight loss in this model. It is equal to the value to the firm without expropriation risk minus the value with that risk, minus the value of the expropriation option. So to evaluate the deadweight loss, we need to know how each of three quantities—the value of the reserve itself, the value of the option to expropriate, and the critical price at which the expropriation could take place—depend on various things like volatility, the slope of the futures curve, and other parameters.

It is necessary to start out with a model of the price of oil. In this case, the Schwartz-Trolle model has three stochastic state variables: the spot price, the slope of the futures curve, and volatility itself. Given that model, the authors have a complicated option valuation problem. They solve this problem numerically using the Longstaff-Schwartz method, which is very powerful, yet relatively easy to implement.

The Schwartz-Trolle model of the oil price is quite complex, and while they can handle the complexity numerically using their simulation approach, this is burdensome, and in my view, probably not necessary. If we are looking at oil in Venezuela or in Ecuador, there is really no futures market. In fact, there is no daily price that one can observe. Instead, the prices are typically negotiated with a limited set of buyers. We are not really worried about very complex derivatives on Ecuadorian oil. Rather, we are looking at a relatively simple derivative, which is the option value of expropriation. As a result, a simpler model of price can probably be used, even a model with just one state variable.

It would be interesting to extend the Schwartz-Trolle model to several reserves or even a continuum of reserves with increasing development costs. Let's say we have ten possible reserves, and we order them based on our estimates of development costs. Using a simpler model of the price process, we are first going to develop the least expensive reserve by the foreign firm. Barring expropriation, when the price rises sufficiently that firm or a different firm will come in, and the next reserve will be developed, and so on. But once expropriation happens, no further reserves will be developed by foreign firms.

By focusing on the cost of development we get two aspects of option value. First, even without a possibility of expropriation there is a very large option value here related to the sunk cost of development and the fact that the price of oil is stochastic. In other words, there is an option value to waiting to see whether the price of oil goes up or down rather than developing the reserve now. The higher price volatility implies less immediate investment even without any expropriation possibility, but it also means a lower likelihood of expropriation at the moment given a fixed price. It raises the value of the expropriation option, and it also raises the critical price at which you would expropriate. It is very important to understand how that works. The option value to the government goes up, but the exercising of the option does not happen earlier; in fact it happens later.

Volatility should clearly affect behavior, in particular investment and expropriation decisions, but it should also affect contract design. So it would be wonderful if there was a way to merge the Schwartz-Trolle model with another paper in this volume, namely, the Engel-Fischer analysis. How does option value, and the parameters that affect option value, affect the design of an optimal contract? A Schwartz-Trolle–Engel-Fischer collaboration (for some future volume) might address that question.

II Country Cases

9 Credibility, Commitment, and Regulation: Ex Ante Price Caps and Ex Post Interventions

Dieter Helm

9.1 Introduction

After the Second World War, the British Labour government nationalized the "commanding heights" of the economy. The core idea was that state ownership would solve the conflict of objectives between public and private interests, and thereby ensure that economic efficiency was achieved. Principals and agents would both be on the same side. Thirty-five years later, the Conservative government embarked on privatizing these nationalized industries, arguing that the change of ownership would ensure efficiency, in the context of competitive markets. Principals and agents might have different interests, but a combination of competitive product markets and, where necessary, regulation would ensure that the agents acted consistently with the principals' interests.

But privatization—like nationalization before it—did not *solve* the core problems of these industries. Rather, it opened up a whole new chapter of contract design and regulation. The economic borders of the state were now to be characterized by new regulatory rules, new taxes, and new supporting institutions. At the heart of the new contractual relationship lay the central issues of credibility and commitment—how the state could design its interventions such that the private sector could invest without being subsequently expropriated.

In the infrastructure sectors of developed economies—energy, transport, and water—the role of governments is pervasive. These industries typically have core elements of natural monopoly, requiring the regulation of prices. The networks are capital-intensive, with high fixed and sunk costs. Short-run marginal costs are typically low, well below average costs, and over long periods technical progress may strand costs. As a result, investors are exposed to expropriation by governments: there is an incentive to promise ex ante that investors will be able to earn at least normal profits but then ex post to intervene to force down prices, claw back profits, and change outputs. It is a classic time-inconsistency problem, familiar in particular in the monetary policy literature, and one that provides the opportunity for governments to be populist.[1]

In partial recognition of the need to commit, in the 1980s the United Kingdom pioneered a new approach to utility regulation, the "RPI–X price cap approach." The idea was remarkably simple and crude: the utilities would be given a fixed-price, fixed-period contract, to be revised every four or five years. With price fixed, profit maximization would be equivalent to cost minimization, and hence economic efficiency would be ensured.

This deceptively simple rule (Helm 1987) has been applied across the UK utilities, in both the private and the public sectors, to industries as diverse as energy, water, telecoms, transport, and broadcasting. Variants of RPI–X have also been applied to a host of private finance initiative (PFI) schemes (notably new hospitals and schools) and a public-private partnership (PPP) has been created for the refurbishment and development of the London Underground. All involve the government contracting with the private sector, using elements of fixed-price, fixed-period contracts.

The core characteristic of the UK approach is that the state contracts ex ante, and thereby undertakes not to interfere ex post within the contract period. It rules out populist interventions. Flexibility is sacrificed in order to maximize efficiency incentives. To give the approach credibility, a number of intermediary organizations—from "independent" regulators to official arbiters—have been created, in the process heralding what has been described as a "regulatory state."

The problems to which this approach is supposed to be a solution are not new. The tension between flexibility and efficiency incentives has dogged the utility sector since at least the nineteenth century, and indeed it proved sufficiently intractable in much of Europe in the twentieth century to necessitate nationalization of most of the core network infrastructures, thereby internalizing the problem within the state sector. In the United Kingdom, the coal, electricity, and gas industries were all nationalized after the Second World War. In the development of North Sea oil and gas, public corporations played a central role in the 1970s, before being privatized in the 1980s.

Experience over the twenty years since RPI–X was first introduced (for British Telecom in 1984) has indicated that the crude fixed-price fixed-period framework is far from robust. The power and scope of regulation have grown, often ex post. Interference within the fixed periods has become commonplace, changing the outputs, adding costs, and even changing the prices.

Two examples illustrate the nature and scale of impacts on credibility: the resetting of the price caps on electricity distribution in 1994–1995, and the windfall tax imposed by the government in 1997. The reasons why the pure RPI–X approach has never lived up to its potential are complex. The purpose of this chapter is to illuminate some of the central issues—notably the conflict between the administrative approach to regulation in the United Kingdom and fixed contracting; the role of populist pressures as a limiting factor to returns; the necessary incompleteness of the contracts; and the pressures from financial markets to shift the regulatory risk to customers (partly in response to such ex post interventions)—and to consider their wider implications for defining the role and borders of the private and public sectors.

The structure of the chapter is as follows. Section 9.2 sets out the origins of RPI–X regulation and the context of privatization, with its multiple objectives—and not just efficiency. Section 9.3 describes the salient framework of the regulatory institutions and in particular the considerable scope for ex post intervention created by the widely drawn general duties of the regulators. Section 9.4 turns to the financial dimensions of regulation and, in particular, the regulatory asset bases (RABs) and the determination of the cost of capital. Having set out the main architecture of RPI–X, the chapter turns to the two examples of ex post intervention—the revision of price caps within periods (section 9.5) and the windfall tax (section 9.6). Section 9.7 then sets out the main implications that flow from these examples, and provides a framework for more efficient ex ante contracts that might mitigate the scope for ex post interventions. Section 9.8 briefly contrasts the experience in the utilities with that of the North Sea oil and gas development. Finally, section 9.9 concludes.

9.2   The Origins of RPI–X and the Privatization Contracts

RPI–X was not some carefully thought out component of the privatization program for UK utilities.[2] It was an afterthought tagged onto the privatization of British Telecom (BT) in 1984, as a stopgap while competition developed. Indeed, it was envisaged that after an initial period of seven years, regulation would wither away (Department of Industry and Littlechild 1983). But what began as a temporary expedient ended up being used for all the main utility privatizations—and all the energy networks. And as it was applied to subsequent cases and with experience, it was developed and modified pragmatically as problems emerged with its application. The very incomplete contract for BT was gradually filled in.

These developments and modifications were set within a wider political context. Privatization in the United Kingdom was itself more an accident of circumstance than a well-worked-out policy. Although the Labour government in the 1970s had begun to sell off British Petroleum, it did not figure in the Conservative manifesto in 1979, and in the first case of BT, it was applied because the earlier attempts to launch a private bond while keeping BT publicly owned failed.

The rationale for RPI–X did, however, fit well with the political objectives of the government at the time (Helm 1994b). Public-sector inefficiency was regarded as the inevitable result of state ownership, and profit-maximizing incentives were deemed essential. At the time, the coal and electricity industries had excess capacity, and it was argued that they had overinvested and were gold-plated. Evidence from a series of Monopolies and Mergers Commission (MMC) reports pointed to investment planning and operating cost inefficiencies.[3] By mimicking the market, making monopolies price takers rather than price setters, profit maximization would, it was argued, be equivalent to cost minimization, provided they were privately owned and hence could benefit from outperformance against the RPI–X contract.

In its pure form, RPI–X was deliberately crude. On Austrian grounds (the dominant economic school of the main advocates of RPI–X),[4] it was deemed hopeless to estimate ex ante the operating expenditure (OPEX) and capital expenditure (CAPEX) costs. Thus the task was to set an arbitrary price cap, and then the utilities themselves would reveal the true costs, and at subsequent periodic reviews when the contract was reset, the prices could be adjusted to pass on the benefits of any observed outperformance to customers. Thus shareholders would reap the returns within periods, but not between them. But its simplicity did not imply completeness—there was little prospect that the other nonprice variables would be left entirely to the private sector's discretion.

Cost efficiency was not the only political objective of privatization. The government also had in mind moving investment programs off the public balance sheet, shifting them from the public sector onto the private—thereby creating, in effect, a *private*-sector borrowing requirement (Helm 2001).[5] The overarching economic framework was set by the medium-term financial strategy (MTFS), which combined monetary targets with targets for the reduction of the share of government in the economy. The MTFS at a time of recession and sharply rising unemployment could not accommodate the investment plans of the nationalized industries. So while the nationalized industries (notably BT) could come up with lots of projects that were net present value positive at the government's internal discount rate, the funds were simply not available. Hence government turned to the private sector— and private balance sheets—to finance investment. This investment requirement was part of the implicit privatization contract—and it turned out, as explained below, to be a crucial element in the windfall tax and the subsequent financial engineering that took place.

By the time RPI–X was applied to the gas (1986) and electricity (1990) industries, there had been much learning-by-regulating, and the crude initial model began to be fleshed out. The simple contracts were filled in. While the Austrian purists could keep to the notion that *any* price cap, if stuck to, would reveal costs, and any resulting excess returns would be temporary, this proved politically impossible to implement. Privatizations were intensely debated, and there was much political and public hostility. Thus to sell the concept to the electorate, politicians were forced to explain why the policy would be in the interests of customers, rather than to the benefit of city institutions, managers, and shareholders. Consumers (and voters) could not easily be persuaded of the merits of the underlying economic incentives. This was made all the more challenging because in a number of industries—notably electricity and gas—prices had been held down in the public sector and hence price levels needed to be adjusted upward in advance of the asset sales.

Thus, from the mid-1980s onward, price caps were set with a view to predicting what the costs of the businesses would be going forward so that expected profits would be limited, and quite quickly it was recognized that the information required to predict and set prices was not much different from that of the rate-of-return regulation it was designed to replace. In particular, regulators needed to estimate the regulatory asset base (RAB), the cost of capital, OPEX and CAPEX, and depreciation. It was also belatedly discovered that profit could be maximized not only by reducing costs, but also by reducing the quality of service, and regulators therefore began to fill in the output specification of the contract too—an element that has led in the electricity and gas industries to, in effect, regulating the security margins.

From this ex ante attempt to estimate the costs came the expectation that the companies would not in fact make large excess profits ex post—setting the scene for the windfall tax later on. The measure of how accurately the price caps had been set was the share price: following on from Tobin's Q, if the prices were set "correctly" the market value of the companies would be equal to the RAB plus a (small) element for expected outperformance. This would be "small," because the scope for coming up with large-scale innovative abnormal cost savings once the cap had been set within the five-year period was limited—unless, of course, the companies had misled the regulator by gaming the price cap negotiations or providing misleading (or even false) information.

The political stage was therefore set for debates about the profits of the utilities after privatization. Excess returns could be blamed on poor regulation or game playing by the utilities. In either case, they could be deemed "unacceptable," and the debate focused on why even if this was the case, customers should have to wait five years before "mistakes" were rectified. There was, after all, nothing special about five years, and prices continually changed in the competitive markets that RPI–X was supposed to mimic.

In the 1990s, these excess returns were used as a wider political symbol by the opposition Labour Party of what they saw as the greed and inequalities that Thatcherism was deemed to have ushered in, and they were reflected in the targeting of the salaries of the "fat cats" who now managed the same businesses they had in the public sector but at much higher salaries (almost all the incumbent management survived privatization because politicians deemed their support for the process essential).

This political focus on managerial returns has remained, and currently there is much political, public, and media comment on the returns to private equity managers. This is not accidental: in the United Kingdom and many European countries, concepts of income equality and fairness are perhaps more firmly embedded in political discourse than in the United States, and the tolerance for inequalities in pay much less apparent (regardless of the outcome in practice). Therefore if returns appeared "excessive" within the five-year contract periods, in the United Kingdom's political culture, there was bound to be a reaction. The fact that these industries were largely domestic and provided essential services added to this perception—one that oil companies in the North Sea escaped by virtue of the perception of the international context. Thus, while, theoretically, RPI–X has some attractions, in industries that are by their nature political, the regulatory regime needed to be crafted to ensure it appreciated these "cultural" constraints—or ex post intervention would be inevitable.

9.3   The Regulatory Institutions and Regulatory Discretion

If RPI–X in its pure form failed from the outset because of the need to try to accurately forecast the costs ex ante, it was also placed in a rather contradictory institutional setting. Unlike the U.S. approach, the UK approach to public administration is not primarily driven by a legal framework and the legal enforcement of contracts and ultimately a written constitution. On the contrary, at least since the great reforms of the civil service in the late nineteenth century, the British have tended to make a virtue of discretion and flexibility, taking a piecemeal and pragmatic approach, without the need to tie down formal procedural rules and rights.

Typically, UK civil servants are required to "pursue the public interest" and are given very wide discretion to carry this out. The discretion granted is intended to be used—indeed, not to use it is typically regarded by politicians and the media as evidence of failure. This approach—which I have elsewhere called "good chaps regulation" (Helm 1994a)—places great emphasis on selecting and educating the "right" people with the "right" values, and then leaving them to get on with the job free from the constraints of judicial review, except where they behave irrationally.[6] It is an approach that is diametrically opposed to the idea of fixed-price, fixed-period ex ante regulation.

The way this administrative approach to public administration was translated across to the regulation of utilities was through the powers and duties directly vested in the individual regulators (Directors General). The exact general duties varied from case to case, but in energy they included the primary duty to promote competition and to ensure that the utilities could finance their functions. A host of secondary duties were added, though the trade-offs between these, and between primary and secondary duties, were never defined and hence left to the discretion of the individuals appointed. As a result, predicting the course of regulation required a study of the individuals' preferences and beliefs, and unsurprisingly, changing the individuals could change the decisions under the same legal and administrative framework. Regulators were independent not only of government, but also of effective legal control.

Thus the UK regulatory system had at its core a contradiction between ex ante RPI–X price caps, on the one hand, and individuals with both ex ante powers to oversee and set the price caps at periodic reviews, and ex post powers to intervene. Over time it was perhaps inevitable that the former would be undermined by the latter. I return to examples of ex post interventions directly in the price caps below. On the wider use of the general duty powers, the duty to promote competition covered in principle almost all activities of the utilities. Some of these interventions were directly on the utilities, through, for example, changing the pricing structures, encouraging contracting out of infrastructure, connections, and metering. Others were more subtle and indirect—by changing the nature of competition between the network users, the predictability of returns could be altered to the core network. The secondary duties came into play too. Social considerations could be placed as burdens on incumbents, with energy efficiency and cross-subsidy measures notable examples.

The significant element of personal discretion was gradually recognized as a problem, and following a review of utility regulation in 1997–1998 (DTI 1998), eventually reforms were introduced in a White Paper (DTI 2000a) and in the 2000 Utilities Act (TSO 2000). The general duties were to be vested in a board rather than in individuals, providing for more checks and balances through corporate governance (rather than through the courts), thereby reducing the element of personal discretion. However, this improvement was offset by making the general duties even broader—now simply the promotion of customer interests. Which customers? Over what time period? And which interests? These issues were left open. Subsequently, a further secondary duty was added—promoting sustainable development. The 2000 reforms also paved the way for the government to give "guidance" in the interpretation of the various duties, but the guidance itself provided hard to draft, and has had at best only marginal effects.[7]

Thus, while the price caps themselves were an attempt to introduce an element of hard contracting into utility regulation, the institutional architecture pushed in the opposite direction. This was a core design failure in the new regime, and unsurprisingly, regulators were keen to show that they were "doing something" with the resources at their disposal—and indeed to increase their budgets over time. They had been deliberately given discretion, and hence it behooved them to use it. Thus they all began to produce "strategies," "initiatives," "action plans," and "strategic reviews," with a view to demonstrating "achievements." Not only was the design flawed, but also the normal bureaucratic incentives would inevitably lead to the ex post powers being used, thereby weakening the ex ante contracts.

9.4 The Financial Dimensions to Regulation—the RAB, the Balance Sheets, Equity Risk, and the Emergence of Financial Engineering

The fixed-price, fixed-period contracting regime was designed to transfer both incentives and risks to the utilities. It was designed to explicitly be the opposite of rate-of-return regulation,[8] which in the United Kingdom at the time was deemed to encourage cost inflation and bias toward capital intensity. The architects were much taken with the Averch-Johnson effect (Averch and Johnson 1962), and wished to avoid its consequences. The fact that several of the privatized industries (notably electricity) were in excess supply meant in any event that the economic focus was more on asset sweating that investment.

More attention at the time was placed on the incentives—less on the risk allocation. In contracting, the residual risk from incompleteness comprises the equity risk, and regulation is a method of allocating the risk across the parties. As long as contracts are incomplete, it will be an enduring feature—equity risk will never go away. It can be borne by taxpayers, customers, shareholders, or some combination of these three. Under pure rate-of-return regulation, the equity risk is with customers, and as a result the utility can be debt financed. Under pure price cap regulation, the equity risk is with shareholders, and hence equity is an important component of the capital structure of the utility. In the case of nationalized industries, and those with state guarantees (in the UK Network Rail and the London Underground PPP companies up to 95 percent), taxpayers absorb the equity risk.

These options illustrate a second point (which will be seen to be important in the windfall tax case discussed below): comparing the cost of capital between alternative ownership and regulatory regimes needs to take account of the residual equity risks. Hence, although a state guarantee leads to a lower cost of debt, it does not follow that this is the true cost of capital.

These considerations feed through to the debate about gearing and the capital structure of utilities, and a further tension between the ex ante price cap approach and the "understanding" at privatization that the purpose of private balance sheets was to finance investment not paid for by customers within the price cap period. Borrowing—and hence increased gearing—was intended to be for physical capital investment.

The government assumed that the ungeared balance sheets at privatization would be sufficient to modernize the United Kingdom's core infrastructures—which it was argued (somewhat in contradiction to the Averch-Johnson argument above) had been neglected in the public sector, due to state budgetary constraints. Once the balance sheets were exhausted, utilities would then, it was assumed, resort to rights issues.

This unwritten part of the privatization "contract" was however open to four core challenges: first, the fixed-price, fixed-period approach did not actually specify the path of gearing, and hence utilities might be free to choose alternative capital structures; second, debt was taxed more lightly than equity—interest was deductible; third, the RAB itself appeared to be protected by the duty to ensure the utilities could finance their functions; and fourth, the use of a weighted average cost of capital (WACC) provided an average cost of capital above the marginal cost of debt and below that of equity. The result was a dash-for-debt, and a decoupling of the gearing from physical capital investment—and in the process of the resulting financial engineering, the returns to shareholders turned out to be much higher than was anticipated at privatization.

The optimal capital structure is a complex subject beyond the scope of this chapter, but it is worth noting that the dash-for-debt in the United Kingdom was the result of the violation of two assumptions in the Modigliani-Miller theorem (under which the capital structure is irrelevant). First, taxation gives a clear bias to debt over equity—and until very recently, the regulators did not claw back the tax benefits. Second, the use of the WACC created a major distortion in the presence of the guarantee to finance functions. It was gradually interpreted to mean that the regulator had a duty to finance the RAB (the shareholders' stake in the utility) and the efficient ex ante projections of OPEX and CAPEX. While the OPEX and CAPEX might turn out differently, and hence there was residual equity risk in running the business, which necessitated an equity element, the (implicit) guarantee to the RAB transferred the equity risk from shareholders to customers. The RAB was therefore pure rate of return. Hence it could be 100 percent debt financed. Add in the RPI pass-through, and the RAB had in effect a risk profile close to an index-linked government bond.

But here the regulation created a major distortion: although there was no equity risk in the RAB, the WACC gave it a return in excess of the cost of debt—proportioned according to the assumed gearing level when the price caps were set. (It also created the parallel distortion that the cost of equity in the OPEX and CAPEX part of the business was not met—the WACC, as an average between debt and equity, was by definition below the cost of equity.)

As a result, a massive exercise in financial engineering was launched, with spectacular returns, and this accompanied the first example of a regulator reopening an ex ante price cap—the first of our two examples set out below. It is an exercise that is not yet complete, because Infrastructure Funds have emerged in the UK buying up utilities at very considerable premiums to the RAB, and well above a Tobin Q–type calculation referred to above. In 2007, during the fourth five-year price cap for water and electricity distribution companies, premiums in acquisitions in the cases of Southern Water and Norweb were around the 30 percent mark over the RAB. From the perspective of the customers, the rates of return expected by acquirers greatly exceeded their costs of capital.

9.5   Revising Price Caps within Period—Ex Post Interventions by Regulators

Regulated utilities were, of course, far from passive when faced with the new regime. The price caps were incomplete contracts that offered a number of opportunities to exploit the unspecified or weakly specified parts. In addition to the financial incentives outlined above, outputs were on occasion flexible, and the periodic reviews themselves could be gamed by strategic timing of efficiency gains and information revelation. Companies had an incentive to overstate costs in the run-up to periodic reviews, and then drive down costs immediately afterward to keep the benefits for the full five years, before they were returned to customers. Conversely, at the end of the period, the incentive was to increase CAPEX, since it would go directly into the (lower-risk) RAB at the periodic review and also higher CAPEX could be used as a signal for a larger ex ante CAPEX contract in the next period. The size of this effect could be very large: in electricity distribution, for example, in the first five-year period, ex post CAPEX turned out at around half the ex ante predicted level.

Within just two years of setting the first price cap for the electricity distribution companies, the whole regime came under challenge and there were significant pressures to intervene. These came largely from the CAPEX side. At the end of the five-year period, when the price cap was reset in 1994 for the second period 1995–1999, the pressures as a result of sharp rises in share prices became so considerable, as to force the regulator to intervene and reopen the price cap in 1995. Thus, before the windfall tax was levied by the government in 1997, the pure fixed-price, fixed-period contract had been breached. That this could happen under the personal supervision of the Director General who was the architect of the RPI–X regime (Stephen Littlechild) further undermined the credibility of the regime—given, as noted above, the personal discretion vested in individual regulators through the general duties. In its pure form, RPI–X died in 1995.

Credibility is an essential feature of the ex ante regime: companies must believe that excess returns will not be clawed back within the period. A wholly new regime without a track record, in the context of an unpopular privatization, and with a general election due by 1992 in which the opposition Labour Party was ahead in the opinion polls and was highly critical of the regulatory regime and the returns of the privatized companies, relied heavily on the conduct of its regulator in these early years to establish a reputation for resisting calls for intervention and adhering to the ex ante principles—to behave in a time-consistent fashion. That he cracked so soon was not perhaps surprising, but it provided a precedent for advocates of the windfall tax to follow.

The problems for the electricity distribution price cap began early in the first period. There was not much experience to draw on to set the companies' OPEX and CAPEX, and there was little clear empirical evidence as to the level of cost inefficiency in the public sector. Furthermore, in difficult political circumstances, it was considered essential to the process of passing the necessary legislation and effecting what at the time were very large equity issues, that the incumbent managers supported the process. They therefore were in a strong position to argue for benign price caps, so that they could personally benefit ex post from the resulting cost reductions.

The scale of the differences between the projected OPEX and CAPEX and the outturns was very large—indeed much bigger than any commentators forecast at privatization. Very roughly, the electricity distribution companies turned out to need about half the workforce their publicly owned predecessors had required to yield the same outputs; and, as already noted, they spent about half the CAPEX allowances.

This scale of apparent outperformance was already evident in 1992, as share prices began to rise as a result of both the higher dividends expected and the failure of Labour to win the 1992 election. Since it was highly unlikely that the difference between normal profits and those witnessed could be explained by extraordinary cost savings that could not have been anticipated at privatization, suspicion fell on the managers for gaming the initial price cap information. It was argued that they were responding not so much to the pure efficiency incentives to run the businesses better, but were reaping the benefits of gaming at the outset. The scale of the returns appeared completely out of line with the sorts of (equity) risks they were running.[9]

A heated debate ensued, and Littlechild argued forcefully that any excess returns should be addressed when the price caps were reset in 1994 for the next period, but not before—otherwise credibility would be undermined. The argument was, however, finally balanced: others argued that the returns were so abnormally high that allowing them to persist risked direct state intervention, as customers rebelled against the argument that they needed to carry on paying an excessive price for three further years in order to have a benefit in the next five-year period and beyond. No convincing argument was provided as to why managers would simply stop trying if there was intervention in 1992— and indeed if they did, others might take up the challenge (at least once the golden shares were removed and the capital market could enforce profit maximization through takeovers).

The price cap for the first period was in fact allowed to run its course, but in 1994 the process of setting the price cap for the next periods was carried out, with an announced new price cap in early August 1994 (OFFER 1994). The process itself had been a fraught one—with the companies providing business plans of their future OPEX and CAPEX, and the regulator using comparative efficiency exercises to try to estimate the true expected costs. Littlechild also had to set a value for the RAB and a cost of capital. For reasons that remain opaque, he allowed a 50 percent uplift on the flotation value at privatization, to set the initial 1990 RAB, and then rolled forward to include the CAPEX. It was a game of unequal players: the companies achieved an outcome that, when announced, led to a sharp rise in share prices that already valued the distribution companies significantly above their RABs. On average, the share prices rose from around £5 to £8 per share.

Unsurprisingly, there followed another intense public debate. The rise in share prices pointed to a value way above Tobin's Q, and since it happened immediately, it could not be the result of unanticipated efficiency gains on behalf of managers operating under the incentives of the fixed-priced contract. For Littlechild, this was a decisive moment in the credibility of the price cap regime: to allow the premiums to stand would require him to hold the line for the next five years, but to intervene would suggest a feedback rule from the share price to the risk of intervention.[10]

His reaction was to try to defend the outcome, and he gave a number of reasons why he believed share prices had risen. The first was the removal of uncertainty that had hung over the sector during the periodic review. The second was the takeover mechanism: now that the golden shares were expiring, it would be expected that there would be a premium for control in the share price (Littlechild 1994).[11] The first was simply implausible—*any* outcome would remove uncertainty. The second was a matter of scale—it could not possibly justify the share price increases.

Neither argument was therefore sufficiently convincing to justify the sheer size of the premium to the RAB. Clearly Littlechild had not managed to get the financial variables right, or to correct for the OPEX and CAPEX errors in the first period. But before this could fully play out, two things happened: the slightly later price controls for the Scottish electricity distribution reviews had been appealed to the Monopolies and Mergers Commission (MMC) (allowing the regulator to use this MMC appeal as a test case) and Trafalgar House had bid to purchase Northern Electric. It was this second event that exposed the fragility of the regulatory regime, and eventually opened the way to the windfall tax on what the Labour opposition called the "excess returns of the privatised utilities."

Northern Electric did not accept Trafalgar House's bid. Instead it embarked on a radical defense strategy. Realizing that the existing assets could be mortgaged, it proposed (in the second defense document) to borrow against the network an amount sufficient to pay out in cash £5 for every share purchased at £2.40 five years previously at privatization. Not only was the strategy executed, but in due course—despite the reduction on revenues as a result of reopening the price cap—the company was subsequently sold for over £7 per share, making a return on the initial investment at privatization of over 400 percent. Few would argue that such returns were commensurate with the risks investors had borne in what is a mature monopoly activity, or were necessary to provide efficiency incentives.

The regulator's response to the increase in share prices following his announcement of the new price cap was to launch a rereview, and thereby violate the core principle of ex ante regulation. As Littlechild explained, "It is relevant to take into account what appears to be widespread public concern about whether the price control proposals are sufficiently demanding on the RECs and whether they represent an appropriate balance between the interests of customers and shareholders."[12] In the meantime Hydro Electric, one of the Scottish companies, had as noted above appealed to the MMC over its proposed new price cap, and the regulator could therefore use its outcome to reset prices (MMC 1995a; OFFER 1995). Even when the price cap had been reset, share prices did not fall back toward a small premium over the RAB, but stayed well in excess, indicating that investors judged the outcomes above that needed just to finance the efficient discharge of functions by companies.

The electricity regulator was not alone in revisiting the price caps ex post. Indeed, compared to the water regulator, he had been relatively robust. In every single year in the first period (again 1990–1995), the water regulator intervened (Helm and Rajah 1994), and after the 1994 periodic review had reset prices for the period 1995–2000, the companies were "persuaded" by the regulator to engage in "voluntary profit sharing," in response to the threat of more explicit intervention. South West Water appealed against this new price cap, and the MMC argued for a sharper cut in the rate of return, rather than a glidepath that had been adopted in the periodic review (MMC 1995b). In effect, the regulator was arguing that companies should ex post reduce returns by lowering the prices in light of an appeal by an individual company and the MMC findings. And back in the electricity industry, a further "deal" was brokered to the effect that when the electricity distribution companies sold their shares in the National Transmission System (in 1996), there should be a one-off £50 rebate to customers. And, again, even after the rereview, the £50 rebate, and the windfall tax, the price level could still be cut by 20 percent at the next review in 1999 (Ofgem 1999a, 1999b).[13]

These messy outcomes of both the electricity distribution and the water periodic reviews undermined the regulators' credibility in sticking to the ex ante contracts. But once the breach had been made, and the companies had revealed their borrowing capacity for purposes other than CAPEX, it was a small step for the government to intervene directly—and to the windfall tax.

9.6   Ex Post Interventions by Governments: The Windfall Tax

The windfall tax represented the largest single ex post intervention in the UK regulatory regime for the core networks since privatization. There had been other changes through legislation that had been profound—notably the liberalization of the supply of gas and eventually electricity, and the consequent breaking of the long-term take-or-pay contracts for gas supply that had underpinned the development of North Sea gas. But these sectors had commodity elements and it could be argued that the promotion of competition was a well-understood underlying policy driver, which investors would have taken into account. Directly extracting additional revenues from privatized monopoly utilities was an altogether more direct act.

The windfall tax on utilities was not strictly a new idea. The Conservative government in the early 1980s had extracted a windfall tax from banks and there had been much discussion of windfall taxes on North Sea oil and gas companies (and many changes to North Sea taxation). But the utility windfall tax came about for a complex set of reasons. Of these, the political aspects were the most important. In the mid-1990s, the Labour opposition was keen to draw a sharp distinction between its more "social" approach and that of Thatcherism. The Labour opposition toyed with the "third way" between capitalism and socialism, and argued that the greed and self-interest that they labeled the Conservative government with would be replaced by a more inclusive approach to economic and social policy. Social justice and economic growth could be combined.[14] It was a deliberately vague and broad political argument, but it had its effect. To give the broad claims meaning to the voters, Labour encouraged the populist claim that a small number of "fat cats" in the privatized industries were gaining undeserved salaries and profits at the expense of the broader electorate. The chief executive of British Gas, Cedric Brown, became a scapegoat for this political argument, and it was a short step to push for these "undue returns" to be clawed back.[15]

To this broader political argument was added a narrower one. The Labour Party had traditionally been stigmatized by the Conservatives as "tax-and-spend" and in the run-up to the 1997 election, the Conservatives were keen to demonstrate that some of Labour's spending commitments were unfunded—and hence that tax rises would be inevitable in the event of a Labour victory. Labour therefore faced an acute dilemma—how could it promise new spending initiatives, and at the same time not raise general taxes? To make matters worse for Labour, they readily expected that the long boom of the 1990s would come to an end, perhaps as soon as 1998.

Labour therefore adopted three strategies. First, they committed themselves to the Conservatives' spending plans. Second, they earmarked specific revenue streams for new commitments. Third, they began to examine the scope for energy or carbon taxes. It was the second that gave rise to the windfall tax. Labour proposed a "New Deal" policy for unemployed young people, and proposed that the windfall tax would finance it. Thus they achieved several political ends neatly: the "private greed" would be dealt with; the young would be helped into the labor market; and general taxes (especially the income tax) would not be raised. As John Prescott, Deputy Leader of the Labour Party, put it more crudely in a parliamentary debate in 1996, "The privatised utilities were sold off cheaply, weakly regulated and allowed to make excess profits. Labour plans to raise a levy to help put the unemployed of Britain back to work, because we believe that is social justice."[16]

It remained to design a tax that would not be susceptible to challenge in the courts, and that could be justified as targeting "excess returns." The former was a very serious problem. Since 1995, a number of the electricity distribution companies had been bought by American utilities,[17] and these new owners, accustomed to the U.S. legal style of regulation, would regard the windfall tax as expropriation of property rights, and therefore might seek legal redress. And in the event that such legal action was to be successful, the careful overall architecture of Labour's funding of its extra expenditure would crumble, and with it their credibility in a macroeconomic sense. (That credibility was indeed so important to the incoming government that it had also granted independence to the Bank of England and created an independent monetary committee (the Monetary Policy Committee, MPC) to set interest rates within its first days in office.)

A complex formula was devised to meet this potential challenge. The windfall tax was described by the Chancellor of the Exchequer as follows:

The Chancellor today announced the introduction of the proposed windfall tax on the excess profits of the privatised utilities. The one-off tax will apply to companies privatised by flotation and regulated by statute. The tax will be charged at a rate of 23 percent on the difference between company value, calculated by reference to profits over a period of up to four years following privatisation and the value placed on the company at the time of flotation. The expected yield is around £5.2 billion.[18]

As a legal construct it survived. As an intervention into the ex ante price cap regime, it was a very serious setback. For if the argument was that the companies had earned excess profits, this had to be established as above the profits that would have resulted from the response to the efficiency incentives in the price caps. Furthermore, to the extent that there were excess profits, this implied that customers had paid too much, and hence the correct response would have been to lower prices—to revise the price caps, as Littlechild had done in 1995, and as happened in the water industry when companies were "persuaded" to voluntarily share profits after 1995. Though there might be considerable overlap between taxpayers and customers, there could be no economic justification in utility regulation for the windfall tax as the optimal remedy. It was even harder to argue that there should be any link between the regulation of utilities and the plight of unemployed young people.

If these linkages could not be sustained on economic grounds, then it remains an important consideration to analyze why nevertheless the windfall tax was—in political terms—successful. And even in economic terms, the companies continued to strive to reduce costs: there is no evidence to suggest any diminution of managerial efforts as a result. As noted at the outset, the contract between the utility shareholders and the government, as brokered in the privatization "settlement," comprised two parts: the formal fixed-price, fixed-period component; and the informal broader contract requiring the modernization of the utility infrastructure, which was used to justify privatization to the electorate. The former might be called the *letter* of the contract, the latter the *spirit*. The UK windfall tax broke the formal contract, and seriously undermined ex ante regulation. But it is less clear that it broke the latter. For, in essence, the informal contract meant that utility shareholders could keep their gains provided that they behaved in a way that served the public interest.[19]

The UK utilities were, as noted above, privatized on the argument that they would invest, modernizing the networks. The balance sheets were ungeared for this purpose. Borrowing was supposed to fit this purpose. Northern Electric had broken with this "understanding," and the subsequent dash-for-debt broke any link between gearing and physical investment. None of this had been contemplated as a possibility at privatization. What the utilities—and especially their new foreign owners—failed to appreciate was that their future would always be political—that they would be allowed to operate provided the outcome was perceived to be in the public interest—otherwise, the terms of the contract would be changed. After the price caps were reset in 1994, few commentators thought they did, and in the media and the broader public debate, they were regarded with growing hostility. The privatization of the railroad industry (and some of the immediate very large capital gains to shareholders—notably in the rolling-stock leasing companies, the ROSCOs) furthered the criticisms.

By 1997, some form of intervention was probably inevitable, and it is possible to argue that had the windfall tax not been levied, the incoming government would have torn up the overall utility framework—rather than, as they did, launching an immediate review and in the end just tinkering with the framework. In other words, the informal contract had been sufficiently violated in the public (and therefore political) eye as to render the windfall tax the lesser evil that could allow the formal parts of the contract framework to persist. And, despite the violations of the ex ante contracts, ex post the companies continued to earn a return in excess of their cost of capital. It was rational therefore to continue to try to maximize profits by minimizing costs, even if some of these profits had been clawed back.

9.7 Developing RPI–X

These two examples—the resetting of the electricity price cap after the Northern Electric takeover defense, and the windfall tax—point to an underlying problem with the pure ex ante contracting approach. The contracts are not only incomplete, but with respect to the RAB, inappropriate. The formal part of the contract operates in the informal context of the wider privatization settlement, and the regulation through a WACC creates the incentives to engage in financial engineering. Add to this poor regulation enabling the companies to game the CAPEX and OPEX ex ante, to produce significant cuts ex post as a result of the strategic revelation of information, rather than through managerial inefficiencies, and reform of the initial crude RPI–X model was inevitable. The issue was whether it would be pragmatic and evolutionary, or revolutionary.

This inevitability does not, however, mean that price cap regulation is doomed to failure, but rather it needs to be designed more sensitively to the implicit aspects of the contract and to take better account of the ways equity risk is assigned. Mechanisms are needed that provide for flexibility when the outcomes price cap regulation produces are so far in excess of normal returns as to stimulate direct political intervention. Whatever the theoretical economic attractions, the political structures simply do not permit pure fixed-price contracts to be written over fixed periods without some scope for ex post intervention. The UK example is extreme in the extent to which there was an attempt to inject great rigidity into the regulatory regime, and it broke badly in the 1990s. Since then interventions have been more subtle, and there have been no more windfall taxes or reopening of price caps, except in the case of collapse (Railtrack and air traffic service company, NATS). Ex post, error correction has become more subtle. The reasons for this less volatile outcome have been a gradual drift toward rate-of-return elements in the regulation, a lowering of the allowed cost of capital, and a lessening of the scope for outperformance. However, the scope for financial engineering remains, reflecting a mismatch between the assignment of equity risk and the price cap incentives.

9.7.1   The RAB and Rate of Return

As argued in section 9.4, the duty to finance functions placed on the regulators has increasingly been interpreted as protecting the RAB. As a result, financing the RAB through debt has been increasingly undertaken by utilities—since, by implication, they face no equity risk with respect to the RAB. This splits the cost of capital experienced by the utilities into two—a cost of debt for the RAB, and a cost of equity for the running of the OPEX and CAPEX aspects of the business. The use of a WACC by regulators, rather than a split cost of capital, has served to reinforce the dash-for-debt.[20]

From the perspective of ex ante regulation, the implication of this trend is that the incentive regime applies only to the operational aspects of the business—the carrying out of investment and the operation of the networks. A flaw in the original approach was to bundle these two activities together, and this was the origin of much of the excess returns (and remains so now). The price cap incentives were intended to encourage the companies to minimize the costs of CAPEX and OPEX by finding innovative approaches to managing the businesses. They were never intended to encourage—and reward—financial engineering.

As a result of the bundling together, the setting of the cost of capital failed to differentiate out the assignment of the equity risk. The equity risk in the RAB lies with the customers, and therefore it is hard to see why any premium should be paid over the cost of debt, and why the ex ante contracting should apply to the RAB—other than an ex ante commitment to ensure that it earns an appropriate rate of return. Thus rate-of-return regulation is the appropriate basis for the RAB, and through the guarantee the regulator provides, it is merely a private funding mechanism, closely akin to the issuing of government bonds. Put another way, the RABs are not really private at all.

On the other hand, the rationale for privatizing the contracts for the OPEX and CAPEX had a clear efficiency grounding, and it is this element of the regulatory contract that would benefit most from the transfer of the equity risk to private shareholders. Indeed, a comparison can be made with the case in which the RAB assets are kept in the public sector, but the government then auctions contracts to the private sector to carry out the business of running and augmenting the assets. This approach is adopted in the French water industry and has been extended to the London Underground. However, in the latter case, the contracts were fixed for thirty years and made inflexible to minimize ex post intervention, in this case by the political authorities in London. Given that the works could not easily be specified for this length of time (and especially now that the system will be substantially affected by a new Crossrail London project to build an east-west line), these long-term ex ante contracts are subject to repeated attempts to make ex post revisions.[21]

The splitting of equity risk between customers and shareholders through the division of the RAB from the rest of the business is an approach that the capital markets have been imposing on UK utilities.

Infrastructure funds have been purchasing public companies and taking them private, using primarily pension fund monies and raising the gearing. The approach adopted has yielded substantial short-term returns through the financial engineering encouraged by the application of a WACC. Nevertheless, the resulting financial structure mirrors the separation out discussed above. RABs are being largely debt financed, leaving a small sliver of equity to cover the risks in the OPEX and CAPEX.[22]

9.7.2 Institutional Consistency with Ex Ante Contracts

Even if the formal parts of the contract had been well specified, separating out the RAB from the operation of the businesses, and focusing ex ante contracts onto the latter, the UK institutional structures would probably still have led to ex post interventions. The reason, set out above, lies in the United Kingdom's administrative approach, as reflected in the "good chaps" regulation that accompanied RPI–X.

At the limit, it could be argued that the UK's public administrative system is peculiarly ill-suited to fixed-price contracts, and that, as a result, it is not surprising that public ownership—and hence internalizing the equity risk in the public sector—has been the dominant way of organizing infrastructure networks and utilities. RPI–X has indeed failed in the railways case, and partly failed in the London Underground, and arguably the water industry has more in common now with rate-of-return regulation.

The institutional response has been to try to insert more grit between the government (and government departments) on the one hand, and regulators on the other. Regulators have been made "independent." This has had mixed results in the UK context—since simply making regulators independent does not answer the further question of: to what purpose? Though it is fashionable in economic theory to separate out objectives from policy instruments, in the energy sector many of the policy instruments remain in governmental hands. Regulation is focused on multiple market failures—externalities, monopoly, complementarities, and social failures—and setting prices requires a detailed specification of precisely what the outputs and services are that are to be provided in return. While in theory there should be as many instruments as targets, and it might be argued that there should be separate institutions and regulators for each market failure, in practice sectoral regulators are required to make the relevant trade-offs. And because these trade-offs are ultimately political, the independent regulators are exposed to the challenge that they have no democratic mandate.

The implications of these considerations are several. It may well be that ex ante regulation is context-specific and in particular that there are greater limits to ex ante contracting in the United Kingdom than in the United States. The United Kingdom's administrative approach—in contrast to the legal and constitutional approach in the United States— may embed flexible ex post interventions into the regulatory process. This creates political and regulatory risk, which raises the private-sector cost of capital. Therefore, a significant element of rate-of-return regulation may be inevitable in the United Kingdom because ex post interventions are likely to be repeatedly witnessed—an irony, given that the United Kingdom invented RPI–X. The equity risk may be best borne by the government (as the controller of these risks) or the customers.

But it also matters considerably how the regulatory institutions are designed. In the United Kingdom, the lesson is that the discretion needs to be bounded by politics and policymakers may need to be more specific in their overarching sectoral policies if ex ante contracting is to be required. This indeed has occurred: the UK government has begun to develop longer-term policy frameworks—a ten-year transport plan, a long-term airport strategy, and a climate change framework for the energy sector (DETR 2000; DfT 2003; DTI 2003b).

9.7.3   The Political Limits to Profits

Ex ante contracting is aimed at economic efficiency. Yet economic efficiency is not the only component of social welfare, and in the United Kingdom the public discourse about profits is conditioned by concerns about social justice and fairness. It is no accident that, as the ex ante contracts revealed high levels of profit and large salary increases, the politicians explicitly pointed to "social justice" as one of the arguments for the windfall tax.

Furthermore, the larger the profits, the greater the pressure to justify them. In the UK case, it is hard to argue that the level of profits was necessary to incentivize the shareholders to exert efficiency pressures on the management, or that the salaries were commensurate with the scale of the management's task.

But if, at the same time that profits and salaries rise, the utilities appear to break the informal parts of the contract—in particular, using the balance sheets *not* for investment, but rather to pay out cash to shareholders—then the political pressures are bound to intensify. Although there were obvious arguments for financial efficiency, it was far from surprising that if balance sheets could be leveraged by shareholders, they could also be by government.

9.8   Interventions in Other Sectors—the North Sea

The striking feature of the regulation of utilities is that there is a formal structure, both in terms of the price caps and periodic reviews, and in terms of the institutions. By contrast, in the North Sea, the interventions are much more pliable and the prospect of ex post intervention has been built into the fabric of the relationship between the state and the private-sector companies from the outset.

The North Sea has been developed in an evolutionary way, with frequent changes. Early on, when the prospects were very uncertain, the government provided a legal framework and a licensing regime—very much as it is doing now with the embryonic carbon capture and storage (CCS) industry. On the gas side, a national champion was used— British Gas—which was granted a monopoly, and offshore companies were required to sell all their gas to it, on long-term contract terms dictated by British Gas. It, in turn, built the National Transmission System, and carried out the conversion from town to natural gas. The model was not, in retrospect, that different from that being developed now in Russia, through Gazprom.

On the oil side, the private companies developed the fields, and the state tried a host of strategies to influence the speed of development and to extract the maximum return consistent with that development. At the end of the 1970s, it tried the nationalized route with the British National Oil Company (BNOC), and BP itself was largely in state hands (although, for revenue reasons, the Labour government at the end of the 1970s started to sell off part of its shares). There followed (after the Conservative government came to power in 1979) the privatization of BNOC and the oil assets of British Gas (Britoil and Enterprise Oil respectively), and a more explicit focus on the tax regime. But, even here, having extracted the state from production, there was little attempt to provide an ex ante stability to the fiscal regime.

The early regime, set out in the 1974 White Paper (Department of Energy 1974) and the Oil Taxation Act 1975, provided for three elements: royalties, petroleum revenue tax (PRT), and corporation tax. The Conservative government abolished royalties on post-1983 fields in 1983, and then on all fields in 2002. PRT was a tax on revenue minus allowed expenses, and a host of other complex offsets. These allowances and offsets were frequently adjusted, and in 1993 the tax was abolished on all new fields and halved on existing ones. Corporate tax rates were frequently changed too, and again allowances were an important element—including, in this case, exploration costs. Losses for other activities were disallowed, so this form of corporation tax was ring-fenced.

In 2002, the taxation regime was significantly changed. This time a new 10 percent supplementary charge on profits included within the corporation tax base was levied, but full capital investment allowances were permitted, in parallel with the abolition of royalties. The rationale was explicitly stated by the government to be the increase in oil prices since 2001 (see HMRC 2006). This same reason was given for the doubling of this supplementary charge in 2005.[23]

These changes were sufficiently frequent to be regarded as "normal." The changes in taxation were not one-off like the windfall tax on the utilities, discussed above. The key difference between the two sectors is that, in the North Sea, the companies had a bargaining chip—their willingness to develop the resources. In the utility case, once CAPEX is complete, given that the marginal costs are very low relative to the average, the scope for ex post expropriation (and hence time inconsistency) is correspondingly large. Short of creating and sustaining a state-owned oil company to work the fields, the government has to find ways to induce investment and production. It can pluck the golden goose, but only so far as the goose is kept alive and healthy. Many other resource-rich countries have chosen the nationalization route—notably in the Middle East, Venezuela, and now Russia. For the United Kingdom after the 1970s, this has not been an option.

Thus, although intervention has been repeatedly ex post, it has been within a basic economic bargaining framework. The companies cannot predict exactly what the UK government will do, but they can rely on the overarching nature of the game, and the need for the government to ensure that production is maximized.[24] It is a luxury that is less directly available to the utilities that are the primary focus of my analysis.

9.9   Conclusions

The British experiment with ex ante contracting has proved less complete or enduring than its advocates forecast. Ex ante contracting requires extremely demanding conditions. It rests ultimately on the credibility of the contractor sticking to the price caps, and the forgoing of short-term interventions. That, in turn, requires a sympathetic institutional architecture. In the United Kingdom, first the regulator and then the government reneged on the ex ante contracts.

It would be easy to conclude that ex ante contracts are therefore hopeless. This would, however, be too extreme. Rather, ex ante contracts can function within well-defined political and institutional frameworks. The political framework includes a specification of the overarching policies and an understanding by the utilities that there are limitations on the level of profits. Blatant financial engineering, in the full glare of media attention, is a strategy that, while in the interests of the specific set of shareholders, is poisonous to the longer-term stability of the framework. Regulation is, after all, a repeated game. On the institutional front, limiting the personal discretion of individual regulators and defining the (political) trade-offs can help to stabilize the framework.

But overriding these political and institutional factors, the ex ante regulation needs to be focused on those aspects of the business to which equity risk is assigned and appropriate. In utilities, this is the OPEX and CAPEX, *but not the RAB*. This splitting of regulation (and the cost of capital—and even the business architecture itself) leads to a more modest role for incentives, and more moderate scope for excess returns. It sorts out the roles of government in setting the policy framework and defining the trade-offs between market failures. It identifies the customers as bearers of the equity risk in the RAB (and hence the sunk, fixed long-term costs of past investments) and the shareholders as bearers of the equity risk for those aspects of the business to which efficient management can make a difference.

Ex ante UK RPI–X, in its pure form, was therefore inevitably doomed to fail, as indeed it did in almost every sector to which it was applied, except perhaps for the regional electricity companies from 1990 to 1994. It remains to be seen whether a more stable ex ante regime can evolve, or whether the UK utilities will in due course collapse back into implicit (or even explicit) state control (as in Network Rail and the London Underground) or rate-of-return regulation.

Notes

Comments to dieter@dhelm.co.uk. Further papers available on www.dieterhelm.co.uk.

1. See also Helm, Hepburn, and Mash 2003 for an application to climate change policy and in particular the setting of carbon taxes.

2. For a subsequent exposition and justification, see Beesley and Littlechild 1989.

3. See MMC 1980, 1981, 1983a, 1983b, 1984, 1985, 1986.

4. See Cockett 1994.

5. See also HMT 1985 for a ministerial statement on the objectives of privatization.

6. See Skidelsky 1983, chaps. 1–3, for insight into the linkages between the state and the leading universities in the development of an appropriate educational framework. Elements of elite education in France play a similar role in developing common values. Hannah 1982 provides a history of how it worked in the electricity sector under nationalization. The government's overall approach to regulating nationalized industries was set out in HMT 1978. Hennessey 1989 explains how the civil service factored the public interest into its architecture.

7. DTI 2000b, DTI 2002, and DTI 2003a set out the painful process of arriving at a (politically) acceptable outcome.

8. Department of Industry and Littlechild 1983.

9. See Helm 1994b and the reply in Littlechild 1994. For the ministerial position at the time, see DTI 1994.

10. This linkage remains part of the regulatory debate—see Competition Commission 2007 on BAA.

11. For the regulator's more general views on the role of takeovers in utility regulation, see Littlechild 1988.

12. OFFER, press statement, March 7, 1995.

13. A more detailed account of the events can be found in Helm 2004.

14. This was the core argument in the "New" Labour project of Blair, Brown, and Mandelson. See Commission for Social Justice 1994; Giddens 1994; Mandelson and Liddle 1996.

15. See Blair 1995 for the then–opposition leader's linkages of the issues. See also Corry 1995a, 1995b, and Corry, Souter, and Waterson 1994 for the broader political and economic arguments at this time.

16. Hansard, November 21, 1996.

17. See Helm 2004.

18. Inland Revenue 1997.

19. It is, interestingly, an argument that in a much cruder context, President Putin was to use against the oligarchs in Russia.

20. See DTI/HM Treasury 2004 and Helm 2007b. See also Bucks 2003.

21. One of the two companies granted contracts, Metronet, collapsed in 2007.

22. In the case of NORWEB being sold in autumn 2007, the contract to operate the business has been explicitly split out as part of the sale, so that the RAB itself will be separately identified and financed. In the earlier case of Welsh Water, it was converted into a debt-only structure and the operation of the business put out to tender. For evidence on BAA's highly geared takeover, see also Competition Commission 2007 and for a critique, Helm 2007a.

23. See Nakhle 2007 for analysis of the impact of these changes.

24. Indeed, this political imperative was so pressing as to lead to the very rapid depletion of the North Sea—at what has turned out to be the period of the lowest oil prices.

References

Averch, H., and L. L. Johnson. 1962. "Behavior of the Firm under Regulatory Constraint." *American Economic Review* 52:5: 1052–1069.

Beesley, M. E., and S. C. Littlechild. 1989. "The Regulation of Privatized Monopolies in the United Kingdom." *RAND Journal of Economics* 20:3: 454–472.

Blair, T. 1995. "Principles for Reform." In D. Corry, ed., *Principles for Reform: New Thinking on Regulatory Reform*, 2–4. London: Institute for Public Policy Research.

Bucks, P. 2003. "Financial Leverage and the Regulator." *Utilities Journal*, Oxera (October): 38–39.

Cockett, R. 1994. "The Road to Serfdom—50 Years On." *History Today*, May.

Commission for Social Justice. 1994. Social Justice: Strategies for National Renewal. Report of the Commission for Social Justice (Borrie report), London: Vintage.

Competition Commission. 2007. "BAA Ltd—A Report on the Economic Regulation of the London Airports Companies (Heathrow Airport Ltd and Gatwick Airport Ltd)." Presented to the Civil Aviation Authority, September 28.

Conservative Party. 1979. *Manifesto*. London: Conservative Central Office.

Corry, D., ed. 1995a. *Profiting from the Utilities: New Thinking on Regulatory Reform*. July. London: Institute for Public Policy Research.

Corry, D., ed. 1995b. *Regulating in the Public Interest: Looking to the Future*. May. London: Institute for Public Policy Research.

Corry, D. 2003. *The Regulatory State: Labour and the Utilities 1997–2002*. London: Institute for Public Policy Research.

Corry, D., D. Souter, and M. Waterson. 1994. *Regulating Our Utilities*. September. London: Institute for Public Policy Research.

Department of Energy. 1974. "UK Offshore Oil and Gas Policy." July 11. London: HMSO.

Department of Industry and S. Littlechild. 1983. "Regulation of British Telecommunications' Profitability." Department of Trade and Industry. London: HMSO.

DETR. 2000. "The 10 Year Transport Plan." Department for the Environment, Transport and the Regions, May. London: TSO.

DfT. 2003. "The Future of Air Transport." White Paper, Department for Transport, December 16. London: TSO.

DTI. 1994. "Speech by Mr Eggar, Minister for Industry and Energy on the Role of Regulators, 21 November 1994." Department of Trade and Industry, press release, P/64/699.

DTI. 1998. "A Fair Deal for Consumers: Modernising the Framework for Utility Regulation." Department of Trade and Industry, Cmnd 3898, March. London: TSO.

DTI. 2000a. "A Fair Deal for Consumers: Modernising the Framework for Utility Regulation: Regulatory, Environmental and Equal Treatment Appraisals." Department of Trade and Industry, January, para 11, p. 7. London: TSO.

DTI. 2000b. "A Fair Deal for Consumers: Modernising the Framework for Utility Regulation: Draft Statutory Social and Environmental Guidance to the Gas and Electricity Markets Authority." Department of Trade and Industry, February. London: TSO.

DTI. 2002. "Social and Environmental Guidance to the Gas and Electricity Markets Authority." Department of Trade and Industry, draft, June. London: TSO.

DTI. 2003a. "Draft Social and Environmental Guidance to the Gas and Electricity Markets Authority: A Consultation Document by the Department of Trade and Industry." Department of Trade and Industry, June 4. London: TSO.

DTI. 2003b. "Our Energy Future—Creating a Low Carbon Economy." White Paper, CM 5761. London: TSO.

DTI/HM Treasury. 2004. "The Drivers and Public Policy Consequences of Increased Gearing." October. London: TSO.

Giddens, A. 1994. *Beyond Left and Right—the Future of Radical Politics.* Cambridge: Polity Press.

Hannah, L. 1982. *Engineers, Managers and Politicians: The First Fifteen Years of Nationalised Electricity Supply in Britain.* London: Macmillan.

Helm, D. R. 1987. "RPI–X and the Newly Privatised Industries: A Deceptively Simple Regulatory Rule." *Public Money* 7:1 (June): 47–51.

Helm, D. R. 1994a. "British Utility Regulation: Theory, Practice, and Reform." *Oxford Review of Economic Policy* 10:3: 17–39.

Helm, D. R. 1994b. "Regulating the Transition to the Competitive Market." In M. E. Beesley, ed., *Regulating Utilities: The Way Forward.* IEA Readings 41. London: Institute of Economic Affairs in association with the London Business School.

Helm, D. R. 2001. "Making Britain More Competitive: A Critique of Regulation and Competition Policy." *Scottish Journal of Political Economy* 48:5: 471–487.

Helm, D. R. 2004. *Energy, the State, and the Market: British Energy Policy since 1979.* Rev. ed. Oxford: Oxford University Press.

Helm, D. R. 2007a. "How Not to Regulate Airports: BAA, the Competition Commission and Regulatory Reform." Commentary, October. www.dieterhelm.co.uk.

Helm, D. R. 2007b. "What Is a Utility Worth?" Commentary, June. www.dieterhelm .co.uk.

Helm, D. R., C. Hepburn, and R. Mash. 2003. "Credible Carbon Policy." *Oxford Review of Economic Policy* 19:3: 438–450.

Helm, D. R., and N. Rajah. 1994. "Water Regulation: The Periodic Review." *Fiscal Studies* 15:2: 74–94.

Hennessey, P. 1989. *Whitehall*. London: Seeker & Warburg.

HMRC. 2006. "Regulatory Impact Assessment for Changes to the North Sea Tax Regime." March. London: TSO.

HMT. 1978. "The Nationalised Industries." Cmnd 7131, Her Majesty's Treasury. London: HMSO.

HMT. 1985. "The Success of Privatisation." Speech by J. Moore, Financial Secretary, Her Majesty's Treasury. London: HMSO.

Inland Revenue. 1997. "Windfall Tax." Press release, July 2.

Littlechild, S. C. 1988. "Economic Regulation of Privatised Water Authorities and Some Further Reflections." *Oxford Review of Economic Policy* 4:2: 40–67.

Littlechild, S. C. 1994. "Chairman's Comments" (reply to Helm 1994b). In M. E. Beesley, ed., *Regulating Utilities: The Way Forward*. IEA Readings 41. London: Institute of Economic Affairs in association with the London Business School.

Mandelson, P., and R. Liddle. 1996. *The Blair Revolution: Can New Labour Deliver?* London: Faber and Faber.

MMC. 1980. "Domestic Gas Appliances: A Report on the Supply of Certain Domestic Gas Appliances in the United Kingdom." Monopolies and Mergers Commission, HC 703, 1979–80, July. London: HMSO.

MMC. 1981. "Central Electricity Generating Board: A Report on the Operation by the Board of Its System for the Generation and Supply of Electricity in Bulk." Monopolies and Mergers Commission, HC 315, 1980–81, May. London: HMSO.

MMC. 1983a. "National Coal Board: A Report on the Efficiency and Costs in the Development, Production and Supply of Coal by the NCB." Monopolies and Mergers Commission, Cmnd 8920, June. London: HMSO.

MMC. 1983b. "Yorkshire Electricity Board: A Report on the Efficiency and Costs of the Board." Monopolies and Mergers Commission, Cmnd 9014, August. London: HMSO.

MMC. 1984. "South Wales Electricity Board: A Report on the Efficiency and Costs of the Board." Monopolies and Mergers Commission, Cmnd 9165, February. London: HMSO.

MMC. 1985. "North of Scotland Hydro-Electric Board: A Report on the Efficiency and Costs of the Board." Monopolies and Mergers Commission, Cmnd 9628, October. London: HMSO.

MMC. 1986. "South of Scotland Electricity Board: A Report on the Efficiency and Costs of the Board." Monopolies and Mergers Commission, Cmnd 9868, August. London: HMSO.

MMC. 1995a. "Scottish Hydro-Electric pic: A Report on a Reference under Section 12 of the Electricity Act 1989." Monopolies and Mergers Commission, June. London: HMSO.

MMC. 1995b. "South West Water Services Ltd: A Report on the Determination of the Adjustment Factors and Infrastructure Charges for South West Water Services Ltd." Monopolies and Mergers Commission, June. London: HMSO, July.

Nakhle, C. 2007. "Do High Oil Prices Justify an Increase in Taxation in a Mature Oil Province? The Case of the UK Continental Shelf." *Energy Policy* 35: 4305–4318.

OFFER. 1992. "Report on Constrained-on Plant." October. Birmingham: Office of Electricity Regulation.

OFFER. 1994. "The Distribution Price Control: Proposals." August. Birmingham: Office of Electricity Regulation.

OFFER. 1995. "The Distribution Price Control: Revised Proposals." July. Birmingham: Office of Electricity Regulation.

Ofgem. 1999a. "Review of Public Electricity Suppliers 1998–2000. Distribution Price Control Review: Final Proposals." December. London: Office of Gas and Electricity Markets.

Ofgem. 1999b. "Reviews of Public Electricity Suppliers 1998 to 2000: Distribution Price Control Review: Draft Proposals." August. London: Office of Gas and Electricity Markets.

Ofgem. 2000. "New Ownership Structures in the Water Industry: A Response to the Director General of Water Services' Consultation Paper." July. London: Office of Gas and Electricity Markets.

Robinson, C. 1981. "What Future for British Coal? Optimism or Realism on the Prospects to the Year 2000." Hobart Paper 89. London: Institute of Economic Affairs.

Skidelsky, R. 1983. *John Maynard Keynes, Volume 1: Hopes Betrayed: 1883–1920.* London: Macmillan.

Utilities Act 2000. London: Her Majesty's Stationery Office.

Commentary

Jeffrey Frankel

Natural resources are once again back in the limelight. In the 1990s mineral commodities were neglected. In the decade of the 2000s, people rediscovered that economies do run on energy and raw materials, that everything cannot be done over the Internet. Helm's chapter and the other chapters in this book address a great theme. What makes these chapters especially interesting is that they focus, in a very nitty-gritty way, on identifying the desirable institutions to deal with commodity booms—what is state-of-the-art, what is best practice—so that resource-rich countries can avoid the mistakes of the past.

This commentary begins by placing Helm's chapter in the general context of the time-inconsistency problem that institutions face. Then it considers the importance of the example of the United Kingdom presented in Helm's chapter. Finally, it motivates and asks a question about attempts at better contracts in practice that are highlighted by the chapter.

Time Inconsistency

A number of the contributors to this volume, including myself, teach classes on aspects of development, in which we talk about the role of "institutions" in determining whether some countries perform better than others. Our students have grounds to tease us, in that we talk about institutions so much but sometimes are not specific enough about what good institutions are. The design of contracts or wealth funds to deal with natural resource cycles is a good example of what they want to hear.

The central theme seems to be the conflict between the incentives that exist ex ante, which is for a government to offer attractive terms so that—whether it is a domestic firm or an outside multinational coming in—it will invest and develop the resources, versus the incentives that exist ex post, which is often to renege on the contract. In particular, if the commodity price subsequently goes up on world markets, governments ask why the company should get all the gains.

This is an area where better design of mechanisms and incentives and institutions can make a big difference. As the introduction points out, the formulation of the problem goes back at least to Ray Vernon. Like Dieter Helm, I think the phrase "time inconsistency" applies. It is a simple idea: the incentive you have to promise ahead of time is different from the incentive you have after the investment has been made.

A classic illustration is the story of Odysseus and the Sirens. The story, of course, is that Odysseus was warned that his ship was going to sail past the Sirens; they sing so sweetly that the sailors would be irresistibly tempted to dive into the water and be drowned. He gave orders to his men to plug their ears with wax, but he wanted to listen. So the captain ordered them to tie him to the mast and no matter how much he begged to be let go, they should not free him. Odysseus hears the Sirens and tells his men to let him go, but they do not because the ex ante commitment is successful.

It is ironic that this metaphor has become best known and best established in monetary theory. Central banks have an incentive to say ahead of time that they will not print a lot of money and will not be inflationary, in order to get price expectations and wages down. After the fact, they have an irresistible temptation to be more expansionary. The lesson is that governments need institutions to tie their own hands, either bodies such as a constitutionally independent central bank or a currency board, or rules like a fixed exchange rate or inflation targeting.

Time inconsistency actually applies better to some areas of microeconomics. Note 1 in Helm's chapter gives a reference on global climate change. This concept of time inconsistency is important, though not widely incorporated in existing analyses of global climate change. Despite all the complications that are in typical models, it has been largely missing. Absent in the design of the optimal path is the idea that governments have an incentive to promise ex ante that, though they will start off slowly, they will cut emissions very sharply in the *second* half of the twenty-first century. But this assurance is not very credible because this set of policymakers is not going to be around in the second half of the twenty-first century. When the time comes it will be expensive for the new crop of policymakers to do it. Furthermore, everybody knows this. Nobody believes the century-long commitment path to begin with. That is a big problem with the economic modeling of climate change.

Time Inconsistency in Utilities in the United Kingdom

The problem of resource contracts is an excellent application of the time-inconsistency problem. The pattern has been repeated many times in many countries: the price goes up, and then the government wants to renege on its contracts. It does not want to give the company all the profits and, in a sense, why should it? Certainly the political pressures are typically very strong. It has become such a familiar pattern that it seems, by now, that contracts ought to have been designed that are robust with respect to this inconsistency. For example, one might have expected contracts in which the parties write in ahead of time, "If the price goes up by X, then the gains are split between the company and the government."

Looking at the UK example is useful. Helm's chapter provides a good review of the British case. It is clearly written; one can learn a tremendous amount on each page, even knowing little about the subject to begin with. One of the reasons to look to the United Kingdom is as a developed country. For a country like Bolivia (chapter 10), it seems likely that the government could write any contract in the world and people still would not believe it because of past history and the institutional roots that are not deep enough. (No offense to Bolivians.) The fear is that such a country would end up reneging. Thus, it is useful to start off with a country where the regulators are supposed to be professional and keep their word, and where they rank high on the indices of Transparency International and the other rankings the political scientists have developed to measure the quality of institutions.

Here the institution is the RPI-X mechanism, which is a fixed-price contract, but only for four or five years, after which it is to be revised or renegotiated.

There is no need to go through and repeat the points that are presented effectively in the chapter. The overall conclusion is that the mechanism has not worked very well. The case study specifically says that this regulation has not worked as well as perceived. First the regulator and then the government reneged on the ex ante contracts. The narrative goes through the two examples of 1994 and 1995 distribution prices and windfall profit taxes. Probably in any country, when there are huge profits, there is political pressure from the public to claw back a share of them.

The chapter discusses some unintended side effects. It says the company violated the implicit contract in shifting its financing composition toward debt. It is not clear whether there in fact was an implicit contract; instead it might be called an unintended consequence. Can you really blame a company—given its incentives, given a rate of return determined by the weighted average cost of capital, and given its responsibility to its shareholders—if it shifts toward debt when that action is more profitable? It may not be appropriate to call this shift "breaking an implicit contract," unless it was discussed ahead of time and the only sense in which it was not explicit is that it was not written down.

One of the reasons the chapter gives for why the RPI-X mechanism has not worked as well as one might hope or expect, is that the UK system is less rule-based than the U.S. system. If one proceeds along the lines that the parties will write down a contract ahead of time and stick to it, maybe that is an arena in which the U.S. approach works better. People are beginning to have doubts about that when it comes to financial-regulation accounting practices. Maybe the European system has some advantages. But in this case, where it is apparently left up to some "good chaps," the answer is not clear. On the one hand keeping your word is a nice British attribute, but on the other hand doing what is in the interests of your citizens is also a good attribute. If one has the discretion it is hard not to use it. And in some sense the government would be just as negligent not to use such discretion as the company would be negligent not to do something in the interest of the shareholders. The whole point is to bind people ex ante so that they do not have that option.

An Open Question: Attempts at Optimal Contracts

One significant aspect of the mechanism to consider is this: it is not clear from the chapter that anything approximating optimal contract design was really tried in Britain. The mechanism is very crude. As the chapter explains, it was not designed to implement some theoretically optimal contract, but arose by historical happenstance. So the first question for experts in this area is, what about some attempts at contracts that build in contingencies? If the price goes up by X, the company gets to keep some of it but some of it goes back to the government. The rule is applied symmetrically if the price goes down.

One predictable response is that there are a lot of contingencies. The price is not the only thing going up and down; there are various other contingencies and it is very hard to write them all in ex ante. Another part of it has got to be that in a situation where the government already has a lot of credibility—for example, when it is ranked high by Transparency International or the political scientists' indices of governance and rule of law—it can withstand a bit more moral hazard without killing off investment. However, for a country without such a good history of institutions and property rights and rule of law, the situation is the opposite. A government could do a great job writing the contingent contract and yet that would not right away establish its reputation and bring in all the investment it wanted.

What is important to find out is if the United Kingdom or other countries have experimented and have learned from their mistakes. The general thrust of the chapter is to present some ideas that did not work. It would be good to hear about some well-designed contracts—not just optimal in theory, but informed by practice—that could be robust and could have some hope of holding up ex post.

10 Hydrocarbon Policy, Shocks, and the Collective Imagination: What Went Wrong in Bolivia?

Fernando H. Navajas

10.1 Introduction

On November 1, 1990 the Bolivian National Congress approved Law 1194 to introduce more private-sector participation in the upstream oil and natural gas sector in Bolivia. The state would retain control, under the umbrella of the state-owned Yacimientos Petrolíferos Fiscales Bolivianos (YPFB), of contracts with international oil companies in a 50-50 arrangement, control both pricing and commercialization aspects of export ventures, and guarantee full state ownership of resources. Exactly fifteen years and six months later, on May 1, 2006, the president of Bolivia enacted Supreme Decree 28701, declaring the nationalization of all fields, a return to YPFB control of all quantities and prices as well as domestic and international commercialization, and provide the government with a heavy take based on explicit royalties of 50 percent plus an additional share tilted in favor of YPFB. Within these fifteen years, Bolivia went full cycle from state control to liberalization and back to state control again. First, an important big bang—within a deeper structural reform process—in the reorganization of the hydrocarbon sector occurred when Law 1689 was approved by the National Congress on April 30, 1996. This modernizing framework established legal and contractual conditions for private-sector involvement upstream, allowing free disposal of production, and a rebalancing of the government take, by reducing royalties to 18 percent for new fields and raising direct income taxation. The response to this policy reform was an unprecedented increase in investment in upstream activities and (at least) a sevenfold jump in certified probed and probable reserves of natural gas.[1] Second, in the context of the 2003 political crisis a subsequent reversion process emerged, involving a national referendum in July 2004 to decide whether to repeal existing hydrocarbon legislation. Third, on May 18, 2005, Congress approved Law 3058, which introduced an additional royalty adding up to 50 percent of sales revenues as well as a scheme for sharing the proceeds with subnational governments and many other stakeholders. These stakeholders ranged from universities and the armed forces to indigenous groups, and the scheme accommodated pressures for the distribution of oil rents.

Figure 10.1 plots the stages just described along with the evolution of the international oil prices. In this story of attraction and partial expropriation of investment this association almost naturally suggests a canonical hypothesis for explaining the policy cycle. At a first stage, faced with the need for heavy investment to comply with a demand-pull export-oriented development of its natural gas base, Bolivia had to provide strong incentives. Later, once such investment had been sunk, and the price of oil (the indexing element in export contracts) reverted to new highs, incentives to renegotiate terms and conditions came to the fore. Thus, huge discoveries followed by oil price shocks triggered a counterreform process once Bolivians presumed that they were facing the last period in a finite-horizon game where, with enough discoveries, there was no point in respecting existing contracts.

While this hypothesis provides an attractive standard explanation, several alternative explanatory factors related to problems in policy design and collective approval for the reform process can be identified.[2] Indeed, the time span chosen in figure 10.1 and the reference to the 1990 reform intentionally call attention to the fact that for many Bolivians the 1996 reform produced an unfair arrangement for national stakeholders. For beyond the evidence regarding actual performance and available options, the political exploitation of this collective perception of an unfair deal proved to be effective in the overthrow of the policy reform regime.

This chapter examines issues related to the reversal of the mid-1990s hydrocarbon policy reform in Bolivia and the evidence on the determinants of the new "populist wave." It focuses on upstream natural gas because this is what the story is all about. It therefore does not cover all aspects of the hydrocarbon sector. Neither does it purport to be an account or a synthesis of the natural gas debate in Bolivia because such a narrative would involve much more historical knowledge than someone outside the process can attain. Rather, the chapter provides an outsider's view of some dimensions that can enrich the discussion of a very attractive case. Section 10.2 describes in more detail the

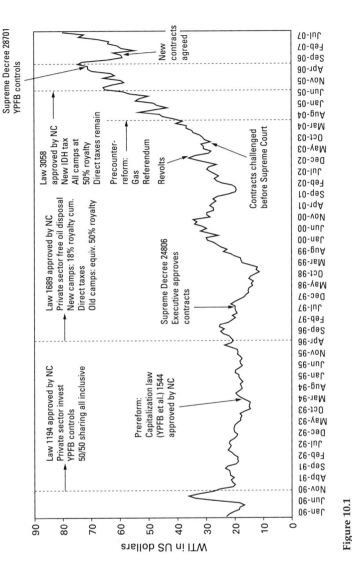

Figure 10.1
Reform and counterreform in Bolivia, 1990–2007

changes effected by the reform and counterreform in the contractual and fiscal framework of the natural gas upstream sector. Section 10.3 develops a central argument of the chapter, namely, that the rebalancing of the fiscal regime adopted in Bolivia—lower royalties, higher taxes on profits—while efficient in terms of investment and production (and even in regard to incentives in well-designed optimal environments; see Rigobon 2006), failed to comply with a latent political constraint that required that fiscal revenue performance should improve after the investment boom. Using a data set from several sources, as well as estimates and assumptions, I simulate the likely path of fiscal revenues for the years between 1995 and 2015 for both the policy reform package and the no-reform policy option. This simulation suggests that uncertainties regarding the net fiscal gain could have been justified. While previous, on the whole positive, assessments (Medinaceli 2003) of the effects of the reform accept that it actually reduced fiscal revenues with respect to the no-reform status quo, my exercise is more counterfactual and speculative, allowing for quantity performance differences between regimes and extending the impacts of changes into the future. I attribute the main policy design pitfall to the expensing allowance embedded in the tax treatment of upstream investments, although I acknowledge that there may have been other problems related to incentives to maximize netback prices of exports. Finally, section 10.4 presents my main conclusions and discusses the limitations and relatively narrow scope of my main quantitative argument as a full explanation of the counterreform in the hydrocarbon sector in Bolivia.

10.2   Reform and Counterreform in the Bolivian Hydrocarbon Sector

Law 1194, enacted in November 1990, replaced a 1972 law and signaled the intention to allow private-sector investment in an otherwise vertically integrated state-controlled monopoly. It opened access to pipeline transmission and downstream sectors while retaining YPFB monopoly control upstream, allowing private-sector entry only in association with this state-owned firm. International private sector interest in Bolivian gas came after a Natural Gas Purchase Agreement signed with Brazil in 1988. This agreement was updated by a new accord in October 1991 that became effective the following year. Thus, a demand-driven export-oriented pattern in natural gas placed Bolivia in the competition to serve the Brazilian market, since Bolivia's historical trade partner, Argentina, was under a "gas-bubble" effect caused by its discoveries in Patagonia. Upstream contractual arrangements took two forms: operation and association contracts. In operation contracts, which were the main type,[3] private companies pursued exploration and production activities under a 50-50 partition of gross production, bore all costs (up to the fiscalization or metering point), and were charged no additional taxes (actually they were subsumed or discounted, which made them irrelevant).

While it is clear that the private-sector firms would receive 50 percent on the production valued at wellhead prices for export or domestic markets (with a methodology set by the Ministry of Energy and Hydrocarbons), the actual government take embedded in the regime was less straightforward because it came out of explicit taxes (paid by both private firms and YPFB)[4] and out of transfers from YPFB to the Treasury.[5] Nevertheless, and in spite of the role of nontax items, the government take operated, in practice, as an ad valorem royalty on the value of production of about 50 percent. In fact, this was the perception of many Bolivians.[6]

In the mid-1990s, international financial institutions in the course of evaluations of the regime pointed to several flaws that required fundamental shifts in policy. A World Bank (1995) loan evaluation report considered the tax regime described above as excessive for a natural gas country that sought access to neighboring countries, which was seen to hinder Bolivian competitiveness. The Bank also considered the existing framework inflexible for upstream operators, most fundamentally restricting free disposal of natural gas (and oil and oil products) and freedom of exports and imports of all hydrocarbons. Beyond this, low performance in the period was also considered in official assessments, since it was judged that the burden on YPFB was too heavy to sustain a dynamic export demand and that new reserves were needed for such a strategy.[7] By 1995, proven (P1) natural gas reserves were 3.8 TCF, while probable reserves added as much as 2.5 TCF, and production capabilities existed but were insufficient for a more aggressive strategy.

The big bang in hydrocarbon policy came in the mid-1990s under the umbrella of a broad, aggressive structural reform process. In fact, the new Hydrocarbons Law—Law 1689—was approved in April 1996, following related or complementary legislation on privatization (so-called capitalization) of YPFB activities,[8] the creation of best-practice regulatory institutions,[9] and a new general tax law.[10] The principles inspiring Law 1689 can be seen by looking at three important dimensions, namely, contractual regulation, taxation, and competition policy. First, the reform adapted preexisting contractual legislation through so-called risk-sharing contracts for exploration and production; and introduced flexibility, in particular the freedom to import, export, and internally trade hydrocarbons (article 5) and freely dispose over (under regulatory supervision) the oil and gas obtained (article 24).[11] Second, the reform changed the tax regime to make it competitive with that of other countries, while meeting "fiscal needs" by establishing royalties (to be allocated to the departments and the Treasury) of 18 percent along with direct taxes[12] and a clear separation between new and old fields so as not to lose revenues or give rise to undue windfall gains. Old fields carried a burden of royalties and taxes amounting to 50 percent of production value, so as to replicate government take under the previous tax treatment.[13] Finally, the reform introduced vertical separation of upstream and transmission, eliminating barriers to entry and guaranteeing open access to pipelines with non-discriminatory pricing surveillance.

While the principles guiding the reform were clear enough and inspired by best practices, readings of the available documents (e.g., World Bank 1995) of international financial institutions (IFIs) working closely with Bolivian authorities show some absence of ex ante risk assessment for the proposed reforms or considerations of potential trade-offs.

First, on the tax regime, the objective of introducing a competitive tax regime may collide (either at the beginning or later in the reform process) with the objective of meeting fiscal needs. The risk here involved ending up with public opinion perceiving a low government take, as eventually occurred. This is particularly so because the term *fiscal needs* means one thing to international investors and financial institutions concerned with fiscal sustainability and another to the polity that makes demands for public expenditures in a poor country. Demands are normally much higher than resources, and the term *fiscal needs* embedded in fiscal sustainability evaluations is not the same as in a political-economy context. Thus, even though a stated objective of the reform was not to affect fiscal revenues it is not clear what the actual target was. If the target was to maintain at least the same level of revenues in dollar terms (as actually happened) in an otherwise booming sector, it is not hard to see how this situation would give rise to political challenges.

The second risk relates to the institutional design of a contract regulation regime. Bolivia followed best-practice recommendations based on an arm's-length approach to establishing so-called independent institutions. In the case of hydrocarbons, this was attempted to promote E&P investment, negotiate and administer contracts, manage E&P data-bank units, and monitor investments. But the risks associated with this approach are that regulatory capture or, even worse, the impact of oil companies on policy decisions above and beyond that of independent regulators, does not necessarily disappear and may be important in practice or from the standpoint of public opinion. This particularly maps onto the tax regime for hydrocarbons since these specialized regulatory bodies provide critical information for the setting of royalties and deductions to the corporate tax (in particular observed investment that relates to the expensing deductions).

The third risk relates to a trade-off between deregulation and government take. The problem to watch here is a likely tension between free disposal, export-import freedom, and deregulated pricing and the risk of being lenient on business practices or contractual provisions that may shift hydrocarbon rents to other (perhaps nonnational) segments of the value chain, leading to low wellhead netback values relevant for government take. Thus, even without the problems in the aforementioned trade-offs, the general public may be reluctant to accept seemingly competitive frameworks that operate by detracting hydrocarbon rents. With a few large projects, as in the case of Bolivia, and given the format of long-term contracting, there is no guarantee that outcomes will avoid business practices that divert hydrocarbon rents.[14] One option is to auction export proposals, but this was not pursued in practice. Even under a contractual density larger than the one observed in Bolivia, contractual provisions, normally unregulated or even unchecked under deregulation, may cause rents to be transferred abroad.[15]

The supply response to the new reforms was impressive, leading to a revolution in the technology and performance of the upstream sector in Bolivia. Six years after the law was approved, Bolivia jumped from less than 6 to about 53 TCF of P1+P2 reserves of natural gas, with a corresponding increase in production capabilities as the country prepared to launch a competitive challenge to go beyond the Gas Sales Agreement with Brazil and toward North American markets. Existing projections in 2001–2002[16] went as far as depicting a path toward 100 MM m^3 day of production, with exports leading the way but also with domestic-market development for industrial projects such as petro-chemicals and Gas-to-Liquids. The aggregate investment displayed in upstream activities during the first years of the reform was also impressive and has been described in many documents and publications.[17] Between 1997 and 2001, upstream investment amounted to about $2.5 billion in an economy with an annual GDP averaging $8.2 billion in the same period. Exports of natural gas rose to become about 20 percent of total exports, or $250 billion.

Despite this evidence, in a society experiencing first fatigue and then open opposition to reforms the political debate soon acquired visible dimensions. The slow economic performance after 1999, because of a sluggish or recessionary regional environment[18] and an economic crisis in neighboring countries such as Argentina (with a demonstration effect used by critics of reform), fueled demands. Many criticisms started to be heard—for example, concerning the absence of a government-regulated development project for natural gas reserves, low netback prices embedded in new large proposed export projects through Chile or Peru, loss of value from moving out segments of the value chain at the expense of those countries or from unregulated lack of separation and pricing of by-products, a challenge to the legal or constitutional status of the contracts stemming from the reform program, and last but not least, the use of a Chilean port in territory that Bolivia lost in the War of the Pacific at the end of the nineteenth century and that left Bolivia landlocked. Growing far left-wing opposition with support from indigenous peoples, representing a new coalition expressing demands for social participation denied for centuries, took solid form in the 2002 general elections (with obvious strongholds in western and densely populated areas of the country). Since then it has cleverly set the political agenda around the natural gas debate.[19]

Thereafter to an outside observer everything looks like pure dynamics around a strong trend toward counterreform. Besides being fragmented and in many cases even doubting the merits of the reform process given the claims against it, urban middle-class groups or the "modern" segments of society rapidly became a minority. Fierce street protests in El Alto—the city above La Paz—were mounted in February and October and led to the resignation of the president and his replacement by the vice president, who remained in office by making concessions and, as a historian and a journalist, by trying to fight an information or propaganda war. Neither accepting some reform design errors, nor organizing seminars on the pros and cons of capitalization and reform, were enough to take the primary agenda-setting role away from the opposition. The attempt to manage the process through an information campaign finally led to a national referendum in July 2004 to revoke Hydrocarbons Law 1689, to propose new legislation in order to raise the government take to an explicit 50 percent and to reconstitute YPFB. Although the president claimed victory in the referendum, a thorough examination reveals serious problems lay ahead for such a strategy.[20] In a fashion parallel to the "gas-war" strategy of the left-wing opposition, latent demands for political autonomy from eastern regions of the country entered the fight for rent distribution. A new law, 3058, was approved by Congress in May 2005, amid attempts to organize a broad national debate that failed in both its timing and opportunity.[21] The law created an additional explicit royalty of 32 percent (called *impuesto directo a los hidrocarburos* or IDH) on the value of production, with a new sharing arrangement for stakeholders that proved detrimental to the position of the Treasury.[22] Worse for investors, the jump in royalties was not compensated (as supported by the president and in some way implicitly included in the referendum questions) by a downward adjustment in direct and other taxes, which were kept as before. Even worse for investors, the law mandated a renegotiation of all existing upstream contracts, after a Supreme Court decision on the issue.

The challenge to the legal status of contracts was a clever attempt to put them in limbo and so to weaken the very foundation of reform. The political constitution of Bolivia in article 139 mandates that natural resources, in this case oil and gas reservoirs, belong in the public domain—that is, they belong to the nation. So moving toward allowing free disposal of oil and gas production had to circumvent a potential legal problem. The draft of Hydrocarbons Law 1689 stated that stocks were national property and delegated to the government the ability to write joint-venture contracts for exploration and production arrangements. These contracts were drafted by the president and approved in August 1997 by Supreme Decree 24806, at the end of the mandate of the administration implementing reforms.

Thus, one of fronts of the "gas war" was directed at exploiting the confusion, either real or in the collective imagination of Bolivians, that SD 24806 had been a way to violate the constitutional mandate, using a contradiction that there could not be private property rights in a flow out of a stock with collective property rights, and that joint ventures could only guarantee the property of the tangible capital added by private contractors but not the oil and gas coming from underground.[23] As we know from the theory of the firm (e.g., Holmstrom 1999), joint ventures need some governance to allow parties to avoid being averse to them because of potential exposure to holdup problems and the interpretation originally given at the time of the reform was in our view somewhat problematic for contracts. But the shot was more direct and ambitious, and the challenge here was threefold. A first challenge was to the property rights on extracted resources and the violation of article 139. A second one was directed at the property rights on the flows and the nature of the joint ventures, as a nonpermanent association that could not establish property rights on produced (i.e., extracted) resources. The final, and most problematic challenge, was the illegality stemming from the absence of congressional approval of the contracts written under the umbrella of Law 1689 and approved by DS 24806. The Supreme Court issued a ruling in December 2003 declaring that there was no constitutional violation. But later, in March 2005, on reconsidering the issue, the Court suggested that contracts should be approved by Congress. That was enough to put them in limbo.

Law 3058 did not change the situation with respect to the free disposal of oil and gas. This final missing piece in the counterreform puzzle came in May 2006, when the newly elected left-wing coalition declared—by way of Supreme Decree 28701—a "nationalization" of all fields, interpreted as granting YPFB full control of commercialization and an additional transitory participation of 32 percent in large fields so as to initiate a renegotiation of existing contracts.[24] What followed was a renegotiation process to sustain committed export contracts to Brazil and to include a new export agreement between YPFB and state-owned ENARSA to expand exports to Argentina. This process is still in a fluid state, because performance has not returned to normal.[25]

10.3   Simulating Counterfactuals: Revenue Performance with and without Reform

Among the many challenges that the reform process faced, perhaps the most visible is the fact that fiscal revenue performance fell below expectations, which triggered criticisms that an unfair deal had been struck in Law 1689. The actual behavior of hydrocarbon revenues stabilized, in dollar terms or as a percentage of GDP, in the second half of the 1990s and in the beginning of the 2000s (in relation to the first half of the 1990s). However, the problem with this evidence is twofold. First, revenue performance was poor considering the jump in production and exports.[26] Second, a visible shift toward indirect taxes on end-users of petroleum products invited the criticism that a shift was occurring out of oil rent appropriation and toward indirect taxes on households and firms.

While some rigorous comparative studies conceded the point that upstream revenues in the new regime underperformed the previous one based on Law 1194 (e.g., Medinaceli 2003), many advocates of the new regime (particularly from the business community) publicly insisted that the total contribution of the hydrocarbon sector to the Treasury had improved much more than just looking at royalties and upstream taxation would suggest. But this was, in the end, an unhappy benchmark. It played into the hands of the opposition's argument that there had been a relative shift from upstream to downstream taxation and that Bolivians were paying through indirect taxes and levies what should have been paid by upstream producers (see Villegas 2004).

My reading suggests that the central issue that needs to be examined in the underperformance of fiscal revenues is the fact that the rebalancing sought in Law 1689, which would shift taxation upstream from royalties to profit taxes, failed to deliver a proper boost to government take by design, calibration, or regulatory capture. While this point has been somewhat overlooked by papers evaluating the hydrocarbon reform, its relevance was explicitly acknowledged in an ex post evaluation report by the IMF[27] and, somewhat implicitly, in public debates in Bolivia.[28] To put it simply, the expensing mechanisms and unlimited carryforward of losses allowed in the profit tax base amounted to an effective reduction of the tax burden (while the investment process was proceeding), and the generous deduction of part of the gross revenues in the tax base of the extraordinary profits tax (surtax) had the same effect, perhaps on a more permanent basis. Throughout the first five years after the reform (1997–2001), profit taxes were on average barely 8 percent of what was collected through royalties on new and old fields. The surtax did not contribute at all.

To assess what could have been behind one of the major determinants of underperformance in government take (one argument for counterreform), I conduct an exercise on the likely performance of fiscal revenues under reform and no-reform scenarios between 1995 and 2015. By "reform" I mean Law 1689, while "no reform" means the scheme under the previous Law 1194. This is a highly speculative and counterfactual exercise since it is based on many estimates and assumptions. I will simulate proxies of the behavior of the reform regime rebalancing toward profit taxes (for new fields) under two alternatives, one that makes few or no allowances for deducting investments and includes strong control over actual costs (or profits) and another that is permissive on both tax allowances and declared costs (or profits). The alternative is the no-reform regime, with the assumption that a 50 percent royalty on a lower production level is sustained.[29]

Table 10.1 summarizes the main assumptions and data inputs used. The appendix shows some basic time series, such as prices and quantities, as well as other auxiliary assumptions used in the exercise. The prices are based on official sources and available data up to 2006 and projections beyond that year that exploit indexing clauses of contracts with fuel products.[30] Thus the same price scenario (for both regimes) is one with high values for exports, while price insulation of domestic markets is assumed to prevail in both regimes (see table 10.A1 in the appendix for assumed values).[31] Quantities delivered for export markets are of course different for both regimes and come from official projections in 2001–2002 representing the reform regime, and for an assumed status quo serving (partially) Brazilian and Argentinean markets, in the no-reform scenario. As for domestic markets, differences again represent a dynamic (reform) versus a stagnant (no-reform) supply response. Overall, the reform regime more than triples the production performance of the no-reform regime, with 116 and 36 million m^3 per day, respectively.[32] The proportion between old and new fields, which is essential for estimating revenues in the reform regime, is taken from data reported in previous studies up to 2006 and then calibrated onward assuming that production increases come from new fields and that old-field productivity declines slowly.

Production costs are assumed to come from a "low" and a "high" type that can be manipulated for tax profit declarations. For the low type, it is assumed that when the wellhead price is $1 per million BTU, production costs are 0.33 cents, and then partially indexed to oil prices. Thus the "base" value of 33 cents per MMBTU changes as prices depart from one dollar per MMBTU, with 33 percent of the difference between observed and the benchmark price (of $1). For the high type, it is assumed that they are 0.50 cents when wellhead prices are $1 per MMBTU, and the adjustment to the base value according to wellhead price changes is computed as before.[33] Investment expenditures to be

Table 10.1
Data set for simulations of fiscal revenue exercise

Variable	Data and assumptions	Sources
Wellhead prices	Annual averages of monthly data for 1997–2005 of export prices and domestic market prices • 1995–1997 and 2006 taken from secondary sources • 2007–2015 projected from price of oil expected path	Ministry of Hydrocarbons sources and López 2007 • Artana et al. 2007 • Catena and Navajas 2006
Quantities	Exports and domestic sales for 1995–2002 same for both regimes. For 2003–2015: • Reform regime: Path "expected" in 2001 delayed one year • No-reform regime: Slow path up to current deliveries to Brazil and Argentina (with no further expansions)	Ministry of Hydrocarbons sources • Ministry of Economic Development 2002 • Artana et al. 2007
New/old fields	Data available for 1997–2001 and 2005–2006 Calibration and extrapolation assuming production growth comes from new fields	Medinacelli 2003 Catena and Navajas 2006
Production costs	Assumed for the exercise. "Low" (L) and "high" (H) types $$c_I = c_i.(1 + 0.3.(p_t - p_0)/p_0).p_0$$ $$c_i = 0.33 \text{ for } i = \text{L } c_i = 0.50 \text{ for } i = \text{H}$$ $$p_0 = 1$$	
Investments	Path assumed on E&P investments from actual data but converging from high values of 1997–1998 to be consistent with assumed production path	Mayorga and Tapia 2006 and López 2007
Royalties	Reform regime 18% on new fields, 50% on old fields No-reform regime: Assumed at 50% on all fields	Law 1689
Profit taxes	25% legal tax (IUE), an additional (effective) 3% due to remittances assumed as from 2005 Tax base: Sales less costs, less investments, less royalties. Only for new fields No-allowance case: No investment deductions and no carryforward of losses Allowance case: Full deductions	Laws 1606 and 1689 Molinedo and Velasco 2006
Surtax	Simulations show only a very small contribution, therefore not included	

used in the deductions of profit taxes (for the reform regime) are assumed from existing historical figures and in line with the quantities projected.

Government revenues from these variables are easy to compute for the assumed no reform scenario, since they simply come out of the 50 percent royalty on sales revenues. Royalties for the reform scenario are estimated according Law 1689 on new- and old-field production. Profit taxes (IUE) depend on the assumptions made about production costs (low or high) and on the assumptions about expensing allowances of investments and about carryforward losses. The tax base for the profit tax also deducts royalties. In all cases, estimates only take new fields into account, because old fields do not pay profit taxes. The tax rate on profits is assumed at 25 percent. An additional 3 percent (effective) on the same tax base is assumed since 2005 to accommodate payment of remittances.[34] Finally, no extra revenue is assumed from the extraordinary profits tax (surtax) because my estimates on collection are rather insignificant, and simulating a different deduction scheme would be highly speculative.

The results of this exercise are shown in figure 10.2, where the evolution of fiscal revenues in current U.S. dollars is drawn for the no-reform scenario and for the two extreme cases of the reform scenario, one where profits are computed at low costs and no allowances are made on investment deductions and loss carryforward, and the oppo-

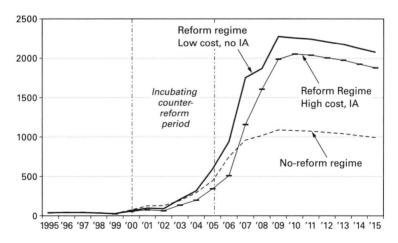

Figure 10.2
Simulating natural gas fiscal revenues profiles in two regimes (in millions of U.S. dollars)

site extreme case where costs are high and allowances are admitted. The path of fiscal revenues shows that given the strong production performance of the reform case, the two variants of reform reach the end period of projections with much higher revenues than in the no-reform status quo. Both reform cases approach fiscal revenues of between $1.8 and $2 billion by the end of the period, after maximum values in 2008–2009 due to oil price dynamics, while the no-reform status quo approaches $1.0 billion. A significant government take difference is achieved under the reform case and the difference should have been considered a good dividend for Bolivians.[35]

However, trajectories show a problematic comparative performance, because the reform case under high costs and investment and loss carryforward allowances significantly underperforms the no-reform case all through the "counterreform incubating period" and up to 2007. Even the reform case with low costs and no allowances underperforms the no-reform case up to 2003 and does not show a significant difference until production jumps along with new export projects.

One can see these estimates as depicting an experiment in the minds of Bolivians assessing the merits of reform for their pocketbooks, with both cases in the reform regime scenario denoting a range of uncertainty of performance, and actual observed performance up to 2004 closer to the low-performance case of the reform regime. It is clear that the role of deductions impinged on a particular dynamic of depressing revenues at the beginning of the reform process. The performance of revenue collection in U.S. dollars under different reforms is affected by the assumed different production performance of reform and no-reform regimes. On the other hand, estimating the effective government take expressed as a percentage of production sales that result from the previous exercise, shows a more problematic picture for reform (see figure 10.3). While one can argue that a reduction of the government take from 50 to 37 percent (of sales revenues) could have been a reasonable strategy for a country trying to compete in natural gas exports in South America in the 1990s, introducing allowances that would lead to a much lower figure could have been equally dangerous for the political sustainability of the reform process. In the high-cost full-allowance case the government take dropped temporarily, reaching a low point of 20 percent in 2005. By that time, the political economy had done its job and the reform regime was a thing of the past.

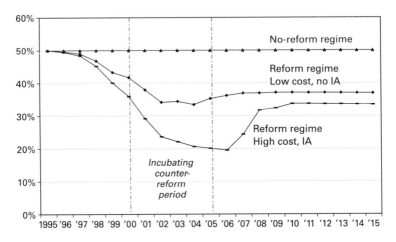

Figure 10.3
Simulating effective government take as percentage of sales revenues

10.4   Concluding Remarks

One tempting conclusion from the previous exercise is that while the
hydrocarbon reform in Bolivia represented an attempt to attract foreign capital by offering a competitive tax regime for a country trying
to establish itself as a potential hub, some pitfalls in policy design created a transitory negative effect on revenue collection. In its early years,
the fiscal regime was not performing on a steady-state path. Actual
revenue performance was surely going to improve up and be much
higher in coming years. But politics does not wait for the steady state.
Thus an erosion of public support was achieved in the end by forces
opposed to reform. The natural conclusion from reading the case from
this perspective would tend to be that "these problems [could have
been avoided] . . . by strengthening regulations in areas such as transfer
pricing and amortizations as well as the institutional capacity of the tax
agency" (IMF 2005, 25).

Even when I have made an effort to qualify the plausibility of such
an explanation, with an exercise that illustrates the problem, a wider
reading of the general case illustrated in section 10.2 would suggest
that this is only part of a broader picture, and so I do not claim to have
presented the ultimate explanation for a policy reversal like the one
observed in Bolivia. Rather, my goal has been to look at a data set to
provide a quantified description of the factors underlying the low gov-

ernment take, which I do believe is a central element of the atmosphere leading to the policy reversal.

Other causes of the policy reversal such as the simple holdup, price-amplified, last-period story, or the political fight between the eastern lowland and western highland regions of the country for the distribution of gains, seem to be secondary and incomplete explanations. The fact that other natural resource sectors, such as mining, outlived the political turmoil and were not part of the counterreform agenda suggest that explanations focused only on ex post opportunism after sunk investments need to be complemented with something else. Interestingly, mining is an activity entirely located in the highlands, where cooperatives coexist with large national and multinational groups, suggesting that the regional perspective could have been important. Also, the opposition to the export-led strategy for developing the natural gas sector might have represented a territorial fight in disguise, because the alternative distribution resulting from domestic industrialization could be more biased toward the more densely populated highlands. But this is a highly speculative argument, since domestic industrialization has other consequences (centralized government control is one of them) that are somewhat difficult to disentangle, and criticisms of an export-oriented development strategy seem to have reflected a more economywide view of the antireform coalition.

Rather, direct evidence suggests that territorial distribution battles over fiscal revenues cannot be used to explain the incubation and development of the counterreform movement, although these struggles emerged later, after the May 2005 Hydrocarbons Law was passed and the resulting sharing arrangements took effect, which created imbalances and triggered conflict. When this fight came to the fore the reform was already history. New tensions and political confrontations have made regions with hydrocarbon reserves (and also other stakeholders) more aggressive in their demands for a share in revenues than what has been historically observed.[36] But this may reflect a defensive strategy in a deteriorated institutional environment where the central government has sought to undermine rights for autonomous administration of departments validated in recent elections.

While alternative explanations will probably suggest themselves to others equipped with better data and methods, I believe that what makes a single hypothesis (like the one developed in this chapter) incomplete is the more problematic picture that emerges from my discussion of the counterreform process in section 10.2. Indeed, the challenge was part of a more general antireform environment under sluggish economic conditions, political fragmentation, and major disruptions in neighboring countries like Argentina. The success of the opposing forces in building a strong antireform coalition rested on their ability to convey to many segments of the population, including segments of the urban middle class, the impression that a status quo that was more favorable to Bolivians—especially with respect to the country's control of natural resources—had been taken away. From this perspective, measures limited to better design of the tax regime would have been too little and too late. Retaliation had become inevitable in even the most favorable performance scenario. Given previous sociopolitical imbalances that had accumulated for decades, given more recent regional imbalances between east and west, and given the fragmentation of formal political parties, it seems that Bolivia had a date with a wider reaction against pro-market reforms. The separation between design-pitfall-induced, shock-induced, or culture-induced reversals in hydrocarbon policy reforms is crucial both for our understanding of such processes and for recommendations for future design blueprints. The Bolivian case shows that all these elements were present, and it is hard to avoid the conclusion that the next opportunity to attempt a competitive leap forward will have to properly address all of them.

Appendix

Table 10A.1 reports basic quantity and price data used as inputs for the simulation exercise. Annual sales revenues come straight from the above figures, taking into account that they are expressed in different units (m^3 versus MMBTU, days versus annual). Production costs are assumed for the exercise and obtained from assuming first unit costs in "Low" (0.33 cents per MMBTU when price $p_t = p_0 = \$1$ per MMBTU) and "High" (0.50 cents per MMBTU when $p_t = p_0 = 1$) cases, along with indexing mechanism for different prices of natural gas. In both cases unit costs adjust by a third of the deviation of prices from the benchmark of $1 per MMBTU (equation (3)).

$$c_I = c_i \cdot (1 + 0.3 \cdot (p_t - p_0)/p_0) \cdot p_0 \tag{1}$$

$$c_i = 0.33 \text{ for } i, I = L \quad c_i = 0.50 \text{ for } i, I = H \tag{2}$$

$$p_0 = 1 \tag{3}$$

Profits, only relevant for computing direct taxes in the reform regime, are estimated by subtracting annual production costs (obtained from multiplying (10A.1) by quantities and taking into account different units and time) from annual sales and considering only new fields. New fields result from historical values of production coming from new and old fields and updated by the production path of the reform regime. Taxable corporate profits (on which to apply the 28 percent rate that includes remittances; see note 34) take into account whether allowances for investment—to be deducted from the tax base—and carryforward losses are introduced or not. For this purpose I estimate investments in exploration and production from values reported in different sources (see table 10.1) and assume a decreasing path of exploration investment that ends in 2009 with $250 million (the maximum are the years 1998 and 1999, with $400 million each year), and a decreasing path of production investment reaching $100 million in 2015. Finally, royalties paid (on new fields) are deducted from the corporate profit tax base.

Government revenues in the no-reform scenario are the direct result of applying a 50 percent rate to the sales revenues. The "Low Cost No IA" path in figure 10.2 assumes low cost from (10A.1)–(10A.3) and no deductions for investments or past losses. The "High Cost IA" uses high costs and assumes allowances and carryforward losses. Effective rates computed in figure 10.3 come from the ratio between taxes and revenues in all scenarios.

Table 10A.1
Quantities and prices used in simulation exercises

Year	Reform regime (units: millions of m3 per day)			No-reform regime			Both regimes Prices (units: U.S. dollars per MMBTU)	
	Exports	Domestic	Total	Exports	Domestic	Total	Exports	Domestic
1995	5.0	2.3	7.3	5.0	2.3	7.3	0.76	0.69
1996	5.0	2.5	7.5	5.0	2.5	7.5	0.80	0.72
1997	4.0	2.7	6.7	4.0	2.7	6.7	0.93	0.83
1998	3.8	2.8	6.6	3.8	2.8	6.6	0.74	0.87
1999	2.5	2.8	5.3	2.5	2.8	5.3	0.68	0.81
2000	5.9	3.0	8.9	5.9	3.0	8.9	1.34	0.93
2001	10.7	3.3	14.0	10.7	3.3	14.0	1.45	0.81
2002	13.4	3.4	16.8	13.4	3.4	16.8	1.19	0.76
2003	25.2	4.2	29.4	15.4	4.2	19.6	1.62	0.74
2004	34.9	13.3	48.2	23.1	4.5	27.6	1.71	0.73
2005	47.6	27.6	75.2	28.4	4.8	33.2	2.18	0.75
2006	48.0	30.7	78.7	30.5	4.9	35.4	3.50	0.75
2007	72.6	30.8	103.4	30.5	5.4	35.9	4.50	0.75
2008	73.1	31.0	104.1	30.5	5.5	36.0	4.78	0.75
2009	83.6	31.2	114.8	30.5	5.5	36.0	5.13	0.75
2010	83.6	31.4	115.0	30.5	5.5	36.0	5.08	0.75
2011	83.6	31.6	115.2	30.5	5.5	36.0	5.05	0.75

2012	83.6	31.8	115.4	30.5	5.5	36.0	4.96	0.75
2013	83.6	31.9	115.5	30.5	5.5	36.0	4.89	0.75
2014	83.6	32.2	115.8	30.5	5.5	36.0	4.77	0.75
2015	83.6	32.4	116.0	30.5	5.5	36.0	4.66	0.75

Sources: See table 10.1 and the main text. Quantities: Reform regime figures are taken from projections by the Ministry of Economic Development of Bolivia (2002), No-reform quantities are assumed. Prices: Historical values up to 2006 are taken from Artana et al. 2007, section 4.2; 2007 is an estimate from secondary sources. 2008–2015 follows an indexed path using data for fuel-oil price forecasts by EIA (2007, table 12, Petroleum Products Prices) for export prices and assumptions of a constant value for domestic market users.

Notes

Special thanks are due to William Hogan and Federico Sturzenegger for their thoughtful review of a previous draft. I also acknowledge useful comments from Fernando Candia (my discussant at the Harvard Kennedy School Workshop) as well as from Daniel Artana, Robert Barros, Marcelo Catena, Gonzalo Chavez, Ricardo Hausmann, Osmel Manzano, and Jeromin Zettelmeyer. This chapter is dedicated to the memory of Guillermo Justiniano, a graduate in economics from the University of La Plata and ministerial reform leader in the attempted modernization of Bolivia in the 1990s. Any errors and misinterpretations are solely the author's responsibility.

1. This is a reasonably conservative estimate that is surpassed by others. On the other hand, it may be somewhat debatable to what extent the increase can be fully attributed to the reforms, since potential reservoirs were already known or expected in Bolivia. For instance, a headline in the Buenos Aires newspaper *La Nación* in October 1990 (see *La Nación* 1990) announced discoveries related to the enlargement of the San Alberto field (one of largest fields in Bolivia, it accounted for about 25 percent of natural gas production in 2005). Thus, it is most likely that a less aggressive reform—or even what I call a no-reform scenario—would have significantly raised reserves in the 1990s.

2. One problem with the simple or straightforward holdup explanation is that other visible, albeit relatively less important, natural resource sectors—such as mining—did not suffer policy reversals of the type and magnitude of the natural gas sector. Thus, counter-reforms through nationalization, contract renegotiation, or even tax renegotiation have not been broader in scope in the time period covered in this chapter.

3. By 1995 there were fifteen operation contracts plus three secondary recovery contracts in twenty-four blocks involving twenty-five private firms. Association contracts, which extended the operation format with a scheme for optional equity participation with YPFB (in which case the state-owned firm became an actual partner with a share in costs and management), were much less preferred, with only three contracts. Finally, YPFB itself was operating in twenty-six blocks. See World Bank 1995.

4. The tax system was formed by 31 percent explicit ad valorem taxes on the value of production consisting of a royalty of 12 percent earmarked for subnational government levels (departamentos; i.e., provinces) and a national tax of 19 percent. There was also a corporate tax of 40 percent, which in practice was considered "a fiction" since it could be completely deducted from the payment of the previous taxes. See Mueller y Asociados 2003 and Medinaceli 2003.

5. The relevant transfer to consider here, for upstream natural gas calculations, is a so-called financial surplus on the exports of natural gas, which worked as an ad valorem transfer. Data in Medinaceli 2003, based on YPFB sources, shows that between 1990 and 1995 this transfer represented on average 31 percent of the value of natural gas exports. Expressed in terms of total sales, it represents an average equivalent royalty of 28 percent for 1991–1995. These average figures overstate actual numbers because they include payments of debt arrears with Argentina, particularly in 1993. For 1995 the equivalent number was 23 percent.

6. Beyond public opinion, professional and academic economists in Bolivia sustained this view, even though there was not an explicit 50 percent royalty. See for example Barja and Urquiola 2003, 8 n. 21: "The 1990 Hydrocarbons Law required that all fields pay 50 percent in royalties, plus a profit tax."

7. Comments and analysis from World Bank evaluations at that time referred to YPFB as a high-cost firm that enjoyed a privileged position because of its statutory monopoly. However, a thorough analysis of upstream (drilling) activities, discovery success ratio, human resources, and its reliability as a partner to private companies does not reveal that YPFB had a disastrous record. This analysis must acknowledge the many constraints faced by YPFB, such as funding limitations, that prevented expansions, as well as evidence of poor management, overhiring, and maintenance of uneconomic units. While it is difficult to separate upstream from downstream operations to get a clear picture, Barja and Urquiola (2003) provide data showing that about a quarter of total employment of YPFB was in the upstream sector and that private firms that took over upstream activities operated with about 40 percent of the labor force.

8. Capitalization was the Bolivian way to accommodate private-sector participation in productive activities. Capitalization Law 1544 was approved by Congress on March 21, 1994, and structural reform loans rapidly followed to support the reform (World Bank 1996), which in oil and gas was completed in 1996–1997. See Barja and Urquiola 2003 for a thorough account of the capitalization process in Bolivia in general as well as in the oil and gas sector. YPFB assets were segmented, reorganized from a modern competitive cum regulatory regime, and partially sold (50 percent) to private investors who gained control. Forty-five percent of the remaining value of the firm was put into a pension fund scheme for Bolivians (represented on the board by the pension fund firms), while 5 percent was handed to the workforce.

9. Under Law 1600 of October 1994 (the so-called SIRESE Law), Bolivia created a regulatory structure for the infrastructure sector with a general superintendancy and five sectoral specialized superintendancies, among them one for hydrocarbons.

10. General Tax Law 1606 of December 1994 established a common corporate tax regime of 25 percent on taxable income for companies involved in exploration, exploitation, pipeline transport, and marketing. It also introduced explicit excise taxes on end-user petroleum product consumption.

11. Free disposal came with constraints to satisfy sales to the domestic market and to honor preexisting export contracts by YPFB. New contracts were allowed to be traded with the acceptance of the regulatory body.

12. First, a corporate tax (IUE) of 25 percent on earnings (less royalties), with expensing of exploration and/or development costs and allowing for unlimited loss carryforward. Second, an additional tax on extraordinary profits (surtax) targeted at companies involved in extractive activities operating large fields. The rate was 25 percent on earnings computed in the IUE less 33 percent of investments and less 45 percent of the value of production at each field (up to a ceiling of $55 million per year). Third, a remittance tax of 12.5 percent of the value of remittances abroad. Fourth, indirect taxes on domestic sales (VAT, at 13 percent, and a tax on transactions, at 3 percent). For a full description in the context of the tax system see Molinedo and Velasco 2006.

13. Old fields faced four tax components. First, a royalty of 12 percent earmarked for departments (provinces). Second, a royalty of 13 percent called National Complementary. Third, a 19 percent participation (called National) to mimic YPFB's share of those contracts. Fourth, a 6 percent share for the Treasury. The first and fourth items were the only royalty components for new fields.

14. This is a rather conjectural argument and relevant only for second-wave export projects toward the Pacific that had to reach Chile or Peru. Evidence of the contractual

performance of the first-wave exports projects—that is, the Gas Sales Agreement with Brazil—fits reasonably within the boundaries of a long-term contracting format, even when some attempts at renegotiation arose at different stages from both sides. Thus, long-term contracting between Bolivia and Brazil has been sustainable (and sustained today), avoiding opportunism or temporal-inconsistency problems. Coordination to build a large transmission system to Brazil that would be the primary way to give value to preexisting and new Bolivian reserves was therefore solved through long-term contracts.

15. For instance, contractual arrangements observed in exports of natural gas from Argentina to Chile had provisions whereby export prices could not deviate much from domestic prices (see Navajas 2008). While this practice enforces a strong cross-border integration (one price) form and has desirable features for integrating markets, it poses a serious challenge for the exporting country if political pressures demand the transfer of hydrocarbon rents in the form of lower prices for domestic users. The trade-off either implies that this practice will create pecuniary externalities to outside buyers or, alternatively, that domestic prices will have to converge to (the price of oil-adjusted) export prices. Either option creates tensions in terms of political sustainability.

16. See, for example, Ministry of Economic Development of Bolivia 2002.

17. See for instance, Barja and Urquiola 2003, Mayorga and Tapia 2006, as well as López 2007.

18. See Calvo 2006.

19. Some attempts to organize a consensus policy framework on natural gas, under the umbrella of a more general call by the Catholic Church in 2001, failed to include this new coalition, perhaps because it was still taking shape. For instance, the document referred to as Ministry of Economic Development of Bolivia 2002 is a kind of Green Paper resulting from a committee with participants from the executive, political parties (except the MAS), the private sector, and representatives from the department of Tarija, where a large proportion of the reserves are located.

20. Ballot results also showed strong opposition to natural gas exports, particularly in Potosí and western departments, reflecting demands for revisiting the whole export-oriented strategy that in some way predates the 1996 reform, since it was implicit in the previous hydrocarbon policy.

21. This attempt took the form of a three-day open-TV debate program organized by private sector organizations, the press, and chambers representing foreign firms. The debate was conducted by a well-known journalist who later in the same year became the vice presidential candidate from the opposition coalition PODEMOS, and included previous ministers, important experts on the issues, political figures, and invited guests from abroad. Prominent figures from the MAS coalition such as the future Vice President Alvaro García Linera and future Minister of Energy Andrés Soliz Rada were part of the debate. The four hours of recorded material from this program (see Amcham Bolivia 2005) effectively document the nature and direction of the natural gas debate in Bolivia in mid-2005.

22. See Catena and Navajas 2006. At the then-projected values of natural gas prices, it also generated doubts about the long-term fiscal sustainability of Bolivia, because delayed expenditures from the sharing mechanism would imply roller-coaster behavior of the fiscal primary surplus.

23. The legal challenge to SD 24806 came in 2003 in a presentation by the MAS opposition to the Supreme Court (Constitutional Tribunal), arguing that articles 59 (requiring congressional approval) and 139 (on the property of natural resources) of the Constitution had been violated and that DS 24806 should be declared unconstitutional and that therefore all contracts were illegal.

24. This sui generis announcement of renationalization also created uncertainty regarding the future of the shares of the new (capitalized) private companies that belonged to the pensioners (due to the capitalization reform) and were under the custody of the pension reform institutions administering universal pension payments out of the dividends of the capitalized firms. (See Artana et al. 2007.) Eventually in 2007 this mechanism had to be superseded by another financial strategy, giving rise to a competition over resources among departments. It is important to point out that the initial 50 percent ownership by Bolivians of the hydrocarbon resources (embedded in assets at the time of capitalization) was diluted as the firms were capitalized and since new discoveries need not come from capitalized firms. This made opposition to counterreform less intense than it would have been if Bolivians had actually owned 50 percent of the ongoing business. Thus, the capitalization scheme acted more as an impact sweetener for the acceptance of the reform than as a permanent, built-in constituency for sustaining reforms.

25. Details of this ongoing process can be found in Medinaceli 2006, López 2007, and Artana et al. 2007.

26. Total fiscal contributions of the hydrocarbon sector were on average $393 million per year between 1990 and 1995, rising to $440 million between 1996 and 2000. However, considering only upstream taxation (i.e., excluding the IEHD) the figure drops to less than $300 million. See Medinaceli 2003, table 9, and Villegas 2004. See also IMF 2005, 24, where estimates of the total hydrocarbon revenues remain rather flat, oscillating between 5 and 6 percent of GDP between 1994 and 2003, with a different composition throughout the period. (Royalties dropped from 5 percent to a bit above 2 percent of GDP, indirect taxes (IEHD) rose from nil to also a bit above 2 percent of GDP, and other taxes (mainly direct taxes) contributed with about 1 percent of GDP.) Data from UPF 2007 show an extension of this pattern in 2003–2004 (with royalties rising above 3 percent of GDP due to higher prices, compensated by a drop in indirect taxes) and a jump since 2004 (due to the compounded effect of higher prices, exports to Argentina, and new taxes (IDH)).

27. See IMF (2005, 24). The comments attributed an initial impact in the "generous (i.e., narrow) definition of 'old' (higher royalties) relative to 'new' fields... [which was]... part of a deliberate strategy to make the capitalization offer attractive." The report added that this risk had been flagged early on to the authorities by the World Bank and the IMF, in a letter in September 1996. It also mentioned the effect on profit taxes of the amortization of large investments and generous deductions in the surtax. Finally, it hinted that "the level of compliance may have declined over time, as the authorities have not adjusted quickly to the new tax system, while oil companies have learned to exploit loopholes."

28. For instance, Carlos Miranda, a former, Hydrocarbons Superintendent in the Hydrocarbons Ministry and long-standing oil expert in Bolivia, voiced the argument in the three-day open-TV debate in La Paz in April 2005 (see Amcham Bolivia 2005): "Royalty is a concept made flesh in our people.... We have to learn from history.... If one looks at the tax regimes we had in different occasions, every time we have gone into the taxation of profits we had had a collision with private firms. Why? Because the state has never had a strong enough administrative capability so as to convince society that the profit taxes being paid were the correct ones.... In a previous administration... [under Law

1194]...we lived a quiet life with a fifty-fifty sharing of gross income and the time we went into discussing profits we had had problems and generated people's mistrust that private firms were cheating us all the time with reported profits."

29. The exercise is necessarily counterfactual because none of the simulated paths ends up representing actual behavior; they are rather best guesses of likely performance. Differences in quantities are in order for long-run scenarios for this kind of exercise. For instance, confronting reform versus no reform under similarly assumed quantities is biased against reform, for one thing one should expect from granting incentives is to have a different supply response.

30. Historical prices (i.e., wellhead) relevant for fiscal revenues up to 2006 are taken from Artana et al. 2007, table 4.2. Projected prices result from indexing 2007 prices with fuel-oil price projections of EIA 2007. Export prices of natural gas in Bolivia are fully contract-driven, and so easy to follow if one uses the partial adjustment indexing formulas with oil products (mainly fuel oils and now diesel) both in the Gas Sales Agreement with Brazil, dated 1996, or in the more recent YPFB-ENARSA contract with Argentina.

31. Prices need not be the same in both regimes for several reasons, ranging from different regulatory and contractual environments to different sales structures and so on. In the absence of robust assumptions to differentiate price regimes, I prefer to use the same path for both regimes.

32. Current production levels are close to ceiling values of the no-reform scenario. Expected new sales to Argentina (about 20 million m^3 day) embedded in the YPFB-ENARSA 2006 contract are not considered in the no-reform scenario. Thus, I am assuming that the no-reform scenario would have eventually reached the current production level (basically thanks to the implementation of the current export project to Brazil, which doubles the 1992 agreement, and to the use of existing exporting transport capacity to Argentina) but without further additions. This is an assumption that may be criticized as too optimistic (or too pessimistic) by pro-reform (by antireform) analysts, but I believe it to be a safe one given the existing or expected reserves in Bolivia before the reform and the slow-motion productivity expected for the no-reform scenario.

33. Under high-type costs and a royalty of 50 percent, production becomes uneconomical at wellhead prices below $1 per million BTU. This is nonbinding according the assumptions of the price path.

34. The tax on remittances has a rate of 12.5 percent on a tax base that is 50 percent of earnings. I assume a payout ratio close to 50 percent.

35. This issue could be made more precise by computing the NPV of revenues in the different regimes. I have skipped this issue since it involves further speculative assumptions regarding reserves and production plans (i.e., monetization of reserves) as well as about discounting. For the sake of my argument, it is enough to note the paths of revenues under different regimes depicted in figure 10.2.

36. Traditional views (see, for example, Lema 1983) in departments (provinces) with large hydrocarbon reserves such as Tarija have defended the historical 11 percent royalty allocated to the producing department (which by the way is similar to the 12 percent observed in Argentina) without explicit claims for a bigger share. This does not seem to be due to the prevalence of a relatively low price of oil. Interestingly, estimates of the expected long-term revenues for Tarija were made in that paper under rather optimistic assumptions concerning the price of oil.

References

Amcham Bolivia. 2005. "Nuestro Gas: Mas allá de la Política." Seminario virtual sobre hidrocarburos en Bolivia. DVD recorded version, April 26, 27, and 28. La Pag, Bolivia: American Chamber of Commerce.

Artana, D., J. L. Bour, M. Catena, and F. Navajas. 2007. "Tópicos Macro Fiscales y Perspectivas de Sostenibilidad Fiscal en Bolivia." RE1-07-005. Banco Interamericano de Desarrollo. http://www.iadb.org/regions/re1/econ/RE1-07-005.pdf.

Barja, G., and M. Urquiola. 2003. "Capitalization and Privatization in Bolivia: An Approximation to an Evaluation." Draft conference paper, February. Washington, DC: Center for Global Development. http://www.cgdev.org/content/calendar/detail/3254.

Calvo, S. 2006. "Socially Responsible Macroeconomic Management." In V. Fretes-Cibils, M. Giugale, and C. Luff, eds., Bolivia: Public Policy Options for the Well-Being of All, chap. 1. Washington, DC: World Bank.

Catena, M., and F. Navajas. 2006. "Oil & Debt Windfalls and Fiscal Dynamics in Bolivia." Economic and Social Studies Series RE1-06-003. Inter-American Development Bank, July. http://www.iadb.org/regions/re1/econ/RE1-06-003.pdf.

EIA. 2007. "Annual Energy Outlook 2008 (Early Release)." Energy Information Administration, U.S. Department of Energy, December. http://www.eia.doe.gov/oiaf/aeo/.

Fretes-Cibils, V., M. Giugale, and C. Luff, eds. 2006. Bolivia: Public Policy Options for the Well-Being of All. Washington, DC: World Bank.

Holmstrom, Bengt. 1999. "The Firm as a Subeconomy." Journal of Law, Economics and Organization 15, no. 1 (March): 74–102.

IMF. 2005. Bolivia: Ex-Post Assessment of Longer Term Program Engagement. IMF Staff Country Report 05/139. April. Washington, DC: International Monetary Fund.

"Importante Hallazgo Petrolero en Tarija." 1990. La Nación (Buenos Aires), October 21, front page.

Lema, M. L. 1983. "Presente y Futuro de los Hidrocarburos en Tarija." Cuaderno de Cultura "C" No. 11, Universidad Autónoma J. M. Saracho, Tarija.

López, C. 2007. "Bolivia's Natural Gas in the Southern Cone." CSIS Conference, Washington, DC, March 16. http://www.csis.org/component/option,com_csis_events/task,view/id,1226/.

Mayorga, E., and A. Tapia. 2006. "The Gas Era." In V. Fretes-Cibils, M. Giugale, and C. Luff, eds., Bolivia: Public Policy Options for the Well-Being of All, chap. 6. Washington, DC: World Bank.

Medinaceli, M. 2003. Sistemas Impositivos Aplicados al Sector Petrolero en Bolivia 1990–2002. December. La Paz: Cámara Boliviana de Hidrocarburos.

Medinaceli, M. 2006. "Sector de Hidrocarburos en Bolivia: Situación y Riesgos Vigentes." Unpublished report, Inter–American Development Bank. Washington, DC: November.

Ministry of Economic Development of Bolivia. 2002. Política de Estado Sobre la Utilización del Gas Natural. July. La Paz: Ministry of Economic Development of Bolivia.

Molinedo, C., and J. Velasco. 2006. "Taxes, Collection Capabilities and Distribution." In V. Fretes-Cibils, M. Giugale, and C. Luff, eds., *Bolivia: Public Policy Options for the Well-Being of All*, chap. 2. Washington, DC: World Bank.

Mueller y Asociados. 2003. *El Régimen Impositivo en el Sector Hidrocarburífero*. July. La Paz: Cámara Boliviana de Hidrocarburos.

Navajas, F. 2008. "Infrastructure Integration and Incomplete Contracts: Natural Gas in the Southern Cone." *Integration and Trade* 28 (January–July): 25–48.

Rigobon, R. 2006. "Lineamientos Generales para los Contratos de Producción de Hidrocarburos." Mimeo.

UPF. 2007. *Dossier Estadístico 1990–2006*. Unidad de Programación Fiscal, Ministerio de Hacienda, Bolivia.

Villegas, C. 2004. *Privatización de la Industria Petrolera en Bolivia: Trayectoria y Efectos Tributarios*. 3rd ed., La Paz: CIDES-UMSA.

World Bank. 1995. *Bolivia: Hydrocarbon Sector Reform and Capitalization Technical Assistance Project*. Report No. T-6228-BO, June. Washington, DC: World Bank.

World Bank. 1996. *Bolivia: Preparation of Capitalization of the Hydrocarbon Sector*. ESMAP, Report No. 191/96, December. Vol. 1. Washington, DC: World Bank.

Commentary

Fernando Candia Castillo

Navajas's interesting chapter is intended to explain why the reform program in the hydrocarbon sector in Bolivia had to be reversed. It concludes that there were design pitfalls in the reform, mainly in the tax regime, but at the same time some cultural traits and a sort of accumulated reaction against pro-market reforms that were bound to end the reform efforts even under the "most favorable performance scenario." Rather than discussing all the propositions and some hypotheses in the chapter, this commentary will focus on a couple of questions that are possibly of critical importance to an understanding of the reform program in Bolivia, and that may shed more light on what worked against the reform program and ended in the nationalization of the oil and gas industry. The commentary begins by asking whether reform in Bolivia was really needed. Then it considers whether high gas exports were due to a generous tax policy that caused the reversal of the reform efforts. After considering these questions, it looks for alternative explanations for what went wrong in Bolivia, narrowing down the list of suspects. Finally, it concludes with policy implications for the future.

The Necessity of Reform

As the chapter points out correctly from the very beginning, one can almost rule out the possibility that the reversal of the reform program was an opportunistic move on the side of the Bolivian government to take advantage of a sharp increase in oil prices, immediately after heavy foreign investments were sunk into this sector. However, it seems that these booming conditions in oil prices helped the reversal. This is probably one of the most important reasons why all foreign investors, after having been "nationalized," remained in the country and accepted new contractual terms, especially higher taxes, that they would not otherwise have accepted.

The goal of this and the following sections is to provide some additional pieces of information that could help create a bridge between the analysis in Navajas's chapter (from an "outsider's view," as he describes his perspective) on the one hand and more of an inside view of what might have gone wrong in the Bolivian case on the other hand. To do this, one should pose a different question: Was the reform needed in the first place? This seems to be a relevant question since the chapter suggests that the status quo (i.e., the application of Law 1194) would have resulted in a better outcome, not only from a fiscal perspective, but also from a political point of view. After all, Law 1194 was already imposing a 50 percent tax on the oil and gas sector, precisely the percentage that was in the "collective imagination" of the population. This would also have been because the gas export contract with Brazil (by far the largest consumption market for natural gas in South America), signed in 1988 and amended in 1991, could have provided enough of an incentive to attract foreign investors into the hydrocarbon sector in Bolivia. Thus the reform process was, to some extent, redundant.

First, one piece of history. Bolivia's attempt to sell natural gas to Brazil dates back more than thirty-five years. There have been numerous bilateral agreements on this subject, but none has resulted in a concrete project. Only in the early 1990s did Brazil agree to sign a preliminary contract to purchase gas from Bolivia. It contemplated the purchase/sale of 16 million cubic meters per day (cmpd), and was subject to an eighteen-month term during which Bolivia was supposed to find the necessary financing for the project; otherwise the contract was to be terminated. Needless to say, Bolivia failed to find financing for that project within the specified period. To make a long story short, after almost five years of failed attempts, no financing and no foreign direct investment materialized to create access to the Brazilian market under those conditions, and under the terms of Law 1194.

It is also important to know that this project was beyond the reach of the Bolivian government. Bolivia's proven gas reserves were around 3 TCFs at that time. However, its great gas potential was suggested by numerous indicators. To confirm this potential, a huge amount of investment in exploration was required. The state oil company, and especially the country, had a heavy burden of debt. (Bolivia had no access to voluntary capital markets; it was eligible only for concessional loans from the official multilateral institutions, and the size and burden of its public debt put Bolivia in the category of a Highly Indebted Poor Country.) To make things even tougher for Bolivia, a contract to export gas to Argentina had already expired, and the amount of gas sold to that country was rapidly disappearing, resulting in a big loss of export revenues for the nation. It was in this context that Bolivia opened its hydrocarbon sector to private participation through a bold reform that included the capitalization of its state-owned enterprise, the adoption of a new hydrocarbon law, the creation of a new and independent regulatory system, and the renegotiation of the 1991 contract with Brazil. It is important to highlight the relevance of the renegotiation of this contract because the amounts of gas sales originally agreed on with Brazil were not enough to make this an appealing project to major players in the industry. Hence, Bolivia renegotiated its contract, increasing the diameter of the pipeline to 32 inches and establishing a larger export quantity, 30 million cmpd (the original contract had been for 16 million cmpd). It also renegotiated the price formula, making it more advantageous for Bolivia.

Taking this review of the story into consideration, it is easy to conclude that the no-reform scenario was not an option for Bolivia. Instead it was compelled to create an attractive environment to develop a sector capable of exceeding its current production levels, which are, by the way, six to seven times the amount it was producing before the reform program.

The reform efforts produced the intended results. Foreign direct investment in the hydrocarbon sector reached unprecedented levels in a short time, and proven and probable gas reserves rose from 5.9 to 54.9 TCF, as figures 10.4 and 10.5 show. After four years of investments, Bolivian gas exports boomed (see figure 10.6). However, this result was not only due to increased quantities, because higher prices also played a role.

The Role of the Tax Regime

Now the question that remains to be answered is whether this result was at the expense of a generous tax regime, which ended up acting as a sort of built-in mechanism to undermine the reform efforts.

It is argued that tax collections performed poorly in the early years of the reform. From figure 10.7 we can see that overall, tax revenues from the hydrocarbon sector improved after the reform. This is quite

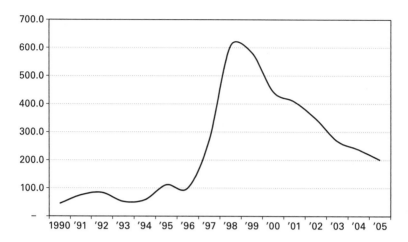

Figure 10.4
Bolivia: Investment in the hydrocarbon sector, 1990–2005 (US$ millions)
Source: Napoleón Pacheco, Fundación Milenio, *Boletín Economico* No. 4, August 2006

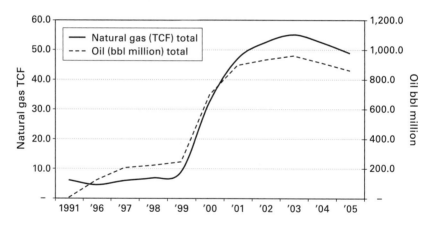

Figure 10.5
Bolivia: Oil and gas reserves, 1990–2005
Source: Napoleón Pacheco, Fundación Milenio, *Boletín Economico* No. 4, August 2006

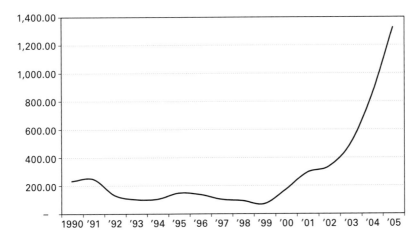

Figure 10.6
Bolivia: Gas and oil exports, 1990–2005 (US$ millions)
Source: Napoleón Pacheco, Fundación Milenio, *Boletin Economico* No. 4, August 2006

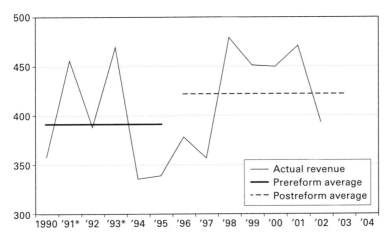

Figure 10.7
Bolivia: Government total revenue from the hydrocarbons sector (in US$ millions)

important from a macroeconomic point of view, although some critics have argued that if there was an improvement in overall tax revenues, it was because the reform shifted the tax burden toward indirect taxes on end users rather than gas-producing companies. This argument does not take into consideration that more than two-thirds (today 85 percent) of gas production is exported, and that a large part of the domestic consumption of hydrocarbons in Bolivia is subsidized.

But the main criticism concerns a comparison of upstream tax revenues, rather than overall revenues. This comparison cannot be done in a straightforward way.

Before the reform efforts, some government revenues were not taxes, but certain variable amounts negotiated by the state-owned company on a case-by-case basis with the companies operating in Bolivia. (This discretionary system embedded more risks than any possibility of a regulatory capture of an independent regulator.) Before the reform, the state-owned company was a fully vertically integrated monopoly. After the reform, upstream and downstream activities were separated, and private participation was incorporated in both sides. Therefore the whole tax system needed to be revamped rather than merely readjusting exiting taxes. To some extent, because of this nontax content in the system, upstream tax revenues before the reform are not fully comparable with tax revenues after the reform.

Navajas criticizes the regime for being too generous to the oil companies on two grounds: it allowed indefinite loss carryforward and a generous allowance for the deduction of investments. Indefinite loss carryforward is close to standard practice in a country that is interested in promoting investments. Investment spending allowances are more debatable, but maybe this issue could be addressed from another perspective, taking into consideration that investment in this sector could not rise indefinitely. The idea of allowing accelerated depreciation at the beginning of the contract period was justified by the fact that in that period all the so-called old fields were going to be making, as it happened, a 50 percent contribution to the state. The production decline in these fields was expected to coincide with the collection of taxes on new fields, with investments almost fully depreciated.

The chapter's counterfactual calculations show that upstream tax revenues in value terms with the reform, both under generous and not-too-generous tax treatment, exceed tax revenues by a large margin in the no-reform scenario. Of course, we know these counterfactual calculations are highly dependent on the underlying assumptions. For instance, it could be argued that production volumes are too generous with the no-reform scenario. It is assumed that Bolivia would be producing the same amounts that it is producing today to supply the Brazilian market and to sell gas to Argentina at the level that the existing pipeline to the latter country permits. These assumptions are highly unrealistic. As noted, the original contract with Brazil, under Law 1194, contemplated half of the amounts exported to Brazil today, and today Bolivia is not realistically in a position to sell to Argentina a tenth of the transport capacity of the existing pipeline. The chapter's counterfactual calculation also considers that the reform scenario would have led to an export volume of 116 million cmpd (almost four times the amount exported today). Although this is very generous with the reform, it probably goes beyond Bolivia's real potential and even Brazil's true demand, and at the same time introduces an investment path that makes it difficult to fully tax this sector even in the long run. A more realistic assumption for the reform scenario could have considered twice the amount exported today, which would have had a tremendous macroeconomic impact in Bolivia.

I also find that the reform scenario is probably hurt by its failure to take the surtax into account, because it was designed precisely to tax large fields like the ones supplying the Brazilian market. Finally, it would have been nice to see the effect of value added taxes as well as transaction and remittance taxes in the upstream component.

The government's take in percentage terms under the chapter's assumptions goes up to 37 percent in the counterfactual calculations. That percentage is well below the expected 50 percent in the minds of Bolivians. One can entertain the question of why it is that for some Bolivians it seemed to be preferable to levy a higher tax rate, say 50 or 60 percent, on a small base, than a smaller rate, say 37 percent, on a larger amount, and collect more money as a result. If this percentage difference empowered the opposition to the reform, some blame rests with the inability to communicate the intended results of the reform. Leaving that issue aside, let's consider only these percentages, regardless of the money collected. It could be shown, for example, that Medinaceli, cited in various places in Navajas's chapter, has calculated that under current price conditions the reform tax regime would have imposed a tax rate of 53 percent.[1] Calculations at the time of the reform showed that the tax could have leveled out in a range between 45 to 52 percent, depending on the fields that would have been in production and the surtax performance. This is something that of course has not occurred, but it shows how sensitive these calculations are to the underlying assumptions.

Alternative Explanations for What Went Wrong in Bolivia

This section is intended to narrow the possible suspects of what went wrong in Bolivia. There is no doubt that things could have been done better or that there is always room for improvement. Conditions change and it is wise for any policymaker to adapt to changing conditions. There is no doubt that under current prices, there is plenty of room to introduce changes. Remember that oil prices were at $20 a barrel when the reform was introduced, and gas prices were at $1 per BTU. At the time of nationalization oil prices were above $70 per barrel, and gas export prices for Bolivia were close to $4 per BTU, without any need to renegotiate contracts but just by applying the same contractual formula renegotiated with Brazil at the time of the reform. However, it could have been possible to take a different approach to the surtax, or even to devise a mechanism in addition to the surtax. For example, Bolivia introduced a complementary tax on the mining sector that varies in direct relation with international prices. This is something that could have been applied to the hydrocarbon sector, too. Could that have prevented nationalization? Maybe not.

So what went wrong? One cannot underestimate the importance of other factors outside the hydrocarbon sector that contributed to the reversal of the reforms, especially in a highly politicized country, and in a region where potential suppliers started to compete to supply gas to the southern cone. Politics played a big role in the reversal of the reforms, which were attacked by both left and right as part of a power struggle and not necessarily because of the defects of the reforms themselves. It is interesting to note that after national elections in 1997, the government that displaced the reformers was a coalition of fierce opponents of the reforms. This coalition ruled the country for five years (1997–2002), with massive support from the international community, especially from the World Bank and the IMF. If something close to a deep-rooted "social imagination" of a 50 percent government take from this sector existed, the reform would have been changed immediately after Sanchez de Lozada's first term. It took ten years for this change to occur. The fact that the reform was not reversed during that time suggests that at least part of the opposition to the reform was rhetorical, and also that the reform flaws referred to in the chapter were not that obvious.

But, just to remain focused on the policies applied in this sector, the chapter is correct in its notion that the lack of stronger institutions is a condition that threatens the performance of these kinds of processes. The independent regulatory system that was supposed to have oversight on this sector was highly politicized. The central government took over some of its functions, and the whole notion of independent regulators was called into question.

One other issue is worth noting: the need for continuity in carrying out public policies. According to Law 1689, oil companies were supposed to invest in the areas that were granted to them as concessions. Otherwise these areas would have been returned to the state and offered to other interested investors. Those obligations were removed by a government decree, without any further attention to the law. The reform also envisaged the functioning of a specialized unit to control and collect corporate taxes from oil companies. That office, funded through international cooperation, was never staffed properly and never delivered a single report on its activities.

Conclusion: Policy Implications

The importance of the collective imagination, beliefs, and myths in a society could not and should not be overlooked. There is no doubt that in a democratic regime one can only attempt to implement policies where there is some social disposition to accept them. That is why the reform process in Bolivia was put forward as an electoral platform that won the 1993 election by a large majority by the standards of that period. But at the same time, one has to be cautious while using those beliefs as a policy guide. Bolivia has nationalized its hydrocarbon sector three times in the last seventy years (in 1939, 1969, and 2006). It has also nationalized its mining sector. But along with a deep-rooted nationalistic sentiment, there is also a strong rent-seeking attitude and a strong belief that the well-being of the country depends on the exploitation of its natural resources. These beliefs produce some contradictory attitudes: on the one hand there is a preference for state control of natural resources, but at the same time there is a predisposition to do whatever it takes to extract as much revenue as possible from the exploitation of natural resources, even accepting private participation.

There is no doubt that in the case of Bolivia there has been a change in public opinion regarding the reform process. Bolivia nationalized its hydrocarbon sector in 2006, with the support of a majority of the population. The new rules governing this sector establish at least a 50 percent government take. Two years after nationalization, investment has stalled, the gas supply for the domestic market is erratic, shortages of gas for domestic consumption have created social protest in the streets, and gas shortages for the manufacturing sector are preventing this sector from growing. Bolivia is complying with about a third of the terms of its contract to supply gas to Argentina and risks having to pay severe penalties to that country. In case Brazil demands the full amount of gas it is entitled to under current agreements (i.e., an additional 2 million cmpd), Bolivia would be incapable of fulfilling its commitments. The government has just appointed the fifth president of the state-owned oil company in two years, and the public is starting to be strongly dissatisfied with the results of nationalization. Sooner rather than later, another shift in hydrocarbon policies will become necessary in Bolivia—hopefully this time a longer-lived shift.

Note

1. Mauricio Medinaceli, "Impuesto Directo a los Hidrocarburos (IDH): Origen maltratos y usos," Coloquios Económicos No. 9, Fundación Milenio, La Paz, Bolivia, December 2007.

11 Urgency and Betrayal: Three Attempts to Foster Private Investment in Argentina's Oil Industry

Nicolás Gadano

In 2007, Argentina's oil industry celebrated its centennial commemorating the discovery of oil in Patagonia on December 13, 1907. Throughout these 100 years, the industry's performance has been insufficient, and oil policies have shown a sharp instability to this day. Two key aspects of the sector's organization, the ownership of oil resources and the responsibility for exploiting them, have been affected by repeated policy changes.

In the early nineteenth century, both issues were clearly defined in the Mining Code, governing the incipient oil activity: the resources in the subsoil belonged to the jurisdiction they were in, either the provinces or the federal government, and the private sector was responsible for the mining activity, explicitly banning the state from carrying it out.

For the last century, these two issues basic to the sector have been raised, heatedly debated in Congress and in the public arena, and eventually modified, giving way to the above-mentioned chronic instability. In this sense, the fight for nationalization and state monopoly of hydrocarbons has repeated itself over and over again in Argentina's recent history.

On the other hand, there have also been periods in which private investment has been permitted, in sporadic episodes of reforms becoming increasingly profound and aggressive, but that have always ended up being reversed, with widespread breach of contracts and other agreements. The same pattern has occurred again and again: the government actively encourages private investment in the oil industry, in cooperation with or even in lieu of the state-owned companies. But over time, arrangements that had been deemed desirable come to be seen as harmful to the national interest, and the international oil companies withdraw from the country amid mutual recriminations. Again the state has to find a solution.

The most recent case in point is the 1990 reform, which brought Argentina's oil industry full circle: ownership of hydrocarbons was in the hands of the provinces (included in the constitutional reform of 1994) and the exploitation of resources in private hands (as a result of the full privatization of YPF, the first state-owned oil company in the world). This reform, of unprecedented size and speed worldwide, began to be reversed after the crisis battering Argentina in 2001–2002, a reversal still underway.

In this chapter I explore the roots of this policy instability, focusing on three cases of incorporation of private investment into Argentina's oil industry: Juan Domingo Perón's attempt in 1954, Arturo Frondizi's oil contracts in 1958–1962, and the industry's reform in the administration of Carlos Menem in the 1990s. In an effort to explain the failed attempts to incorporate private capital into the industry and the reasons for the renegotiation and cancellation of contracts between the state and the oil companies, I leave aside the external framework in order to focus on internal issues.

I am not suggesting that international events are not important in explaining the performance of these three reforms. The evolution of world oil prices, which sometimes leads to opportunistic behavior of governments against private companies, has probably been a relevant factor, at least in some of these episodes. Oil-producing countries usually attract private investment from abroad when oil prices are low, but tend to change the rules of the game when prices go up and investments have been made, in order to get a bigger proportion of the oil rent.[1]

In ideological terms, the international spread of ideas affecting the organization of the oil industry and the role of the state could also shed important light on the events in Argentina. Oil industry history shows waves of ideological assumptions about nationalization and privatization that spread throughout the world, particularly in Latin America and other developing areas. The late 1950s and the 1960s were politically stable for the oil industry (the "Golden Age of Oil" before the shocks of the 1970s).[2] The reform and reversal that we have seen in Argentina in the last fifteen years has been part of a regional process.

I believe that international events played a secondary role in these policy changes, which were mainly driven by domestic political forces. In any case, this chapter does not try to develop a full explanation of the reform reversals. Focusing on Argentina, it attempts to understand how domestic issues could strengthen or weaken these reforms, always subject to internal and external shocks and resistances that could affect their extension and sustainability.

Thus, I have found two common domestic characteristics in the reforms that I believe worth highlighting: they are implemented in the context of a macroeconomic emergency as well as a crisis in the industry, and in every case they are "betrayal" episodes, since the increasing share of private capital in the oil industry has meant that the government officials involved were clearly moving away from their campaign promises and previous stances on oil policies. The "urgent and treacherous" nature of the reforms does not necessarily explain the reversal of policies, but it is not insignificant when it comes to evaluating the results and their sustainability over time.

The common thread of the rulers' "betrayal" in the three cases studied in this chapter leads us to ask ourselves the reasons for such behavior. The answer is simple: in Argentina elections are not won by promising the privatization of the oil sector. The social consensus on Argentina's oil problem, built throughout the sector's 100-year history, is quite close to nationalism, a preference for state-owned oil, and resistance to the participation of foreign companies in the exploitation of resources.

In section 11.1, following a brief summary of the historical development of Argentina's oil industry, I outline the three episodes touched on earlier. Then, in section 11.2, I describe their shared characteristics and analyze the treatment that such issues have received in the literature, as well as their impact on the institutional design of the relevant initiatives. In section 11.3, I consider the reasons for "betrayal" and trace the genesis of the ideas and beliefs underlying Argentina's oil nationalism. Finally, in section 11.4 I offer some concluding thoughts.

11.1 Perón, Frondizi, Menem: Three Projects Involving Private Capital Incorporation into Argentina's Oil Industry

Argentina has never had an absolute monopoly on its oil industry, but the presence of the public sector has historically been very important. Private companies, on the other hand, have commonly played secondary roles, boosted at times by the opening up of the state quasimonopoly.

In this section, following a brief summary of the initial historical development of Argentina's oil industry, I focus on three attempts to incorporate private capital into the sector: the 1954 Peronist program, the oil policy of Arturo Frondizi's administration (1958–1962), and the opening, deregulation, and privatization process carried out under Carlos Menem's administration (1989–1999).[3]

The three cases have had wide political repercussions, took place under democratic governments (no small matter in the unstable Argentina of the twentieth century), and were set in motion by presidents of great significance in Argentina's modern history.[4]

11.1.1 The Initial Development of Argentina's Oil Industry

While the initial attempts to find oil in Argentina date back to the late nineteenth century, the industry's official history begins in December 1907, when a team of employees from the national government found oil on Patagonia's coast.[5]

At the time, legislation in force made no distinction between oil and other minerals.[6] The state (federal or provincial, on the basis of the location of the oil fields) had jurisdiction over the subsoil, and the private sector was responsible for the exploitation through perpetual mining concessions without any royalty payment to the government.[7] The growing importance of oil as a natural resource, key to the defense and economic development of Argentina and other countries, made the authorities override the Mining Code regulations, giving rise to the world's first state-run oil enterprise.

Thus, private companies—both local and international—lived with an increasingly strong state-owned organization known as Yacimientos Petrolíferos Fiscales (YPF) from 1922 on. The downstream activity was in the hands of major international oil companies (primarily Standard Oil of New Jersey and Shell), but the building of a large refinery in La Plata allowed YPF to successfully compete in the retail business. The participation of private local companies in the upstream activity began decreasing with the advent of the major international oil companies. In most cases, Argentinean oil entrepreneurs preferred to give up their role, turning their fields over to foreign companies in exchange for a fixed entry payment and a production royalty. These transactions were not well received by the government, which did not benefit from the growing oil revenues. In this context, the authorities supported YPF in its attempt to prevent international private companies from appropriating oil areas with the most potential. YPF's reserves in the federal and provincial oil territories improved its position.

In the second half of the 1930s, the passage of specific legislation affecting the oil sector and YPF finished consolidating the quasistate monopoly in oil and gas exploration and exploitation. Private companies, which had concessions under the old mining legislation, were not expropriated. But the impossibility of working in new areas condemned them to slow decadence. The share of private companies in Argentina's oil production dropped from a maximum of 63 percent in 1934 to just 11 percent in 1953. In that very year, 68 percent of the processed crude belonged to YPF, a percentage that was only 35 percent in 1937.[8]

Argentina's leaders had decided to boost the state's role in the oil industry. Private companies, mostly foreign, continued to operate in Argentina, but in more secondary positions, subordinated to the state-owned company. One of the key objectives of oil policies—self-sufficiency—became more and more elusive. By the late 1930s, 25 percent of total oil consumption was imported.

In 1939, the outbreak of the war in Europe and its negative impact on trade and financial flows worldwide highlighted YPF's difficulties in meeting Argentina's energy needs by itself. Fuel consumption had to be rationed, great quantities of cereals and oilseeds were consumed as fuel, and YPF was so strained that it consumed most of its capital once the war was over. Postwar restrictions on the purchase of raw materials and equipment limited the recovery of the state-owned company even further. Oil production reached a plateau and consumption growth had to be met with increasing imports.[9] The oil sector was in the midst of one of the main macroeconomic problems that Argentina faced in those years: the stop-and-go cycles.[10] It was responsible for a large share of total foreign currency needs and having a very high income elasticity, it contributed to worsening the situation in economic recoveries.

11.1.2   Perón and the Agreement with Standard Oil of California

Catapulted into politics by the nationalist military coup of June 1943, Perón became president of Argentina in 1946. During the first years of his administration, he supported oil nationalization policies and the state monopoly of hydrocarbon resources—an approach consistent with the general orientation of Peronist economic policies.[11] "Oil policies should be based on the very same principles as those on which economic policies rest: the absolute control over subsoil richness by Argentina and their rational and scientific exploitation by the state," the official documents stated.[12] The nationalist and statist approach even crept into the National Constitution by means of a reform implemented by the Peronists in 1949, which declared oil and gas fields "imprescriptible and inalienable property of the nation," thus blocking any participation by the private sector.[13]

In Perón's second term in office, however, his economic policy took a turn toward more pragmatic and less ideologically biased positions, even in oil policy. Having ruled out reductions in domestic expenditure as a way of adjusting the economy to the external shock, the encouragement of foreign investment became a key point in economic policy: "the government found out that its initial nationalism could clash with the defense of popular living standards, and that having to make a choice, it would go with the latter."[14]

In the oil sector, the Peronist government chose to negotiate new investments with major international companies, including those that were already operating in Argentina (Exxon and Shell). In mid-1954, a special commission made up by members of the executive branch, the state-owned YPF oil company, and the legislative chambers was set up and entered into dialogue with private companies. The strategy was to incorporate private companies in areas with potential for oil, but barely explored. That approach would make it possible to focus YPF's resources on areas where reserves had already been discovered, which demanded large investments in infrastructure and development. The constitutional restriction did not allow granting private companies exploration and/or exploitation concessions, which was circumvented by signing service contracts with YPF.

As late as May 1955, President Perón signed the first contract between YPF and California Argentina, a subsidiary of Standard Oil of California (SOCAL, today's Chevron), and sent it to Congress for ratification. The contract granted the company exclusive rights over an unexplored area in the province of Santa Cruz, which was initially 49,800 square kilometers, for a forty-year term, with a possible five-year extension.[15] The company signed firm exploration commitments for the initial four-year period, and on the basis of the outcome, it could decide to continue the operation, without receiving any compensation for expenses incurred. If the phase of commercial exploitation got underway, California was to give the crude oil to YPF at a price linked to international oil prices (East Texas). The company also had the option of using its oil in a new refinery, which could be built if oil production exceeded one million cubic meters per year. Crude oil exports were only considered in a fully supplied domestic market scenario. This contract could be seen as an early antecedent of a production-sharing agreement (PSA); after the recovery of production costs, and through a combination of general and specific taxes, profits on the operation were shared on a fifty-fifty basis between the state and the company.[16]

The agreement between YPF and California—the first in a series of arrangements with private companies—was signed by an embattled Peronist government; Perón was overthrown in September 1955. The contract was criticized by the entire political spectrum opposing Perón, from the communist left to the nationalist right. It was terminated shortly afterward because of its failure to be ratified by the legislature and it was never implemented. Discussions with other private companies to consider agreements similar to those signed with California were also called off.

11.1.3 Frondizi's Oil Contracts and Illia's Cancellation of Contracts

Arturo Frondizi, a young and dynamic Radical Party leader who had led the opposition to Perón, denounced the contract with California Argentina as "the physical embodiment of vassalage"; he won the presidential election in February 1958. His oil program, implemented at an overwhelming pace from the very beginning of his term, revolutionized the Argentina's oil sector.[17]

From a legal perspective, Frondizi delivered on his campaign promises and supported a hydrocarbon nationalization law to fill the void resulting from the elimination of the constitutional reform by the Peronists. But in practice he implemented a massive incorporation of local and foreign private companies into the local oil industry through service contracts with YPF.[18]

In line with the Peronist strategy some years before, some of the contracts assigned areas in which there were no antecedents to hydrocarbons, so that the companies had to focus on geological studies, seismic records, and exploration-well drilling.[19] The agreements included additional elements favoring the state-owned oil company, such as the building of an oil pipeline to be operated by YPF, and the granting of foreign currency-denominated loans.

Another group of contracts focused on areas in which the state-owned company had already uncovered oil and gas reserves. In such cases, the agreements were intended to increase production immediately and develop fields so as to incorporate new reserves. These contracts, signed by international and local companies, would be the most significant in terms of impact on production.[20] In 1963, five years after the contracts were signed, they represented more than a third of Argentina's total oil production.

The contracts ranged from twenty to forty years, and all provided for the gradual reduction of the territory allocated. In every case, YPF continued to be the owner of the fields and of the oil produced. The state company's commitment was to acquire the oil at a certain price linked to the international reference price. In general, the companies assumed minimum investment risks and the exploratory risk in the case of unexplored areas. The transfer of all the equipment and installations to YPF once the contract expired was also provided for.

Additionally, YPF signed drilling contracts with three foreign private companies in order to speed up the production pace of its own fields.[21] The contracts, concentrated on the south side of the Comodoro Rivadavia oil field, included the drilling of 2,100 wells in just four years. YPF committed itself to paying a fixed amount per meter drilled, and another fee for the time spent in oil well services. The payments could be adjusted by "cost variations," and were paid partly in pesos and partly in foreign currency.

In 1960, with all contracts fully in force, there were 102 active drilling rigs in Argentina, a number surpassed only by Canada and the United States at that time. The outcome was impressive in production, but poor in terms of new discoveries. The exploration contracts involved significant investments in the first three years in force, but no significant hydrocarbon discoveries were made. In terms of production, the program soon reached the targeted outcome: oil self-sufficiency. Oil extraction increased from 5.6 million cubic meters in 1958, to 15.6 cubic meters in 1962.

In March 1962, however, Frondizi was overthrown by a military coup. After several months of political instability, new elections took place in 1963, with restrictions mostly affecting the Peronist Party.

The new president, Arturo Illia, used the nullification of the oil contracts signed by Frondizi as a key issue in his election campaign.[22] A few weeks after taking office, Illia declared the contracts "null and void of absolute nullity" on the grounds of state security reasons, improprieties, pointing to flaws in contract procedures, the omission of public bidding, economic damage to the Treasury, simulation of the real legal nature of the agreements (that were presented as contracts with YPF, but in practice they were similar to oil concessions) and also the new president's campaign promises.[23] The presidential decrees assigned YPF the responsibility of the contractors as well as their employees. A special Investigating Commission was set up in the Lower Chamber, whose conclusions supported President Illia's position.

President Illia's decision led to lawsuits involving private companies, YPF, and the national government. Despite the weight of the arguments represented by the decrees of cancellation, as time went by the government decided to negotiate out-of-court settlements with the companies, acknowledging, in every case, the investments made by the companies. Only two of the most important development contracts extended beyond the Illia administration, which was overthrown in June 1966 by a new military coup. The new authorities renegotiated the contracts, allowing these two companies to continue working on the development and exploitation of the areas assigned under Frondizi's administration.[24]

The cancellation of the contracts reduced the activity in the oil industry and affected production. The total number of drilled wells, which had reached a peak of 1,615 in 1961, dropped to 503 and 557 in 1964 and 1965, respectively. Oil production stagnated at around 15 million cubic meters per year throughout Illia's presidency, and the net imports of oil and derivatives, which had dropped to just US$31 million, tripled in two years. The fact that several U.S. oil companies were affected by the cancellation and renegotiation of contracts also led to a sudden deterioration in the bilateral relationship between Argentina and the United States.[25]

11.1.4 Menem's Reforms

Carlos Saul Menem was elected president of Argentina in May 1989. The Argentinean economy was in dire straits, experiencing a hyperinflation crisis shortly after he assumed the presidency, with deep economic, political, and social consequences. Forced by circumstances to take office before schedule, Menem set in motion a controversial transformation process of the country's economy that would extend throughout the 1990s.

The oil sector was not isolated from this transformation process. Three decrees signed by Menem in 1989 unleashed the process of privatization and deregulation of the industry, which was to be completed some time later with the sale of the state-owned company, YPF, through an international IPO.[26] The 1989 decrees went deeper into private participation in oil production by means of the renegotiation of YPF's existing service contracts, transforming them into exploitation concessions in favor of private companies. These concessions were based on the 1967 Hydrocarbons Law and lasted for twenty-five years (with an eventual extension of ten years). The government take was 12 percent royalties for provinces where oil areas were located. The federal government's share of the oil rent was limited to its income tax revenues. The state-owned company was forced to put up for bidding secondary (low-production) areas and to enter into partnership with local and foreign private companies in its main oil fields.[27] All these areas were also converted into oil concessions.

The transfer of productive areas to private capital was accompanied by significant changes in the regulatory framework that increased the value of such assets, ensuring compliance with market discipline in the sector. Domestic prices of crude oil and fuels were deregulated and moved toward export/import parity. Foreign trade was opened up and the free availability of crude and foreign exchange for producers/exporters was guaranteed. Restrictions on the installation and operation of refineries and gas stations were also abolished, and new rules of open access for the transportation of crude and byproducts were set forth.

For the unexploited fields, a bimonthly bidding scheme for all areas with oil and/or gas potential, open to all local and international companies, was set. The scheme, named "Plan Argentina," prioritized the granting of exploration authorizations to those companies that offered the largest investment in the areas in question.

The process was completed with the privatization of the two state-owned companies in the sector: YPF and Gas del Estado. The privatization of YPF had various stages. Turned into a private corporation, it went through a transformation plan that included the sale of nonessential assets and the firing and/or outsourcing of some 40,000 employees out of 50,000 existing before Menem took office. All YPF's oil and gas areas were converted into concessions. Congress then authorized the privatization of up to 80 percent of the company's capital stock. Most of YPF's shares were sold on the local stock exchange and on international markets, mainly to funds and retail investors. The state initially held 20 percent of the stock, but by the end of the decade, pressured by fiscal deterioration and adverse shocks in the international economic environment, it sold its share to the Spanish company Repsol. After being forced by the bylaws to make an offer for the whole company, Repsol became the owner of close to 100 percent of YPF.[28]

The privatization of Gas del Estado took place by dividing the state monopoly into ten companies: two transportation and eight distribution firms, all sold to the private sector. Assuming free competition in the gas-production sector, the transportation and distribution segments were regulated by a new regulatory agency (ENARGAS). The price of gas for consumers was defined as the sum of the wellhead price plus the transportation and distribution fees, adjusted periodically and reviewed every five years in order to incorporate productivity improvements and new investments required by the system.[29]

Like the Frondizi experience, the industry's transformation led to a sudden expansion of production. Oil production grew from 26 million cubic meters in 1989 to 49 million in 1998, and that of gas increased from 66 to 105 million daily cubic meters in the same period. Oil reserves increased from 249 million cubic meters in 1990 to 448 million in 1999. Those of natural gas rose from a minimum of 516 billion cubic meters in 1993 to 748 billion in 1999.

Argentina became an important exporter of hydrocarbons. Exports exceeded 18 million cubic meters per year in the case of oil (36 percent of total production), and almost 20 million cubic meters daily in natural gas.[30] The process included significant investments in oil and gas pipelines linking Argentina with neighboring countries, mainly Chile.

At the end of 2001, Argentina's economy went through a deep crisis that resulted in a sharp devaluation of the currency, default on the public debt, and the restructuring of deposits and loans in the financial system. The crisis also reached the energy sector, which was affected by measures initially linked to the emergency, but that as time went by became permanent initiatives, constituting a process of reversal of the reform of the 1990s still in force and whose future direction is difficult to forecast.[31]

The free availability of foreign exchange for exports was limited by the foreign-exchange controls. The distribution of the oil rent was affected by taxes on exports at variable rates, which amounted to 45 percent in the case of crude oil. Natural gas prices were reached by the "pesification" of contracts set forth by the law of economic emergency, and have remained virtually frozen for residential consumers.[32] Consumer prices of gasoline and diesel, while formally set freely by companies, have in fact been almost frozen after an initial increase. Even when no nationalizations and/or expropriations have been carried out, the deterioration of the environment has led to an incipient withdrawal of foreign investors, whose reach is still hard to determine.[33]

11.2 The Common Features: Urgency and Betrayal

The three experiences of incorporating private capital into the Argentinean oil industry summed up above have their own characteristics. In the case of Peronism, it was an attempt that never materialized. Frondizi's program experienced a quick surge with significant effects on the sector's development, but it was reversed in a relatively short time (around five years). With President Menem, the changes were deeper and longer lasting; we do not yet know the final outcome of the "counterreform" we are going through these days.

International factors seem to have played a role in the Menem case, but not in the two previous episodes. International oil prices were stable in the mid-1950s and were decreasing in real terms when Illia suspended the Frondizi contracts. While oil privatization in Argentina in the 1990s was part of a broader wave of reforms that reached most emerging economies, the cancellation of the California Argentina contract and Illia's decision were basically internal events, not influenced by any international ideological movement.

But in all three cases we can find common internal characteristics that seem relevant when it comes to explaining the outcome of the three episodes commented on: the reversal—partial or total—of the policies of liberalization, allowing the entry of private capital into the industry.

11.2.1 Crisis and Reform

The first common element is urgency. In every case, government officials decided on the incorporation of private capital as a reaction to an industry and/or macroeconomic crisis that required drastic and immediate action.

In the case of Peronism, the crisis in the external sector that affected the Argentinean economy in the 1940s meant Perón was confronted with a difficult dilemma: either the availability of foreign exchange was adjusted, diminishing consumption and investment, or expansion was financed with the dollars from foreign investment. Naturally, Perón ruled out any kind of recessive adjustment and opted to openly encourage the entry of foreign capital into the Argentinean economy. The oil sector, stagnant because of YPF's technical and financial deficiencies that limited access to the reserves discovered in the northern part of the country, was one of the first areas of the economy to experience the change in policy. The election was not a capricious coincidence: imports of liquid fuels, in constant growth, represented close to a fourth of total imports, and the expansion of the sector required sophisticated equipment not produced in the country.[34]

A similar scenario, under even worse conditions, was the context of Frondizi's initiatives pertaining to the oil sector. Oil production was growing at a lower rate than that of consumption. Despite the attempts to recapitalize the company, YPF did not seem to be in a position to lead the much-needed expansion of the industry.[35] In 1958, when Frondizi took office, imports of crude had increased by 63 percent relative to 1955—the last year of the Peronist government—and represented 57 percent of domestic consumption. On a macroeconomic level, the crisis in the external sector continued to be the key element of the "structural crisis" that the ECLAC had diagnosed in the work ordered by the military faction that overthrew Perón. With exports practically stagnant, the increase in imports put pressure on the current account, leading to larger and unsustainable imbalances. Imports of fuels represented 21 percent of total imports.[36] In a state-of-the-union address, President Frondizi highlighted the "emergency situation" the country was facing and the need to find "immediate solutions," to justify his shift in terms of oil policies.[37]

The urgency is even more remarkable in the reforms of the 1990s. The energy sector, particularly the oil industry, was facing a severe crisis. A World Bank report, written shortly before Menem took office, emphasized that "although self-sufficiency in energy has been a long-term important Government objective, this goal has not been achieved. Crude oil production has fallen steadily since 1981. Crude oil production rates in recent years have exceeded additions to the resource base, with consequent depletion of this most essential resource to a critical level from which it will be difficult to recover."[38]

Over and above the energy problem, the economic situation in which Menem took office was so critical that the inauguration date was moved forward, in a context of hyperinflation and serious social upheaval. With this starting point, the process of structural reforms was conditioned by the need to put an end to the macroeconomic instability, especially in the first years of the Menem administration. The political background of the new president, linked to the most populist groups of Peronism, added a reputational problem that limited his chance of reversing the crisis, forcing him to overreact in his structural-reform initiatives. In the case of the oil industry, the design and timing of the first steps of the reforms—the transfers of areas to private investors and the deregulation and opening of the sector—did not respond to oil-industry considerations, but to the objective of obtaining financing for a public sector that had to do away with the inflationary tax, and simultaneously gain credibility in the face of a distrustful local and international business community.[39]

The positive link between crisis and economic reforms has been underlined on several occasions in the literature on political economy, and it is not exclusive to the oil sector. The basic idea is that a crisis can unlock reform processes when payoffs to the different economic agents involved are modified and resistance is reduced.[40]

In the case of industrial reforms like the one we are dealing with here, however, the association between emergency and reform may have some negative dimensions. To the intuitive idea stated by Sturzenegger and Tommasi (1998) that "things have to get bad before they get better," we can oppose another folk saying: "The urgent displaces the important." A process designed and executed in the urgency of a crisis is not likely to be the best process when analyzed from a long-term perspective.

It is worth pointing out that we are talking about crises that not only affect the oil sector, but that also extend to a macroeconomic level. Thus, the macroeconomic urgencies can determine the design and speed of the implementation of reforms, leaving industry-related considerations in a secondary role. By way of example, the privatization of the state-owned company may be decided on as a source of financing to cope with a short-term fiscal problem, leaving aside a deeper analysis of efficiency, income distribution, and industrial organization.[41]

But over and above the negative effect of this trade-off in efficiency (analyzed by Canovas and Gerchunoff in the Argentinean case), I am interested in pointing out the link between the emergency conditions and the social legitimacy of the reforms, as well as the utilization of inappropriate legal vehicles.

The incorporation of private capital into the oil industry, whether through contracts or the privatization of areas and/or the state-owned company, has always been a controversial type of reform, with great public repercussions. The fact that it is implemented under emergency conditions and in a very short period of time, fuels the idea that such changes are forced on society without appropriate discussion and evaluation.

In this sense, invoking the emergency situation as a way to make the reform feasible is a double-edged sword. It may ensure the approval of the reform in the short term, but the implicit message sent to society is that such a reform would never have been carried out under normal circumstances, or at least it would have been implemented differently. And when the state of emergency disappears, the social legitimacy of the reforms can fade away fast. Pernice and Sturzenegger (2003) showed that privatization was very popular when Menem took office in 1989, but this support began to decline early in 1992, when the hyperinflation crisis was over and the economy was on a growth path again.

In the 1990s, the structural reforms in the hydrocarbon industry throughout Latin America varied in scope and complexity. Just as there were countries that made great progress in the opening, deregulation, and privatization of their markets (Argentina and Bolivia are the most obvious examples), others such as Brazil were much more cautious and respectful of institutional mechanisms.[42] While in the former group we find initial crisis conditions, the latter have developed their reforms under much less pressing circumstances.[43] Not by chance, the former are those showing clear signs of reversals in policies put in place in the 1990s, while the latter show a much higher degree of stability.[44]

11.2.2 Betrayal

The second feature shared by the three programs commented on is the "betrayal" by their players. By encouraging the entry of private capital into the oil industry, Perón, Frondizi, and Menem reversed their previous stances on oil policy, presented to voters during the election campaign. In all three cases, rulers with a reputation clearly associated with nationalism and statism took a large shift in favoring the opening of the country to foreign investment.

Peronism always had nationalistic and statist rhetoric in economic and energy matters, to the extent that in 1949, it incorporated the "inalienable and imprescriptible ownership" of hydrocarbons into the national constitution. While by the end of his term Perón tried to give a new and more pragmatic meaning to the concept of oil nationalism, the contract with California Argentina was turned down by the Peronism base, and even by some members of the Peronist Party.[45] To many Peronists, the contract "betrayed the Justicialist principle of economic independence."[46]

The "betrayal" of Arturo Frondizi is probably the most dramatic. One of the staunchest opponents of the private-contract policy proposed by Perón, Frondizi published a famous book titled *Petróleo y Política* (Oil and Politics) in 1954. In the book he reviewed the history of Argentina's oil industry in a nationalist fashion and supported the exclusion of private companies, arguing that "countries putting up with the measures taken by imperialist monopolies in certain natural resources should nationalize such resources, turning them into the property of the people. The exploitation of nationalized natural resources, that is to say, property of the people, should be carried out by self-sufficient national, provincial, communal agencies or cooperatives."[47] On May 22, 1957, only one year before he took office, his proposal on oil policy was to "declare as a National Decision YPF's monopoly in everything related to the oil issue."[48]

That is perhaps why his speech on July 24, 1958, announcing a "battle of oil" based on the signing of contracts with private companies, went over badly with both friends and foes. "When we could read the contracts, we became aware that what was initially presented as the battle of oil was in fact an unconditional surrender to imperialism," wrote an advocate of oil nationalism.[49] As Szusterman (1998, 202) points out, "What to Frondizi and his closest aides was the symbol of an absolute revolution, to many of their followers became the symbol of betrayed hopes."

A parliamentary committee set up some years later to investigate the contracts reached the following conclusion: "The oil policy followed by the former president, Dr. Arturo Frondizi, meant a betrayal of the Argentine people, who elected him on the basis of statements, principles, and commitments made by him while he was running for office. His attitude is aggravated by the fact that, while in speeches and writings he continued to adhere to a consistent platform, this committee demonstrates in the following pages that he was quilty of doublespeak and disloyalty when he preached and carried out, at the very same time, negotiations incompatible with the policies promised to the people who voted for him."[50]

Carlos Menem, on the other hand, had developed his political career with a populist and nationalist discourse, consistent with the traditional Peronist creed. He managed to become the presidential candidate representing Peronism by running on a populist platform and defeating the Social Democratic wing of the party. Later he campaigned with demagogic promises such as large salary increases and a "productive revolution," and by opposing the privatization of state-owned companies.[51]

The shift in his oil policy, part of a deeper change in economic affairs and international policy, generated criticism both from the opposition and from his fellow Peronists. With the process of reforms and privatizations, Menem betrayed his electoral mandate and broke the bond linking him to the Peronist base. "The Argentine people believed. The betrayal was unbelievable," stated a recent supporter of Argentinean oil nationalism.[52] As time went by, a large part of society came to see Menem as "a big lie, a fabulous fraud."[53]

Like the connection between crisis and reform, "betrayal" is not a new issue nor is it exclusive to the oil sector.[54] In a Schumpeterian concept of democracy, those who have reached power in a free competition by means of the popular vote have the right to carry out the policies they deem appropriate. Unexpected but fruitful reforms may be accepted and betrayal can be forgiven.

"Betrayal," taken as the abandonment of electoral promises, can be legitimized ex post on the basis of the outcome of the policies implemented. For those who see democracy from a point of view that minimizes the issue of representation, the link between promises and governance is not really important because the focus is on results. A crisis that broadens the leeway of leaders to move away from electoral promises could make this process of retrospective social validation of policy shifts easier.

In the political economy literature dealing with reforms in Latin America, Tommasi and Cukierman (1998) developed a model that explained why market-oriented reforms could be implemented by political parties that have always supported the opposite policy position. With asymmetric information between the government and voters, a certain policymaker—in this case we could say a center-left one—that knows more than the public about the outcomes of the reforms, has more credibility to influence the average voter in order to carry out reforms belonging on the opposite side. So, if he is persuaded to change his previous position on the subject, he will be the only one able to unblock the reform process.[55]

In the Tommasi/Cukierman model, the identity of the reformer seems crucial to getting the reform done, but irrelevant in terms of the outcome and the sustainability of the reform, which is assumed to be successful and stable.[56]

I feel more comfortable looking at these Argentinean "betrayals" under the theoretical framework that Guillermo O'Donnell (1997) has labeled "delegative democracy"—new democracies that show features differentiating them from traditional representative democracies. In a delegative democracy, the elected leader can choose the policies at whim, without the restrictions inherent in institutionalized democracies: "Government measures do not have to bear any resemblance to the campaign promises; 'Wasn't the president authorized to rule as he saw fit?' But when the leader shifts and breaks political representation, leaving aside institutions and other branches of the state, he also bears the sole responsibility for the success or failure of his initiatives."[57]

Stokes (1999) disagrees with O'Donnell and justifies the "welfare-to-efficiency" policy switches in Latin America in the 1990s by claiming that government officials "violated mandate representation because they thought voters' beliefs were wrong and that it was in voters' best interests to pursue policies that were ex ante unpopular." In Stokes's model, politicians know what the best policy is but do not say it because, given society's beliefs, they would lose the election. But they also know that those social beliefs can change on the basis of the outcome of the policies carried out; they implement reforms not included in the electoral mandate so that they can later obtain an ex post validation in the following election, in a sort of "retrospective accountability" that ensures the democratic representation whose absence O'Donnell points out. In Stokes's view, "Remaining faithful to campaign promises, at least for some Latin American policy switchers, would have meant governing in a way they considered bad for citizens; it would have meant failing to represent."[58]

Going back to the case of Argentinean oil, the ex post legitimacy of the "betrayal" seems to be a very risky bet. The freedom to decide what to do that the ruler in O'Donnell's "delegative democracy" enjoys also entails assuming the entire burden of responsibility for the outcome of the policies adopted. In case things do not go well, the agents and social sectors that were betrayed and/or excluded in the reform process will deny all responsibility, leaving up to the leaders the difficult task of defending their actions or accepting blame. The leap from high popularity to the demonization of leaders may be as fast as it is dramatic, as we can see from the fate of the presidents surveyed in this chapter.[59]

It is worth mentioning that Argentina's experience in the oil industry shows that the success of the reform, critical to its ex post legitimacy, is not only related to the improvements in the industry's efficiency and energy supply. To society, both the overall economic performance and the political evolution of its players are determining factors. The cancellation of contracts in the Frondizi administration, for example, does not reflect the evolution of indicators of the oil sector, but the overwhelming failure of his political project. The criticism of Menem's reforms in the oil sector arose after the economic and political crisis in late 2001 and is part of a global questioning of the Menem administration. In addition to domestic economic and political issues, changes in the sector's international context (basically significant price increases) may also alter ex post social perception of the outcome of the reform. Oil-revenue distribution policies between the state and private companies that might have been accepted if prices had remained stable, may be opposed fiercely in a higher-price scenario. If the reform is exclusively attributed to a ruler, and its social legitimacy depends entirely on its results, it is highly likely that the process will become volatile and will not withstand the threat of reversal.

11.2.3   Institutional Fragility and Corruption

Limited by the urgency of the situation and by their own previous position on oil policy matters, the three leaders analyzed here did not have complete flexibility to use the optimal institutional framework design for the reforms implemented. The agreements signed by Perón and Frondizi very much resembled the traditional exploration and exploitation concessions. But constitutional and legal restrictions, previously supported by both presidents, forced them to sign the agreements as if they were service contracts with the state-owned company.[60]

With Frondizi and Menem, we find that the executive branch concentrates decision-making power and extends its reach into other areas of the state, behavior consistent with Carey and Shugart 1998, which identifies urgency as one of the factors that might impel legislators to prefer executive decree to standard legislative procedure. During the Frondizi administration, the contracts were signed by the "presidential delegate" appointed at YPF, a sort of trustee who did not consult the board or the technical departments. Also, the agreements were closed, without any public bidding, thus creating a fragile institutional framework for the reform.[61]

The first stage of the privatization of the oil-industry assets in the Menem administration was carried out under the shelter of the Administrative Emergency law, which delegated wide powers to the executive branch and was approved under pressure by Congress in July 1989, a month in which consumer prices rose by 196 percent.[62] The deep deregulation and opening of the oil sector were based on three presidential decrees, and the attempts to reform the hydrocarbon law failed throughout the ten years Menem was in power. Some parts of the current oil legislation (passed in 1967) were weakened, such as the maximum limit of five exploration permits or exploitation concessions for one company.[63] In the privatization of gas transport and distribution companies in 1992, while the reform was based on a law, the quorum for its passage was reached because the Peronist Party incorporated at least one fake lawmaker.[64]

The way policies are implemented is not irrelevant in terms of the outcomes. As Dal Bo, Foster, and Putterman (2007) empirically confirm with their experimental work, institutions can have an intrinsic effect in addition to their instrumental effect. A certain policy will have different outcomes depending on whether it is democratically selected or exogenously imposed on agents.

If we have on the one hand leaders who under emergency circumstances betray their voters by means of not fully democratic procedures, and on the other hand foreign oil companies whose bad reputation dates back to the writings of Ida Tarbell about John D. Rockefeller and Standard Oil, it is no wonder that such procedures were clouded by accusations and rumors of corruption.

The ghost of corruption, never confirmed, hovered over the agreements signed by the three presidents. Kaplan, a left-wing nationalist author, suggested the "participation of high-ranking politicians of different factions of the Peronist Party" in the ownership of SOCAL's Argentinean subsidiary.[65] The Frondizi administration was accused of laying the groundwork for the contracts "within the framework of profound immorality and corruption" by the legislature's Special Investigating Committee, set up during the Illia administration. Frondizi himself was accused by the lawmakers of asking oil companies for support during his presidential campaign in exchange for the promise to award them contracts. The public perception of systematic and widespread corruption in the Menem administration dates back to Menem's early years, and became deeper after he left office.[66] Specifically with respect to the oil industry, Gadano and Sturzenegger (1998) have shown a lack of transparency in the contract renegotiation process and its implications.

Suspicions of corruption, present in the link between private oil companies and the leaders involved, can reinforce opposition to private investment in oil. If we consider a scenario such as that tested by Di Tella and MacCulloch (2004), in which corruption reduces the attractiveness of pro-capitalist policies and moves the electorate to the "left," we would see that ideologies favoring oil nationalism and opposing private companies have to deepen and become widespread, making the magnitude of the eventual "betrayal" even worse."[67]

Corruption can play a significant role in terms of public support for reforms. Lora and Panizza (2002) show that in the 1990s, disillusionment with privatization in Latin America is strongly correlated with the level of corruption perceived in the privatization process. The authors conclude that public opinion is negative toward privatization because it has been carried out without an adequate institutional framework.[68]

Overselling the reforms has also been identified as a factor explaining reform fatigue. If initial expectations are too high, the results will probably be disappointing.[69] In this sense, the natural tendency of politicians to oversell their proposals would be higher when they have to justify a sudden shift in their position on a certain issue (oil policy), and when they need to present the reform as the only way to overcome a deep economic crisis.

In sum, in the three episodes reviewed, we observe that the reform is introduced in an emergency context, by leaders who "betray" their voters and their own history, through the use of formal and contractual instruments not up to par and suspected of corruption. This combination creates a fragility that jeopardizes the survival of the reforms over time. This may not be enough to cause a reversal, which could be triggered by other internal and/or external factors. But it will surely undermine the reform's sustainability by reducing the social legitimacy of changes that, for most of the public, do not reflect popular beliefs and have been enacted by leaders with a different mandate.

11.3   Why Betray? The Ideology behind Argentina's Oil Nationalism

Assuming that market-oriented reforms and private investment in the oil industry are advantageous and that politicians are aware of this, the obvious question is why they do not promise these reforms and explain their reasons for doing so in their campaigns instead of betraying the voters. The answer is very simple: because they would probably lose the election.[70] In a bout of brutal sincerity, former president Menem admitted it in public with these words: "Had I said what I was going to do, no one would have voted for me." Alvaro Alsogaray, a well-known Argentinean supporter of market-oriented policies who was Minister of Industry in the government that overthrew Perón, said that a few months before the election he invited Frondizi to lunch, and the radical leader told him: "I agree with you in everything we have talked about. But being political, I cannot say that to our people. I have to 'get there.'"[71]

But then we should ask ourselves, as Stokes does: "Why did citizens hold erroneous technical beliefs in the first place?" Obviously, it is not easy to identify the process by which ideas and beliefs are created in a society. In a paper explaining the resistance to reform in Argentina, Pernice and Sturzenegger (2003) argue that preferences and beliefs are endogenous to the social structure. Societies with a low and/or unfair distribution of income will tend to support redistributive policies and state interventionism. Argentina has had one of the world's worst economic and political situations in the last century, so not surprisingly, the prevailing social beliefs are completely at odds with market-friendly policies and economic reforms.

In the case of Argentina's oil policy, what took place throughout the twentieth century gives us clues as to how oil nationalism—an ideology consistent with state monopoly and opposed to the participation of foreign private companies—did not achieve positive results in practice, but gained ground in the realm of ideas.

One of the first documents expressing the core ideas of Argentina's oil nationalism—and probably Latin America's—is the well-known 1913 letter by engineer Luis Huergo, who was then head of Argentina's state oil exploitation agency, which was later to become YPF.[72] In an explosive memorandum to his superiors in the government that justified a budget request for an amount fifteen times higher than what was allocated the previous year, Huergo launched a frontal attack against American oil companies, in particular Standard Oil.[73] The unsavory reputation of Standard Oil was not a figment of Huergo's imagination. A few years earlier, the American journalist Ida Tarbell had described the monopolistic practices of John D. Rockefeller's company in a series of articles in *McClure's Magazine* that contributed to the dissolution of Standard Oil in 1911.[74] It is important to stress that in those years, Argentina had a very rich and dynamic economy. According to Pernice and Sturzenegger's (2003) hypothesis on belief formation, the Argentinean people would have been supportive of free-market competition policies. But even when oil trusts had a similarly negative reputation in Argentina and the United States, the ways chosen by both societies to fight against these trusts were quite different: more competition in the United States, a powerful state-owned company in Argentina.

Going back to Huergo's memorandum, this document warned about the risk of appropriation of Argentina's oil resources on the part of foreign interests, and denounced the complicity of some sectors of the local political and economic establishment. In the memorandum we can find the main ideas associated with oil nationalism in Argentina, which in the course of time would become consolidated through other publications, speeches, and political platforms, and that went on to shape the prevalent ideas in terms of oil policy. These ideas are the following:

1. The country has very significant oil resources, higher than those usually mentioned, and sufficient to ensure its energy supply.

2. The major international oil companies conspire along with their governments to appropriate those resources and are willing to use every means available to do so.

3. These companies have local accomplices in every social class (companies, government, press, and so on), which they corrupt with generous bribes.

4. The best defense and protection of oil resources, equivalent to the defense of national sovereignty, is nationalization and a state monopoly. Other schemes would only help companies appropriate these natural resources unfairly.

Drawing on these ideas, oil nationalism would play a major role in the 1927 presidential campaign, which propelled the Radical strongman Hipólito Yrigoyen into office. It is important to underscore that by then, just about every private company with local capital that had been given exploration permits and production concessions in oil areas, had transferred its rights and assets to international corporations in exchange for the payment of royalties on production. This "defection" of Argentinean oilmen, who used to be entrepreneurs but became mere rent seekers, had a major impact on the public discussion of oil policy. The debate between public exploitation and private exploration became a dilemma between national exploitation—through the state-owned company—versus foreign exploitation.[75]

To a growing part of society, the defense of the state oil monopoly became synonymous with the defense of the national interest. Taking advantage of the parliamentary debates on new oil legislation, "pro-Yrigoyen" Radicalism was the first political group to make nationalization and state oil monopoly crucial issues in the mobilization of the electorate.[76] Though they cannot only be attributed to oil issues, the election results tend to confirm the effectiveness of the strategy: Yrigoyen won the election with 60 percent of the votes.[77]

From that moment, oil nationalism was omnipresent in Argentina's main parties and campaign promises from both left and right. In 1946, Perón reached office by means of nationalist promises, although his opponents from Unión Democrática promoted the nationalization of energy sources. Some years later, influential socialist leader Alfredo Palacios won his position as senator for Capital Federal with the motto: "Not even a drop of oil for foreign capital."[78]

Simultaneously, major international oil companies started to be perceived as enemies of the national interest and democracy.[79] From 1930 onward, foreign oil companies were accused of taking part in almost every military coup affecting Argentina in the twentieth century.[80] Curiously enough, in the military movement that overthrew Perón in 1955, oil was identified as the driving force for the coup both by the president removed from office and by his enemies, in both cases from a nationalist perspective.[81]

Summing up, despite the fact that oil self-sufficiency promised by the nationalists was not fully reached until the end of the century—and with the contribution of private capital—in Argentina's oil industry the nationalist and statist ideas won the battle against advocates of the sector's deregulation and privatization. In this context, carrying out a political campaign promising the privatization of the sector would have meant political suicide at a minimum. With no betrayal, there was little room for market-oriented reforms in Argentina's oil industry.

11.4 Conclusions

In Argentina, the three best-known market-oriented reforms in the oil industry have ended up in contract renegotiations, public disillusionment, and reversals. International factors do not seem to have played a significant role in the first two episodes. In the last one—Menem's reform and its ultimate rejection—oil privatization was part of a broader process of reforms, in the context of a regional/global trend toward free-market policies. The reversal also has regional characteristics.

Panizza and Yañez (2006) analyze the reasons for the discontent with economic reforms during the 1990s in Latin America and conclude that the backlash against reforms is mostly explained by economic performance. The authors consider Argentina "a striking example of the importance of macroeconomic factors" in explaining people's attitude toward reform. The decline in output observed in Argentina between 1997 and 2002 explains 80 percent of the drop in support for privatization in the country.

But since 2002, Argentina has shown strong economic growth, and it still has the lowest support for privatization in the region. Surprisingly, between 2005 and 2007 the country's GDP grew 18 percent, but support for privatization fell from 25 to 19 percent.[82] In the same period, support for privatization in Latin America rose from 31 to 35 percent on average. Thus it seems that in the case of Argentina, it is "not only the economy"; other factors help explain why people have turned against the reforms. Pernice and Sturzenegger (2003) cite public beliefs and worldview as key factors in accounting for the instability of market-oriented reforms in developing societies like Argentina. Socioeconomic characteristics have induced negative attitudes toward free-market policies. Unless the reforms could rapidly modify these characteristics, such deep-rooted beliefs would surface again.

My analysis of the three attempts to foster private investment in Argentina's oil industry suggests that the supremacy of a nationalist and state-property ideology undermined any possibility of market-oriented reform, leaving space only for "policy switches" resorted to in an emergency context. This led to inappropriate legal procedures, darkened with accusations of corruption.

Recent work on the political economy of reforms suggests that crises may be a necessary context for the implementation of change, and that "betrayers" are necessary evils that then become validated on the basis of the results. Leaders most closely identified with the policy that needs to be changed, and the least plausible according to their track record and ideology, should be regarded as the most appropriate to do it. But if we decide that "urgent and treacherous" reforms in the oil sector lack the necessary social legitimacy to survive local and/or external circumstances favorable to the reversal of policies, a policy recommendation would be to stop perceiving crises as the right opportunity for reforms, and "traitors" as the right people to carry them out.

The institutional fragility of so-called delegative democracies and the enormous power delegated to the head of the executive branch may create the illusion of being the proper scenario to take shortcuts, implementing fast and deep reforms. In representative democracies, the decision-making process is usually slower and more incremental, not prone to radical changes. The reforms emerging from this process, however, will not depend on the political fortunes of just one person or group, and will enjoy the support of a strong process of institutionalization that will stabilize them over the course of time when errors and/or changes in the environment arise.

Mexico's oil industry, an eternal candidate for reforms enabling the participation of private capital, is a Latin American case to consider. Some still think that "things should get worse in order to get better," and imagine ambitious reforms as a consequence of a crisis in Mexico's energy sector.[83] Taking into consideration Argentina's experience, and what oil means to Mexico's national identity today, the most logical strategy seems to be to encourage very moderate changes, widely discussed by every political group and supported by great public consensus. The Brazilian case is a good example of moderate reforms that are relatively stable as time goes by and that allow the country to reach oil self-sufficiency.

No wonder that in the cases analyzed we find reforms made possible through fragile legal instruments, which then prove to be easy to attack when reversal emerges. In an emergency situation, and when voters feel betrayed, is difficult to put in motion the state institutional system (legislative bodies, consulting technical agencies, and so on) to obtain legitimate approval for the reforms. But the impact of the reforms will be probably different when decisions are not democratically approved, and are imposed on society by a group perceived as not representing the public interest.

The shaping of the economic ideas and assumptions of a society is a complex process, often involving incremental changes. Instead of taking the shortcuts that a crisis offers, we should accept the need to traverse the long, tedious but surer path of the bureaucratic process, building a consensus for reform. This process is probably the only definitive way to change social beliefs about the oil industry, reducing resistance to private investment.

The possibility of implementing fast and deep reforms may be tempting. But, in sum, as O'Donnell points out, "No matter what the advantages of these measures for a country at a given moment are, their sudden adoption does not favor in the least public trust in democracy and its institutions. It is difficult to believe that preaching something and doing the opposite is not destructive to the public trust in institutions and the democratic system."

Notes

I thank Pablo Gerchunoff, Ernesto Dal Bo, Marcelo Leiras, and Marcos Novaro for their useful comments. I also appreciate comments and sugestions from Louis Wells (discussant), Rafael Di Tella, Federico Sturzenegger, William Hogan, and all the other conference participants.

1. International oil prices in real terms were stable in the Perón years (1950–1955), and decreased under Frondizi (1958–1962). The average price of oil in the United States was $2.90 per barrel in 1959 and $2.94 in 1968 (see Yergin 1991). In recent years, oil prices (West Texas Intermediate barrel) have climbed from a minimum of $11, to close to $100 in 2007.

2. See Yergin 1991 and Maugeri 2006.

3. When I say private participation, I mean direct control of oil field operation by private companies, through oil service contracts or oil concessions.

4. The leading role of democratic governments elected by citizens in the attempts to privatize the oil industry shows that oil nationalism has been more influential among the military than among civilians. In the last military dictatorship (1976–1983) there was a slight attempt to incorporate private capital in the exploration of new oil areas after the passage of Law 21.778, in April 1978. The outcome, however, was not very significant.

5. This section is based on Gadano 2006.

6. The Mining Code passed in 1886 was applied.

7. State-run mining exploitation was banned by the Mining Code.

8. In 1953 Argentina produced 4.5 million cubic meters, while consumption in refineries totaled 8.4 million cubic meters.

9. Oil imports increased from 910,000 cubic meters in 1946 to 3.9 million cubic meters (46 percent of total consumption) in 1953.

10. See Díaz Alejandro 1970.

11. On the Peronist economic policy, see Gerchunoff 1989 and Gerchunoff and Antunez 2002.

12. *Política Argentina del Petróleo*, brochure from the Industry and Commerce Ministry, 1949.

13. Text of article 40 of the 1949 Constitution.

14. Gerchunoff and Antunez 2002, 177.

15. The contract provided for the automatic and gradual release of the area involved until a minimum area of 5,000 square kilometers had been released by the end of the twentieth year.

16. See Rumbo 1957 for a detailed description of the contract. The first fifty-fifty oil contract had been signed in Venezuela in the 1940s. See Yergin 1991.

17. See Petrecolla 1989 for an analysis of Frondizi's economic strategy.

18. Law 14.773, passed in November 1958, stated that the fields were "exclusive, imprescriptible, and inalienable assets belonging to the national state," and banned concessions in oil areas.

19. The companies with which these contracts were signed included Shell, Esso, Union, Continental, and Marathon.

20. The international companies were Pan American, Loeb Rhoades (later Cities Services), and Tennessee. The local ones were Astra and Cadipsa.

21. These foreign firms included two U.S. companies (Southeastern Drilling Company and Kerr-McGee Oil Industries), and a subsidiary of the Italian ENI (SAIPEM).

22. In addition to what Illia promised, the cancellation of oil contracts was in the platform of most political parties competing in the election, and was also supported by different Peronist groups. See Tcach and Rodriguez 2006.

23. Decrees 744/63 and 745/63. The former dealt with exploration and development contracts, and the latter with drilling contracts.

24. The contracts that survived were with Cities Services and Pan American. The latter continued to exploit a 4,000-square-kilometer area known as "Cerro Dragon" (Dragon Hill) on the boundary between the provinces of Santa Cruz and Chubut. The renegotiation provided for the total handover of the area to YPF in 1978. Nowadays, Cerro Dragon continues to be operated by Pan American Energy (a partnership between the local firm Bridas and BP Amoco, the continuation of the original Pan American). The company has just been granted a new early controvertial extension of its contract by the provincial authorities.

25. See Tulchin 2007.

26. Decrees 1055, 1212, and 1589 of 1989. For a more detailed analysis, see Gadano 2000.

27. See Gadano and Sturzenegger 1998 for an ex post evaluation of the renegotiation of contracts and the bidding of YPF's areas in the 1990s.

28. The state still holds 1,000 shares that entail veto rights over the company's critical decisions.

29. Gadano 2000.

30. Other products, such as gasoline, diesel, and lubricants, also showed increased exports.

31. See Navajas 2006.

32. Emergency law 25.561.

33. Examples of this process are the exit of National Grid from Transener, that of Sempra Energy from natural gas distribution companies, and the sale to a domestic investor of the stock Electricité de France held in Buenos Aires City's electricity distributor, Edenor. In the oil sector, Repsol YPF sold 14.9 percent of YPF S.A. to a local partner, and Esso has begun a process of sale of its assets in Argentina.

34. See Gerchunoff and Llach 1998.

35. After Perón's fall and the cancellation of the contract with California Argentina, the new authorities implemented a "Reactivation Plan" of YPF, with hardly any success.

36. See Díaz Alejandro 1970.

37. Szusterman 1998.

38. World Bank 1990, Executive summary, ii.

39. See Cánovas and Gerchunoff 1995.

40. See Sturzenegger and Tommasi 1998.

41. This seems to have been the case in 1999, when the government of Argentina sold 20 percent of YPF to the Spanish company Repsol and maximized the sale price by allowing the buyers to take control of the company.

42. With the 1995 constitutional amendment and Oil Law 9478/97, Brazil broke the monopoly of Petrobras and laid the groundwork for a moderate deregulation and incorporation of private capital into its hydrocarbon industry. See Campos Filho and Pires 2005.

43. In her work on Latin America, Palacios (2003) shows how reforms made less progress in countries where the oil sector and state-owned companies were strong suppliers of foreign exchange and financing, while processes were deeper in the case of undercapitalized sectors and state-owned companies in dire financial situations.

44. According to "Latinobarómetro" data, mentioned in Lora and Panizza 2003, Argentina and Bolivia are among the countries in Latin America where support for privatization has dropped by the largest amount.

45. Peronist representative Eduardo Rumbo (1957) was one of the few leaders who tried to conceptually justify the "new" oil nationalism.

46. Gerchunoff and Llach 1998.

47. Frondizi 1954, LXII.

48. Statement by Arturo Frondizi in the National Committee of UCRI, May 22, 1957; quoted in Gómez 1963, 262.

49. Casal 1972, 103.

50. Ruling of the Majority of the Investigation Special Committee of Oil Matters of the House of Representatives, Order of the day No. 394, 1964.

51. See Novaro 2006, Bernal 2005, and Stokes 1999.

52. Bernal 2005, 117.

53. Novaro 2004, 201.

54. In their book *Eloge de la trahison*, Denise Jeambar and Yves Roucaute go as far as to identify betrayal as an essential need on the part of modern democratic states.

55. Alejandro Gómez, elected vice president of Argentina in 1958, identified in his 1963 book—in a very negative way—the exclusive "ability" of Frondizi to develop the reform: "Frondizi had led a life of struggle and devotion that deserved all our consideration and respect. He was the only man that could sell us out, given how we trust him. And he did it" (Stokes 1999, 120). Gómez did not support Frondizi's oil policy, was accused of leading a coup against the president, and resigned his position in November 1958.

56. The paper was published in the late 1990s, before the crisis and the reversal of the market-oriented reforms in Argentina. Menem's reform is described as an "extensive and

quite succesful transformation of Argentina into a market-friendly economy," a characterization difficult to accept today.

57. O'Donnell 1997.

58. Stokes 1999, 126. President Frondizi would surely have agreed with Stokes's hypothesis. "It was said that the president's oil policy was absolutely the opposite of what citizen Frondizi had claimed in his book *Petróleo y Política* (Oil and Politics). I am happy to highlight this. The real option for the citizen filling the position of president was very simple: either he held onto his theoretical ideas and oil continued diminishing underground, or oil was extracted with the aid of foreign capital in order to improve our balance of payments and adequately feed our industry. Either the intellectual prestige of the author of *Petróleo y Política* was kept intact, or the country was kept intact" (Frondizi 1963, 8).

59. Menem's case is a real example. As Stokes underscores, Menem enjoyed high popularity in the 1990s and was reelected in 1995. After the 2001–2002 crisis, however, he became the most condemned Argentinean leader. In August 2007 he ran for governor of his home province, La Rioja, which greatly benefited while he was president of Argentina, but he came in third in the election.

60. The contract with California Argentina and the Frondizi agreements were characterized as "covered concessions." See Canessa 1958.

61. In this sense, Frondizi's contracts are a good example of how decisions are made in delegative democracies: "a frantic decision making process, real *decreetism*" (O'Donnell 1997).

62. Law 23.696 authorized concessions and associations in YPF's areas but did not allow for its privatization. Ferreira Rubio and Goretti (1998) analyze the 1989 Administrative and Economic Emergency laws in the terms of the classification of Carey and Shugart 1998.

63. Article 34 of the Hydrocarbons Law 17.319 stipulates that no company can hold more than five exploitation concessions. The YPF privatization law (24.145) allowed that this ruling would not be applied to the company's concessions.

64. It is law 24.076. The case was known as the "scandal of the phony representative." It is necessary to say that Menem had managed to control the Supreme Court, by increasing the number of members and appointing five of its nine members.

65. Kaplan 1957, page 60. Engineer Julio Canessa, appointed by Perón to head YPF in the 1940s, said "extremely powerful forces" worked against the national interests regarding oil during the Peronist era.

66. See Novaro 2004.

67. Di Tella and MacCulloch 2004. What they call left-wing stances might be better defined in Argentina's case as Latin American populism, which includes elements of nationalism, statism, and anti-imperialism.

68. In their 2003 paper about structural-reform fatigue, Lora and Panizza note that corruption plays a key role in the recent rejection of privatization policies in Latin America. But corruption in these countries is not new. It is a structural problem, deeply rooted in society and not exclusive to a certain period of time. In this sense, corruption has probably offered a good rationale for rejecting privatization, and people find it self-serving to associate corruption with privatization. See Pernice and Sturzenegger 2003.

69. See Panizza and Yañez 2006.

70. Using information on various Latin American countries, Stokes (1999) demonstrates that the fear of losing the election has led candidates to hide their true intentions.

71. *Viento Norte* magazine, no. 49, p. 1; quoted in Gómez 1963.

72. The authors who have quoted Huergo's memorandum include Scalabrini Ortiz (1940), the socialist Julio V. González (1947), Frondizi (1954), Rumbo (1957), Alascio Cortázar (1969), Casal (1972), Kaplan (1972, 1974), Mayo, Andino, and García Molina (1976), and Bernal (2005). The memorandum was also quoted by advocates of oil nationalism in other Latin American countries—for example, Brazilian General Julio Horta Barbosa, president of the Conselho Nacional do Petróleo. In a speech given at the Military Club of Rio de Janeiro in July 1947 (quoted in the YPF's *Bulletin of Oil Information* in January 1948), Horta Barbosa reproduced various paragraphs from the memorandum, highlighting the *"mystique around the direct management of the oil industry by the State"* existing in Argentina.

73. Huergo said: "The acts of Standard Oil are judged everywhere as acts of pirate users, ruthless, led by an ex-priest who began leading millions of families of his own countrymen to devastation and grief, and who, like an octopus, has extended his tentacles everywhere, accumulating incredible fortunes of thousands of millions of pesos, amassed with tears and human blood, which has the government and the institutions of his country on the rack, and which introduces corruption, civil war and national disaster in other countries" (quoted in Gadano 2006, 42; also see Buchanan 1973).

74. The accusations of Tarbell, similar to those of Huergo ("fraud, corruption, bribery, coercion, outright terror"), were the beginning of a permanent hostility toward the oil industry from a significant part of the American public. As a recent article in *The Economist* points out, "Flagellating the oil business is one of the America's proudest traditions" (*The Economist*, January 19–25, 2008, 36).

75. Local oil firms reappeared with Frondizi as YPF's contractors, and as the owners of the new oil concessions in the 1990s. By the end of the century, most of them had sold their companies to international oil firms, repeating the process of the early 1920s. This behavior could lead us to think in terms of a cycle for local entrepeneurs in the oil industry. First they get close to the governement, start as contractors, and build up their companies. When the oil industry becomes open to foreign capital, they sell their firms to the big international oil companies. And then they wait for the following nationalization/ expropriation to start again from the beginning, as the new "national bourgeoisie." This hypothesis implies that local firms could be a strong factor favoring the reversal of reforms. In the episodes analyzed here there is no clear evidence of this behavior. In the Illia reversal, some of the contracts were signed by local firms (Astra, Cadipsa) and were also affected by Illia's decision. In Menem's reform, almost all local firms were sold to international companies before the reversal (Astra and YPF to Repsol; Pérez Companc to Petrobras; San Jorge to Chevron), but it is difficult to prove that they influenced and supported the government in its reversal policies.

76. See Buchanan 1973.

77. The "cause of oil" was effective electionwise not only for Yrigoyen, but also for a split in the Socialist Party that supported Yrigoyen's project in Congress, and that obtained an overwhelming electoral victory. See Gadano 2006.

78. Rein 2006.

79. The seeming tension between oil resources and democracy is not an Argentinean issue. In a 2001 paper using cross-national data from 113 states between 1971 and 1997, Michael Ross finds that "oil does hurt democracy," particulary in poor countries.

80. See Gadano 2006. The accusation of coup mongering over international oil companies has spread throughout other Latin American countries. In Brazil, for example, it was President Getulio Vargas himself who in his "Testament Letter"—written before he committed suicide—denounced conspiring groups and interests that might have attacked him as a result of the creation of the state-owned oil company Petrobras.

81. In statements to *Tempo* magazine of Milan, February 9, 1956, quoted in Kaplan 1957, Perón claimed he had been overthrhown by a pro-British "oil coup," similar to the coup that a few years earlier had overthrown the Iranian government that had nationalized oil. According to Perón, "The purpose was to prevent Argentine oil resources from being exploited so as to contribute to the strengthening of the country's industrial base." In turn, the president of the Revolución Libertadora, General Aramburu, stated a few weeks after the coup: "The main purpose of the revolutionary movement was the threat looming over the oil industry." See "Message to the People of the Provisional Presidente General Pedro E. Aramburu on the Commemoration of the Day of Oil," December 13, 1955.

82. According to Latinbarómetro 2007, only 19 percent of respondents in Argentina think that privatizations were beneficial for the country, compared with 35 percent for the regional average.

83. See, for example Palacios 2003, 29: "In Mexico, incentives to reform are more likely to come from demand pressures or from a demand generated energy crisis within the country."

References

Alascio Cortázar, Miguel M. 1969. *Burguesía Argentina y Petróleo Nacional.* Buenos Aires: Editorial Avanzar.

Bernal, Federico. 2005. *Petróleo, Estado y Soberanía: Hacia la Empresa Multiestatal Latino-americana de Hidrocarburos.* Buenos Aires: Editorial Biblos.

Buchanan, James E. 1973. *Politics and Petroleum Development in Argentina: 1916–1930.* Ph.D. dissertation, University of Massachusetts.

Campos Filho, Leonardo, and Adriano Pires. 2005. *A Abertura do Setor Petroleo e Gas Natural: Retrospectiva e Desafios Futuros.* Mimeo.

Canessa, Julio. 1958. *La Real Situación Petrolera: Abastecimiento de Combustibles.* Buenos Aires: Editorial Colombo.

Canovas, Guillermo, and Pablo Gerchunoff. 1995. "Privatizaciones en un Contexto de Emergencia Económica." *Revista de Desarrollo Económico* 34(136): 483–512.

Carey, John M., and Matthew Soberg Shugart. 1998. "Calling Out the Tanks or Filling Out the Forms?" In John M. Carey and Matthew Soberg Shugart, eds., *Executive Decree Authority.* Cambridge: Cambridge University Press.

Casal, Horacio. 1972. *El Petróleo.* Colección La Historia Popular. Buenos Aires: Centro Editor de América Latina.

Dal Bo, Pedro, Andrew Foster, and Louis Putterman. 2007. *Institutions and Behavior: Experimental Evidence on the Effects of Democracy.* Working Papers, 2007-9, Brown University Department of Economics.

Díaz Alejandro, Carlos F. 1970. *Essays on the Economic History of the Argentine Republic.* New Haven, CT: Yale University Press.

Di Tella, Rafael, and Robert MacCulloch. 2004. *Why Doesn't Capitalism Flow to Poor Countries?* TBS/DP04/5. London: Imperial College, University of London.

Ferreira Rubio, Delia, and Matteo Goretti. 1998. "When the President Governs Alone: The Decretazo in Argentina, 1989–93." In John M. Carey and Matthew Soberg Shugart, eds., *Executive Decree Authority,* Cambridge: Cambridge University Press.

Frondizi, Arturo. 1954. *Petróleo y Política.* Buenos Aires: Editorial Raigal.

Frondizi, Arturo. 1963. *Petróleo y Nación.* Buenos Aires: Editorial Transición.

Gadano, Nicolás. 2000. "Determinantes de la Inversión en el Sector Petróleo y Gas en la Argentina." In Daniel Heymann and Bernardo Kosacoff, eds., *La Argentina de los Noventa.* Buenos Aires: Eudeba / Cepal.

Gadano, Nicolás. 2006. *Historia del Petróleo en la Argentina.* Buenos Aires: Edhasa.

Gadano, Nicolás, and Federico Sturzenegger. 1998. "La Privatización de Reservas en el Sector Hidrocarburífero: El caso de Argentina." *Revista de Análisis Económico* 13(1): 75–115.

Gerchunoff, Pablo. 1989. "Peronist Economic Policies, 1946–1955." In Guido Di Tella and Rudiger Dornbusch, eds., *The Political Economy of Argentina, 1946–83.* London: Macmillan.

Gerchunoff, Pablo, and Damián Antunez. 2002. "De la Bonanza Peronista a la Crisis de Desarrollo." In Juan Carlos Torre, ed., *Nueva Historia Argentina: Los Años Peronistas (1943–1955).* Buenos Aires: Sudamericana.

Gerchunoff, Pablo, and Lucas Llach. 1998. *El Ciclo de la Ilusión y el Desencanto."* Buenos Aires: Ariel Sociedad Económica.

Gómez, Alejandro. 1963. *Política de Entrega.* Buenos Aires: Peña Lillo Editor.

González, Julio V. *Nacionalización del Petróleo.* Buenos Aires: Editorial El Ateneo.

Jeambar, Denise, and Yves Roucaute. 1988. *Elogio de la Traición.* Barcelona: Gedisa.

Kaplan, Marcos. 1957. *Economía y Política del Petróleo Argentino 1939–1956.* Buenos Aires: Editorial Praxis.

Kaplan, Marcos. 1972. *Petróleo, Estado y Empresa en Argentina.* Caracas: Editorial Síntesis Dosmil.

Kaplan, Marcos. 1974. "La Primera Fase de la Política Petrolera Argentina. (1907–1916)." In Revista de *Desarrollo Económico,* 12(45) Buenos Aires.

Latinobarómetro. 2007. *Informe Latinobarómetro 2007.* Santiago de Chile: Corporación Latinobarómetro.

Lora, Eduardo, and Ugo Panizza. 2003. "The Future of Structural Reform." *Journal of Democracy* 14(2): 123–137.

Maugeri, Leonardo. 2006. *The Age of Oil: The Mythology, History, and Future of the World's Most Controversial Resource*. Westport, CT: Praeger.

Mayo, C. A., R. Andino, and F. García Molina. 1976. *La diplomacia del petróleo (1916–1930)*. Biblioteca Política Argentina No. 24. Buenos Aires: Centro Editor de América Latina.

Montamat, Daniel. 2007. *La Energía Argentina: Otra Víctima del Desarrollo Ausente*. Buenos Aires: Editorial El Ateneo.

Navajas, Fernando. 2006. *Energo—Crunch Argentino: 2002–20XX*. FIEL Working Paper No. 89. Buenos Aires, FIEL.

Novaro, Marcos. 2004. "Menemismo, pragmatismo y romanticismo." In Marcos Novaro and Vicente Palermo, eds., *La Historia Reciente: Argentina en Democracia*. Buenos Aires: Editorial Edhasa.

Novaro, Marcos. 2006. *Historia de la Argentina Contemporánea*. Buenos Aires: Editorial Edhasa.

O'Donnell, Guillermo. 1997. *Contrapuntos: Ensayos escogidos sobre autoritarismo y democratización*. Buenos Aires: Editorial Paidós.

Palacios, Luisa. 2003. *An Update on the Reform Process in the Oil and Gas Sector in Latin America*. Tokyo: Japan Bank for International Cooperation.

Panizza, Ugo, and M. Yañez. 2006. *Why Are Latin Americans So Unhappy about Reforms?* IADB Working Paper No. 567. Washington, D.C.: IADB.

Pernice, S., and F. Sturzenegger. 2003. *Cultural and Social Resistance to Reform: A Theory about the Endogeneity of Public Beliefs with an Application to the Case of Argentina*. UTDT, mimeo.

Petrecolla, Alberto. 1989. "Unbalanced Development, 1958–62." In Guido Di Tella and Rudiger Dornbusch, eds., *The Political Economy of Argentina, 1946–83*. London: Macmillan.

Randall, Laura. 1993. *The Political Economy of Brazilian Oil*. London: Praeger.

Rein, Raanan. 2006. *Juan Atilio Bramuglia: Bajo la sombra del Líder. La Segunda Línea de Liderazgo Peronista*. Buenos Aires: Ediciones Lumiere.

Ross, Michael L. 2001. "Does Oil Hinder Democracy?" *World Politics* 53, no. 3 (April): 325–361.

Rumbo, Eduardo. 1957. *Petróleo y Vasallaje: Carne de Vaca y Carnero contra carbón más petróleo*." Buenos Aires: Ediciones Hechos e Ideas.

Scalabrini Ortiz, Raúl. 1940. *Política Británica en el Río de la Plata*. Buenos Aires: Editorial Plus Ultra.

Schumpeter, Joseph A. 1950. *Capitalism, Socialism, and Democracy*. New York: Harper.

Stokes, Susan. 1999. "What Do Policy Switches Tell Us about Democracy?" In A. Przeworski, S. Stokes, and B. Manin, eds., *Democracy, Accountability and Representation*. Cambridge: Cambridge University Press.

Sturzenegger, Federico, and Mariano Tommasi. 1998. *The Political Economy of Reform*. Cambridge, MA: MIT Press.

Szusterman, Celia. 1998. *Frondizi: La política del desconcierto*. Buenos Aires: Emecé.

Tarbell, Ida M. 1904. *The History of the Standard Oil Company*. New York: Macmillan.

Tcach, Cesar, and Celso Rodriguez. 2006. *Arturo Illia: Un sueño breve*. Buenos Aires: Editorial Edhasa.

Tommasi, Mariano, and Alex Cukierman. 1998. "Credibility of Policymakers and Economic Reforms." In Federico Sturzenegger and Mariano Tommasi, eds., *The Political Economy of Reform*. Cambridge, MA: MIT Press.

Tulchin, Joseph. 1990. *Argentina and the United States: A Conflicted Relationship*. Boston: Twayne.

World Bank. 1990. *Argentina Energy Sector Study*. Report No. 7993-AR. February. Washington, DC: World Bank.

Yergin, Daniel. 1991. *The Prize: The Epic Quest for Oil, Money, and Power*. New York: Simon & Schuster.

Commentary

Louis Wells

Gadano's chapter valuably undertakes the task of explaining the changes in private—domestic and foreign—investors' roles in the Argentinean oil industry by focusing on events internal to Argentina. This approach differs from many studies of changes in business and government relations in the oil and other mineral industries, most of which draw heavily on shifts in the international industry. Existing studies turn particularly to vertical integration and disintegration, access to technology, and firms' control over markets, but also to changes in beliefs about foreign involvement that have spread from country to country.

Argentina, more than many other oil-producing countries, lends itself especially well to this approach. Until recently, it was not a petroleum exporter and thus not inevitably tied into what was largely a vertically integrated global industry for many decades. Thus, the control that the major international oil companies exercised over market access elsewhere was not relevant to a country where production was overwhelmingly consumed locally. To be sure, the country might well have needed the technology that the major oil companies held, but the facts that its oil was onshore and the country could acquire refining technology from the major companies seem to have made Argentina relatively immune to the power of the international oil giants.

Although Gadano's chapter explicitly recognizes that international factors might have played a role in some of the changes in business-government relations in Argentina's oil industry, it could have asked whether the country was as isolated from international events as the story implies. Although vertical integration and control over technology by the international players may have affected Argentina less than other countries, the correlation between events in Argentina and those occurring in other producing countries is unlikely to be accidental. The shifting ideological positions of the developing countries with respect to natural resources were influenced by changes in the structures of raw material industries, but it is likely that ideologies also took on a life of their own and affected governments that were less dependent on multinationals. Diplomats and academics in Argentina were, like those in other developing countries, influenced by the ideas of *"dependencia"* and "national sovereignty over natural resources" that swept through the developing world, especially in the 1960s and 1970s. Similarly, Argentineans were hardly immune to the ideology and international pressures for privatization that emerged out of the Thatcher and Reagan years and that permeated aid and multilateral institutions and even academia in the late 1980s and subsequently. Argentinean nationalizations and privatizations were of course products of domestic political events, but those events were almost certainly influenced by what was happening elsewhere, as the timing strongly suggests. It would be nice to understand better the vehicles through which ideas were transmitted across borders and into domestic political actions.

One wonders why Argentina turned to foreign investors at all to develop its petroleum resources, at least before the 1980s. In the very early years, production seems to have been largely private, but by domestic interests. The chapter hints that foreign firms, however, may have controlled the downstream market inside Argentina. Some measures of the degree of control would be helpful, but of course those may simply not be available. The chapter does not explain whether the control—whatever its degree—was exercised because of possession of proprietary refining technology or marketing skills, or something else. Whatever the source of foreign influence, the reader is left to wonder whether control by multinationals over downstream markets meant prices for producers that squeezed out domestic private firms. The large oil companies were certainly willing to exercise their power when they could. This or some other explanation is needed for the increased foreign influence after initial local development.

For much later periods, the author implies that foreign investment was needed to supply the funds to develop new output in Argentina. Yet, if the technology was available and the state petroleum firm could gain access to foreign markets, foreign direct investment would seem to be a very costly way to develop petroleum. Direct investors demand high returns, much higher than the likely borrowing rate for the state oil company or the government. For sure, as reported above, the prevailing ideology had changed and likely affected Argentina's decision.

And privatization could serve as a source of money for a cash-strapped government, as it did elsewhere, even if that money was very costly in the medium or long term. There may have been additional, unexplored reasons for seeking foreign investment, of course.

The author calls the policy changes in Argentina "betrayals." Politicians promised one set of policies at election time and then followed another once elected. If the policies actually implemented were in the national interest, *betrayal* seems a strong word. The chapter does not make a convincing case that any of the "betrayals" were contrary to the national interest (nor that they were in the national interest, for that matter). There are no data in the chapter on the economic returns to Argentina from the different policies. The author does point out that production levels increased under recent privatizations, but provides no analysis of the overall benefits from that increase. To be sure, once private capital was in control, nationalizations might have discouraged subsequent attractive foreign investments. Limited evidence from elsewhere, however, suggests that investors are surprisingly undeterred by takeovers of other investors. The costs of foreign investment were certainly high, and perhaps the costs of nationalizations were also high. How the costs compared to gains, however, is not addressed in this chapter.

More data will be useful in pushing the ideas further. For example, data must exist on production levels at various times, how much of each stage of the petroleum industry was private (domestic or foreign) at various points in the story, how much of the output was exported, and perhaps what percentage of "profits" was captured by Argentineans under various arrangements.

Of course, the chapter does not and cannot answer every question. Given the long relative isolation of the Argentinean petroleum industry from the world market, the country provides an opportunity to focus on the internal political processes that influenced the relations between the Argentinean state and the private sector in petroleum. The author exploits that possibility. The reader can wonder how much of the change described was influenced by events elsewhere, but such a rich description of the internal political process is rare and very worthwhile.

12 The Political Economy of Oil Contract Renegotiation in Venezuela

Osmel Manzano and Francisco Monaldi

12.1 Introduction

"We're not Communists; I'm not whatever-his-name-is in Venezuela," stated Ed Stelmach, the premier of the Canadian province of Alberta, when criticized for the province's increase in oil royalty rates (*New York Times*, October 27, 2007). He argued that the high oil prices justified a higher royalty rate and at the same time wanted to distance himself from the radical politics of Venezuela's president Hugo Chavez, who had forced the renegotiation of oil contracts in earlier years. In fact, as the quote implies, ideology has frequently been invoked as the main factor explaining the cyclical waves of resource nationalism in the developing world. In this chapter we challenge such view.

Production contracts between the Venezuelan state and international oil companies (IOCs) have always been revised by the government before their expiration date. This chapter explores the political economy of this erratic relationship between IOCs and the Venezuelan state, asking the following question: Given the high costs involved in contract renegotiation, why have Venezuela and the oil companies been unable to develop more sustainable agreements? In other words, how is it that, nearly a century after the founding of the Venezuelan oil industry, contract renegotiation remains a perennial feature of state-IOC relations? We hypothesize that, even though ideology sometimes plays a role, the primary causes include the absence of an appropriately progressive tax regime as well as structural features of the oil sector.

These features are extremely high rents, high sunk costs, high initial risks, and volatile prices. We argue that the nature of the development cycle in the petroleum industry and the persistent oil price cycles ensure that the pendulum of power swings back and forth between the state and the IOCs, making the development of contracts that can survive the entire arc difficult. In fact, as the cases of renegotiation in Canada, the United Kingdom, and other developed countries show, the phenomenon is not restricted to the developing world.

Since its beginnings in the 1910s, the Venezuelan oil industry has undergone three major periods of contract renegotiation. (1) In 1943 all existing oil concessions were transformed into new concessions based on a new law with tougher fiscal terms and more government control. (2) In 1958–1976 the concessions approved in the 1940s and 1950s, based on the 1943 law, were the object of significant increases in the government take through a systematic rise in the income tax rate applicable to the oil activity and through the approval of additional surcharge taxes. These changes increased the government take on profits from about 50 percent in the 1940s and 1950s, to more than 65 percent in the 1960s and a maximum of 94 percent in the 1970s. In 1975 the oil industry was nationalized. (The nationalization law was approved by Congress on August 1975 and took effect on January 1976.) (3) Finally, after the successful reopening of the oil industry in the 1990s, in 2004–2008 the government once again forced the renegotiation of the oil contracts, increasing royalties and taxes and transforming the contracts into mixed enterprises (joint ventures) with government control (including state ownership of 60 percent or more of the capital), implying a partial renationalization of the oil sector. The chapter shows that to a significant extent these renegotiations were the result of the prevailing lack of progressivity in the tax structure, which made governments increase taxes in periods of increasing rents. In addition, the way the renegotiations were conducted during the 1960s and 1970s, as well as in 2004–2008, had a significant component of opportunistic expropriation, generating high uncertainty in property rights and causing investment decline.

The oil industry has some structural features that strongly influence the way the institutional framework and the political economy of the sector evolve.[1] (1) There are important rents generated in oil extraction. Governments naturally attempt to appropriate a significant share of those rents. (2) Oil extraction requires a major proportion of sunken investments. Once the assets are deployed the government can change the rules of the game, leaving the investor little choice but to acquiesce. (3) There are high geological risks involved in oil exploration, whereas in the phases of field development and production these risks significantly decline. As a result, contractual frameworks designed to promote investment in exploration have often been ill-suited for the later phases if significant oil reserves have been developed. (4) The oil price in the international markets has been volatile, especially since the 1970s, and as a result oil rents have also been quite volatile. The volatility of rents makes it challenging for fiscal systems to capture the oil rents under different price scenarios. The way oil-dependent countries manage the ensuing fiscal volatility can also affect the contractual framework. This chapter discusses how these attributes of oil exploitation interact with the country's institutional environment to explain the political economy of contract renegotiation in Venezuela.

The above characteristics of the oil sector, combined with the lack of effective progressive tax systems and a weak institutional framework, have generated episodes of contract renegotiation, especially whenever oil rents go up significantly. The fact that contractual and fiscal systems do not appropriately take into account price contingencies implies that when the oil price rises steeply, an increasing share of oil rents is retained by oil companies—that is, frameworks are not progressive. Consequently, governments have had powerful incentives for contract renegotiation or nationalization. Moreover, after large investments have been sunk, if the government reneges on the contract, the producer would still have an incentive to continue operating as long as it can recover operational and nonsunk costs. As a result, high sunk-cost industries, like oil extraction, have been tempting targets for quasirent appropriation.[2] Figure 12.1 illustrates this point more dramatically. The changes in the rent—price minus cost—per barrel in the period $t - 1$ are indicated on the horizontal axis. The vertical axis shows the changes in the government take in t. As the figure demonstrates, the relationship is positive.[3] As will be shown, these changes were mostly due to discretionary actions by the government, rather than automatic triggers from progressive taxation systems. Consequently, it seems that in Venezuela, most of the institutional changes and contract renegotiations have been generally associated with distributive issues. These results seem to suggest the need for a better design of the revenue-sharing arrangements between the government and oil firms.

In this chapter we review the three episodes of oil contract renegotiation in Venezuela: 1943, 1958–1976, and 2004–2008. We show that these episodes had some common elements, like significant sunken assets deployed in the successful development oil reserves, a politically favorable environment for renegotiation, and the existence of increasing rents in the context of nonprogressive contracts, which generally

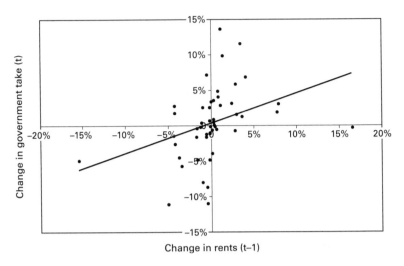

Figure 12.1
Changes in oil rents and government take
Source: OPEC, Ministry of Energy and Mines (MEP), and own calculations

did not incorporate the different prices contingencies in an effective manner.

The chapter is structured as follows. Section 12.2 provides a theoretical framework to analyze oil contract renegotiation in the context of a weak institutional environment. Section 12.3 describes the early years of the oil industry in Venezuela when there was contractual stability, as a background to the renegotiations that occurred later. Section 12.4 analyzes the renegotiation that occurred under the Law of 1943. Section 12.5 evaluates the concessions approved in 1943–1957, under the framework provided by the 1943 Law, and the significant changes in the investment bargain that occurred in 1958–1976, including nationalization. Section 12.6 discusses the contracts signed under the oil reopening in the 1990s and the forced renegotiation that occurred in 2004–2008. Section 12.7 provides some concluding remarks.

12.2   The Political Economy of Tax and Contract Renegotiation in the Oil Industry

Several features of the oil sector make it susceptible to contract renegotiation. In the first place, significant rents exist in oil exploitation. In theory all rents can be captured by the state—which typically has sovereign control and property rights over oil reservoirs—without affecting long-term production.[4] In practice, significant rents are often kept by the producer. The problem arises from the fact that in general, tax and contractual frameworks are not very progressive. As a result, when there is a considerable increase in the international oil price, there are incentives for the government to renege on deals made when the oil prices were lower.[5]

As we explain in the following sections, the core element of the Venezuelan oil tax structure has been the royalty. This has also been the case in many relevant oil-producing countries.[6] The main problem with the royalty is that it is not well suited to capturing rents. Suppose that oil sells for $10 per barrel and costs $5 per barrel to produce. Additionally, assume that the government wants to get 50 percent of the net income (profit). In this case out of the $5 in profits, the government would take $2.50. Given that the royalty is basically a gross revenue tax, the rate should be set at 25 percent. Consequently, for each additional $1 increase in oil prices, the government will take $0.25. This implies that the marginal tax rate is actually lower than the average tax rate.[7] As a result, a royalty-based tax structure is not progressive.

The introduction of an income tax only partially solves the problem. Oil production is a capital-intensive industry. Moreover, besides the typical cash outflows on building and machinery, petroleum firms have to invest in exploration and development of new oil reserves. Consequently it is bound to have the same problems faced by all other capital-intensive industries with the standard type of income taxation. In particular, it will be affected by how the issues of depreciation and the cost of capital are dealt with in the law.

Leaving aside the issue of depreciation, let us return to the previous example. Suppose that for the production of one barrel a year, an investment of $10 is made and the opportunity cost of that capital is 10 percent. This would imply an additional cost of $1 for each barrel. If the government wants 50 percent of net income, but capital costs are not considered in the income tax, the government would ask for $2 out of the $5 of "operational revenue." Consequently it will set up an income tax rate of 40 percent. However, for each additional dollar of increase in oil prices, the government will take $0.40. Therefore, again the marginal tax rate is actually lower than the average tax rate.

As we will point out throughout this chapter, this is a key issue affecting oil contract renegotiation in Venezuela. A fundamental question is: Why have there not been effective attempts to establish more progressive tax systems that consider capital costs and try to capture the rents more efficiently? There are different arguments to explain this:

1. *The institutional knowledge available at the time when the original contracts were designed.* As we will point out, the terms of the Venezuelan contracts were not different from those in other similar countries. Consequently, even if Venezuela was not an innovator in oil contract design, it was not a laggard either.

2. *The structure and timing of the contracts.* Even when contracts did include capital costs and profit-sharing for the government, the contracts were designed based on a low-price scenario. Furthermore, as we will show, prices went up before the clauses set to increase the government take kicked in.

3. *Principal-agent considerations.* Contracts that try to include capital costs in order to make taxes more progressive tend to have problems associated with regulations on the rate of return.[8] In particular, firms might try to invest more or make costs look higher in order to avoid taxes. Consequently, royalties are seen as a way to induce efficiency from the point of view of the government (Mommer 2002).[9]

4. *Fiscal income stability considerations.* Fiscal income from royalties is less volatile than income from more progressive taxation schemes. As a result, policymakers prefer royalties whenever they have trouble setting up sound fiscal stabilization mechanisms.[10]

5. *Heterogeneous agents.* More recently, one of the challenges of the Venezuelan tax system has been the existence of different types of oil fields. Consequently, the tax system has to deal not only with issues regarding the progressiveness related to the oil price, but also to the progressiveness related to field productivity. In this regard efficiency issues might imply that the tax schedule should not necessarily be "progressive" toward rents.[11]

A second important feature of the oil industry is that a large proportion of the investments are sunk costs—that is, assets that are immobilized even before revenues start being collected. For example, seismic studies, exploration and production wells, and pipelines are sunken investments. Once deployed, the ex post value of these assets in alternative uses is very low; as a result significant quasirents exist that can be appropriated (Klein, Crawford, and Alchian 1978).[12] The operator would do better by continuing to operate as long as it can recover operational and nonsunken assets, even if it cannot recover the sunk costs. As a result, the government, or other actors, may expropriate the quasirents by opportunistically changing the conditions of investment, including the taxes and regulations. The political benefits of opportunistic reneging are high. In the short term the government can extract significant fiscal resources or transfer them to the domestic consumers of energy, without a significant impact on oil production (Monaldi 2006; Manzano and Monaldi 2008).

A third feature is the existence of high geological risks in the exploration phase provides incentives for governments to offer attractive deals in order to attract private investment. However, when exploration is highly successful, the incentives for ex post renegotiation by the government may be significant. Contracts typically do not incorporate mechanisms allowing the government to capture the large rents that arise after significant new discoveries. As a result, even in the initial phase of production, there has been a tendency to observe changes in the fiscal and contractual conditions after the discovery of major hydrocarbon reserves that significantly increase the net present value of the project.[13]

In addition to the existence of appropriable quasirents, hydrocarbon production is risky because world oil reserves are concentrated in underdeveloped countries with weak institutions and high political risks. As a result, governments have trouble committing to allowing investors to recover their sunken investments. If the political benefits of reneging are high and the short-term costs low, only strong domestic institutions or effective external enforcement would provide credible property rights. In fact, throughout the history of oil and mineral investment in developing countries, external enforcement played a significant role—for example, when a cartel of oil multinationals existed that could coordinate punishment and the hegemonic powers enforced international property rights (Lipson 1985). However, after the rise of the independent and state-owned oil companies, and the increase in the sovereignty of many producing areas under development starting in the 1960s, the capacity for external enforcement greatly diminished. The ensuing massive nationalizations of the 1970s dramatically changed the structure of the oil market, making the exporting countries very powerful players. More recently, multilateral arbitration, investment treaties, and loans guaranteed by oil export receivables, have provided a limited degree of external enforcement (Monaldi 2002). Still, in some cases (e.g., Brazil, Chile, Norway), domestic political and regulatory institutions have provided credible commitment to foreign investors in high sunk-cost sectors (Levy and Spiller 1996).

The reputational costs of reneging on sunken investments are high when the governments are eager to attract new foreign investment (particularly in the same sector). Thus, expropriation is less likely when a new cycle of investment is being initiated, either because production is beginning or there was a long period of disinvestment (possibly due to previous expropriation), or because the government does not have the necessary fiscal resources to invest. In contrast, after long periods of high investment and rising revenues (and reserves), or when the government has plentiful financial resources, the likelihood of expropriation increases.

Governmental incentives to renege also depend on the discount rate of politicians. In the presence of weak institutional frameworks, episodes of economic and political instability induce high discount rates, which make the reputational costs of reneging less relevant. The short-term benefits of expropriating the oil industry, combined with the existence of high discount rates have made the oil industry a very tempting target in the past. For example, as a result of the Argentinean economic crisis of 2000–2002, the government reneged on oil contracts.

Volatile oil prices generate volatile oil rents. We have already argued that fiscal systems have a hard time capturing oil rents in different price scenarios; as a result, price volatility is particularly problematic. In addition, in the particular case of oil-dependent exporters, volatility may create macroeconomic and fiscal instability, unless stabilization mechanisms are effectively implemented, which has typically not been the case. As a result, oil-dependent governments might be tempted to renege on oil companies when oil prices fall and the governments face a fiscal crisis.

In summary, the oil sector is very susceptible to contract renegotiation because of its unique characteristics. These include large rents without progressive taxation systems, high sunk costs, geological uncertainties when contracts are awarded, reserves concentrated in countries with weak institutions, and volatile rents due to volatile prices. Given these characteristics, governments with oil and gas reserves are likely to be in a better position to renegotiate and increase the government take and their control over the industry if

1. They have higher oil reserves and higher prospectivity (likelihood of finding oil and gas in exploration). IOCs would be interested in entering and staying in this type of country.

2. They have the financial resources to finance the needed oil investment (due to high oil revenues or access to international financial markets). In contrast, when governments are in dire need of financial resources, IOCs are needed.[14]

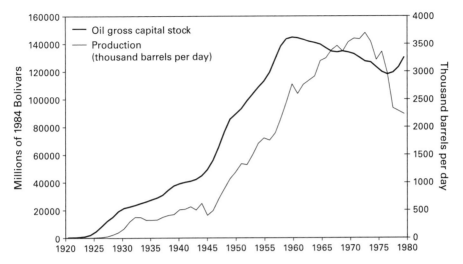

Figure 12.2
Capital stock and production (1920–1980)
Source: Asdrúbal Baptista, *Bases Cuantitativas de la Economía Venezolana 1830–2002*, and own calculations

3. It is the end of an asset deployment cycle, after a successful investment period, when there are significant sunken assets and little new investment is required.

4. The price of oil in the international market is quite high and oil rents are large.

12.3   The Early Years of the Oil Industry and the Rise of Foreign Investment: Low Taxes and External Enforcement Mechanisms (1909–1943)

Oil exploration and production began early in the twentieth century with the first significant concessions approved under the 1909 Mining Law. Production became economically significant in the 1920s. Oil became the country's largest export by 1927, and by the 1930s Venezuela was the largest oil exporter in the world. Production in 1929 reached 370 thousand barrels per day (BPD) (e.g., compared to around 120 thousand BPD in Mexico). That same year, oil fiscal revenues became the largest item in the government's budget and have always been since (Baptista 1997). Figure 12.2 shows the increasing trend of oil production in 1920–1943, with some changes: the rapid initial growth, the slowdown produced by the worldwide Depression of the 1930s, and a short dip produced by World War II. The figure also shows the equally rapid increase in the capital stock of the oil industry, with similar slow-downs produced by the events mentioned above.[15]

General Juan Vicente Gómez autocratically ruled Venezuela from 1909 until his death in 1935. Gómez came to power, backed by U.S. support, after ousting his nationalistic predecessor (General Cipriano Castro), who had systematically confronted the U.S. and European powers. Gómez was, therefore, particularly careful not to oppose important U.S. interests. Even though the government, as it became aware of the tremendous geological potential of the country in this period, aimed to increase the fiscal income from oil by systematically approving new laws with increasingly higher tax rates, it always backed down from reneging on the original contracts made with foreign investors. Each new law only applied to the concessions approved afterward.[16] Contract sanctity was the basic principle defended by the U.S. and British diplomacy at the time, drawing from the prevailing doctrine of international contract law (Philip 1982; McBeth 1983).

Oil exploration had started at the dawn of the century in a climate of high geological uncertainty. Very significant investments were made before oil began to be profitably extracted. To attract investment under these inhospitable initial conditions, the original legislation was very favorable to investors. The first significant oil concessions were approved under the Mining Laws of 1909 and 1910, which provided a very liberal regime, emphasizing, as stated by the introduction to the law, "the security provided to the operators of the concession" and operational freedom "because the fewer obstacles the better." The landowners, by decision of the Supreme Court in 1912, did not have any property rights over the mining concessions given in their land.

Table 12.1 presents a summary of the fiscal conditions under each law approved between 1909 and 1942. Over this period, the contracts were structured as *concessions* lasting thirty to fifty years (depending on the law), during which the concessionaire company had the right to explore, produce, and export oil from a certain area, generally subject to (1) a *royalty*—that is, a percentage tax over gross revenue, which started at 1 percent and was successively increased to a maximum of 15 percent; (2) a *surface tax*, in bolivars (Bs.) per hectare per year (with different amounts assigned for the exploration and production phases); (3) an *exploitation tax* in bolivars per ton of oil extracted (typically Bs. 2 per ton); (4) an *export tax* (only since 1926), Bs. 2 per ton of exported crude; and (5) an *initial surface tax* (similar to a signing bonus) according to the number of hectares assigned to the concession (typically Bs. 2 per hectare or a total of Bs. 1,000, whichever was higher). The specific concessions were governed by contracts that had to be in accordance with the parameters established by the law applicable at the time of the approval of each concession. No other taxes different from those established in the concession contracts could be levied ex post, a principle that was systematically upheld by Venezuelan courts until 1942.

The Mining Law of 1909 established a royalty of 1 percent of gross revenue and a surface tax of Bs. 0.5 per hectare of the concession area. The Mining Law of 1910, under which significant concessions were approved, increased the royalty to 3 percent, established a production tax of Bs. 2 per ton of mineral produced, and raised the surface tax to Bs. 1 per hectare. The mining laws of 1915 and 1918 increased the royalty to a range of 8 to 15 percent depending on specific conditions (such as distance to the port and distance between oil wells, but generally the minimum rate was applicable), although it eliminated the production tax (per ton) and significantly reduced the surface tax.

The first Petroleum Law of 1920 confirmed the state ownership over oil reserves and increased the royalty to 15 percent (25 percent on state-owned lands). The Law of 1922 effectively reduced again the royalty to a rate between 7.5 and 10 percent depending on the oil field, but set at a minimum royalty of Bs. 2 per ton. A law in 1926 introduced a tax on crude oil exports of Bs. 2 per ton (which remained in place for the rest of this period). Finally, the last rate change in this period occurred in 1930 when the royalty was increased back to 15 percent and the production tax was eliminated.

The general tendency toward increasing oil taxes in this period is unmistakable. Espinasa (1995, 10) summarizes it well: "As the state got conscious of the rent-generation potential of oil, there was an increasing tension between the nation, requesting a higher rent, and the companies resisting it.... The evolution of the legal framework...was reflected in the seven laws approved between 1920 and 1935, each one representing a gain in the oil rents appropriated by the state."

However, it is important to emphasize that during this period (1909–1943) the new—generally higher—tax rates did not apply to the concessions that had been approved before, only to those approved when the specific law was in effect. As a result, by 1942 a significant proportion of the Venezuelan production was paying royalties as low as 1 to 3 percent. For example, according to McBeth 1983, the main concessions of Shell were approved under the 1910 law (which set a

Table 12.1
Taxes on oil production in each law (1909–1942)

	Royalty	Surface tax	Export tax	Other taxes
1909 Mining Law	1%	Bs. 0.5 / ha yearly.		Landowners' payment: one-third of profits.
1910 Mining Law	3%	Bs. 1 / ha yearly.		Landowners' payment: one-third of profits. Exploitation tax: Bs. 2 per ton or Bs. 1,000 per concession.
1915 Mining Law	8%	Between Bs. 0.01 and 0.02 / ha yearly.		
1918 Mining Law	8%	Between Bs. 0.05 and 0.1 / ha yearly and eventually between Bs. 2 and 5 / ha yearly.		
1920 Hydrocarbons Law	15%	Bs. 5 / ha yearly.		Initial superficial tax: Bs. 1,000 on receiving the concession. Minimum exploitation tax: Bs. 1,000 yearly.
1921 Hydrocarbons Law	15%	Exploration: Bs. 0.05 / ha yearly. Exploitation: Bs. 5 / ha yearly.		Initial superficial tax: Bs. 1,000 on receiving the concession.
1922 Hydrocarbons Law	Between 7.5% and 10%	Exploration: Between Bs. 0.01 and 0.05 / ha yearly. Exploitation: Bs. 2 / ha the first three years. Bs. 4 / ha the next twenty-seven years and Bs. 5 / ha the last ten years.		Initial superficial tax: Bs. 0.1 / ha for exploration contracts; Bs. 2 / ha for exploitation contracts.
1925 Hydrocarbons Law*	Between 7.5% and 10%	Exploration: Between Bs. 0.01 and 0.05 / ha yearly. Exploitation: Bs. 2 / ha the first three years. Bs. 4 / ha the next twenty-seven years and Bs. 5 / ha the last ten years.	Bs. 2 per ton.**	Initial superficial tax: Bs. 0.1 / ha for exploration contracts; Bs. 2 / ha for exploitation contracts.

1928 Hydrocarbons Law	Between 7.5% and 10%	Exploration: Between Bs. 0.01 and 0.05 / ha yearly. Exploitation: Bs. 4 / ha the first three years. Bs. 5 / ha the next twenty-seven years and Bs. 8 / ha the last ten years.	Bs. 2 per ton.	Initial superficial tax: Bs. 0.1 / ha for exploration contracts; Bs. 2 / ha for exploitation contracts.
1930 Hydrocarbons Law	15%	Exploration: Between Bs. 0.01 and 0.05 / ha yearly. Exploitation: Bs. 4 / ha the first three years. Bs. 5 / ha the next twenty-seven years and Bs. 8 / ha the last ten years.	Bs. 2 per ton.	Initial superficial tax: Bs. 15 / ha for exploitation contracts.
1935 Hydrocarbons Law	15%	Exploration: Between Bs. 0.01 and 0.05 / ha yearly. Exploitation: Bs. 4 / ha the first three years. Bs. 5 / ha the next twenty-seven years and Bs. 8 / ha the last ten years.	Bs. 2 per ton.	Initial superficial tax: Bs. 15 / ha for exploitation contracts.

*Includes the 1926 Buoy Law that set the tax on exports.
**Reduced to Bs. 1 per ton soon after its enactment, but increased again in 1928 (McBeth 1983).

Table 12.2
Oil taxes as a percentage of gross revenues (1922–1935)

Year	Oil taxes (% of gross oil revenues)
1922	10.6
1923	9.2
1924	7.2
1925	5.7
1926	4.8
1927	5.0
1928	7.2
1929	5.6
1930	5.7
1931	12.1
1932	8.4
1933	10.8
1934	12.7
1935	13.2
1922–1935	**8.4**

Source: McBeth 1983 and own calculations.

3 percent royalty). As a result, Shell's tax payments were proportionally significantly lower than its share of total oil production. As can be seen in table 12.2, covering the period 1922–1935, total oil taxes as a percentage of gross oil revenues were on average 8.4 percent and reached a maximum of 13.2 percent in 1935, well below the 15 percent royalty rate that prevailed during a significant part of this period. For the period 1936–1942, when we have data on oil profits, the government take from the total oil profits was 38.8 percent. As we note later, after the 1943 contract renegotiation, the government take was significantly increased to levels above 50 percent of total oil profits.

If the government wanted to obtain additional fiscal revenues from the oil industry, the oil legislation provided incentives to authorize additional concessions instead of simply raising taxes. Since changes in the oil laws did not apply to previously signed concession contracts, in order to obtain higher fiscal revenues after the tax rate was changed in the law, new concessions had to be approved. As will be shown, the Hydrocarbons Law of 1943, which forced the renegotiation of all contracts, also changed this principle, opening the door to additional future renegotiations. After 1943, the easiest way to get additional revenues was by changing the tax rate.

The method of allocating concessions in this period was nontransparent and the source of significant corruption. General Gómez often gave oil concessions to friends, relatives, and other well-connected intermediaries, who in turn sold them to international companies, obtaining handsome profits, including in many cases a *private* royalty for the remainder of the concession. After the death of the dictator in 1935, this was one of the main sources of criticism of the legality of the concessions.

Two key questions arise from the analysis of this period:

1. Why were oil concessions given on such favorable terms for operators (especially at the beginning)? All concessions in this period were characterized by long contract periods; the impossibility of changing, adding or renegotiating taxes; and a fiscal structure that was highly regressive to profits. Moreover, the concessions approved before 1915 had to pay royalties of just 1 to 3 percent, rates significantly lower than those approved later (with a 15 percent royalty rate).

2. Why, before 1943, did governments abide by the contracts and not try to renegotiate them or expropriate the companies? Until 1943 the government and the domestic courts respected the sanctity of the contracts despite strong incentives in the last part of the period to change the terms.

To answer the first question it is important to remember that the first concessions were approved before significant oil discoveries had been made. Geological risks were very significant and large investments had to be made before any considerable level of exports could be reached. The country lacked any oil infrastructure and there were significant political risks. Venezuela had defaulted on its external debt in 1902 and was the object of a blockade by England, France, and Germany that was only lifted after U.S. intervention. The high risks intrinsic in these investments had to be compensated by potentially high returns and some institutional guarantees against expropriation. Contract credibility required sticking to the principle of contract sanctity, and specifically to the rule that no additional taxes, aside from those in the concession contract, could be levied.

Note that after 1914–1917, when some big oil discoveries in Lake Maracaibo were made, fiscal conditions for new concessions were significantly tightened. As the government became aware of the potential profits to be made in oil extraction, it offered concessions with higher government take. Moreover, Venezuelan concessions followed the

Table 12.3
Marginal tax rates (1909–1941)

Concession year	Marginal tax rate (%)	Concession year	Marginal tax rate (%)
1909	1	1926	10
1910	3	1927	10
1911	3	1928	10
1912	3	1929	10
1913	3	1930	15
1914	3	1931	15
1915	8	1932	15
1916	8	1933	15
1917	8	1934	15
1918	8	1935	15
1919	8	1936	15
1920	15	1937	15
1921	15	1938	15
1922	8	1939	15
1923	8	1940	15
1924	8	1941	15
1925	10		

evolution of the Mexican oil concessions, which were initially given on even more favorable terms to investors. Still, one might wonder why fiscal terms were so regressive in both Mexico and Venezuela. As table 12.3 shows that the marginal tax—the tax rate for an additional dollar of profits—paid by the concessions approved in 1909–1942 was quite low, especially in the initial years. If an operator was lucky enough to have concessions approved in 1909, it had to pay only 1 percent of the revenues arising from an increase in the price of oil. Of course it also typically made a riskier investment with less geological information. In contrast, the operator of a concession approved in the 1930s had to pay 15 percent on the dollar, when the oil price increased. The production and export taxes, charged in bolivars per ton produced, and the superficial tax, charged on hectares of land in use did not capture any additional rent in the event of a price increase, and therefore did not have any effect on the marginal take. These taxes were highly regressive to profits. The capacity of the production tax to capture rents was also affected by inflation and the real exchange rate, since it was set in nominal bolivars. A devaluation of the bolivar implied that the companies paid a lower percentage of their profits in this type of tax. Moreover, we have already discussed the lack of progressiveness of the royalty. However, to a large extent the regressivity of the tax structure might be explained by the fact that at the time developing countries generally did not implement more sophisticated royalty structures (such as a sliding scale), and initially they did not have the administrative capacity to implement a more progressive tax such as the income tax.

As to why the government respected the initial contractual terms, the key explanatory factors seem to have been the following: (1) production in the country was concentrated in a very few companies, members of the "seven sisters" cartel, which could credibly retaliate in concert in the event of contract reneging; (2) the United States and Britain on occasion served as external enforcers in tandem with the companies based in their countries; and (3) in the early period before there were significant sunken investments and before successful exploration had added reserves, there were few incentives to expropriate (low benefits, high reputational costs); only after significant production and reserves were in place did the incentives to renegotiate increase (Lipson 1985; Philip 1982; Monaldi 2002).

In particular, reputational costs rose because of the emergence of a relatively stable and effective international oil cartel.[17] In Venezuela, oil concessions were initially exploited by a variety of companies but by the late 1920s they were increasingly consolidated into two: (1) Standard Oil of New Jersey (later known as Exxon) through its affiliate, Creole, and (2) Royal Dutch Shell. By 1937, 92 percent of the Venezuelan oil production was extracted by these two companies. The international cartel plus the dominant position of the world's two largest companies locally made reneging on the part of the government potentially very costly. The companies and their governments successfully defended the principle that the state could only charge the taxes that had been established in concession contracts (Monaldi 2002).[18]

In sum, in the early part of this period (1920–1943), many of the industry characteristics that we described in section 12.2 were not conducive to renegotiation, for several reasons. First, the industry was in its infancy; consequently, little investment had been sunk and the sector needed further development. Second, there were important geological uncertainties in the early years. Third, prices were relatively low and stable.

However, taxation was not progressive, and in the latter part of the period some of the sector features started to provide incentives to renegotiation. At the time, the commitment to avoid revenue expropriation seems to have been guaranteed by the prospect of high reputational costs and by external enforcement mechanisms (U.S. enforcement and enforcement by the cartel of oil producers). Domestic legislation served to codify the external enforcement mechanism. As a result, the large investments in exploration and development required for the takeoff of the Venezuelan oil industry were made and Venezuela became the largest exporter of oil in the world.

12.4   The 1943 Hydrocarbons Law: The Renegotiation of the Original Oil Concessions

After Gómez's death in 1935, his successors—General Eleazar López Contreras (1936–1941) and General Isaías Medina Angarita (1941–1945)—slowly opened the political system, making it more inclusive. The opposition, led by the left (the Communist Party and the Social Democratic party, Acción Democrática) began to play a significant role. Oil was a key element in their political discourse. They demanded a review of all oil concessions signed under Gómez, asserting that many of those concessions were illegally assigned. Moreover, they pushed for the collection of back taxes, arguing that the companies had not appropriately paid them, and for an increase in the government take on oil profits. Partly responding to those pressures, Medina's government, after extensive negotiations with the oil companies and with the participation of the U.S. State Department, promulgated a new oil law and renegotiated all the concessions.

The Hydrocarbons Law of 1943 is a landmark in the history of Venezuela's institutional oil framework. The Venezuelan government took advantage of the Allies' desperate need for oil in World War II and the shadow of the Mexican nationalization, to renegotiate the terms of the oil concessions with the foreign companies. On this occasion, the U.S. government pressured the companies to settle with Venezuela (Machado de Acedo 1989). The objective of winning the war prevailed over safeguarding the property rights of the companies. The outcome of these negotiations was a law that increased the government's share of the oil profits from around 40 percent to above 50 percent (see figure 12.3). It initiated what was known in the industry as the 50-50 deal to split oil profits between the state and the companies.[19] The opposition leaders from Acción Democrática called the law a sellout to the foreign multinationals, since it validated everything that had happened in the

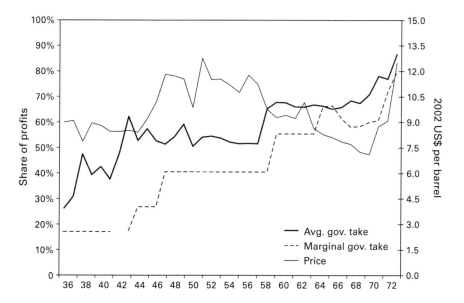

Figure 12.3
Price and government take (1936–1972)
Source: OPEC, Ministry of Energy and Mines (MEP), and own calculations

past. It did not charge the companies for the unpaid taxes and confirmed their ownership of concessions that were illegally obtained. (Espinasa 1995; Mommer 1989; and Tugwell 1975).

The 1943 law unified under a common legal framework all the contractual concession deals made in the past. It established—for the first time—the requirement that oil companies would be subject to corporate income taxes on top of any oil-specific taxes. The law creating the income tax had been approved a year earlier, setting the rate at 12 percent. In addition, the Hydrocarbons Law established a 16.66 percent royalty tax on gross revenue (similar to the highest landlord royalty in Texas). The total government take on profits was in line with what companies in the United States paid (Mommer 1989).

By recognizing the validity of this law, the oil companies were accepting the sovereign right of the Venezuelan state to charge taxes on the companies' profits and to change the income tax rate in the future. The oil companies realized that this would be a powerful instrument for future expropriation, so they opposed it fiercely. They insisted that their fiscal obligations should be contractually fixed.

In exchange for the full application of this tax increase, the 1943 law gave the companies a long-term planning horizon and a transparent tax regime. It renewed all concessions for forty years, increasing the life of many concessions that were going to lapse soon, and provided for the renewal of concessions after twenty years (in 1963). It also gave the companies sounder legal rights over their concessions. This was an important compromise in favor of the companies since one of the objectives of the politicians, in the government and the opposition, had been to act retroactively against the companies whose concessions were claimed to be legally tainted.[20] The state also agreed to forgo indemnification from previous tax evasion. Moreover, in 1944 and 1945 the Medina government approved substantial additional forty-year concessions, which covered more land than all the concessions previously granted (Tugwell 1975). The fact that new concessions, under these new terms, were signed in the 1940s and 1950s with significant success, including important signing bonuses, seems to show that the 1943 law provided enough incentives for new investments.

After the increase of 1943, taxes remained relatively stable during the period 1944–1958. The state's share of total oil profits remained on average just above the 50-50 benchmark established in 1943 (see figure 12.3). Both the companies and the Venezuelan state benefited from an increase in the international price of oil in the mid-1940s and most of the 1950s (see figure 12.3). The oil price hike generated an increase in the companies' profits across the 1950s (before and after taxes, given the relatively stable distribution). Similarly, oil fiscal revenues increased dramatically, by 190 percent in real terms between 1950 and 1958. The 1943 bargain originally provided the stability required for a very significant expansion of the oil sector. Additionally, there was "institutional stability." Except for a brief three-year democratic interregnum (1945–1948), the oil companies confronted a military regime led by General Pérez Jiménez (1948–1958). Pérez Jiménez was clearly aligned with U.S. interests and benefited from a hemispheric preference given to the Venezuelan oil exported to the United States.[21] Furthermore, in 1956 and 1957 the government auctioned significant new oil concessions, from which his government received signing bonuses totaling $675 million (Tugwell 1975; Mommer 1998).

Between 1944 and 1958, the annual growth rate of the net capital stock of the oil industry was on average 14.3 percent (see figure 12.2).[22] Production grew at an average annual rate of 19.5 percent in the same period. Espinasa (1995, 12) summarizes the period: "Clear and stable distribution rules and a long investment horizon created the conditions for what can be called the golden age of oil activity in the country (1944–58), multiplying investment and production to respond to the demand expansion of the post-war period."

In summary, in this period most of the conditions conducive to contract renegotiation were present: important sunk investments, ex post realization of low geological risks, and a tax structure that was not progressive. This was aided by very special international events (World War II), which diminished the effectiveness of external enforcement (i.e., the threat of the costs imposed by the oil cartel and U.S. intervention). As a result, increasing taxes became an attractive strategy for the government. Nevertheless, because the law provided some stability to the sector and profitability was preserved, the new conditions still made investment attractive, and due to the good business prospects in Venezuela, international oil companies (IOCs) did not leave but actually increased investments in the country.

12.5   Tax Renegotiation and Nationalization (1958–1976)

In 1958, after the failed three-year experience in 1945–1948 and after ten years of dictatorship, Venezuela's democracy was finally established. Acción Democrática, the Social Democratic Party led by Rómulo Betancourt, regained its majority support and won the first elections. The precarious democratic regime immediately faced nondemocratic challenges from the left (guerrillas) and the right (military coup attempts). Fiscal resources were needed to satisfy the many demands repressed by the previous regime and confront the enemies of the democratic regime.[23]

Furthermore, the market conditions were changing and the oil fiscal rules were still not progressive. On the marginal dollar of economic profits—that is, resulting from higher prices and/or lower costs—the government retained only 40.4 percent. This was mostly due to the low income tax rate, which was set at the same level as for nonoil activities. Additionally, independent oil companies, with no ties to the seven sisters, obtained a considerable portion of the 1950s concessions, debilitating the cartel's grip in Venezuela and around the world. Unfortunately, in 1957, the price of oil started to decline, and it continued to do so (in real terms) for the following decade (see figure 12.4). The decline in prices in a period of high-demand growth is widely attributed in the literature to the aforementioned oil cartel's loss of control over the oil market (Adelman 1972; Yergin 1992). To avoid the decline in fiscal expenditures brought about by the oil price decline,

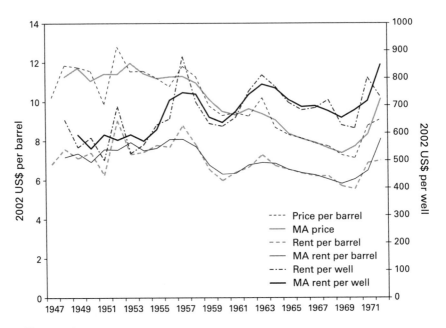

Figure 12.4
Operational rent (2002 US$), price minus operational costs
Source: Petróleo y Otros Datos Estadísticos, various years

Venezuelan politicians decided once again to extract additional rents from the tempting target of the multinational oil companies.

However, it is important to differentiate between price behavior and economic rents and also between rents per barrel and rents per well. Figure 12.4 shows the evolution of the price of oil and alternative measures of rents, per barrel and per well. *Rents* are defined as the difference between the producer's revenues (price multiplied by quantity produced) and the operational costs. For all the variables we present the actual value and the "trend" calculated by moving averages. Although trend prices decreased 6.6 percent between 1950 and 1958, operational rents per barrel went up 4.5 percent and rents per well increased 25 percent. This situation was driven by lower costs (around 20 percent lower) and higher productivity (production per well was also around 20 percent higher). Furthermore, as Manzano 2007 notes, the stock of capital per well was also decreasing.[24] Though this is not a measure of capital costs per barrel, it does suggest that the capital costs per barrel, or at least per well, were decreasing. Consequently, the total economic rent was indeed increasing.

This increase in rents was mostly due to technological advances and discoveries. As argued in Cuddington and Moss 2001, the 1950s and 1960s saw important advances in the evaluation of hydrocarbon-bearing rock formations (e.g., well logging and testing). These technologies stem from advances in geochemistry, stratigraphy, and fluid system sciences. Also, important new discoveries of major reservoirs were made in Venezuela.[25] These large fields implied lower average costs.

Against this backdrop, we have seen that the government's share was either constant or decreasing. In fact, as we can see in figure 12.3, after 1943 the government take fell even though prices increased.[26] Only when the brief democratic government of 1945–1948 increased the income tax rate—for the whole economy—did the government's share increase. The figure shows the main reason for this behavior: lack of progressivity. During this period, the marginal take was below the average take. Therefore, the system was not progressive in terms of higher economic profits.

Finally, it is important to mention the institutional setting. The Hydrocarbons Law of 1943 sowed the seeds of what later turned to be a dead-end distributive confrontation between the state and the companies. Quoting Karl (1997, 88), "The new law introduced a process of fiscal extraction through bargaining between the companies and the state. Once concessions were replaced by this new form of taxation, the granting of access to land that had proved so beneficial to both parties gradually was substituted for a zero-sum negotiating game over relative shares of profits from the industry. . . . In the long run, it even created powerful incentives for state authorities to organize forms of cooperation among contending domestic social groups in order to enhance their bargaining power vis-à-vis the companies, who were especially vulnerable as nationalistic targets." This law eliminated the most important domestic legal restraint against expropriation, establishing sovereign taxation as opposed to contract provisions as the way to determine the state's share of profits.

As a consequence, the prevailing tax and institutional structure gave incentives to the political leadership to increase the government take. In fact, the most dramatic early episode of confrontation occurred just before Betancourt took office. The civil-military junta that governed the country after Pérez Jiménez was overthrown unilaterally decreed an increase in oil income taxes. The government's share of profits rose from 51 to 65 percent (see figure 12.3). The Decreto Sanabria, as it was known, marked the first time an increase in oil taxes was completely unilateral (not even discussed with the companies) and distinct from the regular income tax paid by other nonoil sectors.[27]

The decree represented a radical break with the 50-50 rule that had been negotiated in 1943 and that had provided stability for more than a decade. Following Venezuela's lead, the same approach was adopted by other oil-exporting countries in the Middle East, opening the door to increases in the government take in these countries. In Venezuela, the decree clearly marked the beginning of a more confrontational form of extraction of rents that would continue up to nationalization in 1976 (Tugwell 1975; Mommer 1989). As figure 12.3 shows, the government take in oil profits stayed just above 65 percent until 1967, when it resumed its upward trend, escalating to a maximum of 94 percent in 1974 and 1975, the two years before nationalization.

Later, Acción Democrática established a policy of no more oil concessions, not renewing the 1943 concessions in 1963 (an option provided by the concession contracts negotiated in 1943); as a result, many concessions would contractually lapse in 1983. During the 1960s, oil policy was not geared toward nationalization, but was generally oriented toward defining alternative arrangements with the oil multinationals, which gave the state more control—including partial state ownership of the industry—in order to eventually replace the old concession system. Higher state control of the industry and a greater share of oil profits, with participation of private capital, appears to have been the goal (Tugwell 1975; Urbaneja 1992).

During the Betancourt administration, in a situation of increased market competition, the companies started giving discounts below the "reference" oil prices. Since that policy of discounts implied smaller declared profits (and oil tax revenues), the Venezuelan government claimed that the policy was a tax evasion strategy.[28] As a result, it negotiated a deal with the companies according to which oil taxes were to be calculated not using actual selling prices, but "fiscal reference prices" (FRPs). Under the agreement, the FRPs were to be negotiated with the companies and set for five-year periods slightly above the usual effective prices. In practice, this was equivalent to an additional excise tax (a tax on the price, similar to the royalty). Table 12.4 shows the evolution of the basic structure of the tax regime in 1943–1975, based on the three main taxes: the royalty, the income-tax, and the surcharge tax (fiscal reference price). The latter two were the key tools for increasing the government take. The government used the threat of increasing oil taxes as a negotiating tool. The administration

Table 12.4
Oil taxes (1943–1975)

Year	Royalty (%)	Income tax (%)	Surcharge tax (FRP)
1943	16.67	12.00	None
1946	16.67	28.50	None
1958	16.67	46.50	None
1966	16.67	47.50	10.64%
1970	16.67	60.00	7.95%
1971	16.67	47.50	8.00%
1972	16.67	47.50	20.08%
1974	16.67	63.50	36.37%
1975	16.67	72.00	27.02%

was anxious to finance its recurrent fiscal deficit. The negotiated agreement on the FRPs came after a partially successful government attempt to pass a legislative package increasing the income tax rates applicable to the oil industry and the rest of the economy. Among other objectives, the government package aimed to collect reparations for the oil taxes not collected in the past as a result of the price discounts given by the oil companies. The bill proposal also contemplated a special additional tax on capital assets (only applicable to the oil industry).[29] In the end, even though the administration did not obtain all that it had proposed, it was quite successful. In addition to the fiscal reference price agreement, the income tax was raised 3 percentage points, and the companies obtained what they thought was a guaranteed five-year period of tax stability given by the FRP agreement (Tugwell 1975; Urbaneja 1992; Espinasa 1995).[30] As a result of the tax "agreement," the government share of operating profits increased from 65.9 percent in 1966 to 68.5 percent in 1967 and 71 percent in 1969.

The first administration of the center-right opposition party, COPEI, began in 1969 under the leadership of President Rafael Caldera. At the beginning, Caldera's approach was to provide a variety of incentives and new investment opportunities for the oil companies to increase investment and production. As it turned out, this strategy did not provide the short-term fiscal resources that his government expected.

Caldera's strategy to induce oil investment was centered on a new framework for creating service contracts between the small state-owned company, CVP, and some foreign multinationals.[31] The opposition in Congress was reluctant to approve the contracts, arguing that they were "hidden" concessions. The politicized debate in Congress made the companies worry that the commitment to respect these contracts was not credible. Still, after lengthy negotiations, a few contracts were signed in 1971 and the signing bonuses totaled $21 million (Tugwell 1975; Mommer 1998).

Applying pressure to the companies to increase production was also disappointing since production was close to full capacity and could only be increased by a meager 3 percent. The government's search for revenues to close the fiscal deficit then reverted to the old policy of maximizing short-term rents from the oil companies. In 1970, Congress passed a law allowing the executive branch to unilaterally set the fiscal reference price. In practice this meant that the executive branch could single-handedly increase the government take by as much as 14 percent. Initially, Caldera's administration did not favor this move because it would hinder its attempt to create the new joint ventures with the oil companies. This enlarged executive discretion for increasing taxes would destroy any credible commitment to the new agreements. However, once the opposition majority approved it and it became law, the executive branch used it immediately to increase the government take in oil profits from 71 to 78.1 percent. In a very short time, the government received around US$200 million in additional fiscal revenues.

Furthermore, many concessions would end in 1983 and the alternative of joint ventures with the state-owned company did not seem to credibly protect property rights in the future (as the failure of Caldera's joint ventures suggested). Knowing that, the government decided to take preemptive action to limit the oil companies' policy of taking all nonessential movable equipment out of the country. As a result, Congress passed the Law of Reversion. A complete inventory of all the companies' assets was taken and they were forced to deposit 10 percent of the total value as a surety to guarantee the reversion of those assets to the state when the concessions ran out. This decision escalated the conflict between the companies and the government. They further decreased production and the president established monetary penalties for production cuts. The Caldera administration ended up abandoning all attempts to look for ways to induce the companies to invest and became openly confrontational. The government decided to compensate for the decline in total oil revenues, due to a 9 percent production loss, with an increase in the government's fiscal take, which reached 87 percent in 1972.

In 1973, the Arab-Israeli War generated a dramatic increase in oil prices. In January the average export price of Venezuelan oil was $3; by December it had risen to more than $10. The government received a windfall of more than $500 million. Oil fiscal revenues increased 30 percent in real terms. During the next decade the price of oil climbed above $30 and the Venezuelan government received more revenues from oil than in all its previous history.

In 1974 power returned to Acción Democrática under the leadership of President Pérez. Although nationalization was not part of his campaign platform, it quickly became the consensus solution to the stalemate that the state–oil industry relationship had reached. In the rest of the developing world a wave of nationalizations was beginning, so it was an evident policy alternative.

Nationalization, in fact, was a relatively conflict-free policy decision. The companies focused more on shaping the nature of the relationship they would have with the Venezuelan oil industry after nationalization and secondarily on the amount of compensation they would receive, rather than on challenging the nationalization decision itself. They were, nevertheless, relatively well compensated with payments of US$1.02 billion and with generous oil distribution and technical support contracts (representing in effect additional under-the-table compensation) for the first few years (Martz 1977).[32] The Nationalization Law was passed in 1975 and took effect in January 1976. A state oil monopoly company, Petróleos de Venezuela (PDVSA), was created as a holding company for all the previous private companies, including two small companies owned by domestic capitalists.[33]

Before we proceed to the summary of this period, two issues remain unaddressed. First, there is a difference between a contract renegotiation and outright expropriation by nationalization and this period ended with the latter. However, we have already suggested that the nationalization was relatively free of conflict since by the time it happened, all parties had recognized that the existing framework was no longer viable. In addition, as we have noted, originally there was no apparent intent to nationalize the industry. Therefore, the relevant fact is that contract renegotiation led to the recognition by most IOCs that they should stop investing and prepare to leave the country.

Some degree of controversy exists about exactly when the distributive conflict deteriorated to the point that nationalization became irreversible. Some authors have argued that the process was triggered in 1958, by the combination of the tax hike and the "no new concessions" policy, which limited the firms' horizons (Tugwell 1975; Espinasa 1995; Monaldi 2002, 2006).[34] Other authors have argued that the tipping point may have been the laws passed in 1970 and 1971— unilaterally setting the FRP and the reversion policy—rather than the *Decreto Sanabria* of 1958 (Manzano 2007). Nevertheless, no one argues that there was no intention to nationalize the industry with the Decreto Sanabria.

A second issue that is not clear is whether a more progressive tax structure would have prevented this conflict. It is evident from the discussion that the amount of revenues received by the government was the central element in the dispute. But we have still not mentioned other significant arguments raised by key policymakers at the time. In particular, Juan Pablo Pérez Alfonso, Acción Democrática's leading oil expert, was concerned about resource preservation. For Pérez Alfonso, oil was scarce—especially in Venezuela—and should be preserved for future generations.[35] However, the Raúl Leoni and Rafael Caldera administrations wanted oil firms to increase production to compensate for the falling revenues due to the lower prices. This objective was clearly inconsistent with this preservation principle. Opportunistic pragmatism prevailed over ideology.

In summary, this period was characterized by some of the key driving forces identified in our theoretical section: large sunken investments in place, low geological risks with high prospectivity, compounded by a nonprogressive tax system in a context of increasing rents. Before 1973, even though prices tended to decline, rents tended to increase due to a significant decline in cost per barrel. A key institutional factor in this period was the precedent of the 1943 law. The acceptance of this law by the IOCs reduced the institutional costs for reneging on contracts. Furthermore, the external enforcement mechanisms provided by the IOC cartel and the U.S. government were weakened by the appearance of independent producers and the rise of resource sovereignty. Thus, even though to an extent contract renegotiation was the natural product of a lack of progressivity in the context of increasing rents, at some point in this period the conflict seems to have turned into opportunistic expropriation, causing investment decline and later production decline. The fact that investment decline only had lagged effects on production, as can happen in oil once investment are sunk and productive oil fields have been developed, implied that the political costs of production decline were not perceived at the time.

12.6   Reopening and Renationalization (1990–2008)

Fifteen years after full nationalization of the oil sector, in 1991–1992, the process of reopening the oil sector to foreign investment ("la apertura petrolera") timidly began with a proposal to offer to foreign oil companies the operation of a few marginal oil fields (operational service agreements, OSA, first round). At the same time, negotiations were initiated to create joint ventures with foreign companies to develop the extraheavy crude reservoirs in the Orinoco Belt. In 1994–1998, during the tenure of the leading advocate of this strategy, PDVSA's CEO Luis Giusti, the process gained momentum and the contracts that support the majority of the projects were signed.

The institutional framework used to reopen the Venezuelan oil sector to foreign investment was fragmented and complex. In part, it was done that way because the government wanted to implement it without paying the political costs inherent in making significant changes to major laws. The administrations that designed and implemented the new investment regime, those of Presidents Pérez (1989–1993), Velázquez (1993–1994), and especially Caldera (1994–1999), did not have a majority in Congress; thus they tried to maximize what could be done without going through a difficult legislative process. PDVSA and the government stretched to its limits the "narrow space" given to private investment by article 5 of the Oil Nationalization Law. Article 5 only allowed private participation in oil production in state "controlled" joint ventures to develop projects of "strategic" interest to the nation. These deals also required congressional approval. To attract foreign investors, PDVSA obtained some favorable interpretations of the law by the Supreme Court (Mommer 2002).

The framework implemented was not based on legislation, as had been the case during the concession system that prevailed in the past. Instead, a contractual framework was put into place in which PDVSA, not the state, was the legal entity that signed the deals with investors. Under this framework, if the government or the legislature, using their sovereign authority, changed the rules governing the investment in a way that had a significant negative impact on the foreign investor and that was not valid under the contract, PDVSA could be contractually required to compensate the investor under some provisions. Moreover, in case the state-owned oil company did not abide by the contract, the foreign investor could request international arbitration (Mommer 2002). Under the contract, PDVSA relinquished any immunity that it might have had as a state-owned enterprise.[36] If Venezuelan courts were not willing to enforce an arbitration decision, foreign courts could attempt to enforce it. Arbitration would be costly and would probably take years to implement, but it provided a potential source of compensation for the companies.

To some extent, the new contractual framework offered PDVSA as a shield, and PDVSA's foreign assets were a "hostage," to protect investors against reneging by state authorities. PDVSA contractually guaranteed that the original bargain with the state would not be significantly modified in the future. If the government did not abide by the deal, PDVSA was contractually required to provide some compensation to the foreign investors.[37] The government of Venezuela had the right to change legislation, rules, and regulations affecting the oil sector, and it could not be legally challenged for doing so according to its sovereign laws. However, the investor could get around the issue of sovereignty by taking legal action against PDVSA, a multinational company with assets and business in the United States and Europe. More than 20 percent of PDVSA's consolidated assets were outside of Venezuela—for example, its U.S. refining subsidiary, CITGO, was worth above $10 billion in 2006, according to our own estimates (Mommer 1998, 2002; Monaldi 2002).

There were three types of contracts. In the appendix we present a detailed description of them. First, there were the Operational Service Agreements (OSAs), which started in 1991, with the first round of auctions, and continued with a second round in 1992 and a third in 1997. In theory these involved mature fields with low production. The idea was that the IOCs invested to maintain or increase production in these fields and were paid a fee per barrel. Nevertheless, the third round of auctions was clearly different from the first two, and the contracts more closely resembled a risk-service contract in which the operator's take decreased with the internal rate of return of the projects (and the state's increased). The original expectation was that oil fields producing a mere 70,000 BPD in 1991 would wind up producing more than 500,000 BPD by 2004. These expectations were more than fulfilled; in fact at its peak in 2005 the total production in OSA fields reached 600,000 BPD. Table 12.5 describes the fields and reserves allocated in the three auctioning rounds of OSA fields. As can be seen, the third round was by far the most important in terms of the amount of reserves allocated. Originally, OSAs were supposed to cover only a few marginal oil fields that required significant new investments in second-

Table 12.5
Operational Service Agreements (OSAs), Oil field auction rounds 1991–1997

Round	No. of oil fields offered	No. of oil fields allocated	Proven oil reserves allocated (million barrels)
First (1991)	9	3	175
Second (1992)	14	13	1,550
Third (1997)	20	18	20,510

Source: Office of the Chief Economist PDVSA (1998b).

ary recovery to increase production and that at the prevailing tax rates paid by PDVSA in the 1990s—a 16.67 percent royalty and a 67 percent income tax—would not have been attractive for the state-owned company to invest in. In all the OSAs the private operator paid the nonoil income tax rate of 34 percent, and PDVSA took charge of the royalties.[38] This type of contract ended up being used more widely, not just for marginal fields. In the third round, and in a couple of ad hoc contracts, more productive oil fields with larger areas were also allocated as OSAs. Under those contracts, operators had more liberty to explore and extract in the areas assigned than in those of the first two rounds.

The government also launched a second type of contract, the extraheavy oil Association Agreements (AAs), to pursue four large extraction and upgrading projects (1993–1997). The mechanism used was the creation of joint ventures between PDVSA and IOCs. Four AAs were approved in extraheavy oil upgrading:

1. Cerro Negro Project, in association with ExxonMobil (originally Mobil) (with a 41.67 percent stake) and BP (16.67 percent) (originally Veba Oel). PDVSA, 41.67 percent.

2. Hamaca (Ameriven) Project, in association with Chevron (30 percent) and ConocoPhillips (originally Phillips) (40 percent). PDVSA, 30 percent.

3. Petrozuata with ConocoPhillips (with a 50.1 percent controlling stake). PDVSA, 49.9 percent.

4. Sincor with Total (France) 47 percent and Statoil (Norway) (15 percent). PDVSA, 38 percent.

The projects added up to a total investment of more than US$15 billion in ten years, with a production of 650,000 BPD by the year 2006.

Given the lower profitability of extraheavy crude-oil extraction and upgrading (relative to the rest of the oil sector), Congress approved an exception to the Income Tax Law to make these projects attractive. The AA projects were taxed at the regular nonoil income tax rate (34 percent) and not the special oil income rate (67 percent until 2001 and 50 percent since then). This modification of the law was approved by Congress. The royalty was contractually determined; it was set at 1 percent for the first ten years and at the regular 16.67 percent thereafter. There was a provision allowing the royalty to be increased earlier if a certain revenue level was reached.

The third category of contracts introduced were the Risk Exploration (RE) Agreements, in eight areas, which were auctioned in 1996 for the right to explore and extract oil. The fiscal structure was based on a royalty of 1 to 16.67 percent depending on the internal rate of return (IRR) of the project, a bidding contractual government share of up to 50 percent of profits (PEG), and an income tax of 67 percent (the royalty and the PEG are subtracted from the profit). The marginal government take was set at 67 percent initially and increased to 86 percent after the IRR threshold was reached. Of these contracts, only three resulted in the commercial discovery of hydrocarbons. The government did not create the joint ventures prescribed in the contracts and postponed any decision on the matter until the renationalization of 2007.

As the previous discussion has indicated, all these new contracts implied changes in the tax structure. It is important to mention that the selection of fields assigned to private investors might not have been what theoretically should be the optimal strategy. The areas given were considered "marginal" areas since they had higher costs or lower value or required higher investment because they had not been explored at the time. As Manzano (2000) argues, these are not the areas where the highest deadweight losses arise from an optimal taxation point of view. Consequently, the areas where the highest welfare gains could have been obtained were not given to private investors, and the "export basket" of Venezuela shifted toward oil, where the government take was lower and less progressive.

To understand why the government implemented the reopening the way it did, it is important to recall three factors. First, just fifteen years before the reopening was implemented, foreign oil companies had been nationalized, after almost two decades of redistributive conflicts with the Venezuelan state. Second, the price of oil in the 1990s was between $10 and $30 in current dollars; at those levels it was harder to attract foreign investors. Third, over this period, the Venezuelan state was confronting a tough fiscal situation with recurrent deficits and a banking crisis that required a bailout of more than 6 percent of GDP,

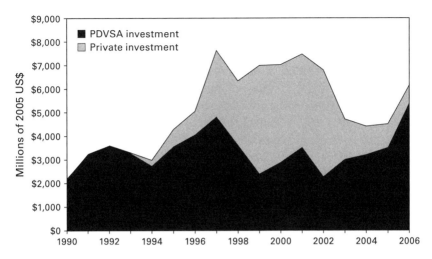

Figure 12.5
Investment in the oil industry (2005 US$ million)
Source: PDVSA, Woodmac, and own calculations

putting pressure on the resources available to PDVSA to carry out investment. These factors made the government very eager to obtain the new investments and made the companies more hesitant to assume risks in Venezuela. As a result, under these conditions the credibility of the framework was crucially important in attracting foreign investors. This situation explains the contractual structure that basically "imported" foreign institutions into Venezuela.

In terms of investment and production, the oil reopening was a major success. As figure 12.5 shows, private investment more than made up for the decline in PDVSA's investment during a period in which the company and the state did not have resources to spare. The total private investment in 1994–2006 exceeded US$25 billion. By 2004, private oil companies were operating close to half of Venezuela's crude-oil production. At its peak in 2004, OSA contracts reached a total production of close to 600,000 BPD. Similarly, Orinoco AA contracts reached 650,000 BPD in 2006. In contrast, in the period 1998–2006 PDVSA's own production declined.

12.7   Renegotiation (2004–2008)

This process was reversed starting in 2004. In the presidential campaign of 1998, Hugo Chávez argued that all the existing oil contracts were illegal, and Alí Rodríguez, his top oil advisor, had been among the most prominent critics of the contracts signed in the 1990s. However, in the first six years of Chávez's presidency, the government did not alter the fiscal conditions in the contracts. In fact, as figure 12.5 indicates, most of the investment and increase in production in these projects has occurred during Chávez's presidency. Moreover, when the president used his special legislative authority to sign the 2001 Hydrocarbons Law, changing the fiscal conditions by increasing the royalty to 30 percent (from 16.67 percent), setting the oil income tax rate at 50 percent, and establishing that the only form of private participation in oil production would be as minority shareholders in joint ventures controlled by PDVSA, the government announced that these changes did not apply to the existing contracts of the oil reopening ("there will not be retroactive application of the law," government officials emphasized).

However, late in 2004 the first forced renegotiation decision was made. The Orinoco Belt extraheavy oil projects (AA) royalty was increased from 1 to 16.67 percent. This was still not a major contractual change in three of the four projects, in the sense that the contracts provided for a royalty increase either after ten years had elapsed or an IRR threshold had been reached, and the threshold was close to being reached in the three projects that had begun earlier. Still, ExxonMobil threatened to turn to international arbitration to establish the principle that the contract fiscal rules could not be changed unilaterally, but they did not do it at this point. This change in the royalty happened after the projects had been in operation for only three to six years (in contracts of thirty to thirty-five years' duration).

In 2005 the government initiated a full-blown campaign to increase taxes on the OSA and AA projects. The tax authority SENIAT imposed tax penalties on the OSA companies for the previous three years totaling $400 million. Then the government established that the OSA projects should have been paying the income tax rate of 50 percent set in 2001 (instead of 34 percent), and that starting in 2005 they would have to pay this higher rate. The Ministry of Petroleum determined that the Orinoco AA had been producing oil above the levels authorized by Congress when the contracts were approved, and that as a result the companies would have to pay the 30 percent royalty (instead of 16.67 percent) on the excess production. The ministry also announced that the fees paid by PDVSA to OSAs would be paid in bolivars, instead of dollars as established in the contracts.

Later in 2006, the Ministry of Petroleum announced that the OSA contracts were illegal under the legal framework that prevailed when they were approved and that they had not been approved by Congress as they should have been. The ministry also argued that under the contracts the oil was too costly for PDVSA and that they were paying lower taxes than they should be paying, by using a variety of accounting tricks. As a result the government announced that the OSA contracts had to "migrate" into new contracts as joint ventures with a 60 percent majority for PDVSA, as prescribed by the 2001 Hydrocarbons Law.

The forced renegotiation of the OSA contracts was implemented during 2006. All the companies except ExxonMobil, which sold its minority stake to Repsol, agreed to begin the renegotiation of the contracts. Some smaller companies only negotiated financial compensation for returning their fields to PDVSA, but most remained as minority shareholders of the new "mixed enterprises." However, in the case of two of the most productive OSA projects—one owned by ENI (Italy) and the other by Total (France)—the operators decided not to sign the agreement. Eventually, Total (which also has a large Orinoco AA project) settled with the government for $250 million. ENI initially decided to go to international arbitration, but eventually settled with the government. The fiscal rules for these new mixed enterprises were set at a 33.33 percent royalty (contractually established) and a 50 percent income tax rate. PDVSA has between 60 and 80 percent of the shares in these new companies. In 2006 the government also approved an exploitation tax (a royalty) of 33.33 percent applicable to all oil projects (Decree 1510). This tax applies minus any other royalty paid by the project, so in practice all oil projects now pay a 33.33 percent royalty.

In late 2006 the government announced the forced conversion of the Orinoco AA projects and the Revenue-Sharing Risk Exploration projects (RE) to the mixed-enterprise format. In 2007 the government took control of all these projects (*nationalization* was the term used). In three of the four AA projects, the main private partner decided to leave and request international arbitration to set the compensation (Conoco-Phillips in Petrozuata and Hamaca (Ameriven) and ExxonMobil in Cerro Negro). Chevron (30 percent) and BP (16.6 percent), the minority partners in Ameriven and Cerro Negro respectively, decided to stay and will keep the same share they had. In the fourth project, the two partners—Total and Statoil—accepted a proportional reduction in their participation (from 62 to 40 percent) under the new conditions. PDVSA, which previously owned an average of 40 percent of the capital and did not operate the projects, now has an average participation of 78.3 percent and operates all the projects. The former AA projects, now mixed enterprises, also pay a royalty of 33.3 percent and an income tax of 50 percent, for a marginal take of 67 percent.

In the case of the RE projects, only three had reported commercial success from exploration, and they were waiting for PDVSA to proceed. Three companies—ConocoPhillips, ExxonMobil, and Petro-Canada—decided to leave, and two of them, ConocoPhillips and ExxonMobil, took the international arbitration route. These three projects will also pay a 33.3 percent royalty and 50 percent income tax for a marginal government take of 67 percent.

After renegotiating all the contracts and promising that the institutional framework would thereafter be stable, in 2008 the government approved a new windfall tax. The tax operates as a surcharge royalty. When the price of the Venezuelan oil basket exceeds $70, the oil companies have to pay a 50 percent royalty for the difference between the actual average monthly price of the basket and $70. If the price rises above $100, a royalty rate of 60 percent is applied to the difference between the actual price of the Venezuelan oil export basket (the weighted mix of crude types exported by the country) and $70.

It is important to note that the windfall tax of 2008 for the first time created some progressivity in the tax structure for prices above $70. For prices below $70 the tax regime remains highly regressive, with a marginal rate of 67 percent for all price levels below that trigger price.

Three main questions arise from this recent episode of contract renegotiation: (1) Was it mainly set in motion by the lack of progressivity in the fiscal framework of the contracts? (2) To what extent could it be considered opportunistic expropriation? (3) Why did the contractual framework, using PDVSA as a hostage and international arbitration as a method of dispute resolution, not deter forced renegotiation? And what prevented the changes from occurring before 2005?

Since the renegotiation of the contracts occurred after a significant increase in the price of oil (see figure 12.6), the lack of progressivity in the fiscal framework of the contracts does appear to have been a catalyst. This is clearly the case with the Orinoco Belt projects and to a lesser extent with the Round III OSA projects (before the higher IRR triggers took effect). However, in the case of the RE and Rounds I and II OSA contracts, the marginal take of the government/PDVSA was quite high. It is important to note, though, that the increased stake of PDVSA, as a shareholder, in all these projects (a partial nationalization) provides the government with a higher marginal take, since they have

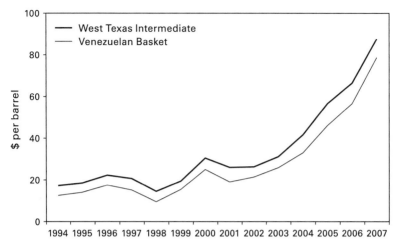

Figure 12.6
Oil price (1994–2007)
Source: Ministry of Energy and Mines (MEP) Statistical Yearbook and MEP Web site

Table 12.6
Marginal government take by type of contract (1991–2007), %

	Before IRR trigger			After IRR trigger			
Contract type	Before 2005	Plus govt. stake	2005– 2006		Plus govt. stake	After 2006	Plus govt. stake
Orinoco AA	34.70	60.82	56.00	45.00	78.00	66.70	92.67
OSA Rounds I and II	100.00	100.00	100.00	100.00	100.00	66.70	90.01
OSA Round III	45.00	45.00	56.00	86.80	86.80	66.70	90.01
Exploration (RE)	67.00	78.55	72.30	86.10	90.97	66.70	92.67

a marginal take of 100 percent in the portion they own. Of course, after nationalization, PDVSA has to take charge of its share of the capital expenditures and costs, and it had to pay some compensation for the assets nationalized, but it is now able to capture the upside of a price increase.

As table 12.6 shows, the marginal take in the Orinoco Belt extra-heavy oil projects (AA) was just 34.7 percent before 2005; as a result, the operators were keeping about two-thirds of the additional rent produced by the oil price increase. By 2005, once the royalty was increased, the marginal take became 45 percent—still relatively low at the prevailing price levels. With the introduction in 2006 of a royalty of 33.3 percent (Decree 1510), the marginal take was increased to 56 percent, and with the conversion to mixed enterprises in 2007, the marginal take became 67 percent (for oil prices below $70, that is, before the windfall tax is triggered). Moreover, since the state has now increased its stake from an average of 40 to 78 percent, it obtains the entire oil price upside from this additional fraction. Taking this into consideration, the marginal take would become 92.7 percent (compared to 60.82 percent, including only the original stake and before the renegotiation). In the case of Rounds I and II of the OSA contracts, the marginal take of the government was close to 100 percent since in those contracts the payment to the service contractor was based on a per-barrel fee, not on a share of profits. Here the marginal take actually has decreased to 67 percent. However, PDVSA's stake escalated from 0 percent to an average of close to 70 percent; therefore the marginal take from that proportion will still be 100 percent. Taking into account the government's take in the new mixed enterprises, the marginal take from this production will now be about 90 percent.

In the case of the OSA Round III, it gets more complex. As explained earlier, these are similar to profit-sharing contracts in which the government take depends on the IRR. In particular, when the IRR is negative, the marginal take is 45 percent. For IRR between zero and 60 percent, the marginal take increases proportionally to the increase in the IRR and the time elapsed. After the IRR surpasses 60 percent, the marginal take remains fixed at a maximum of 87 percent. We do not know the IRR level of all these projects for certain, but our understanding is that the majority were somewhere between 0 and 60 percent. Therefore the average marginal take will probably rise with the new contracts, but in the long run it would have been higher with the old contracts. However, again if we add the PDVSA shareholding stake, the marginal take rises to about 90 percent.

Finally, the RE contracts were highly progressive. Most of the companies that won in the auction process offered 50 percent the highest possible "government take on profits" (PEG) parameter. Only three of those projects offered a PEG lower than 50 percent. The marginal take at the beginning of those projects would have been 67 percent, and after the first billion in gross revenues it would have increased with the return on assets (ROA) until it reached a maximum of 86 percent. It is important to note that the marginal take for these projects was actually reduced in 2007, with the conversion to mixed enterprises. However, it is also true that PDVSA took a stock participation of 60 percent or more in the three projects, when the original contracts set the maximum at 35 percent. Again, the compensation for this increased participation, at book value with some discounts, represents an additional appropriation. Taking into account the higher PDVSA stake in the projects, the resulting marginal take rises to 92.7 percent (compared to 78.6 percent before the renegotiation, with the maximum stake allowed by the old contract of 35 percent).

From this analysis we can conclude that in the case of the Orinoco Belt AA projects and to some extent the OSA Round III projects, the lack of progressivity of the fiscal framework created the conditions for renegotiation of the fiscal terms in the context of a very significant increase in oil prices, such as the increase we have seen in the last four years. Since these two types of contracts involved more than 80 percent of the privately operated production, it is understandable for the government to propose a renegotiation of the whole fiscal framework of the sector.

In the case of the OSA Round I and II contracts, the marginal take actually has been reduced, so the lack-of-progressivity rationale does not work. But there is an important issue with these contracts. As explained before, and in more detail in Manzano 2000, it is expected that what the government pays includes the capital cost. However, tax codes tend not to include capital costs or if so, they do it imperfectly. This is also true in the Venezuela tax code for the oil sector. Consequently, at least from the point of view of taxes, these fields had a higher cost when the rules of the OSA contracts were applied than if the regular rules for PDVSA were applied.

Not surprisingly, the government claimed that in those contracts the cost per barrel for PDVSA was higher than the cost in the projects they themselves operated. Nevertheless, it is important to remember that these oil fields were among the least productive in the country and private investment was able to massively increase production. The government as an operator may be able, at least in the short run, to have a higher average take per barrel, but it will also take more production risks and, as shown above, the marginal take will decrease because now the private partners share oil profits.

In the case of the RE contracts, the marginal take will clearly decline, so there is no justification for renegotiation on progressivity grounds. As noted, these projects have not entered into production and the government is taking operational control and a larger stake, without market-value compensation. Now the government will face more production and price risks. Paradoxically, with the contract renegotiation, the private partners will face a lower marginal take, and the total marginal take, including the government stake, will just go up slightly. Still, renegotiation may be justified as an effort to put all oil projects into the same institutional framework.

Granting the importance of a lack of progressivity as a driver in the renegotiation of AA and OSA Round III contracts, it is key to acknowledge that the way the forced renegotiation was implemented and the conditions under which the government acquired ownership of the assets have a significant component of opportunistic expropriation. Instead of just renegotiating the fiscal framework for the future, the government asked for back taxes for the previous three years. Moreover, in the forced renegotiation of a government majority stake in all the contracts, the firms were offered well below the market (or net present value) price of the projects, even calculated using the new, harsher tax structure. For example, Wood Mackenzie, an oil consultant group, concluded that in the OSA contract renegotiation investors were compensated for less than half of the remaining value of the project, when the government acquired a 60 to 100 percent stake in 2006. Eurasia Group, a political risk consultancy, reports that Total and BP received, as compensation for their OSA project of Jusepin (with a production of 35,000 BPD), US$250 million, less than half of the estimated market value of the project (at $580 million). ENI initially filed for arbitration with ICSID in November 2006, when the government refused to pay market value (estimated at US$1 billion) on another OSA (Dación, with a 60,000 BPD production), it eventually settled before arbitration for much less.

In the case of the AAs, the magnitude of the assets expropriated is more dramatic. When the state seized the Cerro Negro AA project, ExxonMobil was reportedly offered book value (with some discounts and a significant proportion not paid in cash) for its 41.6 percent stake, instead of the market value of an estimated US$2.3 billion (Wood Mackenzie, personal communication).[39] As a result, the company filed for arbitration at the ICSID in September 2007. Similarly, Conoco-Phillips has filed for arbitration to obtain compensation for its stake in two AA projects (50.1 percent of Petrozuata and 40 percent of Ameriven) with an estimated market value of US$7.2 billion (Wood Mackenzie, personal communication). In February 2008, PDVSA reached an agreement with Total and Statoil over Sincor, to pay these companies US$1.1 billion for their stake, which was valued at twice that amount by UBS. Moreover, the payment will be done partly in incremental production from the project. This is in line with what the government has consistently offered: book value compensation and not fully in cash.

It is important to mention that the AA contracts contain an explicit clause detailing the price that should be paid for a stake in the project. Before operation, the value of the project was to be determined by the sum of the capital provided by all the partners plus the interest obtained but not paid. After the initiation of operation the value should be calculated using the net present value of the discounted cash flow after taxes for the remainder of the project. The calculation guidelines are detailed in the contract. For example, interest rates applicable were based on U.S. Treasury bill rates and so on. This type of clause seems to offer a powerful tool to the firms that filed for international arbitration.

Chevron and BP retained the same stake and simply accepted the new terms of the mixed enterprise arrangement (with a PDVSA majority). Even though under the new contracts they have to face a significantly higher government take and have significantly fewer prerogatives (including losing the possibility of international arbitration), they will receive almost no compensation for the renegotiation. Finally, in the case of the RE projects, ConocoPhillips, ExxonMobil, and Petro-Canada did not accept the terms of the new contracts and are filing for arbitration.

From the previous analysis a set of questions arise: Why did the institutional framework not deter expropriation? Why did expropriation not happen before, if it seems so attractive to the state? Why did most companies acquiesce? And why did a few file for arbitration? The answer to the first question seems to be that the institutional framework in place imposed significant penalties for the reneging of contracts, but not enough to compensate for the benefits accruing after the dramatic increase in oil prices. The contracts were honored during the first six years of the Chávez administration for three main reasons. First, the price of oil was much lower in 1999–2002. Second, the AA projects were not completed until 2002; therefore, not all the investments had been sunk and expropriation was less attractive. Third, until the oil strike of 2002–2003, in which Chávez took full discretionary control of PDVSA, the company remained autonomous and was much less willing to take steps toward expropriation because of the reputational costs this strategy implied. Moreover, in 2003 the government needed the IOCs to help it get production back up after the dramatic fall that occurred during and after the oil strike. As soon as these three factors changed, the government started the renegotiation process, in late 2004. As the price of oil went up the conditions proposed became harsher and the government got the upper hand in the negotiations. The companies were now in a very weak negotiating position to use the institutional framework to deter expropriation.

It is important to note that only two companies, ExxonMobil and ConocoPhillips, decided to use the dispute resolution and enforcement mechanisms provided by the contracts. All the other companies accepted the harsh renegotiation terms offered by the government. The explanation for that outcome, we believe, is twofold. First, from the standpoint of the project, once most investments have been sunk, the return from the proportionally significantly lower investments and operational costs that will be spent in the future is quite high. Even under the considerably higher government take in the AA projects, minor new investments in existing projects should be profitable for oil prices above $40. Note that the new 67 percent marginal take (for prices below $70) still allows the investor to capture 33 cents on each additional dollar in the price of oil. The windfall tax approved less than a year after the contracts were renegotiated makes this conclusion less compelling. Under the 2008 tax structure, profits still might be made in existing projects, but large new investments will probably not be attractive. Second, Venezuela is one of the very few countries with abundant oil reserves that is currently open to foreign investors. The IOCs do not have many other attractive alternatives, so it does not make sense to leave Venezuela (when the costs of reentry will probably be high), especially because they expect to be offered new deals in the future. Our interpretation is that the two companies that left did so because they wanted to send an international signal that they would not accept compensation of less than half the market value of their projects; they did not believe that under the current government they would be offered attractive new deals; and taking the previous two points into consideration, they believed what they would obtain in arbitration would be attractive enough and enforceable.

The future reputational costs stemming from the way the renegotiation was handled, in terms of decline in future investments and the damage to PDVSA's commercial standing, are more difficult to assess. A survey of oil executives by the Fraser Institute puts Venezuela in the worst relative position (just above Bolivia) in terms of the oil industry's Regulatory Climate Index, Tax Regime Index, and Fiscal Terms Index (Angevine and Cameron 2007).[40] However, the short-term horizons of government officials, typical of oil-dependent countries, imply that reputational costs, even if they materialize, might not be a sufficient deterrent when the short-term benefits are high enough (e.g., because of the high oil prices) and the short-term costs (e.g., production decline) are low.

In summary, during this cycle of reopening and renationalization we again saw conditions conducive to renegotiation: major sunken investments in place, high prospectivity, and a dramatic increase in oil rents because of the increase in oil prices, all in a context in which some contracts did not have a progressive tax structure. However, there are two novel characteristics in this period. First, the institutional weaknesses that generated a commitment problem were supposed to be mitigated by the use of foreign institutions. Nevertheless, and it is still too early to reach a definite conclusion, it seems that the short-term costs were not very significant, because when the rules changed, most companies decided not to use the external enforcement mechanisms. For the majority of the companies, at the current stage of the projects and under the prevalent market conditions, it was apparently preferable not to invoke the clauses that protected investors—potentially losing a lucrative operation—and instead to accept more stringent fiscal rules and below-market compensation. This result shows how, in this type of sector in certain situations, sophisticated contractual agreements designed to protect private investors might not have enough teeth. However, if ExxonMobil and ConocoPhillips obtain a favorable arbitration decision for something close to the reported market value of their projects, amounting to as much as US$7 to $9 billion, PDVSA and the Venezuelan government would bear significant costs, which could set a major precedent for the external enforcement of investment commitments in the oil industry.

Second, in some of the contracts, the tax structure was indeed progressive, but progressivity was triggered only after certain thresholds of profitability were reached. However, oil prices increased before those thresholds were reached and the conflict ensued. The tax structure did not effectively consider the possibility of a rapid and dramatic increase in prices such as the increase that actually occurred. We cannot be sure if in a counterfactual scenario in which tax rules would have been progressive, contract renegotiation might still have happened. In such a scenario, the government could have

opportunistically taken advantage of the increase in oil prices to renegotiate other contractual issues (for example, international arbitration)
or to nationalize. The objective being not to obtain more rents but to
tighten control over the sector, as would be expected of a radical left-
wing government.

Instead we argue that the lack of progressive taxes during an oil
price boom made contract renegotiation a dominant strategy for the
Chávez administration, as would be the case for any other more moderate government. In other words, no matter the ideological content of
the government, we expect that some form of contract renegotiation
would have happened during the boom, as in fact it happened in
many other countries, with different ideologies, around the world.

We are more confident that in a counterfactual scenario of low oil
prices and with little sunken assets recently deployed, it would have
been very hard to implement contract renegotiation or nationalization
—even for a radical left-wing administration such as Chávez's. Without the incentives and opportunity to expropriate, ideology would not
have made a major difference.

It is important to mention that the tax regime under which the contracts were renegotiated in 2005–2007, before the creation of the
windfall tax in 2008, was even less progressive than the previous tax
regimes. A marginal government take of 67 percent at an oil price
above $100 was too low, given that an additional dollar at those price
levels is way above the range of prices that makes investment profitable. As we have shown, even some of the reopening contracts had
higher marginal takes. Therefore there was a clear economic rationale
for creating a windfall tax, as we had suggested in earlier drafts of this
chapter. On the other hand, the regressiveness of the tax regime and
the high level of the royalty imply that for low price levels the government take would be extremely high, making investments unattractive. According to a study by Cambridge Energy Research Associates
(2007), published before the windfall tax was approved, the tax regime
generated a government take of 94 percent at an oil price level of $55
per barrel (for the West Texas Intermediate (WTI), a reference crude).
At a price of $25 the operator would lose money (the government will
get all the profits), and at a price level of $80 the government take
would be 87 percent (this increased with the windfall tax). The break-
even price for new investments with the new Venezuelan tax regime is
estimated at $44 per barrel (for the WTI). The new regime contrasts, for
example, with the one set in 2007 in Ecuador, which was progressive at
all price levels.[41]

12.8   Concluding Remarks

In general, the literature on the Venezuelan oil sector has focused on ideological explanations and, consequently, attributes most of the historical episodes to the ideological debates and the winners and losers of such debates (Espinasa and Mommer 1992; Espinasa 1995; Mommer 1989, 2003). Even though ideology might have been important in framing the policy options, in this chapter we have argued that the distributive conflict and the lack of an effective tax system, which would allow the government to effectively collect rents, should not be overlooked. In addition, incentives intrinsic in the oil sector make the industry a tempting target for expropriation, and as a result, commitment is difficult to enforce under certain circumstances, such as in periods of high oil prices, especially after high sunken investments have been made and the government is not urged to attract investment.

Furthermore, our analysis implies that, contrary to traditional accounts that emphasize particular ideologies or geopolitical conditions, incentives are the key drivers of contract renegotiation and expropriation around the world. That is, the episodes of expropriation that have characterized the oil sector have been driven by the recurrence of powerful incentives generated by the interaction between the structural characteristics of oil development—including oil price cycles—and the presence of weak and ineffective institutional environments for capturing oil rents.

We have analyzed three periods of contract renegotiation in Venezuela: 1943, 1958–1976, and 2004–2008. In all of them, it is evident that the tax structure in place lacked an effective form of progressivity, leaving the government with a small share of the oil profits. However, the last two contract renegotiation periods have also generally been associated with some form of opportunistic expropriation and nationalization.

The government has taken advantage of the stronger negotiating position provided by high oil prices and favorable geopolitical conditions to expropriate revenues and assets. The way contract renegotiation has been executed, particularly in the last two episodes—generating uncertainty over property rights and leading to state ownership, which has its own problems—has had negative consequences for investment and growth.

Venezuela has not been alone in changing the terms of oil deals whenever oil rents increase. Elsewhere we have shown how it has been a trend not only in the Latin American region but in developed countries around the world (Manzano and Monaldi 2008). For example, in the recent cycle of high oil prices, countries as diverse as the United Kingdom, Canada, Russia, China, and Algeria have toughened their fiscal terms (Cambridge Energy Research Associates 2007). This shows that the problems of a lack of progressivity and credible commitment are widespread. However, the way the contracts have been renegotiated around the world has led to different outcomes, sometimes generating high regulatory uncertainty and creating unattractive fiscal terms at lower oil prices. In other cases, as in Venezuela in 1943, renegotiation did not affect sustained investments in the sector.

The country has witnessed cycles of investment and expropriation, partly caused by the lack of an appropriate institutional framework for managing the changing environment—a framework that would allow the state to capture the rents without impeding the development of the full potential of the oil industry. As we have argued elsewhere, state ownership of the oil industry has not been free of episodes of revenue expropriation by the government; in fact the problem often gets worse with state control than with private operation (Monaldi 2002, Manzano 2007). Therefore, the search for an institutional framework that solves the lack of progressivity and the political economy challenges implied by the particular characteristics of the oil sector would have to continue.

Appendix: The Oil-Reopening Contracts

This appendix describes some basic features of the three types of contracts used during the oil reopening in the 1990s. All three types were eventually forcedly renegotiated in 2004–2007. This section is based on: Office of the Chief Economist PDVSA (1998a, 1998b, 1998c, and 1998d).

Operational Service Agreements (OSAs)

OSA contracts were the first type to be implemented. Typically, mature oil fields with low production were auctioned. The blocks allocated had proven reserves, and so geological risks were relatively low. But there was still uncertainty over whether production could profitably be increased, which introduced some risks. In the first two auctioning rounds, the agreements would be classified as *service contracts*, in which the operator was reimbursed for capital investment and in addition received an operational fee per barrel (which covered operational costs and generated the profit). The operational-fee formula provided incentives for increasing production and as result the operator shared some production risk, but the price risks and the upside were largely obtained by PDVSA and the government. In contrast, in the case of the third-round auction, the contracts were clearly *risk-service contracts*, more akin to a *profit-sharing* or *production-sharing contract*. In this case the companies received a fee based on the market value of the additional oil produced. The fee varied inversely with the internal rate of return of the project, introducing some degree of progressivity. Therefore, the operator kept a larger share of the risks and rewards.

Round I and II OSA Contracts

In these two rounds, the oil fields were auctioned on the basis of a combination of two parameters: the lowest *operational fee per barrel (Opfee)* offered, and the highest minimum three-year initial work program guaranteed. PDVSA paid the operator a total fee consisting of the sum of two different values: the *capital fee*, to reimburse investments and interests on nonrecovered capital expenses, and the *operational fee per barrel*, which covered the operational costs plus a profit. The fees had the following characteristics. First, they were set and paid in U.S. dollars to eliminate exchange-rate risks. Second, the operational fee was indexed using the U.S. energy CPI index. Third, the contracts established a *maximum total fee (Maxfee)*, set for each field taking into account the type of crude extracted, and designed to allow PDVSA to cover the royalty it had to pay to the government plus some margin. This *Maxfee* was thus adjusted using a basket of reference crudes. If the total fee in a year exceeded the *Maxfee* the operator had a credit for next year. The existence of the *Maxfee* implied that the contractor faced risks if the price of oil declined significantly, as it did in 1998. Fourth, the formulas for the total fee, particularly in the second round, provided incentives to increase production. Fifth, for tax purposes, the companies declared the operational fee as taxable income and subtracted the applicable costs, using a 34 percent income tax rate.

The contracts' duration was twenty years, which could be extended to thirty years. Under OSAs, all contractual disputes could be settled through private arbitration. In the first round, any disputes could be settled by private arbitration in Venezuela. In the second round contracts were still subject to private arbitration in Venezuela, but they specified the use of the International Chamber of Commerce (ICC) rules. This is in contrast to the third round, in which international arbitration was established.

These contracts were highly progressive. The marginal government take (including what was kept by PDVSA) on an increase in the price of oil was very high, close to 100 percent, since the total fee did not increase with the price of oil. The price of oil mainly served as a cap on the fee when the price went down. Still, the government argued in 2006 that the cost per barrel to PDVSA in these contracts was too high, between $12 and $14 per barrel (probably the result of cost adjustments using the U.S. inflation and real exchange-rate appreciation). However, this figure implies that, using an estimated actual cost per barrel for the operator of $4 to $7, the operator was obtaining a pretax profit of about $7 to $10 per barrel and a net profit of about $5 to $6, a profit per barrel well below the amount obtained in other contracts.

Round III OSA Contracts

In the third round implemented in 1997, the parameter to auction the fields was an initial signature bonus in a closed bid. The auction was a success, with investors offering higher bids than most analysts had expected. PDVSA collected payments for US$2.2 billion (equivalent to about 20 percent of oil fiscal revenues in that year and more than 2 percent of total GDP). Analysts were surprised by the high bids offered. For example, Repsol offered $300 million for an oil field that most analysts had valued at around $150 million. Almost all oil fields offered were allocated for significantly higher amounts than originally expected by industry analysts (El Universal, June 4, 1997).

In this case, the amount paid to the operator was determined based on the net incremental value (NIV) of production and the internal rate of return (IRR) of the project. In practice this implied that the contract was similar to a profit-sharing contract. The NIV was essentially the value of oil produced minus costs, royalties, and an administrative fee. The operator take on the NIV varied with the IRR according to the following criteria:

100% of NIV when IRR < 0%

K% (65%–52.5%) of NIV when 0% < IRR < 60%

30% when IRR > 60%

where $K = y + Tq(x - y)$

$y = (1 - (1 + r)^*\text{IRR})$ where $r = $ royalty rate $= 0.1667$

$x = 0.75 - 0.75^*\text{IRR}$

$Tq = $ an adjustment variable based on the time elapsed

The operator still had to pay income tax at a 34 percent rate and PDVSA paid the royalty (16.67 percent). The marginal government take in these contracts was progressive with respect to the IRR. Before the IRR of the project reached 0 percent the marginal take was 45 percent, and after the IRR exceeded 60 percent the marginal take reached a maximum of 87 percent. For IRRs higher than 0 percent and lower than 60 percent, the marginal take increased from 45 to 87 percent in direct relation to the IRR and the time elapsed.

In the third round, "definitive and irrevocable" international arbitration in the city of New York was specified, using ICC rules. Stipulations included the following: "The decisions of the arbitrage tribunal must be obeyed and are binding for both parties" and "the enforcement of the sentence can be processed by any court with competency in the case without reviewing the substance of the case." Further, "The parties renounce any appeal of the arbitration decision," and PDVSA "abdicates any legal immunity of jurisdiction" that it may have as a state-owned company or "any immunity against executive embargo of its assets" (Office of the Chief Economist PDVSA (1998b)).

Extraheavy Oil Strategic Association Agreements (AAs)

In order to develop the Orinoco Oil Belt, the largest reservoir of extraheavy oil in the world, significant investments had to be made (US$12–15 billion). The low-quality characteristics of this crude (very low gravity of around 8–9 API grades, high viscosity, and high sulfur content) required a costly upgrading process that made it less profitable than the typical oil production in the country. To upgrade this crude into marketable heavy or synthetic (medium-gravity) oil, specialized highly capital-intensive oil upgrading refinery plants had to be constructed in Venezuela. Therefore, the proportion of sunken costs in this type of project was significantly higher than in other oil projects and capital recovery took longer. Each project required investments of from $2 to $4 billion. All were thirty- to thirty-five-year contracts.

To develop these projects the government decided in the early 1990s to create joint ventures with foreign companies that could provide capital, know-how, and technology. These joint ventures were approved using the option provided by article 5 of the Nationalization Law, which permitted joint ventures with foreign investors under the following conditions: (1) the state has to be guaranteed "control" in the joint venture (but article 5 did not precisely define control or how it should be achieved); (2) the association needs to have a specified duration (it cannot be unlimited); and (3) Congress has to approve the basic legal framework for the associations (Congreso de la República, 1975). The Venezuelan Congress accepted a lax interpretation of the meaning of *control* (and the Supreme Court upheld that interpretation). It required PDVSA's approval, in a control committee, for "important" decisions. The "regular" decisions had to be approved by a simple majority of the capital shares. The marginal take in these contracts was relatively low at 34.7 percent before the IRR trigger set in, and moved up to 45 percent afterward.[42]

These contracts included an interesting clause on tax stability. If the projects faced an act by a state entity or the government having a significant negative effect on their earnings (or those of private shareholders), and such an act represented "discriminatory" treatment not applicable to all companies in the country, the private investors would be compensated by PDVSA. Such discriminatory acts included a change in the income tax or dividend declaration, or the possibility of maintaining the money obtained from the sale of oil in a foreign currency. The compensation would occur in the same fiscal year and would be the maximum between 25 percent of the negative economic impact or a proportional fee based on the oil price. However, the clause established that the compensation would not apply in case the price of oil (Brent crude reference price) went above $25 (adjusted for inflation).

International arbitration in the city of New York using the ICC rules was the method for settlement of disputes in AA (as in OSA Round III). Again, any competent tribunal could execute the arbitrage's decision, without reviewing its substance. The dispute could be taken to the ultimate arbitrage at the International Center for Settlement of Investment Disputes (a World Bank–sponsored institution). (Office of the Chief Economist PDVSA (1998d)).

Revenue-Sharing Risk Exploration (RE) Agreements

Revenue-Sharing Risk Exploration (RE) Agreements are the third type of arrangement used in the oil opening. These contracts are the least relevant in terms of economic impact because none of them has entered the production phase yet. However, it is interesting to analyze why they were also renegotiated. Under RE some areas were auctioned for exploration by the foreign companies. In case exploration was successful and commercial, extraction of oil would be done in a joint venture with PDVSA (which could choose a share of participation between 1 and 35 percent of the stock). In 1996, ten exploration areas were auctioned, of which eight were allocated to fourteen companies (some in multiple association).[43] Here the bidding parameter was not a present cash payment but the share of state participation in profits (PEG) offered by investors.[44] The auction process was very successful. Analysts were surprised by the fact that five of the winners of the auctioned areas offered the highest possible state share of oil profits. In order to determine some tied bids, an additional cash bonus payment was offered. The bonuses added to a total of US$245 million. As in the case of AA, RE contracts had to be approved by Congress under the conditions for private investment provided by article 5 of the Oil Nationalization Law. The duration of these contracts was thirty-nine years, and they offered an extension in case there was a curtailment in production because of a government decision. This type of contract offered some guarantees to foreign investors similar to the others reviewed above (to AA and OSA Round III agreements).[45] (Office of the Chief Economist PDVSA (1998c)).

Notes

We are grateful to Ramón Espinasa, Ricardo Hausmann, William Hogan, Dorothy Kronick, Roberto Rigobon, Federico Sturzenegger, and participants in the Harvard Conference on Populism and Natural Resources and IESA's Research Seminar, for helpful comments and advice. We thank Giancarlo Lazzaro, Manuel Lepervanche, and Stefania Vitale for excellent research assistance. We are also grateful to Harvard's Kennedy School, IESA's International Center for Energy and the Environment, and Stanford's Hoover Institution for funding this project.

1. Some of these features are shared with other sectors to different degrees, but the oil industry is one of the few in which their combined effect is significant.

2. In addition, contract renegotiation has sometimes been, at least partially, driven by the corrupt approval of the original contracts and by the presumption of tax underpayment because of informational asymmetries in the context of poor regulatory institutions.

3. The correlation coefficient between the changes in oil prices and the changes on oil taxation—the variables pictured in the figure—is 0.35 and statistically is different from zero.

4. A definition of rent is the excess revenue above the opportunity cost of the reproducible factors of production (i.e., labor and capital). Mineral rents can be the result of the natural lower costs of extraction or higher quality of certain mineral reservoirs, compared to the marginal producer; these are known as differential rents. In addition, rents can arise from monopolistic restrictions on access to the mineral reservoirs or from output restrictions by cartels.

5. In this case, the increase in government take may only be capturing the additional rents provided by the increase in oil prices and not expropriating the quasirents (see below). Still, the prospect of contractual changes increases the risk for investors.

6. Until 1943, it was actually the only mechanism—except for the land tax and other minor instruments—used to collect revenues. After 1943, the government started collecting an income tax. Nevertheless, it was only in 1958 that the income tax rate for the oil sector began being set at a higher level than the regular tax rate for the nonoil sectors.

7. Manzano 2000 and Manzano and Monaldi 2008 present a formalization of the arguments given by these examples.

8. See Train 1991.

9. In this regard, a partial solution to this problem is to have a royalty with a sliding scale based on the oil price. This will have the "efficiency" aspect of the royalty combined with a progressive tax system. These types of royalties are being introduced in new contracts around the world but were not common in the past.

10. See Rigobon (chapter 7, this volume) for a comprehensive treatment of this issue.

11. Manzano (2000) argued that changes in the tax system based on "effective tax rates" might not be the same as changes that try to address efficiency. Therefore, with the "reopening" of the oil sector to private investors in the 1990s, fields that got tax breaks because they had a higher "effective tax rate" might not have gotten such breaks if the concern was to reduce deadweight losses in the tax system.

12. A definition of quasirent is the difference between the ex ante and ex post opportunity cost of the production factor. In contrast to rents, if the quasirents are extracted from the producer, long-run production would be affected. The operator would continue operating in the short run as long as it can recover operational and nonsunk costs, but it would not redeploy sunken assets—that is, it would not invest.

13. This phenomenon is labeled the "obsolescing bargain" in Vernon 1977.

14. Depending on the availability of domestic human resources, technology, and know-how, governments may have more incentives to attract IOCs.

15. Changes in the real exchange rate also affect this measure of capital stock.

16. A couple of laws allowed for the older concessions to be voluntarily transformed into the new conditions if the companies considered them more favorable.

17. The seven sisters (as the cartel was eventually known) were led by the three major companies, Standard Oil of New Jersey (later Exxon), Royal Dutch Shell, and Anglo-Persian (later BP). After the Achnacarry Accord of 1928, these companies agreed to keep their share of production relatively constant in each country in which they operated (out-

side the United States). Marketing quotas were widely put in force and were specifically agreed to throughout Latin America.

18. Philip (1982) and McBeth (1983) agree that, during the first two decades of production, foreign companies were able to enforce the oil contracts even without asking for help from their home governments. They claim that the economic costs of reneging were more significant than the threat of military or political intervention.

19. During the brief democratic experience of 1945–1948 the law set a minimum government take of 50 percent of profits, so if the sum of taxes and royalties did not add up to that percentage, a surcharge tax was charged.

20. After Gómez's death the government took legal action against some companies, asking for damage compensation for the illegal benefits they had obtained in their concession contracts. Some were settled out of court, but in other cases the Supreme Court of Venezuela ordered the companies to pay. For example, in 1938 Mene Grande (Gulf) paid $10 million (Tugwell 1975).

21. The short-lived democratic government instituted a special surcharge tax to guarantee the 50-50 distribution of profits agreed to in 1943. If the total government take did not reach 50 percent, an additional tax would be levied to reach 50 percent. Pérez Jiménez maintained the application of this surcharge tax (Tugwell 1975).

22. If we compare that period with the preceding and following fifteen years, we see that there was an average annual rate of growth of 3.2 percent between 1929 and 1943, and a negative rate of −2.19 between 1959 and 1972; we exclude 1973 because it is the year of the first spike in oil prices due to the wars in the Middle East.

23. Ames's (1987) study of fiscal politics in Latin America found evidence suggesting that at the beginning of a regime there is a tendency to increase fiscal spending to win support and increase the likelihood of the.

24. In 1956, prior to the auction of new concessions given by Pérez Jiménez, the stock of capital per well was 13 percent lower than in 1948.

25. Between 1950 and 1958, ten fields considered "giants" at the time were discovered (Oritupano, Dacion, Boca, La Paz, Agusay, Zapatos, Los Claros, Centro, Morichal, and Lamar).

26. Prices increased 20 percent between 1943 and 1946, but the average government take fell from 60 to 50 percent.

27. The decree produced an irate response from the foreign oil companies. The president of Standard Oil of New Jersey (later ExxonMobil) was forced to leave the country after publicly voicing vehement anger over the implementation of the policy. Partly in retaliation against the decree, the U.S. government eliminated the preferences given to Venezuelan oil, putting Canada at a relative advantage (Hellinger 2000).

28. A significant proportion of the oil exported was sold to subsidiaries; thus government officials had good reason to feel suspicious. According to Adelman 1995, in reality the companies were giving the discounts and it was not merely a tax evasion strategy.

29. The companies organized a common front with the domestic private sector to oppose the income tax increase. The government then attempted to split the opposition and negotiated separately with the oil companies. Simultaneously, the government threatened domestic capitalists, hinting that if an agreement with the oil companies could not be reached; domestic taxes would have to be increased even further.

30. The companies agreed to pay Bs.700 million in reparations to settle the "discount" controversy (much less than the amount originally claimed by the government). In exchange, the companies were given immunity against all tax reparations in the past, and the oil capital asset tax was not approved.

31. The operational service contracts, as these joint ventures were called, were a way around the problem of providing foreign companies with secure (although limited) property rights over new investments, without reestablishing the old concession system. Concessions were not ideologically feasible anymore (they would not get passed in Congress) and at that point did not guarantee any rights to investors. The foreign oil company would operate as a service contractor signing a private contract with CVP. Risks were shared and the state fiscal participation was contractually enforceable in Venezuelan courts.

32. The accounting value of the capital stock at the time was around $12 billion but most concessions would legally have expired in six years, with all capital reverting to the government free of charge.

33. A retired multinational oil executive we interviewed argued that, due to the dead-end nature of the conflict, the nationalization solution was almost promoted by the oil multinationals. Their goal then became to obtain lucrative distribution agreements that they thought would be more stable.

34. After its peak in 1959 the net capital stock declined systematically for almost twenty years, until the downward tendency was finally sharply reversed in 1977–1978, after nationalization (see figure 12.2). Espinasa (1995) and Monaldi (2002, 2006) argued that the combination of regulatory and fiscal changes in the political context of the period helped push the companies out of Venezuela and to the more competitive oil fields of the Middle East. Production did not fall until 1971, but as Monaldi contends, this is typical of high sunk-cost sectors in which there is a significant lag between investment decline and production decline. In such a case, quasirents may be expropriated and production could still continue going upward for a while.

35. Venezuelan reserves were supposed to last less than ten years. However, the prospect of depletion was itself partly a result of the lack of investment in exploration.

36. In all the new contracts, PDVSA explicitly waived its sovereign immunity. The clear waiving of immunity is important, since any business owned by the Venezuelan government is considered an agency of the Venezuelan state and entitled to immunity from U.S. courts according to the U.S. Foreign Immunities Act, unless such immunity is explicitly waived. The immunity granted by that law would have precluded attachment of PDVSA's assets to enforce a judgment.

37. Under this structure, PDVSA's management—which had a history of being committed to honoring the contracts—provided the first line of defense against expropriation. PDVSA's financial and operational autonomy would have made it costly for governments to force the company to violate its contracts; otherwise, it could risk suffering significant reputational costs. In contrast to the sovereign Venezuelan state, PDVSA was an independent multinational company, governed by contract law, with investments, joint ventures, and long-term contracts in foreign countries. Therefore, before Chávez took control of PDVSA in 2003, there was a significant additional limit to reneging, provided by the autonomous management's resistance to break the contracts.

38. An illustration of the importance of PDVSA's role as a buffer is provided by the way the royalty tax was set. Many of these oil fields were only profitable at the lowest (1 per-

cent) royalty rate (Mommer 1998). The ministry could set the royalty rate in the range of 1 to 16.6 percent. Since the royalty could be set at the government's discretion in the case of oil produced by contractors, it was impossible to commit with foreign investors to such a low rate (1 percent) for the twenty-year contract period. The OSA arrangement solved this commitment problem by making PDVSA the party responsible for paying all royalties. This is particularly important because changing the royalty is one of the most common methods of revenue expropriation.

39. The payment offered by PDVSA has not been officially revealed, but some estimates put it at less than half the market value (personal communication).

40. The survey covered fifty-four oil-producing regimes all over the world. Eighty-two percent of those surveyed answered that the regulatory uncertainties in Venezuela "will cause them not to invest" or "are a strong deterrent to investment." Twenty-four percent answered that the new tax regime in Venezuela "will cause them not to invest" and 35 percent answered that it "is a strong deterrent to investment." Similarly, 42 percent answered that the fiscal terms "will cause them not to invest" (Angevine and Cameron 2007).

41. The new Ecuadorean tax regime is progressive to the oil price, that is, higher prices generate a higher government take. The government take is 59 percent at an oil price level of $25 per barrel (for the WTI), 72 percent at a price of $55, and 75 percent at a price of $80. As the price increases above $80, the government take keeps rising (Cambridge Energy Research Associates 2007).

42. The AA projects are constitutionally (article 9) exempted from local or regional taxes, since they (as opposed to OSA) are considered oil projects. They are also exempted from the value added tax in the preoperational stage. If for any reason this situation changes, PDVSA would have to compensate foreign investors.

43. Twenty-nine offers from forty-four investors associated in twenty-three consortia were received (Office of the Chief Economist, PDVSA 1998a and 1998b).

44. Participacion del Estado en las Ganancias (PEG).

45. First, the companies were exempted from local and regional taxes. Second, a contract clause provided for compensatory damages in case there was a discriminatory act by the government (not of general applicability). Third, the contracts provide final and binding international arbitration in the city of New York, using ICC rules (RE contract, PDVSA 1996, 61). Again, PDVSA irrevocably agreed not to invoke "immunity from jurisdiction of any court or from attachment in aid of execution of any other legal process...with respect to itself or its assets" (Office of the Chief Economist PDVSA (1998d)).

References

Adelman, M. A. 1972. *The World Petroleum Market*. Baltimore: Johns Hopkins University Press.

Adelman, M. A. 1993. *The Economics of Petroleum Supply*. Cambridge, MA: MIT Press.

Adelman, M. A. 1995. *The Genie out of the Bottle: World Oil since 1970*. Cambridge, MA: MIT Press.

Ames, Barry. 1987. *Political Survival: Politicians and Public Policy in Latin America*. Berkeley: University of California Press.

Angevine, Gerry, and Bruce Cameron. 2007. *Fraser Institute Global Petroleum Survey*. Vancouver: Fraser Institute.

Anzola, Oswaldo. 1997. "Régimen Impositivo Aplicable a las Asociaciones Petroleras. La Participación Municipal." In I Jornadas de Derecho de Oriente, *La Apertura Petrolera*. Caracas: Ediciones Funeda.

Arrioja, José Enrique. 1998. *Clientes Negros, Petróleos de Venezuela Bajo la Generación Shell*. Caracas: Editorial CEC.

Baptista, Asdrúbal. 1997. *Bases Cuantitativas de la Economía Venezolana: 1830–1995*. Caracas: Fundación Polar.

Cambridge Energy Research Associates. 2007. "Nationalization—Liberalization Cycles in Latin America." Presentation at IESA, Caracas.

Centro Internacional de Energía y Ambiente, IESA. 2006. *Venezuela: La Energía en Cifras*. Caracas: IESA.

Cuddington, John, and Diana L. Moss. 2001. "Technological Change, Depletion, and the U.S. Petroleum Industry: A New Approach to Measurement and Estimation." *American Economic Review* 91 (September): 1135–1148.

Eljuri, Elisabeth, and José Ignacio Moreno. 1998. "Los Convenios de Asociación para la Exploración a Riesgo y Producción de Hidrocarburos Bajo el Esquema de Ganancias Compartidas." In Juan Cristóbal Carmona Borjas, ed., *Temas de Derecho Petrolero*. Caracas: McGraw-Hill.

España, Luis Pedro, and O. Manzano. 1995. *Venezuela y su Petróleo: El Origen de la Renta*. Caracas: Fundación Centro Gumilla.

Espinasa, Ramón. 1995. "Ideología, Marco Institucional y Desarrollo del Sector Petrolero." Ms., PDVSA.

Espinasa, Ramón, and Bernard Mommer. 1992. "Venezuelan Oil Policy in the Long Run." In D. Fesharaki, ed., *International Issues in Energy Policy, Development, and Economics*. Boulder, CO: Westview Press.

Guasch, Luis, and P. Spiller. 1999. *Managing the Regulatory Process: Design, Concepts, Issues, and the Latin America and Caribbean Story*. Washington, D.C.: World Bank.

Haber, Stephen, Armando Razo, and Noel Maurer. 2001. "The Rise and Fall of the Mexican Oil Industry in the 1920's." Ms., Stanford University.

Hellinger, Daniel. 2000. "Nationalism, Oil Policy and the Party System in Venezuela." Ms., Webster University.

Karl, Terry. 1997. *The Paradox of Plenty: Oil Booms and Petro-States*. Berkeley: University of California Press.

Klein, Benjamin, Robert Crawford, and Armen Alchian. 1978. "Vertical Integration, Appropriable Quasi Rents and the Competitive Contracting Process." *Journal of Law and Economics* 21: 297.

Kobrin, Stephen. 1985. "Diffusion as an Explanation of Oil Nationalization: Or the Domino Effect Rides Again." *Journal of Conflict Resolution* 29, no. 1 (March): 3–32.

Levy, Brian, and Pablo Spiller. 1996. *Regulations, Institutions and Commitment: Comparative Studies on Telecommunications*. Cambridge: Cambridge University Press.

Lipson, Charles. 1985. *Standing Guard: Protecting Foreign Capital in the Nineteenth and Twentieth Centuries.* Berkeley: University of California Press.

MacDonald, Andrea. 1998. "Challenges in the Financing of International Oil Operations." In Theodore Moran, ed., *Managing International Political Risk.* Oxford: Blackwell.

Machado de Acedo, Clemy. 1989. *La Reforma de la Ley de Hidrocarburos de 1943: Un Impulso a la Modernización.* Caracas: OESE.

Manzano, Osmel. 2000. *Tax Effects upon Oil Field Development in Venezuela.* Working Paper Series No. 2000-006. Cambridge, MA: Center for Energy and Environmental Policy Research, MIT.

Manzano, Osmel. 2010. "Venezuela after a Century of Oil Exploitation." In Ricardo Hausmann and Francisco Rodríguez, *Venezuela: Anatomy of a Collapse.* University Park, PA: Penn State.

Manzano, Osmel, and Francisco Monaldi. 2008. "The Political Economy of Oil Production in Latin America." In *Economia* 1(1): 59–98.

Martinez, Anibal. 1980. *Gumersindo Torres.* Caracas: Ediciones Petroleras Foninves.

Martinez, Anibal. 1986. *Cronología del Petróleo Venezolano.* 4th ed. Caracas: CEPET.

Martinez, Anibal. 2000. *Cronología del Petróleo Venezolano.* Caracas: FONCIED.

Martz, John. 1977. "Policy-Making and the Quest for Consensus: Nationalizing Venezuelan Petroleum." *Journal of Interamerican Studies and World Affairs* 19(4): 483–508.

McBeth, Brian. 1983. *Juan Vicente Gomez and the Oil Companies in Venezuela, 1908–1935.* Cambridge: Cambridge University Press.

Mommer, Bernard. 1989. *La Cuestión Petrolera.* Caracas: Ediciones Tropykos.

Mommer, Bernard. 1998. *The New Governance of Venezuelan Oil.* WPM No. 23, April. Oxford: Oxford Institute for Energy Studies.

Mommer, Bernard. 1999. "Venezuela, Politica y Petroleos." Proyecto Pobreza. Caracas: UCAB.

Mommer, Bernard. 2002. "Venezuela: Un Nuevo Marco Legal e Institucional Petrolero." In *Revista Venezolana de Economía y Ciencias Sociales* 8(2): 201–207. Caracas: UCV.

Mommer, Bernard. 2003. *Petróleo Global y Estado Nacional.* Caracas: COMALA.COM.

Monaldi, Francisco. 2001. "The Political Economy of Expropriation in High Sunk-Cost Industries." Paper presented at the annual meeting of the American Political Science Association, Boston.

Monaldi, Francisco. 2002. "Government Commitment Using External Hostages." Paper presented at the annual meeting of the American Political Science Association, San Francisco.

Monaldi, Francisco. 2006. "Inversiones Inmovilizadas, Instituciones y Compromiso Creíble: Implicaciones sobre la Evolución de la Inversión en la Industria Petrolera Venezolana." In J. Pineda and F. Sáez, *Crecimiento Económico en Venezuela: Bajo el Signo del Petróleo.* Caracas: Banco Central de Venezuela.

Moran, Theodore, ed. 1998. *Managing International Political Risk.* Oxford: Blackwell.

Moreno, Aurora. 1998. "La Participación del Estado Venezolano en la Explotación de la Riqueza Petrolera." In Juan Cristóbal Carmona Borjas, ed., *Temas de Derecho Petrolero*, Caracas: McGraw-Hill.

Moreno, José Ignacio. 1997. "Estado Actual de la Aplicación de la Política de Apertura Petrolera—Asociaciones Estratégicas Establecidas." In I Jornadas de Derecho de Oriente, *La Apertura Petrolera*. Caracas: Ediciones Funeda.

Office of the Chief Economist, PDVSA. 1998a. "Asociaciones Estrategicas de la Faja del Orinoco." Ms.

Office of the Chief Economist, PDVSA. 1998b. "Convenios Operativos." Ms.

Office of the Chief Economist, PDVSA. 1998c. "Esquema de Ganancia Compartidas." Ms.

Office of the Chief Economist, PDVSA. 1998d. "Marco Legal, Institucional y Fiscal del Sector Petrolero en Venezuela. PDVSA y sus Filiales." Ms.

Philip, George. 1982. *Oil and Politics in Latin America: Nationalist Movements and State Companies*. Cambridge: Cambridge University Press.

Philip, George. 1989. *Petróleo y Política en América Latina: Movimientos Nacionalistas y Compañías Estatales*. Mexico: Fondo de Cultura Económica.

Rodríguez, Luis R. 2000. "The Political Economy of State-Oil Relations: Institutional Case Studies of Venezuela and Norway." Doctoral dissertation, Oxford University.

Rodríguez, Policarpo. 1974. *Características y Evolución de la Inversión Petrolera en Venezuela*. Caracas: UCV.

Train, Kenneth. 1991. *Optimal Regulation: The Economic Theory of Natural Monopoly*. Cambridge, MA: MIT Press.

Tugwell, Franklin. 1975. *The Politics of Oil in Venezuela*. Stanford, CA: Stanford University Press.

Urbaneja, Diego. 1992. *Pueblo y Petróleo en la Política Venezolana del Siglo XX*. Caracas: CEPET.

Vallenilla, Luis. 1998. *La Nacionalización del Petróleo Venezolano (1975–1998)*. Caracas: Ediciones Porvenir.

Vernon, Raymond. 1977. *Storm over Multinationals*. Cambridge, MA: Harvard University Press.

Vernon, Raymond. 1981. "Sovereignty at Bay: Ten years after." *International Organization* 35(3): 517–529.

Yergin, Daniel. 1992. *The Prize: The Epic Quest for Oil, Money, and Power*. New York: Touchstone.

Commentary: Not Just a Distributional Matter

Ramón Espinasa

The main contentions of the chapter by Manzano and Monaldi are that the "renegotiations were the result of the absence of an appropriately progressive tax regime, which made governments increase taxes in periods of increasing rents" and that nationalization was a consequence of the way the renegotiations were conducted, "generating high uncertainty with respect to property rights as well as declining investment."

The thrust of my comments is that in both expropriation episodes in 1975 and 2006–2007, the government, as representative of the nation-state owner of the natural resource, had the explicit aim of directly assuming control of oil production. Nationalization was an objective per se, not only a consequence of the way the government increased taxes. It will be argued that even in periods of falling rents the government increased taxes based on other than strictly economic considerations. These considerations fall into the realm of ideology, institutional development, and political economy rather than into the realm of rational economic decision making.

My commentary highlights the role of history in the process of contract renegotiation leading up to the expropriation of assets and nationalization of the oil industry. It narrates the history of Venezuela's oil industry in three chronologically ordered sections, with references to ideology and nationalism where appropriate. First, the period from the turn of the twentieth century to 1958 is characterized by Venezuela's lack of political power and knowledge about oil relative to the power and knowledge on the part of the international oil companies (IOCs). Second, from 1958 to 1975 the country takes advantage of resource scarcity and alliances in the Organization of Petroleum Exporting Countries (OPEC). This period concludes with the nationalization of the industry through the formation of Petróleos de Venezuela, S.A.

(PDVSA). The third section covers the period from 1975 to 2007 and chronicles the rise and fall of PDVSA.

Asymmetry of Knowledge

When the first oil concessions were awarded at the turn of the twentieth century, Venezuela was among the less developed countries in Latin America. During the nineteenth century the country had been decimated by bloody federal wars. The Gómez dictatorship finally centralized the country under a single rule and created the conditions for the construction of a modern nation-state. A century ago Venezuela was a backward rural country ruled by weak and unsophisticated elites.

In contrast, the oil companies that were awarded and retained the bulk of the concessions, Standard Oil and Shell, were among the more powerful and sophisticated international companies in the United States and Europe. Thus, when the first concessions were awarded a century ago, the asymmetry of information, knowledge, and bargaining power favored the oil companies to the detriment of the Venezuelan nation-state. This is the reason for the extremely favorable conditions given to the companies under the first concessions.

For Venezuela, it would take time to learn about the profitability and the more technical aspects of the oil business, as well as to become aware of the potential of the country's endowment of hydrocarbon reserves. It would also take time to develop institutions to implement the national oil policy—a policy that in turn was the outcome of an ideology regarding what to do with the sudden source of wealth. The backwardness of the country left few options but to utilize such wealth to develop the country—to "sow the oil." The growing national consciousness regarding the profitability and potential of the sector and the extremely favorable conditions afforded the companies by those first concessions explain the succession of laws increasing the government take until the settlement around the 1943 law.

The 1943 agreement between the Venezuelan government and the IOCs catalyzed by the U.S. government had two great virtues. On the revenue side, it maximized government take when conditions similar to those prevailing in the United States between private landowners and the oil companies were achieved in Venezuela. The distribution of revenue between companies and landowners in the United States was the only reference point for Venezuela, and the government did not have the political power to go beyond that threshold at the time. On the industry side, the 1943 agreement not only created the conditions for production to increase fivefold by the end of the 1950s, but forced the companies to build refineries in Venezuela to process the national crude. By the late 1940s, the Shell and Creole refineries in the Paraguana Peninsula came online; combined, they remained for many years the largest refining complex in the world. It was not just the distributional side. The government also had in mind the downstream development potential.

After World War II the first contingent of Venezuelan nationals was sent by the government to American universities to be trained as petroleum engineers. On their return, these engineers nourished the National Directorate for Hydrocarbons (Dirección General de Hidrocarburos or DGH) at the newly created Ministry of Mines and Hydrocarbons (Ministerio de Minas e Hidrocarburos or MMH). The national counterpart of the foreign oil companies would develop and become stronger over time. In the early 1950s the first Schools of Petroleum Engineering were founded at both Universidad del Zulia and Universidad Central de Venezuela. Professionals trained by these universities fed both the government and the oil companies operating in the country. Thus, the original asymmetry of knowledge in favor of the companies was gradually offset. It was not just that the country could work out better distributional deals, but it gradually developed the skills to eventually take national control of the oil sector.

The Suez crisis generated a price hike in 1958. Venezuela seized the opportunity to increase the government take over and above the 50-50 split implicit in the 1943 agreements. From then on for more than a decade, prices would slide as competition increased in the world petroleum market as new concessions were awarded to independent companies in Venezuela and the North African countries. If the government take had remained constant as a share of operational surplus, government revenue per barrel would have fallen.

Venezuela had to resort to more ideological arguments to defend the take per barrel in absolute terms at the expense of the companies' profits as prices fell throughout the 1960s. The argument would be *scarcity*. Venezuela would demand a larger rent per barrel, not arguing in favor of excessive profits but in terms of the finite amount of reserves of a nonrenewable source of energy vis-à-vis growing world demand.

However, unless other developing oil exporting countries had acted accordingly, Venezuela concluded it would not have had enough power to defend the rent per barrel. Thus Venezuela was a key actor in founding OPEC and was most instrumental in the policy the organization followed throughout the 1960s, leading to the price hikes of the second half of the 1970s, when the OPEC members assumed unilateral control of production and, in most countries, expropriated the assets of the operating companies.

Both points, the role of ideology and the importance of the international context in the process leading to nationalization, are missing in Manzano and Monaldi's account.

Control: Scarcity and International Context

In 1958 Venezuela signed the Cairo Gentlemen's Agreement, which preceded the founding of OPEC in Baghdad in September 1960. Venezuela's Minister of Mines and Hydrocarbons, Juan Pablo Pérez Alfonzo, was crucial in creating the organization. Venezuela and Indonesia were the only non–Middle Eastern countries among the six founding members. Venezuela had a leading role: at the time Venezuela alone produced more crude oil than the entire Middle East and was perhaps the nation-state with the most mature institutions and the most advanced oil legislation. The founding members of OPEC concentrated the bulk of the world's petroleum reserves outside the United States at the time, and this is still the case fifty years later. Being able to coordinate with Middle Eastern producers would greatly enhance Venezuela's political strength in relation to the oil companies.

OPEC would become a forum for the governments of the member nation-states to exchange information and eventually coordinate policies aimed at increasing benefits from the exploitation of their petroleum reserves. OPEC strengthened the bargaining power of the individual members vis-à-vis the powerful international petroleum companies. It became an oligopoly of nations owning the bulk of world reserves that could confront on equal terms the oligopoly of the seven largest oil companies that had dominated the international oil market since the 1920s, with one big difference. While the oligopoly of companies was becoming weaker due to increasing competition from independent companies, the oligopoly of owner nations would become stronger over time.

Throughout the 1960s, OPEC emerged as a mechanism for coordinating policies particularly regarding increases in government take through a continuous process of leapfrogging among member countries. Each country would demand for itself better conditions than those achieved by any other. Demanding a growing rent per barrel in spite of falling world oil prices was based on an ideological rationale: the nonrenewable nature of oil reserves and the relative scarcity of that resource in the face of exponentially growing demand in the 1960s. This premise was developed by Juan Pablo Pérez Alfonzo during Rómulo Betancourt's presidency and was subsequently adopted by democratic governments in Venezuela as well as by other OPEC members.

The argument regarding scarcity complemented the idea of sowing the oil. Demanding a larger rent per barrel was justified on the premise of depletion of a nonrenewable natural resource and the need to serve as a financial instrument to develop the nonoil economy. The rationale of scarcity not only justified increasing the government take as described in Manzano and Monaldi's chapter, it can also be cited as a reason for the policy of "no more concessions." Perhaps more importantly, acknowledgment of scarce resources offered a justification for failing to renew (at the midpoint) the forty-year concessions awarded under the 1943 law. All concessions would revert to the state in 1983. From the early 1960s on, the companies had a fixed horizon for their investments in Venezuela.

By means of conservationist policies implemented through the DGH at the MMH, the philosophy of no more concessions also allowed the government to put pressure on transnational corporations to restrain production. These public institutions would become ever stronger as they increased their know-how and produced more highly skilled personnel. The foreign oil companies reacted to growing pressure by the Venezuelan government by sharply curtailing investment and drilling activity while maximizing the extraction rates throughout the 1960s. Net investment was negative and the number of employees was slashed by half, yet production increased by 50 percent from 2.4 Mbd in 1958 to the historical maximum of 3.6 Mbd in 1970. As a consequence of the lack of investment, production had collapsed to 2.4 Mbd by 1974. Productivity per well had increased as foreign companies intensively exploited existing fields up to 1970, only to decrease sharply thereafter. Throughout this period Venezuela exercised pressure on the foreign companies to restrain production. The government aimed at indirectly controlling production to enforce its declared conservation policies. The net outcome was to increase oil rent per barrel at the expense of production capacity.

Lack of investment also led proven crude oil reserves to fall through-out the 1960s, from 17 billion barrels of proven reserves in 1960 to 14 billion barrels in 1970. Measured with respect to yearly production, the decline in proven reserves was even more acute. Between 1960 and 1970, the remaining production horizons went down from seventeen to ten years. Thus, the hypothesis of scarcity became a self-fulfilling prophecy.

There was an exception to the no-more-concessions policy that con-firmed the state's intention to directly control production. In 1960, the government created the state-owned Corporación Venezolana de Pet-róleo (CVP), which needless to say was not subject to the no-more-concessions policy. Nonetheless, a decade after its creation, CVP produced just a small fraction of total crude output.

Under the leadership of Venezuela in the 1960s, the OPEC countries developed the concept of control of production as a sovereign right derived from their ownership of reserves. Their objective was to exer-cise the sovereign right to administer the development of their reserves. But the companies would not easily yield to such demands. In the end, the control of production as an expression of their sover-eign property rights to the reserves would be the focus of the struggle by the OPEC member countries—a struggle that ended in state control of the foreign companies' productive assets in the mid-1970s. Perhaps the most important document produced by OPEC in the 1960s, Resolu-tion XVI.90 of 1968 titled "Declaration of Petroleum Policy in Member Countries," explicitly states that the goal was to provide for direct con-trol of production by the respective nation-states.

By the early 1970s, OPEC was consolidated as an oligopoly of resource-owner nation-states. They coordinated their oil fiscal policies to appropriate as government take any increase in the price of oil that derived from a very tight market from 1970 onward. The OPEC oligop-oly became stronger not only because it was able to coordinate policies much better, but because each of the individual member countries had become institutionally strong enough to exercise its property rights to the crude-oil reserves.

On the other hand, the oligopoly of international petroleum compa-nies (the so-called seven sisters) that had ruled the petroleum market since the 1920s was becoming weaker for two reasons. First, as men-tioned above, increased market competition as concessions were awarded to independent companies translated into falling prices in spite of exponentially growing demand throughout the 1960s. Second, as the countries became stronger, the companies faced growing resistance to their attempts to move freely in the OPEC countries. The case of Venezuela, as described above, was played out in other countries as well.

This translated into both increasing government take at the expense of lower company profits per barrel and the companies gradually losing control over crude-oil production in the OPEC countries. Falling profits per barrel, and growing institutional pressure in the OPEC countries, led the international oil companies to invest below what was needed to keep pace with fast-growing demand. This resulted in a very tight oil market and rising prices from 1970 onward. A lack of spare capacity made the market particularly vulnerable to supply disruptions triggered by political events. A first example of how much the relationship between the owner states and the producing countries had changed was the confrontation between the Libyan government and Occidental in 1970—a confrontation won by Libya.

However, the event that meant the de facto control of oil production by the governments of the OPEC countries was the embargo by the Middle East oil exporters following the Arab-Israeli war of October 1973. Prices that had already more than doubled after 1970, quadrupled following the embargo. All of the rent derived from this price increase was appropriated by the respective governments. Perhaps more important, from then on, the owner states assumed control of oil production in their territories. The expropriation of productive assets was just a matter of time and convenience in different countries.

The oil industry assets were nationalized in Venezuela on January 1, 1976. The transition from foreign to state ownership and control was seamless. Three reasons can be advanced to explain such a nontraumatic endgame. First, for all practical purposes the management and workforce of the foreign companies operating in the country were Venezuelan nationals. After six decades of oil production in the country, the industry had become national. The oil industry had changed as much as the country itself. Second, the expropriation process and value of assets were negotiated with the representatives of the international oil companies. Third, nationalization was the outcome of a widespread national political consensus. Representatives from across the political spectrum supported the state's effort to take control and seize the property of the oil industry.

However, nationalization did not end the inevitable tension between the owner of the natural resources and the oil-producing companies regarding control of production and distribution of rents. That tension would persist within the Venezuelan state between the government and the state oil company PDVSA. The second part of Manzano and Monaldi's chapter is devoted to analyzing the renegotiation after 2004 of the contracts signed between PDVSA and private oil companies in the 1990s. However, the discussion requires examination of the process leading to the demise of PDVSA in 2003. What happened to PDVSA after 1999 is completely overlooked by the authors. On the contrary, it is my understanding that the renegotiation of contracts after 2004, leading to the expropriation of private oil companies in Venezuela in 2006–2007, is a direct consequence of the fate of PDVSA. The third section of my commentary gives my interpretation of the process leading to the demise of PDVSA as a framework for the discussion of the renegotiation process described by the authors.

The Rise and Fall of PDVSA

One of the keys to understanding the success of PDVSA, until its demise a few years ago, is that the industry's structure was left untouched as inherited from the transnational corporations. From an operating standpoint, the only thing that changed on January 1, 1976, was the name of the affiliates.

At the beginning, PDVSA, the holding entity, was exclusively oriented toward coordinating and consolidating activities of the vertically integrated companies, each of them transformed into an affiliate of PDVSA. The board of the holding corporation was shaped by political realities. In the case of the operating companies, the boards were the result of an eminently technical orientation. Government control over the oil industry was at arm's length.

From a legal perspective, PDVSA and its affiliated companies were corporations subject to private law, with the Republic of Venezuela as sole shareholder. They were governed by commercial regulations, such as the Code of Commerce applicable to the private sector. Their budget and financial outcomes were approved at a shareholders' meeting, where the Minister of Energy and Mines represented the sole shareholder. The nationalized oil industry was governed and run as a commercial company. The affiliated companies retained the corporate structure of their foreign predecessors and kept following their systems and procedures regarding operations, personnel management, finance, commerce, and all other corporate functions. The systems of internal checks and balances were also respected. In the process of rebuilding the nationalized oil industry, it is particularly relevant to highlight that the personnel, with their vast accumulated experience, were retained and empowered.

The role of PDVSA as a holding company was to coordinate the activities among the different vertically integrated affiliated companies. Not coincidentally, the functional units at PDVSA mirrored those existing in the affiliates and were known as Coordination of Production, Manufacturing, Commerce, Finance, Planning, and so on. The multiple affiliates were born from diverse corporate cultures: European corporations, such as Shell, or U.S. corporations, such as Creole, Mobil, or Texaco. One of the first tasks that PDVSA had as a holding company was to homogenize different systems and procedures. With this internal experience, PDVSA had the opportunity to implement the best international practices.

First Phase: Consolidation
The first phase in the development of PDVSA aimed at stopping the deterioration of the productive infrastructure and consolidating the corporation from a functional standpoint. It was necessary to stop the decline in production and refining capacity caused by more than fifteen years (since the early 1960s) of lack of investment by the transnational corporations. This first phase lasted for some fifteen years, until the end of the 1980s. By then the national refining system had been modernized and upgraded with a sustainable capacity of around 1.4 Mbd. The sustainable capacity of crude-oil production was stabilized and consolidated at around the 2 Mbd mark.

The intense and successful exploratory campaign after nationalization was as important as reversing the downward trend in production. While scarcity had become a self-fulfilling prophecy, investment in exploration yielded a massive increase in reserves. By the late 1980s, proven reserves increased more than fourfold, reaching close to 60 billion barrels. The first assessment of the massive agglomeration of hydrocarbons in the Orinoco Heavy Crude Basin was as important as the increase in proven reserves. The perception of scarcity turned into one of plentiful and unlimited endowment of oil reserves and other energy sources. From the perception of scarcity and finitude of the availability of reserves that were thought to last for only ten years at the time of nationalization, in just fifteen years Venezuela was faced with a radically different reality: a superabundant stock of reserves that would sustain capacity, at current levels, for centuries to come.

Ten years after nationalization, by the mid-1980s, it became evident that incremental crude-oil production would be mostly in heavy and sour crude, difficult to dispose of. Thus, PDVSA envisaged a strategy to secure incremental refining capacity overseas that could take in larger amounts of the heavier and sourer crudes. This would be accomplished either by strengthening long-term contracts with independent refiners or purchasing and upgrading refineries in Europe first and the United States later. This *internationalization strategy* led to the vertical reintegration of the Venezuelan oil industry worldwide, which has proven extremely successful over time.

The revenue distribution framework was also unchanged after nationalization: the royalty rate was at 16.7 percent, the income tax rate at 67.7 percent, and the surtax, known as the *Export Fiscal Value* (EFV), remained at 20 percent. The EFV was the result of calculating the income tax over a reference price 20 percent above the true market value. At the prevailing prices and cost structure postnationalization, the Venezuelan tax structure for its oil business translated into a government take of around 90 percent of the operational surplus and 75 percent of the total oil revenue. To finance PDVSA's investment, the Venezuelan government set aside 10 percent of gross petroleum revenues. Over and above this savings, up to the late 1980s, PDVSA financed its investments by retaining the profits from its commercial operations.

Second Phase: Expansion
By the early 1990s PDVSA had been consolidated as a first-class world oil corporation. Staff levels slashed by the transnational corporations in the years prior to nationalization were restored, and personnel were trained to meet the highest international standards. The reassessment of the endowment of reserves made clear that, on the resource side, there was no limit to growth. Besides, declining oil production in the United States, coupled with growing consumption, exponentially increased imports in Venezuela's natural export market. The opportunity for growth was obvious. Throughout the 1990s, PDVSA seized that opportunity under the so-called *expansion strategy*.

The limits to growth were set, first and foremost, by savings to finance investment. Thus, PDVSA pressured the government to reduce the fiscal burden. The corporation argued in favor of retaining a larger share of revenue, without drastically modifying the fiscal structure in order to make it politically feasible. The proposal put forward was to eliminate the EFV surtax. The initiative was accepted by the government and passed by Congress in 1993. As a consequence of the new deal, PDVSA was able to grow throughout the 1990s.

Engineering capacity and access to technology also set limits to growth. In order to grow over and above the limits set by financing, technology, and engineering to the potential of the country's huge reserves base, PDVSA developed the *opening strategy*. Either as contractors for or in association with PDVSA, private capital was allowed into the oil sector within the limits set by the 1975 Nationalization Law. Private companies came back, first through *service contracts* to develop marginal fields and after 1995 through *strategic associations*, to develop and process the extraheavy Orinoco reserves. The contractual conditions and the outcome of the opening strategy are described in detail in Manzano and Monaldi's chapter.

By the late 1990s, the outcome of the expansion and opening strategies was evident: PDVSA crude-oil production had increased by 75 percent, to around 3.4 Mbd, and refining capacity overseas was on the order of 2 Mbd. This, together with domestic capacity, yielded a worldwide refining capacity of about 3.3 Mbd. PDVSA had become one of the top world oil corporations.

The National Oil Policy Debate after Nationalization
Parallel to PDVSA's achievements as a world-class corporation, an ideology vindicating the oil industry arose over time. For decades up to nationalization the oil industry had been portrayed as evil. The foreign oil companies were seen as the curse that destroyed the productive values inherent in the rural, preoil society. A bucolic but premodern nation was transformed as the country's huge oil reserves were developed throughout the twentieth century. The oil industry created poles of development in eastern and western Venezuela that attracted large crowds of rural workers. The expenditure of the oil rent by government in the capital and urban centers completed the transformation of a rural into an urban society. The appreciation of the real exchange rate with the massive inflow of foreign exchange destroyed agricultural export activities. The premodern rural society resisted the modernization and urbanization processes and blamed oil, particularly the international oil companies, for the destruction of the idealized rural country

left behind. Before nationalization the prevailing view was that the only role for oil in national economic development was as a source of revenue for the development of the nonoil sector—to sow the oil—which was consistent with the thesis of scarcity and imminent exhaustion of the reserves and the end of the oil era at the time. However, after nationalization Venezuelan society gradually became aware that oil was not only rent to finance government expenditure but a powerful industry demanding national value-added labor, goods, and services.

In short, nationalization had lifted the veil that had hidden the productive relationship between the oil sector and the national economy. The first point to realize is how integrated the industry was in the national economy, no longer the enclave it was at the beginning. It was not only that the entire workforce was made up of Venezuelan nationals, but most of the inputs for crude-oil production and processing were manufactured in Venezuela. The national oil industry—PDVSA and the private national companies supplying goods and services—developed a nationalistic consciousness. There was shared national pride in making PDVSA a world-class industry. This feeling spread and society gradually became aware and proud of the vitality and international importance of the national oil industry. Significant sectors of society were persuaded of the virtuous relationship between the oil industry and the rest of the national economy.

PDVSA became an important actor with a unique profile in the dynamics of the Venezuelan economic policy debate. It developed its own position regarding the role of the oil sector. Like the rest of the national oil sector, PDVSA demonstrated that the oil industry had a very important role to play in Venezuela's economic development. The national oil sector led by PDVSA argued that investment in the oil sector should be a high priority; without oil production there would be no significant national income.

From the PDVSA perspective, it was argued that investment in the oil industry should be the priority in the distribution of oil revenue between government and industry. The government take should be subordinated to the savings required to finance investment. Furthermore, given the gradual exhaustion of the aging Venezuelan fields, growing investment was needed over time just to sustain production. To facilitate greater investment in the oil sector, the government take should be reduced. The historical tension between the resource owner and the industry for the distribution of revenue now emerged in the Venezuelan state, between PDVSA and the rest of the government. PDVSA would demand a larger amount of resources to invest and, given the level of revenue, this should be at the expense of the government's oil fiscal revenue. PDVSA's arguments were persuasive. It also had the political clout to induce Congress to eliminate the EFV surtax. More important was the reduction of both the royalty and income tax rates to make the strategic associations for the development of the Orinoco extraheavy oils economically viable.

PDVSA became a major world oil corporation and also an important actor within the national oil policy debate. The strength of PDVSA was built on two main tenets of Venezuela's oil policy after nationalization. First, PDVSA had the autonomy to pursue its commercial goals with governmental control at arm's length, confined to supervising industry performance at shareholders' meetings. Second, the government take was adjusted to give PDVSA the savings to finance investments to sustain and expand capacity, according to approved plans.

Thus PDVSA had a life of its own and its own views on the role of the oil sector in the future of the country. Furthermore, PDVSA was endowed with the corporate discipline necessary to achieve its policy goals. It also had both the human and material resources essential to successfully implement those actions.

Lower government take per barrel to favor investment in the oil sector had a political cost for the oil industry. It was not only the distributional issue but also the internationalization and opening strategies that were at stake. Sectors of the public were averse to what was perceived as too large a degree of autonomy and political power for PDVSA. These sectors opposed the internationalization strategy, arguing there was a trade-off between domestic government revenue and overseas investment. The argument was that PDVSA generated the savings to purchase and upgrade the international refining and marketing network at the expense of government take in Venezuela.

Those against the opening and expansion of the oil sector were opposed as a matter of principle to measures that would reduce the rent per barrel to finance PDVSA investment or make the development of the Orinoco heavy crude feasible. They believed that the state should demand a minimum rent per barrel for the natural resource over and above normal taxes. This amount should not be subject to negotiation and had to be the same for all projects. These sectors argued PDVSA should be under tighter government control. The nature and intensity of these arguments evoked those made against foreign oil companies in the process leading to nationalization. Several parallels were drawn between PDVSA's management and the ways of the international companies prior to nationalization.

During the 1980s, as PDVSA kept a low profile and investment in the oil sector was low and prices high, the debate around PDVSA remained a minor policy issue. However, it took center stage in the 1990s. Oil prices dropped and investment increased, while at the same time the corporation intensified its public profile to argue in favor of the expansion and opening strategies. When the political sectors opposing oil policies after nationalization seized power in 1998, the winds turned against PDVSA.

The Demise of the National Oil Industry
From the outset, the new government made clear its intentions to tighten control over the oil industry. The natural tension between the resource owner, represented by the national government, and the industry—PDVSA—increased exponentially. The issue of control was at the center of this dispute. For twenty-five years, PDVSA had enjoyed a high degree of autonomy within the institutional framework set up around the Nationalization Law. But leading to the eventual breakdown of the institutional setup, cracks began to appear in the relationship between the government and the PDVSA professional management in at least four areas.

First, personnel management became a problem. Since nationalization, the government had never interfered in the operational structure of PDVSA. PDVSA had inherited and adapted the best international practices regarding personnel management from the IOCs, and appointments were made on the basis of professional merit. But from the beginning, the new government exerted pressure on the hiring process at different operational levels. The demands for appointments were not based on merit and credentials; the rationale was political allegiance. The government pressure to appoint personnel on this partisan basis caused increasing friction in different PDVSA operating regions around the country.

Second, fuel was supplied internationally on the basis of noncommercial considerations. For PDVSA, behaving as a commercial corporation was a legal duty. As noted, the company was subject to private, commercial law. For the sake of geopolitical considerations, the new government pressured PDVSA to sell oil to specific customers below market prices, particularly in the Caribbean basin. Thanks to what was known as the San Jose Pact, Venezuela, together with Mexico, had supplied crude oil under preferential terms to the Central American and Caribbean countries for many years. In the case of Venezuela, according to the terms of the pact, the subsidy was assumed by the government and not PDVSA. After 1998, the new political regime insisted that the relative loss in commercial terms had to be assumed by PDVSA, not the government.

Third, there was an increase in the government take and a consequent reduction of investment below the minimum required to sustain capacity. The government made clear from the outset that the priority use for profits would not be investment by PDVSA but to finance government expenditures. This was particularly the case in the early 2000s, when relatively low prices set a ceiling on profits, implying a trade-off between the government take and PDVSA investment. Further, the profits from PDVSA's overseas investments—which traditionally had been reinvested abroad—began to be remitted to Venezuela. These profits were transferred to the government. Investment to sustain production capacity or to upgrade refining was no longer a priority.

Fourth, PDVSA4s labor force and resources were increasingly used for purposes not appropriate to the petroleum industry. The new government forced PDVSA to assume social responsibilities and activities not related to its commercial functions. Undertaking these tasks at the expense of core industrial activities caused the gradual deterioration of its infrastructure.

All four practices—interference in appointments, noncommercial supply practices, underinvestment, and the allocation of resources to noncore activities—were increasingly demanded by the government, escalating the friction with the PDVSA professional management. PDVSA employees were under unprecedented pressure and tension. True, the government—acting on behalf of the nation—was the owner of PDVSA and could impose its will. But, there was a traditional set of corporate values that collided with the government will.

As the first signs of these problems began to emerge, a significant number of leading managers voluntarily resigned in 1999. There was a truce in 2000–2001, but in 2002, the situation rapidly deteriorated. To set limits on what they perceived as undue interference by the government, PDVSA professional management became organized. In April 2002, key managers were publicly fired by the president of Venezuela, only to be rehired weeks later. However, both parties involved in the controversy were on a clear collision course.

What began as a short-term strike at the administrative headquarters in early December 2002, evolved into a long-term nationwide strike. The strike became irreversible after a few days, forcing production and refining to shut down. It lasted until the end of February, when the government was able to recover partial control of oil production, refining, and marketing. However, half of PDVSA's employees never returned to work, among them the majority of managers and top technical employees.

PDVSA has never recovered from this loss. The corporation was decimated after the strike. The company's most valuable asset— knowledge accumulated through formal training and years of experience—was lost. The strike was a breaking point. From then on, PDVSA ceased to be an oil corporation. It lost all autonomy and fell under direct governmental control. This was attested by the appointment of the Minister of Energy and Petroleum as the CEO of PDVSA.

The Venezuelan government assumed full control of the corporation. The arm's-length control structure set up during nationalization was dismantled. Once the resistance offered by the PDVSA professional management was erased, the government saw fit to use the company's human and financial resources at will. At every level, appointments were based, first and foremost, on political allegiance, not technical expertise. Ever larger numbers of employees and financial resources were allocated to a number of non-oil-related activities. Just one indicator should suffice: at present, PDVSA's expenditures on social programs are on the same order of magnitude as expenditures on the oil business operations, around $15 billion per year. Thus, for a great number of activities unrelated to the petroleum industry, PDVSA has become an operating branch of the national government.

PDVSA's investment in oil activities is very low for two reasons. First, the corporation lacks the engineering capacity to realize the same investment level as the average in the 1990s. Second, PDVSA is left with minimal savings from profits, as attested by the fact that in 2005– 2007 its international debt rose by $16 billion. As a consequence of both the dismantling of the operational structure and very low investment levels, crude-oil production by PDVSA is at present one-half and oil exports one-third what they were ten years ago.

Once the government assumed direct control of PDVSA, taking over control of the operational contracts and strategic associations was just a matter of time. It was not done immediately because these ventures secured a minimum output, and the government had its hands full bringing PDVSA back to minimum operational levels. Once it controlled PDVSA, the government expropriated the assets of the private companies and assumed control of the operational contracts in

2006 and of the strategic associations in 2007. It was an outright expropriation.

To conclude, the government has dismantled the national oil sector of Venezuela. It will take a radical change in policy orientation, a long time, and huge financial resources to recover what has been lost. Most importantly, it will require recovering the most valuable resources lost during this process of destruction—the human resources that left the oil sector and the country.

III   Conclusion

Epilogue: Populism and Natural Resources Workshop November 1–2, 2007

Bijan Mossavar-Rahmani

When Bill Hogan suggested I participate in this conference and do the wrap-up, my first inclination was to say no. Bill has talked me into this role in other meetings and, invariably, the task has been challenging. I have had to sift through every paper and sit through every session, something I, and probably a good number of the rest of you, seldom do. And this role involves not only sitting still and listening, but also trying to make sense in real time of what is said.

Still, on further reflection, I decided to accept the challenge, principally because I believed that this workshop would offer a unique learning opportunity on a topic that is again becoming central to the business that I am engaged in as the chair of an international oil and gas exploration and production company. That expectation, that I would come away better informed for my participation here, was more than met.

Not that the topic of resource populism was one with which I was unfamiliar. I have long been exposed to this topic. In fact, I have heard it debated and have thought about it and even lived it for more than fifty years, longer I suspect than anyone else in this room. This is not just a reflection of my age or of my career path, but of my family circumstances.

For when I was a toddler in Iran in the early 1950s, my great-uncle, Dr. Mohammad Mossadeq, was a popular and populist prime minister, who demanded a greater piece of the oil pie and proceeded to nationalize the oil industry to get it, but was quickly removed from power through a coup engineered by the CIA but inspired by the concessionaire, then called Anglo-Iranian Oil Company and now BP. The memory of that coup is not only alive for my family, but continues to haunt, to this day, relations between Iran and both Great Britain and the United States.

I am not going to try in twenty minutes to summarize or critique or supplement what was contained in the papers presented over the past two days; the discussants did an excellent job of that at the end of each session. Rather, I see my role as providing an industry perspective, and in particular, I would like to look forward and give some shape to the context in which resource populism might unfold, whereas the workshop papers largely looked back.

Specifically, what is the oil market likely to look like in the short and medium term and how will resource populism play out? And in particular, how might the international oil companies respond?

The first thing that will set the conditions for, and shape the future of, the market is the price of oil. Over the last couple of days the price of marker crude has approached $95 a barrel and $100 oil is only a nudge away. This is uncharted territory. Should these prices be sustained or fall back by a third or even as much as half, we will still be witnessing a sea change in the consensus view that existed among governments and companies as little as two or three years ago, when prices were expected to continue to fluctuate in terms of dollars per barrel in a range between the high teens and, say, the midthirties. Only the brave and the foolish dared go beyond this range in their price forecasts.

Many of the production-sharing contracts or other contract forms that have now been challenged or are under attack by host countries, as we have been discussing, were negotiated in and for that price environment. It simply did not occur to the drafters of these contracts that oil prices in this decade could approach or exceed $100 a barrel.

Conventional wisdom and the experience of the 1970s, 1980s, and 1990s held that higher prices, if they came about, would result from some short-lived, geopolitically induced spike, and that prices would settle back as supply and demand responded and as the geopolitical event passed or was dealt with.

This is not the place to analyze why prices have defied those expectations or projections, though I do want to underscore that there is now growing sentiment that what has taken place, however unexpected, has been a fundamental shift toward a world of higher oil prices. But to what level and for how long nobody knows, of course. Some of you may have read in yesterday's newspapers a quote from the chief economist of the International Energy Agency to the effect that the seemingly unstoppable advance of oil demand in such markets as China

and India has led to what he described as an "earthquake" in his thinking. I quote: "We may see very high prices that will come to a level
where the wheels may fall off." I think he was referring to the global
economy.

In a world of $100 oil or even $50 oil, the rush by host countries to
renegotiate and in the extreme, to renege on, contracts is understandable, even unavoidable. Every week seems to bring a fresh announcement by yet another country of an intent to renegotiate a project's
fiscal or operating or ownership structure. Your research project here
on resource populism is hugely timely and important.

I will not dwell on what changes might result in the language and
terms of the various contracts because each contract will change in a
different respect and also because the papers presented at this workshop, and in particular the country case studies, provide some possible
guidance on this point.

What I would like to emphasize is that in addition to slicing the pie
differently, higher prices and the resulting aggressive populism have
other consequences that we have only lightly touched on, but that matter very much.

First and foremost, for the large Western oil companies, the growing
wave of resource populism will lead to a push—or a pull—out of a
growing list of seemingly inhospitable developing countries and a
flight to safety to politically more friendly havens. But projects in those
areas—the U.S. deep offshore Gulf of Mexico or Canada's tar sands
and shale oil—are technically very difficult and require high prices to
be commercially viable, so the flight to safety is also one away from
easy prospectivity.

Plus, as several of you have noted, the growing pace of resource
populism is a global phenomenon, and not even politicians in Western
countries can resist the pressure and the fiscal appeal of doing something. Even the United States wants a bigger piece of the action; the
federal government raised royalties on new Gulf of Mexico deepwater
leases to 16.7 percent last January from 12.5 percent, the first increase
in fifteen years, and then again announced just this week a further royalty increase of 2 percent for offshore leases to be offered next year.
These hikes are modest under the circumstances, and importantly, the
United States left royalty rates on existing leases alone—unlike the Canadian province of Alberta, which just increased its royalty rate for its
oil sands projects, applicable to existing projects as well as new ones.

Libya, too, joined these two in the same month by announcing it was renegotiating contracts signed only a year or two ago. Libya, Canada, and the United States: The Axis of Weasel.

The shift of the oil companies out of some developing countries will come not just because governments extract more favorable fiscal terms but also because national oil companies, flush with cash and with access as a group to a staggering 80 percent of the world's oil and gas reserves, and the attendant bragging rights, have gained the confidence, if not necessarily the wherewithal, to strike out further on their own.

The track record of the national oil companies, with one or two possible exceptions, and Brazil's Petrobras is one of them, has not been impressive. Resource nationalism is not just about shifting the balance of power between companies and governments in favor of governments, with the latter getting a bigger slice of the pie from existing projects. To the extent that it means the departure of even some oil companies, it means less exposure to investment, project-execution management skills, and technology—and at a crucial time when project-execution management skills are in very short supply, together with nearly everything else in the exploration and production chain, from steel to people to equipment.

Already, some of the world's historically important producing countries are in decline. Mexico, Venezuela, and Iran are prime examples. All three are hotbeds of resource populism. Two other fellow travelers, Russia and Kuwait, are stagnant in production terms. But while production is in decline or stagnant in these countries, their oil revenues have shot up because of higher commodity prices, reducing the pressure to take some corrective action. At the global level, the full effect of this stagnation has yet to be felt because over the past decade other countries aggressively sought out the international oil companies, and higher production from such sources as Nigeria, Kazakhstan, and Angola is making up some of the difference. But the contagion is spreading and this year, two of them, Kazakhstan and Nigeria, are threatening to twist the terms. Angola cannot be far behind.

Yesterday, Ramón Espinasa introduced some very useful historical perspective and color when he talked about the interplay between Venezuela's role in the 1960s in the creation of OPEC and what was going on inside the country in government–oil company relations. Osmel Manzano went as far as to suggest that in the 1970s, in the evolution of the world oil market, OPEC was the elephant in the room.

True, but the fact that OPEC was mentioned only twice in passing here in two days, and in a meeting on resource populism no less, underscores the shrinkage in the stature and importance of the organization. And that is not likely to change. I expect that in the coming years, we will see new elephants in the room. One is technology. Another is the environment.

It is the technology elephant that I would like to talk about this afternoon. How technology evolves, through whose initiative, and how it will be supplied and under what terms will be critical to the shape and structure of the oil market. Resource populism is not just about restricting access to new oil through exploration; it is about limiting production growth in existing fields at a time when technology enhancements make it possible to find and produce oil more efficiently than even a decade ago—and in a safer, more environmentally benign manner. But the skills and experiences required to deploy and utilize these technologies are spread thin within the national oil companies.

The international oil companies, meanwhile, are recognizing more and more that it is not through their access to funds but through technology and project management that the industry can differentiate itself and wield its competitive advantage. Accordingly, they are stepping up investments in technology, not just to deal with the more difficult and remote projects they are increasingly engaged in, but as a way of wedging their way back, eventually, into traditional producing regions.

Historically, research-and-development spending in oil was very low relative to the size and scale of the industry, and while it has recently picked up, it remains a pittance. Last year Microsoft spent nearly 15 percent of its revenues on research and development versus just over 3 percent for General Motors but only 0.2 percent for Exxon-Mobil. In absolute terms, Microsoft and General Motors spent around $7 billion each last year versus one-tenth of that sum or only $700 million at ExxonMobil.

But these figures may be misleading because considerable oil research and development is taking place, except that it is no longer the exclusive domain of the oil companies per se. For example, Schlumberger, the Franco-American oil service provider, on whose board Adrian Lajous sits, while a fraction of ExxonMobil's size, this year is planning to spend as much, if not more, on research and development than ExxonMobil. And it is seemingly getting results. In one measure of how the service companies are edging out the oil companies, the service companies in recent years have filed twice as many technology patents. And these service providers now do much of what the oil companies used to do, from geophysical assessments to reservoir modeling and field development. But in a political sense, they are doing so under the radar and in more palatable collaborative arrangements where the clients, whether international oil company or national oil company, call the shots and the service companies provide just that—service for fees. They are offering these services at the client's own expense and risk, but also control, and without the necessity of sharing the upside.

An active, aggressive oil services industry to which many functions can be outsourced by national oil companies no longer in need of risk capital threatens to marginalize the oil companies by relegating them to a role as intermediaries. And as I noted earlier, their response has been to move to regions and political jurisdictions where national oil companies do not exist and where the national oil companies of other states will not tread. Another response has been to beef up research-and-development spending. A third option is to acquire the service companies themselves and to bring their proprietary technologies, staffs, and equipment into the oil companies, and by the way, block access to the national oil companies and force them to again go through the oil companies as gatekeepers. Thus there is periodic speculation, for example, that ExxonMobil or other large players might buy Schlumberger or other service companies. True or not, such speculation underscores the importance of access to proprietary technology to the future of the oil business.

I close with two further thoughts. First, are the international oil companies and their governments reconciled to their much constrained role in the market and their reduced access to resources? Mark Wright yesterday suggested gunpoint diplomacy to access resources was very nineteenth century. Really? Never mind what took place in Iran just over fifty years ago. Today, countless millions of people around the world, including, I suspect, most Americans, would list access to oil as the primary reason the United States is in Iraq. I might not personally concur in that view. But there is no doubt in my mind that in the event of the Mother of All Expropriations, a takeover of Saudi Arabia's oil fields by Osama Bin Laden sympathizers, the U.S. military would invade that country and secure and operate the oil fields. Farfetched? That is just what happened when Kuwait was invaded by Iraq. When it comes to oil, there are lines in the sand defining just how much resource populism is ultimately permissible and where and by whom.

And second, having painted a picture of change, I conclude as I began by again drawing on my age and my own experiences in the oil arena: I have witnessed again and again, and am now a firm believer in, the commodity resource cycle. Eventually oil prices will weaken as they work their way through supply and demand, and the market dynamic we are seeing today will work in reverse. With each cycle, we never land precisely where we started but close enough for the terrain to be recognizable.

Appendix: Populism and Natural Resources Workshop

Harvard Kennedy School, Cambridge, Massachusetts, November 1–2, 2007

Participants List

Rawi Abdelal
Associate Professor of Business
Administration
Harvard Business School

Philippe Aghion
Robert C. Waggoner Professor of
Economics
Harvard University

George-Marios Angeletos
Associate Professor
Department of Economics
Massachusetts Institute of
Technology

Ashley Brown
Executive Director
Harvard Electricity Policy Group
Harvard Kennedy School

Fernando Candia Castillo
Petromina LLC

Daniele Cesano
Giorgio Ruffolo Fellow in
Sustainability Science
Harvard Kennedy School

Ananth Chikkatur
Research Fellow
Energy Technology Innovation
Policy
Harvard Kennedy School

Gustavo Collantes
Research Fellow
Energy Technology Innovation
Policy
Harvard Kennedy School

Akash Deep
Senior Lecturer in Public Policy
Harvard Kennedy School

Rafael Di Tella
Joseph C. Wilson Professor of
Business Administration
Harvard Business School

Eduardo Engel
Professor of Economics
Department of Economics
Yale University

Ramón Espinasa
Consultant, IDB, and former
Chief Economist, PDVSA

Ronald Fischer
Department Ingeniería Industrial
Universidad de Chile

Jeffrey Frankel
James W. Harpel Professor of
Capital Formation and Growth
Harvard Kennedy School

Nicolás Gadano
Senior Economist
Repsol YPF

Eduardo Garcia
Head of Institutional Relations
Repsol YPF

Jóse Gómez-Ibáñez
Derek C. Bok Professor of Urban
Planning and Public Policy
Harvard Kennedy School

Ricardo Hausmann
Director
Center for International
Development
Harvard Kennedy School

Dieter Helm
Professor
Department of Economics
University of Oxford

William Hogan
Raymond Plank Professor of
Global Energy Policy
Harvard Kennedy School

Godstime James
Giorgio Ruffolo Doctoral Fellow
in Sustainability Science
Harvard Kennedy School

Tarun Khanna
Jorge Paulo Lemann Professor
Harvard Business School

Maurice Kugler
Visiting Professor of Public Policy
Growth Lab Fellow
Center for International
Development
Harvard Kennedy School

Adrian Lajous
International Consultant
Petrometrica, S.C.

Henry Lee
Jadiah Family Director,
Environment and Natural
Resources Program
Harvard Kennedy School

Louisa Lund
Program Director
Energy Policy Programs
Harvard Kennedy School

Osmel Manzano
Senior Research Economist
Country Department—Belize,
Central America, Mexico,
Panama, and Dominican
Republic
Inter-American Development
Bank

Francisco Monaldi
Director, International Center on
Energy and Environment
Instituto de Estudios Superiores
de Administracion, IESA

Bijan Mossavar-Rahmani
Chairman
Mondoil Corporation

Erich Muehlegger
Assistant Professor of Public
Policy
Harvard Kennedy School

Fernando Navajas
Chief Economist and Executive
Director
Latin American Economic
Research Foundation, FIEL

Robert Pindyck
Mitsubishi Bank Professor in
Economics and Finance
Sloan School of Management
Massachusetts Institute of
Technology

James Ragland
Director, Ecomonic Research
Group
Aramco Services Washington
Office

Roberto Rigobon
Associate Professor
Sloan School of Management
Massachusetts Institute of
Technology

Daniel Schrag
Director
University Center for
Environment
Professor of Earth and Planetary
Sciences
Harvard University

Eduardo Schwartz
California Professor of Real Estate
and Professor of Finance
Anderson Graduate School of
Management

University of California, Los
Angeles

Andrew Seck
Business Planning and Support
Manager
EPW Americas
Shell Exploration and Production
Company

Federico Sturzenegger
Lecturer in Public Policy
Harvard Kennedy School

Lawrence Summers
Charles W. Eliot Professor of
Harvard University
Harvard Kennedy School

Laurence Tai
PhD candidate in Public Policy
Harvard Kennedy School

Anders Trolle
Assistant Professor
Department of Finance
Copenhagen Business School

Gloria Visconti
Mid-Career MPA student,
Girgio Ruffolo Fellow
Harvard Kennedy School

Louis Wells
Herbert F. Johnson Professor of
International Management
Harvard Business School

Nils Wernerfelt
Research Associate
Harvard Kennedy School

Mark Wright
Assistant Professor of Economics
Department of Economics

University of California, Los
Angeles

Richard Zeckhauser
Frank Plumpton Ramsey
Professor of Political Economy
Harvard Kennedy School

Jeromin Zettlemeyer
Assistant to the Director
Western Hemisphere Department
International Monetary Fund

Index